ALL THE WAY TO MOBILE

Securing the Erie Canal as a Competitor and Regulator of the Railroads in the Age of the Trusts

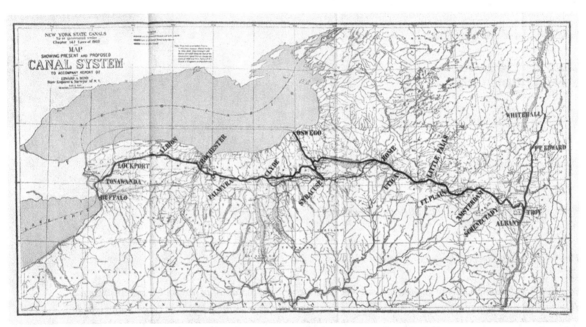

Map of the old canal with changes for the proposed barge canal added (See www.eriecanal.org)

Ernest A. Rueter

authorHOUSE®

AuthorHouse™
1663 Liberty Drive
Bloomington, IN 47403
www.authorhouse.com
Phone: 1-800-839-8640

Published by AuthorHouse 8/2/2012

ISBN: 978-1-4184-5339-8 (sc)
ISBN: 978-1-4184-7041-8 (e)

Library of Congress Control Number: 2003096447

Pictures courtesy of New York State Museum, Albany, N.Y.

This book is printed on acid-free paper.

In Memory of William Hills Gorham
1861-1935
Son of George C. Gorham
and
Grandfather of the Author

Loading Ships for Liverpool from Canal Boats and the New York Central and Hudson River Elevators at the foot of Sixty Second Street, North River – from Frank Leslie's Illustrated Newspaper, April 5, 1879

PREFACE

The year 1877-1878 will always stand as a seminal date in the development of the nation's transportation. On the railroad side of the matter, the four trunk lines running west from the east coast to Chicago formed a cartel in order to set rates among themselves. Within a decade the cartel had seventy member companies and Congress voted that price fixing was illegal. On the waterway side of the matter, New York business leaders in 1877 began to discuss the benefits of making the Erie Canal free of tolls. The question would reach the public in the fall election of 1882 and voters in the metropolitan areas strongly endorsed the Free Canal Amendment.

In comparing these two systems, it behooves an investigator to use information common to both. Here we shall cut to the chase by comparing the amount of commodities, measured in bushels, borne by each of the contenders, presumably accurate since they were important to the commodity exchanges. This approach is particularly important since many accounts of the canal tend to trivialize the system rather than showing that traffic on the canal at times was quite robust.

I came upon this course of history largely through biographical interests in my great-grandfather, George C. Gorham (1832-1909), reporter, politician, and colleague of Conkling. Gorham had settled in California in 1849 and his editorials in 1861 may have helped to keep California in the Union; then he became one of the first eight owners of the Central Pacific. While failing to win the governorship in 1867, the following year he became Secretary of the U. S. Senate. By 1873 he had sold out his Central Pacific shares and the next year showed his anti-monopoly colors by successfully promoting California governor Newton Booth for the U. S. Senate on the Anti-Monopoly ticket.

Gorham was a devoted supporter of New York Senator Roscoe Conkling (1829-1888) and during the Garfield administration he was editor of the party paper, *The National Republican*. He was also looking to return to the post of Secretary of the Senate. There was no question that both Conkling and Gorham held views antagonistic to those of the president and his supporters. If Gorham had won back his old office that would have placed a Grant supporter in a position he would have occupied as long as the

Republicans held the Senate. As shall be seen, he was too much of a freewheeling activist for some members of the Senate to take the risk of re-electing him to his old post.

What has happened since Garfield is that historians have found their own reasons for discounting Conkling and Gorham. In the period of mourning after the attack on Garfield, however, certainly the policy process continued. Solutions were advanced that would have long-range consequences. Conkling would live to see the canal revitalized in 1882 by the Free Canal Amendment, and the canal continue to serve as a surrogate in the absence of a federal regulation.

Gorham's fate in the new Garfield administration was set in mid-January by his own response to Jay Gould's consolidation of the telegraph industry. Within days of Gould's consolidation, Gorham in order to keep the rates down wrote at least one editorial in favor of a government telegraph system. Very soon, James Blaine made the suggestion to Garfield that management in the postal contracting office warranted an investigation, a move that would put Gorham on the defensive. The head of the contract office was the largest owner of Gorham's paper. The Department of Justice investigated. In 1898, however, the department dropped the inquiry due to the lack of evidence for either criminal charges or a civil case for recovery of funds.

I realized that I had a story here due to some experiences I was having. In the 1960s I had lobbied in Indiana for the civil rights bill, as well as for state court reform. I also briefly taught public policy at the Gary extension for Indiana University. From my reading of the century before, I believed that popular biographies simply failed to add up. My principal historical work was a policy study by Lee Benson, *Merchants, Farmers, and Railroads* (Harvard Press, 1955). The Library of Congress provided me with a microfilm set of Gorham's paper. My further good fortune included coming across the work of Professor Edward O. Laumann at the University of Chicago and his associates in their studies of not only elites (*Networks of Collective Action, A Perspective on Community Influence Systems,* with Franz U. Pappi. Academic Press, N. Y. 1976) but also the policy process (*The Organizational State, Social Choices in National Policy Domains,* with David Knoke. University of Wisconsin Press, Madison, 1987).

My credentials include a major in American history at Carleton College, Northfield, Minnesota, and degree from Eden Theological Seminary, St. Louis. I also have a master's degree in the sociology of organization from Purdue University. I have published one non-juried article in the field, "Non-Canal Counties' Support for the Free Canal Amendment," *Bottoming Out, The Journal of the Canal Society of New York State,* Syracuse, 1995, No. 31, pp. 10-19.

I very much appreciate the helpful suggestions I received from the late Professor John Simon of the Ulysses S. Grant Association, Southern Illinois University, Carbondale, Illinois; from Professor Clifford Clark, Department of History, Carleton College; and from Professor Vincent de Santis, Department of History, Notre Dame University, who graciously allowed me to make presentations before three meetings of his seminar. A meeting with Professor Edward O. Laumann of the Department of Sociology, University of Chicago, along with one exchange of letters, proved very helpful.

I am also thankful for the careful attention given to my manuscript by my copy readers Kathleen Mullen and Dee Nuechterlein, both of Valparaiso, Indiana, and my copy editors Deborah Kenotic of Leveret, Massachusetts, Catherine O'Callaghan of Dummerston, Vermont, Deb Schulz of Bellows Falls, Vermont, and Judy Myrick, Joanna Nomer Rueter, and Fran L. Hansen, all of Brattleboro, Vermont, and Jennifer Holan of Westminster, Vermont. Further thanks go to the staff at AuthorHouse.

I am especially grateful to my wife, Jeanne, for her patience in enduring this long study; to my late brother John Gorham Rueter and his wife Betty for financial support, as well as to our two sons, Robert and Allen. Robert introduced me to the work of Professor Edward Laumann, and Allen, a computer specialist, helped me review some 7,000 U.S. Senate committee assignments from the 40th Congress to the 49th (1867 to 1887). It has been Professor Laumann's interpretation of networks that has allowed me to show that Conkling played a much different role than convention has held. The finding here is that the Senator had a very good grasp of the transportation policy and always defended his constituents' advantages in the redundancy provided by the Erie Canal.

CONTENTS

TABLES

CHAPTER I

The Foreshadow of President Theodore Roosevelt's Antitrust Drive: The 1882 Vote on the Free Canal Amendment.

When Midwest farmers harvested their dry grains and took them to a local eleva-tor, their produce was not packaged, handled with handcarts, or otherwise processed. Indeed, handling was minimal. Those local elevators were emptied into railcars that made their way to deep-water ports where larger silos and empty ocean-going ships waited to be filled. For the grain trade the milling was completed at Buffalo and the commodity was in the form of flour thereafter.

Much of the heartbeat of New York life in the Gilded Age was set on capturing this traffic to the seaport whether it arrived either by rail or by smooth-bottomed canal boats traveling over the level water of the Erie Canal and the Hudson River. A canal boat drawn by two mules could handle as much as a ten-car railroad train and, although slower, was obviously more economical. In the mid-1870s the New York Central Railroad opened a line of huge elevators or silos at 62nd Street on the East River. Toward the end of the decade--just as the railroad cartel was launched in order to fix prices among the member railroads—the new cartel director, Albert Fink, explained in detail in a letter to Senator William Windom of Minnesota how each spring the opening of the canal with its lower rates made the rails across the country follow suit by lowering their rates. Thus the canal navigation season made the canal a regulator of the rail rates.

Each of these systems went through metamorphoses, including changes in carry-ing capacity, financing, and business model. Railroad corporations introduced larger railway cars and the state of New York responded by enlarging the waterways to host larger canal boats. The rails were privately financed and operated on lands given by state franchises while the canals had state financing. The business model for the canals included state supervision over the competitive canalers. The electorate opted by a wide vote in 1882 to completely remove tolls. In the end, the adoption of the Interstate Commerce Commission Act of 1887 made the railroads' price-fixing illegal and each of the railroads was thrown into competition with one another just as each canal boat owner was in competition with all others.

While many observers have noted that the competition between the rails and the waterways may have had the appearance of a battle between the titans in good Gilded Age form, they have too easily concluded that the battle produced an example of Joseph Schumpeter's "creative destruction." The technological metamorphosis was actually not that dramatic. All that happened was a change in the design of the ships hauling the product. The canal boats made with smooth bottoms were designed to move on level waters across the canal and down the Hudson River, so the later, larger ships were designed with smooth bottoms to travel on the relatively level St. Lawrence Seaway. Ships were enlarged but they still had smoothed bottoms and were meant to travel on level waters. In the earlier case, each of the canal boats took on its total cargo at Buffalo of 3,000 tons, while in more recent times, the ocean-going vessels loaded up farther west in the Great Lakes, such as at Chicago, Portage, Indiana, and a few other ports, with a load of 20,000 to 25,000 tons. By the mid-1920s, the Army Engineers' improvements on the Mississippi basin also preempted the traffic that had gone by way of the Erie Canal. Meanwhile, at the old outlet in New York City observers had to note that there were no longer canal boats in the harbor and no longer the huge New York Central elevators on the East River shore at 62nd Street. Both systems of grain transport in the port, the canals and the rails, had lost out. The deep-water port of the city had lost to inland deep-water ports and was now bypassed.

While it was technologically advantageous, the popular sentiment supporting the canal system remained strong far into the Twentieth Century. The public in 1882, by a vote of more than 70% and greater in New York City, supported the Free Canal Amendment. Theodore Roosevelt was a witness to the entire episode since he had won his first election to the State Assembly in 1881 when the Democrats seized control of both houses of the legislature for the first time since the Civil War. Roosevelt again came to the fore as governor in 1898–1900 when he gave attention to businessmen who persuaded him to support the plan for a new barge canal and in 1903 the electorate gave massive support for the $101,000,000 bond issue.[1] Rather than the story of the competing systems being an illustration of Schumpeter's "creative destruction," it was a story of Arnold Toynbee's concept of "challenge and response" and the value of the European model of utilizing both rails and canals.

In 1881 and 1882, to get the proposal of the free canal to the electorate as an amendment to the state constitution, the legislature had first to pass enabling resolutions in successive sessions. The first time was in the summer of 1881; then came the tumultuous election of November 1881, and Roosevelt's election to the Assembly during the Democratic sweep. By mid-1882 the assembly passed the resolution a second time by a vote of 74 to 53, with Democrats voting 55 for and 19 against, and the Republicans voting 19 for and 34 against, with the young Theodore Roosevelt voting with the Republican minority. In the state senate, the Republican support proved negligible; while 18 Democrats were in favor only 4 Republicans were. Ten Republicans were opposed.[2]

The Prevailing Question of Competition Versus Consolidation

The conventional account of political history for those times emphasizes the alleged corruption and the victory of civil service reform against the bosses. A second look at public affairs, however, does show a continuing thread of jockeying over the question of competition and consolidation. While the Rockefeller trust stood as the stellar example of an industry consolidation, the formal leadership for the policy of competition came from the report filed in 1873 by Senator William Windom of Minnesota on routes to the seaboard. The Windom report stressed the combined work of rails and waterways, pointing out that an east-west axis included the Great Lakes and the Erie Canal while the north-south axis included the Mississippi basin. The report also urged the technical improvement of double tracks and warned the public about the intentions of the wealthiest investors of the country. In New York by 1877 and 1878 many business leaders were convinced they had a creditable model for the canal and began discussing the free canal option. In 1885--twelve years after Windom's report--when the Senate took up the question of a select committee for interstate commerce, such leaders as George Hoar of Massachusetts and Nelson Aldrich of Rhode Island told the Senate how impressed they had remained with the work Windom had done.

Assisting Windom in preparing the report was a civil engineer by the name of Joseph Nimmo, Jr. As a result of his contribution, Nimmo was named Chief Statistician to cover railroad affairs, and occupied a new post at the Treasury Department. Albro Martin, author of the recently published *Railroads Triumphant*, has written that Nimmo produced "a series of reports that are a priceless source of information on the rapidly evolving American transportation system in its most critical and formative years."[3]

One lasting statement from Nimmo found in the 1873 report embraced his views of competition.

> The beneficent law of supply and demand where it operates most freely may not secure systematic justice, and yet the whole world concedes that, as far as it is operative, it secures substantial justice. This is all that can be expected in the present condition of human affairs. Competition may not make all things even, but it affords a nearer approach to equitable dealing among men than any substitute, which has yet been proposed for the nations laws of trade. The very instability of competition is the surest safeguard of public interest.[4]

One of the greatest tributes to Nimmo later came from Charles F. Adams, Jr., who although in early 1880 on behalf of the cartel in testimony before a House committee had criticized the notion of competition, nonetheless in later years in publishing a revision of his own book, *Railroads: Their Origin and Problems* he included Nimmo's quote above.

Another leader on the question was Texas Congressman John Reagan who came to serve as chairman of the House Commerce Committee and was a fierce defender of the notion of competition. Shortly before the 1880 Republican National Convention he released his committee's report of the meetings where Adams had testified a half-year earlier. What he had to say may show one of the contending views of the conflict then dividing the New York Republican Party. Reagan wrote,

> It is urged by at least two of the ablest representatives of the railroad in-
> terests, Mr. Adams and Mr. Fink, that the idea of competition must be
> eliminated from the railroad problem before it can be satisfactorily and
> properly adjusted. . . . I look upon this as the most dangerous theory, which
> has been advanced.[5]

In 1885 the Senate established the select committee under freshman Shelby Cullom, former three-term governor of Illinois. His committee joined with Reagan's in a tour of eight cities to gain testimony and in the end, it was the House Democrats, presumably un-der Reagan, who insisted on the provision in the ICC legislation prohibiting price-fixing.[6] That prohibition is worth mentioning here to demonstrate that the idea of competition, rather than consolidation, was the preferred state of affairs. It was not until 1890 that the Sherman Antitrust Act was passed, the leverage that Roosevelt later used. But by 1887 and the ending of price-fixing the political culture was already set.

In this panoply of leaders, two others should also be included. They were former governor Democrat Horatio Seymour and his brother-in-law Roscoe Conkling. Some authorities acknowledge that they had worked together earlier, but not later in their ca-reers. It will be seen that Seymour kept abreast of the legislative developments, usually making his views known in person at the annual meeting of the Canal conference, or at least sending letters there to be read. Conkling carried his share of the responsibilities by mentioning the role of the canal as regulator in the latter part of the 1870s.

Perhaps no politician in the Gilded Age has a sorrier legacy than New York's Senator Roscoe Conkling due to his standoff with both President Rutherford B. Hayes and President James Garfield. The late Professor John Simon, editor of the U. S. Grant papers, told me that the New York senator has become regarded as the "quintessence of evil." The conclusion depends largely on the method of analysis. As shall be seen, the conventional view of Conkling has contributed mightily to obscuring any consideration of what he actually did, especially in matters of transportation policy. Without that aspect of the story, the dispute over transportation cannot be well understood. It is my intent here to track the senator's public career in order to flesh out the policy narrative. A hint of Conkling's trouble may have come from his consistent support for the canal in the face of little enthusiasm among his fellow Republicans for the project.

An almost equal effort has been expended over the years in trivializing Roscoe Conkling's career. One often-used quote comes from Ohio Senator John Sherman's note to President-elect James Garfield shortly before his inauguration. The note said Conkling "never interests himself in anything but personal antagonisms . . . he never rises above a Customs House or a Post Office."[7] Other investigators have tried to show some appreciation of Conkling but their comments have usually been one-dimensional. Matthew Josephson, in his book, *The Politicos*, wrote that Conkling spoke with "the voice of the powerful financial groups of New York City."[8] Ken Burns carried forward the same view into the present generation by stating in his 1990 PBS documentary entitled *The Congress* that "Conkling was for big business and the railroads. They made the country great."[9] These one-side appraisals may have derived from a victory Conkling won in an 1882 Supreme Court decision very favorable to the corporations, which has been taken as a lens through which to judge his entire career.

More importantly these statements, whether by Josephson or Burns, propel a "convention" or judgment, that Jeffrey Mason describes as "present[ing] as an absolute . . . [so as] to remove it from scrutiny. It endures as long as those who use it question neither its validity nor the process through they developed it."[10] Such conventions begin as simple statements and can be referred to as *ipse dixit,* defined by the Oxford English Dictionary as "An unproved assertion resting on the bare authority of some speaker." In this account the conventions extend much further than merely the public career of Senator Roscoe Conkling. As shall be seen, they also serve to obscure the function of the Erie Canal. Through the work of sociologist Professor Edward O. Laumann and his associates one can show a political process that works reasonably to reconstruct the career of Conkling, the peculiar function of the Erie Canal he sought to protect, and the political process behind it all.

An Overlooked Defense of Conkling

Conkling was a conservative on the currency question, though he had questions about the national banking system. Often, he appeared as an independent, such as on the canal question. If the more broadly held convention has been that the senator favored the corporations and financial institutions, one clear dissent came from Lee Benson, who published his account of the Anti-Monopoly League in 1955. Benson was highly honored for his work, but other authors in later works have not referred to his judgment about Conkling. Benson wrote,

> There is little or no evidence that [Conkling] had been subservient to the corporations, or quick to respond to the dominant (*sic!*) interests' wishes on issues which really aroused the people and upon which professional politicians might best be cautious . . . Conkling as a professional politician whose main asset was popular support, was not averse to posing as the sword-bearer of the people on properly dramatic and important occasions.

. . . It was guessed at the time that Conkling was shrewd enough to see that an Anti-Monopoly wind was blowing and set his sails accordingly.[11]

Benson was not alone in this view. Editor Edwin Godkin in the June 9th issue of *The Nation* offered his observation about "Mr. Conkling's ability to play the part of an Anti-Monopolist champion in politics and a Monopolist lawyer in the court."

As shall be seen, one of the key methods that the supporters of the convention about Conkling continue to use is one-sided treatment of occasions that raised questions at the time. A chief example comes from the state convention of 1877 when reformer George W. Curtis appeared saying, in support of endorsing the president's Civil Service Order Number One, that the administration was at "war" with the leaders of the New York party for failure to support the administration. What is remembered about the incident is that Conkling took the podium to scold the emissary and made a reference to "men milliners," a comment that shook many at the convention. Later, in a response no authority has used, Conkling denied that there was any "war" but rather always a willingness to discuss with the executive the desirability of "retracing his steps." His answer covered experiences with both Lincoln and Grant and proves to be an interesting tour into oral history.

Added to the usual one-sidedness of the criticism is the confidence that there is no more to say. When his most disturbing encounter was with President Garfield, additional weight against the senator is gained through assuming that the president was innocent and the senator at fault. Thus, the senator was the "quintessence of evil." For our part, a better story can be cast by showing how these actors played their parts in the contention over competition and consolidation.

Chapter I

The Foreshadow of President Theodore Roosevelt's Antitrust Drive: The 1882 Vote on the Free Canal Amendment

1   Grasso, Thomas X, "Who is the Father of Today's New York State Canal System?" *Bottoming Out, Journal of the Canal Society of New York State* (No. 38, 1998, pp. 22-34. Professor Grasso has served as volunteer president of the Canal Society and as a professor at Rochester Community College.

2   The vote for the free canal resolution is found in *NYT,* March 24 (Assembly) and April 6th (State Senate), both in 1882.

3   Martin, Albro, *Railroads Triumphant: The Growth, Rejection and Rebirth of a Vital American Force.* New York: Oxford University Press, 1992, p. 191.

4   Nimmo, Joseph, Jr., *First Annual Report on Internal Commerce of the United States,* Treasury Department, Washington, D. C.: Superintendent of Documents, 1873, pp. 88–91.

5   *CR*, 46th Congress, 2nd Session, Vol. X, Part IV, June 1, 1880, p. 4026.

6   Google: *Interstate Commerce Act of 1887,* Section 5.

7   Sherman, John, to Garfield, January 23rd, 1881, *Garfield Collection*, LC, quoted in Allan Peskin, *Garfield,* Kent State University, Kent, Ohio. 1978, p. 557. Margaret Leech and Harry Brown write, "When the Customs House was in the greatest port in the nation, a state political boss could not afford to rise above it." *The Garfield Orbit*. New York: Harper and Row, 1978, p. 230.

8   Josephson, Matthew, *The Politicos.* New York: Harcourt, Brace, 1938, p. 109.

9   Burns, Ken, *The Congress*, PBS, 1990.

10   Mason, Jeffrey D. *Melodrama and the Myth of America*, Bloomington, Indiana, University Press, 1993, p. 188.

11   This quote is a composite of footnotes by Benson. See Benson, Lee, *Merchants, Farmers, and* Railroads (Cambridge, MA: Harvard University Press, 1955), page 285.

CHAPTER II

The Triumph of "The Sir Walter Disease"
And the Trivializing of the Erie Canal

The leaders of business and government contending in the transportation dispute might have settled matters by agreeing to meetings. The *New York Times* expected them and foresaw an "ordeal." As reasonable as that approach sounds—it almost happened in September of 1878—it did not work that way. Rather, people on each side played to engage both supporters and opponents. Each side exploited opportunities as they arose. The term "play" is particularly apt, as both sides made the most of the Gilded Age theatrical fashion of melodrama. It called for deprecating their opposition in the hopes of gaining the upper hand. It was the theatrical form of the "putdown." The winner could come out righteously superior. The medium of melodrama had been most popularly staged in Harriet Beecher Stowe's *Uncle Tom's Cabin*. The victim slaves and the evil slave driver were the central characters. It had exhilarated audiences who called for more. The story is told that when Mrs. Stowe appeared on the street walking along a crowd often formed following behind her. It was as though they were going to a hanging and wanted to be the witnesses.

The success of dramatists enticed politicians to mimic them by risking casting a spell over audiences from the stump. Take George W. Curtis's address to the 1877 New York Republican state convention when he announced that the new administration was at "war" with the state leadership. He had just seen President Rutherford B. Hayes. The trip north gave him time to settle on the medium of melodrama to make his point. Conkling ends up on the wrong side among historians who recall only the facts that fit the conclusion.

The Wide Appeal of Melodrama in 19th-Century America

Both conservatives and progressives could raise up melodramas. Webster's defines the form as a "dramatic piece characterized by a sensational incident and violent appeals to the emotions, but with a happy ending." When staged in the early 1880s, the focus was on the death of Garfield. The reprieve was by civil service reform. As the vision, of course, was ubiquitous another melodrama unfolded.

Choices of politicians on the stump included whether one wanted policymaking or just melodrama. One can observe that in the policy arena players on either side discounted their opposition in colorful and devastating language. Such evidence is hardly the final word; it merely shows that contention was the best course for the moment. The path of politics can lead in the end to adjusting competing interests for the good of the whole. Melodrama is something else. The course of melodrama differs from policymaking in that in melodrama one party aims at permanently damaging its opposition— exactly what happened to New York Senator Roscoe Conkling. In a melodrama, the hero stands for good and drives out evil. The turmoil ends, and, lo, he has brought society back to the previous state of affairs. In policymaking, the players contest by defending their respective interests lest their institution(s) collapse. They make some adjustments. Since the positions have been altered, the *previous state of affairs does not return.*

Jeffrey D. Mason, in his 1993 study of Gilded Age theatrical melodrama, including *Uncle Tom's Cabin*, describes the difficulties of melodrama; it is a

> world composed of binary oppositions. Individuals are either wholly good
> or wholly evil, and it is this Manichean vision that most obviously char-
> acterizes melodrama and expresses the fundamental faith of the middle
> class. Melodrama is the arena wherein hero and heroine contend against
> villains and the forces of virtue ultimately defeat the forces of evil.[1]

The southern cause, reinforced by Sir Walter Scott's legends, tried this course but finally failed. According to Mason, the myth of melodrama, foreclosing history from yielding new permutations,

> presents the ideal American society as a structure built on [the indi-
> vidual, family and community], and it *firmly denies* that the interest of
> anyone could undermine those of another. . . The entire motion of myth
> is return; return to what was or return to what is imagined, but always
> return to what should be . . . Change is actually a matter of return and
> restoration, that history is static . . . Melodrama is actually atemporal.[2]
> (Our emphasis.)

Ulysses S. Grant's appeal, "Let us have peace" might have struck the popular melodramatic chord. The James Garfield story, reconstructed by the reformers, left a legacy of light dispersing the darkness. No good report of his foe, Roscoe Conkling, would be allowed.

After the Civil War, similar sentiments emerged from among the advocates of northern industrial progress. One prominent bearer of the medium was Senator James

Blaine of Maine, the hope of many for the presidency. Closely associated with railroad interests, Blaine cast the issue of government interference in business as a struggle of good versus evil. Transportation leaders did deal with the Garfield administration. In order to understand what happened an investigator needs to move beyond the rhetoric that disregarded those connections.

While contenders may struggle fiercely, only they recall the real contention because melodrama covers them out front. In the transportation field rate wars did force some merchant shippers out of business. Low rail rates did draw business from the canals. Canalers did take the opportunity to undercut rail rates. The New York City commercial class highly favored competition while the railroaders sought to end it. A new equilibrium did arrive. Once we pull aside the curtain of melodrama and show the dispute behind the scenes, we can dwell on the backstage settlements.

The Philadelphia Centennial Exposition and the Promise of Progress

Imparting additional excitement to post–Civil War politics, men faced daunting problems in the industrial process. They exercised their creativity and became inventors, casting wonder and awe among the public. To be sure, during the period, the canal artisans also slowly improved their old technology. Much more dramatic, however, was the parade conducted by the new industrialists. They showed their new applications of steam and electricity and raised popular applause. Along the route they showed their machines in the tents at the 1876 Philadelphia Centennial Exposition. With a railroad rate war in progress, nearly everyone could afford to get there. The milling throng reacted much as the English had in the 1850s to their great World's Fair. The common experience was a new level of thrill, showing fairgoers new talents to exploit, new ways of cooperating, and the promise of a new age. Just consider the advent of the popular use of electric lights: manufacturing could expand to two or three work shifts a day without increasing plant size, and new profits could quickly accrue.

What the fair offered the crowds coming to Philadelphia were the fundamentals of progress. Everyone simply had to see the exhibit in the Agricultural Hall. There they beheld the tall, double-piston Corliss steam engine, the most advanced model of the technology, which the Rhode Island company had shipped to Philadelphia. They saw whirling drive shafts and pulleys, with revolving and slapping belts running from the Corliss to the other exhibits. Witnessing the huge machine and its extensions, visitors submitted to the catechism of the new systems thinking,[3] and saw that each component had its place, each fitting into the energy hierarchy. They could have left the exhibit pursued by a resonating, contagious martial air, making them ponder what place they could fill in the patriotic columns of industrial cooperation marching toward the prosperous future. From that exhibit forward the term "progress" would have an undeniable appeal.

The Centennial Exposition filled a void in the American experience. They had recently seen the collapse of an older vision, what Walter Nugent has called economic liberalism. Its explanations had done well in filling in the crevasses between socioeconomic groups and smoothing over the differences. The bond market collapse in 1873, however, found economic liberalism wanting for no more complex reason than that it had failed to predict the collapse. The market panic gave the railroad bonds a drubbing, and as bankruptcies spread the days of economic liberalism were numbered. Self-interest replaced the easy business talk. Nonetheless, its more stubborn adherents continued to pick over the old ideological debris, thinking some of it was still useful.[4] In the higher atmospheres of the advanced clarions of industrial growth, however, the new systems thinking now blew forcefully, shaping the currents below. Inventors with new patents gave rise to new monopolies, becoming a visible sign of the new spirit of the society. No less important was John D. Rockefeller's business model for a trust that promised great wealth for those who could apply it elsewhere. Social Darwinism came to set the pace and write the script describing what was happening.

In 1879, Congress finally managed to settle the postwar disparities between different currencies. Foreign investors again showed more interest. The markets recovered smartly and railroad stock prices vaulted. In 1881, for example, the *Graphic* reported, "A little less than three years ago, in September, 1878, the entire issue of the Louisville and Nashville stock was worth at current prices $3,041,300. A day or two ago, also at current prices, it would have taken $19,196,000, and this after a stock dividend of one hundred percent."[5] Stock prices in other railroads had exhibited similar spikes. Rufus Hatch, a New York trader, thought foreign demand for grain had prompted American stock prices.[6] In those flush days, the owners of the railroads in the Chicago cartel, including the New York Central, the Erie, the Pennsylvania, and the Baltimore and Ohio, welcomed other companies to their membership. The cartel and its pooling of freights and rates gave a new foundation to interstate transportation.

Meanwhile, the field hands with their scythes retreated in the face of the more costly mowing and threshing machines. The iron puddlers in their crossroads blacksmith shops gave way to huge steel factories. The educated occupations became professionalized. Most bankers now belonged to the new American Bankers' Association (ABA), an association of individuals rather than organizations. Railroad accountants and locomotive engineers formed their own associations. In academia, historians and sociologists did as much. The leaders of the revolution in occupations believed that government at all levels should organize the civil service similarly on the basis of merit rather than favoritism and family. From industry to occupations, melodrama set the lighting on the stage. In many ways, the country, once in the shade, sometimes even in darkness, transmigrated into a period of light and progress. Anyone who resisted faced attacks from the righteous in their impatience, and was soon crowded to the wall.

The Righteousness of Justice Stephen Field

High above these quickening currents stood U.S. Supreme Court Justice Stephen Field, whose decisions had a melodramatic cast giving them wide appeal among capitalists. Field had gone west in the gold rush days and become the mayor of Marysville, California. Moving up in California politics, Field, a Democrat, won appointment to the Supreme Court by President Lincoln. His message favored the *laissez-faire* camp by sharpening the contrasts between light and dark, good and evil. R. G. McCloskey claims that for Field

> The dividing line between good and evil remained always clear and sharp in his mind; the relationship between them was fixed. It was an "eternal verity." Those who proposed action that violated this clear dichotomy were not merely wrong, they were outrageously wrong; they were sinners. A profoundly moral tone pervaded many of his judicial utterances; legal issues were stated in ethical terms; "right" rather than precedent tended to be the guiding consideration. In addition, conjoined to this preoccupation with normative questions was a remarkable sense of certainty concerning the answers. Field did not believe something to be right; he knew it to be and the self-righteousness thereby generated was a dominant feature of his juridical personality.[7]

With a respected jurist casting such intoxicating dichotomies and the popular mind demanding as much from its icons, whether in politics or in the theater, it is not surprising that leaders of all sorts joined the parade. Since Field was a lifelong friend of Gorham, my great-grandfather, the stories about the jurist percolated up through my family's recollections. My mother recalled her father's impression that "Field was God."

The Righteousness of Congressman James Garfield

Field was the son of a minister, and James Garfield became a preacher with the same cast of mind. Garfield's biographer, Allan Peskin, writes,

> To Garfield the hard money doctrine was more than true; it was virtuous as well. Even though he had left the pulpit he still tended to think in terms of moral imperatives. In this sense, the issuance of greenbacks was a fiscal sin that had to be atoned for through economic suffering. Greenbacks were not merely impolitic, they were immoral: "the printed lies of government." It was axiomatic in Protestant theology that one sin begets another in the *slippery slide* of damnation . . . To Garfield, sound currency was more than a political issue, it was more than an intellectual theory; it had an element of the apocalyptic about it.[8] (Our emphasis.)

Nineteenth-century Protestant apocalypticism could have fueled the prevailing love for melodrama, as actors, politicians, and preachers united to pursue the "good" and scorn the "evil." Although the nation had formally declared a separation of church and state, religious influences in its everyday affairs continued. Raised in a religious culture, the public servants could switch in a flash to play the theologian.

The Righteousness of Anglo-Saxon Gentlemen

The elite believed that what they produced in the marketplace proved their own moral superiority. A new people were appearing. E. Digby Baltzell in *The Protestant Establishment* notes how they were held in awe:

> In so many ways, the year 1882 was symbolic of both nineteenth century confidence and the shape of things to come in the twentieth. As the year opened, the great and the powerful gathered for a dinner at Delmonico's restaurant in New York to honor the visiting British sociologist and Social Darwinist, Herbert Spencer, who had scientifically "proved" the Anglo-Saxon gentleman's Natural Fitness to rule the world.[9]

In this spirit, the main actors took on new obligations. In foreign affairs, for example, the thrust became colonialism and "the white man's burden." From beginning to end, the elite betrayed a new arrogance, leading to many errors. In domestic affairs Shelby Cullom, Governor of Illinois and a U.S. Senator and first chairman of the Senate Committee on Inter-state Commerce, recalled "the high railroad officials they avoided being called before us . . . They considered the railroads superior to the laws of Congress . . . they . . . were the most arrogant set of men in this country."[10] First had come the failure of the liberal economic rhetoric in 1873 due to the bond market collapse. Then in 1879, economically, came the sharp rise in railway stock following resumption. That suggests that the key monopolists filled the rhetorical void and assumed the status of economic sages. For Garfield the sage would be railroad financier Jay Gould, owner of the *New York Tribune* as well as the consolidated Western Union, and connected to the president through the "premier" James Blaine and the editor Whitelaw Reid. In other words, Garfield would have no council of economic advisors. He would depend instead upon what market circumstances had turned up. Those circumstances would be defined by Gould, Blaine and Reid, or, for that matter, also by John Hay, a broker for John D. Rockefeller.

In the transportation policy struggle, the new elite overlooked the canal industry. Improvements there were often proposed and frequently effected. That industry, however, got none of the applause showered on railroading, telecommunications and electronics. Historians have failed to realize that by remaining intact with its simple technology of homemade boats and state-owned locks, the old canal system invariably had an impact on railroading. Conkling remained their defender. In the survey of new technology, however, academics have largely rejected Conkling. He had to camp in the shadows. They did not perceive that he took a seat on a stone that would become the cornerstone of the economy, a functional canal contributing to permanent competition.

Mark Twain's Protest against Sir Walter Scott's Influence

Fed all his life on the melodrama of Sir Walter Scott—but fighting it off as much as he could—Mark Twain found the vision disgusting. It was a throwback to pre-Napoleonic times, and hardly a herald of progress. Perry Miller, tracing the plain style in American literature in his *Nature's Nation*, summarized,

> The respectable South, like Tom Sawyer, had been brought up on Sir Walter Scott. Twain's rancor came out most explicitly, far more than his "humorous" method usually permitted, in Chapter 44 of *Life on the Mississippi* in 1883, revealingly entitled "Enchantments and Enchanters." The French Revolution and Napoleon, he declares, whatever their crimes, broke the chains of the *ancien regime*, leaving the world their debtor for services to liberty, humanity, and progress. Then came the enchanter Scott, to set the world "in love with dreams and phantoms; with decayed and swinish forms of religion; with decayed and degraded systems of government; with silliness and emptiness, sham grandeurs, sham gauds, and sham chivalries of the brainless and worthless long-vanished society." Had it not been for Sir Walter, the character of the Southerner—"Southron, according to Sir Walter's starchier way of phrasing it"—might have become wholly modern, but Scott so debauched the mentality of the region that "he is in great measure responsible for the war." Cervantes had swept the "chivalry silliness out of existence"; Ivanhoe had restored it. Southerner Mark Twain could never cease to lament; the work of Scott was unqualifiedly "pernicious." In case any should miss the point, in 1889 [Twain] caused the Connecticut Yankee to plant nineteenth-century mines under the mail-clad hosts of medieval chivalry and blew them to pieces.[11]

According to Francis-Noel Thomas and Mark Turner, writing in our times, in their *Clear and Simple as the Truth*, Twain thought that melodrama greatly damaged how Americans perceived their condition.

> Mark Twain identifies a particular style as the *central catastrophe* in American intellectual history. Beginning from the fixed verbal phrase, "the beauty and the chivalry of New Orleans," Twain traces the surface marks of what he calls "the southern style" back to their sources in a complex of ideas he calls "the Sir Walter disease"—a conceptual monstrosity combining contemporary observation with an atavistic chivalric ideal derived from Ivanhoe. Twain demonstrates that the faults of the Southern

style have nothing to do with verbal skills. When a Southern writer is not enchanted by Walter Scott's "sham chivalries," he is capable of "good description, compactly put." Verbal blemishes at the surface derive from systemic intellectual disease at the core. "The beauty and the chivalry" is a surface eruption of an intellectual disease whose effects are only incidentally verbal—in Twain's account, this underlying conceptual stand was also "in great measure responsible for the war."[12]

The antediluvian Scott had corralled southerners in paroxysms of heroic efforts, and the tendency was elsewhere in the nation. It gave opportunistic politicians like James Blaine, in his reliance on Scott, a ready popular hubris to nurture.

The Commercial and Financial Chronicle's Measure of New York Opinion on the Canal

The contagion of melodramatic euphoria was hardly total. Some New York canal supporters showed themselves especially immune. In 1877, shortly after the Philadelphia Centennial Exposition, the *Commercial and Financial Chronicle* was especially clear regarding its position. Decades later Lee Benson thought the *Chronicle* "afforded a good insight into the evolution of metropolitan public opinion."[13] The paper noted that views about the canal divided into four camps. It left to the last the camp touching on the melodramatic vision.

> There has been no time in the history of the Erie Canal when the matter of its success and its relations to the commercial prosperity of the State and city were of such importance or seemed so closely dependent upon the adjustment of tolls, as at present. Yet, there are four classes of persons in the State: First, there are very many indifferent ones, comprising the population of the counties not bordering on nor intersected by the canals, who trouble themselves nothing at all about the subject so long as they are not called upon for any taxes on account of the canals; then there are the high-toll men, who hold that the canals should not only be self-supporting, but should yield also some slight revenue to the State, and that reducing tolls for the sake of attracting traffic is a ruinous policy; next we have the low-toll men, some of whom would gladly see the canal ultimately made a free route, but who all agree, at present, that low tolls are indispensable and are the surest means of reviving canal business.

Lastly came the many fair goers returning home transfixed by a new moral imperative of technological celebration. These would be the proto-Schumpeterites, who saw the process of creative destruction even before the economist came up with a name for it. The *Chronicle* editor believed such people unfortunately just did not understand.

Finally, come those---perhaps not many in number---who look with positive disfavor rather than indifference at the canal, thinking that the question of competition with the rail is already closed, and that the artificial waterway belongs to a bygone age, and the great ditch of DeWitt Clinton might as well be abandoned to decay as a curiosity of progress.

To be sure, a charging knight with a lance at full gallop might overcome one evil after another. He could set a model for the leaders of industry in that role bringing progress as they succeeded in marketing one new technical application after another. When matters got down to the performance of the canal with the rails, it was an entirely different matter. The editor of the *Chronicle* challenged the canal opponents who refused to see gains for the old waterway.

We have space only for discussion of the immediate issue now raised between the low-toll advocates and their opponents upon the apparent results already of the large reduction made last May . . . [Compared to shipments by rail] it is . . . plainly no argument against low tolls to say that they have thus far not succeeded in producing an increase of tonnage during the seasons when all tonnage has declined and the grain movement is reduced . . .

It appears that the railroads have been far the heaviest losers of grain traffic, so that the canal has relatively gained, and that it has made an absolute gain during the last month . . . We see . . . no reason for the charge that low tolls have failed; on the contrary, they have given already hints enough of success and the real season of business is yet to come.[14]

Canal advocates had good statisticians.

In support of a freestanding canal system, the Board of Trade, according to the *Times* of February 14, 1878 (a year before the Hepburn committee hearings) voted unanimously to make the canal free. A. B. Miller had made the motion. Miller, a warehouse operator, had been a conscientious activist for years. He had served on several committees of the Cheap Transportation Association. For years he served as chair of the New York Chamber of Commerce's canal committee.

Miller had developed an envied reputation for annually providing the statistics on shipments of grain by canal and by rail. One source was possibly the weekly and monthly reports found in the *Herald* where comparisons were made against the same week or month a year previously.

The saliency of the topic of the free canal for the merchants would appear the next month. Miller reported on federal statistician Joseph Nimmo's long disquisition calling for both a free port and a free canal.

Senator William Windom's Statistics on Water and Rail Traffic

In early June 1878, another advocate of waterway transportation came to the fore, Minnesota's Senator William Windom. He reported to the U.S. Senate on the improvements in traffic on the Erie Canal. He stated that in the previous year reducing the cost of transportation of a bushel by a half cent had attracted freight off the railroads. He said,

> During the season of 1876 the canal carried 28,841,100 bushels of grain, while for the corresponding period of 1877, under the reduced tolls, it carried 43,712,500 bushels, being an increase of 14,871,400 bushels more than in 1876 [a 50 percent increase], caused by the reduction in cost of only one-half cent per bushel. That the large crop of 1877 did not cause this increase on the canal will appear from the fact that the total amount received at the seven principal seaboard markets that year was less by 10,516,031 bushels than in 1876. It was merely a transfer of freight from the railroads to the canal, for the former lost what the latter gained. [T]hat reduction . . . turned the wavering balances in its favor.[15]

Furthermore, farmers shipping their surplus grain found the waterways a better bargain than the rails. Windom cited an annual report from the Illinois Central Railroad telling his colleagues "the railroads have to play a losing game in their efforts to compete with the water [ways]." In the report, the Illinois Central admitted

> The outlays made to increase the carrying capacities of the railways have been improvident, and since the reduction of the tolls upon the Erie Canal by the State of New York, cheap water communications is *so firmly established* that the effort to take freight by rail during the summer months has failed as indicated by the reports of several of the leading railways. During the contest, freight was carried in large volume at about half of the actual expense incurred.[16] (Our emphasis.)

Windom warned that if the farmers had to pay railroad rates for shipping grain, the higher cost would cut into their profit, limiting their ability to purchase finished goods from the East. Therefore, the entire economy would slow. These developments in 1877 and 1878 came to vindicate Windom's report of 1876 justifying the rivers and harbors appropriation signed by President Ulysses S. Grant.

Charles F. Adams, Jr.'s Statistics on Water and Rail Traffic

In his self-education, Charles Adams often came to early conclusions he left uncorrected. In writing about the Erie Canal, he remained oblivious to what Miller and his New York Chamber of Commerce friends believed, what Windom had disclosed in the Senate, and what the *Chronicle* had published. While Conkling and other New Yorkers from time to time visited the Welland Canal in Canada to understand the Erie Canal's competition, during the 1878 discussion of the canal, without making a field investigation, Adams rendered an opinion.

> It is more advantageous at all seasons to forward nearly every description of merchandise by rail than at least by canal. Accordingly, the amount of agricultural products carried by rail from west to east, as compared with that carried by water, had gradually increased until at the close of the year 1876 it amounted to more than half the whole quantity moved. In 1873, the proportion was 29.8 percent moved by rail, [compared] to 70.2 by water; in 1874, it was 33 percent by rail, to 67 percent by water; in 1875, it was 41 percent by rail to 59 percent by water; and at last, in 1876, it was 52.6 percent by rail to 47.4 by water.

Thus the water traffic, according to Adams, missed first place by just five percent. That led him to note, "The struggle was no longer between the railroads leading to New York and the Erie Canal, but between railroads leading to different seaboard points."[17] He failed to recognize what most other observers had failed to say in trivializing the canal. The decline of volume on the canal did not disturb the canal's role in keeping rates down.

In the minds of the *Chronicle* editors, Adams would probably have qualified as a prime example of

> those--perhaps not many in number--who look with positive disfavor rather than indifference at the canal, thinking that the question of competition with the rail is already closed, and that the artificial waterway belongs to a bygone age, and the great ditch of DeWitt Clinton might as well be abandoned to decay as a curiosity of progress.[18]

Sweeping aside not only the *Chronicle's* opinion, the merchants' unanimous vote for a free canal and Windom's report, Adams missed a big chance. Through his 1878 volume he failed to impress New Yorkers more familiar than he with the state's transportation business. Where he had a chance to build support, he lost it. He had developed only his own statistics. He failed to examine the statistics of others, even those of the cartel manager, Albert Fink.

The Hepburn Committee Weighs in on the Canal

Adams failed to realize that the canal nonetheless continued to set the rates. The canal ran alongside the New York Central in the Mohawk Valley. The Erie Railroad also paralleled the canal at some points. When the canal opened each spring, the Central and the Erie had to drop their rates to win traffic. Next, most likely the other companies with terminals at Philadelphia and Baltimore had to drop their rates. Adams' view in 1878 made no dent in the Hepburn committee's 1880 report that the cost of water transportation [by canal and the lakes] from Chicago to New York determines the rate of rail transportation, and the rate of rail transportation from Chicago to New York is the base line upon which railroad rates are determined and fixed throughout the country.[19]

Despite the volume of traffic gained by the rails, the canal remained the tail that wagged the dog.

John F. Stover's Statistics on the Canal

Some investigators in the field of transportation have written off the importance of the canal without so much as a doubt. Many of them, while mentioning the canal business, also show how quickly canals fell into disuse following the Civil War. John F. Stover's volume for The Chicago History of American Civilization, edited by Daniel J. Boorstin, *American Railroads,* is a case in point. Stover wrote in 1961 that

> Some of the great increase of railroad traffic in the late nineteenth century was at the expense of the nation's rivers, waterways, and canals. The Erie Canal had outlasted all the other man-made waterways but was losing out to rail competition by the end of the Civil War. The fierce railroad rate wars of the seventies proved to be the final blow. By 1876 more than four-fifths of all grain received at eastern ports came by rail.[20]

Missing from Stover's calculation is the Hepburn committee's claim (1880), repeated in the first ICC report 1887, that the canal and water routes from New York to Chicago set the base rate for railroads throughout the country. The canal's rates remained vastly disproportionate in influence compared to the volume it lost.

Albro Martin's Comments on the Erie Canal

In 1992, Albro Martin, in his *Railroads Triumphant: The Growth, Rejection, and Rebirth of a Vital American Force,* did the same thing. He asserted that "by the 1880s the railroads ruled supreme, and even the Erie Canal was crumbling into ruin."[21] In case the point was missed, Martin later reiterated that the "Erie Canal after the Civil War . . . soon crumble[d] . . . into the ditch."[22] Thus, Martin and Stover dwelt with Adams in the "creative destruction" camp in a never-never land. The figures used by the people who knew the canal were entirely different.

Statistics from A. B. Miller on Water and Rail Traffic in Grains, the Navigation Seasons of 1881-1885

Regardless of Adams' views, canal supporters were confident. At the 1886 Canal Convention, ten years after the Philadelphia Exposition, A. B. Miller, chair of the Chamber of Commerce canal committee, laid out the figures on grain shipping. They showed that from 1881 to 1885 the canal gave the rails a good run. They trended in the same direction as the report from Buffalo:

> Philadelphia received 89,525,832 bushels of grain, Baltimore 144,881,572 and Boston 93,818,935, while New York received by canal 179,161,232 by railroad, 292,001,808 and coastwise 9,940,388; total 418,404,517 bushels. [The three sub-figures for New York add up to 480 million, probably an interpolation that made for a 15% difference.] Thus, the canal receipts at New York were larger than the gross receipts of [each] of the competing ports.[23]

Converting Miller's figures to percentage shares of the total 800 million bushels shows the Erie Canal, open but seven months a year, carried more than one-fifth of the total, while the rails, open 12 months a year, carried the rest.

Table 1. A. B. Miller's Five Year Report Expressed in Percentages

New York total		59.4%
Railroads	36.0%	
Canals	22.0%	
Coastal	1.2%	
Baltimore		17.9%
Boston		11.6%
Philadelphia		11.1%

Although New York lines led the rails, the New York canal came in second and managed to carry twice as much as either of the railroads going to Boston and Philadelphia, making the competition between canals and the rails quite robust. Figure the calculation for the rails on a 12-month basis and for the canals on a 7-month basis, and one finds that in the warm season they were equal. The two New York rails, open 12 months a year, together carried each month on average 3 percent of the annual total of eastbound grain. By comparison, the Erie Canal, open only during the seven warm months of the year, carried 22 percent of the annual total, or also 3 percent a month.

Horatio Seymour's Statistics on the Canal

At the Canal Convention of 1885, the elderly Horatio Seymour summed up affairs since the free canal vote of 1882 and gave a rousing call for the future.

> Before the canals were made free, it cost three times as much to carry cargoes from Chicago to New York as it did afterward. The balance of trade against our country before the removal of tolls was $800,000,000.

After the canals had been made free in eight years, the balance was $1,300,000,000 in our favor. The commerce of the canals has made us one of the most prosperous nations on the earth. We find that the wisest among us have fallen short in our estimates.

[T]he men opposed to the canals desired their ruin and have failed in their object. A glance at the railroad stock lists will show that the enemies of the canal have been defeated, and they alone are the losers. [Applause.] I believe there is a brighter outlook for the canals in the immediate future that will enable them to carry larger cargoes and do business on terms that are more advantageous. Today you are here to declare with one voice, that our canals must and shall be sustained. [Applause.] Men who seek to impair their usefulness or to destroy them must encounter determined and earnest men who will sustain the canals, and thus do their duty to their country.[24]

After the Free Canal Amendment passed in 1882, shipping on the slower canal had an advantage. Miller noted, "The average rate of canal freight for 1884 was .27 of a cent per ton per mile, against .34 of a cent per ton in 1883. The average rate of freight on the railroads for all classes of articles shipped in 1884 was .74 of a cent per ton-mile, against .845 of a cent per ton in 1883."[25] The major adjustment between the two institutions consisted of the canal giving the best price for bulk goods while the rails gave the best service for finished and half-finished goods.

The Free Canal Amendment not only cut shippers' costs by two-thirds, but also bested the costs by rail. That adjustment, however, hardly left railroaders satisfied. The in-house legends about their technological superiority kept them waiting for weaknesses to appear in the canal system as an excuse to put it out of business. Yet on July 23, 1885, the *Times* acknowledged that the canal regulated the rails in the matter of shipping grain, adding, "The only other method of control when competition fails is regulation by Government authority." Thus, the canal served for a period as a hedge or surrogate until the arrival of the era of federal regulation. New Yorkers had hardly built canal for such a purpose, but when circumstances dictated the new role of the canal as a surrogate, the publicists and politicians gave that new role popular expression and the canal came to serve the nation adequately for the time being.

The Opening of the Navigation Season of 1886

The above report by Miller covered the years through the 1885 season and he added new figures about what was happening in the beginning of the 1886 season. During May, June and July the grain arriving at New York was by canal, 15,136,350 bushels; by rail, 11,200,327 bushels and coastwise 174,140 bushels, showing that the canal alone brought, up to August 1, 3,761,883 bushels of grain [24 percent] more than was received by all the railroads, river and coastwise routes combined.

Table 2. A Short Term Table by A. B. Miller

Three months (May, June & July), 1886, Bushels delivered to N.Y.		
Conveyance	Number of bushels	
Canal	15,136,350	57%
Rail	11,200,327	42.2%
Coastwise	174,140	.6%
Total	26,510,817	98.8%

The Times editorialized:

> Nothing would justify the abandonment of the canals except demonstration that they had ceased to be of substantial value to commerce. The contrary of this is still capable of easy proof. During the season of navigation the canals carry a larger amount of grain and other bulky commodities than all the trunk line railroads with which they compete, and at materially lower rates . . . they compel the latter to make lower rates than they otherwise would, which is shown by the fact that those rates are increased during the season of closed navigation. If the canals were thrown out . . . the railroads would undoubtedly gain, but it would be at the expense of the communities they serve.[26]

The Navigation Season of 1887

Table 3. A Short Term Table by A. B. Miller

Seven months of 1887, bushels delivered to N.Y.		
Conveyance	Number of bushels	
Canal	45,688,100	68%
Rail	20,934,400	31%
Total	66,622,500	99%

The rails carried about one and three-quarter million bushels a month over a twelve-month year and the canals carried six and one-half million bushels per month over a seven-month navigation season or over three and a half times more than the rails.

After all the figures were in for the following navigations season of 1887 the canal supporters had even more to cheer about. The year 1887 was an exceptionally good one, with the canals carrying slightly over twice as much as the rails. The *Times* noted, "When we consider that during the season of navigation more grain is brought to this port by canal boats than by all the railroads put together, we can appreciate how much the supremacy of New York as a grain-exporting city depends upon the waterways."[27] The final count for 1887 showed the canal had delivered 45,688,100 bushels to the New York port, while the railroads had delivered 20,934,400.[28] While the first report of the Interstate Commerce Commission in 1887, as shall be seen, recognized the role the canal played in rate setting across the nation, academicians have been less likely to concede the point, even overlooking the great spike in canal performance that year. They have missed the fact that the free canal had become the competitor and regulator of the railroads in the days of the trusts. According to Adams' logic, from these statistics he would have had to say that the canal was back in the competition. The proto-Schumpeterites would have to overlook these figures in order to sustain their point about new, superior technology overcoming old, inferior technology.

The Business Culture of Trusts

As the American economy teemed with mergers, overcoming competition, in the railroad industry one major exception stood out and that was the continuing competition between the roads and the canal. Elsewhere monopolization was running at full tilt, as Henry D. Lloyd, of the *Chicago Tribune,* noted in the June 1884 issue of the *North American Review.* After discussing the coal and milk industries, Lloyd listed others:

> Other combinations, generally successful, have been made by ice men of New York, fish dealings of Boston, western millers, copper miners, manufacturers of sewer pipe, lamps, pottery, glass, hoop-iron, shot, rivets, sugar, candy, starch, preserved fruits, glucose, vapor stoves, chairs, lime, rubber, screws, chains, harvesting machinery, pins, salt, type, brass tubing, hardware, silk, and wire cloth, to say nothing of the railroad, labor, telegraph and telephone pools, with which we are so familiar.[29]

The leaders of these industries would comprise the advanced social class and keep the model popularized.

Lee Benson's 1955 Statistics on the Canal

The unique canal subculture, however, remained muffled, and the railroad view, heralded by Adams, Martin and Stover, had greater influence. In a 1991 article written about reinvoking tolls to raise revenues to build tourism on the canal, the *Times* again took up the Schumpeter interpretation. The paper told its readers "New York voters banned tolls on the Erie Canal in 1882 in a futile effort to stop the loss of canal traffic to the railroads."[30] Miller and Seymour would not have agreed. Neither would Lee Benson. In his 1955 study of the eastbound traffic, Benson asserted:

> The Erie Canal continued to carry significant quantities of grain right down to 1890, particularly wheat during the peak seasons of movement, and during the uneasy rail truces that broke out from time to time. But, its proportionate share of the tonnage dropped rapidly. Water rates also dropped to all time lows, but even the most drastic cuts could only enable the canal to hold its own for a number of years and then to fall rapidly behind.[31]

Before another decade passed, New Yorkers came to the rescue of their European vision. In 1903, voters, by a wide margin, strongly supported the $101,000,000 bond issue to reconstruct the system as a barge canal. That event, however, no longer has a strong impact on the common imagination. What has happened in conventional American historical thinking, the Schumpeter concept of creative destruction, has displaced historical observation. Lost to the public memory are the vitality of the canal as an institution, its adjustments with railroading, and the sustained support it won from inside and outside of the state from Hatch, Seymour, Conkling, Nimmo, Thurber, Windom, the merchants, the *Commercial and Financial Chronicle,* and later Theodore Roosevelt. As shall be shown, several organizations, such as the Produce Exchange, the Board of Trade, and the Chamber of Commerce—all principal actors in the 1882 campaign for the Free Canal Amendment—came forward on the policy arena during Roosevelt's governorship to initiate the support leading to the adoption of the 1903 bond issue.

In those days the railroaders, dominating the storytelling, not only missed the place the canal continued to hold in New York opinion. They also missed the indisputable fact that the canal rates for grain were better than the rail rates. However, the railroad promoters had only themselves to blame. In 1881, the reform journal *The Nation* complained about the anti-monopolists' proposals for railroad regulation. Godkin complained, "The difficulty with the Anti-Monopoly League and the whole granger school of agitators seems to be that they will not study out their subject."[32] The same may be said of the railroad enthusiasts' view of waterways and the canals, beginning with Charles Francis Adams, Jr. He and others could have taken time to make a field trip and on-site inspections of the canal system, and to read the pertinent literature. That would have given him a more accurate picture of the canal's function, but he did not. Since a policy study seeks to understand both sides of a conflict, it has to avoid granting veracity to the criticisms cast by one side against the other. A generic model for a policy conflict can make a place for the interests and tactics of both sides and can show the support for the canal. The model visually would represent an arena with contenders lined up on opposite sides.

Republican Factionalism in the Gilded Age: The Pro-Trust Side

While canal and railroad authorities talked past one another, the politicians handling policy hardly did better. In the Republican Party, factions arose under the umbrella of a great melodrama. Overlooked among academics who have covered the period, the political factionalism came close to reflecting the split between the contenders in the transportation dispute. On the one hand, canal advocates supported a state-owned institution that had a long history appreciated mostly by New Yorkers. On the other hand, the trunk-line supporters since 1877 had succeeded in cooperating on rate-fixing and were very likely excited about forming a master merger the likes of Rockefeller's oil empire. Therefore we had on the one hand the simplicity of the canal system faced off against a monster railroad system, albeit no more than a prospect in the minds of its supporters.

Most of the accounts of the Garfield administration fail to reflect the intensity of the views of the people around the president-elect. As we read of the factionalism around President Garfield, we learn that Senator James Blaine of Maine became secretary of State. However, we do not read that he represented railroad interests even though he had recently given stellar leadership in opposition to the Thurman sinking fund bill. We learn that Garfield named William Robertson Collector of New York but not that Robertson, too, represented railroad interests.[33] He was an attorney for Vanderbilt and won a prominent state senate post allowing him to influence legislation on transportation matters. Robertson did vote for the free canal while his allies on railroading supported the opposition. Conkling's conviction, stated from the stump, that the canals could provide sufficient regulation for the railroads has hardly ever been mentioned, if at all.

The Republican Party factionalism of 1880-81 emerged from roots of several years. The two factional leaders, Blaine and Conkling, ever since they served together in the House during the war, had been irritating one another. When House Speaker Schuyler Colfax became Vice President under Ulysses S. Grant in 1869, Blaine succeeded him as Speaker. In 1872 the party faced a difficult split. Four years earlier, most Republicans had looked forward with satisfaction to Grant's coming administration. When those four years closed, Grant's alleged errors left many Republicans in doubt. They switched to an independent movement endorsing the Democratic candidate, Horace Greeley, editor of the *Tribune*.

The majority of Republicans nevertheless gathered around Grant and proceeded into the campaign. Conkling, then a senator from New York, set tongues wagging by trumping Greeley's claim to war-time loyalty. He knew of Greeley's prewar talks with the southerners. It seems that a returning southern senator had told Conkling what in 1861 Greeley had told him. Greeley had said that southerners by a majority vote in their states could leave the Union and Republicans would not object. Thinking Greeley spoke for the Republican elite, some southerners proceeded to leave, only to find that the North would go to war to get them back. In his 1872 campaign address, Conkling repeated this story before the nation, hanging shame on Greeley for an unnecessary war. Many voters who were cool toward Grant decided that the only thing left to do on Election Day was to sit out the election. If the independents thought that the first Grant administration had been a catastrophe, their own campaign against the general was an even greater one. Grant took the country by a landslide, leading the independents upon what Gorham often referred to as their "journey of political discovery."

At the opening of the next Congress, Speaker of the House Blaine gave the factionalism new life, denouncing the Grant administration and thereby making himself the titular head of the Republican "independents," known also as "half-breeds." In 1875 President Grant would recommend passage of the "force bill" and near the end of the session it was defeated with 20 House Republicans, including Blaine and Garfield, joining the Democrats. The Democrats took over that year, and then, just prior to the 1876 Republican convention, Blaine became a senator from Maine. When Blaine ran for the Republican nomination, Roscoe Conkling, Stephen Dorsey, and George Gorham produced a piece alleging his corruption in railroad affairs, a charge that, along with the Mulligan letters, stuck to him like pitch for the rest of his public career.

Republican Factionalism: The Antitrust Side

The ambitions of Blaine and Gorham soon collided. Among the political elite, Gorham already had a flamboyant career, coming to political fame first in California. Arriving there from the East at age sixteen in late 1849, Gorham grew up in the school of practical politics and journalism. He had quickly associated with a group of politically ambitious new arrivals and became clerk to Mayor Stephen Field. They were living together in the same rooming house![34] In 1861, a major figure on the Union side,[35] Gorham may have served well by writing editorials in the *Sacramento Union* persuading Californians to stay with the Union. Also in the same house were "the Welsh-looking fellows," John P. Jones and William Sharon, both later serving as senators from Nevada. [A frontier story held that while there, a neighbor named Murphy disturbed the three by regularly beating his daughter. They formed a *"posse* to go in and make old Murphy stop from keeping that child screaming." The young Murphy girl would become Mrs. William Sharon!]

While an early owner of shares in the Central Pacific Railroad,[36] for whom he lobbied, Gorham in 1867 became the Union Party candidate for governor.[37] For a running mate, Jones, his friend from the rooming house, ran for lieutenant governor. The Carson City (Nevada) *Daily Appeal* described Gorham as "a master of logic, wit and satire," and "as full of information—literary, political and general—as an egg is of meat. Opposition brightens him and makes him a terrible enemy . . . [The campaign] will be the sensation of the State for a long time."[38]

In 1867, the railroad to the east was under construction. The question of Chinese labor was much in the fore. Gorham knew what Charles Crocker, one of the owners of the Central Pacific, needed in the way of labor, and had watched Judge Field issue opinions beneficial to the Chinese. He took a similar position in the campaign, explaining to his Platt Hall audience in San Francisco,

> Because I am opposed to the coolie system, I am not the enemy of its victims. I believe in the Christian religion, and that rests upon the universal fatherhood of God and the universal brotherhood of man. The same God created both Europeans and Asiatics. No one man of whatever race has any better right to labor, and receive his due [?] therefore, than has any other man.[39]

The audience failed to applaud. Next, the Democrats lampooned Gorham for his multi-racial politics, and he lost the election to Henry Haight. Gorham trailed the ticket while his running mate Jones headed it--but still lost.

Some figured that Gorham had a chip on his shoulder. In 1877, Judge Field astutely observed that Gorham's "success as a public man would have been greater, had he been more conciliatory to those whom he differed from in opinion."[40] Twelve years later, the *Washington Post* put a different slant on Gorham's strong character. In 1889 he gave a memorial address in Washington on Roscoe Conkling and the paper observed,

> Mr. Gorham, like Mr. Conkling, is of a fearless, aggressive nature, who has no opinion that he cares to conceal—none that he lacks courage to express . . . as Mr. Conkling was never known to employ tergiversation or deceit to compass an end, and never paid an obsequious price for his friendships, we may rest assured that George Gorham will not allow his personal likes or dislikes—the fervor of the one or the intensity of the other—to disturb the equipoise of his judgment, even in writing the epitaph of a friend.[41]

Since Senator Charles Sumner of Massachusetts saved a copy of Gorham's Platt Hall address, it could have figured in Gorham's becoming secretary of the Senate.[42] Gorham's association with the Central Pacific Railroad, while hurting him in California, probably proved an asset in Congress, where caucus members realized he could serve as a reliable information link to his adopted state. In Washington, in the midst of President Andrew Johnson's dispute with the radicals over tenure of office, Secretary of War William Stanton barricaded himself in his office and Gorham brought him food.[43]

Sometime early in the 1870s Gorham sold his Central Pacific shares back to the Big Four, and in time he became an anti-monopolist. The bond market shock of 1873 led many people to change their minds about railroading. That year Garfield gave his anti-monopoly address, warning of the railroads' control of government but approving their consolidation as a federally regulated utility. About the same time Conkling arranged his committee seating, as shall be seen, probably to give him a survey of what was transpiring in the industry. The bond market collapse had brought a great change in the political contours of the country. Only one year later, in 1874, Gorham supported Governor Newton Booth for the Senate on the Anti-Monopoly ticket. Booth won.

In Washington Gorham authored a pamphlet on railroad regulation for members of the California legislature. Apparently in 1873–74, the railroads had argued that, since Congress had done so much for them without the consent of the states, they came under only federal law. On the other hand, Gorham argued, the California state constitution provided that corporations could be established under uniform law but that such law "may be altered from time to time or repealed." Gorham emphasized that the reservation affected the entire relation between the state and corporations and placed under legislative control all rights, privileges, and immunities derived by its state charter. Gorham opined:

> This question of the right of the legislature to regulate freights and fares is now pending in the United States Supreme Court. It has never before been directly presented to that tribunal. The decisions I have quoted very clearly point to what they must decide. Arguments are yet to be heard. The railroad people will probably exhaust all their rights, under the rules of the Court, to prevent the cases from being submitted in time to have a decision rendered while the several State Legislatures are in session. With this situation as a pretext, it may be the purpose of some pretended friends of public rights to advocate non-action in the California legislature at the present session. They will be urged by the Railroad managers to serve them, by saying that "the question is in the courts," and that while it is pending no legislation had better be had. As a citizen I should regret this postponement, and should say to members of the legislature: "Look at the decisions already made, and ask yourselves if anybody will believe you have an honest doubt as to what the Supreme Court will say when it can be.[44]

Gorham, secretary of the U.S. Senate, was pursuing the daring strategy of urging the state to adopt regulation before the *Munn v. Illinois* decision!

Blaine and the Stalwarts

Despite a circular against him, James Blaine managed to win notable support in the 1876 Republican National Convention. His nominator, Robert Ingersoll, thrilled his delegates with a spectacular address and, alluding to Sir Walter Scott, presented Blaine melodramatically, with his record of censuring the Grant administration, as the "plumed knight." Stalwarts O. P. Morton and Conkling had a siege of bad blood between them and did not unite the friends of Grant. Troubles in the Grant camp, however, did not assure victory for Blaine. The convention ended up nominating R. B. Hayes rather than letting the factionalist Blaine win the prize.

In 1880, Blaine prepared for another run for the party nomination but found that his southern support, which in 1876 had been quite encouraging, in 1880 had turned to Grant. Gorham possibly had a hand in that shift. At the midterm elections of 1878, with all the advantages gained as head of the Republican Congressional Campaign Committee, Gorham conceivably held out the hope to southerners that Grant would support biracial politics. Further, the recurring evidence that Blaine had railroad support, especially after his opposition to the Thurman sinking fund act, blunted his popularity. While in 1876 he won the title as "the Plumed Knight," later by opposing the sinking fund act he had lost some of his luster. By 1880 he took on the title of "Gould's errand boy."[45] Again, in 1880 the major factions in the Republican Party managed to keep each other from winning the nomination.

Blaine entered the new Garfield administration as secretary of State still troubled over his loss at the convention. As his predecessor, Evarts, had done for Hayes, Blaine used his office to help the new president with New York patronage. Ready to wreak vengeance on his foes, he told friends he would do nothing "to build up Conkling, Cameron, or Gorham."[46] Peskin writes, "Blaine was obsessed by patronage matters and used his influence with the President to punish Grant's friends and reward his own."[47]

Leaving aside the partisan struggles, there was one other topic that could have moved Garfield to follow a factional course. There was the beguiling prospect that the nation's railroads might adopt the model that John D. Rockefeller's Standard Oil Trust had perfected in the oil industry in Ohio. Significant portions of New York businessmen, however, were antagonized by what Rockefeller had done. As the anti-monopoly movement grew in response to both Gould's telegraphy consolidation and the promise of railroad consolidation, members worried about Rockefeller's work inspiring other segments of the economy, forcing out some of the less hardy businesses in New York with the corresponding loss to the city's tax base. In 1881 Senator Conkling appeared to represent that anti-Rockefeller sentiment, and Garfield may have cast himself on the opposite side. Six years later, when Shelby Cullom of Illinois made his report in the Senate on inter-state commerce, many businessmen were still upset with the oil czar's practices. The feeling was so high that Cullom attacked Rockefeller in his report. Rockefeller got the message, as shall be seen, because after the vote in support of the inter-state commerce bill, Rockefeller trimmed his tactics.

Blaine Arranges a New Melodrama for Garfield

After Garfield's election, James Blaine brought forth a new melodrama. This one was based not on saving "the Lost Cause," nor on the new technology and overlooking the canals. Rather, it was derived from his own wounded career mixed in with the prospect for his own personal redemption by supporting anything the railroaders wanted.

Blaine believed that he had to keep Conkling and his stalwart allies at arm's length. Blaine very likely understood the coming legislative scenario for the Adams bill and the belief among some that it could end up as a railroad trust. What was needed was a very firm executive hand in the process. He began working on that objective in the post-convention period plausibly through two lines of reasoning with Garfield. One was based on comparative statistics of the recent convention and election. The other was based on an economic forecast. First, Blaine wrote Garfield that his own supporters could be committed to him for a second term. Blaine claimed that his own faction at the 1880 convention ranked first. Looking back over the figures from the general election, Blaine conjured the numbers. They showed that a high proportion of the districts going for Garfield in the November election had earlier gone for him at the Chicago convention. That is, the southern delegations could not be counted upon in 1884 to help with Garfield's re-election. From that comparison he found reason to believe that his own faction was the stronger. Blaine failed to mention that if New York had not supported Garfield, he would not be writing him. Showing his own advantage in all the numbers in his December 16th letter to Garfield, Blaine made a compelling claim. He claimed that his own support "represents the reliable strong background of preferenced friendship and love on which your administration must rest . . . men who will labor for your success, and who will demand your renomination." Garfield would find such an appeal hard to resist. While the president-elect had eschewed thoughts of a second term, Blaine went right ahead and mentioned the prospect. Garfield apparently found himself paying more attention.

Blaine's second line of thought may have secured the deal. It was possibly adopted from what Jay Gould often repeated. The capitalists had often held that any political interference in business would set off a market decline. By using the mantra, the capitalists could keep the politicians circumspect, and it would be decades before economists came up with more sophisticated explanations for market changes.

In 1880, when meeting with Garfield the day after the August Fifth Avenue Hotel meeting, Gould very likely took the opportunity to assert the belief that political intrusion into the market would harm business. If so, the implication was that Garfield ought to discourage such a course. And after the 1880 election Blaine could have built upon that view by adding that politics was divided between the "good" men and the "bad" men. All this pointed to the fact that the sounds from the Hepburn hearings of 1879 were still hanging over the business community. A division appeared. While earlier in the decade Joseph Nimmo had written that competition was the best assurance of justice, men of consequence saw much greater gains in the course that Rockefeller had taken. It was time for Garfield to make a choice. A dream in mid-January would disclose just how uncertain Garfield was at the moment.

Both of these lines of thought would have put Blaine in an enviable position guiding Garfield. They suggested that, as Henry Adams had described only a year earlier in his anonymously published novel *Democracy*, "The truth was that Ratcliffe [Blaine?] had now precisely ten days before the new Cabinet could be set in motion, and in these ten days he must establish his authority over the President so firmly that nothing could shake it."[48] The rumors reached Gorham, who could not believe his ears. On January 29, 1881, he took the opposite view, claiming "Senator Blaine . . . is falsely represented as being engaged in securing absolute power over General Garfield in order that he may thereby wreak vengeance on the Republicans who supported General Grant." Blaine, enthralled by Sir Walter Scott, probably had in mind the motive depicted by Wordsworth in *"Rob Roy's Grave."* "That they should take, who have the power, and they should keep who can."[49] That power apparently depended upon Blaine creating in Garfield's mind a hope for re-election and then casting himself and his suggestions as the pathway to achieving that end.

Blaine had to be sure that Garfield would see the line drawn between the good and the evil. So without the least shame, he described in his letter to the president-elect the party leaders who had defeated him at the last two party conventions. Before Garfield named him secretary of State, Blaine turned on the stalwarts, calling them evil.

> All the desperate, bad men of the party, looking as longingly to the restoration of Grant as the Cavaliers of England in the time of the Protector looked to the return of the Stuarts, ready for any Mexican invasion [or] Caribbean annexation and looking to excitement and filibustering and possibly to a Spanish war as a legitimate means of continuing political power for a clique, are harmless out of power and desperate when in possession of it. [Finally, came the reformers:] the unco-good, the worst possible political advisors, upstarts, conceited, foolish, and vain, without knowledge of measures, ignorant of men. Shouting Shibboleths, which represent nothing of practical reform. Noisy but not numerous, pharisaical but not practical, ambitious but not wise, pretentious but not powerful.[50]

Blaine was riding the self-congratulation and arrogance of the new industrial elite. Here he was applying it directly to the incoming administration. Just perusing such alarmist prose, Garfield would have scrambled to defend the city gates against all comers. Blaine's view certainly would not have encouraged harmony enough for intra-party cooperation. On December 23, 1880, he acknowledged Blaine's line of thought in his diary: "Important letter from Blaine today—may have marked influence on his future and mine." While Garfield accepted Blaine's definition of the problem facing his administration, he also placed the stalwarts on the outside. Probably he felt that politicians could move in and out of such a mode without paying a price. The irony would be that New York City would become a hotbed of anti-monopolism, the home of the "bad" people. In 1884 Blaine without a blush would appeal to that vote, the "bad men" of 1881. Further, in 1884 the critical failure of his campaign was that, as Gorham would point out, he would have no southern states to make up for a loss of New York.

Who would lead and who would not quickly became evident to Conkling as he commented to his New York acquaintance J. H. Bailey, in a letter dated January 9, 1881.

> Political affairs look oddly. Genl. G. is being presented unwisely and hurtfully I think and entangled in advance. Those who are thus engaged act without warrant I trust, but the instances are becoming so numerous and various that men's opinions and actions must be affected. Indeed unpleasant frequency of proof shows how much and how needlessly serious misunderstandings are astir. I am anxious for the best, and the best seems easy and natural, but so far the signs are not flattering altogether.

By the end of the month, Conkling was much more certain. Writing to Colonel J. Schuyler Crosby on January 25, he said, "Your wishes have not been forgotten or neglected, but my efforts have amounted to nothing, as you know nothing from me finds consideration with our present Masters. Mr. Hayes is not only filling every place but reaching ahead into his successor's term."[51] The tone of Conkling's correspondence was hardly as bellicose as Blaine's, intimating the accumulating energy on the half-breed/monopoly side of the party.

To keep Blaine's support in the Garfield camp and the economy on the proper course the question of personnel became important. The most favorable reserve of top-notch personnel was in the railroad companies. Godkin's thought correlated quite well with Blaine's and expressed it as the imperative for the good men to enter the civil service:

> Most of the executive . . . talent of the country is now employed by the "monopolists." The great railroads, for instance, use the most effective means yet devised in any part of the world to get the best men into their service and to keep them there. They carefully select their employees in the subordinate position; they give them tenure during efficiency, and sure promotion and good pay in return for marked zeal and long service. They have, in short, just the kind of servants the Government ought to have but the government has a kind of servant that no money-making corporation would employ, and who, when pitted against the corporation servants in any kind of competition, naturally go to the wall.[52]

By the end of January, five weeks before the inauguration, the phrase "bad men" had become common in Washington. Gorham commented, "The Republican Party seems to be divided into two factions. The one concedes equality of rights within the party, the other frowns on all who triumph over it as 'bad men.'" Dark days for the administration were foreshadowed in Gorham's further remark. He wrote, "General Garfield has wisely refused to allow his name to be used as a makeweight in senatorial struggles within the party. He may well consider whether he shall not prevent it from being so used against the party itself."[53] The independents of 1872 had not only recovered from their embarrassment over Greeley but they also now assumed management of party affairs, beginning with defining the victors of 1872 as "bad men" and preparing for a battle.

Blaine's antagonistic definitions, just as he was entering the cabinet, suggested warfare. As sociologists John P. Heinz, Edward O. Laumann, and their associates point out in their volume, *The Hollow Core,* the selection of heavyweights (Blaine) could cause particular alarm and caution among all the prospective opposition. [The same would apply to Gorham's taking the editorship of the party paper. His elevation as a "boss" in Washington must have startled some people.] Gorham's unemotional observation that Garfield could act against the party itself meant that he saw the possibility a month prior to the inauguration that a new melodrama was about to unfold. The new elite held in their hands the power of the melodramatic process. They could make dispensations casting others in the light or the dark. An English monarch can dispense a knighthood to about anyone and elevate his status in the eyes of all. A Roman priest can dispense a wafer to a member to symbolize restoration by grace. The U.S. Constitution forbids the dispensing of titles, but Americans demand other dispensations. Politicians are ready to give them. Blaine suggested that Garfield dispense the title of "good" on the industrial elite, and Garfield willingly accepted the advice.

An investigator should not have difficulty in describing the scene--at least plausibly describing it. It is a matter of trying out different hypotheses. The hypothesis here is that the issue between the factions was competition between businesses versus consolidating single industries. While Adams had made quite a case for consolidation in his 1878 volume, Rockefeller in the oil industry showed what abolishing competition could do. On the other hand was the competitive culture of the New York harbor, handling almost two-thirds of the nation's commerce. It also had the competitive waterway up the Hudson River and across the Erie Canal to Buffalo. The investigator should find the material for such a story embracing both sides. The material would include describing events as well as how the players on either side interpreted them. Nothing obligates the investigator to give total credence to either set of views. If some of the players saw the entire affair as melodrama, the investigator should report it but is not obligated to take the same view. What has happened is that an exception was made for the story involving Garfield and Conkling. The position Garfield held and the manner of his death has virtually dictated generation after generation that investigators enter the arena expecting a melodrama exonerating the president. It is not even considered that Garfield may have said and done things which finally undercut his own position.

The drumbeat rolling forth from his alarmist "premier" likely helped keep Garfield in line with the story. The battle between the factions, however, was hardly over a foreign venture such as Caribbean annexation. It was only for solutions in domestic transportation where it was up to Blaine and his half-breed friends to run interference. They could easily foresee the outcome. Congressional approval would vault the credit of the cartel

33

and the buying out of sundry railroads would proceed. By comparison, the object of the New York stalwarts and merchants was hardly as grandiose. They simply wanted regulation of railroads and wanted to use the canal as backup since that would provide all the national regulation they thought necessary.

That struggle over regulation has faded from popular memory. All that remains is the distant haze of battle through which we still hear the clash of two characters: Conkling supported by his ego, and Garfield supported by his backbone. The practical check upon the new administration, of course, was no more difficult to understand than the fact that the party platform had given no guidance to either course. Indeed, some people on his side detested the entire idea of having a platform. If the platform failed to give clear instruction, other less visible sources would provide it, as events seemed to dictate.

Reid and Gorham, the Labelers on Either Side of the Drama

Melodramatic excess is easy to see in the process of "labeling." Someone on each side labels who is in the right and who in the wrong, who is good and who is bad. Laumann and Knoke write, "Certain actors may come to be specialized as ideological labelers who 'clarify' the meaning of a particular controversy for the participants by the stands they take. [They] serve to mobilize sympathizers and antagonists based on ideology, irrespective of the event's substantive content."[54] The benefit for the investigator follows from the discipline of tracking the labeling from both sides; he lays the ground for being more objective. In the factional fight of 1881, Whitelaw Reid and Gorham served as the labelers on either side. The juxtaposition of their editorials alerts the reader to the possibility of objectivity, as each side becomes a conspiracy discounting its foe. Labeling takes on its own life. The two papers contain a treasure trove of insults thrown at one another.

One might also expect to transcend such rhetoric and identify substantively what the actors had in their sights. To do so, an investigator has to look in the lobbying around a legislative body where interests were at play. He takes note of the options of either side. He further notes whether either side anticipates any reconciling. Some interests are seeking only to defend their position, while others are projecting great plans that need defending. The scene may also include thoughts of exclusion. A president can become as defensive as the key lobbyists surrounding him. They can make him their key lobbyist. The standard coverages of Garfield present him as defensive but often with no explanation. The explanation could plausibly come from adequately describing the links around the president. Admittedly Garfield had close ties to Whitelaw Reid, editor of the *Tribune*, and reinforced those ties by giving *Tribune* reporter E. V. Smalley a desk in the White House. Since financier Jay Gould owned the paper, describing the linkages is simple. In the course of time, the peculiar wants of the Reid-Gould elite would become clear. Not only would the railroader have wanted the national consolidation, but by mid-January he had brought to pass a consolidation between three telegraph companies. His behavior from that moment forward warrants reading it as that of a defensive monopolist. Garfield soon took steps to help protect the interests of the man he had met at Reid's home just a few months earlier. On the other side, the star route system with its headquarters in New York City became a subject of investigation by the new administration. If the investigation could show the incompetence of the postal system, Gould's new telegraph consolidation would be less subject to either a buyout or competition from a federal system.

A clue about substantive content comes from focusing on the desires of the major players outside the White House. What did Gould and other railroaders and their supporters such as Blaine and Reid want? What did they not want? What did the merchants want? What did they not want? On the issue of national banking, due before Congress in 1882, a variety of wants were in play. What did the bankers want, and what did they not want? What did the president want and not want? What did potential opponents, such as old Jacksonians and the greenbackers, want and what did they not want? Similar questions could be addressed to the Republican stalwarts and half-breeds. Answers come by tracking the influence aimed at defining the problem (implied in proposed legislation and appointments) and in defining who could take part (implied in naming the committee to handle the legislation or the advocates who won the administrative posts).

The clique around Reid continued relentlessly with its version of the story. Later Reid's biographer, Royal Cortissoz, faithfully passed on Reid's labeling of Conkling just as Jeffrey Mason in his study of nineteenth-century drama said it was done. "It is precisely as in a play," wrote Cortissoz. "With action and counteraction, the interests of the central personage, Garfield, are alternately advanced and threatened, the climax is postponed, and, here, *Roscoe Conkling is always the villain of the piece.*"[55] If this play were staged, catcalls would arise from the audience. At the end, the curtain would drop followed by great applause. Reid and his biographer and friend, relying on that complaint about Conkling, were captives of the model of theatrical melodrama. Without a blush they applied it to politics and did so for years. Blaine had had a good student in Reid. (Our emphasis.)

Reid was probably correct in blaming Conkling. Reid's stock portfolio probably included railroad equities. As Seymour reminded the delegates at a canal convention in the mid-1880s, the railroad stock had gone nowhere. Of course, Reid would blame Conkling, the man who had done as much as any to frustrate the plans for the great railroad trust. Further, what was wrong with Conkling was that he then expounded on the utility of regulation by the canal system. There—along with the proper role of experts—was the nub of the factional fight. On one hand, the Erie Canal each of the seven months it was open bore 3 percent of the nation's grain production east. On the other hand, right alongside the canal, the rail companies operating twelve months a year also carried 3 percent of the annual total each of those months. Throughout the canal continued to set the rates for the rails. In the end, the rails could not prevail. Even after the depression of the 1890s railroads were badly hampered, creating a bottleneck in transportation and remaining poor investments. Roosevelt would seek to solve that logjam by more expenditure on waterways and by legislation allowing the rails to compute the cost of doing business.

Casting the Legacy of the Factional Fight: Conkling's Reputation

Reid's status in the upper echelons of Gilded Age society presented him with frequent chances to cast Conkling as a lower form of the species. He had no sense of humor about the matter. In polite conversation, whenever he recalled the Garfield administration, he probably repeated his old saw that Conkling remained "the villain of the piece."

In a business environment that continually launched and applauded new trusts or combinations, the adventurous capitalists sitting at the peaks of those creations could look down with pity on the poor railroad system, forced into competition by the New York voters and by congressmen with affinities for pork barrels in advancing river and harbor appropriations. In the ancient fable the fox, disappointed that he could not reach the grapes, withdrew from trying by saying that they were not any good anyway. In this incident Reid, unable to affect a legitimized trust, escaped disappointment by saying that the chief politician, Conkling, was evil. Unrestrained, he found it easy to repeat his refrain and could count on a chorus of approval.

The Cartel Elite Around Garfield

In Reid's audience were Cortissoz, his biographer, and also a number of other writers, artists, and reformers, many of whom associated with cartel leaders. The latter, along with Reid, had witnessed the Garfield administration. There was the reform postmaster from New York City, Thomas James, known for his excellent administration of the New York post office. Even Europeans came to visit. James became Garfield's postmaster general. He made cuts in the star route service, and with those and other savings granted mail contracts to Vanderbilt's New York Central, overcame the deficit of the department, and reduced postage from 3 cents an ounce to 2 cents. Then James benefited from the revolving door. After leaving office, Vanderbilt named him president of his Lincoln National Bank on Vanderbilt Street, a post he held for the rest of his working years.[56] At the party conventions George W. Curtis, the civil service reform leader, often took a seat next to Chauncey Depew, who was not only attorney for the New York Central Railroad but also chair of the cartel. Depew had supported Greeley in 1872 and joined the Democratic ticket to run for lieutenant governor but was now a *bona fide* Republican. Then there was Charles Francis Adams, Jr., the lobbyist for the cartel, who made the trip down from Quincy, Massachusetts, two or three days a month to work at the cartel office, always finding time to walk over to the offices of the *Nation* and pay a visit to editor Edwin Godkin and then note the visit in his diary. As for John Hay, once President Lincoln's secretary and a friend of Garfield and Blaine, he had married into a Cleveland family that handled the brokerage business for John D. Rockefeller.[57] The point is that all these people probably knew one another, in the culture of trusts. They all had occasion to find themselves within earshot of Reid when he melodramatically characterized players in the Garfield administration. Thomas James, Chauncey Depew, Charles Adams, and John Hay were there to vouch for anything Reid said.

Since Henry Adams mentions Theodore Roosevelt a few times, one can assume that they moved in the same circle. It is interesting, however, that whereas Roosevelt broke from the convictions of that social circle and, following his merchant inclinations, entered trust busting, Henry Adams never mentions the matter of competition and consolidation. What was the payoff? Was it that in the heyday of trusts as the newly wealthy in America sought indigent European princes to marry their daughters, they also invited them to their social functions with the Adams brothers, the descendants of the early presidents? Then Theodore Roosevelt came along and took the punch bowl away! While they would associate with T.R., they did not appreciate his greatest act.

Getting the Story of the Evil Conkling into the Schools

Demonizing Conkling in high circles might have provoked a contest among his detractors. The reformers had the social setting allowing them to weave together an extensive story, disdainfully recalling the details. One of the best efforts of discounting Conkling appeared in articles written by E. Benjamin Andrews, president of Brown University in Providence.

Printed in 1895–96 in *Scribner's*, eight years after Conkling's death, the articles appeared under the title *"The History of the Last Quarter-Century in the United States."*[58] In covering the Grant and Conkling years, Andrews first cites arguments that the anti-third-term delegates brought to the 1880 convention. The accompanying pictures emphasize Conkling's meanness toward Garfield and the apparent consequences. The first picture shows Conkling lecturing or scolding Garfield at Riggs House. The next pictures show Garfield's ambulance train to Elberon, and then Garfield's remains lying in state at the Capitol, and finally Garfield's funeral car arriving at Cleveland. The pictures exploited the popular grief and targeted Conkling as the culprit. Finally, Andrews mentions the passage of the civil service bill and the launching of the Civil Service Commission. He makes only a passing reference to William Windom and his record on anti-monopolism, completely overlooking the growing cooperation among the boards of trade that led in 1887 to the prohibition against pooling of rates. Probably because of the ubiquity of trusts in 1895, nothing was said about how during the Garfield administration the anti-monopoly movement became so strong that it influenced the fall elections of 1881. It would then influence the vote on the Free Canal Amendment in 1882.

Andrews was rewarded. In 1897, he became a standard authority when Charles Scribner and Sons published his serial article as a four-volume *History of the United States, from the Earliest Discovery of America to the Present Time*. School libraries for years to come would carry on their shelves Andrews's four-volume set with a coverage telling youth what darkness Conkling had once cast over the republic.

The magazine articles appeared just as the civil service reached the final stage of reform set by the 1883 Pendleton Act. Godkin wrote in the July 1896 *Atlantic Monthly* that "this year the final transfer of the whole civil service, including the 85,200 places, to the merit system has been made." Therefore, reformers could again cast Conkling as the "villain of the piece" as reformers celebrated the victories of their long, good fight. Now persons of merit occupied most of the posts in the federal government, an almost perfect reflection of the employment process used by the great industrial trusts.

The success in demonizing Conkling is evident in what history departments failed to do upon Roosevelt's launching on trust busting. Francis Thurber was still living and even testifying before Congress. In 1881, his organization, the Produce Exchange, was one of the first to champion Conkling's reelection. But no academic seems to have talked to Thurber about those turns of events. Nor did they record that in 1882, early in Roosevelt's first term in the state assembly, he took the opportunity to support competition by voting for the free canal resolution.

While Andrews's volumes must have appealed to the younger readers, when in 1921 they became adults they could read again in *Scribner's* chapters by Chauncey Depew. He had outlived most of the people involved in the great disputes of the 1870s. He had served as a long-time president of the New York Central and president of the cartel, and also as a two-term U.S. Senator from New York. Assembling his recollections that became a single-volume biography, he was "very critical of Conkling."[59] Depew, however, never mentioned Conkling's frustrating the plan to create a cartel-friendly committee to handle the Adams plan for a trust. The cartel leaders and their friends stuck to their story. They had no competition in the world of literature. The public accepted the explanations, failing to suspect what they did not know.

The railroad leaders like Reid and Depew always took their complaints against Conkling seriously. Demonizing Conkling had almost become a cottage industry. A less melodramatic account would include that fact. The birth of competition in the Roosevelt administration had required a lengthy gestation period—two decades, as it turned out—and in fairness the story of its conception deserves to be told. Unfortunately, the celebrated leaders around Garfield largely favored monopolism, consolidations, and trusts. Hindsight should at least lead to the admission that they failed in promoting a great railroad consolidation. They talked like winners but they lost on their plans for a trust and were among the losers. They remained unhappy about public hearings such as the Hepburn committee had held in 1879. Then they had to endure the Cullom hearings beginning in 1885 and going nationwide. They were completely disgusted that they could not, as shall be seen, proceed surreptitiously to achieve legitimate, national consolidation. They apparently thought that any open discussion would lead to their defeat. They had simply wanted the wrong thing and could never admit it. Therefore an assessment of that story should help take much of the venom out of the scapegoating of Conkling. Conkling had truly got under the skin of railroad interests. They could never quite get over it.

The Evil of Conkling Updated

Recent standard treatments of Conkling continue to assume Reid's views. The most recent history of New York State, published by the state historical society, as well as the biography written by David Jordan, tacitly agrees with Reid in casting events as pure melodrama, blaming the suffering on Conkling, the villain. What his critics at the time overlooked was that although in 1878 the Customs House employees won freedom from patronage control, the senator nonetheless won reelection with the Republican legislative candidates, receiving a 70,000-vote majority. They also overlook that he never asked Hayes or Garfield for an appointment. Yet the repeating of the story of the senator's control of political spoils continues. Further, it was Conkling's defense of Chester Arthur, Alonzo Cornell and William Merritt, all dropped from federal offices, which led to the reformers' accusation that he was a spoilsman. A report from the Collector's office, however, showed that Conkling's sponsorship figured in the appointment of only three of the 1,200 office holders.[60] Yet the most recent edition of the standard text on New York State history carried this summary on Conkling:

> A handsome man of undeniable ability, an artist in the use of in-
> vective, and a master of spread-eagle oratory, Conkling subjected his
> Republican followers in New York to a degree of discipline that would
> have won him rapid advancement in the armies of Frederick the Great.
> He shunned theories and principles, despised reformers, and believed the
> spoils system was the cornerstone of party government. In what has ac-
> curately been termed "the age of the spoilsman," *Conkling was the greatest
> spoilsman of them all.*[61] (Our emphasis.)

Garfield's biographer, Allan Peskin, similarly characterized Conkling in a biogra-phy of the senator (The American National Biography, published by Oxford University Press for the American Council of Learned Societies, 1999). The view taken here is that scholars have not availed themselves of research methods that could bring into question the customary view of Conkling's career. Such methods would include noting his com-mittee associations over time and letting that evidence leave the inference regarding what took his interests, and whether it qualified him for having views about policy, such as transportation. When one focuses on the larger policy questions, however long they took to settle, some balance appears. Authors also do not offset Conkling's reputation by reference to his work on goals set by the Anti-Monopoly League, an independent or bipartisan organization.

The reformers' philippic has continued. Henry Adams has a character complain to reformers that "you want us to take [civil service reform] at your own price, but you lecture us on our sins if we don't."[62] Conkling was not inclined take civil service reform at their price and subsequent generations have been lectured on a list of his sins. The reform crowd comprised a number of very righteous persons and in time they entered into the realms of hubris to reap their own rewards.

One may wonder about the motives of Conkling's critics. Given that the reformers had a close association with the monopolists, perhaps their charges against Conkling had utility in glossing over the losses suffered by their monopolist allies. An accusation that Conkling "shunned theories and principles" consigns him as a policy-maker to irrationality. That can exempt investigators from reporting the senator's part in adjusting economic institutions. Their demonizing him and trivializing the canal suggests—by never referring to the canal's lower rates—that his actions foreclosed financiers' opportunities for huge returns on investments. The Rockefeller model was as big as life, and one can plausibly assume that railroad leaders were straining at the harness to get on with the work and achieve the same model. They, however, could not get around Conkling. His steady defense of the state institution that provoked national competition has not been worth the mention. If the financiers had complained publicly of those losses, they would have fallen under general disapproval. It was easier to malign Conkling. Conkling's biographer, David Jordan, carried on the convention in 1971, alleging that the troubles between Garfield and Conkling had not the least bit to do with policy––a bold assertion requiring examination. Jordan concluded:

> The assault upon the president stretched the Republican Party to its greatest extreme. The amazing thing is that, when analyzed, this split was not one of issues, or of *policies*––it was mainly one of personalities––and, more than any other was, Roscoe's *[sic!]* Conkling's personality. Almost unaided, Conkling severed the Republican Party.[63] (Our emphasis.)

Jordan's observation cannot stand up to the fact that Garfield sided with the cartel in its quest for approval. Conkling thwarted that goal and thus created a policy conflict.

Challenging the Conventional Thought Regarding Roscoe Conkling's Reputation

Such a verdict has at least four difficulties to surmount. First, Jordan undertakes the troublesome task of trying to prove a negative, that policy had no part in it. Second, investigators have overlooked events recorded in the daily press and private collections that need acknowledgment. Most surprising, Jordan writing in 1971 makes no mention of Benson's conclusions written in 1955.

Third, understanding Garfield's naming William Robertson collector is easy because policy influences such nominations. As G. Calvin Mackenzie has explained in *The Politics of Presidential Appointments:*

Public policy concerns are the dominant topic in the confirmation process and the dominant factor in most confirmation decisions. The Senate considers a number of things in formulating its confirmation decisions, but no other single issue is as pervasive or as determinative as its concern over a nominee's likely impact on public policy. Even when senators cite other reasons as their basis for opposition to a nominee—and they usually do—often that is just a disguise for their displeasure with his political philosophy or his views on important policy issues.[64]

The fourth difficulty arises from the circumstances in the unfolding conflict. The railroad leaders, most importantly, were gripped by institutional strain including the fear of bankruptcy, and plausibly by high hopes of an industrial trust seen in the Rockefeller model. Their preoccupations would have influenced any string of events that can fit into the scenario.

Getting to the core of the process of conflict, Laumann and Knoke's concepts rely on the work of the functionalist Talcott Parsons. His point was that the actors are bound together in a *common fate*. In the transportation dispute of the 1880s the common fate of the railroaders and canalers was geographical. The two were in the same business and they were traveling side by side across central New York and down the Hudson River within sight of one another. If investigators recognize this paralleling of the institutions, they can assume for themselves a perch giving them the elevation of objectivity. From that perch they can observe how matters on the two sides worked out.

Parsons' master theory of functionalism, Laumann and Knoke wrote in the 1980s, anticipates the behavior of institutions in policy conflicts:

In Parsons' succinct definition, a social system is a plurality of actors [the merchants, canalers, and the railroaders] interacting based on a shared symbol system [derived from the transportation system]. Membership in any social system under analysis is substantively defined by a criterion of mutual relevance and common fate that stipulates the basis on which *members are to take each other into account in their action (i.e., keep each other in mind).* That is, the basis of their mutual relevance to one another or their common orientations to some shared reference point [such as the transport of products to market whether by rail or by a parallel canal system] serves to mediate their interdependence. . . . A national policy domain is, therefore, a set of actors with major concerns about a substantive area [transportation], whose preferences and action on policy events must be taken into account by other domain participants.[65] (Our emphasis.)

With each side using the same Mohawk Valley and Hudson River to get to and from New York, certainly they had to *keep each other in mind* and one would expect some degree

41

of disharmony, episodes of outmaneuvering one another, and disputes or conflict. Each side of the transportation dispute, according to the record derived from reports and news articles, is replete with remarks showing what each thought of the other. For example, in the Hepburn hearings, Vanderbilt mentioned that the canal regulated the railroad rates. Later an associate protested that the company would not announce rates for customers because the canalers would undercut them. When the Hepburn committee issued its report in the late winter of 1879–1880 it included a statement detailing in poignant terms its wrestling with the common fate of the two carrier systems.

> New York possesses the key to the situation in the Erie Canal. While the committee made no attempt to investigate the relation of the railroads to the canal, and sought to lessen their labors by avoiding this question, the canal, like *Banquo's ghost*, would not down; we were compelled to meet it at every point and turn of the investigation.[66] (Our emphasis.)

Less observable facts also pointed to the mutual relevance of the two systems. As the tonnage showed, shippers had some advantages in using the canal. Each side would have been interested not only in keeping its share but also in gaining more from the other. Second, leaders on each side knew that their physical plants suffered from overcapacity. The rails were underused much of the year and the canal was frozen five months a year. They also had to use revenues to pay off debt, and their opponent might actually press them so badly that the debt could become troublesome as a forecast of bankruptcy. They needed to reach some resolution adjusting their practices, and an investigator can find that point by working backwards.

In addition, the policy dispute appeared on two levels. The matter required a settlement at both the state and national levels. When judging the course taken by any of the players, one must grant that each of them had in mind the consequences for New York as well as the nation. Also, options taken at either the state or national capital might well foreclose options taken at the other level.

A third feature concerns what I describe as the no-straight-line character of policy development. Benson observed that as Francis Thurber, a wholesale grocer and head of the Anti-Monopoly League, abandoned one proposed policy position for another, Chauncey Depew, the chief attorney for the New York Central and president of the cartel, was right behind him, occupying the position just abandoned. This illustrates the difficulty in tracking policy development. However pleasant it is to discover that an advocate on one side or the other had very early proposed a solution that led straight to the end, it often does not work that way. Straight lines are often interrupted by a more subtle and pervasive factor.

The Peculiarities of a Policy Scenario: Agreeing on the Participants and on the Problem

Within the concept of the scenario process, Laumann and Knoke hold that two variations are always occurring. Those two are how the leaders define the problem and who they believe should help to solve the problem. In the lobbying before committees of legislatures, the contestants continue disputing whose testimony is relevant and what the real problem is. Laumann and Knoke summarize that

> membership in a policy domain is a continuing collective social construc-
> tion by the domain actors. Membership is the outcome of continuous nego-
> tiations between the consequential actors currently forming the elite, who
> seek to impose their preferred definitions and requirements for inclusion,
> and various excluded non-elite actors, who seek the right to participate in
> collective decision making for the subsystem as a whole.[67]

A consequential actor is one in a position where he can command a broad range of material and/or human resources. He effects binding decisions in his or her sphere and is taken into consideration by other consequential actors where, with them, he may do the same. Among the railroaders, Vanderbilt and Gould were the consequential actors, while among the merchants there were Francis Thurber, Lucius Chittenden, Simon Sterne and others. After the Hepburn committee hearings the railroaders finally decided they wanted to talk only among themselves. They narrowed support down to a small group that included Blaine and President Garfield. That course was not the only one open to them. Often when a legislature passes a law, it becomes apparent that it had broad and diverse support, a prerequisite the cartel decided not to meet. The administration, insufficiently alert to these properties of lobbying, came to the aid of the cartel.

When they found themselves blocked, rather than retreating and planning to enter the arena again with more forethought and more allies, that is "run up the hill again," the promoters of the railroad trust turned their energies upon those who seemingly stood in its way. Conkling became the target. Other heads did not roll. Charles F. Adams, Jr., soon left the cartel staff and took a prize job as president of the Union Pacific. During the lobbying of 1880 and 1881, as disclosed in his posthumous autobiography, he had taken his instructions from cartel manager Albert Fink. While they had done a very poor job of planning and executing their lobbying, these two men did not suffer accordingly. Rather blame settled on Conkling.

The unpredictability in defining both the problem and the eligible participants leads not only to rejecting the no-straight-line concept of policy-making. It also prompts considerable skepticism about who indeed has been in charge. According to Heinz, *et al.,* in long-drawn-out policy scenarios no one party proves to serve as the permanent leader.

> The interest structures of the domains share many organizing principles.
> Most prominent among these is the *absence of a centrally positioned group* of

43

elites that is capable of coordinating or integrating disparate interest group demands. Our findings indicate that the structure of interest representation reflects and, quite probably, contributes to the uncertainty of the policy-making process.[68] (Our emphasis.)

In the transportation policy dispute of the Gilded Age some of the players, chiefly the railroaders, presumed their leadership in the policy scenario was permanent, and although they tried to enforce that presumption, they failed. Following the Republican convention of 1884, the party advanced sharply in assigning formal responsibility through following former governor Shelby Cullom's leadership in the Senate.

Applying Parsons' theory to historical evidence from the Gilded Age frees an investigator to use it to make a new start. Original source material still matters. Much of it, however, comes from the public realm. Garfield had an immense private collection, and by comparison nothing in the stalwart camp matched it. Stanley Hirshson has noted, "Unfortunately, since New York Republican leaders like Conkling, Platt, Arthur, and Morton left only insignificant manuscript collections, it is impossible to ascertain more than the general business reaction to their tactics."[69] I believe, however, following Talcott Parsons' thought and etching a line between the railroad interests and the canal interests competing for the traffic in grain that came down the Mohawk Valley, that I can show the general business reaction to the stalwart tactics. Each of those interests had kept the other in mind, and Parsons' theory helps to locate a "community of antagonism" between the two. The investigation depends upon culling the interactions of the contenders in railroading and canalling from government reports, news reports, editorials, and expressions from consequential actors and thereby trumping the absence of helpful private collections.

Further, some investigators have complained that history does not appear on the front pages of newspapers but in the financial columns at the back. What will become evident is that a reader can even find history in the center of the paper, in the editorial columns. Clues there can prompt an investigator to make profitable surveys into private collections. For example, at the time, the press often discussed Adams' views on regulation, alerting any later investigator to discover whether his private papers might illuminate his work even more. Further, since the center of the study is on the prospects for various options—the canal on the one hand and a trust on the other—what Adams and others had to say about either helps to make the story. Among the cartel leaders, Adams and Fink had quite different judgments about the value of the canal!

Since Jordan, Conkling's biographer, holds that a split in the Republican Party occurred due to Conkling's personality, the task here is to show where policy conflict, and not merely personality, had defined results. Presumably, the split would appear in the next election. To be sure, the party that in 1880 had carried New York State quite well for Garfield fractured a year later—so badly it lost both houses of the state legislature to the Democrats. Conkling, out of office for about half a year, took no part in the fall campaign. Such evidence leaves more questions than answers. How could one ex-senator have so much influence in a state campaign as to give the Democrats the state legislature for the first time since the Civil War? The suggestion is that the party destructed due to institutional conflicts rather than a personality conflict, and that the nature of the institutions bore upon transportation systems, which the voters recognized were in crisis and needed adjustments. The League had identified the railroaders as the most intransigent in the legislature and organized every district to oust them, and the public followed their suggestion.

In some quarters the popular legacy of conventional Gilded Age thought virtually mandates that the educated public regard the stalwarts as among the "bad" people. When this view is blended in with the reputation of President Grant conclusions are no better. The modern American mind has become hardened to any ambiguity in that respect. I believe, however, that there has been a simple disciplinary error committed by some historians who, for example, have not followed through on the charges of rank thievery made against the Grant administration. The error consists of not discovering whether anyone in that generation finally accepted the charges as true. A case in point comes from the testimony of Senator Shelby Cullom of Illinois made in 1891. Cullom was a lifelong admirer of Grant and had helped nominate him at the 1872 convention. At a celebration in Pittsburgh, reported in the *Post* on April 30, 1891, Cullom said of the Grant administration:

> The losses to the Government by theft, fraud and defalcation under his administration were in the first term only $1.50 on each [$] 1,000 of Government funds and in his second term only $1.01, while in Jackson's last term these losses amounted to $11.18, in Van Buren's to $12.19, in Harrison's and Tyler's to $14.49, in Polk's to $10.35, in Taylor's and Fillmore's to $8.77, in Pierce's to $9.61, in Buchanan's to $8.77. This showing, says Houghton, indicated that while the revenues had increased more than five times, the losses on equal sums had diminished more than ten times.

That should still all the critics of the Grant administration then and now as to its alleged thievery. Anyone in those old audiences of reformers, however, whose righteous indignation kept them from staying around to hear the results would have harbored enough rhetorical fuel to keep politics quite warm with calumny. Needless to say, they fanned the flames of melodrama. Houghton's analysis brought the story to a close, and that should have ended the matter. New generations of historians, however, keep coming along with their students; together they focus on the opening charges and overlook the facts as finally discerned. What the modern reader needs, but has not always received, is an assurance on a given policy topic that the reporter has brought his report to an endpoint, to a close. The disciplines set forth by Laumann and his associates give promise of doing just that. The conclusion in this instance should be that President Grant was

45

charged with a great deal of corruption, but in the end most of the allegations were without substance, and the question remains regarding the character of the parties first making the charges.

What follows is a full discussion of the melodrama of the time and its encroachment upon politics. Melodrama exacts a price. Believers assume that the focused issue is much more important than anything else that could possibly be imagined. There is the error, generic in nature. Since melodrama starts out with only part of the world accounted for, the excluded may come back to haunt, bite or otherwise devour the celebrated cause. The insurance against that happening comes from letting the real winners become the storytellers later. Their temptation consists of keeping up the solitary issue. Recollection leaves us with the belief that the most important consequence of the Garfield administration was the adoption of civil service reform. Certainly the assassination of Garfield antagonized significant segments of the population, and the reform of the patronage system answered that weakness. Unfortunately, the reform victory overshadowed the concurrent victory in the field of transportation where the trashing of trusts went so far as to prohibit cartels from setting rates. It is as though the American consciousness despises any competition for the melodrama it agrees has won the field. Other issues—in this case transportation—ranked with civil service reform. Honest treatment does not mean that they were competitive. Rather it sees them as organic; the moves in any camp have to be held in tension with the rest. I treat the transportation question as an authentic policy dispute and not merely an echo of the old anti-monopolism of the Jackson days. The weakness of the continuing reform tradition is that its supporters in the modern era following Adams, such as Stover, Martin, and Jordan, uniformly fail to mention that the canal, no matter how low the volume of grain, could undercut the rates charged by the rails. Conkling accepted that and supported it. The facts of the transportation dispute show events running from the dispute over the free canal up to the antitrust activity of Theodore Roosevelt.

Chapter II

The Triumph of "the Sir Walter Disease" and the Trivializing of the Canal

1   Mason, Jeffrey D. *Melodrama and the Myth of America.* Bloomington: Indiana University Press, 1993, pp. 18f.

2   Mason, pp. 191, 195.

3   "Americans during this period constantly made spatial and functional distinctions, and rigorously differentiated among various types of enterprises, peoples and tasks. . . . The criteria for each category were fixed, and all its elements were treated as if they were representative of that type . . . (B)ecause each component varied in capacity and quality, each had to be assigned its proper function or position in the machine; relationships had to be systematized in a hierarchical fashion. Only in that way could processes, activities, and society operate smoothly and at peak efficiency. In this view, the country's processes, activities, and social structures were systems of discrete, fixed hierarchically arranged parts." Marcus, Alan I. and Howard P. Segal. *Technology in America: A Brief History.* New York: Harcourt Brace Jovanovich, 1989, pp. 139f.

4   "The rhetoric that served to bind social groups together in the pre-1873 period fragmented . . . Previously thin cracks among groups widened into major cleavages. . . . A view of society in which several large economic groups were understood to share common goals and work with each other toward civilized progress, began to polarize into a dualistic social interpretation opposing capital versus labor. . . . by 1879 society had polarized . . . rhetoric had deteriorated from a system of potential social intercommunication to the reflex slogans of group self-protection. The money question turned Arcadia into a battlefield." Nugent, Walter. *Money and American Society, 1865 – 1880.* New York: The Free Press, 1968, pp. 176, 266–268.

5   *NR,* June 2, 1881.

6   *NYT,* August 3, 1881.

7   McCloskey, Robert Green. *American Conservatism in the Age of Enterprise, 1865–1910.* Cambridge, MA: Harvard University Press, 1951, p. 88.

8   Peskin, Allan. *Garfield.* Kent, OH: Kent State University Press, 1978, pp. 264f.

9   Baltzell, E. Digby. *The Protestant Establishment: Aristocracy and Caste in America.* New York: Random House, 1964, p. 27.

10 Cullom, Shelby M. *Fifty Years of Public Service: Personal Recollections.* Chicago: A. C. McClurge & Co., 1911, p. 319.

11 Miller, Perry. *Nature's Nation.* Cambridge: Harvard University Press, 1967, pp. 272f.

12 Thomas, Francis-Noel, and Mark Turner. *Clear and Simple as the Truth: Writing Classic Prose.* Princeton: Princeton University Press, 1994, p. 204.

13 Benson, Lee. *Merchants, Farmers, and Railroaders.* Harvard University Press, 1955, p. 237.

14 *Commercial and Financial Chronicle (Chronicle),* July 14, 1877, pp. 28f.

15 *Congressional Record (CR),* 45th Cong., 2nd sess., Vol. 7. June 10, 1878, p. 4358f. Washington, D.C.: Superintendent of Documents.

16 Ibid., *CR,* p. 4363.

17 Adams, Charles F. *The Railroads: Their Origin and Problems.* New York: Putnam's, 1878, p. 162.

18 *Chronicle,* July 14, 1877, pp. 28f.

19 *NYT,* January 23, 1880.

20 Stover, John F. *American Railroads.* Chicago: University of Chicago Press, 1961, p. 172.

21 Martin, Albro. *Railroads Triumphant: The Growth, Rejection and Rebirth of a Vital American Force.* New York: Oxford, 1992, p. 12.

22 Ibid., p. 241.

23 *New York Herald,* August 26, 1886. On August 20, 1885, the *Times* quoted Miller as saying "The Erie canal delivered at the port during the season of navigation 37,501,424 bushels of grain while the total receipts by all railroads were 28,049,020—an excess in favor of the canals by 9,452,404." A year later on August 26, 1886, the *Times* quoted Miller saying "statistics showing that the receipts of grain in New York by canal for the first three months of navigation had been nearly 4,000,000 bushels more than was received by all the railroads combined."

24 *NYT,* August 20, 1885.

25 *NYT,* January 28, 1885.

26 *NYT,* July 5, 1886.

27 *NYT,* July 30, 1887.

28 *NYT,* March 11, 1899.

[29] *North American Review,* June 1884, p. 549.

[30] *NYT,* November 6, 1991.

[31] Benson, p. 38.

[32] *The Nation,* April 21, 1881, p. 273.

[33] Benson noted that early accounts of Conkling covered only the political struggle and not the larger context about "the underlying differences between Half-Breeds and Stalwarts. Robertson's employment by Vanderbilt, Chauncey Depew's affiliations, etc., also do not figure into these treatments" (Benson, p. 285, f.n. 32).

[34] At his rooming house Mary Murphy would become Mrs. William Sharon. "There met at Washington city Jones and Sharon in the United States Senate, Gorham, Secretary of the Senate, and Field on the Supreme Bench—all out of the same boarding house." *Washington Post,* February 14, 1889.

[35] Field, Stephen J. *Personal Reminiscences of Early Days in California,* privately published, 1877. p. 39. (Published again in 1893 with a new chapter by George C. Gorham telling of the assassination attempt on Field.) Author's copy.

[36] Lavender, David. *The Great Persuader.* Garden City: Doubleday, 1970, pp. 215, 260, 283.

[37] Davis, Winfield J. *History of Political Conventions in California,* 1849–1893. Sacramento: California State Library, 1893, p. 247.

[38] *Oakland Tribune* quoted in the *Carson Daily Appeal,* Carson City (NV), July 27, 1867. Author's copy.

[39] Gorham, George, *Address.* Platt Hall, San Francisco, Gorham Collection, Sacramento: State Library. July 10, 1867. Author's copy.

[40] Field, p. 39.

[41] *Washington Post*, February 14, 1889.

[42] Harvard Library general catalog, see "William Sumner."

[43] Author's conversation with Harold Hyman.

[44] Gorham, George C. "The Power of the Legislature of California to Regulate the Rates of Freights and Fares over Railroads within the State." Washington, D.C.: National Republican Printing House, 1876. Author's copy.

[45] Klein, Maury. *The Life and Legend of Jay Gould.* Baltimore: John Hopkins University Press, 1986, p. 174.

[46] Gorham to William Mahone, March 19, 1888, *Mahone Collection,* Duke University, Durham, NC. In 1882, Chandler, secretary of the Navy, tried to get Blaine's support for Gorham. Mrs. Blaine wrote her daughter, "Mr. Chandler is here, and sits

here now, bowing to the storm which your Father is invoking anent [in the face of] the appointment of Gorham to the Secretaryship of the Senate." H. B. Blaine, *Letters of Mrs. J. G. Blaine,* letter dated November 29, 1882, Vol. 2, pp. 63f. Chicago: The Microbook Library of American Civilization, Library Resources, 1971.

47 Peskin, p. 553.

48 Adams, Henry. *Novels, Mont Saint Michel, The Education.* New York: Library of America, 1983, p. 94. While the novel *Democracy* was first published anonymously, Henry Adams later acknowledged authorship.

49 Wordsworth, William. *Complete Poetical Works.* Philadelphia: Porter & Coates, 1817, pp. 242f.

50 Blaine to JAG, December 16,1880, *Garfield Collection, LC.*

51 These two pieces of correspondence by Roscoe Conkling are found in the New York Historical Society.

52 *The Nation,* January 27, 1881, pp. 55f. "The Consolidation of the Telegraph Companies," Vol. XXXII, January to June 1881.

53 *NR,* January 29, 1881.

54 Laumann, Edward O., and David Knoke. *The Organizational State.* Madison: University of Wisconsin Press, 1987.

55 Cortissoz, Louis, *The Life of Whitelaw Reid,* New York: Scribner's, 1921, Vol. II, p. 45.

56 *NR,* Nov. 2 & 5, 1881.

57 Dennett, Tyler. *John Hay: From Poetry to Politics.* New York: Dodd, Mead, 1933, p. 102.

58 Andrews, E. Benjamin, "The History of the Last Quarter-Century in the United States." *Scribner's,* September 1895, Vol. XVIII, pp. 267–289.

59 Chauncey Depew, *Charles Scribner's Sons Magazine,* Vol. 70, July-December, 1921, pp. 667–670; "Roscoe Conkling," in "Leaves from My Autobiography," pp. 664–676.

60 *NR,* August 1, 1881.

61 Ellis, David, et al. *A Short History of New York State.* Ithaca: Cornell, 1957, p. 363.

62 Adams, Henry. *Democracy.* New York: The Library America, 1983, p. 32.

63 Jordan, David M. *Roscoe Conkling of New York: Voice in the Senate.* Ithaca: Cornell University Press, 1971, p. 407, 437.

64 Mackenzie, G. Calvin. *The Politics of Presidential Appointments.* New York: The Free Press, 1981, p. 169.

[65] Laumann and Knoke, p. 9f.

[66] *NYT*, 1880. From January through March the Hepburn Committee had several meetings. The *NYT Index* carries about a half column of citations for the topic and committee.

[67] Laumann and Knoke, p. 12.

[68] Heinz, John P., Edward O. Laumann, Robert L. Nelson, and Robert H. Salisbury. *The Hollow Core: Private Interests in National Policy Making.* Cambridge, MA: Harvard University Press, 1993, p. 22.

[69] Hirshson, Stanley. *Farewell to the Bloody Shirt.* Indiana University Press, 1962, p. 286, fn. 14.

CHAPTER III

The Information System For Transportation Policy, 1873–1881, Developed by Senators Conkling and Windom

The Evidence of a Problem Solving Culture in the Senate

In mid-nineteenth-century America, a policy leader wanting to move a major policy idea forward could use an idealized format. He could follow the model for the transcontinental railroad with its several stages. First, the delegates at a national convention adopted a platform plank in support of the idea. The project was so broadly popular before the 1860 national conventions that the delegates confidently approved it. Second, if the party with that platform wins the election, the next step falls to the president. In the instance of the new railroad, the new president in the third stage would make an appropriate comment. The question of the location of the route was left to President Lincoln and he named Omaha as the eastern terminal. Finally, a committee in Congress would draft a resolution for adoption by the rest of the members making it a mandate for their action. In this idealized format, higher levels of authority provided the leverage for the lower levels to get on with their work. So it went from the delegated convention then to the platform plank and next to the electoral majority and to the president and finally to the Senate committee.

The executive message was, of course, marked for special attention or handling. Network analysts have discovered that sub-elites (committees in Congress) would meet their responsibilities by handling the executive requests efficiently, most notably by pairs of members. This special function of sub-elites was first discovered in the twentieth century by sociologist Clyde Mitchell among elite sub-groups in Africa.[1] Edward Laumann and his associates discovered it again in the 1960s in Germany. Our investigation of arrangements in the Gilded Age Senate shows that members also followed the practice.

The key was that pairs of members on one sub-elite show up as members of another sub-elite and serve as transmitters of information between the two groups. The importance of the pairing is found in its ability to corroborate information. To grasp what was afoot, one can imagine a visitor to Washington in order to follow the work of specific committees. Any visitor who observed committee meetings would have seen enough of the outward evidence of the practice to surmise that some plan was in the works. If he had first visited a meeting of the committee on Pacific railroads and then attended a meeting of the committee on finance, he would have noted something special. He would have noticed that two of the members seated on the committee on finance also had taken seats on the new Pacific railroads committee. Likewise, he would have noticed that two members seated on post offices and postal affairs appeared at meetings of the new committee. Finally, if he had attended meetings of military affairs he would have seen the same thing happening.

These arrangements were not by happenstance. They were intended. At the outset, the members on the new committee on Pacific railroads did not intend to develop their case for the railroads out of whole cloth. They purposely sought out in other committees the resources and affiliations important to their new work. What the committee slate in the *Congressional Globe* shows is that the railroad committee promoters decided that they needed other members chiefly from the three committees. Those committees were finance, post offices and post roads, and military affairs. Just how important those committees were regarded is found in an additional twist. Any member coming from one of those committees brought along with him a committee peer. The consequence was that when the two showed up, the new committee knew that any information either one reported could be confirmed. The new committee thereby proceeded with confidence in its accuracy, a practice that would have helped increase the accuracy of the foundation of the new work. The network analysts have called the evidence of the practice *redundancy*.

The importance of the practice of redundancy was underscored when, for whatever reason, a vacancy occurred on the Pacific railroad committee and a replacement for the former occupant had to be found. The important point is that the nominators would restrict themselves to selecting a replacement from the same committee that first sent the former incumbent. This part of the practice meant that the new person would continue to transmit information from the old source that was as easily corroborated as before. No interruptions. The analysts have called the continuing link between the committees *duration*. The flow of information trumped the individuals passing it along.

Such a practice in the Senate subculture should encourage an investigator. When he reads the names in the slates of committees in the *Congressional Globe* or the *Congressional Record* he can make profitable comparisons. The inclination is to observe whether the various regions are represented on the committee under study. Another comparison can be made. That is whether session after session any other committees are also represented by pairs. Where there was a change in personnel, the new member probably came from the same committee that sent his predecessor. When congressmen took care in making these arrangements those steps had benefits, not the least of which was the information management provided the guidance regarding where the replacement came from. The appointment of the replacement would add authority to the managed or transmitted information. The committee would be less likely to have to brook competition, interference, or delay from other sources. Such arrangements among high-level elites should give investigators promises of quite an advance in a scholarly understanding of systems.

In the Senate career of New York's Roscoe Conkling, a reading of the committee slates shows that this process was in effect. Where his name appeared also appeared the names of other members from the upper Mississippi states of Wisconsin and Minnesota. One should not have difficulty understanding such evidence. At the time those two states constituted the nation's breadbasket—the states of Kansas and Nebraska would later take the leadership—providing a surplus in grain for the ready market in Europe. The national outlet for shipping was New York City, which as the principal commercial city—the rank that the city of New Orleans would later take—shipped the surplus of the harvest from the upper Mississippi off to Liverpool. By sitting on committees with Conkling, senators from the breadbasket states had a special confidence. They were observing information important for the functioning of the flow of traffic by water or rail. The further inference is that Conkling's continuity with these links from Congress to Congress meant he thought them important.

Of the benefits of redundancy, Laumann and Pappi wrote a century later:

> The presence of these multiple mediators provides a number of alternative paths by which information about activities and objectives in one subclique can be communicated to the other. The redundancy in the connections joining the subcliques can be seen to strengthen the ability of the clique as a whole to respond coherently and promptly to diverse challenges originating at different points in the elite system. The impact of idiosyncrasies in the characteristics of individual mediators that serve to filter or bias information flows is considerably reduced under conditions of multiple mediating pathways. The multiple mediators, drawn from diverse institutional areas, also increase the likelihood that specialized information from a given institutional sector will find suitable channels to flow from one subclique to the other, even in the face of the personal animosities of the two key influentials.[2]

Heightening the importance of his associates in the Senate, as we shall see, Conkling probably made use of his own relatives in his information system. He had a brother Fred who always sat in a high post at the Chamber of Commerce. He also had a nephew, Horatio Seymour, Jr., working at the state engineer's office, which had responsibilities for receiving reports from both the railroads and the canal. The Senator, from just these links, appears to have had an information system that kept him well informed. The civil service reformers, however, raised so much criticism about his public career that their professional descendants have set aside any evaluation of these arrangements.

Once the information network was in place, members began to work on the exchange of information, and they worked toward a reputation of honesty. Laumann and Knoke further note:

> To be of any value, information must be relevant, timely, and trustworthy. Every actor is thus dependent to a varying degree on other interested actors for crucial pieces of information that tell it, among other things, when critical events affecting its interests are going to occur or have happened and often with what potential consequences. No actor, however well endowed in organizational resources, has a monopoly on all the information relevant to its concerns. Moreover, even if an organization is the sole source of certain information of relevance to a policy decision, it typically gains nothing from that monopoly until it communicates that information to relevant others, who must be willing to accept its trustworthiness. Herein lies the reason for the remark often made by our informants that reputation as an honest, reliable source of information is an essential asset for an effective [read: "influential"] claimant organization.[3]

Conkling would emphasize the importance of honesty at different junctures—the opening of his campaign speech for Garfield and his warning to his supporters at Albany knowing that the district attorney was working on reports of bribery. These reminders to others would have represented his part in maintaining his information system, and expecting others to do as much.

An Example of Redundancy and Duration in a Senate Committee: The Pacific Railroads Committee

Before covering Conkling's information system in further detail, a return to the system for the transcontinental railroad the previous decade will prove instructive by comparison. Beginning in 1863 the Republican leaders of the Senate, in organizing the committee on Pacific railroads, provided a pristine example of an information network in the Gilded Age Senate. What associations Conkling later developed, reported in Table 2, followed on the habits of the Senate culture, shown in Table 1.

While both parties before the war had adopted planks favoring the transcontinental railroad, the occasion for organizing the standing committee came later—after the construction project had begun. Work had proceeded into Kansas and then ran into difficulties. Subsequently, the Senate organized the committee. Once in place, it could possibly get better cooperation out of the departments in Washington. They would overcome their difficulties, and the project in the West then resumed. Table 1 displays the evidence of using pairs of members, redundancies, traveling between committees for a period beginning in 1863 and running over the subsequent 8 years, just beyond the closing of the construction. To repeat, the special arrangements in the committee on Pacific railroads detail the practice used later by committees where Roscoe Conkling sat, and used again on two other occasions important to the story line here.

In order to set forth this longitudinal study, I first had to discover when the *Congressional Globe* first carried the name of the railroad committee along with the names of its members. As a rule committee slates appeared in the record near the opening of a congress. Next, I prepared a card for each member of the body. On the card I included five or six items of information. I wrote on the card the member's name, party, and home state, the name of the committee he chaired, and the names of the other committees he sat on as well as their chairs, and the states and parties of those chairs. Sometimes I added other information I thought necessary, such as his seniority by the congress he entered. Then, I compared the cards to discover those members who served together on pairs of committees. Finally, I repeated all of the steps for each of the subsequent Congresses until I had reason to stop. The following cards for just two members of the Senate show examples of their assignments in 1863 to both the Pacific railroads committee and the finance committee:

Committees for John Conness of California:

On Finance under William P. Fessenden of Maine, also

On Post Offices under Jacob Collamer of Vermont, and also

On Pacific Railroads under Jacob Howard of Michigan

Committees for John Sherman of Ohio:

Chair of Agriculture, also

On Finance under Fessenden of Maine, also

On Patents under Edgar Cowan of Pennsylvania, and also

On Pacific Railroads under Howard of Michigan

From just these two cards, the extra pathway for information is apparent. Conness and Sherman served together on the two committees of finance and Pacific railroads, allowing the conjecture that together they sat on both committees in order to pass specialized information back and forth. It is likely that the two men were critical in helping both the Pacific railroads committee and the U.S. Treasury in scheduling bond issues authorized by Congress. The arrangement to link the two committees was not merely for one Congress but for several. It showed the continuing importance, for example, of the flow of information from the U.S. Treasury to the committee.

Table 4. The Duration and Redundancy in the Seating of Senators on the Pacific Railroads Committee, 38th through 41st Congresses, 1864 through 1869.

Associated Committees:	Congress / Year			
	38th 1864[1]	39th 1865[2]	40th 1867[3]	41st 1869[4]
Finance	Sherman, OH	Sherman, OH	Sherman, OH*	Sherman, OH*
	Conness, CA	Morgan, NY	Morgan, NY	Fenton, NY
Military Affairs	Howard, MI(Chmn.)	Howard, MI(Chmn.)	Howard, MI(Chmn.)	Howard, MI(Chmn.)
	Morgan, NY	Brown, MO	Wilson, MA*	Wilson, MA*
	Brown, MO			Abbott, SC
Post Offices	Collamer, VT*	Conness, CA	Conness, CA	Ramsey, MN*
	Conness, CA	Ramsey, MN*	Ramsey, MN*	
Public Lands	Harlan, IA*			
Indian Affairs	Harlan, IA		Harlan, IA	Harlan, IA*
	Brown, MO			
Judiciary	Howard, MI	Stewart, NV	Stewart, NV	Stewart, NV
	Trumbull, IL*			
Agriculture	Harlan, IA			
	Sherman, OH*			
Mines		Conness, CA*	Conness, CA*	Stewart, NV
		Stewart, NV	Stewart, NV	
Library	Collamer, VT*		Morgan, NY*	
Audit		Brown, MO*		
Public Bldgs		Brown, MO*		
District of Col.			Harlan, IA*	
Education			Harlan, IA*	

Notes: 1) Chairs of the sending committees are marked with an asterisk. (*). 2) Throughout the period Senator Howard of Michigan was chair of Pacific Railroads. 3) The left-hand column shows the names of the associated committees that sent members to the main committee. 4) The underlined committee names are those first mentioned by Senator William Gwin of California under the previous Democratic control.

Sources:
[1] Thirty-Eighth Congress: 1st session; *The Congressional Globe (CG)*, Volume 34, Part 2, 101f, January 6, 1864.
[2] Thirty-Ninth Congress, 1st Session, *CG*, Vol. 36, Dec. 6, 1865.
[3] Fortieth Congress, 1st Session, *CG*, Vol. 38, page 12, March 7, 1867
[4] Forty-First Congress, 1st Session, *CG*, Vol. 41, page 27f, March 8, 1869.

This array of names is of those Republican senators who in an eight-year period, from the 38th through the 41st Congress, served on the Pacific railroad committee. Since the committee had to depend on a number of other committees for important information, the leadership assigned a pair of members from no fewer than three other committees:

finance, military affairs and post offices and post roads. When the committee assembled for a meeting, one of each pair could transmit needed information while the other one could corroborate it. In addition to the two members from finance that likely linked to Treasury, two senators who also sat on the committee on post offices and postal roads would have worked on information about the right of way across the territories and the carrying of mail to settlers. Finally, the two senators who also sat on the committee on military affairs would likely have managed information from the War Department about the necessities of moving troops, munitions and supplies.

Notably, whenever a member dropped off the committee, a successor from the same sending committee replaced him, assuring the durability of the original inter-committee connection. This array does not disclose the size of the workload imposed on each member, but filling a subsequent vacancy leaves the inference that the connection was important. Senator Conness of California apparently represented finance on the Pacific railroads committee, and when he left, Senator Edwin Morgan of New York, another member of finance, immediately replaced him. When Senator B. Gratz Brown of Missouri, apparently representing military affairs, left the railroad committee, Henry Wilson of Massachusetts from military affairs took his place.

Further, because these three committees each sent two members to the Pacific railroads committee, the committee assured it could reduce any bad blood between the committee members. The problem cited by historian David Donald that "senators are such prickly and egotistical persons that alliances among them tend to be short-lived" was largely mitigated.[4] From the table it is obvious that Senators Howard, Sherman and Harlan had an eight-year association. Rather, in this critical work of the Senate the prickly egotists might have found that they needed help in understanding new, complex transportation problems and they learned their lessons because of the assurances that they could win corroboration for all incoming information. In brief, the committee would have believed that the information was too important for a single intermediary to handle. Redundancy helped the Pacific railroads committee skirt the idiosyncrasies of the actor's personality as well as assure a rapid advance in knowledge for all the actors. With most members helping one another advance in understanding, committee life became a school or a seminar.

In addition, the Pacific railroads committee could respond quickly and confidently to comments from other significant sources in and out of the government. As a result, it probably supervised many adjustments. With its growing authority, the committee became a clearinghouse for the transcontinental project. Note that in the 40th Congress, when the project was coming to a close, members from the first three supporting committees were chairs of those committees. The other member of each of the pairs was the number two member of the supporting committee. That flank of six made it easier to gain greater compliance from the respective departments. The arrangement would have relayed the confidence of the Senators and increased the public confidence in the entire work just as the great accomplishment came to a conclusion.

Petitioners on later policy would not always follow the sequence of steps. Party platforms had supported the plans for the transcontinental railways. U. S. Grant would later support water transportation. The Garfield administration reversed the course as major supporters discounted platforms. When the railroaders of 1881 tried to win congressional approval for their national consolidation, they made the attempt without first winning support from the 1880 platform. They also persuaded Garfield not to mention the issue in his acceptance letter. In spite of the promoters skirting the party platform and the candidate's acceptance letter, they kept pressing their legislation. To make sense afterwards of what had happened in the Garfield administration, publicists relied on melodrama.

Party leaders, however, made sense by taking another course. They had enough wit and regret to bring matters back to the protocols of affecting a hierarchy of announcements. At the top level was the pronouncement by the Court as well as one by President Chester Arthur. They provided the leverage for the next step down: Convention managers, "retracing their steps," installed a plank on the topic in the party platform and the convention delegates endorsed it. That convention action on the platform, next gave the leverage to party leaders in the legislative body, the Congress, when it convened, and they took the responsibility to assign the issue to the proper committee. Party leaders, now responsible to both the platform and the executive, had assumed control of the issue and they named the committee members with freshman Shelby Cullom as the committee chairman. Finally, the committee began its work by touring the country to take testimony. There is a hint here about the return of balance between the petitioners (lobbyists) on the one hand and the elected policy makers on the other. The politicians were completely in control since it was clear that the special interest group had not named the committee members as they had tried to do in 1881. Thus, the national convention of 1884, and subsequent Congress, turned out quite differently from the 1880 meeting and subsequent Congress.

The Numbers

Members of the U.S. Senate appear to have worked consciously within a range of numbers. First, the Senate custom usually compelled members to select only *four* committee assignments and let all other opportunities go. Second, they were sometimes involved in forming *pairs* between committees to corroborate information. Third, these links persisted over *several* Congresses. Fourth, when anyone left a committee, someone who could make the same link for the committee, whether to another committee, a state, or a region, most often filled the vacancy. Such persistent patterns of Senate organization should give any investigator confidence about the source material with which one has to work. In 1963 historian William O. Aydellotte wrote that quantitative study could challenge prevailing views.

> An orderly arrangement of the evidence is a major step toward coming to terms with it . . .. As we work into a problem, we sometimes find that certain information proves usable in ways not expected. The very nakedness of the results, the intolerable character of the discrepancy of this kind, is a stimulant to reformulation and may also give a good indication of the direction in which it can be attempted.[5]

How essential was a Committee Hierarchy?

The practice of the caucus allowing the doubling up of members between committees apparently had very little to do with the so-called structure. The job was to get a report to the floor of the chamber and have it sustained. In getting there they could always draw upon others momentarily as they saw fit. Authority came from their command of the facts along with the public demand to do something. A formal structure could not assure such desired results when it came to the presentation of their report on the floor. Members, indeed, may have believed that information management was much more significant than structure. Investigators may miss the priority altogether. For example, historian David Rothman has written, "In the decade and a half after Grant's inauguration, neither Democratic nor Republican organizations ordered Senate proceedings . . . unity was not achieved through the systematic use of organizational machinery."[6] Such a system would probably have had an executive board of senators making assignments and supervising the work of the committees. However, network analysts have repeatedly found information systems, irrespective of their setting in a hierarchy. The analysts assert *"organizations strive to reduce uncertainty, information costs, and opportunistic behaviors of members by creating relatively stable channels of information and thereby develop certain norms of the game."*[7](Our italics.) The evidence of these efforts may appear in either a hierarchical or flat, non-hierarchical organizational environment. Rather than being a predictable feature of some specific organizational model, the circumspection aims at making inter-organizational relations more stable. Indeed, the committee arrangement made for efficiency. Any oversight by a board would have made work less efficient. Similarly, another habit of thought among historians shows a preference for hierarchical thinking. That is, the expectation has been that senior members chaired committees. The evidence, however, provides many examples of the opposite. The expectation works only with modification.

Again and again, members of an elite subclique (legislative committee) expected to reduce uncertainty in the way they handled information. They sought to reduce the time they had to wait for information mediated through some third party. The same principle is found in industry where, for example, employees of one company, with management approval, establish direct communication with employees of another company. They proceed without a third party or a hierarchy having to supervise. Employees of a rolling mill may then develop direct communications with employees of a manufacturing firm. Information can then flow back and forth between the men on the floor of the rolling mill and men on the floor of the stamping plant. There is no interference. They improve their product in ways not imagined by the engineering departments or managements.

Warren Bennis, former president of the University of Cincinnati, writing in 1966 of future organizations, could just as well have been writing about the Senate response to the transcontinental railroad a century earlier:

> These will be task forces organized around problems-to-be solved by groups of relative strangers with diverse professional skills. The group will be arranged on an organic rather than mechanical model; they will evolve in response to a problem rather than to programmed role expectations. . . . Organizational charts will consist of project groups rather than stratified functional groups. [8]

Examining the Pacific railroads committee of the 1860s, network analysis could plausibly conclude that the members of the U.S. Senate had arranged a quite mature form of organization. Their aim was getting the job done. They sought concurrence on their reports from the rest of the Senate. Their methods were not only functional to transcontinental transportation but also capable of sustaining their own integrity from Congress to Congress. In the immediate postwar period the Congress was not necessarily more primitive and inept in its organizational arrangements than later, say in the 1890s. Legislators usually create the necessary bureaucracy to get their work done in a usable form for others.

Later, they may have to pay the cost of watching their creature, a project or a department, dominate them, the creator. But then the Senate can always assert its rights of the pursuing oversight, even to the point of restricting an overzealous executive. All that the caucus needs to do is divide work into the committees of jurisdiction mirroring the spending departments. In addition, two members from each committee on jurisdiction would also serve on the larger oversight committee. The oversight committee has the power to command the attention of the principal departmental officers. Congress would not regard itself as the final arbiter on the effectiveness of oversight, but rely on a free press to help to get to the bottom of things. Whatever obstructs a free press should have Congress's attention. Offsetting the prospect of scandal, the caucus would arrange committees to assure that members would work with corroborated information.

In the nation's history redundancy began very early. The Constitution provided that each state sends *two* persons to the U.S. Senate, and that the legislative branch has two houses. Early on, some state official carried the practice into transportation management. In "Connecticut . . . as early as 1803 . . . an act was passed providing *two* commissioners should be appointed annually for each turnpike in the state, with powers to inspect and compel repairs."[9] That would have assured authorities and other parties that the commissioners easily corroborated information. The pair would more likely give fair treatment, make rapid decisions and lessen the chance that an idiosyncratic personality would grandstand or sabotage the process. By the time Congress got to the business of the Pacific railroads, leaders simply assumed that arranging for pairs was the way to handle the matter.

Conkling's Committee Experience

In the New York–Upper Mississippi Valley Senate coalition this phenomenon has obvious importance for investigators. If one tracks two or more Congresses to discover a legislator's own choice of committees, they may conclude that any continuity had some importance for the legislator. Discovering that importance is the challenge. If they also note that he travels in a pair between committees, there may be further significance for the assignment as an information network. Should investigators come upon reasonable explanations that free them from indulging in prejudices against the legislator they need not continue pejorative treatment through mere convention. In the face of Conkling's continuous cooperation with members from the Upper Mississippi states there can be the inference that he had an interest in the transportation policy or was not just interested in patronage.

Seeing how senators of the 1860s organized their workload, we can better understand the wisdom of the Senate culture guiding the committee arrangements involving Senator Roscoe Conkling of New York. When still in his first term, he had already shown a marked sensitivity to the peculiar needs of his state when he managed to become chair of the committee on revision of the statutes. At that time the New York Bar Association was first organizing.[10] Under the law, commissioners set to work to produce volumes that would have proven very useful in the New York attorneys' offices. When he won re-election in 1873 and transportation difficulties arose he was ready to make links to important sources of information that would keep him on top of affairs.

Conkling committee arrangements existed during two major crises in transportation. The first entailed complaints from farmers in the upper Mississippi Valley while the second entailed the port of New Orleans as a competitor in exporting. At first, the difficulty in the mid-1870s consisted of getting the surplus grain from the upper Midwest to the east coast. The farmers in the upper Mississippi valley often faced extortionate rates that took most of the incentive out of farming. Benson wrote in 1955:

> The cry for low freight charges and transportation regulation spread nationwide. Angry outbursts in the Old Northwest against railroad policies simply sounded one variation on a general theme. Yet, two points deserve stress: nowhere did agitation attain greater intensity during the early seventies than in the upper Mississippi valley [Wisconsin and Minnesota]; in-

tense agitation there undoubtedly had a catalytic effect upon developments elsewhere.[11]

In the upper Mississippi valley farmers' livelihoods were endangered. In response, an early step taken by Congress consisted of collecting and evaluating information. First, Senator William Windom of Minnesota, elected to the Senate in 1871, formed the select committee on transportation routes to the seaboard that appeared on the committee slate at the opening of the 43rd Congress. It included Conkling, Sherman, and others. Very early the committee went to Canada to appraise alternative routes to Europe. They were on their way home when the bond market failed, sending some railroads into bankruptcy. Their collapse had a ripple effect with companies that had extended them credit, bringing many more companies into financial embarrassment.

The collapse of the bond market, in turn, set off a new chain of events in railroad organization that raised more controversy. Since a bankrupt company could hold off paying interest on its debt, it could lower its freight rates, threatening the financial strength of the stronger companies. To protect themselves, some of the stronger railroads colluded to keep their rates up, causing consternation among the shippers. Rate wars among the rails had given the shippers market competition, which the owners detested. In short order, two opposing camps formed––the shippers and the railroaders.

Second, Senator Roscoe Conkling reacted along the line of those with whom he took committee seats. He apparently aimed at gaining critical information about the transportation problem. From 1873, in the 43rd Congress forward, Conkling and a senator from a neighboring state, either New Jersey or Vermont, joined members from the upper Mississippi valley. They straddled two committees; in the 44th Congress onward, three committees. The arrangement lasted at least six years. Obviously, New Jersey's Senator Frederick Frelinghuysen, former state attorney general and ambassador to London, would have had an interest in the port of New York. The Senate could expect him and the New Yorker to have settled most of their differences before their committee brought anything to the Senate floor. After Freylinghuysen left the Senate, a Vermont member from Burlington, George Edmunds, joined the committee. He would have been sensitive to the shipping needs, first of all, of Burlington businesses. Their lumber exports used sailboats convertible to canal boats that would go from Lake Champlain at Whitehall into the Champlain Canal and down the Hudson River to Albany and New York City. Secondly, the same senator would have had an interest in the great Vermont quarry industry that regularly sent blocks of stone down to New York City and on to other parts of the country for use on public and private buildings.

It is not immediately apparent how influence on the committee on the judiciary and the committee on commerce would benefit grain, timber and granite shipments to New York City. What happened was that Conkling had a choice to make. As a New Yorker in the Senate he could be assured that the caucus would recognize the state delegation's proprietary claim to defined committees. The caucus would grant seats to

New Yorkers on no fewer than four committees: judiciary, commerce, foreign affairs, and finance. Conkling may have been reluctant to leave any of these apportioned seats to join a new committee on inter-state commerce. Rather, the other interested senators joined him on his committees of special interest to his state. When he had to talk with those men about matters other than his committee mandates, they had the cover to carry on conversations.

Together from that vantage point they could survey information on transportation matters important to themselves and the port of New York. The judiciary committee would excel in passing railroad legislation such as the Thurman Act, covering the Pacific railroads' debt. The commerce committee would handle work on appropriations for rivers and harbors. Therefore, some tie to transportation matters prevailed from where Conkling and his allies sat. Comparing the decision-making clique of the Pacific railroads committee with the arrangements on Conkling's committees, it appears that the earlier committee brought specialized interests from finance, military affairs, and post offices to one place in the railroad committee. The arrangements around Conkling entailed spreading a decision-making clique over several committees with no formal central point of collaborating on focused information. Conkling's information system came under duress in 1881 when the cartel sought to have Congress pass its legislation simply because that was the route that previous railroad legislation had traveled.

The alliance around Conkling may have found that they attracted important information due to the broad mandates of the several committees. Foreign affairs had to deal with treaties and tariffs. Commerce had to pay attention not only to customs houses but also to appropriations for rivers and harbors. Judiciary had take up nominations for the court. As members of the Senate sought to win both nominations for acquaintances to the bench and appropriations for rivers and harbors for their states, they might have had to discuss their preferences with the members around Conkling. In exchange Conkling and his allies might have won information and agreements from them. The members in the rest of the Senate very likely felt the influence of this sub-elite and tailored their requests to fit the requirements. While Conkling has left a record of giving "spread eagle" oratory, he could have also, through the requests he and his allies received, enjoyed "spread eagle" surveillance over the Senate.

The great change in American transportation in 1879 occurred with the entry of New Orleans as a rival to New York. Over the long term, that threat proved quite irregular since the Mississippi, as a means of transport, was not always reliable. In the early 1870s, as previously mentioned, the Senate had to monitor the difficulties between farmers and railroads in Minnesota and Wisconsin, leading to the rivers and harbors appropriations. During some seasons, shippers found it impossible to use the Mississippi River efficiently: low water all down the river created more shallows, often forcing boatmen to lighten their loads. Ice jams could also create many seasonal dangers. At New Orleans they had to break bulk to flatboats in order to take the product to oceangoing vessels anchored in the Gulf. Understandably, the great harbor at New York remained the more reliable and efficient port. Canal boats coming down the Hudson River could come along side of oceangoing vessels for unloading. In 1879 the scene changed dramatically when J. B. Eads successfully completed sluicing out the mouth of the Mississippi River. That project not only made New Orleans available for ocean shipping but also the city of Memphis up river. That would mark the beginning of inter-city rivalry between New York and New Orleans.

Table 5 shows the Republicans on Conkling's committees. At the outset is shown the judiciary committee from which the alliance often drew its members.

Table 5. The Duration and Redundancy in the Seating of Roscoe Conkling, 40th Congress, 1867 through 47th Congress, Executive Sessions, 1881.

Congress/Year	Committees		
	Judiciary	Commerce	Foreign Affairs
40th/1867	Edmunds, VT		
	Frelinghuysen, NJ		
	Conkling, NY		
41st/1869	Edmunds, VT	Conkling, NY	
	Conkling, NY		
	Carpenter, WI		
42nd/1871	Edmunds, VT	Conkling, NY	
	Frelinghuysen, NJ		
	Conkling, NY		
	Carpenter, WI		
43rd/1873	Edmunds, VT*	Conkling, NY	Conkling, NY
	Frelinghuysen, NJ	Frelinghuysen, NJ	
	Conkling, NY	Howe, WI	
	Carpenter, WI		
44th/1875	Edmunds, VT*	Conkling, NY*	Conkling, NY
	Frelinghuysen, NJ	McMillan, MN	Frelinghuysen, NJ
	Conkling, NY	Cameron, WI	Howe, WI
	Howe, WI		
45th / 1877	Edmunds, VT*	Conkling, NY*	Conkling, NY
	Conkling, NY	McMillan, MN	Howe, WI
	Howe, WI		
46th / 1879	Edmunds, VT**	Conkling, NY**	Conkling, NY
	Conkling, NY	McMillan, MN	Carpenter, WI
	Carpenter, WI		
47th/1881/Dem.*	Edmunds, VT**	Conkling, NY**	Conkling, NY**
	Conkling, NY	McMillan, MN	Pendleton, OH
	Pendleton, OH		
47th/1881/Rep	Edmunds, VT*	Conkling, NY*	Conkling, NY
	Conkling, NY	McMillan, MN	Edmunds, VT
	McMillan, MN		
Notes: * Committee chair ** Ranking minority member *** Slate not adopted			

Sources:
40th Cong., 1st sess., *Congressional Globe, CG*, Vol. 38, March 7, 1867, p. 12;
41st Cong., 1st sess., *CG*, Vol. 41, March 8, 1869, p. 24;
42nd Cong., 1st sess., *CG*, Vol. 44, Pt 1, March 10, 1871, pp. 33f;
43rd Cong., spec. sess., *Congressional Record (CR)*, Vol. 1, December 4, 1873 p. 56f.
The Congressional Record succeeded *The Congressional Globe* in 1873;
44th Cong., spec. sess., *CR*, Vol. 4, Pt. 1, March 9, 1875, pp. 8f;
45th Cong., 1st sess., *CR,* Vol. 6, March 9, 1877, p. 39;
46th Cong., 1st sess., *CR,* Vol. 9, Pt. 1, March 19, 1879, p. 15f.;
47th Cong., spec. sess., *CR*, Vol. 12, March 10, 1881, p. 5. Democratic slate for Senate committees not adopted. In this Democratic slate the committee on judiciary also included Ben Hill of Ga., and John Sherman of Ohio; *CR*, 47th Cong., spec. sess., Vol. 12, March 18, 1881, pp. 33f;
47th Cong., spec. sess., Adopted; *CR* Vol. 12, March 18, 1881, p. 33;

This table shall be the most significant in developing the story line here. It shows that Conkling found a way to continually associate with peers from the breadbasket states which shipped grain to New York and thus created an economic benefit for the port.

Senators Roscoe Conkling of New York and Frederick Frelinghuysen of New Jersey initiated this information network in 1873 when they took seats on both judiciary and foreign affairs. Concurrently, two men from Wisconsin, Timothy Howe and Matthew Carpenter, joined the same committees. Conkling and Freylinghuysen could together meet with Howe and/or Carpenter to get a clear picture of what was happening in the grain states. As Table 2 suggests, through his committee seating Conkling had, over a period of the next three congresses, easy access to at least two senators from the upper Mississippi states. It was an arrangement that would have allowed him to obtain corroborated information important to New York harbor interests. In the Congress that convened in 1873 Conkling began the association with upper-Mississippi senators the same year that William Windom formed his committee and made his report, a report that stood in high esteem even a dozen years later.

In 1875, halfway through Grant's second term, Angus Cameron, speaker of the Wisconsin House, defeated Carpenter, who had been holding a seat on judiciary, for the Senate. In a shuffle, Howe moved from commerce to judiciary while newcomer Cameron took the seat on commerce which Howe had occupied. Cameron would remain on Conkling's commerce committee for only one Congress.

In the U.S. Senate, Windom's committee on transportation routes to the seaboard would soon report and President Grant would announce his views on the matter. In the second session of the 44th Congress, Windom became chair of appropriations, enabling him to monitor expenditures for river and harbor improvements.

In the 45th Congress, Samuel McMillan of Minnesota, a former state Supreme Court chief justice, was the first Minnesotan in the alliance. Simultaneously, Senator Cameron of Wisconsin left the commerce committee to become chair of transportation routes, a committee where Windom remained a member.

For the 46th Congress (1879), Carpenter defeated Howe in the state legislature and took both of Howe's committee seats in Washington. McMillan's continuance meant redundancy was maintained for the upper Mississippi group. In the 47th Congress, Senator Edmunds of Vermont responded to the alliance by sitting on foreign affairs with New York's Conkling for the first time. McMillan of Minnesota, already on commerce, joined Edmunds and Conkling on judiciary. There was, however, no longer a pair of members from the upper Mississippi valley serving around Conkling.

In 1881, President Garfield selected Senator Windom, chair of appropriations, to serve as secretary of the Treasury. To succeed Windom in the Senate, Governor John Pillsbury of Minnesota named A. J. Edgerton, a former member of the state railway commission.

With the death of Garfield, Windom resigned from the Treasury, and returned to Minnesota. He was re-elected to the Senate to take the seat he had recently vacated. He took Conkling's seat on the Judiciary committee. His return to the U. S. Senate reflects positively upon the consistency of opinion in his own state legislature during this 1881 crisis period.

Conkling could also make use of additional information links, largely because businessmen in the state were so well organized and informed. The members of the Chamber of Commerce of New York each year received their copies of the organization's annual report. About half of the report consisted of a summary of exports and imports for the state. Apparently Joseph Nimmo compiled part of the report in the office of the chief of statistics in the Treasury. Some information on items was reported for the last three years while other information was reported for each of the past ten years or more. Any business leader in the city who kept himself abreast of Nimmo's annual reports could have helped the chamber, as a lobbying group, deal quite intelligently with the state's congressional delegation. The organization appears to have taken Nimmo's suggestions for improving the functioning of the port quite seriously. The merchants formed committees at the chamber addressing special difficulties he named. Thus it could be said that while New York senators or the Treasury officials had influence over the port, Joseph Nimmo had as much if not more.[12]

The Apparent Effect of Conkling's Committee Assignments on His Political Behavior

The relations in the senate alliance probably had an effect upon Conkling's political behavior. Some authorities might have believed that a person like Roscoe Conkling was under no constraint from those with whom he worked. If so, that increases the likelihood that authors can treat him melodramatically. He can be consigned as the evil one who deserves defeat and relegation beyond the pale. On the other hand, if one grants that a work group, such as a legislative committee, has importance for most of its members, another scenario unfolds. The membership of Conkling's committees could have shared a common interest explaining the course he took. That course often resulted in criticism from some groups in the state. Laumann and Knoke as well as others may see a cause-effect relation here. We follow Laumann and Knoke who wrote in 1987 that:

> First, we assume that corporate entities—such as trade associations, professional societies, labor unions, public interest groups, government bureaus, and *congressional committees*—are the key state policy-domain actors. Natural persons [such as an individual legislator] are important only insofar as they act on behalf and at the behest of these collectivities.[13] (Our emphasis.)

In the committee setting Conkling was known by the company he kept.

First, before giving plausible examples of how Conkling's committee associations influenced his behavior, some additional considerations are in order. Since New York commodity brokers owned well over half the grain en route to the city via the canal, Conkling could have paid attention to them. After his resignation, the Produce Exchange was one of the first groups to call for Conkling's re-election. From them, he could have learned what they thought about keeping rates low so that the commodity business in New York City remained more secure. The senators from the upper Mississippi states, by their affiliation on committees with Conkling, probably had their attention brought straight to the center of the New York economy. In exchange, they probably brought Conkling's attention straight to the center of the great grain-producing region of the upper Mississippi River. Interestingly, about two decades later, when President Theodore Roosevelt opened his first antitrust case, it was aimed at an upper Mississippi railroad monopoly, Northern Securities. That singular attention given by both Conkling and Roosevelt to the upper Mississippi River states, the nation's breadbasket, underscores just how much in those days commerce to the city depended on the eastward flow of grain.

The broadest generalization is that New Yorkers favored waterway traffic and praised Grant for his support. Anyone traveling across the country in the nineteenth century, in the absence of later transcontinental highways and airlines, had to rely on rails and waterways. Whereas the canals had operated for several decades and adopted improvements along the way, the railroads, established about the same time, did not turn to notable consolidations until about the 1860s. One great stimulus was "Commodore" Cornelius Vanderbilt's consolidating routes to Chicago. He had imaginings that some day flowers would grow in the bed of the Erie Canal. In time, his New York Central line achieved state-of-the-art operations, with not only the best equipment but also double tracks allowing traffic in two directions at once. The Vanderbilt family held most of the stock, making the Commodore, and then William, the head of a family-owned business. Without a widely representative board of directors to influence decisions, Cornelius and William were left to act autocratically if they wished. Some time after William's death in the mid-1880s, large amounts of stock were sold to insurance companies and charities.

A broad-based board was formed, allowing the company to become more responsive to the public.[14]

From the 1830s through the Civil War, the canal had poured wealth into New York. Settlements along the waterway grew into towns and then into cities. Canal receipts often exceeded all other state revenues. The canal made such a spectacular display that other states thought they could do as well, and canalling became quite the fashion. Indiana, for example, took on debt to build a canal, but as the rails grew, the canal found it hard to compete either in business or in lobbying. The Indiana canal pulled the state into bankruptcy and, like those in Illinois and Ohio, closed.

By the late 1870s, some New Yorkers wondered aloud whether their canals would close. Perhaps the rails were merely tolerating the canals. While canal supporters remained unfazed by reports of the greater share of traffic going to the railroads, they settled for competition in the bulk farm commodities. A key railroad leader, cartel manager Albert Fink, described the canal's advantage when he explained that each spring on the opening of the canal the railroads had to drop their rates to stay competitive. The practical consequence was that the profits from the freight on either carrier spread more widely to the shippers.

Several incidents strongly suggest that Conkling's Senate alliance had an effect on his behavior. In his annual message to Congress on December 1, 1873, Grant's mentioning the need for waterways could have been political cover for Conkling's new Senate alliance. Laumann and Knoke could classify the president's comments as a statement of preferences for specific policy options. Grant said that the "lack of cheap transportation" had contributed to the "recent panic [1873] and stringency" and he claimed that the nation needed an improved system of rivers and harbors. Grant declared that:

> This would be a national work; one of great value to the producers of the West and South in giving them cheap transportation for their produce to the seaboard and a market; and to the consumers in the East in giving them cheaper food particularly of those articles of food which do not find a foreign market, and the prices of which, therefore, are not regulated by foreign demand.

Grant had waited for the details in the long-expected Windom report on routes to the seaboard. On August 14, 1876, he signed the Rivers and Harbors Appropriations Bill, putting the government in a position to ensure waterway competition for the growing railroad industry.[15] Positions in the alliance soon opened up. In midsummer, Lot Morrill left his position as chair of appropriations and became secretary of the Treasury. Windom then left his post as chair of the transportation routes to the seaboard committee, and took over the appropriations committee, where he had been second in rank.[16] That put him in a position to monitor the spending on his plan, which Grant had approved. At that moment the Senate seemed to take the attitude that great measures could be turned over to their authors to execute. Accordingly, Sherman, who had worked out the plan for resumption, was made the secretary of the Treasury to execute the task. Along with Windom, Conkling, as chair of commerce, would also have a hand in internal improvements. The New Yorker became especially critical of appeals by many congressmen to improve waterways that were not much more than trout streams and hardly navigable.

There was another occasion of Conkling aiding his western allies having to do with an appointment to the Supreme Court. During the 44th Congress, when it was learned that the president was considering corporate attorney William Evarts as Chief Justice, Conkling intervened. Evarts not only had served as attorney general in the Johnson administration, but also more recently had helped the corporations in preparing their defense against the granger laws, which were then reaching the Supreme Court. Grant agreed with Conkling not to name Evarts and instead nominated Morrison Waite. The new chief justice would soon write the decision favoring the granger laws in *Munn v. Illinois.* Waite's work on the Court would have been completely consistent with the views of the men from the granger states. Plausibly, their influence within the New York–upper Mississippi alliance led Conkling to oppose fellow New Yorker Evarts on their behalf. Of course, the Waite appointment antagonized capitalists who would not have applauded Conkling for sidelining Evarts.

Conkling also would have his attention attracted by the New York bureaucracy, where the chief anchor interesting to him was in the post of surveyor and engineer. That post was important to both the railroads and the canals and was occupied by his nephew, Horatio Seymour, Jr. (1844-1907). In December 1874 Seymour became the state assistant surveyor and engineer. His father had been the wartime Democratic governor of New York and a well-known canal advocate. Young Seymour in 1867, as Whitford points out, had graduated from the Sheffield School of Engineering at Yale and was a member of the American Society of Civil Engineers. From 1867 to 1874 he had done survey work for several railroad companies and for a coal company.[17]

Seymour's office required that both the railroads and the canal file regular reports. It would not be surprising if the young Seymour passed the information on to Conkling. In those reports evidence might have appeared showing questionable stock issues. From all his sources of information, Seymour came to believe that changes in the rates of canal tolls had a direct bearing on just how far west the frontier would extend. He believed that if the tolls were dropped, new western frontiers would be opened in order to grow grains for the New York market. He announced:

> Reduction [in canal fees] in carrying to the seaboard will increase largely the area from which grain shipments can be drawn. Abolishing the westward tolls will pay the freight on a bushel, and this will add a strip of territory 50 miles wide, extending through Minnesota, Iowa, Kansas, Nebraska, Missouri, and Dakota, which now cannot send grain to market

at all, or must send via New Orleans. This region is equal to producing 100 million bushels, or more than the canals carried in 1880.

In 1877, Democrat Seymour won the statewide election as the state engineer and surveyor. He won the office again in 1879 despite the fact that it was a strong Republican year. That second victory may have been brought by a stroke of whimsy. New York Republicans posted Howard Soule, a known corruptionist, on the ballot.[18] While authors of the reformed tradition still fault the stalwarts for having slated Soule, the nomination also suggested that Conkling correctly believed he could steer the criticizing "scratchers." He had to opt for some political theater to keep them from sitting out the election. It is plausible that he needed to trump all other considerations in order to maintain an information network through a qualified and reliable blood relative. In fact, the scratchers came out in numbers, crossed party lines, and cast a protest vote against Soule and for Seymour, making Conkling's nephew the only Democrat to win statewide that year. What may have been important was not Conkling's effrontery in supporting corruptionist Soule but that Conkling's information network through his nephew remained intact.

Conkling's attention to his western allies may also have been evident during the currency debates. Much to the disgust of hard-money easterners, Conkling submitted petitions in favor of silver (along with a few petitions for gold). The petitions probably showed his western allies that their soft-money position had adherents in the East. Some New Yorkers became quite hostile to Conkling for the petitions. During the course of the currency debate, the New York Clearing House decided not to deal any further in silver.

Similarly, Conkling apparently exercised some influence in helping his friends win seats on committees. The silverite John P. Jones of Nevada, entering the Senate in 1873, two years later, apparently with Conkling's help, joined the finance committee. From Conkling's perspective that committee could have been too single-minded in support of the gold standard. True to his custom, Conkling sought to provoke a good discussion among the opposing interests on the committee.

Conkling's Views on the Erie Canal

Our conclusion is that Conkling had a strong interest in transportation binding him to allies in the West. Further, his public statements were consistent with that interest. In the mid-1870s, Senator Conkling, who only rarely came back to a topic a second time, expressed his views on the Erie Canal on at least three occasions in the *Times*. His first comment appeared shortly after the opening of the 43rd Congress, just as two Wisconsin senators joined his committee network. His second comment appeared after his nephew joined the office of state engineer and surveyor.[19] A third mention appeared in the 1880 campaign address for Garfield.

Conkling's view would have supported the necessity of market competition, even though it meant state ownership in order to achieve it. After the canals thawed in the spring and were "bottomed out" by workers scooping out the mud and trimming the banks, the boats began to move, providing a fleet of canal boats competing with the rails. Too numerous to combine or consolidate, they competed among themselves. A similar phenomenon appeared later on American highways when independent truckers did not combine or consolidate and kept rates low. Most important, in 1874 in his first comment on the canal, Conkling accurately projected that in five years (1879, the year of the Hepburn investigation) the policy discussion would come to a head. He made this forecast before the annual dinner of the New England Society in 1874, just a year after his Senate alliance formed:

> At this moment the times are full of signs and warnings for New York, threatening her commercial and material supremacy. I speak to those who know better than I the things, which might here be said; let me allude to one of them: "Clinton's Ditch" was dug to bring products of one part of this State to another. Soon this great work of statesmanship and forecast transcended its mission, and bore to the sea from western states a traffic greater than that of the River Rhine, flowing through seven sovereignties in the heart of Europe. The Erie Canal, enriching and draining vast regions, poured like a golden river into the city of New York.

> Transportation can be cheapened; it will be cheapened, and the tracks will be marked anew for a colossal commerce. Shall New York have it? Shall Canada have it? Shall Pennsylvania and Maryland have it? Who shall have it?

> Men hear me who will do much to decide the question. Terminal facilities in this city, elevators, harbor accommodations, seagoing opportunities—these are factors in the problem, as well as canal or railway policy and advantages of route. Here is a huge unfinished work for this State and this city, and he who lives for five years will see a vast stake won or lost by what shall yet be done or left undone.

> The subject urges itself upon us in a double aspect. Laying aside the inquiry who shall profit by handling an untold traffic, the matter of cheap transportation touches the prosperity of the West, and whatever touches the prosperity of any section or State of the Union touches the prosperity of New York. Nothing affecting the welfare of any community in the nation can be without influence on this metropolis. There is not a state or city in all our borders which can be blighted without shriveling us. The bonds of every State, the bonds of the railways that gridiron the West and the South, are held in great sums in the East and in the North. Whatever wounds any member of the Union, we feel also; whatever fertilizes and enriches the most distant field invigorates this Commonwealth.[20]

Among other things, the senator had in mind the legendary conflict between the cities of Boston, New York, Philadelphia, Baltimore and New Orleans for the transatlantic trade. Since New York had such a disproportionate share of the total U.S. commerce, about two-thirds, a loss of traffic might not seem important to New York but the loss could provide a bonanza gained by a smaller port. Thus, other cities had the motive to take any commerce they could. When New Orleans began taking trade away from New York at the end of the decade, they did so with little apology. Rather, they were quite gleeful to take the trade. In such a political atmosphere of envy, how would the senator fare, especially if he did not have an ally in the White House, as Grant had been?

Although in the foregoing passage Conkling focused on the effect of western prosperity on the bond market, within a year he returned to the transportation issue, discussing "combination," or monopoly, probably disclosing the views of allies on his Senate committees along with Windom heading the committee on transportation routes to the seaboard. In the second address, he said:

> The Erie Canal has brought untold wealth to this city. However, much of it is slipping away. The sea end of the canal is blocked by want of elevators and terminal facilities. Philadelphia, Baltimore, and Montreal are draining off through other channels the seagoing products of the West. Grain and other bulky freights are handled more cheaply at these other ports than here. This subject needs attention, and interwoven with it, of course, is the preservation of the canals themselves.

> The canal is the only sure reliance against railway combinations to raise freights. A waterway is cheaper than a railway for bulky commodities, and the Erie Canal, running parallel with the Erie and Central roads, is during seven months of the year their competitor, and is the one power preventing such high rates of transportation as will drive to other routes a portion of the commerce due to us.

> This matter should be watched more closely than ever now, because of the law which last Winter made its way through the Legislature and received the signature of the Governor. Before this act came into being, the statutes expressly forbade any consolidation between the Erie and the Central Roads, and forbade the Directors of one to be Directors of the other. Here was a partition built between the two, to make them rivals. However, the act of last winter is an act of repeal, and now the same men may be the Directors of both roads. Freight combinations have free course now, and unless combinations were intended, it is not easy to see the purpose of this legislation. This gives us new reason to be wary of hostility to the canals.[21]

In using the term "combinations," Conkling showed that he was aware of his constituents' understanding of changes in railroad organization. He also showed that he realized that the railroads and canals had each other in mind and were subject to a common fate. From the perspective of a policy scenario, what is interesting is whether Conkling, here identifying with the canal side of the issue, would continue to support it.

Conkling's Attitude after Grant's Presidency

As Grant's second term ended, the *Times* noted that Conkling became more ill tempered. New York had great advantages in transportation, and plausibly the senator knew that he would never again have such favorable executive support. As the convention and campaign season began, Conkling had at least three options, each appearing and then fading. For a moment, a Grant third term had been a topic, but that soured quickly. Next, Conkling was nominated at the Cincinnati Republican National Convention, probably in the hope that as president, he could give New York continuing influence over transportation affairs. This came to naught when the convention gave him fewer than 100 votes. The party instead turned to Rutherford B. Hayes. Conkling's next opportunity appeared when the national election results led to the dispute over the vote count between Hayes, an Ohio Republican, and Samuel Tilden, a New York Democrat. If Tilden won, a person open to New York interests would again occupy the White House. Perhaps showing his preference, Conkling scoffed at the news that the Republicans could count on election returns from Florida. He then supported a plan to create a special commission to review the Electoral College votes. When the Tilden candidacy finally failed, Conkling lost his last option. In 1877, the *Times* noted the change in his attitude.

> For years past, Mr. Conkling was always assumed to be the most courteous of men, the pink of chivalry. Did he wish to attack an opponent upon the floor of the Senate, he did so with a delicacy of polite consideration, which was worthy of all commendation. His enemy was always "his distinguished friend," "the learned gentleman on the other side," "the deeply-read Senator," or "my gifted colleague who has just taken his seat." Since his defeat at Cincinnati, however, the Senator seems to have been studying other methods. It is evident that he is now trying to be natural, but it is to be regretted that as yet he has only succeeded in displaying a woeful lack of that dignity and tact which the people have a right to expect from a man in his position.[22]

Conkling's attitude illustrates Laumann and Knoke's point that the behavior of an actor in a policy domain depends partly on the "characteristics of the policy domain and the nature of the controversy in which policy deliberations are taking place." As Conkling's place in the Senate alliance turned disappointing, he became grim and offensive. Hayes seemed to turn against him. Now secretary of State, Evarts, aside from his foreign policy duties, could help Hayes with New York appointments. Then the president issued Civil Service Order Number One, curbing office holders' participation in party management. Subsequently, Hayes dismissed Chester Arthur and Alonzo Cornell from posts in the Customs House.

The Tiff between Curtis and Conkling at the 1877 State Convention

Everything blew up at the 1877 state Republican convention. George William Curtis, proponent of civil service reform and friend of the administration, appeared at the meeting to win support for Civil Service Order Number One. Although Conkling's friends argued that state conventions often failed to toe the line on presidential requests, Curtis took upon himself the task of scolding the state leadership:

> The President has taken up the war against the evils and abuses of civil service. Now, Sir, it is a serious and a hearty war. The question is, whether in the war which he has thus begun—whether . . . we will support the President of our choice . . . One of the great mischiefs of the civil service as we have seen it, and especially, Sir, in the State of New York, is that interference with the freedom of elections against which all the great statesmen lifted up their voices.[23]

The comment raised the hackles of Conkling, Platt, and their peers. It was tantamount to a governor today sending a representative to a faculty meeting at a large state university to announce, "The governor has taken up a war against the evils of the tenure system." Not knowing what would come next, the atmosphere would have become electric. Conkling rebuked Curtis by dismissing "men milliners" taking part in politics. (Ironically, Conkling was one of the fanciest dressers of the time.) The two men tried to put this matter behind them and in the subsequent state convention were at peace, but that moment of peace hardly meant that others would forget the comment.

A reasonable opinion on the incident, of course, would require hearing both sides of the story. It began after the 1876 national convention, when Conkling irritated the Hayes camp because he did not take to the stump. To some, it looked as if he was sulking, bringing him under criticism from both friends and foes. Finally, in response to Curtis's attack, he gave his explanation. He had contracted malaria in 1876 and decided to fight it by taking a rest cure abroad. At the state convention Conkling's explanation not only proved touching but also disclosed his preferred style of consulting with presidents, suggesting the manner he would want to follow in the new administration:

> Surely, no Republican in this State has made war on the present Administration to my knowledge. It cannot be denied that wanton assaults have been made [on us] . . . . If the convention will pardon a personal allusion, I will illustrate this in my own case, though other cases are not less marked. We hear unmeasured denunciation of men holding

office—taking part in political campaigns. Last year I was an officeholder, as I am this year, and malarial disease contracted in Washington disabled me for months. It was out of the question to undertake the labors of a canvass, but contrary to the positive injunction of my physician, I attempted to address my neighbors on the issues of the day, and the attempt gave sufficient caution against its repetition. Because I did not and could do no more, I, as an officeholder, have been bitterly denounced far and wide to this day, and by the same men who now insist that every man in office who even signs a notice of a convention shall be degraded and removed, so flagrant is it deemed, of a sudden, for officeholders to take part in the work of the Republican Party.

[Since then] no utterances, hostile to men or measures, have proceeded from me; not a straw has been laid in the way of any man or of his ambitions or schemes. But, still I have been the object of persistent assaults and misrepresentations, coming, it so happens, from those claiming to speak especially for the National Administration. On returning home, a few words of greeting could not be spoken to neighbors and personal friends of both parties, without drawing down bitter and scornful denunciations for not making a political speech endorsing the policy of the administration. Not a word of reply has escaped me . . . I deeply regret all these things, insofar as they are personal and aimed at individuals. They are of little consequence as far as they are the acts of those who heretofore deserted and betrayed the Republican Party [in the election of 1872], and are now striving to make it subserve their personal advancement . . .The future will test the sincerity of all concerned in this respect.

Mr. Hayes, when inaugurated, deserved from the party which supported him just what Mr. Lincoln and Gen. Grant deserved at the outset of their Administration. What is that? Fair, friendly, and dispassionate consideration of his acts. Wherever he is right he should be sustained. Wherever he is misled by unwise or sinister advice, at a proper time and in a proper spirit, dissent should be expressed. This right of judgment is the right of every citizen. It is a right which, in common with others, I exercised personally, and in the seats . . . in the national councils under the administrations both of Mr. Lincoln and of Gen. Grant. Neither of them ever objected to this. Both were thankful to any man who, in good faith, stated reasons corrective of their action. They never deemed an honest difference of opinion cause for war or quarrel, nor were they afflicted by having men hang around them, engaged in setting on newspapers to hound every man who was not officious or abject in fulsomely praising them. They sometimes made mistakes, too, and they manfully corrected them, and retraced false steps in the presence of the whole people more than once. Who has the right to suppose that Mr. Hayes will in these respects differ from his illustrious predecessors?[24]

If historians fail to mention Conkling's complete response to Curtis, then the convention delegates' embarrassment due to Conkling's comment on "men milliners" has to be marked down as a loss to the senator. On the other hand, recognizing Conkling's full response gives grounds for a later surmise: as he later waited for a response from President Garfield regarding a nomination, what might have been passing through his mind?

The Interest of Conkling's New York Constituency in the Canal

Momentum for Conkling's alliance recovered in early 1878 as his committees received new information. On February 13, 1878, at a meeting of the New York Board of Trade, A. B. Miller, chair of the Board's committee on canals, offered a resolution favoring a free Erie Canal. The board adopted it unanimously and without debate.[25] At the board meeting the following month, Miller read a report from Joseph Nimmo of the Federal Bureau of Statistics, who also advocated a free canal:

> The writer begins with the assertion that Montreal will never be able to compete with New York City for her commerce, and the prediction that the Welland Canal will not help it against the aid afforded to New York by the Erie Canal. He next advocates the policy of making the latter canal free, and suggests that another good thing to do would be to make New York harbor as free as those of Boston, Philadelphia and Baltimore. On this point he offers numerous arguments, and quotes some statistics which he received several years ago from Col. Edward Hincken, who adds: "Although the Port of New York owes its prosperity to commerce, there is no state in the Union that has done so little to encourage it as New York. Its commerce has grown up in the face of the enormous sums paid yearly to the Commissioners of Emigration, Commissioners of Quarantine, enormous rates of pilotage, and unserviceable wharves, for which large sums are fleeced out of vessel owners."

> Gen. Nimmo says, "The United States tax on gross receipts from passengers and on profits has been removed, but yet the remaining taxation at New York would, according to this statement, be 10 times as great as at Liverpool." If you throw into the scale wharfage, harbor dues, and the various legitimate and illegitimate exactions upon vessels, you will probably realize the fact that the wheels of commerce are clogged at New York in a most extraordinary manner. Gen. Nimmo cites the case of the Allan Line of steamers, which was recently prevented from making New York their United States terminus by the great charges and were forced to

go to Philadelphia. He also speaks depreciatingly of the exorbitant charges imposed upon the Long Island packets, and quotes from Gov. Robinson's last message to the effect that it is probable many of these charges would not be sustained under recent Supreme Court decisions.

A free canal and a free harbor are objects worthy of special interest at this time. Twenty years ago New York occupied the position in commerce of a sort of *cul de sac*. The superiority of her advantages for both the import and export trade of the United States was so marked that no special effort was needed to prevent commerce from being deflected to rival ports. However, it is not so today. The equipoise of trade is now exceedingly delicate. A very small difference in price or in cost of transportation or handling, or a slight detention or annoyance, will not only turn trade from the door of the merchants but from the harbor of a city.[26]

Twice in two months the Board of Trade had taken up the issue of the canal. Such attention could only mean that the question among New York merchants had become quite salient. Taken together with Conkling's alliance with senators from the upper Mississippi Valley, there can be little denying how important the topic of water traffic was becoming.

Cartel Manager Albert Fink Provides Information to Senator William Windom

In a few weeks, another member of the alliance, Senator William Windom, had an announcement. He had obtained important information about the Erie Canal's value to the nation from railroad cartel manager Albert Fink. The senator had written the cartel manager asking him to describe the effect that the spring opening of the canal had on railroad rates. Fink's reply was important because it constituted transmitting information from a consequential leader on one side of the regulation issue to a consequential leader on the other side. Since Windom as head of appropriations might influence outlays for levies, jetties, and breakwaters important to railroads, Fink would hardly have wanted to deny the senator his request. Because Fink's answer to Windom proved so important to New York interests, Conkling in his stump speeches for a third term may not even have had to mention the matter. What Fink explained was that the canal opening, beyond helping New York canal rates, had a ripple effect across the nation. Windom read Fink's sensational letter to the Senate:

In your letter of April 29 [1878], you asked me to explain the effect of the opening of navigation on the lakes upon the rates of transportation charged by railroads extending from the West to the interior of the Gulf States. You are aware that when the rates are reduced between Chicago and New York on account of the opening of the canal that this reduction applies not only to Chicago but to all interior cities (St. Louis, Indianapolis,

Cincinnati) to New York. If that was not the rule, the result would be that the roads running, say, from Saint Louis, Indianapolis, and Cincinnati to Chicago would carry the freight to Chicago, from which points low rates would take it to the East and leave the direct road from the interior points to the seaboard without any business. Hence, whenever the rates are reduced on account of the opening of navigation from Chicago and lake ports, the same reduction is made from all interior cities, not only to New York, where the canal runs, but also to Philadelphia and Baltimore. Although the latter cities have no direct water communication with the West, yet they receive the benefit as far as railroad rates are concerned, the same as if a canal were running from the lakes direct to these cities. [If these cities did not respond,] the business would all go to New York.

The reduction of the rates from Chicago and Saint Louis to Baltimore causes a reduction in rate on shipments via Baltimore to Atlantic ports––––Norfolk, Wilmington, Port Royal, Savannah, Brunswick and Ferridandina, &c––––and from there into the interior Atlantic Gulf States–––Augusta, Atlanta, Macon, Montgomery, Selma, &c. The roads running from Chicago and Saint Louis via Louisville and Nashville or Memphis and Chattanooga to the same points are obliged to follow the reductions made via the Baltimore route, and which were primarily made on account of the existence of the Erie Canal and the opening of navigation.

The same way about the westbound business. When rates are reduced from New York to Chicago, the roads from New York to Louisville reduce their rates on shipments by way of Louisville to Memphis, Nashville, Montgomery, Selma &c., and the southern transportation lines via Norfolk, Wilmington, Charleston, Savannah, &c., have to reduce their rates to meet those made by the northern lines to the same points.

It appears from the above statement that the Erie Canal and the lakes exercise their influence over the southern country until it reaches a line where low ocean rates made in the Gulf cities––Mobile, New Orleans, and Galveston––exercise their influence upon the rates to the adjacent interior points, so that it may be said that all the rail rates are kept in check by water transportation.

There need be no fear that extortionate rates will be charged by railroad companies; on the contrary, the fear is that water competition will be so effective as to prevent railroads from securing paying rates.[27]

Fink's letter confirmed what Conkling had said in 1875 and what anyone closely associated with canal business could have observed: "a waterway is cheaper than a railway for bulky commodities." It is likely that his allies from Wisconsin and Minnesota confirmed the facts. Therefore, Fink's letter would have quickly impressed business thinking in New York and secured greater credibility for the alliance of senators in Washington. Later Fink was often credited with a slogan that opening the canal each year reduced the rates all the way to Mobile.[28]

Fink's detailed explanation became accepted doctrine of policy groups. The early 1880 report from the Hepburn committee had noted, "The cost of water transportation from Chicago to New York determines the rate of rail transportation, and the rate of rail transportation from Chicago to New York is the base line upon which railroad rates are determined and fixed throughout the country."[28]

By 1887, the view had become commonplace. The first report of the Interstate Commerce Commission (ICC) read as though it was paraphrased from the Hepburn committee report: "The great free Erie Canal [cannot] be ignored; it influences the rates to New York more than any other one cause, and indirectly, through its influence upon the rates to New York, it influences those to all other seaboard cities, and indeed to all that section of the country."[29] It is worth repeating that in neither of these reports is there any hint of Schumpeter's vision of "creative destruction" of the canals due to the railroads' technological superiority. The volume of traffic on the canal may have changed from year to year, but the rate paid by the railroads came under the influence of the rates charged by the canal boats.

It is also worth summarizing that the scholars in railroading who have brought up the issue of the canal have uniformly overlooked both the official reports from the Hepburn committee and the first report of the Interstate Commerce Commission. They also overlook where it said that waterways set the rates for the rails, first explained by cartel commissioner Albert Fink in his reply to Senator Windom, head of the Senate appropriations committee. That oversight has to be marked up as one of the casualties of sectionalism. Within the state both parties gave significant support to the waterway's vitality, but on the outside of the state observers simply did not realize what was happening.

The state canal system had gone through several permutations, some much more easily recalled than others. From the 1870s onward, the canal had taken on the function of a surrogate for a role the federal government had yet to assume. The canal benefited the nation and persisted in the role until the price board law supported by President Theodore Roosevelt demonstrated that the ICC had become the federal alternative to the canal. In such a role, New Yorkers waited for the federal government to catch up to the service that New York so easily provided the nation. In retrospect, New Yorkers, unable to win the railroaders' support for a state system of regulation, initiated a campaign for their waterway venture without laying a hand on the railroads. The voters would show by a massive vote margin for the free canal that they had clear views on the policy question. What remained was for the railroads to respect such a popular definition of the state's commercial preeminence.

Curiously, in April 1878 Fink's letter appeared in New York papers and in the *Congressional Record*, before Charles Francis Adams, Jr. published his volume. Although Fink had urged Adams to write his book, Adams did not incorporate Fink's view of the canal. More curious is that Adams wrote that the canal was no longer significant in the competition. In the end, Fink's views and not Adams's influenced the reports of the Hepburn committee in 1880 and the ICC in 1887. That is, members of the cartel leadership were of two minds on the role of the canal, a fact that would confuse their position in lobbying for the approval of a national railroad trust.

With the new facts on the canal exposed to the public, Conkling in the election of 1878 did not have to mention the problems of the canal and suffered no weakness. While some interest arose in Congress about the Reagan Act providing federal regulation for the railroads, New York was already imposing national regulation by merely letting the canal be the canal.

The Canal Boatmen's Complaints Against the Railroads

Still, the canal advocates believed that the railroads crowded them unfairly. The boatmen complained to the Hepburn committee, "It is apparent that the policy of the railroads chartered by the State has been to wipe out the canals [and to] seek to overthrow them by a system of special rates, on condition that the shipper send none of his goods by canal at any season of the year."[30] A large number of boatmen, avoiding the winter freeze on the canal, docked their boats in the New York harbor, giving them access to important city events throughout the winter. It would take years, however, to get their complaints on the public agenda. Although, like the railroad express companies before them, the railroads issued "through bills" for one another, they refused to transfer them to the canals. Canal historian Whitford wrote:

> The conflict between rails and canals extended beyond competition in rates. The Terminal Commission established at the end of the century reported that "The railroads have always refused to either pro-rate or through-rate with canal carriers but, on the contrary, have only been willing to receive freight brought to them by canal boats in the most un-usual and expensive manner, such as by forcing them to discharge their freight at places other than railroad wharves, and then team it to the railroad wharves, instead of allowing them to come directly to the railroad wharves, and there discharge their freight. By refusing, on the other hand, to deliver freight to canal boats at their wharves, they have been able to prevent them from carrying large quantities of freight that would other-wise have been shipped by the canals."[31]

Chapter III

Conkling and Windom's Information System
For Transportation Policy, 1873–1881

1   Mitchell, Clyde, ed. *Social Networks in Urban Situations: Analyses of Personal Relationships in Central African Towns.* Manchester: Manchester University Press, 1969.

2   Laumann, Edward O., and Franz U. Pappi, *Networks of Collective Action.* New York: Academic Press, 1976, p. 115.

3   Laumann, Edward O., and David Knoke, *The Organizational State.* Madison: University of Wisconsin Press, 1987, p. 191.

4   Donald, David. "The Congressional Equation," in *Sociology and History: Methods,* edited by Seymour M. Lipset and Richard Hofstadter. New York: Basic Books, 1968, p. 247.

5   Aydellotte, William O. "Notes on the Problems of Historical Generalization," in *Generalizations in the Writing of History, A Report of the Committee on Historical Analysis of the Social Science Research Council,* ed. Louis Gottschalk. Chicago: University of Chicago, 1963, p. 175.

6   Rothman, David. *Politics and Power, The United States Senate, 1869–1901.* Cambridge, MA: Harvard University Press, 1966, pp. 88–90.

7   Laumann and Knoke, p. 34.

8   Bennis, Warren G. "The Coming Death of Bureaucracy" in *Think Magazine.* Armonk: IBM, 1966, p. 16.

9   Wood, Frederic J. *The Turnpikes of New England.* Boston: Marshall Jones, 1897, p. 34. (Our emphasis.)

10 Burrows, Edwin, and Mike Wallace. *Gotham: A History of New York to 1898.* New York: Oxford University Press, 1999, p. 968.

11 Benson, Lee, *Merchants, Farmers, and Railroads.* Cambridge, MA: Harvard University Press, 1955, p. 24.

12 *Annual Reports of the Corporation of the Chamber of Commerce of the State of New York* are found at the New-York (City) Historical Society, New York City.

13   Laumann and Knoke, p. 9.

14   Depew, Chauncey M. "Speech of . . . at the Congress of Railway Employees," Chicago, February 24, 1899. Evanston: Transportation Library, Northwestern University.

15   Hull, William J., and Robert W. Hull, *Origin and Development of the Waterways Policy of the United States.* Washington, D.C.: National Waterways Conference, 1967), p. 24. See also President Grant's *Annual Message* to Congress, December 1, 1873, *CR,* 44th Cong., 2d sess., Vol. 5, Pt.1, pp. 28f.

16   *Congressional Review (CR),* 44th Cong., 2d sess., Vol. 5, Pt. 1, December 6, 1876, pp. 46f.

17   Whitford, Noble. *History of the Canals.* Albany: State Engineer, 1906, p. 1164. The biography for Horatio Seymour, Jr., in Whitford's *History,* 1906, p. 1164, reads as follows: " . . . born Jan. 8, 1844, at Utica, N. Y.; graduate of Sheffield Scientific School, of Yale University, Class of 1867, the degree of M. A. being conferred some years later. Member of the American Society of Civil Engineers."

18   Hoogenboom, Ari. *Outlawing the Spoils: A History of the Civil Service Reform Movement, 1865–1883.* Urbana: University of Illinois Press, 1968, p. 175.

19   *New York Times (NYT),* December 23, 1874; October 23, 1875; October 9, 1879; and September 18, 1880.

20   *NYT,* December 23, 1874.

21   *NYT,* October 23, 1875.

22   *NYT,* November 10, 1877.

23   *NYT,* September 27, 1877.

24   *NYT,* September 27, 1877.

25   *NYT,* February 14, 1878.

26   *NYT,* March 14, 1878.

27   *CR,* 45th Cong., 2nd sess., Vol. 7, June 10, 1878, pp. 4358–4367.

See also Whitford, Noble. *History of the Barge Canal of New York State.* Albany: State Engineer, 1921, p. 20.

28   *NYT,* January 23, 1880.

29   *Interstate Commerce Commission Report, 1887.* Washington, D.C.: Library of Congress, p. 674.

30   *NYT,* June 24, 1879.

31   Whitford, p. 187; also p. 366.

CHAPTER IV

Albert Fink, Cartel Manager; Charles Adams, Lobbyist; and James Garfield, Legislator

Obviously once the railway building got underway, the consequences were frenetic, giving promise to both the wealth and destruction of communities. This pattern would presage the rise of later technologies, such as the automobile in the twenties and computing and the Internet in recent years. At the time Henry Adams wrote of everything related to railroading as overwhelming the republic. "The generation between 1865 and 1895 was already mortgaged to the railways, and no one knew it better than the generation itself."[1]

States had responsibility largely through franchising corporations. Legislatures could decide how much stock a company could issue. The excitement caused by railroading led to oversubscribing bond issues and that led to the crash of the bond market in 1873. States could not help much with bankruptcy. Congress fine-tuned the bankruptcy law and could improve the national debt by passing the resumption act. Concurrently, the larger companies resorted to collaborating among themselves to set rates and stave off their own bankruptcy. In both Iowa and the south cartels were founded for that purpose. In the northeast the companies at first tried the Saratoga agreement, which soon failed. Then, employing the founder of the southern cartel, the railroaders enlisted Albert Fink, a civil engineer by training, in 1877. His job was to settle down the industry by enforcing their agreements about rates. Fink built a massive, national staff located at the major terminals. They checked and reported the rates that the member railroads were charging. He then had the authority to bring the deviant members into line.

In retrospect, the companies, knowing they needed supporting legislation, were not proficient in dealing with the public. The political mechanism which they needed, the legislature, they looked upon with cynicism. Not until 1885 were Courts, the owners, and the politicians able to bring the industry under some uniform surveillance. That was through the organization of the Senate committee on inter-state commerce chaired by Senator Shelby Cullom of Illinois. It would be another twenty years before the Court would agree to the arrangements by approving the rate setting functions in the Interstate Commerce Commission. What would plague the industry all those years was the absence of a common understanding among the policy arena's leading lights. The Erie Canal fortunately continued to operate as a competitor and regulator of the railroads, allowing the country and the companies to settle down and figure out how to use what they had created for railroad regulation.

Reaching the phase when the Cullom committee provided a formal setting, discussion resorted to tried and true legislative practices. The committee work fell back upon use of the *hierarchy of announcements.* Once the Court ruled that states had no jurisdiction over interstate commerce, the Republicans took the matter from there. Arthur mentioned the matter in his annual report given in December 1883. At their national convention of 1884 Republicans adopted a convincing plank stipulating that Congress had the responsibility to proceed. Next came the announcement of the formation of the Senate committee. (Our emphasis.)

In 1880 and 1881 railroad leaders disregarded the protocols that sustained the integrity of the Congress, and pursued their own course. The railroaders' behavior could be traced into New York City life. The city that handled almost two-thirds of the nation's commerce was gripped in the late 1870s by the fear of the collapse of the tax base and the inability to pay on municipal bonds. City leaders were convinced that the rail companies and their arbitrary rate setting were part of the problem. Assembly leaders decided upon a hearing, which proceeded with mixed reviews. Afterwards a bill to form a regulatory commission got nowhere. No such difficulty had appeared in the neighboring states of Pennsylvania and Massachusetts. Again, it was lucky for New York that they had the Erie Canal serving as a surrogate, creating a margin for error until policy makers could get their matters settled. What followed was a record that few could regard as honorable.

While Senator Roscoe Conkling explained that the state-owned canal gave the railroads sufficient competition to regulate them, the cartel manager, Albert Fink, had performed an invaluable service by explaining in detail to Senator William Windom of Minnesota, a leader in transportation policy, just how well that regulation by the canal had worked. The disputants could have used Fink's letter as a starter for negotiations between the two systems, the canals and the rails. But that is not the way it worked. Other players in the policy arena––William Vanderbilt, Jay Gould, Collis P. Huntington, and Albert Fink himself––sought regulation by another option. They sought regulation, building on their cartel, by congressional approval of a plan of great moment, a national consolidation. The benefits were obvious. Such a trust could have more easily raised money than any single member railroad might have. The pace of buy-ups of existing roads would have quickened. Economies of scale could have been gained. The speculation in railroad building would probably have been muted. The obvious drawbacks included headquartering the new business in New York where it would have diminished the relevance of smaller, older institutions.

One benefit would be internal discipline. Each of the member companies had its own agents in the communities across the country soliciting business. They were often tempted to undercut competing agents, and if they did, they could set off a price war violating cartel agreements. Under a national consolidation, the managers could have exercised much more discipline over their agents dealing with shippers. What plausibly came to excite the entire industry was the prospect that one day they could do as Rockefeller had done in the oil industry, form a trust or single company, abolish competition altogether, and enforce discipline in their own ranks and rate regulation for shippers. The improved discipline would have added handsomely to company profits.

When the year 1881 opened, two outstanding events regarding consolidation occurred. Charles Adams's plan for industry consolidation arrived in the House of Representatives. Next, Jay Gould in a daring move consolidated three telegraph companies, giving hope to the railroaders that their system could be next. Many people thought it was quite easy to imitate what John D. Rockefeller had done in Ohio with the oil industry. Unfortunately for the consolidators, since August the anti-monopolists had been organizing in anticipation of such eventualities. The growth of New York opinion became pronounced, and Senator Roscoe Conkling decided to throw a block in the way of the consolidators by denying them seats on an all-important senate committee. Following that move the president insulted Conkling by naming his nemesis, railroad attorney William Vanderbilt, as collector of the port. The conclusion is warranted that rather than the nomination being the centerpiece of the Garfield administration, the distinction should go to the cartel's lobbying failure. It took time to clean up that debacle. From March of 1881 until March of 1885, when the Senate approved Cullom's committee, not much was done. Favorable political influences had to be corralled to get the work moving again.

Charles Adams's Assistance in Lobbying

Adams's 1878 volume, *Railroads: Their Origin and Problems,* had launched the lobbying for the railroad trust. Adams was a self-educated railroad expert. In 1869 he had helped found, and then manage, the Massachusetts commission. He wrote articles about what he was discovering in the "railroad problem." He also gained new authority for the commission since he saw to it that the Massachusetts legislature continued to grant authority in investigating and reporting. The greatest gain came in 1876, when "the legislature then placed the entire system of accounts kept by the corporations under the direct supervision of the board."[2] Cartel manager Albert Fink had encouraged him to write the book, and later invited him to join the cartel staff. Adams would follow up his book in February 1880 with testimony before Reagan's commerce committee. No less importantly, Adams and Garfield enjoyed a decade-long association, largely through sporadic correspondence on railroad legislation. The *Times* once mentioned the association between the two, but unfortunately, none of the standard accounts of the Garfield administration has done so.

Adams believed that if the Massachusetts model were adopted in western states, it would help lessen the popular distrust. Iowa was the first to make the move. Whether other states gladly made the move comes under some doubt due to the comment by William Z. Ripley just before passage of the Interstate Commerce Commission Act in 1887. He said, "Only a few companies . . . such as the Pennsylvania, the Union Pacific and the Louisville and Nashville, had indeed attempted to systemize their accounts."[3] In the face of all the trumpeting about the superiority of railroad management in comparison to government management, this record of the poor development in railroad accounting might have prompted more modesty.

The system Fink managed covered the trunk lines running from the east coast to Chicago. Seven years later, in 1884, Fink recalled his frame of mind at the time when he took up cartel leadership in an effort to stabilize the market:

> Recognizing that damaging effects of ruinous competition and sense-less wars of rates the railroad managers of the country in their endeavors to correct these flagrant evils have taken the only step in their power, namely, to co-operate for the purpose of establishing reasonable and proper tariffs that avoid unjust discrimination, and to adopt the proper measures to see that these tariffs are strictly maintained alike to all shippers for like service. This is the primary object of the association of railroads known as the Joint Executive Committee and the Trunk Line commission. To satisfactorily attain this object, I may state here, is a most difficult problem, requiring an organization, in fact, a regular government of the railroads, with rules and regulations to which the different railroads have to conform. The great dissatisfaction that existed in 1876 and part of 1877, during a prolonged railroad war, will be remembered, and also the efforts made by the Chamber of Commerce of this City and their call for State and national legislation to put a stop to a state of affairs so disastrous to the commercial interests.
>
> In July 1877, the trunk lines carrying the westbound traffic from New York, recognizing the justice of these complaints, and each unable to control the tariff individually, formed an association and agreed that each company would thereafter strictly adhere to the established tariffs, which were then considered reasonable and just: that all underbidding on the part of one railroad against another by secret rates and rebates should cease; that no unjust discrimination should be made between shippers. For the purpose of better carrying out this object, and to remove the motive for underbidding and payment of rebates, an amount of the traffic considered equal to that which each trunk line would carry under maintenance of equal rates was mutually conceded to each company. This, however, is

merely a subsidiary measure of no importance to the public, the only of which is the maintenance of published tariffs.[4]

Fink ascertained early on that the public was chiefly interested in published tariffs, but some New York Central officials did not want their rates published lest the canal men undercut them.

This collectivity of the railroads would soon meet up with another collectivity representing the canal business. Laumann and Knoke's assumption in their research design, namely a "social perspective, which assumes that supra-individual structural arrangements among these corporate entities," must be taken into account "in formulating an adequate explanation of policy event participation."[5] Legally the canal came under the purview of the state legislature. Beyond that its administration was altered by amendments to the state constitution adopted by the voters. Practically speaking the canal system was under the stewardship of the century-old Chamber of Commerce. Some elected officials such as Conkling with his information links to westerners in the Senate, to his brother in the city, and to his nephew in the state engineer's office also figured in. The conventional view that Conkling was merely a patronage manager is actually distracting because it blurs his full role in the changing scene.

Adams's Preference for Legalizing the Railroad Cartel

The year 1878 found Fink urging Adams to collect his articles for publication, which he did under the title *Railroads: Their Origin and Problems*. Next, Adams joined the cartel staff; a move that suggested that the cartel endorsed his views. When he went to meetings with the cartel board, in addition to the railroad presidents, there would have been Albert Fink as the executive director and Chauncey Depew, attorney for the New York Central and chairman of the cartel board. Inasmuch as the greatest railroaders had recruited Adams to their circle, a respected expert who hailed from one of the nation's aristocratic families, the selection was nothing less than new money employing old money.

In early 1880, expanding upon his views in the 1878 volume, Adams testified before Reagan's committee. He next had his testimony published, suggesting that his cartel allies wanted to target specific audiences, probably the rest of the railroad industry. In February 1880 he told the House committee that Fink "simply proposes to legalize a (pooling) practice, which the law cannot prevent, and, by so doing, to enable the railroads to confederate them in a manner which shall be at once both public and responsible."[6] This assertion was made at the opening of the political season running up to the national convention in June of 1880, putting everyone in the chaotic industry on notice regarding what the key leaders in the industry were thinking.

Other railroaders had often expressed that prospect, as Stephen Ambrose relates in his coverage of Leland Stanford of the Central Pacific:

Stanford wanted consolidation and monopoly. He once said he expected to "see the time when there would not be more than five great companies in the United States," and he especially wanted one single railroad. "If all the roads were operated as one road," he said, "they could regulate prices lower than today and make money, while now they don't make money."[7]

Adams's confidence in the inevitability of consolidation, "which the law cannot prevent," arose partly from his apparent faith in the three-stage Hegelian dialectal process of business. It had three parts that followed from one another: 1) development, 2) competition, and 3) consolidation. His confidence rose also from the knowledge that the great financiers were taking steps to effect the final goal. Adams observed,

> Contrary to the general and popular conviction, an increasing number of those who have given most thought to the subject, whether as railroad officers or simply from the general economical and political points of view, are disposed to conclude that, so far from being necessarily against public policy, a properly regulated combination of railroad companies, for the avowed purpose of controlling competition, might prove a most useful public agency. . . recognizing the fact that the period of organization is now succeeding that of construction, these persons are disposed to see in the regulated combination the surest, if not, indeed, the only way of reaching a system in which the advantages of railroad competition may, so far as possible, be secured; and its abuses, such as waste, discrimination, instability, and bankruptcy, be greatly modified if not wholly gotten rid of . . . .

> Commodore Vanderbilt ['s] . . . vast property, in the peculiar shape in which he left it and as it is now handled, seems to be little else than an accumulating fund devoted to bringing about consolidation of railroad interest on the largest possible scale. The New York Central is the basis upon which this superstructure rests. The Vanderbilt interest in the property is so great that practically the earnings of this road, instead of being dissipated among innumerable stockholders, as is the case with the other trunk lines, are continually applied to securing the control of other and connecting lines . . .

> While this is going on in the East under the Vanderbilt lead, two other and precisely similar "one-man" combinations are assuming shape, the one in the central region of the country West of the Missouri [under Gould], and the other one on the Pacific slope [under Stanford and Huntington]. They, also, are built upon the principle of devoting the

earnings to the development of business, and to the support of stockholders. Accordingly competition does not now exist within the sphere of influence of these combinations, and its existence is rapidly becoming impossible; for, as soon as it makes itself felt the competing [railroad] line is bought out of the way. In this way the Union Pacific combination now controls seven corporations owning and operating 3,000 miles of track in the heart of the continent----an absolutely controlling interest----while on the western coast the Pacific Central occupies an even more commanding position. . .

By its originators, it is confidently claimed that, if properly developed and recognized by legislation, it would afford a complete and practical solution of the American railroad problem.[8]

These three players in railroading were a formidable group. William Vanderbilt headed the largest company in the country. Jay Gould's total holdings came to 52,000 miles of track or half the trackage in the country. Collis Huntington would soon open a project in Virginia giving him a single road from coast to coast all on his own property. With the railroad combinations progressing, the middle stage of the business dialectic--competition--became as rare as iron puddlers in the new steel mills. Adams observed how the three great railroaders were investing their profits in more purchases rather than in dividends, giving every reason to believe that the plan for a single national railroad trust would soon materialize.

Aspects of the Transportation Industry in the Late 1870s and Early 1880s

The history of the railroad industry from the Civil War through 1882 falls into three periods. From 1860 to 1880, track mileage had increased from roughly 30,000 to 100,000 miles, a rate of expansion difficult for any nation to digest. Financing was supremely important, and changes in market conditions set the three periods. The threshold between the first and second periods was the 1873 bond market crash, and the third period began in 1879, when the nation returned to the gold standard.

In the early period, railroad mileage increased everywhere and companies often faced problems with the public. In the West, the great transcontinental Pacific railroads were completed in 1869. In the East, heading the New York Central, Cornelius Vanderbilt bought up some companies and soon provided one through line with a double track to Chicago. Because of trouble in the upper Midwest, where railroads had boldly raised rates, Senator William Windom of Minnesota ventured into government planning by forming a new Senate committee on transportation routes to the seaboard and in time produced a report. Finally, the Adams brothers entertained the nation with a story of the corrupt Erie railroad in their memorable book, *Chapters of the Erie*. Railroading had seized the public's imagination.

In the second phase, beginning in 1873, the bond market collapse forced some companies into bankruptcy. That left others looking into the abyss. Cooperation among the large corporations soon materialized. In explaining the cooperation, in a passage important to Laumann and Knoke in identifying a policy scenario, Adams declared, "Capital is trying to protect itself; and will succeed in doing it. The *stress* of competition has been too great, and in its own way is resulting in combination."[9] (Our emphasis.) Adams' use of the term "stress" fits perfectly into the sociologists' use of the term "institutional strain" to characterize an important phase in a policy scenario: a consequential leader's foreseeing that his institution is approaching a slippery slope. Accordingly, institutional strain drives the leaders toward some resolution, the next phase in the policy process. In the case of the railroaders, the solution rested in following the iron law of the business dialects, taking them on the course of continued consolidation and to the final standing as a single, regulated national utility.

The Management and Political Style of Albert Fink

A fair appraisal of the political scenery at the time has to justify consequential actors. They were people who, according to Laumann and Knoke, influenced decisions in their own realm and had a bearing on the broader field of interest. This definition fits with Laumann and Pappi's *positional* approach in understanding influence or power. Influential leaders are those who may or may not have *reputations* as powerful people. Or, they may or may not be concerned with *issues*. They, however, certainly occupy an *institutional position* giving them influence. One of the most conspicuous incumbents was the German-born engineer Albert Fink, who emerged in the railroad industry and proved decisive in molding the cartel members into a strong interstate association. Others had to take them into account. When Fink retired from his post in June 1889, the *Times* ran a long story about him, describing him as

> . . . a man of striking personal appearance. He is of large figure and has a massive head and hair, mustache, and chin whiskers of silvery gray. His railroad career has been a continued success and it has been a long one. He was born in Lauterback, near Frankfort-on-the-Main, Oct. 27, 1827, and was graduated at the Polytechnic Institute in Darmstadt, where he studied architecture, in 1848. A year later he came to this country and began his railroad career as a draughtsman in the office of the Baltimore and Ohio Railroad.

Fink designed the bridge over the Monongahela River and other bridges from Grafton to Parkersburg. As a consultant he designed the bridge at Norfolk, a bridge at Nashville, and "the great bridge over the Ohio at Louisville." This engineering output would certainly have given him credence.

In 1865 Mr. Fink was made General Manager of the Louisville and Nashville, and in 1870 he was elected its Vice President. After the financial crisis of 1873 the evils of unrestrained railway competition forced upon his mind the necessity of a remedy. [Fink's L & N Annual Reports 1873–4 attracted nationwide attention as they served as a "lesson in railway economics and a carefully prepared defense of railroad rate-making policies with an eye to the experience of railroads in the granger states."[10]] This led him to devise his plan for the creation of the Southern Railway and Steamship Association, and in 1875 he resigned his office in the Louisville and Nashville Company and became manager of the association, with the title of General Commissioner. He came to New York in June 1877 with the intention of going at once to Germany for a visit, but after his arrival here Messrs. Vanderbilt, Garrett, Jewett, and Scott, then the presidents of the four great trunk lines, had a conference with him and asked him to remain in this City and attempt the organization of a pool of the west-bound traffic of these roads on a plan of division of the tonnage similar to the one he had succeeded in putting into operation in the South. He stayed there, formed the great trunk-line pool, was made Commissioner of the pool, and when the inter-State commerce law made it necessary to call it "association" instead of "pool," Mr. Fink was officially titled Trunk Line Commissioner instead of Pool commissioner. His expert testimony on railroad management before various committees forms an important chapter of American railroad history.

It was doubted that the presidents of the railroad companies would accept Fink's retirement. His response on that question suggests how he had met many other controversies among the cartel elite.

By some well versed in matters relating to the association its acceptance is regarded as extremely improbable. Mr. Fink has been a valuable man to the roads in his association. He was the adviser, the peacemaker, and sometimes the polite and diplomatic dictator to the Presidents in their various controversies. He was a great adjuster of difficulties. He chided where chiding was necessary; he bridged many a yawning chasm, and was the mouthpiece between the public and the association. No matter how stormy the meeting or how conflicting the interest, when the Commissioner was asked for the details he always took an optimistic view of things, and told of the harmony that prevailed.

Ten days later the presidents agreed to Fink's retirement, issuing a press release stating:

The trunk line Presidents accepted the resignation of Albert Fink, Commissioner of the Trunk Line Association, yesterday. They did it because there was no other course left them. Mr. Fink insisted on resigning. No long vacation would suit him. He wanted out of the business, and he gave them to understand that he meant what he said in his letter of resignation. The Presidents know Mr. Fink well enough to understand that when he is in earnest about a thing they do as he says as a rule.[11]

Adams paid tribute to Fink in his 1878 volume by writing, "[The] trunk lines [are] held together only by the personal influence and force of character of one man—its commissioner, Colonel Fink."[12] Fink was a consequential actor who successfully derived influence from both his character and the position he occupied.

The Cartel's Early Troubles with Pooling of Rates and Income, 1877

Shortly, to ensure profits, the trunk lines pooled their receipts and allocated agreed-upon portions of the total back to the participating companies. The New York Central and Erie railroads each received 33 percent; the Pennsylvania 25 percent; and the Baltimore and Ohio 9 percent.[13] From the outset, the lines to New York charged a premium because that route was longer from Chicago than the routes to Philadelphia and Baltimore. The merchants protested that the extra cost constituted rate discrimination. Later they came to realize that, as the *Times* would write in 1885, "the restraining effect of the canal route is wholly in favor of New York and materially limits the possibility of discrimination against her."[14]

The pooling agreement was exactly the kind Fink was hired to arrange. Purportedly it helped the members fend off bankruptcy. But, with its small share, the B&O suffered an unintended consequence that had almost exactly the opposite effect. To cut costs, the B&O management reduced employee wages at the same time the federal government was contracting the currency in preparation for the coming resumption of specie payments. Feeling the currency stringency, the B&O's employees immediately went on strike, and employees in other companies followed. The strikers turned to rioting and destroying property, especially in Pittsburgh. Ramifications were widespread. While the stringency of the currency now illuminated poverty, political interests were choosing sides. On July 27, 1877, the *Tribune* argued that inflationists were robbing the creditors, the grangers were robbing the transportation companies, and the trade unions were robbing the laborer, who wished only to work. "The whole process of larceny weakened respect for law and led to bloody scenes which had just horrified the nation."[15]

On the policy scene, a stall came in Congress's dealing with the silver bill, an amendment to the resumption bill of 1875. The House had passed Richard Bland's silver bill twice, giving the bond market a startle. The reluctant Senate finally decided to take it up. Thus, in the country now gridironed by rails, one policy question, attempts at railroad cooperation to secure their income, bore on another policy question, the lack of liquidity in the currency.

The third phase in railroad history began in January 1879 with the resumption of specie payments. Secretary of the Treasury John Sherman had purchased enough gold to "make a show" of supporting the greenback circulation on a par with gold. Coincidentally, farmers' harvests, good in America and poor in Europe, had just the right balance to spur both American railroading and waterway traffic. Foreigners increased their investments. The railroaders envisioned even bigger plans. In this sunny business climate not only did the three titans of railroading look to judicial relief from the regulation in some of the western states, but they also looked to congressional approval of their consolidation into a national railroad trust.

The better days, however, hardly meant that the public lost interest in the roads. Skepticism had arisen when it was discovered that to achieve economies of scale, Vanderbilt and Rockefeller had signed contracts on oil shipments to the east coast. The agreement undercut going rates and forced some New York business houses to close, threatening the New York tax base. On attorney Simon Sterne's urging,[16] the New York assembly authorized a select committee, the Hepburn committee, to investigate the collusion. Hearings ran into the summer of 1879, with the record of the hearings becoming a best seller. The committee reported in early 1880. While the state legislators and owners concluded they needed improved state and federal regulation, Vanderbilt added the caveat that Congress should act first.

By 1879–80 the Chicago cartel, only two years old, had become strong.[17] Fink invoked a much-needed discipline. Thomas S. Ulen has written, "The cartelists recognize[d] the incentive to cheat and establish[ed] an internal policing mechanism with penalties for violating the implicit cartel contract." In 1879, the cartel announced, "each line has put up $300,000, or has agreed on that penalty, in case of violation of the compact."[18] How well this penalty worked remained to be seen. They also formed a Board of Arbitration, comprising experts from the industry. It began its work in June of that year, at the height of the Hepburn investigation. Besides making a place for Adams, the board seated David A. Wells and John A. Wright. The former had published in transportation economics, and the latter had served as the general freight agent for the Baltimore and Ohio and had investigated the cartel's eastbound rates in 1877.

A New Professional Class in New York City

With New York City handling most of the nation's commerce, the companies in the railroad industry, including the cartel, set up their headquarters there. "All trunk lines," Adams observed, "whether they terminated there or not, had offices in New York, and were in steady competition for the merchandise shipments to the West from that place."[19] He also noted that as the companies tried to settle on eastbound rates. "In February and March 1878 a succession of meetings were held which were attended by the representatives of no less than 40 different corporations operating some 25,000 miles of road, or about one-third of the whole system of the United States."[20] Later, in 1881, Fink called a meeting and sent out invitations to 42 companies involved in traffic from the east coast. Representatives of 25 railroads showed up.[21] The railroad companies were so cooperative in scheduling their traffic with one another, that Joseph Nimmo, Chief of the Bureau of Statistics, could write, "There are over 100,000 miles of railroad in the country extending into almost every town, and so closely connected as to be operated practically as one line, so far as shipments from one road to the other is concerned."[22]

The railroads' headquartering themselves in New York City meant a new professional class had settled there. The political consequences were bound to become evident as they strengthened the half-breed faction of the Republican Party. On the other side of the question, the Cheap Transportation Association and the Chamber of Commerce could each show a membership of far over a thousand members. Once the Hepburn hearings had aroused the public, the railroaders tended to act defensively as one. Within a year, they were taking precautions to keep the public out of their affairs. They even went so far as to try to place Vanderbilt's attorney and cartel president, Chauncey Depew, in the U.S. Senate. In New York City, politics and social life often mirrored each other. In politics the half-breeds tried to beat the stalwarts, and in the city's social life the new money contested the old.

Fink Brings Adams to the Cartel

Fink, and through him the railroaders, seemed to give Charles Adams more attention whenever political events demanded it. Fink, on the job since June 1877, began talking to Adams in November about adapting his Massachusetts plan to the federal level.[23] He urged Adams to summarize his many articles in a book, and six weeks later, Adams wrote in his diary, "began looking over my r. r. articles to prepare a volume for permanence."[24] In another six weeks, he was well on his way,[25] completing his manuscript in July.[26] Next, Congress, anticipating that the two Pacific railroads would not be able to meet their debts by the 1890s, brought up sinking fund legislation. Almost concurrently, Secretary of the Interior Carl Schurz urged Adams to accept a nomination to the Union Pacific's government board of directors. On March 23, 1878, Adams agreed, and he attended his first meeting on June 3rd.[27]

Then came the greenback victories in the 1878 election. That raised the specter of inflationist policies and anti-monopolism making railroad debt harder to pay. Since 15 greenbackers won election to the House, railroad leaders felt they had to shore up their defenses. By month's end, Adams wrote in his diary that Putnam's "had already disposed of an edition of my 'Railroads,'"[28] suggesting an impressive response among railroaders. On November 22, 1878, sixteen months after the riots, Fink interviewed Adams about joining the cartel's board of arbitration.[29] Six months passed; the Hepburn hearings had convened. Finally on May 2, 1879, Adams noted in his diary, "I met my colleagues on the Board of Arbitration and the joint executive committee of the trunk lines."[30] One and one-half years had passed from the time Fink first encouraged Adams to write a book to the time he joined the cartel staff. The long delay suggests Vanderbilt's caution about letting outsiders into the business, especially if they had been as critical as Adams had been in 1869.

His new work took Adams to New York City twice a month, requiring a train ride of seven hours each way. He ordinarily stayed in the city about three days. His salary was $10,000 per year. Adams and two other experts from the railroad industry demonstrated what a national regulatory board could be. Adams became so trusted that he even arbitrated a case with Vanderbilt by correspondence.[31]

In *Railroads: Their Origin and Problems*, published in 1878, Adams presented views quite changed from those of 1869. Then he had criticized Cornelius Vanderbilt, but nine years later he voiced not a word of disapproval. In nine years, he had switched from critic to promoter. He now approved of William Vanderbilt's plan to consolidate the northeastern railroads.[32] He also honored Fink's cartel management.[33] At the end of his life, however, when he looked back at his years in railroad work, he proved quite selective in recalling the volumes he had written. At the time of his death in 1915, the antitrust actions of Roosevelt had prevailed for over a decade. Adams had come to follow the new fashion. In his posthumously published autobiography, he wrote warmly about the 1869 book that he and his brother had written. There was, however, not a word about his 1878 volume promoting a railroad trust, nor his follow-up testimony before the Reagan Committee in February 1880 when he excoriated the idea of competition. The closest he gets in his 1915 recollection to the 1880–1881 events is to say that he had only done what cartel manager Albert Fink had told him to do.

Adams's Prize Contribution: The Sunshine Law

Several aspects of Adams' 1878 volume were significant. The most famous was the "sunshine law." It was a method for quickly completing convincing investigations. The *Times* explained it as a process consisting of "investigations and reports of a commission [that] would create a public opinion which would induce the roads to remove existing cause of complaint without compulsion."[34] One aspect was missing in the *Times'* definition. The paper failed to say that the sunshine law required promptness in execution.

Early in 1877 Adams had become convinced of the correctness of the method. He counted it as a success that "more than counterbalanced all my shortcomings elsewhere."[35] Three decades later he recalled the one persuasive incident that would become his hallmark. He wrote

> I refer to our action and report on the strike of engineers on the Boston and Maine railroad, in February 1877. On that occasion our Board rendered a really considerable public service, putting a sharp stop to a rapidly

increasing epidemic, and courageously laying down some very salutary doctrines, which were productive of lasting effects. That was twenty-three years ago; and there has not since been a strike of railroad train operatives in New England. I wrote the whole of the report, at Quincy, during the evening, which followed the hearings. My associates adopted my draft the next day, without the change of a word; it was immediately published; and, as a leading member of the Legislature—General Cogswell, of Ipswich—afterwards remarked to me: "It cleared the air like a thunder clap. . ." I told the story in a paper entitled Investigation and Publicity as Opposed to Compulsory Arbitration, read before the American Civic Federation, and then printed by me in pamphlet form. The Roosevelt Commission on the Pittsburgh Anthracite Coal Strike of that year formally adopted my views, and recommended accordingly; but nothing came of it . . . Perhaps I ought to have followed it up; made in fact the following of it up my life work.[36]

That one-night inspiration in 1877, for avoiding a railroad strike, led elsewhere. It became grounds for his proposal for national legislation. In his early 1880 testimony Adams told the Reagan committee:

You should not approach the case [a complaint against a railroad] with defined theories as to cause and effect—a whole statute book, the quack legislator's pillbox, in hand . . . I object simply to legislating in advance of investigation—to perpetually inverting the order of things . . . Penal legislation will be necessary—should follow and not precede investigation. The concrete cases should first arise and be made the subject, not of slow and profitless litigation, but of swift inquiry on the spot; and from these concrete cases the body of general legislation should gradually be developed.[37]

This was the voice of Yankee pragmatism. Adams meant to build legislation upon what, in more recent times, is called the case study method of analyzing management difficulties. Business schools have since made the subject their core curriculum. The method allows for surveying one case after another. The random collection of identifiable railroad troubles, followed by summarizing them according to their commonalities, can uncover additional work to do. From that collection, investigators could recommend legislation or other rules. So Adams would complain that investigation had to precede legislation, and that the grangers usually got it backwards.

Adams's Early Standards for Participation in the Policy Scenario

In addition to the commissioners adopting proper investigative procedures, Adams argued that only qualified people should conduct them. That provides a confirmation of Laumann and Knoke's view that, in a policy scenario, there are "continuous negotiations between the consequential actors currently forming the elite, who seek to impose their preferred definitions and requirements for inclusion."[38] It will become evident that in this Gilded Age story the elites often failed to discuss their position or view before they acted. Often they acted and then explained afterwards. In the pejorative, these associations were often known as "rings" such as the "canal ring." The practice ranged all the way up to the White House.

The debate was wide ranging. Vanderbilt, for one, was certain that only railroad experts should take part. On the other hand, the western grangers believed that they had to be heard. Much to Adams' disgust, the grangers thought that almost anyone was qualified. He finally quoted George Stephenson, the English railroad founder and policy advocate, who had written:

> What we want is a tribunal upon these subjects, competent to judge, and willing to devote its attention to railway subjects only. We do not impute to Parliament that it is dishonest, but we impute that it is incompetent. All we ask is that it shall be a tribunal that is impartial and that is thoroughly informed; and, if impartiality and intelligence are secured, we do not fear for the result.[39]

The task of selecting commissioners consisted of avoiding incompetence by enlisting people who were "thoroughly informed." For Adams, that could be a railroader. It could even be a non-expert, a leading member of the business community who used the railroads.

In Massachusetts in the late 1870s a commission seat was reserved for a business representative. Adams had to come to its defense. The state legislature was in a retrenchment mood and to save money it sought to reduce by one member the size of the commission. On February 20, 1879, only months before the start of the Hepburn hearings in New York, Adams wrote to Charles Osgood, the chair of the legislative oversight committee, that:

> Whether, under certain conditions, the number of its [the commission's] members could not be reduced without impairing its efficiency, I am not clear. As public boards go, however, I do not see how it could. It was originally organized to consist of one engineer, one representative of the active business interests of the community, and one person of legal training to act as its mouthpiece, and to attend to its legislative duties. This organization has been steadily continued to the present time, and seems to me wise, and to have in it nothing superfluous. In the first place, an engineer is essential. If the Board did not contain one, it would have to employ one. His services are in constant requisition. In the second place, some well-informed and largely acquainted representative of business circles is very

necessary to enable the Board to accomplish desired results. In fact, these results have usually, in the past, been brought about through directly dealing with presidents, members of boards of directors, and influential men of business. They are so being brought about today.

Just as New York legislators were planning the Hepburn committee hearings, Adams added prophetically:

> If the Committee will imagine a similar board elsewhere—in New York, for instance—they will at once see why this is necessarily the case. The matters coming before it are not *per* questions of law and of fact; they involve many practical considerations: and, to deal with these successfully, it is, above all, necessary to know whom to apply to, and how to reach them. This will always continue to be the case; and, so long as it is so, the aid of some capable businessman will be essential. As to the legal adviser and general mouthpiece, the commission could not get along at all without one.[40]

Adams was arguing not merely for selecting men who knew railroading. He wanted men of different competencies in railroading. They would complement one another. He opposed the notion that just any person was qualified to do the job. He expressed shock that the western granger commissions refused to take even one person who had company experience. The grangers feared that such appointees might side with the companies. For the same reason, the grangers appointed commissioners for terms of one year only. Grangerism had proved such a powerful force in the Midwest that it influenced legislative action. In 1875 the Minnesota state legislature elected a new U.S. senator from the state supreme court, Justice Samuel J. R. McMillan. On the bench he had found the state granger law constitutional. *(John D. Blake and others vs. Winona & St. Peter Ry. Co, Minnesota Reports, 1872–73, pp. 362–376.)* On entering the Senate he joined Conkling on the commerce committee, and later took a seat on the judiciary committee.

Some authorities infer that following the Supreme Court decision the granger movement slowly disappeared. Illinois, however, did not follow the trend. In 1877, Governor Shelby Cullom received a recommendation from the legislature asking that the Railroad and Warehouse Commission be closed down and the law repealed. Cullom replied with suggestions to strengthen the body. He argued that "The mere fact that a tribunal is there, that a machinery does exist for the prompt and final decision of that class of question put(s) an end to them. They no longer arise." The doubt about the utility of the state commission was set aside.[41]

In his 1878 volume, Adams, taking no account of the Illinois experience under Governor Cullom, excoriated the entire granger effort:

In America, there are not many specialists, nor have the American people any great degree of faith in them. The principle that all men are created equal before the law has been stripped of its limitations, until in the popular mind it has become a sort of cardinal article of political faith that all men are equal for all purposes. Accordingly, in making up commissions to deal with the most complicated issues arising out of our modern social and industrial organization, those in authority are very apt to conclude that one man can do the work about as well as another. The result is what might naturally be expected; and the system is made responsible for it. All this received pointed illustration in the case of the granger commissions.[42]

Dissent came from Joseph Nimmo, Chief of the Bureau of Statistics, who made his views known at about the time that Adams appeared before the Reagan committee. Nimmo argued that the granger commissions had some redeeming qualities:

> Experience has proved that certain of the restrictive measures adopted a few years ago by the Legislatures of some of the western states were, in their practical workings, detrimental to the producing and commercial interest of the country, and at the same time injurious to the railroad interests. Nevertheless, the legislative acts regulating freight charges which have been adopted in this country have generally had salutary influence as have resulted rather from their moral influence in restraining and preventing abuses than from their effect in enforcing the right and correcting wrong. The railroad companies have been constrained to explain the principles upon which their freight tariffs are based, and thus the public have been enabled to gain much valuable information as to the distinction which exists between just and unjust discriminations, and between practices which are based upon economic considerations and sound commercial principles and such as are indefensible and therefore constitute abuses of the rights and privileges conferred upon the companies.[43]

Probably with Nimmo's views in mind, in January 1881 New York business leaders objected to the Adams plan just as it appeared on the House floor. They complained that it made no room for business participation. It depended too much on railroad experts. Therefore, from the moment of Adams's first discussion with Fink until the merchants rejected the Adams plan, Adams accepted a critical change. The old money man from Quincy met Vanderbilt, the new money man, finding that he discouraged non-experts from deliberating with him. Adams faced new circumstances. In Massachusetts, he was explicit with Osgood about the necessity of business participation in regulation—it had taken a decade of work on the Massachusetts commission to come to that conviction—but in New York he found that he had to bow to his host's view of the matter. Years

101

later in his autobiography, he may have referred to having backed down on the point. He confessed, "I made some mistakes of judgment, and bad mistakes. Frequently, I proved unequal to the occasion. More than once, I now see, I was lacking [in] firmness, and even in courage. I did not take the position I should have taken."[44]

Regardless of what he had written to Osgood, Adams would nevertheless still accept Fink's invitation to join the cartel's staff. He could have declined and taken the next train home, denying the cartel leadership the blessings of the old aristocracy. On the other hand, if Adams had decided to exclude public members, he could have suppressed the Osgood correspondence. Indeed, his saving the piece in his collection, and its printing as a formal legislative document, may reflect his later regrets.

Adams on Government Ownership

On another policy front, Adams thought that the government should not establish businesses to assure competition, a practice popular in Europe. This practice was, however, also popular in New York where the canal was integral to the economy. Adams objected.

> The English, the Belgian, the French, and the German are the four great railroad systems. In their political relations, they are divided into two groups by a broad line of demarcation. On the one side of that line are the systems of the English-speaking race, based upon private enterprise and left for their regulation to the principles of laissez-faire, the laws of competition, and of supply and demand. On the other side of the line are the systems of continental Europe, in the creation of which the state assumed the initiative, and over which it exercises constant and watchful supervision. In applying results drawn from the experience of one country, which present themselves in another, the difference of social and political habit and education should ever be borne in mind. Because in the countries of continental Europe the state can and does hold close relations amounting even to ownership, with the railroads, it does not follow that the same course could be successfully pursued in England or in America. The former nations are by political habit administrative, the latter are parliamentary; in other words, France and Germany are essentially executive in governmental systems, while England and America are legislative. Now the executive may design, construct, or operate a railroad; the legislative never can. A country, therefore, with a weak or unstable executive, or a crude and imperfect civil service, should accept with caution results achieved under a government of bureaus.[45]

Any New Yorker with knowledge of the state's economy would have had to wonder what Adams had in mind. It was pure ideology that could not adapt to the facts as they existed.

Finally, Adams was sure that the new arrangements for railroading required some external force. Voluntary alliances invariably fell apart. The industry's culture was for Adams a troubling sight.

> Order is not easily established in any community, which has been long in a state of anarchy. . . demoralization becomes general; the tone of the individual deteriorates. This is what now is the matter with the railroad system in America. Lawlessness and violence among themselves, the continual effort of each member to protect itself and to secure the advantage over others, have, as they usually do, bred a general spirit of distrust, bad faith and cunning, until railroad officials have become hardly better than a race of horse-jockeys on a large scale. There are notable individual exceptions to this statement, but, taken as a whole, the tone among them is indisputably low. There is none of that steady confidence in each other, that easy good faith, that *esprit de corps*, upon which alone system and order can rest. On the contrary, the leading idea in the mind of the active railroad agent is that someone is always cheating him, or that he is never getting his share of something . . . Peace is with him always a condition of semi-warfare . . . Under such circumstances, what is there but force upon which to build? A Caesar or a Napoleon is necessary. . . . Then will come the combination of a few who will be sufficiently powerful to restrain the many. The result, expressed in a few words, would be a railroad federation under a protectorate.[46]

Given the mob rule that occurred during the spring 1877 railroad strike, some of the public was ready for a Caesar. Delegates gathering for the summer conventions of 1880 even looked for one in their presidential candidate. The right person could not only satisfy public opinion. He could also lift the industry out of its disarray. Certainly, a national railroad trust modeled after Rockefeller's work would reduce chaos in the industry.

The Prospects for Passing Congressional Legislation

Vanderbilt may have thought that Congress could handle the legislation. If Congress did not adopt the legislation he wanted, he would rather have nothing. Convinced that the railroads had not achieved sufficient coordination and harmony, Adams warned against rushing matters. "This process [of national consolidation] is unlikely to prove a rapid one," he wrote, "for order is not easily established in any community which has been long in a state of anarchy."[47] His forecasts would prove quite accurate.

Garfield's Association with Adams

Adams's call for a Caesar could have impressed James Garfield, who had entertained thoughts of the presidency. The Ohioan took a new view that bound together railroading and one of his favorite topics, national banking. He had a long record of supporting the gold standard. In 1878 a particular turn of events led him to blend his hard-money views with the necessities of the corporations. The ordeal of the silver debate ended in February 1878. It was followed by a surge for greenbackers in the midterm elections. Gold advocates became alarmed that greenbacks would replace national banknotes with worthless paper money. That would drive out gold and foreign investments. Toward the end of the 1878 campaign season a great effort had to be made to save the forthcoming resumption (making paper dollars equivalent to gold by backing them with enough gold in the Treasury).

In a celebration of resumption, on New Year's Day 1879, Garfield was featured at a Chicago rally hosted by Thomas Nichol, founder of the Honest Money League of the Northwest. Nichol had recently impressed easterners by helping defeat soft-money Republicans in Wisconsin.

Garfield told his audience that resumption achieved needed continued protection. He implied that three bonded institutions had to stand together: the banks, the railroads, and the U.S. Treasury. He warned that:

> The most dangerous indirect assault upon resumption is the attempt to abolish national banks, and substitute additional greenbacks in the place of bank notes. The effort will call to its support the sentiment, which to some extent prevails against moneyed corporations [railroads]. Should the attempt succeed it will inevitably result in suspension of specie payment [at the Treasury].[48]

Garfield had brought railroading into his equation for securing resumption of specie payments. He was able to build on Adams' view of consolidation entailing: 1) eschewing permanent competition, 2) placing experts over the process of regulation, 3) waiting for investigations to lead to legislation, 4) winning legitimacy for combinations as a hedge against bankruptcy, 5) drawing a line against government ownership, and 6) looking for a Caesar to shape up both the political atmosphere and the unwholesome behavior within the industry in order to achieve national consolidation. A seventh point was now added: Corporations (railroads), national banks, and the Treasury had a common interest in staving off the fashions of soft money.

Garfield's Visit to Adams's Home

During the 1870s Adams and Garfield were in touch with one another. They may have first met in 1869 with Henry Adams inviting the Ohioan to the family home. Garfield had just gotten help from his patron, Hugh McCulloch, the first controller of the currency and then secretary of the Treasury in the Johnson administration. McCulloch had helped Garfield move up that year to a House committee chair. Henry urged Charles to take an interest in the man.

> Wells and Garfield are coming to Boston. I have invited them to Quincy. We will have Atkinson too, and Greenough, and cut out our work. Garfield will talk about a railway schedule with you, for his census—which is a bore. So get ready to help him, for he may help you some day. He may never come up, but he probably will swim pretty strong.[49]

Garfield's Correspondence with Adams

Garfield and Charles Adams next exchanged letters in 1873, the year that the bond market crash brought turmoil to railroading. Garfield thought it time to speak up on the topic and prepared an address on railroad regulation. In his address he quoted Adams at least three times while raising the specter of monopolist influence in politics. What bothered Garfield the most was their heavy-handedness in the political arena. In the end, Garfield favored a national, regulated utility, that is, a regulated monopoly.

> [Some] insist that the system has overgrown the limits and the powers of the separate States, and must be taken in hand by the national government, under that provision of the national Constitution which empowers Congress to regulate commerce among the several States. When it is objected that this would be a great and dangerous step towards political centralization—which many think has already been pushed too far—it is responded that, as the railway is the greatest centralizing force of modern times, nothing but a kindred force can control it; and it is better to rule it than be ruled by it. (Burke Hinsdale in *The Works of James A. Garfield*, Vol. II, 1882, pp. 46–49. The cover letter on a copy to Charles F. Adams, Jr., dated May 31, 1873, in the Garfield Papers, Library of Congress.)

With this sentiment expressed, Garfield could hardly be classed as an anti-monopolist.

Sending his address to Adams, Garfield pointed out in his cover letter, "I am preparing an article a portion of which will be devoted to the discussion of railroad corporations and their future relation to our politics. *Will you do me the favor to tell what is the latest thing you have written on the subject?*"[50] Adams could not reply immediately. The following October, however, he wrote the Ohioan in a generous spirit, "Should you in the approaching session desire on any point to avail yourself of any suggestions in my power to offer you, I hope you will not hesitate to call upon me—you will always find me most ready to respond to the extent of my ability."[51]

As generous as Adams appeared to be, he would apparently not send Garfield a copy of the letter to Osgood in defense of naming a business representative on the state commission. With that in hand, if Garfield had a mind to, he could have urged cartel leaders to moderate their objections to non-experts. Garfield, so gladly accepted into the hard-money elite, was left bereft of the resources they had developed. What if Garfield, in January 1881, had leaked to the press Adams's letter to Osgood? Likely the prospects of the legislative landscape would have taken on a more positive aspect.

Adams's Legislative Suggestions to Garfield

In 1877 they were in touch with one another again. The Democratic Congress was considering the Republican Garfield as Speaker of the Democratic House.[52] Adams wrote in his diary, "Prepared and sent to General Garfield a bill for natl. r. r. comm."[53] Adams might have expected that if Garfield became Speaker, he would give his bill to the appropriate House committee. Garfield, however, did not become Speaker.

A year later, railroad accidents loomed large in the public mind. The *Times* reported that Adams and Garfield had come up with a better method of investigation. It seems to have fit Adams's parameters for the sunshine law. Their solution required removing accident investigations from court delays or coroners' juries. Rather, the Army Corps of Engineers, following the example of the Massachusetts Railroad Commission, would give the matter immediate attention. On February 26, 1878, the *Times* editorialized, "We are extremely glad to note that Mr. Garfield has again brought to the attention of the House of Representatives the measure introduced by him at the instance of Mr. Charles Francis Adams. . . . We bespeak for Mr. Garfield's measure the early and earnest attention of Congress."[54] The leadership assigned the bill to the committee on railroads and canals. Its course, however, is unclear. With the Democrats controlling the House and with experts out of favor, the bill could have simply died in committee. If Congress had passed the bill, it might have kept a door open for a cartel law to come later. After his election in 1880 and before his inauguration, Garfield could have pressed the lame duck Congress to pass the bill. More importantly, by the *Times'* discussion everyone knew that Garfield and Adams were working together.

Adams seems to have influenced Garfield further in 1878 during the debate on the Reagan regulation bill. When discussing the bill, Garfield appears to have used Adams's analogies in criticizing it. Biographer Allan Peskin mentions Garfield's "proud advocacy of the Reagan bill,"[55] but in his diary, Garfield wrote that he voted for the bill with "some hesitation."[56] On the House floor, Garfield objected that the Reagan bill too quickly brought complaints to the corporations. Similarly, Adams wanted to avoid a quick recourse to the courts, the exasperating practice among the western commissions. Adams had written, "In the West the fundamental idea behind every railroad act was force—the commission represented the constable."[57] Likely using the analogy, Garfield told the House, "I regret that those two central sections of the bill have been wreathed about by so much verbiage of a common law indictment."[58] In the two men's criticism one term was lacking. It was "grand jury." Either Adams or Garfield could have said with disdain, "The grand jury would issue a common law indictment for the constable to deliver to the railroad." Adams did not support the Reagan bill because it reversed what he considered the proper order of investigating first and then legislating. While Garfield could see Adams's point, he still supported the Reagan bill.

Many might have realized that Garfield was Adams's man in the Congress. The Adams brothers probably knew it. The *Times* probably knew it. The only trouble was that the relationship had not been productive. Adams's railroad bill had not emerged from the House. The plan for the Army Corps of Engineers to take over investigations of railroad accidents had not materialized. With Adams moving to the cartel in 1879 and Garfield moving up to the Senate, it remained to be seen whether they would work together in the near future.

Chapter IV

Albert Fink, Cartel Manager; Charles F. Adams, Jr.,
Lobbyist; and James Garfield, Legislator

[1]   Adams, Henry, *Novels,* etc. Library of America, 1983, pp. 939f.

[2]   Adams, Charles. *Railroads: their Origin and Problem.* New York: Putnam's, 1878, p. 140.

[3]   Gilchrist, D. T. "Albert Fink and the Pooling System," *Business History Review,* Vol. 34. Cambridge: Harvard University. 1960, p. 29.

[4]   *NYT,* Jan. 15, 1884.

[5]   Laumann, Edward O., and David Knoke, *The Organizational State.* Madison: University of Wisconsin Press, 1987, p. 9.

[6]   Adams, Charles F. Jr. *The Federation of the Railroad System, Argument . . . before the Committee on Commerce of the United States House of Representatives on the Bills to Regulate Interstate Railroad Traffic,* February 27, 1880. Evanston: Transportation Library, Northwestern University, p. 9.

[7]   Ambrose, Stephen. *Nothing Like It in the World: The Men Who Built the Transcontinental Railroad, 1863–1869.* New York: Simon & Schuster, 2000, p. 246.

[8]   Adams, Charles, *Railroads,* pp. 186f, 195–197.

[9]   Ibid., p. 179.

[10]   Gilchrist, p. 29.

[11]   *NYT,* June 18 and 28, 1889. Fink died April 8, 1897. See Gilchrist, p. 28.

[12]   Adams, Charles, *Railroads,* p. 191.

[13]   Ulen, Thomas Shaman. *Cartels and Regulation: Late Nineteenth Century Railroad Collusion and the Creation of the Interstate Commerce Commission.* Ph.D. diss., Stanford: Stanford University, 1979, p. 259.

[14]   *NYT,* July 23, 1885.

[15] Baehr, Harry W., Jr. *The New York Tribune since the Civil War.* New York: Octagon Books, 1972, p. 182.

[16] *NYT,* April 20, 1878.

[17] *NYT,* August 10 and 12, 1881.

[18] Ulen, p. 187.

[19] Adams, *Railroads,* p. 173.

[20] Ibid. p. 177.

[21] *NYT,* August 10 and 12, 1881.

[22] *NYT,* November 21, 1881.

[23] Adams, Charles F., Jr. *Diary,* November 20, 1877. Boston: Massachusetts Historical Society.

[24] Adams, *Diary,* January 8, 1878.

[25] Ibid., February 22, 1878.

[26] Ibid., June 25 and July 5, 1878.

[27] Ibid., March 23 and June 3, 1878.

[28] Ibid., November 22, 1878.

[29] Ibid., November 22, 1878, and May 2, 1879.

[30] Ibid., May 2, 1879.

[31] Ibid., January 4, 5, 9, and 14, 1882.

[32] Adams, *Railroads,* pp. 194f.

[33] Ibid., p. 191.

[34] *NYT,* January 28, 1880.

[35] *Adams, Charles Francis, Jr., 1835–1915, An Autobiography.* Boston: Houghton Mifflin, 1916, p. 174.

[36] Ibid., 1916, pp. 174f.

[37] Adams, *The Federation of the Railroad System,* p. 9.

[38] Laumann and Knoke, p. 12.

[39] *NYT,* February 26, 1882. George Stephenson (1781–1848) began experimenting with railroad locomotives in the second decade of the nineteenth century and by 1825 had produced his best model for demonstration.

[40] Adams, Charles F., Jr. to Charles S. Osgood, chair, Joint Committee on Railroads, Massachusetts legislature, February 20, 1879, in relation to the "Organization,

duties, compensation, etc., of the Board of Railroad Commissioners" (Mass. Documents, House, No. 225, item 124) in the *Collection of Charles Francis Adams, Jr.* Boston: The Massachusetts Historical Society.

[41] Cullom, Shelby, *Fifty Years of Public Service.* Chicago: A. C. McClurge & Co., 1911, p. 308.

[42] Adams, *Railroads*, pp. 132f.

[43] *NYT,* February 19, 1880.

[44] Adams, *Autobiography*, p. 174.

[45] Adams, *Railroads*, pp. 115f.

[46] Ibid., pp. 193–195.

[47] Ibid., p. 193.

[48] *NYT,* January 3, 1879.

[49] Adams, Henry, to Charles F. Adams, Jr. June 22, 1869, in *Letters of Henry Adams, 1858–1891,* Worthington Chauncey Ford, ed. Boston: Houghton Mifflin, 1930, pp. 162f.

[50] Garfield to Charles F. Adams, Jr., May 31, 1873, *Garfield Collection, LC.*(Our emphasis.)

[51] Adams, Charles, Jr. to Garfield, October 1, 1873, *Garfield Collection, LC.*

[52] Woodward, C. Vann. *Reunion and Reaction, The Compromise of 1877 and the End of Reconstruction.* Boston: Little, Brown, 1951, pp. 171–173.

[53] Adams, Charles, *Diary,* January 27, 1877.

[54] *NYT,* February 26, 1878. Garfield had introduced the bill (HR 3384) on February 18, 1878.

[55] Peskin, Allan. *Garfield.* Kent State University Press, 1978, p. 497.

[56] Garfield, James. *Diary.* Edited by Harry James Brown and Fredrick D. Williams. East Lansing: Michigan State University Press, 1981. Vol. 4, p. 155, December 11, 1878.

[57] Adams, *Railroads*, p. 138.

[58] *CR,* 45th Cong., 2nd sess., Vol. 7, Pt. 4, May 9, 1877, p. 3406.

CHAPTER V

The Midterm Election Campaign of 1878: Republicans Rally against the Greenback Surge

The hard-money contingent in Congress would face passage of the twenty-year rechartering bill in 1882, an off-year campaign when no presidential candidate would top the ticket to keep discipline. They would manage to so organize the committees that the soft-money parties were greatly reduced in influence.

Smarting after the silver votes in early 1878, the gold advocates managed to turn the November midterm campaign against the greenback. Subsequently, they displayed a new prowess in the Senate organization, bringing more western members to their view of matters. After his inauguration, President Garfield would do his part by replacing government department heads who had helped in the 1878 campaign. When the banking bill emerged for a vote in 1882, these combined efforts in the Senate and in the White House would prove to have a salutary effect for the hard-money cause.

The second matter in the coming administration was the effort by major railroad owners to win congressional approval for the Adams plan to consolidate the companies into a single trust. While this effort failed, at least it testified to the post-resumption availability of money to carry out the project. With both banking and railroading coming before Congress in 1881 and 1882, it is best to take a long look at the run-up to those dates.

Going back to the creation of the hard-money currency provisions of the Constitution, it is worth noting that the U.S. Constitution gave Congress authority over the currency backed by gold and silver. It also gave Congress authority to issue "greenbacks" in cases of emergencies, such as wars. Three decades earlier the Congress approved a charter for the National Bank organized at Philadelphia. President Andrew Jackson, however, found it monopolistic and undemocratic, too often interfering in electioneering, and closed it down. Jackson's action gave a spur to state banking with all the attendant problems of exchange rates across the country. At the outbreak of the Civil War the Democrats left Washington. The old Whigs, now Republicans, made a new majority, and seized the chance to authorize "national banks." They would depend on gold in private hands surrendered to the government for notes. Notes were usable in all states and would boost interstate trade, being free of exchange rate difficulties.

Hugh McCulloch was a patron of the system. He remained important because he made a protégé of Congressman James Garfield, helping Garfield at the end of the 1860s in winning a committee chairmanship. When the banking bill first arose, McCulloch was a Fort Wayne Democrat. He went to Washington to oppose the legislation, stayed, and became the First Controller of the Currency lodged in the Treasury. He then canvassed the country for businesses to enter banking and had the most fortune in the New England states. In both the Johnson and Arthur administrations he would serve as secretary of the Treasury.

The banking bill provided for deposits of at least $100,000 in gold at the Treasury, exchanged for bonds. The bonds were presented at the Controller for bank notes designating the name of the bank of origin. Owners retained control over their circulation, having the right to pull their reserve out of the system. The legislation put a tax on state banking, driving many of those companies out of business. Massachusetts would go so far as to declare that there could be only one state bank. That state provision, of course, placed significant influence on their members of Congress to defend national banking.

During the war the government also printed greenbacks. The quartermaster corps would use them to buy supplies. In small-town America nearly every family had a pig in its back yard under contract to be sold to the government to feed the troops, making the currency widely used. The catch was that if a debtor tried to use the paper to pay back a bank loan, the banker usually objected. The banker would rather do business exclusively in gold and gold notes.

From the moment he entered President Hayes' cabinet in 1877, Secretary of the Treasury John Sherman pressed forward in a campaign of selling U.S. bonds to underwrite the coming resumption of species payments. Following the British example, he planned to "make only a show" of being able to redeem greenbacks. Still he had to reduce the total circulation of currency, which, in turn, caused stringency across the country. With less cash in the economy, businesses had less to borrow from the banks. Laborers faced reduced wages. In the end, once the gold standard was reached, foreign investors returned and the economy turned up.

The most sensitive segment of the country proved to be the railroads and their employees. The railroads faced difficulties in borrowing and the workers were strapped for cash. One incident illuminated the entire scene. In 1877 the recently formed cartel and its pooling agreement gave the B & O only nine percent of the freight and receipts. The next day the company, verging on bankruptcy, reduced wages, prompting a strike not only at the B & O but also throughout the rest of the industry. (At the other extreme, the New York Central immediately granted wage increases and managed to remain free of strikes.)

For the twenty-first-century reader, the dimensions of the currency question are not easily understood. The first thing to appreciate is that a wall of legislation now separates us from the politics of the currency question. Ever since the 1913 passage of the Federal Reserve Act we have lived in a different world because Congress no longer exercises direct authority over the money supply. To make head or tail of public policy requires later generations to honestly descend into the *esoterica* and discover that it had importance for our forbears, who would win office and who would not.

As shall be seen, New Englanders held an inordinate share of the gold reserves. Needless to say, leaders of the region after the war wanted to get back to a gold standard as soon as possible. England had done the same at the end of the Napoleonic Wars, and it was popularly believed that consequently England enjoyed great prosperity over the subsequent decades. To make the shift, the English had to endure a momentary bump in their economy, but it was soon over and forgotten. In the United States, however, the process hit a snag. On December 18, 1865, the House of Representatives, remembering what the greenback advocates had promised during the war about their extinction with the coming of peace, voted 144 to 6 in favor of "contracting the circulation with a view to an early resumption of specie payments." Secretary of the Treasury Hugh McCulloch proceeded to extinguish greenbacks, but as liquidity faded, business groups complained and McCulloch suspended the operation.

The bond market crash of 1873, prompted in part by oversubscription of railroad bonds and a departure of foreign investors, refueled interest. In 1875 Congress finally passed the Resumption Act to take effect in January 1879. Between those dates polarization increased with increasing economic stringency. As first greenbackers pressed their case, and then the silver interests came to the fore. The great railroad strike of 1877 seemed to further push the partisans to get on with a solution. In early 1878 a silver bill was passed as an amendment to the Resumption Act. But, as shall be seen, it opened up a new opportunity for greenbackers, making the midterm elections of 1878 a harrowing experience for the gold advocates. Several greenbackers entered Congress.

Garfield as an Early National Bank Advocate

One strong advocate for hard money from the outset was congressman James Garfield of Ohio. He displayed a grasp of the problem and insisted on finding a solution. Tracking Garfield on the subject can help to explain some of the opportunities he took for the cause once he became president. Speaking on the need to contract the currency which McCulloch had failed the year before, Garfield painted an 'either/or' picture for the House of Representatives:

> The greenback currency was issued only as a war measure, to last
> during the necessities of the war, then to be withdrawn, and give place to
> the national bank currency.

The war is now ended; and unless we mean to abolish the national bank system, and make the government itself a permanent banker, we must retire from the banking business, and give place to the system already adopted. Unless gentlemen are now ready to abandon entirely the national bank system, they must consent that ultimately the greenback circulation shall be withdrawn, and that the notes of national banks shall furnish a paper currency, which, together with gold, shall constitute the circulating medium of the country.[1]

Garfield would often return to this theme, especially to improve national banking. In the House he had served on ways and means, and won the chair of banking and currency, a post from which he could speak with some authority. One thing he did was to investigate the gold panic and the part that financier Jay Gould played in it. Next, he assumed the chair of the House committee on appropriations and then served four years as chair of the House committee on the census. He brought an unusual discipline to these tasks, leading fellow committee members into intensive studies of the committee mandates, turning the committee work into seminars often followed by some articles to magazines. His work on the census even brought him the opportunity to address the Social Science Association.[2] He gained a reputation for being deliberative with public issues, and some in the country may have thought that he would do the same as president.

Garfield's Study of the Distribution of the Currency

Turning to the quantity of currency, Garfield told the House that he sought an answer to the question, "How is the country now supplied with currency?" Looking over the figures to measure the *per capita* distribution, he divided the banking figures for both 1860 and 1869 by the 1860 census figures, and by regions, and ran a comparison. He found that since the outbreak of the war New England had advanced far beyond the rest of the country. He said that the six New England states, under the euphemism "the East," had bank resources amounting to:

. . . $33 1/3 for each inhabitant. Compared to the 1860 figures, New England had experienced an increase of one hundred and thirty-three percent. By contrast, in the Southern and Southwestern States the circulation had reduced eighty-eight percent.[3]

As he noted the sharp contrasts, the prospect of inter-sectional unrest gripped Garfield's mind. It could easily undo the banking system—some greenback leaders even foresaw a civil war that would unite the South and West in a fight against the Northeast. He voiced his alarm:

It ought to be understood everywhere that the great injustice done to the western and southern portions of the country by the present distribution of banking facilities is so flagrant that it cannot much longer be endured; and if the wrong is not soon righted, the overthrow of the national banking system is imminent.[4]

Through legislation he proposed redistributing bank circulation. Garfield added:

> If we hope to thrive by perpetuation of the great wrong done to the South and many portions of the West by refusing this distribution, you gentlemen must take the responsibility. I have done what I could to remedy the evil.[5]

Four years later, Garfield had to admit disappointment, telling the House, "the $54,000,000 was issued so slowly that even today four and one third millions of that amount has not been taken by national banks in the States that had less than their proportion of circulation."[6]

New England's High Economic Status

The 1880 Census, sorted as Garfield did, reported that New England continued to stand head and shoulders above the rest of the economy. The region was at the top not only in banking but in other measures of the economy as well. One might have expected in modern debates and studies that this persistent and skewed pattern in the regional distribution of wealth in America would figure in, but it has not. The results are mixed. Over the subsequent decades New Englanders would not have wanted their region pointed out as exceptional, but, on the other hand, it is difficult to understand some of the national politics at the time unless one does just that.

To begin with, commonly accepted definitions of regional boundaries have been lacking. While Garfield distinguished the six New England states as "the East" for their relatively great wealth, there is no agreement among later investigators on the regional boundaries. Others combined the six states with the five states from the Middle Atlantic region and called it the northeast.[7] I treat New England separately, partly because, as a studious politician, Garfield recognized the situation and its plausible consequences. I also treat New England separately partly because I have found through an application of the sociogram method of analyzing preferences among group members, that Senate New Englanders won special recognition in the Senate organization and held it at least until 1913.

The popular interest in silver arose in the 1876 apparently following a two-day address in the Senate by Nevada's John P. Jones, which catalyzed the question only to put backbone in the gold advocates.[8] The popular support for hard money was no longer difficult to muster in the New England region. Allen Weinstein noted in his 1970 study that to New Englanders of modest means, most of whom never owned a resumption bond, the silver movement appeared to be a continuation of earlier "repudiationist" campaigns to undermine the federal government . . . nowhere in the country was opposition to remonitization [of silver] more intense than among the rank and file agrarian and rural New England voters of both major parties.[9]

Comparing and contrasting the size of banks in the region to similar statistics across the country may explain the strong, popular New England response. Only eight percent of the nation's population lived in New England, but the region benefited from over a third of the national banking. Banks in the region were not only more numerous but also larger than elsewhere. There was one bank for every 7,000 persons in New England, compared with one bank per 21,000 persons elsewhere in the country. Understandably, the average New Englander had a greater opportunity to do business with individual national banks, and from their familiarity with the greater density of national banks they were more likely to favor the federally franchised institutions.

When it came to banking leaders discussing with their congressmen the prospects for their institution, it stands to reason that the New England bankers, managing banks twice the size of those in the rest of the country, would have seen little reason to take their cues from the outside the region. By the same token, their larger size would have kept outsiders from understanding them. Too much outside influence in the banking legislation could cause considerable damage to the region's economy.

Inter-regional discussion was difficult to promote. Conkling may have tried. In 1875 silverite John Jones of Nevada, a friend of Conkling, having entered the Senate in 1873, became a member of the committee on finance. On the other hand, in 1877, Senator Justin Morrill of Vermont took the opposite tack. Morrill, after several years of subordination on the finance committee to inlander Sherman, never again accepted a subordinate committee seat under an inland senator. Rather, to the end of his career Morrill took his secondary seats under freshmen senators either from New England or from other coastal states. There may have been a trade-off here. If those freshmen looked to Morrill for endorsements for a re-election, they likely had to please him by not endorsing inlanders' views. Morrill could stand free of the inland soft-money influences and unequivocally represent the New England hard-money culture, easily winning the title of "father of the Senate." Concurrently, according to Cullom of Illinois, Hoar of Massachusetts was always pressing for New England men to fill the vacancies in the bureaucracy. The energies of the New England delegation were devoted in no small part to keeping the initiatives with their own region.

The exceptional character of New England banking showed that providence had been good to the region. The entire economy was far ahead of that of the rest of the nation. Industry thrived there in part because its rainfall exceeded rainfall elsewhere and the rain combined with the hilly geography made it possible to store quantities of water.

Rivers and streams had driven waterwheels for years, especially since the 1840s. Louis Hunter writes, "As of 1880, the six states of New England possessed 33 percent of the developed water power of the United States, although occupying but 2 percent of the nation's land area."[10] Remnants of 3,000 millponds can still be found there. In addition, the Puritan emphasis on thrift and hard work led not only to shipbuilding that changed models every year but also to munitions works, textiles, milling and other examples of inventiveness. In the 1870s, investments in steam power advanced, benefiting from the growth of skilled labor employed in earlier milling. This steam power economy had come to depend on the rapid movement of money from investors and lenders to businesses and back again. After the Erie Canal opened, New England agriculture proved less profitable and the region abandoned much of that business to the West.

Economic reports for 1880, summarized in Table 3, show that on 4 measures calculated *per capita,* the New England region stood in the vanguard of 1) industrial horsepower, 2) value added in manufacturing, 3) bank notes (Garfield's interest), and 4) ownership of U.S. bonds. On a per capita basis, the neighboring Middle Atlantic States were no match. *Bankers' Magazine* in January 1881 was the first to issue the data on bond purchases, drawing upon the Census data that would become public much later. Their early publication could have supported the hard-money interests as Garfield prepared to take office.

Table 6. Per Capita Measures of Wealth of Selected Regions of the United States, 1880.

Region	Horsepower per 1,000	Mfg. Value Added Per Person	Value of National Banknotes Per Capita	No. of Private Holders of U.S. Bonds Per 100,000 Ppl
New England	185	$105.70	$34.11	664
Middle Atlantic	98	66.10	10.73	248
Balance of Nation	45	14.14	2.85	55
National Average	69	36.80	7.18	146

Sources: Tenth Census, 1880.
Column 1: Power Used in Manufactures, Table 1, p. 9.
Column 2: Albert W. Niemi Jr., State and Regional Patterns in American Manufacturing, 1860-1900 *(Greenwood Press, Westport, CT, 1974), p. 183.*
Column 3: Tenth Census, 1880, compared with the report of the Controller of the Currency.
Column 4: Annual Report of the Secretary of the Treasury, 1880, p. 85, and Tenth Census, 1880, Valuation, etc. Ownership of the Debt. Table IX(*exclusive of DC residents and private corporations).*

New England residents enjoyed a more industrialized and urban economy than did the average person in the rest of the United States. New England industrial horsepower per 1,000 persons reached 185 or nearly twice the level of 98 found in the 5 Middle Atlantic States. Contributing to this advantage were the many small and large manufacturing firms along the several New England rivers. Correspondingly, value added through industry stood 60 percent greater in New England than in the Middle Atlantic States. National banking wealth per capita was more than 3 times greater than in the region immediately to the south, and bond purchases were over 2 times greater than in the Middle Atlantic region. Any combining of the data from New England with the Middle Atlantic regions minimizes the gains New Englanders had made during the war years and makes it difficult to explain the region's position on the politics of the Gilded Age.

The contrasts between New England and the remainder of the nation were even more striking. Horsepower was 4 times greater; manufacturing value, 7 times greater; and banking strength and bond purchasers, 12 times greater. Understandably, the difference between the New England economy and the rest of the country made that region a world unto itself.

Southern New England was especially strong in banking. In Massachusetts, the banks held $44 per resident; in Rhode Island, $55 per resident; and in Connecticut, $32. By contrast, the national banks in New York, the nation's leader in commercial activity, worked with about $11 per state resident; the other Middle Atlantic States operated at about the same level. On an institutional basis, New Englanders, especially those in the lower three states, had the most to protect in national banking and would have had a greater affinity among themselves than with New York.

William Graham Sumner's Explanation of Demands for Currency

Easterners might have found that sociologist William Graham Sumner of Yale had explained their good fortune. In his work of 1874, *A History of American Currency*, Sumner suggested that intensity of local economies set the demand for money. He divided those economies into urban and agricultural. He maintained that in the intense urban economies, cash reached a high velocity and less cash became necessary, but in rural economies where cash was needed only seasonally, more was needed. Sumner's views, one can surmise, became familiar in decision-making circles, when he wrote of paper currency:

> The whole story . . . goes to show that the value of a paper currency depends on its amount . . . This amount, of course, is relative to the requirements of the country for performing its exchanges. What the requirement is, however, no man can tell. There is no rule for finding it. It does not depend on population, or wealth, or the amount of the exchanges. It bears no fixed relation to any known or ascertainable quantity. An agricultural country wants more, for the same population and wealth, than a manufacturing country. A sparsely populated country wants more, other things being equal, than a densely populated one. A country in which the means of communication are poor wants more, other things being equal, than a country with good means of communication. It is idle to attempt to compute it at so much per head, or so much per thousand of wealth.

Currency is economized also by banking arrangements and clearinghouse processes; railroad extension and all facilities of communication reduce the requirement.[11]

The weakness of Sumner's explanation was that he minimized the upcoming rapid improvements in technology. While other regions had a much later start in getting their economies going, the advance of steam power to drive not just railroad engines but also factories would begin to level the playing field for industrial America. Chicago and other Midwest cities relying on stationary steam power would soon boom. The advent of electric power at the turn of the century would launch the nation into a full-dressed industrial revolution capped off by the building of hydroelectric dams after World War I.

At the time, the maldistribution of bank notes disturbed Garfield, and he kept making his views public. During the controversy over silver in 1876, in a strong appeal to hard-money interests, Garfield wrote an article for the February issue of the *Atlantic Monthly* summarizing the hard-money position and presenting a glossary of soft-money arguments. He stressed that the currency had to be international, a point that soft-money advocates could not understand. He also held that the currency had to be immunized against congressional whimsy. For Garfield, national banking met both requirements.

The Increasing Stringency Leading up to Resumption, January 1, 1879

As the solution of resumption remained out of reach, the delay probably led to political polarization as seen in the division in the Republican Party over silver. In the 1870s, the greenback question remained before the public, but more interest arose around silver advocates after they charged that the government was conspiring to reduce the silver circulation. The country, caught between the rock of 1873 business failures and the hard place of preparing for resumption in 1879, fretted over options. The silver debate lasted some time, and, as Weinstein's tables suggest, Midwestern Republican congressmen increasingly turned to support silver. Northeastern gold advocates became more and more isolated.

Table 7. Votes by House Republicans on the Silver Question, Late 1870s.

Legislation	Date	For Silver	Against Silver	% For
Reagan Amend.	March 30, 1876	23	64	26 %
Landers Amend.[17]	June 28, 1876	25	36	41 %
Kelly Motion[18]	July 24, 1876	34	37	48 %
Bland Bill[19]	December 13, 1876	44	34	56 %
Bland Bill[20]	November 5, 1877	66	24	73 %
Matthews Resolution[21].	January 28, 1878	74	56	56 %
Source: Allen Weinstein, *Prelude to Populism: Origins of the Silver Issue, 1867-1878* (Yale, New Haven, Ct., 1970): Reagan Amend. Table 1, pp. 110f; Landers Amend. Table 2, pp. 112f; Kelly Motion, Table 3, pp. 120-122; Bland Bill, Table 4, pp. 192f; Bland Bill, Table 5, pp. 238f; Matthews Resol. Table 8, pp. 314f.				

Discussion: In a matter of two years—from the Reagan Amendment to the Matthews Resolution—support for silver among House Republicans tripled from 23 to 74.

After a passage of the Bland bill by the House, congressman Richard Bland of Missouri reflected on that unrest and the legislative process at a meeting of some New York bankers and brokers. They had come down to Washington to object to the act and Bland told them that

> If I were in debt five years ago a hundred dollars, the wages of my labor, worth one dollar a day would pay the debt. Today, by the reduction of the volume of the circulating medium, you have so reduced prices, till labor is worth only fifty cents a day . . . If I know the people I represent throughout all the West—and we had a little experiment last summer [the great railroad riots], when there was an uprising from one end of the Union to the other—promises were made that this financial matter would be attended to, and the people should have some relief; and these people went home, and are looking to Congress.

> But I tell you that if you put on the screws much further, and reduce this people much further to the necessities, when their uprising comes again, there is no power in this government to put it down again, and instead of your bonds being paid in gold, they will be wiped out with a sponge! [12]

The riots ended in August 1877. Financial discussions continued to sweep through the country. In November 1877, three months in advance of the legislation, Hugh McCulloch warned in the *North American Review* that resumption would "drive [gold] out of the country."[13] Nonetheless, the House passed the Bland Silver Bill a second time, leading to the momentary suspension of bond trading. The Senate Republicans finally agreed to take up the matter at the second session of the 45th Congress, opening in December 1877. That month the Republicans shuffled committee seats to enhance the influence of the New England delegation.

Throughout these public discussions and legislative debates the senators from New England, joined by a few others on both coasts, uniformly favored the gold standard. Most of the rest of the country opted for silver. Advocates on either side testified to the morality of their own positions and the evil of their opposition. The money question had created another community of melodramatic antagonism laying the ground for the later rise to the stump of William Jennings Bryan.

Senate Hard-Money Advocates Arrange Committees to Conserve National Banking

Apparently, the New Englanders were not only aware of their states' differences from the rest of the country's economy. They also appreciated their advantages in the

Republican caucus, and they soon showed the ambition to press it. While the votes in the Senate against their hard-money position came largely from the inland members of both parties the New Englanders had their work cut out for them. They had to bring some of the inland Republicans to their side. Even though the Democrats dominated committees during the last two years of the Hayes administration, the New Englanders managed to keep an eye on affairs by granting most of their delegation ranking minority seats on a minimum of two committees each. When in 1881, the Democrats again almost took over the committees, the slate shows that at least one New Englander sat on each of the committees.

As it turned out, by 1881, the Republicans took control of the committees and the New Englanders managed to achieve their objective by seating the senior inlanders under them on their committees. One can assume that these inlanders heeded the New Englanders' interests if they wanted support for their own legislation.

The New Englanders had in 1877 first attended to committee arrangements for Roscoe Conkling. They placed him under chairmen from New England, which would have led him to hesitate to oppose their legislation. He took seats under Senator George Edmunds of Vermont on the judiciary committee, and Senator Hannibal Hamlin of Maine on foreign affairs. Indeed, on behalf of the gold advocates he may have tried to take leadership against the Matthews Resolution; if he did, the effort proved a failure.

The interest in maintaining this system of surveillance over Conkling clearly appeared in 1881 when Hamlin decided not to run for reelection and left the chair of foreign affairs open. Most observers would have expected the next senior member to move up to the chair. The record, however, shows that another New Englander who had no prior experience on that committee, Ambrose Burnside of Rhode Island, filled the vacancy. His selection probably helped the New England delegation keep a redundant link to Conkling. Similarly, in another committee arrangement redundancy trumped seniority. Henry Dawes of Massachusetts, with no prior record of experience on the committee on Indian affairs, was nonetheless given the chair. Justin Morrill of Vermont probably had a hand in the assignments for Burnside and Dawes since both had just won their second term elections and previously chaired lesser committees where Morrill had also served. That is, Morrill had found them trustworthy on those committees, and they presumably would accept the role taken by New Englanders to keep an eye on the western members.

Some of the Lobbying for the Silver Bill

With the coming of the New Year of 1878, McCulloch, who wrote in November that resumption would drive out gold, finally saw the silver bill's benefits. In fact, he now began claiming that the silver bill's failure would bring dire results, and he urged early adoption. In a shrill letter to Garfield dated January 30, 1878, he wrote that if politicians let the silver debate extend into the fall elections, victory would go to the inflationists.

121

They would "repeal the National Banking System, pass anti-resumption legislation, and issue large amounts of additional greenbacks, and engage in other actions worse than silver."[14] McCulloch's new goal was to get the matter off the public agenda.

The Ferry Amendment: Instructing the Treasury to Conserve Greenbacks Exchanged for Hard Money

As the silver debate ended in February, those legislators, hoping to cool public clamor before the November midterm elections, were in for a rude surprise. A Pandora's box soon opened for greenbacks and wafted all the way into the early fall elections, as Garfield would explain to his wife. In executing the proposed silver bill, the Treasury, of course, would receive the greenbacks in exchange for silver. However, the legislators had failed to instruct the Treasury on what to do with them. Senator Francis Kernan of New York offered an amendment that became the third section of the Silver Bill, calling for the Treasury to cancel the received greenbacks. Senator Thomas Ferry of Michigan, a state with some greenback activity, amended the amendment, replacing the word *canceled* with the word *reissued*.[15] The Ferry amendment passed 42 to 25. As the record of proceedings was confusing, the same proposition was passed later as the Fort bill.[16] That bill (HR 4663) forbade "the further retirement of U.S. legal tender notes." On May 28, 1878, the Senate passed it by a vote of 41 to 18. That was margin enough not only to override a presidential veto and encourage the greenbackers but also to scare the gold advocates into rising to the battle.

Table 5 reviews a portion of the Senate Republicans' roll call vote on the Ferry amendment. Not shown to the left of the table is the block of New England senators uniformly voting against the amendment. Not shown to the right are the Republicans from the South or the West, where national banking activity was minimal (under $1 per capita). These senators uniformly voted for the greenbacks. The table shows that the battleground was among the votes of other non–New England Republicans from the Midwest and coastal areas. Shown here is whether, in Washington, they supported or opposed the position of the New Englanders who sat over them.[17] Giving evidence of the influence of committee chairs over their members, the New England chairmen of committees won the concurrence from other members from outside the region who took half or more of their secondary seats under New Englanders.

Table 8. The Vote of Some Non–New England Republican Senators on the Ferry Amendment (to conserve the supply of greenbacks at the Treasury) by both the Geographical Location of Their Home States and the Frequency of Their Seating on Committees Chaired by Senators from New England.

	Proportion of secondary seats under New England Chairs			
	<u>Half or more</u>		<u>Less than half</u>	
Vote	Seaboard	Inland	Seaboard	Inland
Nay(Favorable to New Eng.)	Conkling, NY, 3/0	Allison, IA, 1/1	Booth, CA, 0/3	
	Mitchell, OR, 1/1	Christiancy, MI, 1/0		
	Sargent, CA, 1/1	Howe, WI, 3/0		
Abstain			Patterson, SC, 1/2	
Aye (Unfavorable to New Eng.)	Cameron, PA, 2/2	McMillan, MN, 2/1	Spencer, AL, 0/2	Oglesby, IL, 0/2
		Cameron, WI, 1/1	Kellogg, LA, 0/3	Teller, CO, 1/2
		Ferry, MI, 2/0		Chaffee, CO, 0/3
				Paddock, NE, 0/3
				Matthews, OH, 1/2
				Kirkwood, IA, 1/2
				Saunders, NB, 0/3
				Windom, MN, 0/3

Probability: The number of names in columns 1 and 2 combined versus columns 3 and 4 combined yielded a chi square of 13.56; 1 degree of freedom, *** < .001.Source: *Congressional Record*, February 15, 1878, *45th Cong., 2 Sess, p. 1110*; *Report of the Controller of the Currency and the Census*. Notes: 1) The non–New England senators selected for this table came from states with at least $1 per capita in national bank notes. 2) The vote was whether to conserve greenbacks received at the Treasury in exchange for gold rather than to destroy them. A vote favorable to New England led them to vote Nay while a vote not favorable to New England led them to vote Aye. 3) Following each name is a ratio showing the number of seats taken under New England chairs by the number taken under chairs from elsewhere; e. g., at the time of this vote Conkling had three assignments under New England chairs and none under chairs from els*ewhere.*

This table is the most important for understanding the formal career of George C. Gorham for it displays in mid-1878 the strong support for greenbacks in the Middle West, which he tried to build upon for the midterm campaign in November of 1878. In columns 1 through 3, 7 out of 14 non–New England senators who came from seaboard states and/or took at least half their seats under New England chairs voted not to conserve the greenback supply. In column 4, all eight senators who came from inland states took less than half their seats under New England chairs. They all voted to conserve the greenbacks. It appears that the senators representing seaboard states more frequently voted with the New Englanders due probably to their own communities being involved in international trade.

This array also shows that committee arrangements tended to influence the behavior of individual senators. Members tended to vote as their chairs did, but not always. Yale sociologist Sumner had predicted as much five years earlier when he claimed that where money turns over slowly (inland areas) more is wanted, while where money turns over rapidly (seaboard areas) less is wanted. Sumner's analysis would prove even more perceptive a few days later when the Congress took up Hayes' veto and no New Englander opposed the veto while no inlander supported it.[18]

The amended silver bill went back to the House. Garfield, perhaps caught up in the euphoria of the moment, endorsed the Senate amendments, saying, "I shall vote for them all,"[19] and became known as a "probationary greenbacker." Senator Ferry's amendment brought the greenback to a new stage, for it assumed "the congressional right to authorize the issue of legal tender paper currency *in a time of no special emergency.*"[20]

While the silver issue seemed settled for the moment, the broader currency question became quite lively. In his 1970 book *Prelude to Populism: Origins of the Silver Issue, 1867–1878,* Weinstein wrote that

> Although monetary standard myths and politics evolved during the brief silver drive of the seventies, the absence of sustained interest by politicians and public alike explains the swift demise of further controversy on the issue for almost a decade following passage of the Bland-Allison Act.[21]

If the question is expanded from "silver drive" to the "money question," one can see that the early passage of the silver bill failed to calm down the currency dispute. As Congress had closed one barn door, it opened another. Greenbackism could have had its strongest surge late in the summer of 1878 only to peak shortly before the November elections.

The rise of greenbackism early in the year had solid footing. A week after Congress passed the Ferry amendment, and before President Hayes vetoed the bill, greenback leaders on February 22, 1878, assembled for a general convention in Toledo, Ohio, north of Hayes's home and south of Michigan, a hotbed of greenbackism.[22] They prepared their message in the face of opinions such as Henry Poor's view of the Ferry amendment that "resumption . . . with the legal-tender clause preserved, is an impossibility," and "government notes can never become the permanent currency of a people."[23] With the legislation carrying the provision to conserve greenbacks received at the Treasury, the Congress overriding the veto must have greatly pleased the greenback leadership at its Toledo meeting.

Treasury Secretary Sherman's Testimony, March 1878, Favoring Greenbacks

Another boon for the greenbackers would come on March 19, when the Senate finance committee heard testimony from John Sherman, secretary of the Treasury. "In a government like ours it is always good to obey the popular current," said Sherman, "and that has been done, I think, by the passage of the silver bill."[24] He told the committee that his strategy followed the British. He believed he did not have to achieve reserves equal to the amount of resumption but had only to "make a show" of meeting the requirements. His second critical view, according to Poor, was his opinion about greenbacks: "Even if the Supreme Court holds them as no longer a full legal tender, they are as much so as a bank-note. If the choice must be made between the two, the common interest would decide in favor of the United States note."[25] In a policy scenario, such a comment from such an official would have had significant weight. The comment amounted to a consequential actor setting a course of policy. In this case, Justin Morrill of Vermont, who had just succeeded Sherman as the head of the committee on finance, would have been more than chagrined. Despite Sherman having given national banks lower status, he reported that the bankers had pledged to underwrite resumption. He told the committee that he had "a written proposition from these gentlemen, and from Mr. [George S.] Coe himself [President of the American Bankers' Association] that if I will give them 4 1/2 percent bonds instead of 4 percents, they will guarantee resumption."[26] Therefore, the bankers were on the line in support of resumption under a Treasury secretary who did not think bank notes qualified as the last resort.

The April Caucus Elects Greenbacker Gorham
to Head the 1878 Congressional Campaign Committee

In the midst of this fluid debate over the currency question, the Republican members of Congress prepared for the fall midterm congressional campaign. They held caucus meetings over several days in April, with 118 House members and 23 senators in attendance. Neither Senator James Blaine nor Senator Roscoe Conkling put in an appearance. The Secretary of the Senate, George Gorham, had authored a piece focusing chiefly on the "southern" problems of postwar racial conflict. The *Tribune* found it "bitter," and thus Gorham's reputation as a bitter writer was launched. The caucus adopted a motion asking President Hayes to drop his Civil Service Order Number One, requiring that "no assessments for political purposes on officers or subordinates should be allowed." Hayes not only complied with the caucus request but also framed the language in the committee's circular, which assured the Government employees that the voluntary contributions—the reformers had always called them assessments—"would meet with no objection in any official quarter."[27] The caucus also expressed hopes of winning the races in 12 to 14 southern districts with black majorities. They elected Gorham as secretary of the Republican Congressional Campaign Committee.[28] In a subsequent circular to government employees, Gorham asked, "Is it 'warring upon the president' to say that the laws should be obeyed, and that to deny a citizen his lawful right to vote is a crime against our system of Government? Is it 'bitter' to say the truth—that this rule is uniformly reversed in the lately rebellious States?"[29] As a California paper had said when he ran in 1867 for governor, "opposition always brightens him," Gorham could not finesse the *Tribune* attack without disclosing his contempt for the source, contempt for the *Tribune's* support in 1872 for the Democrats. Gorham could have simply said that the failure of critics to join the debate about Southern outrages only showed that they conceded his point.

In the election campaign, Gorham took positions on two additional party policies. First, standing on earlier party platforms, he made a strong appeal for citizens' rights in the South and was pleased to tell Republicans that he was one of the remaining radicals in the party. Second, riding the tide of the currency controversies, Gorham encouraged greenback support. In his favor was the vote in Congress supporting the Ferry amendment on greenbacks as well as the stunning defeat of Hayes's veto along with the secretary of the Treasury's comments favoring greenbacks over bank notes. Gorham's "voluntary" assessments proceeded in the departments quite well. Such supervisors as Sherman at Treasury put his name at the top of the sheet circulating through that department. The practice certainly looked like coercion. Other department supervisors also took lists to circulate. That put Gorham close to the center of the operations throughout the city. At his disposal he would have had a network that linked the government employees organized by states, the help of senators to motivate them, and several pro-greenback newspapers in the city.

Henry Poor's Campaign Book: A Rejoinder to Secretary Sherman

Secretary of the Treasury John Sherman had already announced his views favoring the greenback and aroused a rejoinder from Henry Poor, a hard-money publicist. Poor foresaw no end to political agitation. Quoting Congressman Richard Bland's statement about the condition of the poor at the time of the railroad strike a year earlier, Poor added, "the condition of the people has not improved. Their sufferings are still as intense as ever. Their indictment preferred against their oppressors has lost none of its force. They are actively organizing in support of the new party, in almost every town and village throughout the land."[30]

Poor's publication could have served as a tutorial for the hard-money campaign. He titled his chapters "What Is Paper Money?"; "Resumption of Specie Payments"; "The Silver Question"; "Legal Tender Currencies"; "The Greenback Party"; and "Method of Resumption." He gave no credence to Secretary Sherman's easy faith, insisting that "the secretary's maxim, that the popular current is to be followed which ever way it flows, is the curse of all popular governments, and threatens to destroy our own." Likely opposing Sherman's probable run for the presidency, he added, "The path that leads to the presidential mansion is white with the bleached bones of aspirants whose only method of reaching it was to commit themselves to the fickle and treacherous current of popular favor."[31]

Gorham's Fund Raising for the Campaign in the Departments

As the clock ticked down to the midterm elections, the parties prepared. President Hayes's suspension of Civil Service Order Number One doubtlessly discouraged the reformers. Several department heads began circulating subscription sheets to their employees. In the next Congress, a select committee examined the alleged fraud.[32] The signature of the respective department supervisor had topped each sheet, and the project was underway. That is, top federal officials solicited employees on government property to give to the campaign fund, an activity soon to be prohibited by law under penalties as a felony. As shall be seen, President Garfield would later give most of these persons special attention. In 1878 the name of William LeDuc, the commissioner of Agriculture, appeared at the top of a circulated list in the Agriculture Department. A pledge sheet passed through the Post Office Department under the name of Thomas Brady, charged with the postal contract office. Another sheet circulated with the name of Jacob McGrew, sixth auditor, at the top and probably went on to postal contractors. Most important, in the Treasury Department, Secretary John Sherman agreed to circulate a sheet with his name at the top. Later, comptroller John Knox testified that in the Treasury were two groups: a "legal tender faction" and a "national bank faction."[33] Secretary of the Interior Carl Schurz closed the doors of his department to the solicitors, but several of his employees nonetheless volunteered. In the end, Gorham reported that he raised $106,000, exceeding any previous campaign. Probably not more than an eighth of the federal employees took part.

In that campaign, Gorham, secretary of the Senate, took on one more task. He helped manage Roscoe Conkling's campaign for a third term in the Senate. Opposition within the New York party was insignificant; neither the Hayes administration nor any New York faction fielded an opponent. Hayes, in the midst of the campaign, did remove the Customs House employees from patronage control. Nevertheless, Conkling won a third term, crossing a threshold no New Yorker would cross again until the 1930s when Senator Robert Wagner won a third term.

Conkling's Dissatisfaction with National Banking

In his greenback thrust, Gorham most likely found political cover from his friend Conkling. The New Yorker was a staunch gold advocate but still held many questions about national banking. Earlier, in 1867, while serving in the House, Conkling had expressed his views in detail:

> Sir, there was once a great deal to be said upon the question of interest and how to save it; a great deal which I once vainly struggled to obtain the privilege of saying in this Hall when the national bank bill was first on its passage; a great deal which has never been answered by the financiers or the statesmen who originated that measure, and I beg leave to say that in my judgment it never will be successfully answered except

by the vested rights which have intervened and the good faith which has become plighted.[34]

A year later Conkling declared his preference for New York banking, a system founded in part on mortgages, giving it an affinity to a currency based on a measure of gross national product:

> When rebellion raised its hand New York had a banking system of her own, matured and perfected by long experience, which supplied the wants of her people, and comported with her vast resources and her great commerce . . .
>
> It was, in my belief, a better system than that under which we are living now. Regarded in respect of these relations to the government, it was free from one contradiction found in the present system, which has not yet been reconciled to the satisfaction of unbiased and discerning men.
>
> The general banking system . . . involves an interest in coin of six percent per annum upon bonds exempt from taxation, paid by the United States to corporations for circulating a currency for which the United States are ultimately responsible, and which currency they might themselves have issued without the expense of one farthing beyond the paper and engraving and the cost of striking it off. I have heard a great many financiers deal with this point, and I have never heard it so disposed of as to make it appear a good fiscal arrangement for the Government of the United States.
>
> New York had a banking system satisfactory to herself, a system carefully guarded, and the people of New York were content; a system guarded against inflation, for, although banking circulation was based upon mortgages of real estate, and so far unchecked in volume, it was also based upon State stock to the extent of one half, which stocks could never be increased a farthing without a popular vote of the people of the State consenting to the increase.[35]

By the time of the campaign of 1878, McCulloch's earlier hope soured, as the financial question could not be kept out of the campaign. Even the Maine Democrats forsook their Jacksonian hard-money legacy. They stated, "We are opposed to the present national banking system, and in favor of a gradual substitution of greenbacks for national bills." To Poor this statement served as evidence of "the decline in the intellectual and moral tone of the country . . . Now, the hard money party of Maine not only wholly departs its principles, but goes for a money infinitely worse than that of the banks."[36]

Maine Republicans soon enlisted James Garfield to come and help in the state campaign to defend the gold standard. Once he arrived there, Garfield betrayed as much panic as McCulloch had earlier in the year. From Lewiston, Maine, on September 2, 1878, he wrote his wife, worried that the greenback craze had now reappeared after he had thought Congress had disposed of it the previous February.

> The political situation here is full of peril and uncertainty. Within the last year, and *notably within the last six months* [subsequent to the February passage of the silver bill with its provision of the Ferry amendment for saving greenbacks as well as Sherman's March testimony], the greenback craze has broken out with the force and spirit of an epidemic. While we were battling with it in the West, New England was free from its ravages; but now, when we have almost reached specie payments, the pest has burst upon Maine like a thief in the night, and no one can foretell the result. I shall not be surprised if it defeats Powers and Reed, and perhaps Hale. Even Frye is thought to be in danger. It spread among the staid citizens like a midsummer madness. You can hardly imagine the welcome, which has met me here by our friends. All other issues are swallowed up in the absorbing question of what money is and what it ought to be. The old questions which I have been discussing during the last ten years are as fresh and new here as the telephone.

> The mysteries of this intellectual epidemic will never cease to be a wonder to me. It is comfortable to feel that in such a fight, I can look back over 12 years of public discussion, and challenge my opponents to find a speech or a vote of mine in conflict with the position now held by our sound money men.[37]

Forgetting his own endorsement of the Senate greenback amendments to the silver bill six months earlier, Garfield now battled evil. He had not seen at the earlier moment that there was a cloud no larger than his hand, but now in his diary he wrote of the "whirlwind," "a regular mania, an intellectual epidemic," and "the greenback tornado."[38] The virus could emerge almost anywhere and it should never be given encouragement.

Garfield's Address at Faneuil Hall after the 1878 Maine Election

In a matter of two days following the greenback victories in Maine, Garfield and Gorham each in public addresses gave their assessments. The former spoke at Faneuil Hall in Boston on September 10, 1878 as a guest of Senator George Hoar, and the latter at the New Jersey Republican Convention in Newark on September 11. Each cut to the chase regarding the future of national banking. Garfield was in favor and Gorham opposed. These differences in 1878 between the two men may have made Garfield cautious about Gorham in 1881.

Garfield gave five reasons for supporting national banking. First, the government had pledged to issue no more greenbacks. Second, banks with notes out would have to redeem them, helping the process of resumption. Third, banks paid taxes of upwards of $16 million. Fourth, abolition of the national bank circulation would mean that the volume of money would depend on acts of Congress instead of the law of supply and demand. Possibly with Congress in mind rather than the future Federal Reserve System, Garfield said, "No group of men are wise enough to . . . regulate the necessary volume of currency." Finally, Garfield told his Boston audience that trade would languish since drafts, checks, and commercial bills based on national banking would disappear. New Englanders were already persuaded of how helpful those banknotes had become for exporting their surplus production by rail across the country.

Further astonished, Garfield also warned about the growth of greenbackism. The movement had been gaining attention. Before Hayes vetoed the silver bill, greenback leaders had met in Toledo. Three months later, Henry Poor had also said, "They are actively organizing in support of the new party, in almost every town and village throughout the land." Ending his address, Garfield referred to the 4,500 greenback "cells" or study groups, some aided by communists (probably German socialists) and the danger that lay in wait.[39] The October issue of the *Bankers' Magazine* emphasized the same point.[40] The eastern conservative leaders soon found that the best way to express their own institutional strain was to raise the prospect of any alternatives leading to communism. That would feed the popular hunger for melodrama and contending with evil, and also free them from considering negotiable options with cooperatives, etc. The state Republican committee ordered 100,000 copies of Garfield's address.[41] They had learned to hold the breach by resorting to fears about national security.

Gorham's Address before the 1878 New Jersey Republican Convention, Newark

The next day the other side of the question was heard when Gorham, secretary of the campaign committee, spoke before the New Jersey Republican convention at Newark:

> The greenback circulation . . . is not merely an obligation of the Government to fall due and be paid, but lawful money of the United States . . . It is important to the Republican Party that it should state clearly its views and record on the greenback question. . . .

> On this money question, there are Republicans who prefer an exclusive national bank circulation. They are few in number in my judgment. There are other Republicans who would prefer to see the national banks abolished and their circulation displaced by greenback circulation. I believe that class to be the most numerous; perhaps because I belong, myself to that class.

We have had during the last 48 hours a great reminder. The battle in Maine has been a reconnaissance, and has shown where our weakness was, and how the forces of the enemy were disposed. . . . Without any criticism whatever on the management of the campaign in the State of Maine, I firmly believe that the party was misunderstood by many who have heretofore acted with it in that State. In the anxiety there to lead out against inflation of the currency and the wild scheme for issuing an un-limited volume of irredeemable paper money they have omitted, perhaps, clearly to state just how far the Republican Party has hitherto gone, and still does go, on the question of greenback currency . . .

There was never any other specie payment in this country than con-vertibility of paper money. (Applause.) We cannot resume in any other kind, because we never discontinued any other kind. But a great many individuals did believe that the greenbacks were to be destroyed in a lump in 1879 . . . The Republican Party has set its face against contraction.[42]

Concurrently, one of the greenback papers in Washington printed an interview with Secretary Sherman. He repeated his March comments to the finance committee: if a choice came between greenbacks and banknotes, the former would prevail.

Gorham's comments at Newark disturbed the hard-money Republicans. Sherman also came under criticism. Jonas M. Bundy, then editor of the *New York Mail,* and later the author of a Garfield campaign biography, found Gorham's address appalling. He believed that Gorham "has done more to alarm Republicans here than anything that has happened in Maine."[43] The *Times* thought Gorham ought to be "transferred to some other sphere of service."[44] It had been a half-year after the February 1878 passage of the silver bill that the greenback surge appeared in Maine. The election in Maine was the peak perchance of the greenback surge.

Congressman Eugene Hale of Maine, chair of the campaign committee, met Gorham in Washington to discuss what he had said in New Jersey, namely that "No man has any right to say of this party, that it favors any diminution of the volume of paper money now in circulation." He had also told his Newark audience that due to the high party vote in Congress for the Ferry amendment, and then the Fort bill, the vote amounted to laying a plank in the party platform. Reviewing matters with Hale after the address, Gorham said that he had not tried to dictate policy to the committee. Hale's inquiry after the fact implied that, prior to his Newark address, Gorham had not checked out his proposed comments with the committee chair. This practice in Gilded Age politics of acting first and then explaining later was endemic.

The campaign next took a decisive turn when Gorham handed the baton to the hard-money advocates. Hale and Gorham agreed that a new committee ought to go West to educate the voters.[45] Secretary of the Interior Carl Schurz and others soon took to the campaign trail, with Schurz speaking in Cincinnati on September 28.[46]

The October 1878 Atlantic Monthly Spurs the Hard-Money Advocates to Action

The October issue of the *Atlantic Monthly*, coming after Poor's criticism of Sherman and Hale's rebuke of Gorham, spurred the hard-money advocates. Its lead article, "Certain Dangerous Tendencies in American Life," sounded a warning about the nation's moral decline in the aftermath of the Civil War. The article challenged the new leadership to lay claim to the role of the older leadership. They had to reassert that patriotic Americans should again recognize that they live in a moral universe. The article claimed that the previous year's railroad strike and pillage had been symptomatic of the decline. It could lead to the defeat of resumption of specie payments scheduled to begin just ten weeks later. The November vote, however, could show a reversal to that trend if only the new leadership rose to its duties.[47]

John Hay of Cleveland, once Lincoln's private secretary and now a member of the Hayes administration and a stockbroker for John D. Rockefeller, was quite enthused about this turn. He wrote Whitelaw Reid, editor of the *Tribune*, that businessmen could win the battle. "Without buying a single vote, a million could be spent to great advantage—and would be the best investment ever made . . .. Money can carry these elections, and rich men are as blind as moles if they do not see it." The hard-money advocates, spurred by Poor and the *Atlantic*, took hold of the campaign. The sudden surge of campaigning at the end impressed Henry Waterson, a Kentucky editor and Democratic politician, who wrote Samuel Tilden, "We see the Republicans deploy like a phalanx. It is enough to make a cat howl."[48]

This extra effort turned the tide. Both New England and New York Republicans outdid themselves in the election by increasing the number of congressmen to the U.S. House. The election results implied that the northeast took the election as a referendum on resumption two months in advance, and the region heartily approved. The earlier vote in Maine had been the greenback high-water mark.

Bankers to the Rescue in Their First Election Campaign, November 1878

Core to the hard-money drive at the end of the campaign were the members of the American Bankers' Association (ABA), a special-interest lobby. Poor's book and the *Atlantic* article may have moved them. Furthermore, they were learning from a recent strategic mistake and now took a new tack. Bankers, not banks, made up the membership. Organized two years earlier, this group had only recently entered politics. The year 1878 marked a great change in what the association expected of its members, and shows just how quickly an interest group can come out of somnolence and become a disciplined contender, forever thereafter having to be taken into account. During the earlier silver debate, the ABA members had been reluctant to lobby Congress to oppose the bill and looked instead to President Hayes's veto to kill the legislation.[49] But that did not work. After Congress succeeded in overriding the veto, bankers realized that they had missed the opportunity for influence. In the fall campaign, they would come much more to the fore. Members of the nonpartisan ABA fanned out into the South and West, visiting with representatives and senators to distribute literature on the bank task and to make their case.[50]

The effort of bankers to build bridges between hard-money interests and westerners paralleled the development in the Senate where New Englanders were taking western senior senators onto their committees. Members of Congress recalled, of course, that in the spring Secretary Sherman had told the House banking committee that the national banks would back resumption. Then, ABA members circulated 340,000 copies of editorials about the repeal of the federal tax on national banknotes. Its Executive Council issued 115,000 copies of journals and pamphlets. Laumann and Knoke emphasize that the private sector (in this case, the bankers) often provides policymakers with information they later need for their work. Emphasizing that transfer creates a debt on the part of the recipients to the providers, Laumann and Knoke state, "Organizations not only mobilize resources but also deploy resources to buffer the environmental threat as well as to make dependent relations of other organizations so that they can ask the latter to join a collective action pursuing their goals."[51] Therefore, the bankers' visits to their senators and representatives would have made the politicians more sensitive to the bankers' interests.

By October 1878, they were under the spur from several sources. Their own magazine had a warning about communists among the greenbacker cells. Both Poor's volume and the *Atlantic* article most likely gave the ABA members confidence enough to campaign for the Republicans. Across the country, bankers in the many communities could enlist other businessmen and together impress the townsfolk with their torchlight parades. The effort may just have been enough in the northeast to increase the Republican delegation. They had made up the phalanxes Waterson knew he saw and prompted the howling cats he thought he heard. Those phalanxes that appeared in towns across the country in 1878 would appear again and again in coming campaigns and mark the business leadership of the Republican Party.

Garfield's Resumption Day Address, Chicago, January 2, 1879

The November election left the hard-money forces with mixed emotions. While the vote strengthened hard-money Republicans in the northeast, reversing the early trend in Maine, it nonetheless added 15 greenbackers to the House. After the election, President Hayes, probably recalling how quickly the Maine Democrats had shifted from the gold standard to paper money, wrote in his diary of trouble ahead. He wrote, "The unpopularity of banks [is] strong enough to be a cornerstone of parties and platforms."[52] While Garfield thought the election beneficial for business confidence, a month later he noted that the greenbackers were more active than ever.[53] Finally, the Republican caucus's hopes to gain several southern seats was totally frustrated, and the House remained Democratic. That disastrous sortie left some hope with Gorham who soon began consulting with Virginia's independent Democrat William Mahone about jumping party traces and coming to the U. S. Senate to vote on the Republican side. The national greenbackers would ask Mahone to be a candidate for vice president, but he declined.

Two months after the election, Garfield spoke on Resumption Day before the Chicago chapter of Thomas Nichol's Honest Money League of the Northwest. He enlarged his cognitive map of the money dispute by suggesting that there were common institutional interests among the government, railroads, and the banks. He warned that sentiment opposed to the corporations and banks could unite, leading to the suspension of specie payment. "The most dangerous indirect assault upon resumption," he said, "is the attempt to abolish national banks, and substitute additional greenbacks in the place of bank notes." This was the same language used by the Democrats of Maine in their state platform and Gorham in his address to the New Jersey Republicans—only on the opposite side.

In the terminology of Laumann and Knoke, the contrast between the two currency systems in the mouths of opposing speakers—Garfield and Gorham—set the common fate that would bind them into a community of antagonism, betraying a cleavage in the party. Garfield's address in Chicago had filled his host Nichol with enthusiasm. He rose and offered a melodramatic resolution that "such practical and enlightened statesmanship may be extended until the entire people of the Republic are educated in questions of political economy, and until false and delusive theories are banished from our midst." For Nichol the Garfield address at the resumption celebration seemed to promise a party house cleaning. In 1881, as he looked to his reelection to Senate office, Gorham would be very aware of the continuing weight of that antagonism.

At Chicago on Resumption Day Garfield had warned, "The (greenback) effort will call to its support the sentiment which to some extent prevails against moneyed corporations [railroads]. Should the attempt succeed it will inevitably result in suspension of specie payment."[54] That sentiment had already shown itself in the railroad strike of 1877, which provoked renewals of specious monetary theories, thus keeping hard-money advocates on edge. Garfield was now casting a new prophecy. It may have followed from Poor's retelling of the continuing troubles of the laboring class. It also followed from Garfield's disturbing experience in Maine. Add to that his new awareness of the continuing greenback activity. In sum, Garfield's thinking was undergoing a change, moving him beyond his earlier anti-monopoly sentiments and his support for the Reagan interstate commerce bill. He may have entertained new options and new alliances. He could see that Adams was projecting a national railroad consolidation. William Vanderbilt would champion it. So would Jay Gould and Collis Huntington. Through the Hepburn hearings of 1879 many leaders were becoming more familiar with the way in which Rockefeller developed his oil trust. It did not take much imagination to see that the railway trust could be built in much the same way. A consolidated railroad system would find easier terms in capital markets, vastly reduce competition, and through more buy-outs have less difficulty in bringing discipline to the industry. The railroaders needed just the right man in the presidency, such as Garfield, who might have seen that a railroad monopoly would have made resumption even more secure.

Within a week of Garfield's speech in Chicago, Nichol wrote the Ohioan that some admirers could run him for president.[55] Nichol soon found himself in the role of companion, troubleshooter, and adviser to the candidate. The Honest Money League moved to Washington. If Nichol was to encourage a party purge, he was now in a much better position to do so.

Garfield won the presidential election and faced the troubles of the hard-money agenda. Once nominated, the buoyant Garfield would tell the nation in his letter of acceptance that all of the dollars were now equal. At his inaugural, however, his tone changed. Once he was elected, the prospects of the next midterm election may have started looming before him. He sought to finesse the banking issue by saying, "Grave doubts have been entertained whether Congress is authorized by the Constitution to make any form of paper money legal tender." Doubtless, Garfield was thinking of the third section, the Ferry Amendment to the Bland-Allison Silver Bill passed over President Hayes's veto in late February 1878. By 1881 Garfield believed that the Court would find that amendment unconstitutional and, if so, that would precipitate a pure return to the gold standard sought since the end of the Civil War.

The prospects for bank rechartering in 1882 were not at all encouraging. The midterm election of 1878, lacking the discipline of presidential candidates at the top of the ticket, not only brought out greenbackers. It had also shown the Maine Democrats equivocating. In 1882 national banking had to face a real test from those two sources. After the 1878 elections evidence surfaced that even Republicans encouraged support from among greenbackers. For the gold advocates the strategic goal was to at least return their foes to the neutral middle ground. Many gold advocates, along with Garfield, suspected only trouble.

Chapter V

The Midterm Election Campaign of 1878:
Republicans Rally Against the Greenback Surge

[1]   Hinsdale, Burke A., ed. *The Works of James Abram Garfield.* Freeport: Books for Libraries Press, 1970; first published in 1882, Vol. 1, p. 190.

[2]   Leech, Margaret, and Harry James Brown. *The Garfield Orbit.* New York: Harper and Row, 1978, pp. 161–163.

[3]   Hinsdale, Vol.1, p. 552.

[4]   Ibid., Vol. 1, p. 551.

[5]   Ibid., Vol. 1, p. 591.

[6]   Hinsdale., Vol. 2, p. 179f.

[7]   Albert Niemi and Louis Hunter defined New England as a separate entity of six states. However, Walter Nugent, Stanley Coben, and sometimes Allen Weinstein grouped the states differently. The sources for this observation are as follows:

1) Albert W. Niemi, Jr. *State and Regional Patterns in American Manufacturing, 1860–1900.* Westport: Greenwood Press, 1974, Appendix, Pt. 26, Per Capita Manufacturing Value Added by Region, 1860–1970, p. 183.

2) Louis C. Hunter. *A History of Industrial Power in the United States, 1780–1930,* Vol. 1. *Water Power.* Charlottesville: University of Virginia Press, 1979, p. 131.

3) Walter T. K. Nugent. *Money and American Society, 1865–1880.* New York: The Free Press, 1968, p. 296, note 4; p. 310, note 5.

4) Allen Weinstein. *Prelude to Populism: Origins of the Silver Issue, 1867–1878.* New Haven: Yale University Press, 1970, p. 194, note 41; p. 215.

5) Stanley Coben. "Northeastern Business . . . " Mississippi *Valley Historical Review,* June 1959, pp. 67–90.

[8]   Weinstein, 1970, p. 60.

[9]   Weinstein, 1970, pp. 286f.

[10] Hunter, p. 131.

[11] Sumner, William G. *A History of American Currency.* Westport: Greenwood Press, 1968; first published New York: Holt, 1874, pp. 221f.

[12] Poor, Henry V. *Resumption and the Silver Question.* Westport: Greenwood Press, 1969; first published by the author, 1878, p. 225.

[13] McCulloch, Hugh. *North American Review,* "The Resumption of Specie Payments," November 1877, Vol. 125, issue 259, pp. 397–404, p. 403.

[14] Weinstein, 1970, pp. 321f.

[15] *CR,* 45th Cong., 2d sess., Vol. 7, Pt. 2, February 15, 1878, p. 1110.

[16] *CR,* 45th Cong., 2d sess., Vol.7, Pt. 4, May 28, 1878, p. 3871.

[17] *CR,* 45th Cong., 2d sess., Vol.7, Pt. 4., February 15, 1878, p. 1110.

[18] Weinstein, 1970, Table 15, pp. 348f. Compare the "New England States" with the "Midwestern States" and the "Border States."

[19] *CR,* 45th Cong., 2d sess., Vol. 7, Pt., 2, February 21, 1878, p. 1279.

[20] *NYT,* April 30, 1881.

[21] Weinstein, 1970, p. 358.

[22] Poor, p. 217.

[23] Ibid. p. 33, and p. 232.

[24] Ibid. p. 20.

[25] Ibid. p. 47.

[26] Ibid. pp. 23–25, 47, 48.

[27] *NR,* April 24, 1882.

[28] *NYT,* April 9, 11, 19, and 25, 1878.

[29] Author's copy, April 6, 1878.

[30] Poor, p. 230.

[31] Ibid. p. 230.

[32] Senate Report 427, 46th Congress, *Select Committee to Inquire into the Alleged Frauds in the Late Elections,* Senator William A. Wallace, Pennsylvania, Chair, pp. 10, 11, and 26.

[33] Redlich, Fritz. *The Molding of American Banking.* New York: Johnson Reprint Corporation, 1968, p. 121.

[34] *CG,* 39th Cong., 2d sess., Vol. 37, Pt. 3, Feb 28, 1867, p. 1664.

35   *CG,* 40ᵗʰ Cong., 2d sess., Vol. 39, PT. 4, June 15, 1868, p. 3153.

36   Poor, footnotes, 230-231.

37   *Garfield Diary,* Vol. 4, p. 110, footnote 213 (letter of September 2, 1878).

38   Ibid., Vol. 4, p. 116.

39   *Garfield Collection,* Vol. 2, p. 586.

40   *Bankers' Magazine,* October, 1878, p. 248.

41   *Garfield Diary,* Vol. 4, p. 118.

42   Gorham, George C. "The Greenback Issue," September 11, 1878, *LC.*

43   Bundy, J. M., to Col. W. K. Rogers, September 18, 1878, Rutherford B. Hayes
     Library, Fremont, Ohio. Bundy's biography is in the *National Cyclopedia of American
     Biography.*

44   *NYT,* September 18, 1878.

45   *NYT,* September 21, 1878.

46   Bancroft, George, ed., *Speeches, Correspondence, and Political Papers of Carl Schurz.* New
     York: Putnam, 1913, pp. 422–480.

47   Harrison, J. B. "Certain Dangerous Tendencies in American Life," *The Atlantic
     Monthly,* October 1878, pp. 385–402. Houghton, Osgood and Co. published a vol-
     ume under the same title by the same author in 1880.

48   Waterson, Henry, to Samuel Tilden, November 29, 1878, in C. C. Tansill, *The
     Congressional Career of Thomas Francis Bayard, 1869–1885.* Washington, D.C.:
     Georgetown University Press, 1946.

49   Weinstein, 1970, p. 267f.

50   *Bankers' Magazine,* September 1878, p. 203.

51   Laumann, Edward O., and David Knoke. *The Organizational State.* Madison: University
     of Wisconsin Press, 1987, p. 346.

52   Williams, C. R., ed., *Diary of Rutherford Burchard Hayes.* Columbus: Ohio Historical
     Society, 1924, entry for November 12, 1878, pp. 509f.

53   *Garfield Diaries,* Vol. 4, November 6 and December 4, 1878, pp. 143, 144, 152.

54   *NYT,* January 3, 1879.

55   Peskin, Allan. *Garfield.* Kent State University Press, 1978, p. 451.

CHAPTER **VI**

The Acme of a Gilded Age Policy Scenario

January 1879 finally brought the day for which politicians and business leaders had long waited. Having restored the gold standard, Congress and the secretary of the Treasury had forced the hazards of wartime financing back into the bottle. At the Treasury, a person presenting greenbacks could receive an equivalent amount in gold in exchange. (Nobody doubted that it could happen, so no one showed up to make the trade!) Confidence among foreign investors advanced, as did railroad stock. Celebration swept the New York harbor. The resumption of specie payments successfully launched a gold-standard economy that would last for over two generations—into the 1930s.

The next major question crying for attention, railroad regulation, affected both the nation and New York City. In New York it remained to be seen which party would have the last word—the owners who had supplied the capital or the state government that had supplied the initial franchises for the railroads. If capital demanded respect so did state ownership of the canals. How that would play out remained to be seen. The role of the canal as a regulator had fully matured by early 1879 as seen in plans of March 2 by the Chamber of Commerce announced by the *Times* for a special meeting on the free canal proposition. Already ex-Governor Seymour and Senator William Windom had agreed to give addresses.

As time passed the major players' views included their seeing changing opportunities. Very few would have held static positions on a topic over a long period. Understandably the leaders at the cartel felt the optimism created by their new organization and the continuing request by other companies to join. The spurt in the economy seemed to give the railroads the confidence they could handle coming problems. In June 1879, cartel members made $300,000 deposits against fines on infractions.[1] William Vanderbilt, President of the New York Central, now occupied an enviably strong position. With the Hepburn committee investigation underway, he began thinking about regulatory legislation, foreseeing that a congressional solution would be most advisable.

During the hearings of the summer of 1879, Simon Sterne thought he understood what the railroaders wanted and did not like it. Sterne said,

> Mr. Fink's remedy for these evils is to create a corporation which shall practically have control of the whole railway interests of the country and divide the business in proper proportions, and shall end all competition by charging a uniform rate which shall be kept in bounds by stringent legislation, which shall also forbid all making of special contracts. The adoption of this plan would deliver us . . . powerless indeed into the hands of such a corporation.[2]

The same thought came from Chester Arthur a few years later when he said, "No individual and no corporation ought to be invested with absolute power over the interest of any other citizen or class of citizen." Leading New Yorkers were simply staggered by the prospects of the collaboration of the corporations.

The Run-Up to a Settlement in 1879

Arriving at the threshold of great promises, the country had gone over a long trek through that slough of financial despondency that began in 1873 and had even troubled the city managers. Rail business dropped but interest payments on their bonds demanded attention according to schedule. Businesses collapsed and unemployment increased, resulting in fewer receipts for city services. Not until 1875 did Congress pass the resumption act, which postponed fulfillment four years, a risk indeed.

The air was thick with complaints, investigations, and proposed solutions. Apparently sensitive to the rise and fall of empires, one of the first to speak out was Governor Samuel Tilden who named a commission to review the "decay of municipal government." Edwin Burrows and Mike Wallace in *Gotham* tell of the commissioners' plan to reduce the problem by reducing popular participation in government:

> Its members included intellectuals and influentials, like *Nation* editor E. L. Godkin and railroad lawyer Simon Sterne, who had been arguing for some years that the root of New York City's problems was an insufficiently fettered franchise. In March, after nearly two years of deliberation, the commission revealed what it thought should be done. It called for a constitutional amendment that would establish a Board of Finance, to be elected solely by men who paid taxes on property worth over five thousand dollars or an annual rent higher than $250. This Board would appoint all financial and legal officers of the city and take control over all municipal revenues and expenditures. The rest of the citizenry could still participate in electing the mayor and Board of Aldermen, but these worthies would be effectively stripped of their power to distribute public

goods and services. The commission's proposals were an instant hit in upper-class circles. The Chamber of Commerce, the New York Stock Exchange, the Produce Exchange, the Cotton Exchange—indeed every leading business organization—endorsed them enthusiastically. So did Astor, Vanderbilt, Dodge, Have Meyer, and the leading newspapers like the *Times*, the *Herald*, and the *Tribune*.

When the Republicans lost the state legislature in November of 1877, the amendment to the state constitution also lost. The Common Council scuttled the plan. The initial sponsors had to content "themselves with the strategic positions in the government and on independent boards and commissions."[3]

The Railroaders Cause Strain Among the Merchants, 1878

In the backwash of the failed proposal for a city finance commission, another specter of the troubles dawned at a gathering of aldermen and business leaders, many of whom could muster many resources of government and business. For the first time one segment of the economy had to take the blame for the myriad troubles. After the meeting on March 2nd Charles Smith, a warehouseman and a founder of the Board of Trade and Transportation, speaking for the assemblage, stated:

> Bad government, enormous taxation, miserably paved and dirty streets, insufficient and expensive terminal facilities, and, more recently oppressive railroad discrimination, all combined, have made New York the most expensive city in which to do business. The time was not far distant when the city would find it hard work to pay the interest on its bonds, and when merchants would have to close their doors and discharge their clerks, porters, and cartmen. Unless the discrimination against New York trade can be stopped, *we shall lose immense business.* (Our emphasis.)

Smith went on to point out that it cost $10 per carload more to handle goods in New York than in Boston, Philadelphia, or Baltimore. Further, New York had 22 commission houses for the sale of eastern-made goods, with sales of $150,000,000. Smith warned,

> Unless the discrimination against New York trade can be stopped these houses must necessarily withdraw . . . we shall lose their immense business unless we see to it that they have equal rights and privileges with other competing points. [4]

This statement of strain by such a meeting of leaders, making them *en bloc* consequential leaders, had the effect of instigating a policy scenario. As Laumann and Knoke write, the complaint "does not become a domain issue until it is recognized as a strain problem by (a) consequential actor(s) in the policy domain."[5] That is, only leaders of consequence can

141

make an authentic assessment suggesting that a *slippery slope* is in the offing. As shall be seen, the most extreme recognition of the city's situation would come in mid-1881 from the Rev. Henry Beecher in his pulpit. Four months later harbor expert E. R. Livermore would spell out the details in a special legislative hearing at the Produce Exchange.

The idea for a board of finance to relieve difficulties in taxation and expenditures for the city had won support across a wide spectrum, including Vanderbilt. The coterie of complainants now narrowed while their cries increased. Smith and his chamber associates, after meeting with city officials, and without the railroaders in attendance, now defined railroads as part of the problem. What had happened was that moving from Tilden's general vision of gloom for the empire city, other leaders now focused upon one player in their midst: Excessive rates were as bad as excessive taxes. Again, the players described their strain in terms of the prospective collapse of their economic institution, the commercial supremacy of New York City. For the moment they felt injustices that required nothing less than organizing a new committee to promote regulation. Smith succeeded in setting up a special committee on railroad transportation in the Chamber, which, according to Benson, "led the city's fight against the railroads for several years thereafter."[6]

Sterne soon offered a railroad commission bill at Albany.[7] A month later Vanderbilt replied to inquiries on the issues from the Chamber of Commerce and the law committee of the Board of Aldermen.[8] Rather than proceeding immediately with Sterne's bill, members of the assembly decided to name a special committee of investigation under Barton Hepburn. Evidence had emerged that the New York Central Railroad under Vanderbilt and Standard Oil Company under Rockefeller had set special rates. What needed examining was not hypothetical but a specific case at hand. Their collusion, shaping business by economies of scale, had not only closed down refineries and forced some New York firms to close their doors, but also, in the end, threatened the tax base by a devaluation of property and the payment of municipal bonds. Since the corporations seemed to violate their state charters, the public needed to know why.

The Hepburn hearings got off to a poor start when the charges made by the merchants, although denied by the corporations, proved true. The hearings ended on an equally dismal note. Vanderbilt could not answer some of the questions to the committee's satisfaction. The merchants were left wondering what kind of creature they were dealing with. Apparently, the committee did not ask the company for written answers to be submitted later. Poor relations between the two sides would shadow the dispute for decades.

Just as city leaders had lamented their condition, so cries for solutions arose among the railroaders. They had tried the Saratoga agreement in August 1873. After that they moved on to the plan for the Chicago cartel, hiring Albert Fink as their manager. Charles Francis Adams, Jr. explained most railroaders' stress when he wrote, "Capital is trying to protect itself; and will succeed in doing it. The stress of competition has been too great,

142

and in its own way is resulting in combination."[9] Without combination the railroads would continue to face the slippery slope. Adams' characterization of the railroaders' interest qualified the condition as a *domain issue*. Now each side had a consequential actor—Smith on one side and Adams on the other—recognizing a strain problem. The merchants' expressed strain meant that their position was not merely a throwback to Jacksonian anti-monopolism. No matter who ascended to office on the state or national level, he would have to deal with the issue and let the chips fall where they may.

Both sides were now recognizably bound in a common fate. Each kept the other in mind. A political battle was developing. Each side sought its own goals while wondering what the other side wanted. Carrying the description one step further, one could say that the two sides were now bound in "a community of antagonism." Once these consequential actors expressed their respective positions, antagonism was better recognized and likely increased. Vanderbilt would express his particular strain at the Hepburn hearings of 1879 when he said,

> I am in favor of a law to punish railroads for going above or below certain rates, to be fixed by the General Government, cooperating with individuals and State Governments; the State legislatures can haul railroads up at any time for the infringement of the law; if Governments would interfere with a shoe-maker or merchant in the conduct of his business, the man interfered with would be likely to sell out and quit business; corporations should have the same rights as private persons.[10]

The ground was now laid for still another person in a consequential position to project a solution. The comments of these lesser figures were building blocks. Laumann and Knoke write that:

> We may find that the organizations first drawing attention to an issue are not the same actors who subsequently propose various policy options or solutions aimed at eliminating or reducing the strain problem and restoring the subsystem to a new equilibrium.[11]

The opportunity would soon arrive after the party conventions.

From the Hepburn Hearings of Early 1879 to the State Party Convention, September 1879

Out of expressed strain, the policy scenario moves forward. Before the factional fight made an appearance, the participants attempted to make adjustments in regulating transportation backed by state and national actions. But first, information had to be gathered. Over the next several weeks, the Hepburn investigation, at which Vanderbilt had appeared on two separate days, completed its initial work.[12] The topic next came before both state party conventions with their platforms on regulation. The Republican convention voted to adopt a regulation plank. The platform made no mention of the alternative proposal for the cartel promoted the previous year by Adams in his book. The subject, however, did not die there. The conventions were followed by public appeals from both the Chamber of Commerce and Vanderbilt for different courses in regulatory legislation. Vanderbilt had replied by urging action in Congress first. Finally, Alonzo Cornell's letter accepting the nomination for governor mentioned regulation. The reappearance of the topic over these several weeks suggests that all of the meetings—the hearings, the platform meetings and the adopting of planks at the conventions, plus the open letters from both sides of the issue and gubernatorial candidate Cornell's letter of acceptance—can be covered as a single event.

Preparing for the state Republican convention, Roscoe Conkling, Thomas Murphy and Chester Arthur contacted delegates. Former collector Murphy was apparently important since many of the Customs House employees under him had remained on the job. The three worked to line up votes for Conkling's candidate for governor, Alonzo Cornell. The candidate's father, Ezra, had been a founder of the Western Union telegraph company in the 1850s and a founder of Cornell University in the 1860s. In early 1881, the son, Alonzo, continued on the Western Union board of directors, serving through Gould's consolidation in 1881.[13]

Arthur, Conkling and Murphy prior to the state convention in recruiting delegates apparently discovered the popular response to the Hepburn investigation and support for the state regulation. From a more general perspective, the canvass suggested what was important about the Collectors office for New York politics. In looking for delegates to the state convention, the leading politicians must have screened both Customs House workers and merchants. Later when Garfield named Robertson for Collector, he placed a man in the post who was the last person Conkling would have wanted to join in a canvass in preparing for a state convention—or Robertson would be the first man to object to conducting such a canvass—and either of these prospects could help to explain Conkling's discomfiture.

At the meeting, Conkling, in his opening remarks, made a passing reference to the anticipated regulation: "Over-production depresses particular industries and localities--the dairy interest in this State, for example. But time and sense and justly-regulated freights will set all this even."[14]

The lengthy platform was taken up. At the end, it carried a paragraph referring to the Hepburn investigation indicating sympathy for the merchants.

> Moneyed and transportation corporations are not alone the works of private enterprise, but are created for public use, and with due regard to vested rights it is the clear province and plain duty of the state to supervise and regulate corporations, so as to secure the just and impartial treatment of all interested; to foster the industrial and agricultural welfare of the people, and with a liberal policy favor the public waterways and maintain

the commercial supremacy of the State. We look to the inquiry now in progress, under the direction of the Legislature, to develop the facts, which will guide to all needed action.[15]

The entire platform passed without dissent. While endorsing the continuing work of the Hepburn committee, it gave no place for endorsing a national railroad trust that Adams had proposed a year earlier.

Then came the balloting for nominees to run in the fall campaign. As it turned out, Cornell's support came not entirely from machine politicians. The news from the Saratoga convention was that a leading reformer at the last minute decided to swing his influence to the candidate bringing several others with him.

> During the early hours of this morning, . . . those who believed that Mr. Cornell was not the best man who could be nominated had every assurance that they would succeed in naming some other candidate. They were, indeed, confident of success, when suddenly it was reported and extensively circulated about the hotels and among the delegates, that Mr. George B. Sloan [Oswego], who had been most prominent as what is called a reformer, who has been looked upon as the very head and front of everything noble, worthy, and honorable in politics, had deserted the men who had trusted and confided in him, and had pledged his vote and influence to Mr. Cornell . . . the back of the opposition was broken. And nearly a score of unpledged delegates, who, like most men, were anxious to be on the winning side, declared in favor of Cornell.[16]

Since the course of political conventions is about as predictable as the movement of mercury on glass, any suggestion that the meeting was machine-dominated simply suffers from inaccuracy. Rather, reformers would make the difference. Conkling's apparent skill was in lining up a goodly number of loyalists. He would hold them in reserve. Next, at the last minute while watching the course of volatile opinion at the convention, he would bring to his side a sufficient number of other delegates to put him over the top.

After the vote on the platform, all that Conkling needed was a majority of votes for Cornell. The majority might show up on the first ballot. Or, since four candidates were in the field, the vote might have to be repeated through one or more additional ballots. It is no mean trick in a four-way race to accumulate a majority of the votes. As it turned out Cornell did seize the majority in the first ballot winning 52 percent of the vote and the next strongest candidate, William Robertson, a New York Central attorney, winning half that amount, or 26 percent. That two-to-one margin over the nearest contender, from an industry just recently the subject of hearings by a state legislative committee, showed solid support for the anti-monopoly sentiment. A winner was declared and it was time to stop voting. Nothing was to be gained by another ballot, which would have only increased Cornell's lead and rubbed the noses of the lesser candidates in their own defeat. That would hardly have helped build post-convention harmony necessary for the coming campaign.

Some historians covering the politics of the summer of 1879 focus on the Republican state convention and conclude that the bare majority of first ballot votes mustered for Conkling's candidate, Cornell, was proof that Conkling had become politically weak. According to this view, the vote presumably forecast Conkling's later fall and the ultimate victory of civil service reform over the patronage bosses. However, to reach this conclusion one had to overlook other matters, chiefly that he apparently depended upon the influence of a reformer.

Conkling must have observed that the delegates arriving at the state convention came well informed about railroad matters. They represented voters who wanted relief from increasing urban costs including taxes and railroad rates. In a year's time, the public had come to see the railroads as part of the problem, and believed that the recently adjourned Hepburn hearings were a step toward a solution. On arrival at the convention and hearing of the Robertson candidacy, the delegates probably recalled that an earlier governor had signed a bill letting the Erie and Central railroads enjoy interlocking directorates. Since the railroad problem remained unresolved at the convention, the delegates would not tolerate placing another railroad advocate in the governorship. If Robertson had succeeded, New York Republicans would have been proposing to place the fox over the henhouse. His view of the character of New York's commercial supremacy would have taken precedence. Two years later when he became collector he could exercise that judgment.

Each side came to the convention wanting something, and Conkling showed that he could play the game down the middle. In promoting Cornell, a member of the Western Union Board of Directors, he could appeal to corporate interests while promoting a platform calling for corporate accountability and thus recognize the widespread anti-monopolism stirred first by Smith's views a year earlier and then advanced by the Hepburn hearings.

The division in the party was still latent. In the convention, matters went quite well. The *Times* reported, "The resolutions were received with cordial favor by the convention and adopted unanimously." While others lost badly in the race against Cornell, none of them spoke up against the regulation plank. Within a year the party conflict arose, marked by Robertson's bolt with sixteen others from the Grant delegation to the Blaine delegation.

Much more, however, had happened that summer. A focus on Conkling alone overlooks the activities of railroader Vanderbilt. First, the railroader had appeared twice before the Hepburn committee. Second, at the convention one of his attorneys, Robertson, contested for governor against Cornell. Finally, within a month Vanderbilt answered a public inquiry from the Chamber of Commerce on desired legislation. That meant that both Conkling and Vanderbilt were to the fore, and their activities helped set the boundaries for the policy scenario.

The Open Letters from the Merchants and William Vanderbilt, September 1879

The leaders on either side who had complained the most convincingly about the problem of transportation soon proposed solutions. About two weeks after the state convention, the railroaders and the merchants made their suggestions public. They tacitly admitted that neither the hearings nor the convention had produced a binding solution. Furthermore, the open exchange of letters between the two sides meant that skeptics could not discount the importance of the regulation plank in the party platform and see only evidence of the onset of Conkling's slide from power. The platform and the exchanged letters were all of a piece, meaning the platform had been right on target.

First, in an open letter on September 18, 1879, a committee of the New York Chamber of Commerce wrote Vanderbilt that:

> The public will justly demand both State legislation to regulate local traffic and Congressional legislation to regulate the through traffic, and that to this end it is desirable that the representatives for the trunk lines and the people should work in harmony.[17]

The merchants were suggesting that the parties should conduct broad negotiations all down the coast between the railroaders and the merchants and brokers.

The next day, Vanderbilt answered publicly:

> I believe that any legislation upon the transportation question by the State, unless based *on general legislation first had by Congress,* will be disastrous to the commercial supremacy and prosperity of New York. The State cannot tie the hands of its roads and leave outside competitors free without working directly for the ruin of its mercantile and industrial interests, and for the growth of other and rival States and seaports. I differ, however, from many other railroad men in believing that Congress might act, which would both benefit the public and protect investors. I certainly will be very glad to meet the Presidents of the trunk lines to discuss the matter, and prepare, if possible, *a bill to overcome the difficulties, and also to meet with the representatives of commercial bodies and arrive with them at an amicable understanding and united action.* This is surely wiser than to put these problems up at auction for politicians to bid up for votes.[18] (Our emphasis.)

Vanderbilt's course struck the *Times* as just the right one to take. The same day the paper carried Vanderbilt's open letter, it editorialized with the following:

Mr. Vanderbilt's reply to the Chamber of Commerce letter is chiefly valuable as an indication of his readiness to change what has been so long the policy of his own and other railroad corporations in dealing with the protests of the public. The Central Railroad, like its neighbor in Pennsylvania and its namesake in California, has *preferred the purchase of legislators and the packing of Legislative committees* to any fair discussion of proposals that it found unpalatable, or deemed injurious to its own interests. As a general proposition, it is quite true that railways are not, and cannot be, antagonist to the public with whom their very existence is indissolubly connected, but railroads are usually managed on the theory that the value of a given amount of transportation depends not so much on the nature of the service rendered as on the necessities of the company and the ability of the forwarder to prescribe his own terms. The methods adopted by Mr. Vanderbilt to sustain the commercial supremacy of New York are not such as have generally recommended themselves to those who are as vitally interested as he is in the prosperity of the city and state, and it is at least something gained when he expresses a readiness to submit to the *ordeal of thorough discussion* the points at issue between himself and the mercantile community, whose complaints he has so long ignored. (Our emphasis.)

It appears that Conkling had orchestrated the preparations for the state convention. He had not only produced a good platform but also prompted a response from the platform's target, William Vanderbilt. Conkling, therefore, should have the credit for having been a good guide to the policy process.

From the larger perspective of policy scenarios, the letters from the merchants and Vanderbilt carried expressed preferences of consequential leaders. The statements fit Laumann and Knoke's standard for crossing a critical threshold. They write: A policy option is the empirical unit [of] act [ion] in the policy process. It consists of a statement made by a policy domain actor [the committee from the nearly century-old Chamber of Commerce and Vanderbilt from the state's largest corporation] or by some other authoritative actor about a socially perceived issue. Most policy options can be cast in the form: "Organization A proposes that authority B undertake action X for reasons Y."[19] Thus, the Chamber of Commerce proposed that the state legislature and Congress pass regulatory legislation. Correspondingly, the president of the New York Central Railroad proposed that Congress first pass regulatory legislation to preserve New York's place in commerce. These activities are characteristic of a policy scenario. Framed in the 1970s, they also appeared in the 1870s.

To recap, the two institutions, the merchants association and the railroad company, perceived a level of strain with a broad base. Smith had mentioned it a year earlier after a meeting of merchants and officials. Adams similarly spoke for the railroaders in his book about strain. The condition was apparent enough to lead to the party platform and to nominating candidates for the post of governor. Therefore, according to Laumann and Knoke's model, a) the statements of strain and b) the emergence of options for solution, in that order, display the unfolding policy scenario. If one accepts these steps in the course of the scenario, one can see that the 1879 convention had more to do with the transportation dispute than has been generally recognized. While the evidence from the convention might suggest that Conkling's strength was declining, the evidence of the convention, along with the hearings and the exchange of letters, shows that affairs had reached a major threshold in adjusting institutional differences.

The capitalists probably understood well that Conkling had been the leading consequential actor who had either orchestrated the developments at the hearings and convention, or at least approved them. Whether he would harvest any benefit from them remained to be seen. Unfortunately, the railroaders developed a proclivity to discount one person, Conkling, for the current turn in events. Often they failed to understand public opinion. While they would be concerned with staving off bankruptcy, they came to focus more on Conkling as the typical politician who could continue to cause them trouble. It would not be a long leap from blaming him to deprecating his motives and then to saying he was merely a patronage monger and "the villain of the piece." The monopolists wanted federal regulation first, in a plan that gave legitimacy to their price-setting arrangements. Conkling wanted the canal protected. He would openly discuss anything in the way of regulation, a course the monopolists were almost assured they could not win. That was a good reason to discount Conkling.

Who would dominate the task of writing the story of these affairs would prove to be another matter. The railroaders, along with the reformers, would dominate the writing of history on the subject.

Henry Demarest Lloyd, the financial editor at Joseph Medill's *Chicago Tribune*, did not like what he foresaw. He thought he saw that the corporate leaders would take steps that would add up to imposing the Adams plan. Watching the stock market, Lloyd caught Gould's purchase of stock from Vanderbilt's company, possibly in order to have a minority interest. He also observed that Vanderbilt had begun interchanging his company's stock for the stock of other companies. Purportedly, he sought a larger community of interest. Shortly the combination increased eastbound rates from Chicago from $3 to $8 a ton, depriving the farmers of most of the recent advances in prices.[20]

According to Lloyd, the Adams plan fell short because it was based only partly on the model of Britain's railroad commission. The plan had left out "authority over rates, pooling, and service." Lloyd thought Congress could "add . . . to the Reagan Bill." Showing his familiarity with Adams' 1878 volume, Lloyd added, "Only in this way . . . could effective national regulation be instituted and the *dictatorial* Vanderbilt-Gould-Huntington attempt to unify the railroads in one great railroad trust be defeated."[21] His use of the word "dictatorial" could have served as a prophecy that the legislative discussions would not only exclude the public but also have punishments attached. That, of course, raised the specter of another dispute over who was permitted to participate. On this policy question, the anti-monopolists could suffer the threat of exclusion even down to the arranging of committees in the U.S. Senate in 1881. Momentum among New Yorkers would shift dramatically in 1882 with broad popular support for the Free Canal Amendment. The momentum for the merchants would increase to the national level in 1885 when Congress organized the Cullom committee that traveled about the country to hear anyone who wanted to testify.

In 1879, shortly after these political actors made their views known, gubernatorial candidate Alonzo Cornell reiterated in his letter of acceptance the Republican Party platform on state regulation. He had nothing to say about the prospect of the negotiations, which Vanderbilt and the merchants mentioned. Cornell wrote that:

> Particular attention is due also to growing dissatisfaction among the farmers, merchants, and other businessmen of the State about railroad and other corporate institutions. Corporations created by law exercise within their charters delegated functions, and are subject to the supervision of the power from which they derive their being. Originally endowed for the public benefit, they have no warrant to discriminate against the rights of any class or portion of the people; especially they should not discriminate against the interests of the citizens of New York and in favor of those of other States. The unexampled development of our State and the country beyond its borders, has, in many instances, vastly increased the value of these franchises, the recipients of which should recognize a just accountability to the sovereignty, which endowed them with such great and valuable privileges. Legislation adapted for the preservation of the rights of all classes, and for maintaining the commercial primacy of the State of New York seems to me manifestly just.[22]

A comparison is instructive between the amount of space in the platform devoted to regulation and the amount of space devoted to the topic in Cornell's letter of acceptance. Although the convention platform included coverage of national issues, and the regulation plank covered in length only about a tenth of the platform message, by the time of Cornell's acceptance letter the public consciousness of the regulation matter may have increased sharply. This might explain why Cornell devoted a third of his letter to the matter. If so, a track of momentum might be traced. The momentum began at the convention when the reformer George Sloan abandoned his friends and announced his support for Cornell. It increased when the public learned of the exchange of letters between the merchants and Vanderbilt. Finally, Cornell captured the excitement by devoting much more space in his letter of acceptance to regulation than the platform had.

This, in turn, could explain Cornell's success in the November election. The scratchers decided that they could not protest this election by sitting it out. They had to turn out to defeat the corruptionist Howard Soule who was on the ballot for the state engineer's position. Among those scratchers who did turn out, a significant number may have bolted their own group to support Cornell, just as reformer George Sloan and his friends had done at the state convention, on the regulation question. President Hayes had dropped Cornell from the Customs House, but the shock it caused must have quickly quieted down. While serving as governor, Cornell must have pleased his reform supporters by the large number of bills he vetoed.

On to the Republican National Convention, Chicago, June, 1880

The *Times* had called for the interested parties to enter into an "ordeal of thorough discussion" but together the parties were unable to take up the challenge. Several matters intervened. Vanderbilt increased some rates that could have cooled interests. Moreover, Vanderbilt noticed that the merchants were also at work on plans to strengthen their hand in the next legislature.[23] He complained of a newspaper announcement: " . . . of appointment of a committee of merchants to foment agitation upon the support or threaten hostility to legislative candidates unless they will pledge an unquestioning support to whatever furthers [their] sentiment."[24]

Vanderbilt decided to adopt the same tactic. He could stave off the merchants trying to trump him in the election. If he won, he could keep the legislature from taking up state regulation until Congress acted. He therefore went into the campaign of 1879 and picked up the expenses of several state senate candidates. Later in August 1881 the *Times* reflected that:

> the railroad companies took the precaution in the canvass [of 1879] to secure a majority of the [state] Senate in their own favor. For two years, the hand of the corporation has been on one branch of the legislature paralyzing its action whenever this subject [railroad regulation] has been before it.[25]

A modern investigator using the policy process to catalogue campaign funding could regard the funding as "strategic action that asserts that a preferred end-state outcome may 'determine' how an actor participates in events leading up to that outcome."[26] When contributors pay off a candidate, they can discourage the candidate from further considering other options. That built inflexibility into the legislative discussions while removing responsibility one step out of the legislature. Becoming a legislative candidate puts a person in quite an odd position, for he curries the favor of voters to win a majority, building up expenses covered by big donors to whom he abdicates his judgment. The process might diminish one's freedom. The paralysis in the policy process would hang over the next president, no matter who it was.

Opposition to Ulysses S. Grant's Candidacy

In the meantime, former president Ulysses S. Grant returned from his widely popular world tour and politicians excited the political scene with talk of another candidacy. Those who opposed him were largely people opposed to a third term, civil service reformers, and railroaders who probably could recall that he had favored competition from the waterways. If Grant entered the White House and the railroad legislation came up, he could have encouraged the discussion, one that had to be postponed until 1885 under Cullom. For the moment, in 1880, the railroaders did not want Grant elected. They decided to try to get around a repeat of the Hepburn hearings and still achieve a national consolidation. In discussing Grant's candidacy, the *Times* of October 2, 1879, reported that a majority of prominent railroad managers "would prefer some other good Republican."

It seems that Vanderbilt recruited Adams to discourage others from supporting the Grant candidacy. While in the state senate races Vanderbilt was taking up campaign expenses of candidates who would serve his purposes, Adams's assignment consisted of helping to stave off the Grant boom at the coming national convention. Adams saw Vanderbilt on October 4, 1879, and on the 14th he saw people in Kansas City "in relation to the Grant matter." On October 17 he noted in his diary that he bet a basket of champagne that Grant would not win re-election.[27] Gorham, in charge of the Grant campaign office in Washington, would later write that:

> From October 1879 until June 1880 the money and men of the railroad monarchs, the organized corporation lobbies in the several States, the reckless and malignant Independent papers which opposed the Republican Party from 1871 till 1876 and gangs of political outlaws and lepers were combined together in one grand organized effort to defeat and destroy the most illustrious citizen of the Nation and the most famous and honored man in the world. . . . The railroad power had determined that Grant would not be a safe man for their purposes. The iron hand of Vanderbilt was stretched out in New York and his strikers, associates and dependents, like Robertson, Wagner, and Sessions, to the number of eighteen, were collared and marched out of the Grant ranks, which they could never have entered had their treachery been foreseen.[28]

The exchange of letters in 1879 after the state convention had left New York stalwarts with the hope of a promising outcome between Vanderbilt and the merchants. Then, in short order, the scene changed—not just the prospects for candidates but for a clarifying substantive question. In his February 1880 testimony before the Reagan committee, which he immediately published, Adams drew a harsh line against all who favored competition.

Adams complained that the popular view of railroad legislation did not reach the core of the difficulty, and he used terms that, I believe, provided the test of politically correct thinking as far as the cartel elite was concerned.

> Almost uniformly, the symptoms have been mistaken for the disease, and the remedies intended to remove the evil have consequently only tended to aggravate it . . . In legislating directly upon [popularly known railroad troubles], therefore, we are merely treating skin symptoms, and the chances will be large that in doing so we will only succeed in making what is already bad very materially worse.

Adams moved on to the prime cause of the "railroad problem" probably exploiting the popularity of the good reports from the Standard Oil Trust's record of overcoming competition in the oil industry.

> Every abuse in the railroad system, so far as the interstate commerce of this country is concerned, can be shown to be the direct, the logical, the inevitable outcome of unregulated and desperate competition, and a mere outward skin symptom of it. [His solution was to let consolidation run its course.] The process of railroad consolidation in this country, if by endless competition it is forced to work out its logical results, will therefore, in all probability, at no distant day produce the one man of combining power. That man will prove himself equal to every emergency, and end by holding in his hand a complete practical mastery of the whole field.[29]

Explaining that the railroads themselves sought to end the Darwinian struggle, he added, "I wish to invoke the assistance of Congress. They are trying to federate themselves." If Adams was speaking for the cartel leaders, they apparently had concluded, banking on the iron law of the business dialectic, that they should proceed and leave nothing to negotiations. Thus Adams built on the views he had presented in his 1878 volume that Vanderbilt, Gould, and Huntington were looking forward to a railroad trust and sought the blessing of Congress. He had explained then that the big three had the financial strength to proceed.

> The earnings of the combinations are continually accumulated in the business. There is no toppling superstructure of debt. . . .[T]he railroad system of this country is now on the threshold of a most active and .unprecedented consolidating development. . . . By its originators, it is confidently claimed that, if properly developed and recognized by legislation, it would afford a complete and practical solution of the American railroad problem.[30]

According to Adams, the politicians themselves comprised the next obstacle, and he harshly faulted the House commerce committee chaired by John Reagan of Texas.

> If you insist on seeing in this growing tendency to federation merely a dangerous spirit of conspiracy which *the law-making power cannot too summarily repress*—in such a case it only remains for you once more to fulminate against it the well-worn phrases of the statute book, while I go home possessing my soul in patience. The stone, which you would thus reject, however, I would make the head of the corner—that Federation of the Railroad System, which you would make a criminal offense, I would use as the basis of my whole railroad legislation . . . Your legislation will be but as a bull against the comet.

> Mr. Fink simply proposes to legalize a practice, *which the law cannot prevent*, and, by so doing, to enable the railroads to confederate themselves in a manner which shall be at once both public and responsible. . . . To advance . . . requires some faith in the force of an enlightened public opinion. In this country, and in the strength of our political institutions . . . you should not approach the case with defined theories as to cause and effect--a whole statute book, the quack legislator's pillbox, in hand. . . . I object simply to legislating in advance of investigation--perpetually inverting the order of things. . . . Penal legislation will be necessary--should follow and not precede investigation. The concrete cases should first arise and be made the subject, not of slow and profitless litigation, but of swift inquiry on the spot; and from these concrete cases the body of general legislation should gradually be developed.[31] (Our emphasis.)

Thus Adams's testimony slammed the door on arranging the "ordeal of thorough discussion" that the *Times* had contemplated. The cartel could go no further. Negotiations were impossible. Name-calling would soon emerge with some adhering to competition becoming known as the "bad men" and those looking to settle the market with trust becoming known as the "good men." So, shortly after the New York Republican 1879 convention the grounds were set for the factional fight that would grip the next administration.

The Times's Criticism of the Adams Plan, 1880

The tone of Adams's testimony did not sit well with the *Times*. On January 29, 1880, the paper promptly responded, and trenchantly noted that the problem was not

> as Mr. Adams chooses to state the question, whether honest and capable men are or are not to be found. The trouble is that in national even more than in local affairs corporate influences may be so employed as, silently and unseen, to control the personnel of a commission. Our experience

with the representatives of the government in the affairs of the Union Pacific illustrates the difficulty. The commissioners and Government Directors may all have been honorable men, judging of them by the average standard, but in some way it has invariably happened that the officers appointed to watch the railroad managers have become their apologists if not their allies. [The granger commissions in the West required short terms to keep them from taking the side of the corporations.] The same result would almost inevitably follow the acceptance of Mr. Adams' nostrums instead of the vigorous legislation, which he deprecates. The commission would not command public confidence, and in all probability would not deserve it.

Mr. Adams places much reliance on the efficacy of public opinion as a means of enabling the commission to restrain, in a certain sense to guide, the railroad companies. Because it is all sufficient in Massachusetts, he infers that it would be equally irresistible all over the country. The premise is too narrow for the conclusion. In fact, we know that public opinion is impotent when it stands in the way of what great corporations suppose to be their interests. Public opinion was of no moment to the perpetrators of the Erie's rascalities. It was not public opinion but the Thurman law, which brought the Union and Central Pacific companies to recognition of their obligations to the government.

Exactly how public opinion has asserted its influence in Massachusetts, Mr. Adams does not explain. We know, however, that in other states public opinion has never prevented the creation of fictitious capital, has never stopped arrangements of the most flagrant character, and has never been acknowledged by the managers of powerful corporations as an arbiter whose dictates they should respect. They have, on the contrary, defied it with impunity. Indeed, we have but to glance at the attitude of the companies in this state in regard to discriminations and complaints, to perceive the folly of relying on anything less than positive law. A commission will have its uses as a supplement to the well-considered and stringent enactment, but to accept it as a substitute for law would be to leave the railroad companies absolute masters of the situation.

That critique amounted to a laundry list enumerating the points that remained to be worked out. The *Times* was still looking for the necessary ordeal. A year later even the members of the Massachusetts Commission would criticize Adams's views.

Adams had an additional reason for attempting to tame the jungle culture of railroading. He had told the committee:

> Our railroad system now resembles nothing so much as a huge mass of eels
> in a tub. It is a tangled mixture of heads and bodies and tails, but which
> tail belongs to which body, and which head to which tail, it is past human
> wisdom to find out. This it is which makes it so difficult for the law and
> the law-making power to deal with; it is not a system, except in name. Let
> it once organize and federate, however, and whether it means to do so or
> not, it renders itself amenable to control. It comes out into the open where
> it can be got at.[32]

This picture of railroad realism, presented by an insider, was all the evidence needed to support sardonic witticisms: Now and then peace broke out among the railroads. The picture would hardly have prompted leaders of the private and public sectors to hasten a solution. The *Times*, however, thought that the attempt should be made. In an editorial, the paper inferred that Adams, honored for his work on the Massachusetts board, had nothing to say about state regulation having a part to play. Perhaps realizing that opportunity was fast passing by, the *Times* said on February 20, 1880:

> A system of reform, to be adequate and effective, must partake of
> the nature of our complex Government, in which the wider interests of
> the Union of States are administered under national authority, and those
> that are limited by State boundaries are administered under State author-
> ity. Our legislators at Washington and at Albany have upon their hands a
> task calling for the exercise of all the wisdom they can command, and it
> cannot long be neglected.[33]

Instead of the mutuality that the paper sought, politics in the next several months would go through a turmoil that had to embarrass everyone. The desired mutuality would not appear until after the Republicans lost the state legislature in late 1881. The state commission bill passed in 1882 and the railroads learned that compliance with state regulation was not so difficult after all. Light would then seem to dawn. Those who had evaded matters earlier swallowed hard and at the 1884 national convention adopted an explicit platform plan that gave Senator Cullom a green light to proceed in 1885 with a new committee.

In New York state politics, in early 1880 the party called a special state convention to name delegates to the Republican National Convention in Chicago. The meeting adopted a unit rule requiring all delegates to vote with the majority, a measure momentarily showing that Conkling had much more strength than at the 1879 meeting. Before too long, however, the railroad contingent bolted taking peers with them from the Pennsylvania and Illinois delegations. Adams would be able to pop the corks on his champagne bottles much earlier than he may have expected to.

Railroad Leaders Criticize the Recent Hepburn Hearings

When in March 1880 the Hepburn committee finally reported its proposed bills, Chauncey Depew appeared as the principal witness for the railroad. Rather than explaining why the company had not proceeded in the negotiations with the merchants as promised the previous September, he turned to deprecating the initial hearings. He claimed that over two-thirds of the traffic from outside the city came from large shippers, and they had not been represented on the Hepburn panel. He also claimed that only a small number of merchants, perhaps ten, supported the drive against monopoly. However, he did not suggest that the committee ought to be reconstituted.

A word is helpful here about the constitution of committees. Just from the resources presented here on this topic it is possible to illuminate the function of a working legislative committee. Depew's complaint that the Hepburn committee did not include a heavy shipper meant that very little testimony would be taken from that class of people. Five years later when Senator Cullom of Illinois organized the committee on inter-state commerce he would include a heavy shipper, Senator Miller of New York. One of his functions probably was to call as witnesses people who were of a like position. Again, Adams had included in his letter to Osgood that the committee needed people who knew how to "reach" other businessmen in the community. Probably, he had in mind the kinds of people who could testify on particular problems. Returning to Cullom's committee formed in 1885, we will note that several members of his Senate committee were from terminal cities (Gorman of Baltimore, Harris of Memphis, and himself of Chicago). Cullom had told the U.S. Senate on March 17, 1885, that he had heard enough from railroad presidents and attorneys and now said that through his new committee he wanted to "go to the people on this question and find out what they want as well as what the railroads want . . ." (March 17, 1885, Executive Session, 49th Congress, *Congressional Record,* p. 57). Certainly, the membership of his committee would be more than assured that users of the railroad would be called. Each of the senators from terminal cities would be able to turn up people who knew what the merchants thought about the railroaders and their services. This particular service a committee member performs in enlisting certain kinds of witnesses to testify will greatly help in understanding the contention in 1881 between President James Garfield and Senator Roscoe Conkling.

The Hepburn committee also heard testimony from another railroad spokesperson, James Rutter. He opposed the "requirement that roads should make their rates public [since that] would enable the canal boatmen to know to a certainty just how much to cut under in order to get the big shippers."[34] On March 18, 1880, at the state assembly committee on railroads, Hepburn recalled during the hearings, "the railroad officers only came before the committee to find fault with this bill, and none of them have made any suggestions or amendments to correct the errors of the bill, if any exist."[35] There was now no doubt that from September 1879 to March 1880 the views of the railroad leaders had taken an ominous turn.

While all this discussion was in the air, it was remarked that even Adams had a new viewpoint showing that he had betrayed his own better judgment gained while serving the previous decade as a Massachusetts commissioner. Thurber recalled that:

> When the bills proposed by the Hepburn Committee for the prevention of railroad abuses were pending at Albany last winter Mr. Adams was quoted on both sides of the same question, and one of the speakers, in commenting on this fact, stated that Mr. Adams had graduated from the Massachusetts railway commissioner at four thousand dollars per year, into a pool-line commissioner at ten thousand dollars per year, and as a commissioner of the pooled lines he entertained very different views from those he advocated when chairman of the Board . . . if he were filling a judicial position, his opinion would be entitled to great weight, but . . . he is virtually counsel for the railroads and naturally advocates their interest. [36]

By April 1880 the merchants' cause began making headway in the state assembly. Both houses adopted four minor bills from the committee. The assembly also voted on the recommended antidiscrimination bill from the Hepburn committee, passing it by a vote of 73 to 35--interestingly about the same ratio by which Cornell had won the nomination for governor. Both votes roughly indicated the loyalty that U.S. Senator Conkling had won in the lower house of the state legislature. The antidiscrimination bill, however, would have trouble in the state senate.

Also, two reports appeared that month involving Gorham. One was his testimony about the conduct of the 1878 campaign solicitations in the departments, repugnant to reformers. The other was his report on the strength of the Grant delegation to Chicago, suggesting a first-ballot victory. His state-by-state count probably gave the foes of Grant a good picture of the work that they had cut out for themselves. In a scenario of action and reaction, the next move most likely came from the railroaders.

Within two weeks of the assembly action and a month before the national convention at Chicago in June, William Robertson, who had lost a bid for the gubernatorial nomination at the state convention, led a "bolt." At the 1880 state convention, Robertson and his allies had pledged to abide by unit rule and vote for Grant. Shortly, however, Robertson led 16 New York Grant delegates to support candidate James Blaine. Conkling was incensed at Robertson and his bolters. Blaine, former Speaker of the House, now a Senator from Maine, had most recently served the railroads by harshly opposing the Thurman sinking fund bill, a service that won him the tag of "Gould's errand boy." The bolt seeped into the Pennsylvania and Illinois convention delegations and greatly weakened the stalwart strongholds. While Robertson argued that national convention delegates should represent their own district's preferences, the bolt could have given his state senate allies help to delay further progress on the assembly's regulation bill until after a new president, who they hoped would be Blaine, took office. Thus the bolt probably helped sideline state legislation until legislation could be had from "Congress first."

Two days before the Republican National Convention opened in Chicago, Democratic congressman John Reagan issued his committee report on the February 1880 hearings. He made several points, showing that he had gotten the crux of monopolists' position, total contempt for competition.

> It is urged by two at least of the ablest representatives of the railroad interests, Mr. Adams and Mr. Fink, that the idea of competition must be eliminated from the railroad problem before it can be satisfactorily and properly adjusted. . . . I look upon this as the most dangerous theory, which has been advanced. . . .

Reagan's observation is elementary to the structure of a policy scenario. He spoke as a consequential leader on the topic in the national legislature and faithfully characterized the views of the opposition that he had to reject. At the moment, Reagan's view may have strengthened the stalwarts at the 1880 Republican national convention. Of longer consequence, the idea that all competition had to be eliminated was no better displayed than in the business practices of Standard Oil Company. Cullom, in his report to the Senate in 1887, would name Rockefeller's company as an unacceptable example of the practice of eliminating competition. That experience, throughout the decade with the oil trust, doubtlessly influenced popular views respecting the advent of federal railroad regulation. In the new legislation, pooling of rates was made illegal.

Adams had further testified that it would take a Caesar to achieve consolidation and that is exactly what bothered Reagan, who said,

> The character of the railroad men he describes as "hardly better than a race of horse-jockeys" are not the kind that should be trusted with vast powers necessary to control and direct the "combined" railroads of the United States. He sees no remedy for existing evils of railroad management but force. He describes with sufficient fullness the character of force he means. It is not the force of law; it is not the force of public opinion; but it is the force, the power of one man, of a Caesar or a Napoleon or a Vanderbilt; the force of personal will wielding corporate powers unrestrained by just laws; "the few who will be sufficiently powerful to restrain the many"; "a railroad federation under a protectorate," and the people and their property securely in the grasp of power, with no hope save such as might come from the charity of lust, or the mercy of avarice.

What angered him were:

159

The people, the shippers, the owners of the many billions of dollars of commerce which is annually shipped over these roads, and who are interested to the extent of 99 percent of its value, while the railroads at most cannot justly be interested in it more than 1 percent. The railroads under a "combination" or "federation," and left free from the restraints of legislation, and having legitimately no more than 1 percent interest in this immense commerce, may control absolutely the rates of freight, may bull or bear the markets at their pleasure, may as to individuals discriminate in freights and charges as they please, allow rebates to whom they please, ruin one city and place and enrich another at their pleasure, and may levy any tax on the commerce of the country which their sweet wills may dictate or their avarice call for.[37]

Ironically, in the course of time, a Caesar would arrive on the scene but on the opposite side. He came in the person of Theodore Roosevelt, whose determined trust busting took businesses in the opposite direction from that sought by Adams and the consolidators. The "bad men" of 1880s who sought competition would become the "good men" of 1900s.

Henry Adams, Charles's brother, in his novel *Democracy* anonymously published that summer, described the days before the convention as part of the policy arena.

In February the weather becomes warmer and summer-like . . . the struggle of existence seems to abate . . . as though all the ice and snow on earth, and all the hardness of heart, all the heresy and schism, all the works of the devil had yielded to the force of love and to the fresh warmth of innocent, lamb-like, confiding virtue. In such a world, there should be no guile—but there is a great deal of it notwithstanding. Indeed, at no other season is there so much. This is the season when the two whited sepulchers at either end of the Avenue [the White House and the Capitol] reek with the thick atmosphere of bargain and sale. The old is going; the new is coming. Wealth, office, power are at auction. Who bids highest; who hates with the most venom? Who intrigues with the most skill? Who has done the dirtiest, the meanest, the darkest, and the most political work? He shall have his reward.[38]

Betrayal and revenge were in the air. In 1881 Gorham described those days before the Chicago convention the previous year and outdid Henry Adams in covering the fierceness of the battle. Gorham held that "Republican Party . . . conventions sent more than a majority of all their delegates to the National Convention favorable to Grant. That is a historical fact which cannot be obliterated." On June 7, 1881, he wrote that:

160

The air was made thick with the noisome stenches of calumny, while the roar and din of imprecations and maledictions suspended all ordinary transactions and forbade all sane reasoning and remonstrance. The basest elements of society—the harpies around Legislatures, the chiffoniers of the press, the criminals fearing arrest, plunderers who had been discovered and disgraced, disappointed, soured, and dyspeptic place-hunters, tatterdemalions ready for any scramble, and desperate adventurers seeking to organize opportunities for public theft, all engaged in a concerted and long-sustained outcry against Grant and his supporters.

The lines from Adams and Gorham describe almost perfectly the news next read at a merchants' meeting on June 9. It was clear from the Chicago convention that the anti-Grant forces had succeeded. Grant had won on the first ballot in 1868 and 1872 but not this time. Now trouble loomed for the anti-monopolists.

The Railroaders and Financiers Allegedly Invoke a Gag Rule, June 1880

The railroaders and financiers had played a long shot and won. In New York, they were exuberant. Like a gang of immigrant stevedores on the docks who had beaten out their rivals on a contract, with their victory they chose to settle old scores and became vindictive. They were ready to enforce a new political order against those who had brought them before the Hepburn hearings. Merchants coming to a meeting of the Board of Trade's committee on railroad transportation were appalled at the gossip that now swept the New York business community warning that a fearsome course lay ahead. It was now claimed, according to the *Times*, that:

> the railroad managers will oppose to the bitter end any and all attempts to control them; that free passes, advertisements, and other favors are being extended to the press more freely than ever before; that a "vigorous political policy will be pursued"; *that expressions upon this subject in political platforms will be suppressed*; that legislators who made themselves conspicuous in behalf of the public, if seeking re-election, will be beaten wherever money can accomplish it, and, in short, that the policy of repressing public opinion will be pursued, instead of making concessions to it.[39] (Our emphasis.)

The article did not report everything that the merchants had heard. It noted that "to reprint it as a whole, would be to take the risk of numerous actions for libel, as a great many persons of wealth and standing (not named below) are mentioned in it by name in anything but a complimentary way." The article's headline nonetheless raised a red flag. "Merchants' Opinions of Mr. Blaine and His Adherents Plainly Expressed." At the newspaper office, someone in a hurry had neglected to cut out all the copy they should have and failed to edit the remark about Blaine from the headline! But the rumored report may have been right on the mark. Years later in writing his recollections, Shelby Cullom, Governor of Illinois, a U.S. Senator, and apologist for the grangers, recalled: "The high railroad officials paid no attention to us . . . they considered the railroads superior to the laws of Congress . . . in those days they were the most arrogant set of men in this country."[40]

According to the rumors heard among the merchants, the new political order would be based on a reversal of the platform of the 1879 state convention. The clauses that brought their intentions to light were "the railroad managers will oppose to the bitter end any and all attempts to control them" and "expressions in political platforms on the subject will be suppressed," recalling the 1879 convention. Thus, the capitalists sought, as Laumann and Knoke assert can happen, "to impose their preferred definitions and requirements for inclusion."[41] Accordingly, the new leadership in 1880 was ready to exclude many people from policy discussions. Adams had marked westerners as incompetent in discussing railroad policy, and New York capitalists were casting New York merchants in the same manner. Those promises Vanderbilt had made to the merchants the previous September had evaporated in Grant's defeat.

The indignant tone of the new alleged gag rule was hardly novel. It may have come from only a fraction of the railroad financiers. Simon Sterne had come away from the Hepburn hearing happy to see that Albert Fink "did not lose his temper trying to justify railroad actions. His arguments made sense and his logic destroyed a great deal of the indictment that the railroads were exercising an irresponsible censorship over the affairs of the business community."[42] Fink saw what the problem was when he said that:

> Many railroad managers still cling to the idea that they are autocrats, as far as the control of their property is concerned, and that they can dictate terms and force compliance, although the dearly-purchased experience of many years should have shown them that this is not the fact.[43]

However, the news items from the *Times* were frightening and gave the merchants more to ponder. Upon Grant's defeat in Chicago, the railroad autocrats had apparently seized the lead in their own alliance, and Fink fell into the minority. Some of the railroad leaders now assuming leadership must have found the Hepburn and convention episode nothing less than disgusting and humiliating. The longer the railroaders thought about it, the more confidently they came to a new rationale not to honor what they had promised.

While some historians recall the 1879 state convention chiefly as evidence of Conkling's declining power, in June 1880 the financiers recalled the Hepburn hearings as an embarrassing public airing of their business management and thus as interference in their affairs. If the rumored gag rule of June 9, 1880 was authentic, it no doubt traced directly back to the discomfiture that the great financiers experienced. They wanted no repeat performances. Historians' emphasis on Conkling's decline in power at the Saratoga convention is a distraction. A win for Cornell on the first ballot in a four-way race was no sign of weakness. It was claimed as a weakness simply to give his foes a point from which they launched their new ascendancy. In fact, the anti-monopoly contingent left the convention very strong because they had a front-page letter from Vanderbilt promising conversations and negotiations. Subsequently, the railroaders reneged. Presumably they saw a way to win without negotiations. What would it be? The handwriting would be on the wall in March with Depew's testimony at the March legislative hearings when he criticized the composition of the Hepburn committee and trivialized the anti-monopoly sentiment in the city. After that matters only went from bad to worse.

The hierarchy of announcements would be badly used. In the case of the Pacific railroads, both parties had first adopted platforms endorsing the project. Next, candidate Lincoln gave his support. Once the Republicans won the election, it remained up to the majority party in Congress, on the next level down from the national convention, to get on with the work through a committee system that was up to the task of handling the detailed information. In the next example, with regard to monitoring western rail traffic from the nation's breadbasket in the upper Mississippi River states to the New York port, President Grant spoke out forcefully on the need for waterway competition with the railroads, and Conkling's committees and Windom took up the task of monitoring. In 1879 the New York party adopted a plan for regulation, but failed to win support for it at the 1880 national convention. Indeed, once Grant was out of the way at the 1880 convention, the financiers appear to have announced a new order by reversing the 1879 state plank and dismissing the value of having a platform. All party guidance was gone, a forecast of the frightful factional fight about to unfold.

Chapter VI

The Acme of a Gilded Age Policy Scenario

1   Ulen, Thomas S. *Cartels and Regulation.* Ph.D. thesis, Stanford University, 1979, p. 187.

2   *NYT,* April 20, 1879.

3   Burrows, Edwin, and Mike Wallace. *Gotham.* New York: Oxford University Press, 1991, pp. 1032f.

4   *NYT,* March 2, 1878.

5   Laumann, Edward O., and David Knoke. *The Organizational State.* Madison: University of Wisconsin Press, 1988, p. 15.

6   Benson, Lee. *Merchants, Farmers, and Railroads.* Harvard University Press, 1955, p. 119.

7   Ibid., p. 120.

8   *NYT,* April 20, 1878.

9   Adams, Charles F. *The Railroads.* New York: Putnam's, 1878, pp. 148, 179.

10   *NYT,* August 30, 1879.

11   Laumann and Knoke, p. 15.

12   *NYT,* August 21 and 28, 1879.

13   *New York Tribune*, June 8, 1881. For coverage of the 1879 convention, see Thomas C. Reeves, *Chester Arthur: Gentleman Boss.* New York: Knopf, 1975, Chapter 8.

14   *NYT,* September 4, 1879.

15   *NYT,* September 4, 1879.

16   *NYT,* September 4, 1879.

17   *NYT,* September 18, 1879.

18   *NYT,* September 19, 1879.

[19] Laumann and Knoke, p. 16.

[20] Destler, Chester McArthur. *Henry Demarest Lloyd and the Empire of Reform.* Philadelphia: University of Pennsylvania Press, 1963, p. 108.

[21] Destler, p. 111.

[22] *NYT,* September 23, 1879.

[23] *NYT,* June 10, 1880.

[24] *NYT,* September 19, 1879.

[25] *NYT,* August 10, 1881.

[26] Laumann and Knoke, pp. 31f.

[27] Adams, Charles. *Diary,* Oct. 17, 1879.

[28] *NR,* June 7, 1881.

[29] Adams, Charles. *Argument . . . before the Committee on Commerce,* February 27, 1880., Ill., pp. 5–7.

[30] Adams, *Railroads,* p. 197.

[31] Adams, *Argument...,* pp. 9, 11.

[32] Ibid., p. 17.

[33] *NYT,* February 20, 1880.

[34] *NYT,* March 11, 1880.

[35] *NYT,* March 19, 1880.

[36] *The Nation,* April 21, 1881.

[37] *CR,* 46th Cong., 2nd sess., Vol. X, Pt. IV, June 1, 1880, p. 4025f.

[38] Adams, Henry, *Democracy,* p. 58.

[39] *NYT,* June 10, 1880.

[40] Cullom, Shelby. *Fifty Years of Public Service.* Chicago: A. C. McClurge & Co., 1911, p. 319.

[41] Laumann and Knoke, p. 12.

[42] Gilchrist, D. T., "Albert Fink and the Pooling System," *Business History Review.* Cambridge, MA: Harvard University Press, 1960, Vol. 34, p. 39.

[43] Ibid., p. 44.

CHAPTER VII

Anecdotes From the Presidential Campaign of 1880

The Republican Chicago National Convention, June 1880, with Ulysses S. Grant running again, was hardly a repeat of the 1868 and 1872 conventions when on the first ballots he swept through to victory. The anti-third-term forces succeeded at the outset in depriving Ulysses S. Grant of a first-ballot victory and the meeting settled down to a deadlock. Senator James Blaine continued to run a close second while others, including John Sherman, trailed. Then it became clear that James Garfield, though not nominated, was winning support simply by having admirably handled his convention duties. He had spoken not only in nominating John Sherman, but also in speaking as chair of the convention rules committee. Conkling tried to win support for some procedures but only managed to exasperate many delegates. When Conkling thought he saw the increasing popularity for Garfield, Sherman's manager passed a note to the Ohioan with the sarcastic question inquiring who was really running for the nomination.

On the thirty-sixth ballot, the convention nominated Garfield as its dark-horse candidate. Responding graciously, Senator Roscoe Conkling called for a unanimous vote, ending his remarks by saying that the zeal found in the convention against one another should now turn to "carrying the lance of the Republican Party into the ranks of the enemy." Naming Chester Arthur as the candidate for vice president offered New York an olive branch.

Once the convention euphoria had subsided, party managers began to wonder whether they had selected a winner. Certainly, the Grant forces would pull their share of the load. On the other hand, Garfield's name was under a cloud from the *Credit Mobilier* scandal, the Louisiana vote count, and Washington paving contracts. The pro-Democratic press, beginning with the *Sun* and its indefatigable A. M. Gibson, had a field day. Graffiti humiliating Garfield was soon smeared all over Washington. Remembering the shadows crossing Garfield's career, Thomas Nast, presumably a Republican, "refused to introduce [Garfield] into his cartoons." While Senator Dawes of Massachusetts was generally pleased with the nomination, he did write one correspondent that "Garfield, good, glorious, and yet—it is an escape. Garfield is a grand, noble fellow, but fickler, unstable, more brains, but no such will as Sherman, brilliant like Blaine but timid and hesitating."[1]

The Fifth Avenue Hotel Meeting and Its Aftermath, August 1880

Early planning for the campaign got underway with party leaders holding a conference at the Fifth Avenue Hotel on August 5. Much is made of the inexplicable absence of Roscoe Conkling, inexplicable only if one fails to note the financiers' alleged gag rule announced June 9th, the uncompleted work on the Hepburn report, and the failure of the Chicago convention to adopt a strong plank on regulation. The usual comments on Conkling's truancy attribute it to his alleged immaturity and pouting.

What has been overlooked is that the meeting at the hotel gave opportunity for the confirmation of a new, emerging political structure. That structure involved two coalitions, one emerging after the other. The first coalition was that mentioned by Leach and Brown in their biography of Garfield and consisted of a meeting the day after the hotel meeting with only Reid, Garfield and Gould in attendance. It was held at Reid's home.

Other Republican leaders in New York must have learned about this session. It was left to those not invited to Reid's home to speculate what the terms of this coalition might be. In retrospect, Conkling's absence credits him with enough sense to avoid becoming prematurely involved in the quickly moving affairs, that is, until he could see how matters fell out. He may have prompted the second coalition.

The evidence of the first alliance came the day after the August hotel meeting when editor Whitelaw Reid drove Garfield to meet Jay Gould, railroad, telegraph, and *Tribune* owner. Margaret Leech and Harry Brown write:

> On the morning after the general conference, the candidate was driven to the home of Whitelaw Reid, editor of the *New York Tribune* and Garfield's chief campaign adviser on New York politics—and a foe of the Conkling machine. There Garfield conferred with Jay Gould whose support was not yet assured. Although there is no record of their conversation, it is probable that one of the topics touched upon was Garfield's attitude toward railroads.[2]

They possibly also discussed the even larger issue of consolidation of the railroads. Other matters could have included Gould's general business plan, including his warnings that any political interference in business could prompt a market decline. Six years later, when he tried to discourage passage of the ICC legislation he broadcast similar warnings. Assuming that he made the same prediction in his meeting with Garfield, he would have dissuaded the candidate from any ventures into the economy. If so, his comment would have been consistent with the alleged gag rule of June 9th. Other markers of achievement in this alliance would include agreements about Supreme Court nominees and ultimately the reversal of the Court's decision in 1877 in *Munn v. Illinois* written by Chief Justice Waite.

The Garfield-Gould meeting could hardly have remained a secret and probably gave New York leaders pause as they wondered where candidate Garfield was headed. He could have met with others after the hotel meeting, such as leaders of the Chamber of Commerce. The following spring the Chamber did invite Garfield to its annual dinner but he declined, mentioning his wife's illness.[3]

The public consternation over monopolists' practices was very high. It is seen in the fact that shortly after the Fifth Avenue Hotel meeting some merchants made new attempts to gather allies to counter anything Reid, Garfield and Gould could plausibly put together. These antagonists, as Parsons, Laumann, and others would explain, were keeping each other in mind, acting in their own interest while reacting to the actions and apparent intentions of the other side. Apparently they were sure that the 1877 decision in *Munn v. Illinois* would come under attack.

Setting aside the threat of the alleged gag rule on June 9, the merchants reached out to a broader constituency. While it was not reported in the *Times* until December 2, the New York merchants began polling their peer organizations across the country about monopoly behavior in August.[4] The poll was preventative and preparatory. The *Times* would finally report in December:

> The Chamber of Commerce in August addressed to prominent men in various parts of the country a circular asking their opinions on some of the chief points involved in the problem of railroad transportation. They sought answers to a series of questions, among which were these:

> How can the prevailing discriminations against individuals and communities be prevented?

> Is it safe to allow railroad managers to follow their new theory of charging, "all the traffic will bear?"

> Ought not the companies to be supervised in the public interest, as banks and insurance companies are, and for more pressing reasons?

> What do you think of companies and managers contributing large sums of money to election expenses or to influence legislation?

> Is it right to water stock [inflating value] through any means by which fictitious bases of value are established?

Is a law just, which limits passenger rates, and if so, should not the principle be extended to freight charges?

What do you think of charges of $4 per 100 pounds from New York to Salt Lake City and only $2.50 from New York to San Francisco?[5]

The supposition can be made that when the Chamber leaders gathered to produce this poll and get the mail out, they also discussed other actions they could take after the New Year to launch a full-scale anti-monopoly movement. This was the second alliance.

Garfield Negotiates with Editor Reid

After the August conference Garfield returned to his home near Mentor and began corresponding with the editor Whitelaw Reid. First Reid wanted to know whether Garfield adhered in the case of *Munn v. Illinois* to the opinion of Chief Justice Waite or that of Justice Field. With that settled, they discussed the money needed to support the Indiana October campaign. While funds would come in from several sources, they were specifically discussing $100,000 raised from principal capitalists, some of whom were also cartelists. According to Robert D. Marcus, "The lines were being drawn on the crucial question, which in this era was not so much *laissez-faire* versus regulation as it was judicial versus legislative control over regulation."[6] Marcus adds that this is the one idea that prevailed among such railroad men as Collis P. Huntington, Cyrus M. Field, and Jay Gould, and bankers like John A. Stewart. In effect, they sought to reduce the role of state commissions and legislative hearings. There had been enough of that in the Hepburn hearings. The alleged gag rule of June 9th suggested that there would be no more. But in the swirl of debate there would be plenty of exhibitions of the *laissez-faire* position.

Marcus also notes that Reid, not trustful of any of Garfield's generalities, won a promise from him in writing: to appoint to the Supreme Court only men "entirely sound on these questions." The candidate made a further pledge to Reid to base his selections "upon evidence . . . satisfactory to you as well as to me." In short, Marcus concludes that Garfield offered Reid and his friends at least a veto over nominations for the high court. Of course, a risk attended this correspondence, the risk of disclosure. Therefore, the question remained whether the correspondence led to intimidating Garfield. He made an agreement with Reid who had yet to retract the false charge he had made eight years earlier in the *Credit Mobilier* affair.

The letters between Garfield and Reid moved through the national campaign office and became "an open secret,"[7] catching the campaign workers' attention. Of course, the workers did not know the content of the letters. When they learned that the donor's bookkeeper would travel to Indiana to keep track of the payouts, they had to suspect that the men had reached some sort of agreement.[8] Since no one was so naive as to believe that Gould made a strings-free charitable contribution, insiders had to wonder what was afoot.

This news from the back room at the Republican National Headquarters did not sit well with the New York faithful. A pall fell over the scene already quieted by the loss of Grant. Then there was the intimidating presence of the factional victors. The railroad elite, comprising three or four dozen companies headquartered in New York City, supported the half-breeds. Also figuring in the mix was the railroaders' control over the state senate. Robertson's bolt from the Grant delegation had stunned them. The firm commitment behind the alleged gag rule of June 9, discouraging concessions to the public, meant that a new order prevailed. The standoff between the factions was unmistakable. One friend wrote Garfield that the two sides in New York sat there "making faces" at each other, likely waiting to see which side he would come down on.[9]

Maine would hold its state election in September, and Ohio and Indiana in October. All of them served as barometers for the November presidential election in northern states. Right off, Blaine's state of Maine went Democratic, doing no better than two years earlier in the off-year elections when the state had a heavy greenbacker turnout. Winning Maine in the primary, the Democrats, holding the Congress for the past two years, now looked as though they could put Pennsylvania Democrat General Winfield Scott into the White House. Republican campaign leaders knew that they had to reverse matters in Indiana and Ohio where elections would be held in October. To do so they had to play their strongest card, orator Roscoe Conkling.

Conkling Tutors Candidate Garfield

By the time Conkling was ready to assume his campaign duties, the rumors about the Reid-Garfield correspondence were well known among the party insiders. The existence of the correspondence had to irk Conkling, for it implied he was on the outside of the circle.

What bothered Conkling at the time was the innuendo about his feelings and views on the candidate. The following June Gorham, a traveling companion with Conkling and Grant in the Ohio and Indiana campaign, wrote his recollection.

> When General Garfield [went] to Washington last summer, soon after his nomination, to arrange his "private papers" he eagerly sought Senator Conkling. [The loss] had created a sense of injury and a feeling of profound disgust in the minds of those who had been thus practiced upon. . . . That the stalwarts would waive the irregularities at Chicago and acquiesce in the nomination no man doubted. General Garfield had no fears on that score. But it was important the wounded enemies, acting from a sense of party obligation, should become hearty friends and enthusiastic in the campaign. Candidate Garfield knew that all through the ranks of the stalwart wing of the party there was distrust of him which must be overcome or defeat was certain. . . . [He sought] the great leader whose slightest word would dispel the gloom and give heart to the men behind

him. He called on the senator, but did not see him alone. The senator returned the call and the candidate was not in. He was riding with Carl Schurz. Further efforts were made to a meeting but without success.

[The] desire of the presidential candidate to make an opportunity, to give promises which the New York Senator had not asked, is meanly perverted by some into evidence that "Conkling was sulking in his tent." He did not occupy his tent when the proper time arrived for him to take the field. He had no interview which censorious people could misconstrue or a defective memory cause to be misreported. He did not put a price upon his party fealty; that had never been with him a subject of barter. He eluded the candidate's pursuit and took no part in the prizes which are now being distributed. This did not prevent the eminently practical nominee for the presidency from protesting his love. To the vice-presidential nominee, General Arthur, to Mr. Platt, and to others known by him to be intimate associates of the senator, he voluntarily declared with great earnestness and particularity that, should he be elected, he would always consult with the senators and with the Republican State Committee in reference to New York matters, and no action should at any time be taken which would be disagreeable to them.

On the day of the Warren meeting General Grant, Mr. Conkling and ex-Senator Simon Cameron paid a visit of compliment to Mentor-- that being the first meeting of the senator and the to-be-President after the Chicago Convention. There were no private conversations between them then, nor at any other time prior to the election. There was no "treaty at Mentor." In brief, there never was at any time either sulking or bargaining by Mr. Conkling. He did what the party expected of him. He grandly led in a campaign for the Republican cause, and on the stump aided greatly to make the people forget the shortcomings of the candidate in the grandeur of the cause.[10]

The candidate had become wrapped in both private deals and high morality that bore on the condition of the party. Conkling went directly to the matter in his opening remarks of September 17, 1880. He said,

A candidate, if he were an honest, genuine man, will not seek and accept a party nomination to the Presidency, Vice Presidency, or Congress, and after he is elected become a law unto himself. Few things are more despicable than first to secure elevation at the hands of a party, and then, in the hope of winning pretentious non-partisan applause, to affect superior sanctity, and meanly to imply that those whose support and confidence were eagerly and deferentially sought are wanting in purity, patriotism, or some other title to respect.

Here was a warning for the coming administration. Conkling could observe the arrogance arising from the likes of the self-appointed Anglo-Saxon elite now ready to rule. All others had to be wary. Conkling was warning against the hubris that attended candidates. On the other hand, in a letter, Blaine would urge that such hubris *should* properly resonate on through the new administration. Conkling had made public the temptation facing the new president a few weeks before Blaine gladly walked him right into it.

In his address, the New Yorker next alluded to the matter of the Reid-Garfield correspondence that had been irritating party insiders in the back room of the national campaign office. [The *Sun* of December 31, 1882 would disclose the contents, a bargain of Gould's contributing in exchange for Garfield nominating Stanley Matthews as Justice. Gorham printed the *Sun* article on the next day, January 1, 1883.] Conkling had let the nation know that:

> *The higher obligations among men are not set down in writing and signed and sealed*--they reside in honor and good faith. The fidelity of a nominee belongs to this exalted class, and, therefore, a candidate of a party is but the exponent of a party. The object of political discussion and action is to settle principles, policies, and issues. It is a paltry incident of an election affecting fifty million people that it decides for an occasion the aspirations of individual men.[11] (Our emphasis.)

Conkling had hit the nail on the head by forecasting the coming melodrama. The comments about the use of private correspondence taking precedence over public platforms did not merely add up to a civics lesson. His remarks administered a rebuke that probably made sense only to the second-tier New York stalwarts. Conkling was tutoring the candidate on how to be one, and, not surprisingly, the relations between him and Garfield became touchy.

In his addresses Conkling made only spare mention of the candidate by name, leading Garfield to complain. The candidate had forgotten that in the 1864 campaign he took the stump and scarcely mentioned President Lincoln's name. Lacking generals who could give him victories in the field, Lincoln had stood before the country as a poor candidate.[12] Thinking he understood Conkling's motives, Garfield, still impressed by the long deadlock at Chicago, wrote to a friend about the senator. Garfield said that the senator and his friends "are more concerned in running Grant in 1884, than they are for carrying the Republicans safely through the contest of 1880."[13] Garfield would remain suspicious of the stalwarts' motives all the way through his visit the next spring with Grant at Long Branch. He was also quite confident about his suspicions. With each man's feathers ruffled, the speaking tour to counter the loss in Maine launched into Ohio and Indiana awkwardly. Another observer of the fall campaign noted that Conkling

> went to Ohio to find the Republicans there had been fighting a defensive fight—explaining De Golfer, *Credit Mobilier*, back-pay, and so on. He changed their campaign into an aggressive one. He made the fight a party one. He ignored individuals at the head of the ticket. He did not bespatter Hancock. He did not plaster Garfield with unmerited praise. He refused all entreaties to go into the Credit Mobilier business and the other things; and thereby hangs a tale. . . . He secured Ohio and Indiana without other help than his own voice.[14]

The sweeping forces in society that caught up many men of affairs were now making their presence felt. In his book *Education,* Henry Adams captured them well.

> The leaders of industry betrayed no sentiment, popular or other. They used, without qualm, whatever instruments they found at hand. They had been obliged, in 1861, to turn aside and waste immense energy in settling what had been settled a thousand years before, and should never have been revived. At prodigious expense, by sheer force, they broke resistance down, leaving everything but the mere fact of power untouched, since nothing else had a solution. Race and thought were beyond reach. Having cleared its path so far, society went back to its work, and threw itself on that which stood first—its roads. The field was vast, altogether beyond its power to control off-hand; and society dropped every thought to dealing with anything more than the single fraction called a railway-system. This relatively small part of its task was still so big as to need the energies of a generation, for it required all the new machinery to be created: —capital, banks, mines, furnaces, shops, power-houses, technical knowledge, mechanical population, together with a steady remodeling of social and political habits, ideas and institutions to fit the new scale and suit the new conditions. The generation between 1865 and 1895 was already mortgaged to the railways, and no one knew it better than the generation itself.[15]

Conkling Tells the Nation His Plan for Railroad Regulation

Not knowing the content of the Garfield-Reid correspondence, Conkling could only wonder if the exchange had a bearing on a plan for railroad regulation. While on the circuit he could not let the opportunity pass to mention again the New York *status quo* option of letting the canal be the canal and provide the national regulation.

> The construction of railways has revolutionized traffic and transportation. Four trunk lines of steel roads, of which the sea ends are Boston,

New York, Philadelphia, and Baltimore, now carry, each one of them, more freight than ever moved on the Mississippi River. The great companion and competitor to this transcontinental movement is the lakes and the Erie Canal. Besides handling a vast traffic, this water route acts as a check on railway freights, keeping them down by force of competition.[16]

If the railroad elite had thought that by imposing their alleged gag rule in June of 1880 they had taken control of the national discussion on regulation, Conkling's comment was an affront not to be overlooked. Their plans would not be safe with him. Probably in a hierarchy of actions, it could not appear that Garfield endorsed anything Conkling did to broaden the discussion of regulation.

After Garfield and Reid settled on the campaign contribution, Reid wrote the candidate on August 31, 1880, with the comment that if he satisfied the capitalists, they "could make a big demonstration at once."[17] On October 5 the Bankers and Brokers Association announced plans for a huge march in New York City, and asked other business associations to join. Six nights later, on the eve of the Indiana election, with Ulysses S. Grant in the reviewing stand, the merchant organizations marched in battalions. Party camaraderie was high and, when leaders on the platform looked down and saw William Evarts, Secretary of State, leaning against one of the support posts, they reached over, grabbed him under his arms and hoisted him bodily up onto the stage. The *Times* headlines reported, "Sixty Thousand in Line. The Most Remarkable Display Ever Seen in the City. 300,000 Spectators."

It all added up to a great turnout for Garfield on Election Day. In an editorial on November 5, 1880, entitled "Political Power of Business Men," the *Times* said,

> The large registration, the heavy vote, and the great Republican gain were due in no small part to the active and zealous part which business men took in support of the party whose success they regarded as important to the material interest of the country. . . This year we have been treated to the spectacle of prominent merchants and bankers and manufacturers, the brains and energy of the business community, marching in street parades, forming political organizations of their own, holding meetings in Wall Street, and taking part in popular demonstrations. They have contributed liberally to the legitimate expenses of the campaign, and, above all, they have registered and voted. The votes which they cast and which they influenced may have determined the result of the national election.[18]

Reid's efforts had produced great results. After the election, the *Times* noted that the city Democratic margin had fallen 12,000, compared to 1876. The grand display in New York may have impressed upon Garfield that Reid had broad influence among New York business leaders.

Who had the most influence in carrying the election would remain a question. In Indiana, the campaign had been so remarkable that it attracted more money than was needed. Of the $100,000 received through Reid, a total of $40,000 was returned, [19] making it impossible for the Reid-Gould clique to claim that their money had won Indiana for Garfield.

Elsewhere business associations played a large part. The bankers had cut their teeth in politics in the 1878 election and Harry Baehr wrote of the 1880 election that:

> Two thousand National Banks, members of the "best banking system ever devised," were organized against the Democratic threat to their institution. And finally in defense of the tariff, "thousands of manufacturing establishments are banded together for mutual defense in a dozen associations." Of such was the Republican organization, and it carried Garfield to victory. [20]

Obviously, the record of these efforts offset any claims that Conkling's speaking tour was decisive for the victory. His message had been that control of the Senate ought to be returned to the industrial states. Therefore he helped re-enforce what the many commercial associations sought to do.

The New York Chamber of Commerce Surveys Peer Groups and Others on Railroad Regulation

The great parade in New York City marked the height of Reid's influence among the city's business leaders. Soon afterward the New York business community would begin experiencing a division. The New York Chamber of Commerce began to receive from business organizations across the country their responses to its August survey about monopolist behavior. One of the most critical replies came from Garfield's good friend, Jeremiah S. Black, the attorney general for President James Buchanan. Black had later joined Garfield on the Camden-Amboy railroad monopoly case and then the two continued as law partners. Their friendship led them in the fall and winter of 1880–81 to purchase a farm across the Potomac River in Arlington with a view of the White House. [21]

Black probably knew, as well as anyone, Garfield's mind on the corporation question, state commissions, and the like. His answer to the poll was one of the strongest, and it appeared in the *Times* on December 2nd.

> The corporations who have got into the habit of calling themselves the owners of the railroads have no proprietary right, title or claim to the roads themselves, but a mere franchise annexed to and exercisable thereon. They are the agents of the State for the performance of a public duty. [22]

According to the *Times*, the railroaders hardly helped their own case by shutting the public out of the discussion on railroad regulation. Their behavior fit perfectly the comment from one of Garfield's friends that, in the New York Republican Party, the factions were sitting there "making faces" at one another. The *Times* could see what these reticent monopolists were doing, and in its comments about Black's views, it forecast the cost to be exacted.

> The principles of our constitutional law being what they are, it is only a question of time that the heavy hand of the State will be laid on corporations which grossly violate their obligations to the communities by whose sovereign will they exist. The most striking feature of the railroad problem is that the corporations show themselves so blind to this fact, and refuse to provide the solution, which would be gladly accepted from them if they had the sense to offer it.

> Meeting the requirements of the rights of both the companies and the public would not be impossible to fulfill. We confess that we have very small hope of enforcing them by Legislative or any Governmental action. But, if they be not voluntarily complied with, it is beyond question that the governments, both State and national, will find themselves driven to take the case in hand, and the railways will find, perhaps when it is too late, that they will suffer far more and worse than they would have done if they had honestly and reasonably undertaken to meet the demands of the public themselves.[23]

That the staid and proper *New York Times* used such language about a premier industry located in its own provinces, however elusive it was, testified to the strain of policymaking just before the new administration entered office.

Francis Thurber Returns to Common Law in the December 1880 Scribner's Magazine

Then the December 1880 issue of *Scribner's* appeared, with the anti-monopolist Francis B. Thurber giving a scorching criticism of corporate attorneys. The time of the appearance of the article suggests that when the Chamber met in August to begin circulating a poll of peer organizations they also determined to further some other activities. They could have asked Thurber to prepare an article for publication. He began by mentioning both the 1874 Windom report on transportation and the 1880 Hepburn committee report———matters which the railroaders had thought they had disposed of. He also came to the defense of the granger legislation, which railroad attorneys had long since discounted. Thurber charged that railroads often reminded western audiences that the repeal of the old granger state laws had proven their inadequacy. He complained that the railroad attorneys had purposely misconstrued the laws. "(M)anagers had made them as troublesome as possible to the public, in order that they might create a reaction in public opinion, and, with the liberal use of money in both elections and the lobby, secured their repeal."[24] But not all had gone the way that the attorneys had hoped. As shall be seen, Governor Shelby Cullom of Illinois had been asked to help repeal some granger legislation. Cullom, however, decided not to, and then wrote out a report to strengthen the law, and succeed in getting it adopted.

On December 17, 1880, while the National Board of Trade was in annual meeting in Washington, the *Times*, picking up on Thurber's views on common law, presented a long disquisition on Chief Justice Waite's decision. "When private property is affected with a public interest it ceases to be *juris privati* only," the paper noted. "The result of the whole reasoning of the Chief Justice is the conclusion that railroad companies are common carriers, using in their business property to which a public interest attaches, and giving the right of public control to the extent of that interest." While in recent times the granger law had fallen out of favor, Black's and Thurber's revival of interest likely explained some political shuffling soon to take place.

Another industry soon came under suspicion. Merchant leaders felt that they had to impede the consolidation plans for telegraph companies; they called for Congress to create a government-owned telegraph system to compete with the private companies but never to merge with them, ensuring permanent competition. The English and Europeans had found this arrangement popular, and reported rates much lower than those in America. Important support for the plan came in November from President Hayes's postmaster general, Horace Maynard.[25] Thurber also weighed in on the question, telling the assembled delegates, now turning in their August surveys about monopolist behavior, what he had learned of the English postal telegraph system. The issue was brought to a vote and the delegates cast the required two-thirds vote, thus supporting an American equivalent.[26]

Early Rumors about Sacking Conkling

By the end of the year, the half-breed or railroad alliance was talking of putting Conkling to one side. The plotting may have been due to his support for the canal or, more broadly, because he encouraged public discussion on regulation. Forty years later, Cortissoz would write in his biography of Whitelaw Reid that the editor had held a party in his home at the end of 1880 and among the guests were Depew, Robertson, and Blaine———all from the railroad elite and none from the commercial elite connected to the Chamber of Commerce. "At a party, plans were laid for the defeat of Conkling, which was desired in any case."[27] Reid was hosting both Depew and Robertson, each in the pay of the New York Central, while others, especially civil service reformers, were conspicuous by their absence. That same evening they discussed who would be *"The* Senator" (Depew, president of the cartel) and *"The* Premier" (Blaine), giving the railroad elite of the city a foot in both the Senate and the Cabinet.

Whatever their reasons, no one could overlook the effort to drive out Conkling. He was thought to be the sole cause of the antagonism felt by the capitalists. As the Garfield administration opened, Gorham was amazed at all the dire warnings about what awaited Conkling. When the crisis finally arrived, he looked back and wrote, "The fact is, as stated by all the administration organs, that the President had prepared his mind for a quarrel with Mr. Conkling, and thought it had better be precipitated at the beginning of his term than to come later."[28] The half-breeds' tacit policy preference was to avoid any discussion of business, and in a hierarchy of preferences, it was left to Garfield as president to execute the steps against Conkling.

Chapter VII

Anecdotes from the Presidential Campaign of 1880

1. Baehr, Harry W., Jr. *The New York Tribune Since the Civil War.* New York: Octagon Books, 1972, p. 198; Hoogenboom, Ari. *Outlawing the Spoils.* Urbana: University of Illinois Press, 1968, pp. 182f.

2. Leech, Margaret, and Harry J. Brown, *The Garfield Orbit.* New York: Harper and Row, 1978, pp. 214f.

3. *NYT,* May 11, 1881.

4. Benson, Lee, *Merchants, Farmers, and Railroads.* Cambridge, MA: Harvard University Press, 1955 p. 220.

5. *NYT,* December 2, 1880.

6. Marcus, Robert D. *Grand Old Party: Political Structure in the Gilded Age, 1880-1896.* New York: Oxford University Press, 1971, pp. 51–53.

7. As late as 1888, the substance of the deal between Reid and Garfield was probably still not generally known. That year Gorham wrote only that some agreement had been made. "Mr. Gould had been extremely liberal, and it was an open secret that General Garfield had in return given a testimonial in writing, and signed with his own name, into the hands of Reid, to be safely kept by him as Gould's security . . . the sum to be paid for it in advance during the campaign was $100,000." George C. Gorham. "Conkling Vindicated," *New York Herald,* 1888, leaflet copy in New York Library.

8. *NR,* September 23, 1882.

9. Norris, James D., and Arthur H. Shaffer (eds.). *Politics and Patronage in the Gilded Age: The Correspondence of James A. Garfield and Charles E. Henry.* Madison: Wisconsin Historical Society, 1970, p. 66.

10. *NR,* June 15, 1881.

11. *NYT,* September 18, 1880. On the Senate floor, March 3, 1879, Conkling had addressed the same point, saying,

    He who now wields the powers deposited by the Constitution with the executive branch of the government was not the nominee of the Democratic Party; he was the nominee of the Republican Party. If he was sincere or honest, he incarnated the creed and the purposes of the Republican Party. He accepted a nomination from a delegated party convention. He stood upon the declaration of principles announced by that convention, and in accepting such a nomination, he took upon himself plain, unmistakable, and high obligations. They were not technically formulated in a written contract. The more sacred obligations of man are commonly not set down and signed and sealed. The requirements of honor and trust are not those usually stated in agreements in writing, attested by a subscribing witness, stamped with a revenue-stamp, drawn technically so as to be good within the statute of frauds, and so as to leave no hole to creep out of.

The more cherished and revered duties are unwritten and taken for granted; they rest in the conscience, the honor and the understanding of those concerned. The trust assumed by one who accepts the nomination of a political organization having a creed and a faith, is of the nature I have mentioned––it is a plain and sacred trust. Whoever cannot subscribe to the creed of a party is bound to say so, and to refuse to become its exponent and representative.

[12] Peskin, Allan, *Garfield.* Kent State University Press, 1978, p. 243 and 501.

[13] Leech and Brown, p. 305.

[14] *NR,* June 9, 1881

[15] Adams, Henry, *Novels,* etc., pp. 939f.

[16] *NYT,* September 18, 1880.

[17] R. D. Marcus, p. 50.

[18] *NYT,* November 5, 1880.

[19] *NR,* September 23, 1882.

[20] Baehr, p. 198.

[21] *NR,* July 20, 1881. Reprinted in *NYT,* July 22, 1881.

[22] *NYT,* November 2, 1880.

[23] *NYT,* December 3, 1880.

[24] Thurber, Francis, "The Railroads and the People," *Scribner's Monthly,* December 1880, pp. 258-265.

[25] For Maynard's view, see *NYT,* November 24, 1880.

[26] *Proceedings of the Eleventh Annual Meeting of the National Board of Trade, Washington, D.C., December 1880.* Boston: Tolman and White, 1881.

[27] Cortissoz, Royal, *The Life of Whitelaw Reid.* New York: Scribner's, 1921, Vol., II, p. 45.

[28] *NR,* June 17, 1881.

Chapter VIII

The Showdown of 1881

After the Christmas holiday, with its break for sweetness and hilarity fading from memory, the country got down to work again. Some of the business sectors bolted out of the blocks as though at the next spring's races. President-elect James Garfield, as the New Year opened, would have had to observe that some business leaders close to him headed enterprises that fell quite short of popular support. As some of his allies in the business world frowned on openly discussing business policy, he had to help them. They plausibly would have considered a good return on their campaign gifts if the president succeeded in diverting public attention from anything they were doing.

The Adams Plan for Railroad Regulation under Fire

Right from the outset of the New Year, coming under fire was the plan Charles Francis Adams, Jr. had submitted for railroad regulation. A year earlier after his testimony before the House commerce committee under John Reagan, the *Times* had been especially critical. Now the new criticism came from a more troubling source, none other than the members of the Massachusetts Commission, which Adams had helped found and then led. In a nutshell, the commissioners let it be known that the Adams plan then waiting in the U. S. House left too much out and weakened his position. The current plan, they claimed, betrayed a disregard for law. A year earlier, the *Times* had faulted Adams's testimony for the same reason: "A commission will have its uses as a supplement to the well-considered and stringent enactment, but to *accept it as a substitute for law* would be to leave the railroad companies absolute masters of the situation." Now the Massachusetts Commission virtually endorsed the *Times*'s criticism. The process of the "sunshine law" standing by itself would not be sufficient. With respect to the Massachusetts experience, the *Times* of January 7, 1881, told its readers that:

> the chief points which in *this* State continue to be disputed in the
> interest of railroad corporations, and which a majority of our senators

last Winter treated as if open to question, are already settled beyond all reasonable controversy [in Massachusetts]. . .

The Massachusetts Commissioners have no doubt that discriminations against individuals and communities are contrary to justice and public right, and should be *prevented by law*. In their State, they are prohibited by heavy penalties, and it is a part of the duty of the Railroad Commission to secure *the enforcement of the law* in this regard.

They . . . condemn the rule of charging "what the traffic will bear," instead of a "reasonable rate" based on the "cost of service". . . it is an indictable offense . . . wherever the common law prevails.

These gentlemen declare themselves decidedly in favor of a railroad commission as a means of securing *the enforcement of the laws* and the settlement of disputes between shippers and the railroads. They regard the English system of regulation as excellent in its working and deserving of imitation in every State. Under that all rates must be public and uniform for like service, and must have the approval of the Commissioners, who exercise a general supervision and act as a tribunal for the settlement of disputes, from whose decision there is no appeal. (Our emphasis.)

Adams's work now betrayed a shift from the model of the English system and appeared to follow the spirit of Justice Field's decisions. They implied that "economic freedom transcends all other consideration."[1] That could mean that the public in defense of its stake had no place in the matter, and that the U.S. Congress should recognize such a privileged status of the corporations. If Vanderbilt was holding out for legislation from "Congress first," what he sought might mean simply codifying the *laissez faire* position. If Garfield favored any part of the railroaders' preferences, leaders favoring the English solution could be defeated.

The New York merchants were also heard from, raising objections for not including a public member. Adams knew better. In 1879, he had urged Charles Osgood, the chair of Massachusetts's legislative oversight committee, to persuade the legislature not to drop the member from the business community for the sake of economy. Prophetically he had urged Osgood to tell the committee on legislative oversight that:

> . . . a similar board elsewhere—in New York, for instance—will at once see why this is necessarily the case. The matters coming before it are not *per se* questions of law and of fact; they involve many practical considerations; and, to deal with these successfully, it is, above all, necessary to know whom to apply to, and how to reach them. This will always continue to be the case; and, so long as it is so, the aid of some capable businessman will be essential.[2]

Furthermore, Joseph Nimmo, the federal chief statistician, saw the silver lining in the cloud of western state regulation and had written a year earlier:

> (T)he railroad companies have been constrained to explain the principles upon which their freight tariffs are based, and thus the public have been enabled to gain much valuable information as to the distinction which exists between just and unjust discriminations.[3]

Perhaps fortified by Nimmo's rejoinder to Adams, the New York merchants in January 1881 stated that they did not

> believe that the operation of railroads is so complex and mysterious that the laws of business, common sense, and fair play cannot be applied to their government, and that only railroad attorneys and experts are capable of forming an intelligent opinion upon this subject. Neither does the committee believe that railroad interests are so privileged that the interests of the public in general should be entirely subordinate thereto.[4]

Showing that they did not appreciate business transacted in economies of scale, the New York merchants further remarked that

> Rebates, which are recognized by the Adams bill, but which are prohibited by the Reagan bill, while they may sometimes be found convenient to the railroad companies, are not consistent with the public interest.[5]

Soon the New York Chamber of Commerce in its mailings to boards in other cities included these complaints from the Massachusetts Railroad Commission. Unfortunately, journalists failed to see the incongruity. Some reporter could have made a trip to Boston and looked up Adams's earlier letter to Osgood and turned in a sensational story to his paper. After all, Adams's appeal to Osgood had been printed up as a legislative document. If, in January 1881, the newspapers had reprinted it, they would have exposed Adams's changing opinions, making it much easier to discount the version of the Adams bill now in the U.S. House.

For months the doctrine that only railroad experts should have a word in drafting railroad regulation remained intact. In August 1881 Gorham spoofed the notion:

> Ten men in the United States confiscate nine-tenths of all the profits made by agricultural and manufacturing industry. This they do by arbitrarily demanding that share as a condition of allowing transportation over the great toll-roads which they have been licensed to maintain. But any attempt to compel them to diminish their extortions might do them injustice. Legislators cannot know the laws of railroading. It takes a railroad expert to adjust the balance correctly . . . . The fixing of rates is

183

so much a matter of grades and curves, bulk weight and value of goods, value of services, fluctuation of business, and a hundred other things, that only the "bold barons" themselves can measure their customers' pockets and exact all the contents. It is because of these great difficulties that the "railroad problem" has to be solved by railroad men themselves. It is better that ten railroad kings should seize upon all the profits of all industry and the "fair return upon capital" invested by others than that, in an effort on the part of all other citizens to retain a little, any mistake should be made against the enterprising ten.

To insure "justice" to themselves in the matter of charges, the great railroad corporations employ men to control politics. They have an eye equally to the conventions of each party, and, without the knowledge or consent of any considerable number of members of either party, they manage to exercise great power over the machinery of both. As the Republican Party was organized by the people to resist the encroachments of the Slave Power, it should be the instrumentality through which the people should crush out the political tyranny and check the hateful extortions of the Railroad Power.[6]

Democrats Threaten National Banking, Leading Over One Hundred Banks to Withdraw from the System in Protest, January 1881

Next, the national banks—the one institution Garfield had so long championed and the one whose leaders in the recent national election had performed so impressively—now felt imperiled by Congress. Some bank leaders decided to hit back with their own stick. The Democrats wanted to refund the national debt at 3 1/2 percent, which was satisfactory. At fault was the Carlyle amendment, a restraint upon making summary withdrawals, which some said was certain to drive national banks out of the system. Warnings came from the *Tribune* on January 16 and 17, 1881 that the amendment would "break down resumption." Decades later Irwin Unger wrote that the victory of resumption in January 1879 had been only symbolic. "The enemy had not surrendered, a fact that was indeed recognized by the more astute among them."[7]

In January 1881, a year before Congress would vote on rechartering of national banks, many bankers, livid about the Carlyle amendment, hardly reached out to find new friends. Almost as though on cue from the *Tribune*, and without prior notice, 137 banks withdrew their circulation of $18,764,434 in bonds and shook the marketplace. While that action reduced the circulation, the rest of the banks virtually halted their loan activity. In the following year's House debate on the banking bill, Samuel Randall, who had served as Speaker of the House from 1876 to late 1881, recalled that "in those thirteen days" those few banks "caused a panic and raised the rate of interest from 4 percent per annum to 1 percent per day."[8] In July 1881, the *Post* would write, it was a "victory for the corporations that bullied the Government and tried to produce a panic."⁹ The withdrawals were likely a case of the banks punishing the politicians for letting the Carlyle amendment get as far as it had.

On February 28, 1881, Gorham commented on the banks' actions as an avalanche of punishment and intimidation:

> It is one thing to have an opinion and to maintain it decently, but quite another thing to threaten penalties which cannot be enforced if Congress shall dare to legislate as its majorities shall deem wisest and best . . . No doubt the fifth section [the Carlyle amendment] was placed there as security against the execution of threats . . . The fifth section is wholly due to the silly system of intimidation which has been in vogue for some years in certain newspaper offices [*The Tribune?*] . . . . Congress must not allow itself to be badgered into injustice and wrong . . .

> A mock panic is easily improvised by the publication of a long list of banks, which have given real or sham notice, the wild shrieking of a pretendedly excited newspaper, and goodly report of "wash sales" in the stock market. These, with sensational headings and knowing insinuations, as though the president were stowed away in a convenient clothes-press, from where he could be made to veto bills or sign them, as directed by the Tappertit having him in charge, and the conditions are supposed to be complete for substituting individual will for legislative judgment.¹⁰

Compared to his 1878 Newark address, in which he had urged abolishing national banking, Gorham's views in 1881 represented a notable change. Again, Gorham wrote in March 1881, "Everybody knows that there was an attempt to bully Congress as to funding legislation, but everybody ought to know that not one national bank in fifteen had anything to do with the reprehensible business."¹¹ Gorham had come to recognize that since the silver debate of early 1878 the banking community had risen from its political quiescence to exercise leadership in the fall elections of 1878 and 1880, and he seemed to have adjusted.

Less than a week before leaving office, President Hayes, in his veto message on the refunding bill, explained that the Democratic bill would have closed down national banking and caused great harm to the economy:

> If the present efficient and admirable system of banking is broken down, it will inevitably be followed by a recurrence to other and inferior methods of banking. Any measure looking to such a result will be a disturbing element in our financial system. It will destroy confidence and surely check the growing prosperity of the country.

185

Hayes was claiming that the Democrats brought national banking right to the brink, allowing the suspicion that in the months to come they might fancy other chances to do so again. That left a question for Garfield: How would he manage to finesse threats to national banking?

The Democrats had time to override Hayes' veto, but they decided not to try. The refunding problem passed on to the Garfield administration, where Secretary of the Treasury Windom, without benefit of Congress, handled it surprisingly well. Rumors circulated that in the panic a conspiracy among the bankers had prevailed, but later John Knox, controller of the currency, denied it. Examining the figures, however, does show an excessive number of withdrawals from some states. Those states that sent at least one new Republican to the Senate had a higher proportion of banks quitting the system. In those states, 5.5 percent of the banks withdrew while in states that sent only Democrats to the Senate, 1.9 percent of the banks surrendered their circulation.[12] In a day when some Republicans running for office had taken support from greenbackers,[13] the panic could have constituted the bankers' shot across the bow, warning the new Republicans in Congress to pay heed to their interests. The withdrawals were like the snapping of a whip, only for its sound effects.

The Consolidation of Jay Gould's Western Union and Two Other Telegraph Companies, January 1881

The next surprise arose from financier Jay Gould, and it raised the question whether, in the Garfield presidency, business interests might have a free hand in the marketplace. In mid-January 1881 Gould, both a monopolist and a campaign contributor, consolidated three telegraph companies into one trust, ending most competition in the industry, an action that the standard accounts of the Garfield administration have not mentioned. It can be shown that what Gould did, and the popular reaction, went a long way in the New Year to illuminate the landscape politically and economically. The consolidation showed the trend of industrial organization away from competition and toward trusts. The trend further helps explain the continued fracturing of the Republican Party into the half-breeds and stalwarts.

At the moment of Gould's winning court approval for his consolidation, fears arose that the country was to see another trust like the one Rockefeller had built in the oil industry. Behind the scenes, among the people around Garfield, a flurry of correspondence broke out. The worry was twofold: 1) being careful about letting some people become insiders and 2) diverting public attention.

In the long view, Garfield would apparently care for Gould's interests. They had talked in August, the day after the Fifth Avenue Hotel meeting. Part of their conversation probably centered upon Gould's conviction that any political interference in the market would possibly cause a market decline. The record shows that through the campaign and into the new administration Garfield stayed away from such issues. In early winter, however, attention was mounting: Postmaster General Maynard and the National Board of Trade both announced that they favored a federally owned telegraph service to compete with the private companies and keep rates down. Whatever ideas Garfield and Gould discussed, one episode stands out as a sure reflection of the capitalist's feelings for the new president. When Gould later learned of the assassin's attack on the president, his reaction was hardly a matter of indifference—in fact, it was quite emotional. The response to the news suggests that Gould and Garfield were seriously involved with one another.

Trader and Activist Rufus Hatch Wins a Temporary Injunction Against Contributor Jay Gould, January 20, 1881

A second cluster of events, evidence of reaction, began January 19. At that time Gould took his plan for consolidation to court, and the account of the judge's approval immediately made front-page news across the country. One of Gould's fellow stock traders in particular, Rufus Hatch, would react with a counter-thrust since he had earlier tried to persuade Gould not to proceed.[14]

No one could discount anything Hatch might decide to do. He was a Republican, a trader, and a promoter of the city's welfare. Years earlier, after heading up a western railroad, Hatch had come to New York and was immediately offered the presidency of the New York Stock Exchange, but he declined.[15] His popularity rose through writing a column on the stock market for the *Times*, describing opportunities for young traders who responded with appreciation by giving him the nickname of "Uncle Rufus." Most troubling to the capitalists was the recollection that Hatch "had attacked Vanderbilt interests in 'Rufus Hatch's *Circulars*,' exposing stock-watering plans of the N. Y. Central R. R."[16] As a market insider, Hatch personified all the evils offensive to the other capitalists and gave them good reason for promoting their new alleged gag rule of June 1880. Those financiers could easily picture Hatch driving public opinion over the same ground, perhaps leading to public hearings inquiring into the Western Union consolidation.

Another worry about Hatch was his avid support of former president Ulysses S. Grant. Early in January 1881 Hatch hosted Grant and the World's Fair committee to discuss the plans for an 1883 fair in Central Park where the great man would be the featured guest.[17] Hatch's dinner party had a decidedly political hue since in attendance were both Stephen Dorsey, a leading star route contractor and fund raiser, and Thomas Murphy, former collector at the port. Grant's appearance at the 1883 fair could neatly fit into an 1884 campaign for the presidency. When Hatch turned against Gould a few days later, it looked like a matter of the Grant supporters working to blend into the antimonopoly movement.

An 1883 fair in New York would bring a short tourist boom to the city. An anticipated surge in passenger traffic should have caught the attention of the railroad companies. The companies, however, declined to contribute and quite reasonably. Had not they gone through considerable trouble before the 1880 campaign to stop Grant at the convention? Would not they look forward to supporting Garfield for a second term? Thus they put a chill on the plans for a New York world's fair and the cartoonists lampooned the effort to stage it in Central Park.

Hatch had another link he could exploit and that was his access to the editorial rooms of the *Times*. That may explain the paper's very long coverage of the telegraph industry history, a story that had been shared at the recent national board meeting.[18] The coverage appeared at the moment when Hatch was trying to persuade Gould not to proceed with the consolidation. The prospect, however, remained a rumor and rumor gave way to news of volatility in the stocks. About a week into the New Year, telegraph stock plunged and then the bulls piled in and raised the prices. In eight days Western Union stock increased from $81 7/8 to $103, or 22 percent; Atlantic and Pacific rose 7 percent; and American Union rose 16 percent.[19]

On January 16, 1881, the Cotton Exchange members called a special Saturday meeting. As New Yorkers, troubled by taxes, they resolved, "Telegraphic tolls were the heaviest tax that existed on the cotton trade."[20] The competitive telegraph lines to distant Philadelphia charged but 15 cents a word, while the noncompetitive lines to nearby Paterson, N.J., received 25 cents a word.[21] Most galling was that the Germans, using their government postal telegraph, paid only a half-cent per word.[22] If the indifferent did not believe that monopolism meant higher prices, little doubt now remained.

In crowded Manhattan Island, businesses' use of telegraphy served an important function in their supply chains. With property at a premium and warehousing costly, many merchants held down expenses by holding down their inventories and ordering half-finished items. A New York merchant could wire a manufacturer or supplier in nearby New England and ask him to forward a half-finished item that would arrive by ship the next day.[23] What the monopolists saw in business-to-business telegraphy were profits. Once the consolidators defeated all objections in court and raised rates, the spread between the costs of immediate wires and the rental on storage space probably narrowed. Understandably, the situation reminded people of feudal times, when outlaws roamed the highways of commerce and exacted tolls. Watching the increased levies on their businesses, the merchants easily called the monopolists the "robber barons."

On January 19, 1881, the telegraph consolidators placed their plan before Judge Barrett. While some estimates pegged the value of the three systems at $15 million and the current stock price set the total value at $41 million, the consolidators wanted more. They wanted to double the value to $80 million. The single telegraph system would serve to support Gould's railroading, with many inter-city telegraph lines running along railroad rights-of-way. It would make his inter-city telegraphy much more secure.

The consolidators had to overcome one weakness of their plan. One of the companies, American Union, to ensure competition, had a charter provision prohibiting consolidation. Knowing the business, Hatch bought 100 shares. Within hours of the consolidators' appearance in Judge Barrett's court, Hatch and his attorney, Robert Sewell, a friend of vice president-elect Chester Arthur, went to the same judge and sought an injunction.[24] The *Times* announced, "Judge Barrett granted a temporary injunction in Supreme Court Chambers yesterday restraining the Western Union, American Union and Atlantic and Pacific Companies. The plaintiff in the case is Mr. Rufus Hatch who is owner of 100 shares of American Union Co. Stock."[25] Hatch lost this first court case, and the judge scolded him for only recently purchasing shares. However, he would win in all his subsequent appeals, except the last. When he finally lost, telegraph rates doubled.[26]

Public Outrage and the Punishment by the Monopolists

Hatch's petition gave merchants hope that they could achieve some relief. Many of them saw the consolidation as a swindle. They understood that their own rates for use of the telegraph services were leveraged right off the expected dividend. Therefore, the higher the valuation, the higher the dividends, which, in turn, meant the higher the rates.

Many New York merchant leaders were outraged at Gould. The *Times* reported that the consolidation "elicit[ed] a storm of fierce denunciation entirely inconsistent with the ordinary reserve of the speakers." Its reporter had interviewed many of them and filed a story showing a wide range of opinions. Some merchants had even begun work "in constructing competition," adding to the stringing of wires running up and down Manhattan streets. President Parker of the Produce Exchange said there could be no question that the consolidation was a "grievous public outrage . . . [but it] had always been the rule not to fight against the inevitable." President Elwell of the Maritime Exchange did not think it would do any good to pass resolutions. "The companies would be foolish if they do not respect public opinion."

Continuing the complaints, Darwin James, who was in the spice trade and secretary of the Board of Trade, said:

> I consider this the highest swindle of modern days and cannot conceive what the end will be unless the check is found in the legislature. To make the public pay dividends on so much water is a proposition that may well call out righteous indignation . . . There should be a reason why American telegraphic rates are not as low, or lower, than those of Great Britain.

The *Times* also noted that:

> F. B. Thurber regarded the consolidation simply as a fresh confirmation of the propriety of the action taken by the National Board of Trade at the annual meeting held in Washington in December last, in response to the report of a special committee on postal telegraph, composed of representative men in eastern and western cities . . . He was for immediate action

in the premises regarding it as the duty of the Government to protect the people from the exorbitant charges of monopolies.

E. R. Durkee, also in the spice trade, was quoted as having said:

I have been a member of the Board of Trade since its formation, and have seen the results of telegraphic and railroad combinations to my utter disgust . . . It is a sort of legalized swindling, and should be stopped by the general Government.

A. B. Miller, in warehousing and chair of the canal committee of the Chamber, said the monopolies:

have full swing in the Legislature, and the people have no voice but are obliged to pay . . . The General Government should have full control of the telegraph lines as they do in Great Britain . . . Let the General Government have the telegraph lines appraised, find out their real value and buy them, just as Great Britain did, and the merchants, importers, and everybody will rejoice.

If boards of trade across the country had failed to reply to the August 1880 survey that the New York Chamber of Commerce had mailed out, they had reasons to do so now. In the poll, they would have noted two relevant questions:

"Is it safe to allow railroad managers to follow their new theory of charging 'all the traffic will bear?' "

"Is it right to water stock through any means by which fictitious bases of value are established?"

Replies continued to come into the New York Chamber of Commerce.

The monopolists entered the fray showing they were ready to fight and punish their opposition. As Laumann and Knoke report, punishment is part of the standard order of the policy process. "Given an adequate monitoring capacity, organizations also differ with respect to the specific resources they control that can be used to reward or punish their supporters and adversaries in the policy-making process."[27] When the bankers felt that they were crowded by the Democrats' refunding legislation, they raised interest rates sharply, thus punishing the Democratic majority. President Hayes finally vetoed the measure. In the telegraph industry, punishment could be expected from Gould. Years earlier when Iowa passed granger legislation, Gould built a road to Omaha but not through that state. It went around through Missouri instead. Now in 1881 Gould's resource for punishment was the Associated Press wire service running directly to newspapers. When a newspaper criticized his consolidation, he simply cut off its wire services. Thurber would tell the 1882 National Board of Trade meeting that Gould's Western Union denied A.P. service to any newspaper that "shall encourage the construction of any competing telegraph company," whether owned privately or publicly.[28] That would be his contribution to maintaining the gag on public debate.

The Telegraph Consolidation: A Spur to Republican Factionalism

Alerted by the December meeting of the National Board of Trade and next by the flurry of news in January, party members found themselves driven further apart. Some harmony had recently prevailed when a bi-factional delegation at the end of December had gone to see Garfield at Mentor, Ohio. They went to develop plans for co-operating with Virginia's independent senator, William Mahone. The Virginian's handling of the state debt raised questions in some quarters. A strain on relations seemed to appear when on January 14, 1881, Gorham denied that he had a deal with Mahone that would return him to the secretaryship.

A week later the party ties began to fray badly. It was about the time when Judge Barrett of the New York state Supreme Court approved Gould's request to consolidate the three telegraph companies. While it added to Gould's vast holdings, others foresaw only increased telegraph rates. Given New Yorkers' objections to Gould's business practices, some half-breeds reacted and veered away from party harmony. They began losing interest in Mahone. While Mahone offered the party a chance to unite and to put pressure on the solid South, the defense of Gould divided the northern party. That relieved the Democrats, sending half-breeds looking for help among the Democrats against the stalwarts!

Garfield's Apparent Response to the Telegraph Consolidation

The consolidation appears to have reverberated in several directions around the First Family–elect. Garfield was in Mentor receiving the daily papers as well as gossip from his wife. Reid, Blaine, and Lucretia were all meeting at Reid's New York home while she was on a shopping trip in the city. Where would Garfield stand? In 1873, he had written:

> The old feudalism was finally controlled and subordinated only by the combined efforts of the kings and the people of the free cities and towns, so our modern feudalism can be subordinated to the public good only by the great body of the people acting through their governments by wise and just laws.

> States and communities have willingly and thoughtlessly conferred these great powers upon railways, and they must seek to rectify their own errors without injury to the industries they have encouraged.

There is plenty of room to speculate about what crossed Garfield's mind. Now that the consolidators had set their value at $80 million, could Garfield have made a suggestion? Or, was he constrained by the alleged gag rule adopted the previous June? Would his contributors take exception to any move he made to assure a more open market? Shouldn't the public know what was happening in the Western Union? Or, was he committed to the Rockefeller model, easily applicable to the telegraph industry?

Wasn't the lack of corporate transparency largely the problem? Several opinion leaders had long complained about the failure of companies to provide reliable reports on their financial condition and what they were planning to do. In 1877 the *Times* had called for legislation that would compel companies to furnish all the details giving a correct understanding of their balance sheets. The paper said that the state should supervise accounting and prevent companies from suppressing information and cooking the books. Such "mismanagement has within the last few months brought ruin on thousands and shaken to its base the public faith in corporate securities."[29] In January 1880 some Hepburn committee recommendations surfaced and the *Times* praised the committee, saying, "There will be no room for the charge of secrecy, and no chance for any cooking of accounts. Everything relating to the affairs of the corporations will be brought to light."[30]

> The need for fuller reports and the importance of enlisting complete information regarding the condition and operations of railroads are so generally recognized that little opposition was to be expected to this measure, not because it is likely to be acceptable to the companies, but because no plausible pretext can be set up for resisting what is clearly a public demand.[31]

The *Nation,* on March 24, 1881, joined in by stating, "Unfortunately, in this country we have no body of reliable railroad statistics." Could Garfield have adopted the views of these authorities and championed reforms? How could he lose? If he had urged business reform, wouldn't that have relieved the tension across the country?

On the other hand, as Blaine had explained to Garfield, Gould and others "represented the reliable strong background of preferenced friendship and love on which your administration must rest . . . men who will labor for your success, and who will demand your re-nomination."

To abide by the alleged gag rule of June 1880, Garfield would have to disengage himself from politicians who saw opportunity in the issues. The appeal to give Virginia's Mahone support may have been a subtle way of enlisting more support for the anti-monopolists. Could Garfield afford to be enthusiastic about the Virginian?

The news that Garfield received from New York could have prompted a dream he had on January 19th, which showed how focused he was on the great city. Because of the advanced press coverage Garfield's mind must have been prepared for the next shoe to drop. For one thing, he perceived that he could not walk the fine line he had projected in his 1873 address. He had then told about "our modern feudalism" being "subordinated to the public good only by the great body of the people acting through their governments by wise and just laws." On awakening on January 20, 1881, the day after Gould had gone to court with his consolidation plan, Garfield wrote out his dream on a slip of paper. He inserted it into a billfold that was fortuitously discovered in recent years by Garfield's biographer, Allan Peskin.

> Last night I dreamed that General Arthur, Maj. (David) Swaim, and I were on an excursion to attend some great ceremonial. We were on a canal packet during the night. A heavy rainstorm came on and in the gray of the morning, Swaim and I awoke just as the packet was passing a point to enter a deep broad basin. We leaped ashore, and on looking back saw that the packet was sinking. Just as it was sinking, I noted General Arthur lying on a couch very pale and apparently very ill. In an instant more, the packet sank with all on board. I started to plunge into the water to save Arthur, but Swaim held me, and said he cannot be saved, and you will perish if you attempt it. It appeared that we were naked and alone in the wild storm and that the country was hostile. I felt that nakedness was a disguise, which would avoid identification in this dream; for the first time I knew I was Pres. elect. After a long and tangled journey, we entered a house, and an old Negro woman took me into her arms and nursed me as though I were a sick child. At this point I awoke.[32]

Two features of the dream stand out. First, ever since the convention, Garfield had assumed that Vice President–elect Chester Arthur could serve as his link to the New York organization. Roscoe Conkling's name never came up. Now with the merchants irate over Gould's consolidation and Arthur so prominent in the stalwart camp, he wondered whether he had to sideline Arthur as well. Or, at another level, Arthur could have stood for the New York City culture in which people were more accustomed to discussing business practices openly, and the dream meant that he could not give that culture recognition.

Second, Garfield probably recognized that he could do nothing openly to help his capitalist contributors. If he did not take shelter under the June 9, 1880, alleged gag rule, he could, as Swaim warned, "perish." If, by the rule, Garfield helped to "repress public opinion . . . instead of making concessions to it," he would make a successful crossing of the River Jordan and enter the Promised Land of industrial trusts. The afterthought about the "old Negro woman" may have meant that he could postpone working on civil rights until shortly before his re-nomination.

Garfield's silence fits into a concept of the hierarchy of announcements based on the concept of expressed preferences as elaborated by Laumann and Knoke. Only in this case, the absence of any direction from the platform meant that there was a hierarchy of silence all down the line. What remained at the highest level, standing in the background for the Ohioan, was the example of the Rockefeller trust near Mentor. Now, at the next level, the move by Gould called for no response. In his dream, Garfield appears to have conceded to the implicit new platform of silence and the new alleged gag rule, realizing that he could not join the stalwarts (Arthur) in the popular outcry lest he be destroyed. If he countenanced any popular cries for corporate reform, he would have attracted a myriad supporters. He would, however, have greatly disappointed his new friends, not only beginning with Gould but also John Hay, Rockefeller's stockbroker, whom he had sought as his personal secretary. In the circumstances, the capitalists had a range of worries. Some of the capitalists apparently thought that if they gave the anti-monopolists an inch they would take a mile. Therefore, open approval or disapproval of the consolidation by any consequential political leaders was out of the question. Outside the formal party structure, the financiers had set the course that party leaders had either to follow or to oppose and take their chances.

Lucretia Garfield has Words about Levi P. Morton

Lucretia Garfield provided the second written piece reflecting how the political actors were lining up. What she wrote to her husband remains important because she mentioned Levi P. Morton's ambitions to become Secretary of the Treasury. As an insider, Morton was probably privy to fund raising activities at the Republican Party's national headquarters and would have known of the passing of some correspondence, if not its content, between Reid and Garfield.

Morton had succeeded in raising campaign funds from among large donors, and in return for his efforts, he concluded that Garfield promised him the post of Secretary of the Treasury. When Garfield heard of Morton's hope for a cabinet position, he denied that he had said any such thing. Given the new circumstances caused by Gould's consolidation, if Morton took an important cabinet post he would probably urge Garfield to make concessions to public opinion. That would have put the president in an unhappy spot when facing his contributor Gould and the champions of Rockefeller. Rather the president's role was to stand as Horatio at the bridge. Morton finally saw the light: with Gould now needing help from Garfield, he realized that he had no chance of becoming Secretary of the Treasury. His sudden realization was relayed back to Lucretia, staying at Reid's. Reid had every reason to alienate Garfield from Morton and took the opportunity to set-up Lucretia to do the job. She wrote her husband that:

> Mr. Reid told me this morning that Morton had been very ugly in his talk about you, using the expression that seems to be so gratifying to the Roscoe Conkling clique, "That Ohio man can not be relied upon to stand

by his pledges" . . . You will never have anything from those men but their assured contempt, until you fight them dead. You can put every one of them in his political grave if you have a mind to & that is the only place where they can be kept peaceable.[33]

Gould consolidating the telegraph system led Garfield and Morton to similar conclusions. Within a day of each other, yet in different places (Garfield in Mentor and Morton in New York) and in different states of consciousness (Garfield asleep and Morton awake), both men concluded that they had to abandon their beguiling plans for the new administration. Garfield believed that he might have to give up the idea that the vice-president, stalwart Arthur, would serve as his link to the New York organization. Morton, another high-ranking New York stalwart, had to give up hope for appointment to the Treasury. Garfield and Morton each drew back from his particular plan, affirming a shared belief that the new administration would have to help protect a campaign donor.

Reid's Response Joined by William Robertson

Another note would come from Albany. After Hatch won his temporary injunction against the telegraph consolidation on January 20, 1881, Reid was off to Albany to see William Robertson, the leader of the bolt from the New York delegation to Chicago. Robertson would write Reid a letter that he would pass on to Garfield, betraying the panic then surging through the half-breed camp. Robertson's letter, taking the long view, arrived at Mentor immediately after the letters from Blaine and Lucretia, saying:

> Aside from other public consideration, I take a deep interest in the success of General Garfield's Administration, because it will be a full vindication of the action of the Independent Delegates from this State to the Chicago convention, and because it will put an end to Imperialism.
>
> Its success will depend to a very great extent upon a right start. The formation of the cabinet will be the groundwork. With this end in view, no one should be put in it that will not have the same fidelity and devotion to General Garfield and his administration that Boswell had to Johnson and Harvey to Webster. No one, whose first allegiance is to another personage, should be allowed to enter it.
>
> Conkling will neither recommend anyone, nor be satisfied with anyone, for a cabinet position who is not absolutely under his control. Conklingism thrives on patronage. The Treasury, Interior, and Post Office Department are regarded as patronage offices. It is not desirable that a Conklingite should fill any of these.

Reid's cover letter reminded Garfield that Robertson had made his nomination possible. Without Robertson's help Grant's candidacy would have ridden roughshod over everyone else. Coming so quickly on the heels of the January 19th telegraph consolidation, the Robertson-Reid correspondence may have offered another cover for Gould's boldness. Robertson and Reid, eschewing any mention of corporate behavior, had reduced matters to the commonplaces of current politics, to personalities and fault finding, by attributing autocracy to a sole actor––Conkling. Whether anyone else was trying to play king-of-the-hill in business (Gould) or in the new administration (Blaine) was beside the point. What plausibly was at stake for both factions was not so much patronage following from winning a cabinet seat, as it was access to information in the cabinet. The information could have been about the administration's legislative proposals on behalf of the monopolists. The half-breeds, apparently in furtherance of the alleged gag rule, sought to dry up every source of information they could.

The warnings to guard against Conkling's imperialism gave the half-breeds greater assurance that they would gain a corner on appointments. In turn, they would gain secrecy over information. At the outset, the letters to Garfield set up a diversion distracting attention from the telegraph monopoly. Robertson's letter fit the scenario that included Garfield's dream of Arthur drowning and Morton's realizing that he would not get Treasury and have access to the cabinet. The letter adds credence to the evidence that the Republican Party split arose out of the half-breeds' defense of Gould's business consolidation. They had to exclude some of the party from information sources lest their leaks fuel a popular reaction.

Former U.S. Treasurer F. E. Spinner's Early Warning about the Prospect of Post Office Scandals

The anti-monopolist forces had a weak flank. The real possibility existed that anti-monopolists would soon propose that the government buy up some of the telegraph system in order to establish permanent competition in the field and bring rates down. That venture into corporate matters, however, was chancy, since the postal staff was under question. Indeed, management was proceeding so poorly, according to some people, that the ground was laid for a scandal. Once Postmaster General Horace Maynard was out of office at the end of the Hayes presidency, his successor, rather than promoting a government telegraph service, would likely have to focus on administrative reform.

The fear of a scandal in postal management was a long time in the making. It was now stronger than ever. Money was scarcer as the Treasury reduced the supply in preparation for resumption. That new shortage led many people of poorer circumstances to move west to begin farming. That migration called for additional mail services and greater government expenditures. Thus, the mounting appropriations raised the suspicion of corruption in the postal contract department. The two previous Congresses had heard from the post office and had agreed to increase appropriations, but an allegedly slack accounting of funds was not explicitly exposed and addressed.

The trouble stemmed from the old law covering the accounting for postal expenditures. Since the War for Independence, all federal departments except for the Post Office Department were required to have their accounting approved by one of two comptrollers in the Treasury department. The Post Office Department had remained exempt. Its special status was probably because during the war the postal system had proven so valuable in linking the colonies up and down the coast. After the war it was one of the first federal departments created. In the Senate, the committee on post office and post roads was one of the first committees established. Since it had been profitable while handling its own budgets and audits, those privileges were continued, making it an exception from the other departments founded later. Of course, the exception was bound to create suspicions, if not problems.

No one could plead ignorance. In 1871 U.S. Treasurer F. E. Spinner had raised a warning in his annual report.

> All other accounts, civil or military, or of whatever branch of the public service, are finally passed upon, adjusted, and settled by either the First or the Second Comptroller of the Treasury. Neither of the Comptrollers has any legal authority to review, decide upon, or in any manner control [over Post Office Department accounts] . . . . The final settlement and the correct payment of these accounts should be under the supervision of a Comptroller, or other proper officer designated for that purpose. As matters now stand . . . this office is not only inconvenienced and imperiled, but it has great responsibilities thrown upon it that do not attach in other cases. . .
>
> It is feared that through the loose, irregular, and anomalous manner in which these accounts are settled and paid, eventually, the Government will suffer serious losses.[34]

By 1881 Congress had still not followed up Spinner's warning with remedial legislation. Or, by some good luck, the mere warning by Spinner could have made postal administrators more circumspect. A large portion of Congress was satisfied with leaving the Post Office Department alone. The surmise is that the less attention given the department, the more likely congressmen would have a ready source of campaign workers and funds.

With the boom in westward migration in the late 1870s, the post office was contracting with 93 stagecoach and river steamer routes. The practice in the department was to issue low-bid contracts and then later "expedite" the services by increasing both the contract services and the contract costs. The most shocking news was that the head of the system, Thomas Brady, had spent a year's appropriation in six months. When some members of Congress objected to Brady's spending, he, in good Gilded Age punishing fashion, cut off some of their services. The question was whether Brady personally skimmed funds for himself. Successful in campaign fundraising in 1878 and in 1880, and showing smart gains in telephone stock, Brady started the year 1881 by building a new home in Washington and becoming a major shareholder in the *National Republican*, where fundraiser Gorham would write the editorials. As Gorham began, he passed up the chance to recommend legislation that would have addressed Spinner's criticism of bringing postal auditing under the controllers at the Treasury.

Thomas J. Brady did have a record in public service warranting respect. Before becoming Second Assistant Postmaster General in July 1876 he had served, beginning in July of 1875, as supervisor of internal revenue for Ohio and Indiana, and then for Kentucky, Tennessee, Alabama, Mississippi, and Louisiana. In this latter assignment, he helped to target the New Orleans wing of the St. Louis whisky scandal before the culprits had stolen the money. Born in Muncie in 1840, at the war's outset he was a Union Democrat, and served the entire length of the war largely in Tennessee. After the war, his father became mayor of Muncie and Thomas Brady purchased the Muncie *Times*. A great ally of Governor O. P. Morton, he served as chair of the Indiana Republican Party for a year.[35] After Postmaster Thomas James asked Brady to resign without cause and the press followed with accusations, a former postmaster general, David M. Key, now judge of the United States Circuit Court at Nashville, told the *Times* that he thought that James' investigation "so far has been inquisitorial and one-sided."[36] The charges did not fit the facts. Gorham would expand upon Key's criticism.

Edwin Godkin's Response to the Alleged Post Office Irregularities

The news of the telegraph consolidation in mid-January triggered a discussion of postal administration, joined in by Edwin Godkin in the January 27, 1881, issue of the *Nation* and by Blaine in a note to Garfield. Godkin criticized the anti-monopolists and speculated that the post office could buy up the consolidated Western Union and offer the country a postal telegraph system. However, first the post office administration needed cleaning up, said Godkin.

> [N]othing is more striking in the discussions which the consolidation has called forth than the small amount of knowledge which outsiders seem to possess of the conditions under which the telegraph business is carried on . . . The managers of the telegraph companies are naturally and inevitably guided in fixing their rates, not by the amount of their stock, but by their estimate of the amount the public will pay for telegraphing instead of writing letters.

> If we are ever to have really cheap telegraphy in this country . . . we must look for it in companies chartered to do business under Government

rules and regulations . . . The promoters of the consolidation between the Western Union and the American Union are freely accused of making the combination in order to sell $100,000,000 of stock to the Government at par in three percent bonds. . . .

The transfer of the telegraph to the Post-Office would, of course, involve the creation in law of a strong Government monopoly . . . We should, in fact, place ourselves in complete dependence, as regards the most important part of the social machinery next to the administration of justice, on an official class for whose wrong-doings the public would be absolutely without remedy, if it continued to be filled as it is now. At present, the United States Post Office is officered and worked as a political machine. [Godkin discusses the political work of Assistant Post Master (sic!) Tyner and James Brady.] It would never enter the head of the present managers of the Western Union or American Union to employ either of these gentlemen in important places in the conduct of the telegraph . . . they would not dare to fill their subordinate offices, with their present responsibility to their stockholders and liability in damages to their customers, with persons urged upon them by Congressmen. . . . It is clear enough from all this that the assumption of the telegraph monopoly by the government would make imperative a radical and final change in the mode of selecting officers to discharge Government business. The entire Post-Office service would have to be assimilated by law to that of the New York Post Office as now conducted by Mr. James.[37]

James did become postmaster general, and Godkin's comments might have hit the mark. If everything had remained equal following the scandal and reorganizing the department, the government could have proceeded to buy the consolidated Western Union. The post office, selecting personnel through a civil service system based on merit, was the place to lodge a new agency.

Blaine's Response to the Alleged Postal Irregularities

Blaine, like Godkin, numbered among those observers who suspected more trouble than promise in the postal contracting office. On the very day, January 20th, when Rufus Hatch won an injunction against the telegraph consolidation, Blaine realized that it was time to impede any popular view Hatch might stir up. While Godkin had warned that "a political machine" managed the Post Office Department, Blaine saw in the mess an operation foisted on everyone else. In a picturesque note to Garfield, he alluded to the pigeons fluttering above the entrance to the post office building, dropping their feces on scurrying patrons not agile enough to escape being innocent targets. Aiming at the evil he saw, Blaine wrote that:

The P. O. Dept in some of its most important bureaus has been a nest of unclean birds under Hayes. Another flock of like color is preparing to take the same roost under Garfield. Your administration must be actually and veritably clean as has that of Hayes been pretentiously and ostentatiously so.

Never mind that fundraising among the postal contractors had helped the campaigns for both Blaine and Garfield. Blaine's quick reaction assured Garfield that the matter was important and that he had a person of consequence in the network between the capitalists and the party who could quickly suggest a solution. Options need promoters, and promoters need rank. Now the administration could conduct a full disclosure of the evils in the Post Office Department and outpace any attention that Hatch might gain in his campaign for a full disclosure of the new telegraph consolidation. Hatch, from the December meeting of the National Board of Trade through to the newspaper coverage in January, had laid the ground for a full discussion of telegraph policy. Instead, Garfield applied the alleged gag rule of June 9 and sidelined the debate. He would open an investigation of the postal system and create a scandal that diverted the nation's attention.

Raising a scandal would give Garfield an earthy opportunity to clean out the "bad men" Blaine had alluded to in his December 16 letter. The difficulty of exposing the "star route" services was that it dragged on for seventeen years. In 1898, as shall be seen, the Department of Justice finally dropped the investigation due to the lack of evidence, a point Gorham had made from the first day! There had not been "bad men" after all.

Donors Placing Obligations on the President-Elect

Garfield was taking steps to benefit Gould more than anyone else. Garfield had let Reid, the editor of Gould's *Tribune,* have a veto over Supreme Court nominations. He had granted a *Tribune* reporter, E. V. Smalley, a desk at the White House. Further, Blaine had suggested that the "star route" services should be investigated right on the heels of efforts at Albany and Washington to give Gould's new telegraph service some competition from a government telegraph. The first agreement about the court nominations disclosed the camel's nose in the administration tent; soon more of the camel would appear.

The proprieties of a presidential candidate taking a large campaign contribution from a donor like Gould could change the office. Winning an appointment to see the president would rest not with the host but with the donor, or his representative. "Access" could mean an open invitation and the assurance that unannounced arrivals, or their representatives, would always be cordially welcomed. The privileges, however, only went one way. Gould did not bring Garfield onto his board of directors. Governor Cornell served on Gould's board, possibly taking the seat that his father once held, but whether he was brought into the loop on Garfield's behalf to share information on the consolidation remains unknown. Rather, Governor Cornell in early 1881 would distinguish himself in his annual message by his silence on recommendations for corporate regulation. Thus, he, like Garfield, was now an associate of Gould, and each in his own way helped minimize attention to regulation.[38]

Garfield apparently saw the need to recognize the anti-monopolists. In New York his old law partner, Jeremiah Black, was emerging as a spokesman for the anti-monopolists. Additionally, for the Treasury, Garfield began considering William Windom of Minnesota, well known in New York as an advocate of competition between the waterways and the railroads. When that news appeared, Blaine demurred. [Blaine seemed to expect a solid line of defense all across the front of the administration.]

The Anti-Monopoly Movement is Founded, January 1881

Running in the same stream of information early in the month was the note about the founding meeting of the Anti-Monopoly League where Fred Conkling, the senator's brother, gave one of the addresses.[39] The implication was that Fred could keep brother Roscoe well informed. Fred, as the annual reports of the Chamber of Commerce show, already held high office in that organization. (Another family connection surfaced in January when a relative of the Grant family in St. Louis came to national attention. He was Chauncey Filly, a manufacturer of stoves, and a delegate to the 1880 convention. In midwinter he was in the midst of casting memorial medallions, sending one to each of the delegates to Chicago who had proven to be a Grant loyalist.) As Garfield looked ahead, he had reason to expect difficulties from the stalwarts, especially if he looked to the prospect of a second term.

In Washington, while half-breeds contemplated a postal scandal, Gorham thought that the focus instead should be upon the Republican opportunities in the South. He wrote that:

> The recent election gave us a national victory. It signified more than a party triumph; it meant peaceful conquest. The Nation spreads her borders in fact as well as in theory. The march of ideas penetrates the South. The ice breaks. Brave and enlightened men stand forth who have long been redeemed from the thralldom of sectional bigotry, and say: "Give us standing-room among the adherents of the Nation and national authority. Do not make hard conditions. We are for the Union, the Constitution, and the enforcement of the laws. We break the chains of tradition, and desire to share in the blessings of the new era." Who will dare reject them?[40]

On January 18, 1881, John Syphax, an African-American in government employment, wrote Gorham of a pending opportunity.

> The colored people do not need any masters to tell them how to act or for whom to vote. Experience, tardy but sure, has at last done the work. Let them go to a convention of their own and calmly determine

for themselves. In this direction they are already moving. A conference of colored men who know the demand of the hour will soon assemble, I am informed, and help intelligently to adjust any misunderstanding. I hardly think any good citizen will fail to approve this movement; but if any doubts exist in the minds of any, many facts can be stated to support the views here expressed.[41]

The stalwarts might have realized that they could benefit from two causes coming to maturity: southern biracial politics and anti-monopolism.

Leland Stanford Breaks the Alleged Gag Rule, January 23, 1881

If the stalwarts gave the half-breeds worries, one of their own, Leland Stanford of the Central Pacific Railroad, confounded them. He would make a statement of his position at the most inopportune time. Stanford, feeling no restraint from the alleged gag rule of June 9, decided to answer the New York Chamber of Commerce's August inquiry. Unfortunately for Stanford, Francis Thurber had just published an article in *Scribner's* looking to the revival of grangerism, repudiated in recent western elections. Thurber had called the readers' attention to the common law supporting the granger cases, noting how corporation attorneys had hoodwinked westerners into throwing the baby out with the bath. Now Stanford came right to that point of granger relevance. He wrote to the Chamber that:

> What you propose in regard to railroad property is, to my mind, on a par with the principles contended for by the Communists, and the agitator Kearny advocated no doctrine in regard to property more atrocious than the principles embodied in the granger cases and the laws, which they sustain.[42]

Two days later, on January 25, 1881, the *Times* turned the full force of the arguments on Stanford.

> [Stanford] maintains that railroad corporations own the property under their control in the same sense and to the same extent as does a joint partnership . . . [H]e must . . . attack the established principles of law, whether embodied in legislation or judicial decrees . . . [I]t is hardly probable that he will succeed. . . . The decisions in the granger cases, which are simply in accord with all existing adjudication on the subject, base the authority of the state to regulate railroads not, as Mr. Stanford assumes on "the number of people with whom the business might be transacted," but on the fact that the business is carried on under a public franchise and widely affects the interest of the public which it is the duty of the State to protect.

With that blast from the paper no one could deny that grangerism was alive and well. Only a month earlier Thurber had made a very persuasive case in *Scribner's*. The *Times* also noticed Stanford's easy reliance on his religion.

> [Stanford] said, "the primary consideration with railroad managers under the observance of the golden rule is their Treasury." . . . When that famous ethical precept is made the basis of the policy pursued for the enrichment of corporate treasuries by the most effectual means its application is exquisitely ludicrous. According to the golden rule of railroads, the highest rates are to be charged for service that can be made profitable. If there is no competition, and merchandise must be moved in order to reach a market, the "primary consideration" demands that as much shall be exacted for carrying it as it will bear rather than reach no market. In other words, the profits of trade must be yielded up to the carrier to the point where there would be no inducement left to continue the trade.

While sightings of the monopolists' behavior had disclosed enough to stir outrage, none of the monopolists had recently voiced their views as confidently as had Stanford. Gould's consolidation gave an indication of the monopolists' intentions, but Stanford revealed their heart. Appearing on a Sunday, the references to the golden rule could have invigorated some Sunday school classes and sermons. At the end of the day, Stanford probably tilted public opinion against the capitalists.

On the same day that the *Times* gave Stanford an editorial whipping, the Republicans in Albany were trying to elect a senator to succeed Democrat Francis Kernan. Railroad attorney and cartel chair Chauncey Depew thought that he had a chance, but his hopes quickly soured and the half-breeds made a deal with Thomas Platt. That left Robertson believing that in the new administration the New York half-breeds would benefit from at least one half-breed. Such confidence on Robertson's part was soon shattered. On January 25, 1881, two days after Stanford's letter appeared in the *Times*, Robertson conceded that Platt, who had won election to the U.S. Senate with half-breed support at Albany, had now turned into a stalwart. Robertson wrote Reid,

> With *two* Stalwart senators and a Vice President from this State, the incoming Administration could in no way, so effectively put our Independent delegation to the Chicago convention in a political metallic casket hermetically sealed, as by placing in the cabinet a stalwart from New York.[43] (Our emphasis,)

The *Times'* reassertion of Chief Justice Waite's 1877 opinion on state regulation proved to have great influence.

It appears that Stanford's reply had two immediate consequences. First, contrary to Stanford's wishes, it put the assembly members on a sound footing for their common law legislation, long stalled since the Hepburn committee had reported. Second, it gave Francis Thurber the victory of the day in debating points. It now blew up such a storm that, when it reached Albany, it wiped out not only half-breed Depew's candidacy, but also probably also any of the pledges Platt had made to that faction. The unexpected joust at Albany between Stanford and Thurber was quick and surprising and left the half-breeds sprawling.

Assembly members who had voted the previous year for a railroad commission would have been elated. Garfield's dream of isolation was not materializing at Albany. His note about the dream said, "It appeared that we were naked and alone in the wild storm and that the country was hostile." What had happened was that since the collapse of the western state regulatory commissions, eastern conservatives had imbibed deeply on Justice Field's pronouncements about economic activity being the highest form of life and about the sanctity of property above all else. Thurber and the *Times*, however, making reference to the common law in the mix, had brought them down to earth. Their house of cards had collapsed and the wind they heard was merely reality filling the vacuum of their own *laissez faire* construction. The hoodwinking that corporation attorneys had given the western commissions was coming back to haunt them at Albany.

Garfield's Perplexities

Garfield, as his biographer Allan Peskin recounts, had gotten himself into fixes before, and he could come through this one as well. For the moment, however, it bore heavily on him. He might have bolstered his spirits by reflecting, as he had in his dream, that now for the first time, he truly felt that he was president. In a day or two, however, he showed a darker demeanor. Possibly what went through his mind was that, in his 1873 address on railroading, he had championed the citizens of free cities in feudal times who had broken the hold of the robber barons. Looking forward to a possible postal scandal, he had little stomach for character assassination or smears. Fully aware of the melodramatic atmosphere, he had written in a recent issue of the *Atlantic* that:

> The earnestness and vigor with which wrongdoing is everywhere punished is a strong guaranty of the purity of those who may hold posts of authority and honor. Indeed, there is now a danger in the opposite direction, namely, that criticism may degenerate into mere slander, and put an end to its power for good by being used as a means to assassinate the reputation and destroy the usefulness of honorable men. It is as much the duty of all good men to protect and defend the reputation of worthy public servants as to detect and punish public rascals.[44]

In addition to resorting to character assassination, he might have to promote the purchase of Western Union to establish a federal postal telegraph system. At what a price––$80 million! Now, in 1881, he was beholden to Gould and Blaine, and their group, and drew back from doing anything that would help the New York philistines against the monopolists. Garfield began to lose his enthusiasm for working on his inaugural address, and looked dourly on his coming duties.

Late in the month, Benjamin Harrison, the senator-elect from Indiana, visited with Garfield. He appeared at Mentor after the president-elect had received a letter from Blaine, two notes from Robertson, and all the hostility Lucretia brought home with her from her New York shopping trip. Harrison was taken aback by the tenor of his visit with Garfield, and on returning home, wrote him a note, saying, "You looked troubled yesterday and I was sorry to see it. It is hard for a real friend to know how to help you. I hope this letter will at least add nothing to your perplexity. The best (?) you aim and then stick by it—the country will sustain you."[45]

The troubled and perplexed Garfield was standing between the capitalists, who wanted no one but themselves discussing their business practices, and the merchants, who were increasingly critical of monopolistic behavior. Each side was trying to reform the other. Almost at that same moment, in New York, the Board of Trade reviewed resolutions condemning the telegraph consolidation. One N. M. Vail spoke excitedly, saying, "If ever we should have a civil war, it will be between the people fighting for their rights on the one side and the corporations on the other."[46] The paper reported on February 1, 1881, that some businessmen had wired the state attorney general for help, pointing out that the new dividends on the Western Union Company would increase by $3 million and calling it an illegal tax. On February 2, 1881, the state assembly passed an anti-consolidation bill and sent it to the senate. The Chamber of Commerce took up the matter on February 3rd, passing their resolutions with only two dissenting votes.

With New York businessmen standing as one, Garfield's outlook was pessimistic. His diarist, Harry Brown, noted that:

> On February 4, visiting Hiram to attend a funeral, he spoke briefly to the students and faculty of the college. "To-day is sort of a burial-day in many ways," he said, "I have often been in Hiram, and have often left it; but, with the exception of when I went to the war, I have never felt that I was leaving it in quite so definite a way as I do to-day."[47]

The Surge of the New York Anti-Monopoly League

The anti-monopoly movement pressed forward toward the new administration like an intrepid glacier. The returns from the New York Chamber of Commerce's August survey of peer organizations were unanimous in support of national regulation, and the December 1880 National Board of Trade meeting mustered the necessary two-thirds vote to put it on record for a federal postal telegraph system. Garfield was putting together his cabinet at the time, and that rising opinion must have given him pause, leading him to take precautions. Running in advance of the rising opinion was his old law partner,

Jeremiah Black. If Black showed up in Washington, Garfield knew that he would represent far more than himself. Figures about the growth of the anti-monopoly movement would not appear until March, but those later figures plausibly showed what was occurring in January. The March 12, 1881, issue of the *Times* would report, "Branches are now established in 25 States, and the mails bring from 40 to 50 letters every day asking for constitutions, by-laws, and instructions. The managers now propose to devote their special attention to the organization of branch societies in the several assembly districts in this city." The spark struck by Gould's consolidation, added to the articles, had quickly flamed up. Concurrently, the position of the incoming administration congealed, as seen in the correspondence about keeping certain types out of the new cabinet. Each side was keeping the other in mind and planning according to their best lights.

In January 1881 the anti-monopoly effort escalated so rapidly that it caused a hiatus in later research. Francis Thurber appears to have been too busy to keep his file of newspaper clippings up to date. That might explain the curious fact that many decades later, when Lee Benson reviewed the Thurber collection, he found no clippings about the Western Union consolidation. No less important, he did not audit the private collection of newspaper clippings by comparing them to the coverage that the newspapers gave the episode. Benson, not realizing that there was a gap, never mentioned the event. Thurber's busy schedule took him before meetings called by the Board of Trade on January 28, 1881, the Anti-Monopoly League on January 29th, and the Chamber on February 3rd, all fueled by a new appreciation of grangerism. He presented proposals that he wanted to take to Albany. The three groups gave Thurber virtually unanimous support.[48] The only dissenting vote was that of William Vanderbilt's son-in-law, Elliott Shepherd, the current U.S. attorney for the southern district. On February 3, 1881, the Chamber of Commerce did adopt a resolution on telegraphy, saying that the federal government should "inquire into and consider if telegraphic lines cannot be constructed and operated in connection with the Post Office Department with greater economy and with better results to the public than by the present system."[49] In 1877, the Board of Trade had hardly been quiet since it voted unanimously in favor of a free canal. In 1881 the Board, the Chamber and the League were voting unanimously on several other questions.

The number of organizations involved was important. In their 1970s study of health and energy policy, Laumann and Knoke tracked the number of organizations and marked attendance at joint meetings, court cases, press mentions, and the like, along with a review by a panel of expert insiders. They named the organizations whose names appeared with regularity as the members of the elite: "217 energy organizations and 156 health organizations as the elite set."[50] In 1881 the increase of the number of organizations from one, the Anti-Monopoly League, to three was just the start.[51] While this movement was launched in January and February 1881, when they recouped their strength late in the coming summer, the number would increase. Furthermore, important for Laumann and Knoke was the fact that some of the same organizations would reappear almost two decades later in lobbying Governor Theodore Roosevelt to address problems of the Erie

Canal. Their appearance in the early 1880s followed by their reappearance twenty years later proves the existence of a persistent two-decade elite in the issue of transportation. This New York City elite antagonized the half-breeds while the stalwarts sought ways to accommodate. While there is simply no way in this study to trace all of the interrelations of the commodity exchanges a century ago in promoting the survival of New York City, by our focus on the fate of the canal we have something of a research surrogate. The historical course of that institution in policy making should help to modify many of the conventions about the institution that have settled down and come to rest in academia.

Blaine's Support for A. M. Gibson, Garfield's Nemesis from The Sun

Blaine and Reid must have observed the surging activity among the anti-monopolists and recognized that it might turn Garfield's head. Therefore they could have plausibly concluded that they had to plan for the contingency of Garfield slipping to the other side. They needed a hedge. Their looking for a way to keep a hold on Garfield possibly explains the strange exchange of correspondence between the two, not discussed in the standard accounts, about making use of the journalist, A. M. Gibson, of the *New York Sun* (Democrat).

Well informed about the postal department management, Gibson could add authority to any new coverage of a postal scandal aimed at distracting the public's attention from telegraph policy. Gibson also knew Garfield's failures and foibles, such as the Credit Mobilier affair, the 1876 Louisiana vote count, and the paving contracts in Washington. During the recent campaign, Gibson had elaborated those stories *ad infinitum,* serving as texts for painting up Washington.

It is possible that Blaine and Reid felt that Garfield's old friend and law partner, Jeremiah Black, might make a harmless visit. Since the New York anti-monopolists were building up Black, who doubtlessly knew Garfield's mind on corporate law, the prospect was more than hypothetical. Blaine and Reid had to be ready to keep Garfield in line. Thus, they decided upon having Gibson in reserve on the sidelines available to nettle the president-elect in the press with his old shames.

Did Blaine and Reid think that the mere threat would hold Garfield in line? Blaine was convinced that Gibson would be trustworthy, if needed, and did not hesitate in laying the groundwork to use him. Peskin writes, "With a perfectly straight face he [Blaine] predicted the direst consequences if his advice should be ignored."[52] Blaine's enlisting Gibson had an echo of the fictional Senator Ratcliffe in Henry Adams's novel *Democracy*, who "avowed that he knew no code of morals in politics; that if virtue did not answer his purpose he used vice."[53]

Fortunately, Gibson wanted the work, and moved astutely to make the connection. In January 1881 he approached George Spencer, former Republican senator from Alabama, now living in New York. He showed him the results of his study of the records of 93 western contracted postal routes having the greatest increases in expenditures.

Spencer referred Gibson to some others he knew, including William Chandler, a Blaine supporter. Chandler, with Blaine, was supporting New York postmaster Thomas James for postmaster general.[54] After seeing Spencer, Gibson talked to Blaine, who referred him to Reid. Reid wrote Blaine about Gibson's strange visit, and Blaine replied, building up Gibson as a fellow Scot and a Democrat who wanted to change parties to improve his status.[55]

New York

Feb. 5, 1881

Dear Mr. Blaine:

A. M. Gibson, the correspondent of *The Sun* for so many years in Washington, is about to leave it, and, curiously enough, applies to me for some work on The *Tribune* and refers to you as to his personal character, good relations in Washington and general squareness. Please write me a confidential letter about him. He could undoubtedly furnish some valuable news, but is he safe? I have not told him that I would communicate with you at all.

Very truly yours,

Whitelaw Reid

Blaine turned over Reid's letter and wrote on the back.

Washington, D.C.

Feb. 7, '81.

My Dear Mr. Reid:

I have tried the man in many ways and consider him in all respects faithful & trustworthy. Indeed his personal fidelity is the strong trait of his character. He has been with a bad lot and against his political convictions has been true to them. His ambition to get into better company is a good sign. His pride is aroused and he is seeking to attain a better status in his profession, which he wisely thinks a connection with the *Tribune* would give. He comes from an adjoining county to me in Penn and is of the Scotch-Irish stock, which I rate so highly and consider superior to every other blood that enters the grand composite of American Nationality.[56] He has a wonderful power in getting hold of secret things & though not a highly educated man writes with ease, force & precision, entirely free from efflorescence. I think he would be a very useful man on your staff, as he possesses the faculty of working almost anywhere and would be ready to do any duty to which he might be assigned. It might seem like a rash experiment to transfer a man from the *Sun* to the *Tribune* but you would recall the incident in the *Heart of Midlothian* when Ratcliffe was made the turnkey of the Tollbooth. It was brilliantly successful.

Very truly yours,

J. G. Blaine

The reference to Ratcliffe in the *Heart of Midlothian*, drawing Blaine back to his love for Sir Walter Scott's melodrama, was a way of saying that a thief could catch a thief. When the cartel needed a diversion, Gibson would be on hand. At the moment, in Garfield's emerging agenda, the president-elect was to initiate the "star route" scandals. If he didn't, Gibson would be on hand and ready to be called to do his bit. Should Garfield quail from his new list of obligations, some old journalistic indictment, or else a newly concocted one, could flow out of Gibson's pen to the high-speed Bullock presses, holding up the pilloried president for all the land to see.

Senator Blaine was moving without caution. Merely a month after he had accepted Garfield's offer to head the State Department and a month before Garfield's inauguration, the senator seemed to be laying in a stock of punishment to be used against his new patron. In his dream, Swaim had warned Garfield that if he were to move to the other side and save Arthur, he might well perish. Garfield, yet to be inaugurated, was now the subject of a squeeze play.

In the light of this exchange of treacherous correspondence, one has to wonder, of course, how Blaine and Reid qualified as champions of Garfield. The same question long bothered Gorham, but on the basis of other evidence. Gorham never tired of reminding his readers that, in 1873 during the Credit Mobilier hearings, Garfield had testified that he neither owned a share of that company nor borrowed money from Oakes Ames. Yet, after the testimony the *Tribune* reported, "James A. Garfield had ten shares." Again, Garfield had borrowed a small sum of money from Oakes Ames and repaid it. The *Tribune* inferred, however, that he had perjured himself. The paper printed that Garfield had "received $329, which *after* the investigation began, he was anxious to have *considered* a loan from Oakes Ames to himself."

What amazed Gorham was that, while in 1873 Reid had malignantly calumniated Garfield without so much as retracting the slander, in 1881 the *Tribune* editor would take up defending Garfield.[57] In early September 1881 Gorham suggested that the New York State Republican convention adopt a resolution "warning the people not to heed the crocodile tears of the *Tribune* over the man to whom it has never apologized for its infamous libel. No Republican ought to admit that paper into his home until it repents . . ."[58] The vote of censure on Reid came a decade later, as he stood on the threshold of office. In 1892 the national convention unanimously nominated him for vice president on the Harrison ticket. By the time of the November election, however, New Yorkers, reminded that Reid had dealt so badly with Ulysses S. Grant in the 1872 campaign, had a different view. Consequently, Reid, who had unanimous support at the convention, saw the New York voters reject the Harrison-Reid ticket, while the nation saw Grover Cleveland take a second term in the White House.

In 1881, in the face of the rising anti-monopoly sentiment, Garfield would not quail. His own thought was apparently anchored in the position he explained in his Chicago Resumption Day address, identifying a community of interests among the railroads, the banks, and the Treasury, all dependent on creditable bonds. His plausible conclusion was that, until resumption was secure with the national bank vote in 1882, no meddling among the parts was safe for the whole.

Republicans Examine Whether to Accept Senator-Elect Mahone of Virginia

The electorate had given Garfield a slim margin and left the Senate divided. The Senate, in March 1881, included 37 Republicans, 37 Democrats, and 2 Independents. The Democrats, in the majority since 1879, thought that the independents would vote with them, giving them continued control of the Senate committees. One of the independents was David Davis of Illinois, once Lincoln's campaign manager, later an associate justice (1862–1877), and now the largest landowner in the state. The other was William Mahone of Virginia. Once a Confederate general, at the Battle of the Crater near Petersburg he stood off generals Grant and Burnside. More recently he had headed a Virginia railroad that went bankrupt. His attorney was Benjamin Butler.

Troubled by the state's exorbitant debt, Mahone entered Virginia politics, forming the Readjuster Party.[59] The debt traced back to Virginia's wartime losses. Reconstruction had covered finances, but only national finances, not those of the state. Virginia came out of the war with the largest debt per capita and had to handle the repair of roads and bridges by its own resources. Adding to the difficulties, in the midst of the war, West Virginia had broken away without so much as asking what its fair share of the debt would be. Understandably, a new party in Virginia called the Readjusters would have found wide popular appeal.

It was found that the numbers of white adherents to Mahone, added to African-American Republicans, made a new majority. Since during Reconstruction Virginians had not felt the heel of northern occupation, race relations in Virginia were better there than elsewhere in the defeated South. The Readjuster movement turned away from any hint of white supremacy, and made headway as a biracial anti-Bourbon political movement. Leaders promised blacks more services, especially from schools and colleges. Compared with the state figures from 1874, the record for the year 1881 showed the following increases: number of schools from 3,902 to 5,382; pupils enrolled from 173,875 to 239,046; teachers from 3,962 to 5,892; colored teachers from 499 to 927; colored schools from 994 to 1,443; and colored pupils from 52,086 to 76,959.[60] In addition to financial improvements for the state and its departments, in 1882 the Readjusters could claim

> they had abolished the whipping post and the lash; they have finally adopted a joint resolution to strike the poll-tax restriction on suffrage from the constitution; they have provided for the erection of an asylum for the colored insane and for the institute of a normal school for colored students.[61]

The Readjusters also took steps toward state railroad regulation.

The Readjuster movement elected Mahone to the Senate and was strong enough two years later to elect another senator, H. H. Riddleberger, an editor and legislator from Woodstock in the upper Shenandoah Valley. As Mahone had to stave off the Virginia white supremacist Democrats, he sought an ally in Senate Republicans. One of his key sources of support was an electorate that believed that the North favored the Readjuster movement. This could be discerned by the views expressed in the northern press. Gorham would give his editorial support, as would other papers, and as an intermediary between Senate Republicans and Mahone, Gorham sought to arrange for the Virginian's reception.

Some Senate Republicans, circumspect about public credit, had their doubts about associating with Mahone. A careful examination was in order. After the 1880 election, Garfield welcomed Gorham to Mentor and asked him to see Mahone on his behalf. The president-elect set about gathering information and opinions. No one wanted the state debt to turn into repudiation. Garfield also did not want the Mahone organization to swallow up the state Republican organization. By mid-December, he was corresponding with former governor Daniel Chamberlain of South Carolina about his views.[62]

At the end of 1880, to obtain further information, Garfield welcomed a group of Republican Party leaders representing both the stalwart and half-breed factions. Garfield's diary entry named as his guests "Senator Cameron, Messrs. Gorham, Smith and Burt." Gorham, of course, was the editorial writer of the Washington paper. Burt (or Burr) was probably a reporter from the *Philadelphia Press*, while Smith was Charles Emory Smith, the editor of that paper.[63] Including Smith, a Blaine supporter, made the delegation inter-factional. They brought with them Mahone's 57-page paper explaining the state debt, and Gorham helped read it aloud. Not pulling any punches on his aggravations with settling the debt, Mahone had made a target of Garfield's longtime mentor and bond dealer William McCulloch. After hearing it all, Garfield remarked that the 57 pages made an "honest document," but that it was certainly "*ex parte*." The question remained whether Mahone's financial plan for Virginia could pass muster. If it could, the Senate Republicans could willingly accept him to their side when they organized in March.

Garfield knew he had to stir up more discussion. As the meeting broke up, Charles Smith promised to take Whitelaw Reid, editor of Gould's *Tribune,* a copy of the paper. On January 7, 1881, Reid wrote Garfield:

> Charlie Smith has been here with the Mahone documents. I have only read the summary and it impresses me as extremely plausible, but probably unfair . . . (it is certainly wholly *ex parte*) in many of its statements. Its descriptions of Ex-Secty McCulloch's actions, for instance, cannot possibly be correct. I will publish, however, a full synopsis of it––the entire document is unreasonably long––and will make a brief article intended to promote discussion in the line you suggest.[64]

Some newspapers published Mahone's document while Reid waited for some opposing Virginians to bring him a refutation.[65] He had to report to Garfield that no one had shown up.[66]

Mahone's widely published paper would hold the field. On January 15, 1881, Gorham reprinted the favorable summary from the *Cincinnati Gazette:*

> The creditor is better off with the debtor (Readjusters) who confesses inability and pays part than with the debtor (Bourbon Funders) who professes his high sense of honor and pays nothing. The Funders can claim no virtue over the Readjusters, and they are the Old Bourbons of Southern politics, while the Readjusters are for bringing Virginia into a line with national supremacy, with human rights, the equality of all men before the law, and general progress of the age.

Suddenly, intruding on all the patience and goodwill attendant to examining Mahone's fitness to win cooperation from the Republicans, the news of Gould's telegraph consolidation rocked the business world. From that moment on, party harmony suffered. Apparently, factional leaders looking to the future decided who was "in" and who was "out" according to their probable stand on the question of business consolidation versus competition in the telegraph industry.

As Mahone had the strongest support from the stalwarts and the stalwarts were concentrated in New York, Garfield appeared to close the door on Mahone. On February 3, 1881, the president-elect wrote a letter severely criticizing Mahone's position. Two days later, the *Tribune* printed a letter from McCulloch raising doubts about Mahone's handling of the debt. The paper seriously questioned whether Virginians were committed to debt paying. An answer came about a half year later when it was shown that Virginia was paying slightly above the national average on assessed valuation.[67] If that answer had come in February, the Mahone movement would have greatly benefited. As Gorham recalled, Garfield had claimed "the question as to whether the Readjuster movement was 'tainted with repudiation' or not was one to be decided by the Virginia Republicans." The Virginia Republicans, in their state convention, assembled on August 10th of the same year, decided that Readjusterism was not "tainted with repudiation."

The chasm in the Republican Party opened immediately after the January 19, 1881, attempt at telegraph consolidation. Within days, a fierce discussion erupted concerning who would have influence over the new president. On January 31st, the *Washington Post,* partial to Blaine, boldly laid out the matter.

> It is arrant nonsense to say that Senator Blaine desires all factions of the Republican Party to receive equal recognition from Gen. Garfield. Mr. Blaine is simply human. If he can pocket the political power and influence of the next Administration himself, he will not share it with other comers.

Reaction to the telegraph consolidation continued to ripple through the country. In Ohio, the state house judiciary committee called for Congress to pass laws regulating interstate commerce. The *Times* again supported a government telegraph system. Also, the New York Chamber of Commerce, following the two-thirds vote at the December national meeting of the boards of trade, resolved that it was time for the government to "inquire into" placing the operation in the Post Office Department. Gorham took up the Chamber's cause and on Thursday, February 3rd his editorial favored a federal postal telegraph just as a postal telegraph bill was presented in the U.S. House.

On Friday, February 4, 1881, trying to minimize party splits similar to those that had emerged in the election of 1872, in the silver debate of 1878 and again at the national convention of 1880, Gorham wrote in the *National Republican* about Garfield's recent campaign:

> Honest Money and honesty to creditors. By this sign we conquered. The President-elect is wedded to this school. It is a poor compliment to him to suppose that he is to be swayed by a Western prejudice against the East just after a canvass in which the West heartily endorsed the very views which at one time it looked upon with some disfavor.

Then came the counter-attack. On the following Monday, February 7, the *Post* carried a warning, sounding like Blaine himself.

> Our neighbor the *Republican*, while running with Garfield, bays with Conkling. This will not do. There is no man colossal enough in intellect or legs to stride the gulf already formed between them. The Republican Party must become either all Blaine or all Conkling—all Cossack or all Tartar.

213

The chasm widened between the "ins" and the "outs," resting in part in the difference between those Republicans who wanted government to provide competition and those who did not, those who saw a role for the state-owned Erie Canal and those who did not, and those who saw the possibility of a government postal telegraph and those who did not. There was no striding the gulf. The piece in the *Post* was right on the mark. In the context of the Gould consolidation, the legislation to examine the matter, and Gorham's position, the question of the substantial difference between the stalwarts and half-breeds is clear. The former were the anti-monopolists while the latter were the monopolists.

Further, the declaration of June 9, 1880, stated that anyone who "made themselves conspicuous in behalf of the public, if seeking reelection, will be beaten wherever money can accomplish it." Since Gorham would soon be a candidate for reelection to a Senate office, he had put himself at risk in the face of the energetic and determined half-breeds. The *Post* editorial further had echoes of the views Blaine had expressed in his mid-December letter to Garfield when he melodramatically characterized the stalwarts as the "bad men," opposed to the "good men" who supported Garfield. Indeed, the issues at stake could easily fall into the melodrama of corporate consolidation against market competition. Democrat John Reagan had no better heralded the gap in his June 1880 report on his committee hearing earlier in the winter. He had written that Fink and Adams had pressed their case by saying that "the idea of competition must be eliminated from the railroad problem before it can be satisfactorily and properly adjusted. . . . I look upon this as the most dangerous theory which has been advanced." By early 1881 the opposition that Reagan thought was necessary had now institutionalized into the Anti-Monopoly League.

The Continued Growth of the Anti-Monopoly League

A firestorm blew into New York in February 1881. It had probably begun in August through a subtle process that Talcott Parsons would later call experiencing a common fate: two opposing groups were connected by the prospect of winning in the coming presidential election and took each other into account. After the party meeting at the Fifth Avenue Hotel when New Yorkers must have learned of Garfield's meeting with Gould, a whole succession of actions followed.

These actions consisted of steps from writing detailed articles to making motions in court that each took expert knowledge. Taken together the actions infer that the actors were working in concert, discussing the political landscape, and taking suggestions from one another. Their polling of peer organizations across the country that began in August, but was not mentioned by the *Times* until December 2nd, was but one dimension of their activity. First, they may have persuaded Francis Thurber, later credited as founder of the Anti-Monopoly League, to prepare an article on the continuing relevance of the 1877 *Munn vs. Illinois* decision by Chief Justice Waite. It had fallen from public attention if not public favor. Thurber wrote the article and it appeared in the December issue of *Scribner's*. The article came out just as delegates from around the country were gathering in Washington for the annual meeting of the National Board of Trade, where Thurber was a prominent member. At the meeting, the delegates heard the long history of telegraph consolidations in the country and cast a vote in favor of a government-operated system to force competition on the industry. Next, in the first week of January, the Anti-Monopoly League was organized in a small meeting. Fred Conkling gave an address.

Rumors about a telegraph consolidation swept the market as prices on the three companies fell and then quickly rose again. The *Times* ran a long story about telegraph consolidation, a story possibly Thurber had used with the December meeting of the National Board of Trade. Rufus Hatch observed Gould's trading in telegraph stock and urged him not to consolidate. He, nonetheless, went to court on January 19th and won a favorable decision. The next day Hatch won a temporary injunction. In that brief period Blaine urged Garfield to consider pursuing an investigation of the "star route" postal system, and Garfield had a bad dream suggesting he was loosing ties with New York.

In mid-January Leland Stanford of the Central Pacific replied to the questionnaire from the Chamber, and the *Times,* relying on Thurber's updating the *Munn vs. Illinois* decision, dismantled Stanford's position.

In the magazine industry, it is still the practice to publish an issue long in advance of the date on the cover. Garfield's friend, William Dean Howells, editor of the *Atlantic Monthly,* published the March issue in mid-February. It included Henry Demarest Lloyd's article, based on testimony taken at the Hepburn hearing in early 1879 about the Rockefeller trust, and created a sensation. The *Times* stated on February 19th that "By far the most important contribution to the magazine literature of the month is H. D. Lloyd's 'Story of a Great Monopoly.'" The League had it reproduced and included it along with the letter from 'Jere' Black, Garfield's law partner, to new members. Lloyd's article would continue to have influence in the progressive movement twenty years later.

On the next day, February 20th, Senator George Edmunds of Vermont, ranking Republican on the Senate judiciary committee—the committee that had produced the sinking fund act which Gould had not yet recognized—went to New York in federal court before Judge Blatchford, and won another temporary injunction against Gould's telegraph consolidation.[68] Readers of the news could have speculated that Conkling, also on the judiciary committee, had encouraged Edmunds to make the move.

The next evening, February 21, a crowd of business leaders assembled at the Cooper Union Institute with Chamber chairman Lucius E. Chittenden in the chair.[69] There wasn't an empty seat in the house. They heard two speeches. One was by Representative John Reagan of Texas, whose interstate commerce bill Garfield had supported; the other, from Garfield's law partner and friend "Jere" Black. While many matters were covered regarding the corporations, noteworthy was longtime activist Chittenden's remark that the situation could not endure for another year. This echoed Vail's remark, less than three weeks earlier, that "if ever we should have a civil war it will be between the people fighting for their rights on the one side and the corporations on the other."[70] Chittenden told his audience, "If there is not some change, and that very soon, the matter would end in a bloody revolt."[71] These leaders perceived that the monopolists were so intransigent that there was no hope of legislative compromise.

In addition, the gathering heard a letter read from Senator William Windom of Minnesota, an ally of Conkling on transportation matters, who some insiders knew was Garfield's likely choice for secretary of the Treasury. Windom stated that corporate power was of "incalculable value as an instrument to execute the will and serve the interests of the public; but, as the imperious ruler of the people it is a most cruel and relentless tyrant."

Moreover, Windom ventured a forecast of a corporate imposed alleged gag rule over all discussion of public affairs.

> The men who wield this stupendous corporate power have grown wiser with the passage of events. Hitherto they have been apparently content to absorb and control the great industrial and material interest of the country by a monopoly of the channels and implements of transportation, but recently new and alarming conditions are presented. They know full well that if people can freely communicate with each other they will see the dangerous tendencies of this power, and organize to restrain it. Hence, in order to lay deep and sure foundations for the maintenance of their power, and defeat the efforts of the people to curb it, they have now seized upon the channels of thought.

> Look at it a moment. One man [Jay Gould?], who controls more miles of railroad than any other in the world, and who is almost daily adding new lines to his colossal combination, now also controls the telegraphic system of the United States and Canada, and is reaching under the sea to grasp that of Europe. Not content with all this, and determined that no instrument of commercial and political power shall elude his grasp, he is (as I learn) also the owner of three out of seven newspapers, which constitute the Associated Press, through the agency of which the news is distributed over the entire country. He may at any time secure the fourth paper, which will give him absolute control over the news, which the people shall receive. When that takes place what will be our condition? What chances will the people then have to resist the encroachments of corporate power? How shall they even communicate with each other on the subject? What opportunity will there be for a fair discussion of the questions?

The daily news supplied to the myriad newspapers must first pass under the supervision of one or two men, who represent the Associated Press, and who are appointed by its owner. They will have full authority, and doubtless will be required to suppress, add to, or color the information thus sent out as may best serve the interest, the ambition, or the malice of the man to whom they owe their places. Hence, the twenty millions of people who read their morning papers at their breakfast tables will daily receive just such impressions as this one man shall choose to give them. Public men and affairs, and business interests and movement, will be seen in the coloring, which shall serve his interests. The legislator who shall then be bold enough to raise his voice in behalf of the people, or to strike a blow in their defense, will be misrepresented, or denied a hearing before his own constituents. The businessman who shall venture to question the divine right of corporate rule will be crushed, and no telegraphic wire of Associated Press will voice his woe or demand redress from his persecutors. The people will find themselves unable to communicate with each other except by the gracious will and pleasure of the autocrat of the wires. Should special correspondents undertake to supply information not deemed expedient to be sent by the Associated Press, they will find that the owner of the wires can supply a ready remedy for such presumptions.[72]

While the conventional discussions of the incoming Garfield administration centered on the president-elect's difficulty in assembling a cabinet, concurrently, as these newspaper clippings indicate, men in and out of politics were engaged not just in a fierce debate about corporate independence, responsibility and the public's right to free speech but also demonstrating that the anti-monopolists would rise to every opportunity with strength and finesse. If it is granted that the anti-monopolists had girded up their loins, then it is understandable why it was that Garfield appeared to be on the defensive.

Chapter VIII

The Showdown of 1881 between the Stalwarts and Half-Breeds

1   McCloskey, Robert G. *American Conservatism in the Age of Enterprise, 1865–1910.* Cambridge, MA: Harvard University Press, 1951, p. 116.

2   Letter of Adams to Osgood, February 20, 1879, *Collection of Charles Francis Adams, II.* Boston: Massachusetts Historical Society.

3   *NYT,* February 19, 1880.

4   *NYT,* January 8, 1881.

5   A Chamber of Commerce report in early January held that the four trunk lines of the cartel had paid Standard Oil $10,151,000 over a period of eighteen months; they omitted mention of the services Standard Oil rendered in return. Out of that payment may have been huge drawbacks that ruined Rockefeller's competition, a practice that the New York merchants did not want to see Vanderbilt extend to other industries.

6   *NR,* August 16, 1881.

7   Unger, Irwin. *The Greenback Era: A Social and Political History of American Finance, 1865–1879.* Princeton: University Press, 1964, p. 405.

8   *NYT,* May 18, 1882.

9   *Washington Post,* July 9, 1881.

10 *NR,* February 28, 1881.

11 *NR,* March 24, 1881.

12 "Report of the Controller of the Currency," *Banker's Magazine,* December 1881, p. 463; the membership roster of the U.S. Senate, 47th Congress, 1881.

13 Marcus, Robert D. *Grand Old Party: Political Structure in the Gilded Age, 1880–1896.* New York: Oxford University Press, 1971, pp. 53f.

14 *NYT,* January 21 and 29, 1881. Hatch contradicted Gould's affidavit.

15 *Who Was Who in America,* Historical Volume, 1607–1896. New York: Marquis *Who's Who,* 1963, p. 239.

16 Ibid.

17 *NYT,* January 15, 1881. Hatch entertained Ulysses S. Grant at his home. Guests that evening included Stephen Dorsey, Noah Davis, Thomas Murphy, C. K. Garrison, R. G. Rolston, Frank Work, and Rev. John Newman.

18 *NYT,* January 14, 1881.

19 *NYT,* January 12, 1881.

20 *NYT,* January 16, 1881. See also Klein, pp. 278–282.

21 *NYT,* January 21, 26, and 29, 1881.

22 *NR,* March 24, 1881.

23 Taylor, William L. *A Productive Monopoly: The Effect of Railroad Control on New England Coastal Steamship Lines, 1870–1916.* Providence: Brown University Press, 1970, p. xiii.

24 *NYT,* January 20 and 21 and February 4, 1881; January 5, 1883. Sewell used Arthur's office for meetings in February 1881; in 1883 President Arthur may have considered Sewell as attorney for the Southern District.

25 *NYT,* January 21, 1881.

26 *NYT,* May 16, 1882.

27 Laumann, Edward O., and David Knoke. *The Organizational State, Social Choices in National Policy Domains.* Madison: University of Wisconsin Press, 1987, p. 37.

28 *Proceedings of the Twelfth Annual Meeting of the Board of Trade,* January 19, 1882, p. 92. Copy at the Library, Champaign: University of Illinois.

29 *NYT,* March 29, 1877.

30 *NYT,* January 14, 1880.

31 *NYT,* March 6, 1880.

32 Memorandum, January 21, 1881, *Garfield Collection, LC,* cited in Peskin, p. 680.

33 Garfield, Lucretia, to J. A. Garfield, January 21, 1881, *Garfield Collection, LC.*

34 *Annual Report of the Secretary of the Treasury, 1871,* "Report of the Treasurer of the United States," *LC,* p. 271.

35 *Biographical History of Eminent and Self-Made Men of the State of Indiana.* Cincinnati: Western Biographical Publishing, 1880, Vol. 1, pp. 92-95.

36 *NYT,* May 6, 1881.

37 *The Nation,* January 27, 1881, p. 55f.

38 *NYT, January* 5, 1881. "As to the broader questions affecting the direct and constant supervision of the railroads by the State . . . the Governor says nothing."

39 Benson, Lee. *Merchants, Farmers, and Railroads.* Cambridge, MA: Harvard University Press, 1955, p. 150; *NYT,* January 7, 1881; *Tribune,* January 7, 1881. In attendance were L. E. Chittenden, F. B. Thurber, Nelson Smith, E. P. Miller, John Keogh, Clarence Lyons, F. A. Stewart, Theodore E. Tomlinson, Homer H. Stuart, A. R. Foot, Wilson Wolfe, William Ward, Stephen B. Brague, and F. A. Conkling.

40 *NR,* January 6, 1881.

41 *NR,* February 1, 1881.

42 *NYT,* January 23, 1881.

43 Robertson, William, to Whitelaw Reid, January 25, 1881, *Reid Collection, LC.*

44 Garfield, James. "A Century of Congress," *Atlantic,* July 1877, quoted in John M. Taylor, *Garfield, the Available Man.* New York: Norton, 1970, pp. 291f.

45 Harrison, Benjamin, to James Garfield, February 1, 1881 *Harrison Collection,* University Library, Bloomington, Ill.

46 *NYT,* January 29, 1881.

47 Brown, Harry James, and F. D. Williams. *The Diary of James A. Garfield.* East Lansing: Michigan State University Press, 1981,Vol. 1, p. lix. See also Vol. 4, p. 540 (text and f.n.).

48 *NYT,* January 29 and 30 and February 4, 1881.

49 *NYT,* February 4, 1881.

50 Laumann and Knoke, p. 12.

51 Benson, p. 154.

52 Peskin, *Garfield,* p. 553.

53 Adams, Henry, *Novels,* etc., p. 165.

54 Leland, Earl J. *The Post Office and Politics, 1876–1884, The Star Route Frauds.* Ph.D. diss. Department of History. Chicago: University of Chicago, December 1964, pp. 130f.

55 Reid to Blaine, February 5, 1881, and Blaine to Reid, February 7, 1881, *Reid Collection, LC.*

56 "Americans of Scottish descent tend to be better educated and have higher incomes than other European-based ethnic groups, according to a new Census Bureau study." Associated Press, May 12, 1982.

57 *NR,* October 20, 1881.

58 *NR,* September 6, 1881.

59 For a discussion of the politics of the Virginia debt, see Tice, James Moore, *Two Paths to the New South, The Virginia Debt Controversy, 1870–1883.* Lexington: University Press of Kentucky, 1974.

60 *NR,* November 6, 1882.

61 *NR,* April 25, 1882.

62 De Santis, Vincent P. *Republicans Face the Southern Question: The New Departure Years, 1876–1897.* Baltimore: Johns Hopkins University Press, 1959. p. 136.

63 Brown and Williams believe that "Smith" was a Virginia Republican congressman who had crossed over to Mahone's party. See *Garfield Diary,* Vol. 4, pp. 516 and 517. Gorham, in his 1888 piece on Conkling, identified "Smith" as the Philadelphia editor.

64 *Garfield Collection, LC.*

65 Reid, Whitelaw, to James Garfield, January 4, 1881, *Reid Collection, LC.*

66 *Garfield Collection, LC.*

67 *NR,* September 19, 1881.

68 *NYT,* February 18, 1881.

69 Chittenden was one of five men who founded the Free Soil party. He had been the first registrar of the United States Treasury under Lincoln. His experience in the antislavery wing of the Republican Party led to his making parallels between the antislavery movement and the antimonopoly movement. Benson, p. 153.

70 *NYT,* January 29, 1881.

71 *NYT,* February 17, 1881.

72 *NYT,* February 22, 1881.

CHAPTER IX

Drawing the Line in Organizing Both the Cabinet and the Senate Committees, March 1881

A mark of Congress's independence is the constitutional provision that each house shall organize itself. That has come to mean the election of their own officers and the naming of members to committees. Some Senate committees are standing or permanent, from congress to congress, while others are select or temporary and end with the end of the congress.

As has been shown, legislators will arrange committees to produce the best information they can obtain on some salient matters. Beginning in 1879 business leaders in eastern ports could not escape observing that the shipping business at New Orleans was gaining at their expense. J. B. Eads had deepened the Mississippi channel, allowing ocean-going vessels to come up the river, not only to New Orleans but also to Memphis. Ocean traffic was now moving to the mouth of the river. The committee on improvement of the Mississippi had seated mostly members from the Midwest. When the Republicans in 1881 took over committees, they added two east coast Republicans. Freshman John Mitchell of Pennsylvania would serve as the committee chair and freshman William Frye of Maine as a member. The work of Laumann and his associate (1976) allows the surmise that the redundancy in a committee (the two members from the east coast) would assist another interested sub-group (the Republican caucus) in gaining corroborated information from the Midwesterners' discussions. The new Senate arrangement allowed those two members to make a very focused examination of what was happening and then consider options for solutions. It serves as an example of consequential leaders coping with institutional strain. From this one example of the sudden appearance of east coasters on the committee, the generalization could be offered that *alterations within committee arrangements from congress to congress serve as a bellwether of some perceived institutional strain in the general economy.*

To spot the sensitivities of the Senate members, one need only compare a new slate of a committee with the previous slate for that committee. In 1881, the slates appeared only days apart. The Democratic slate, much like the Democratic slate for the recent lame-duck session, appeared on March 10th, and the Republican slate on March 18th. The sharp change in the March arrangements for the Mississippi River committee would not make an impression on the public until the papers told the story later in the summer. Both the *Times* and the *Post* would carry stories describing dangers for New York in the loss of shipping to New Orleans. Although senators understood the crisis in March, the public would be about a half year behind. By the time the public became aware, New York was in the midst of the early-winter election season. The public shock over the loss of traffic to New Orleans, challenging the city's commercial supremacy, would precede the devastating defeat of the New York Republican Party in the state legislature. Since the monopolists had exercised a proprietary claim over the legislature, the only way in which the public could free itself from that burden was to give the majority of seats to the opposing Democrats.

As shall be seen, in addition to watching the boom at New Orleans, easterners took steps to monitor the West on another matter: the currency. The silver debate (1876–1878), followed by the greenback surge in the off-year election of 1878, apparently led the hard-money advocates to defend their position. They would do so by forming committee hegemony over the western Republicans. Given the fact that Midwest Republicans in 1878 had supported silver and the reissuance of greenbacks, in 1881 this new arrangement was a counter strategy. New Englanders had to prepare for the vote on rechartering national banks the following year.

When James Garfield entered the presidency, he had both the currency question and the transportation question to deal with. When the Congress dealt with the silver question in 1878 the hard-money advocates gave hardly any hint of a strong defense. In 1878, the loose alliance of congressional delegations from the South and West had demanded a return to silver coinage. The northeasterners, much more involved in an advanced economy, opposed it. The sharpest division appeared when President Rutherford B. Hayes vetoed the silver bill in February 1878. The New Englanders as a block supported the veto, and the inlanders as a block opposed it, revealing what Laumann and Knoke refer to as a *cleavage* around an event in the policy arena.[1] Any political strategist in 1881 would have had to concede that such a vote could occur again and should be prevented. As shall be shown, in the executive session of the 47th Congress (March 1881), the hard-money advocates brought their hegemony into full flower. When in 1882 the currency question rose again in the form of the banking bill, rather than polarizing the Republicans as in 1878, most of the inland Republican senators voted with their chairmen from New England giving the Senate party a moment of unity.

Garfield in His Inaugural Address Shows a Harsher View toward the Currency

The path taken to currency stability was not at all straight or clear. After the 1880 convention, James Garfield, in his letter of acceptance, had mentioned the currency matter, taking a congenial attitude. Garfield told the nation that it had now

> close(d) with honor the financial chapter of the war . . . Our paper currency is now as national as the flag, and resumption has not only made it everywhere equal to coin, but has brought into use our store of gold and silver. The circulating medium is more abundant than ever before, and we need only to maintain the *equality of all our dollars* to insure to labor and capital a measure of value from the use of which no one can suffer loss. Any violent changes or doubtful financial experiments should not endanger the great prosperity, which the country is now enjoying.[2] (Our emphasis.)

In this comment, Garfield, manager of Sherman's 1880 presidential campaign, may have picked up some of the Treasury secretary's opinions, expressed in his 1878 testimony before congressional committees. Godkin of the *Nation* read Garfield's letter and must have shook his head, writing that the candidate "has here only too faithfully copied the ambiguity of Mr. Sherman."[3] Joining Godkin's show of disgust, the Massachusetts party at its September 1880 meeting registered its disappointment, likely catching Garfield's attention. The Bay Staters' platform held that gold and silver were unequal in value. They believed that it was absurd to talk about paper currency as redeemable in equal terms; and they urged the repeal of the silver bill.[4] This Massachusetts action suggested that the state party had found the Chicago platform not explicit enough. It seems that the national platform, or Garfield's letter of acceptance, had about as much standing in Massachusetts as the 1879 New York platform on corporate regulation had had with the national party in 1880. It had about as much standing, for that matter, as Hayes's Civil Service Order had had in 1877 with the New York party. In this casual anarchy, the future was left to the daring and persistent, and factionalism was the name of the game. More specifically, factionalism consisted of a plethora of elites who acted on their own and then perchance consulted others. By the time Garfield delivered his inaugural address, he had dropped his Shermanesque views on the currency for a more austere position. Obviously alluding to the Ferry amendment to the silver bill of February 1878, he reported that "grave doubts have been entertained whether Congress is authorized by the Constitution to make any form of paper money legal-tender. The notes are not money."[5]

The **Tribune's** *Criticism of Garfield's Nomination of Windom for Treasury*

The absence of a strong focus in the new administration showed up in the naming of the Secretary of the Treasury. To keep affairs on the straight and narrow Blaine pressed his own plans for the cabinet and committee. When Garfield named Senator William Windom of Minnesota as secretary of the Treasury, Blaine dissented. Windom would have been remembered for his report on transportation. Waterway advocates had great respect for his careful approach to their cause, especially how he had won a reply from railroad cartel manager Albert Fink about the opening of the Erie Canal each spring lowering railroad rates across the country. Then, just two weeks before Garfield's inauguration, Windom had issued a challenge to telegraph consolidator Jay Gould, Blaine's patron, by describing how the new telegraph consolidation could enforce an alleged gag rule on any political discussions.

On the Windom appointment, the *Tribune,* owned by Gould and serving as Blaine's spokesperson, took exception. The newspaper thought that Windom was the wrong man to have an influence upon corporate (railroad) policy. With the Adams plan in the wings, Windom would sit too close to the sidelines. An answer to Reid's paper came from Gorham:

> The *New York Tribune* assures the country that although "it has been thought by some that Secretary Windom's views in regard to the treatment of corporations would prove injurious to important railroad and other enterprises," there need not necessarily be any fear that those much oppressed interests will languish, for says the great corporation organ, "the treatment of all questions of that nature will rest, not with the Secretary of the Treasury, but with Secretary of the Interior Kirkwood, or with Attorney General MacVeagh. . . ."

Gorham next quoted from Windom's recent letter to the New York meeting:

> The individual citizen is impotent to contend with this gigantic and rapidly growing power. Governmental authority, State and Nation, alone is competent to restrain its aggressions and correct its abuses . . . This organized gigantic corporate power can only be kept under proper restraint by the organized power of the people, expressed through their State and National Governments. That such governmental power exists and may properly be exercised I have not a particle of doubt. It is plainly written in our Constitution, and had been unequivocally declared by the Supreme Court of the United States. [Francis Thurber would later reiterate the favorable ruling by Chief Justice Waite.]

Gorham asked whether

> the *Tribune* mean[s] to be understood as lecturing General Garfield for appointing Mr. Windom, because of his views on the subject referred to. *Is it sure that it is safe to open the great struggle, the coming of which seems inevitable?* Is the history of the slave power [with a gag rule] about to be repeated? Will the corporations not be content with present conditions? Will they insist

upon *conformity with their views in every department?* Are those for whom the *Tribune* speaks ready to follow up its covert sneers at Secretary Windom by demanding a *drawing of the line for and against them?* [enlisting "good men" and alienating "bad men."] On which side would they find the President? Let them find their answer in his past utterances.[6] (Our emphasis.)

What Garfield had actually objected to was not a national utility for regulating the rails; he objected to the supporters' heavy-handedness in achieving it.

Also, moving over the new Washington perspective was an atmosphere left by the half-breeds' announcement of the previous June––"the policy of repressing public opinion will be pursued, instead of making concessions."[7] For Gorham, it meant a coming "great struggle." Caro Lloyd, brother of the famous financial columnist on the *Chicago Tribune*, wrote: "You are on the right side of the great fight that is coming."[8] The Anti-Monopoly League president, Lucius E. Chittenden, had recently foreseen the prospect of a "bloody revolt."[9] In June 1880 Reagan, chair of the House committee on commerce, had put his finger on the polarization when he scoffed at the claim by the monopolists that competition had to be disposed of. Remarking about the fierce standoff between the two factions on corporate privileges and governance, Gorham was neither impertinent nor exaggerating the case. By mid-May, Garfield would describe the standoff in similarly extreme language. What has been missing in the accounts of the Garfield presidency is a method of research that could capture the legitimate strain between great interests. We suggest that policy analysis is up to the task, having the means of setting aside the temptation of the usual recourse to character assassination and the like.

Next on the Docket, Arranging Senate Committees

In the U.S. Senate the confident Democrats proceeded to organize committees, not expecting that Virginia's independent Senator William Mahone would break to the Republican ranks. The half-breeds around Garfield felt the same way. Fully certain that they would organize the committees, the Democrats presented a slate on March 10 and had it printed in the *Congressional Record.*

One interesting change came with the committee on foreign affairs, strongly suggesting that the incoming secretary of State, James Blaine, would have wanted a friendly panel. On their slate the Democrats proposed three new Republican members all of whom were Blaine supporters. There was Eugene Hale of Maine, a former member of the House and Blaine's campaign manager; John Mitchell of Pennsylvania, an attorney and recent half-breed victor in the Senate race at Harrisburg; and John Miller of California, interested in the government completing immigration negotiations with China and hailing from a Blaine state at the last convention. The surmise is that those new Senators were named because Blaine had asked the Democrats to include them on the committee.

It was not unusual for a cabinet member to look out for his friends. In *Democracy* Henry Adams, tracking Ratcliffe [Blaine?], wrote:

> During these early days of every new administration, the absorbing business of government relates principally to appointments. The Secretary of the Treasury was always ready to oblige his colleagues in the cabinet by taking care of their friends to any reasonable extent. The Secretary of State was not less courteous.[10]

Blaine was doing Ratcliffe one better. He lined up committee seats for his loyalists and would probably later oblige other cabinet members to help them with their patronage. Trying to guard against cabinet members bothering one another on appointments, Garfield heeded Secretary of the Treasury John Sherman's advice that "one rule is essential to your comfort, that the head of one Dept. shall not meddle with or interfere with appointments to office in another Dept." Garfield's biographer Allan Peskin has added, "This seemed reasonable, and at his first cabinet meeting Garfield laid down just such a rule. Blaine, however, acted as if the rule was not intended to apply to him."[11] Precisely! In this new administration, Secretary of State Blaine, getting ready for the star route scandal, was probably conferring with Attorney General Wayne MacVeagh about a place for Garfield's calumniator at the *Sun,* A. M. Gibson!

Arranging the Democratic slate for foreign affairs probably gave Republicans Hale, Mitchell, and Miller special advantages. It put them in a position of being able to ask Blaine for patronage appointments, giving them more favorable state organizations and a better chance for re-elections after six years. Blaine, in return, could expect these three to assist him in adopting his policies. But adding three freshmen to the foreign affairs committee was quite strange, since seats on that panel were usually reserved for seniors. No less strange was that the sole Republican senior remaining on the Democratic committee—since Carpenter had died the previous month—was Blaine's nemesis, Roscoe Conkling. If the New Yorker discounted Blaine's views and proposals in the meetings on foreign affairs, the three freshmen could come to his aid, making Conkling an irrelevancy.

The Contrast between the Two Plans for the Judiciary Committee

A very marked contrast appeared between the slates that the two parties prepared for the proposed judiciary committee. Both plans to a great extent came out of New York City—the first from the office of the cartel located at 346 Broadway and now in its fourth year. The second plan for judiciary more likely represented Conkling's associations with the Chamber. They represented the activities plausibly launched in August after the party's Fifth Avenue Hotel meeting, all leading to the midwinter surge in interest for common law. Apparently behind it was Francis Thurber, who had produced an article on common law in the December *Scribner's* followed by the *Times's* January criticism of Stanford on the same grounds. Then came Gould's telegraphy consolidation in mid-January and Lloyd's mid-February *Atlantic* article about Standard Oil, both giving a spur to Thurber's effective organizing of the new Anti-Monopoly League. The range of quickly changing opinion, plausibly due to the *Times*'s application of Thurber's views to Stanford's line of argument, could have been reflected in the election of a new U. S. Senator at Albany. One day the half-breeds thought they had lined up Thomas Platt. In very short order, however, Robertson, in writing a letter that Reid sent to Garfield, identified Platt as one of two stalwarts and warned Garfield about that faction's intrusions into the new cabinet. At the same moment, Levi P. Morgan realized that there would be no room for him in the new cabinet plausibly because that coterie had to protect Gould's venture into consolidation: local, New York opinion would not be welcome.

Not only had the cartel leaders and the Chamber leaders failed to reconcile their differences before they left New York City for Washington, the record suggests that nowhere else in the committee structure had the dispute over transportation become so formidable as it would be for the Senate judiciary committee. During the previous decade, the judiciary committee had won eminence in that field on two occasions. In 1881 it must have been assumed that the issue had to go there. In 1873 when the U.S. Senate learned that federal funds for the Pacific railroad had gone into bribing the Kansas state legislature's election of U.S. Senators, the Senate refused to seat the two men. In that debate, the judiciary committee, on a motion by Conkling, won the right to review the work of both the Interior Department in distributing land to the railroad companies and the Treasury Department in distributing bonds.[12] That move pleased the northeastern electorate, troubled by the flood of land grants to the railroads, while in the Senate the move undercut the standing of the Pacific railroads committee. Next, in 1878 the judiciary committee competed with the Pacific railroads committee on the legislation for the Pacific roads sinking fund. The judiciary committee's version won out. Competition broke out again in 1881 when the question arose about the degree of hospitality that the judiciary committee would show the Adams plan awaiting action in the House. The Democrats answered the question by naming additions to the committee that would have given the Adams plan a very favorable reception. The parties were already jockeying on a matter. Benson notes "Early in 1878, in an attempt to stir up sentiment favoring national legislation, the New York Board of Trade and Transportation circulated a petition calling upon Congress to appoint a joint committee to investigate the workings of the American railroad system."[13] Again, in 1881, while committees were being settled on, the Baltimore Board of Trade wrote the New York Board, as reported March 8, that:

> " . . . The national railroad commission recommended by the railroad interests is very questionable and we would rather recommend a commission composed of members of both houses of Congress, to investigate the whole matter, and report whether, in their judgment, any such regulation is necessary, and, if necessary, to urge the passage of a law or

laws forcible in provisions, equitable in effect, and preventative against present and growing abuses."

As it turned out, this idea prominent in New York and Baltimore turned out to be the one that was followed. In 1885 the Senate approved the new Cullom committee on interstate commerce, which joined with the Reagan committee from the House, and together they toured the country soliciting everyone's opinion on regulation. The Republican judiciary committee in 1881 could have become just the right one to match with the House commerce committee and comprise a joint committee. In March 1881, there appears to be no evidence that the cartel lobbyists contacted the Republicans to discuss their preferences for judiciary committee membership just in case the Democrats failed to organize the Senate.

Traces of Adams's Hand in the Democrats' Senate Plan for the Judiciary Committee

The Democratic plan for the judiciary committee in 1881 was all monopoly and Adams appears to have made the arrangements. Adams had first promoted his plan for railroad consolidation through his 1878 volume. In early 1880 U.S. House commerce committee hearings he elaborated on it. The committee brought the plan to the House floor early in 1881 along with the Reagan bill and an alternative. Apparently, Adams and Reagan could not agree on compromises. Not only did the merchants of New York object to Adams's plan because it made no room for merchant participation, but also the New York Chamber of Commerce mailed merchants around the country the Massachusetts Railroad Commission's criticism of Adams's new version. That warning should have provided the cartel promoters with cause for caution. Undaunted, the cartelists still sought a friendly committee in the U.S. Senate. When Blaine talked to the Democrats about seating his friends on foreign affairs, he may also have spoken to them about the membership for judiciary.

The Democratic plan for seating new committee members on judiciary almost certainly carried the stamp of cartel staff member Charles F. Adams, Jr. Apparently how he viewed matters in 1881 would not appear until a year later in a Boston address on a proposed federal commission. Our comparison here of his 1882 comments on *commission* membership, with the names proposed in 1881 for *committee* membership, persuades us that Adams exercised influence at the earlier date.

Unfortunately, too much time passed before Adams came to the point about commission membership. Before the Reagan committee over a year earlier, Adams had only alluded to the arrangements.

> That men qualified to do the work on hand can be obtained under
> proper conditions, the corporations themselves demonstrate by their daily
> action. Their officials, as you have good cause to know, serve them ef-
> fectively and well; —they understand their business and they do it. If the

government cannot get equally good service in the same field, it had undoubtedly best leave the work wholly undone, and patiently allow events to take their course . . . I argue that it is useless for the government to move in the matter in the way I have endeavored to point out, unless it is prepared to move through agents who, understanding well their business, also, from the outset, *command not only the confidence of the public but the respect of the railroad corporations* . . . If this subject cannot be approached in a spirit at once large, liberal and patriotic, it had better—much better—be left alone.[14] (Our emphasis.)

These comments proved not direct enough. In his 1882 Boston address, Adams came much closer to the point, failing only to say that he had used the same ideas when in 1881 he helped put together the Democratic plan for the judiciary committee.[15] Quoting the English leader in railroading, Stephenson, Adams said in 1882 that:

What we want is a tribunal upon these subjects, competent to judge, and willing to devote its attention to railway subjects only. We do not impute to *Parliament* that it is dishonest, but we impute that it is *incompetent*. All we ask is that it shall be a tribunal that is impartial and that is thoroughly informed; and, if impartiality and intelligence are secured, we do not fear for the result.

First, Adams would tell his 1882 audience that on the three-member tribunal "one member of the board must possess a thorough knowledge of constitutional law, and be qualified to draft most difficult statutes." He warned that the commission needed protection from corporation lawyers; they could easily drive a locomotive right through any ill-conceived legislation. Matching that standard, not just for the commission but also for the membership of the Senate judiciary committee, in 1881 Adams had urged the Democrats to seat Ben Hill of Georgia on the judiciary committee. Hill had demonstrated his competence as counsel before the Supreme Court for the plaintiffs in Pacific railroads case *(U.S. Reports, Supreme Court, Vol. 99. October Term, 1878, The Pacific Roads Sinking Fund Case.* Reported by Wm. Otto, Boston, 1879), a challenge of the Thurman sinking fund acts.[16]

Hill's personal interest in joining the judiciary committee would have derived from his prestige in handling the defense in the sinking fund case, giving him a virtual open road to proposing a better settlement for Jay Gould. Once the committee work got underway, he could have served as the cartel's general utility legislator. Indeed, Gould was in arrears in meeting payments to the sinking fund. Klein notes: "Since its passage (of the Thurman Act) in 1878 the Union Pacific had ignored the payment provisions, preferring to gamble on either a negotiated settlement or victory in the courts."[17] When Garfield and Gould met in August, the railroad financier could have mentioned that he wanted to pay less. Then, just before the organizing of Senate committees in March, according to Gorham's 1888 account, Garfield and Hill visited and the latter may have accepted the assignment if he were named to judiciary.[18] If Hill took up the committee duties and offered a new sinking fund bill, his service for Gould would have given the railroader a magnificent return on his $100,000 campaign contribution. In addition, Hill could have helped the committee call as witnesses other railroad attorneys who were of the same mind on railroad organization as he was.

The second regulator, Adams told his Boston audience, must be "a railroad specialist—a practical man fully informed as to the way in which railroad work is done." Matching that standard in 1881, Adams appears to have persuaded the Democrats to name freshman Senator George Pendleton of Ohio, president of Kentucky Central Railroad. Pendleton would leave the Senate six years later known for his promotion of the civil service reform legislation. In addition, Pendleton on the committee could assist in calling as witnesses other railroad presidents to testify, especially those from the South, whom Albert Fink, the cartel manger, must have known quite well.

Finally, Adams said, a member was needed who is "trained to treat cause and effect, to handle statistics, to be sure that the remedy proposed will reach the evil complained of." The Democrats selected Senator John Sherman of Ohio, a Republican whose keenness in statistics was legendary. He had served as the chair of the finance committee and then as Secretary of the Treasury. As a working ally with President Garfield and Senator Sherman through his vast connections from having served as Secretary of the Treasury he could have helped the committee enlist any number of people to testify. Independent Senator David Davis of Illinois, formerly on the U.S. Supreme Court, would serve as chair. On March 11 the *Times* carried a report on the Democratic slate. The great railroaders, William Vanderbilt, Jay Gould, and Collis Huntington, thinking ever since 1878 of a national railroad trust blessed by government concurrence, probably warmly approved it. This committee plan, however, did not include a merchant representative, which Adams in 1878 had told Osgood was so important.

The railroaders were not the only parties interested in reconfiguring the judiciary committee. Conkling, quite competent in corporate law, would have looked at the Democrats' proposed slate and calculated what it meant. One trouble with it was that it would have changed the character of his alliance with the grain shipping states. For the past six to eight years, Conkling had joined members from Minnesota and Wisconsin on commerce, foreign affairs, and judiciary to monitor the transportation business to New York. With the Democrats' incursions into judiciary and Blaine's designs on a friendly foreign affairs committee, the grain shipping alliance would have had less cohesion.

While the Democrats scrupulously arranged the judiciary committee, public opinion hardly supported the new slate. The cartel had not conducted a reasonable campaign for the Adams bill. Leading proponents of the legislation did not find broad support. Their public image was in poor repair. At the Hepburn hearings, Vanderbilt did not seem to know how his company was run. Gould was in arrears on the sinking fund. The Board of the Massachusetts Railroad Commissioners severely criticized the bill Adams had proposed for the national level. In addition, in his 1878 book, Adams had completely discounted the role of the Erie Canal; thereby they failed to grasp the structure of New York transportation. Further, with his antagonistic attitude toward the western state railroad commissions, he could hardly appreciate the way corporate attorneys had hoodwinked westerners, persuading them to overturn their state granger legislation. In early 1881, grangerism rooted in English common law was making a strong comeback. Disregarding the place of a state commission concurrent with a federal commission, the Adams bill did not merit a rubber stamp. The only support for the bill came from railroaders. It had received poor press, and in a poll by the New York Chamber of Commerce, boards of trade across the country leaned toward the Reagan bill. In addition, both Massachusetts and Pennsylvania had reported effective state commissions operating under law,[19] while the New York railroaders still debated such an idea. Proponents of state commissions might have seen that a federal commission was premature until New York had its own state commission.

In March 1881, it was too late to round up support for the Adams bill. It was arriving in the U.S. Congress long past the time for the interested groups to discuss it. On the positive side, the judiciary committee members could have the long-awaited ordeal of thorough discussion over the substance of the legislation. Whether they would want to adjudicate the differences between the factions without first testing relevant public opinion was a question. Again, the new members on the committee might have easily persuaded some of the old-timers, like Conkling and Edmunds, to approach railroad problems on a case-by-case basis. Whether they could proceed, however, with legislation that legitimated a national consolidation remained a more difficult matter. After all, journalist Lloyd had earlier asserted that the railroads would attempt to dictate the legislation. This suspicion gained strength from Garfield's later invoking a requirement of "letters of introduction" from senators opposed to Robertson. If the Adams bill had made its way onto the Senate floor, Garfield could have invoked the tactic of "letters of introduction" to win Senate passage. In spite of the popularity of the Reagan bill among the boards of trade, the president could have made open discussion and popular support irrelevant. The atmosphere surrounding the reception of the Adams plan had all the marks of the promoters' great hopes that a consolidated railroad system would soon match the industrial marvel recently achieved by John D. Rockefeller in the oil industry, a trust intensely managed at the top, covering the entire nation, and reaping great wealth for the owners. With such an end in mind, the railroaders could have thought that they were warranted in dropping most of the customary protocols to get there.

The Senate postponed taking up the Democratic slate. The Republicans would now have a chance to meet the standard that Conkling had set in his campaign speech, i.e., since the South now represented one-fourteenth of the nation's economy, its senators should not have control of the Senate committees. To reach committee organization, they recruited Virginia's Mahone and used Vice President Arthur's vote even though he was not a member of the Senate. Over the weekend, they began putting their own slate of committees together.

The Canal Option for National Railroad Regulation

While the elite in Washington jockeyed for influence over cabinet and committee appointments, in the transportation debate the remark in the Hepburn report still stood that "the canal, like *Banquo's ghost*, would not down."[20] On February 2, 1881, the *Times* editor wrote:

> Aside from the bulk of grain, which they have brought to this port, accounting last year to more than 70,000,000 bushels, they have been a powerful check upon extravagant charges by the railroads. *The state owning the canals and the 5,000 boats floating upon them belonging to many different proprietors, any pooling or other combination opposed by the public interest is impracticable.* The reduction of the State tolls has been followed by a great increase in the volume of traffic, which was 6,4621,290 tons last year, against 1,743,320 in 1876 . . . There is one difficulty in the way, which can be removed only by a change in the Constitution. The amendment of 1874 restricts the amount to be expended upon the canals of the State in any one year to the receipts of the preceding. As the tolls last year amounted to only $1,164,567.92, it is evident that any surplus over the expense of management, which is to be anticipated, would be entirely inadequate for such changes and improvements of those recommended. (Our emphasis.)

What was known and when did they know it? It was common knowledge in New York City that the current railroad pool could not proceed with confidence as long as the Erie Canal was open with all the boats on it running at competitive rates. Young Seymour had plans for increasing the traffic. He wanted to raise the canal banks so that they would accommodate larger ships, allow steam towing, and drop all tolls in order to compete with the anticipated Canadian Welland Canal. This was known, as the *Times* demonstrated a full month before Garfield's inauguration.

In Washington, with the Democrats planning to stack the judiciary committee with railroad experts to pass the Adams plan, the New York press began suggesting that the canal was already the national regulator and additional federal regulation was unnecessary. *The Commercial and Financial Chronicle* addressed the question at least twice. On March 5 the paper argued,

> That the canals should be retained, valued, appreciated and improved, under a policy of less stint and more enlarged views, we entertain no doubt. That this will be the policy adopted, now seems sure. They are not only of almost incalculable commercial advantage to the State and the

nation directly, but their improvement will be of indirect advantage to the public. We hear much nowadays about railroads oppressing the people. There can be no competition, it is said, under which railroad charges can be regulated———they are a law unto themselves———so we must regulate them by legislation. Here, however, is an absolute check to "railroad extortions," as they are called, if we choose to use it.[21]

Yet, the New York state legislature could not move on canal improvements. The proposal to allow steam towing went nowhere. It has never been the habit of legislators representing an interest, such as railroading, when voting on a matter opposed to their interest, to recuse themselves. As Vanderbilt had picked up the expenses of enough state senators to protect his position, the Astor bill failed, an event that before the year ended would come back to haunt the railroaders. On March 9, just as the U.S. Senate prepared to take up the Democratic plan for organizing committees, state Senator William Astor, a firm ally of Conkling who had business on the canal, said in Albany,

> A clause of the Constitution prohibits the use of public funds, and provides, in effect, for the gradual ruin and ultimate abandonment of the canals. [Due to low summer rates,] the canal earnings are thus reduced to a minimum, and consequently there can be no improvements of any adequate, or even considerable, nature. Upon this point the State engineer says in his report, 1880: "A single disaster, an unfavorable season may cut down the tolls so that they may not be equal to the cost of opening next year." In this event, no matter how small the deficiency may be, the Legislature is not allowed to give one dollar to save the canals from destruction.[22]

On the same day that Astor's ominous comments appeared in the *Times*, the paper's editor wrote in the same foreboding spirit about the fall elections:

> The most active influence at Albany is, now as always, that of corporations whose interests are touched by contemplated legislation. The Senate being the smaller and more manageable body is, naturally, the instrument with which the agents of these corporations work for the obstruction of inconvenient legislation. Yesterday's adverse report on the bill permitting steam towing on the canals and its accompanying facilities for cheap freight transportation by railroad, would seem to indicate that the Senate continues to be less sensitive to public opinion than corporate pressures. The dealing of the upper house with the Telegraph Consolidation bill is . . . another evidence of similar disposition . . . With a large majority in both houses, the Republican Party has a certain obvious responsibility for the

results of the session and unless these are a good deal more creditable than at present can be anticipated, *the party is very likely to suffer.*[23]

In Washington, the railroaders had worked with the Democrats to seat more senators with interests in railroading on the judiciary committee. In Albany state senators with railroad affiliations controlled the state senate on canal matters. Further, executives at both levels were reticent about making references to corporate regulation. Governor Cornell and President-elect Garfield had very little to say. A year earlier in February 1880, as Adams testified before the Reagan committee, the *Times* had lectured the leadership that astute treatment of the transportation question was needed at both Albany and Washington. Now in early 1881, there was hardly a sign of such an attitude.

The popular remembrance of Conkling's career is that he had a dispute with President Garfield and that led to the president's death. Therefore, it was Conkling's fault. Conkling's biographer adds to the story that the difference between the men was one of personalities—chiefly Conkling's—and had nothing to do with policy.[24] In the face of that version, here was the *Times* a week after Garfield's inauguration saying that railroad policy at Albany would have everything to do with party defeat in the coming November election. That is, the railroad leaders quieted their own apprehensions of their institution approaching a slippery slope by managing to corral a majority in one house of the legislature. They did not appreciate, however, that at the next election, they and their party would suffer losses. All of the half-breed correspondence with Garfield simply overlooked the more certain troubles arising for the closer 1881 state election and focused on the more distant prospects of trouble at the 1884 national convention.

Within a week of the *Chronicle's* first editorial on the canal, the paper returned to New York canal policy. The editorial compared the support for the canal in Albany and the railroaders' plan for legislation in Washington, recalling the opinion of the proto-Schumpeterites four years earlier.

A few seasons ago—about the time when the reduction of tolls in 1877 went into effect—the current feeling, at least with quite a respectable number, was that the canals had served their purpose, and might as well be allowed to go to decay, as no longer fit to compete with railroads. We hear scarcely anything of this now. There has been a decided turn in public opinion on the subject, and the policy of maintaining and developing the waterways seems to be fully determined upon. Probably the success of the low-tolls experiment, which was begun in 1877 under the unfavorable circumstances and against the opposition mentioned in our article last week, has had not a little to do with bringing about this change. A still more potent influence has probably been the growing jealousy of the railroads. There can be no combination on the canals and lakes—-competition will always be unrestricted there. It is becoming understood that developed water communications must bring into play a natural law of competition which will regulate charges more exactly and infallibly, as well as more wisely, than all statutes that can be framed. This natural law can neither be repealed, nor evaded, nor abused.[25]

The *Chronicle* editor was urging that the Erie Canal was sufficient to the task of national regulation and that a new federal bureaucracy was unnecessary. From that paper's view, the U.S. Senate Democratic slate for the judiciary committee looked forward to a federal law creating such a bureaucracy that would have to assume its own risks. Among those risks was that some future Congress might repeal it. Or, the new bureaucracy could set up standards that could be evaded. Worst of all, that bureaucracy might abuse its position. Happily, the state had a bird in hand, the canal, forever freeing the matter from such troubles, leaving the other options as two birds in the bush (the Reagan bill or the Adams plan). For a brief period, in early March 1881, minds were being made up, and the most attractive option in New York was the *status quo*.

The New York Anti-Monopoly League in Full Flower

Concurrently, while U.S. Senate Republicans caucused to work out plans for taking over the Senate committees, the March 12, 1881, *Times* carried a report on the dramatic growth of the Anti-Monopoly League.

> Branches are now established in 25 States, and the mails bring from 40 to 50 letters every day asking for constitutions, by-laws, and instructions. The managers now propose to devote their special attention to the organization of branch societies in the several assembly districts in this City. One was formed in the First District on Tuesday night . . . Another was formed in the Twelfth District on Thursday night . . . Another will be formed in the Third District next Tuesday night, and thereafter the managers intend to organize at the rate of one district every two nights until the 24 are completed. The managers have distributed 40,000 copies of their "Appeal to the Public" and are preparing for distribution of 20,000 copies of secretary of the state [sic] Windom's letter and Mr. Lloyd's article on the Standard Oil Company in the March *Atlantic*.

The press coverage for the canal and the anti-monopolist causes had been right on the mark, coming just as the U.S. Senate was considering committee organization. By comparison, the press for the cartel plan was defensive. While occupying the pinnacle of American attention, they detested anyone bothering them. The monopolists had written in another journal pleading "to be let alone," and the *Times* had to remind the companies that they should not shudder at penal legislation. "The argument in favor of criminal legislation is not that all men are thieves and all humans deal in robbery, but that the community should be protected against exceptional crime, and that no instances should be permitted to pass with impunity."[26] Governor Cullom of Illinois had used the same argument in rejecting the request to repeal inactive granger legislation.

After the U.S. Senate Democrats made public their plan for committees on March 10, one can imagine Conkling in Washington, copies of the *Times* and the *Chronicle* in hand, circulating among his peers in the caucus rooms. He could boast of the canal as a key regulator of the railroads, as the papers said, and he could minimize the Adams plan. In turn, since New York handled two-thirds of the commerce, a strong showing of New York opinion was hard to rebut. Blaine, earlier in the year, had described the stalwarts as "bad men" set on Caribbean expansion. When it became clear that the stalwarts only wanted to save the nation from a new federal bureaucracy in the belief that the canal could do the work of regulation, Blaine had not a word to say. No less critical, no evidence exists that Garfield made a fair appraisal of the options discussed in the papers. While he had been quite circumspect about gathering information on the Virginia debt question, neither he nor Adams made field trips regarding the canal nor did they ask for help in assembling information from New Yorkers.

Over the weekend, the Republicans settled some matters. First, they decided to accept Mahone's vote to organize committees. All Mahone wanted in exchange was for the Senate to elect Gorham, H. H. Riddleberger, and Charles Johnson to fill the posts of secretary of the Senate, sergeant at arms, and clerk respectively. In turn, Gorham would commit the Senate patronage to work in Mahone's Virginia campaign.

Gains and Losses for the Railroaders in Senate Judiciary Matters

On Monday, March 14, high drama unfolded in the Senate. First, the Senate received President Garfield's nomination of Stanley Matthews for the U.S. Supreme Court.[27] Hayes had submitted the same name, but it had died in committee. Matthews, a former senator from Ohio, had served as an attorney for the Union Pacific and in 1878 the *Times* had condemned him as a spokesman for Gould.[28] The new nomination probably surprised Conkling for he had told Gorham that Garfield informed him in their February meeting that he would not resubmit Matthews.[29] Unfamiliar with Garfield's promise to consult with Reid on court nominations, the New York senator had taken Garfield's February comment as binding. Now, in a flash, Conkling had to conclude that the new president was not as good as his word. Furthermore, the Democratic judiciary committee would likely approve the Matthews nomination as the first step in making the court friendlier to the railroads.

On the face of it, the Matthews nomination proved quite awkward, since it put too many attorneys for the Pacific railroads in the mix: Senator Hill and Stanley Matthews had both served as corporate attorneys. Hill had defended the companies before the Supreme Court on the Thurman Act and would take a seat on the committee approving the nomination of Stanley Matthews. The *Times* on March 15 found the Matthews nomination "injudicious and objectionable . . . without excuse." In addition, Conkling probably considered the fact that the railroaders had not budged on the state commission bill at Albany. Therefore, to proceed with the Democratic plan in Washington for the judiciary committee would mean that they would have a combined influence through both the New York Senate and the U.S. Senate.

To cast his opposition to the Democratic slate, Conkling turned to humor. Remembering the popular charges against him as the chief of the spoils system, Conkling may have decided that turnabout was fair play. Anyone could see that Ohio was getting too much. Garfield of Ohio was nominating Matthews of Ohio for the Court. Recent news from Columbus told that Ohio legislators found they could not curb the new Western Union monopoly; [30] and Lloyd's article in the March *Atlantic* had criticized Ohio's Rockefeller. Conkling could not resist reaching back to some of his repartee with the former Senator Thurman of Ohio, who had referred to Ohio as the "land of the law and of erudition."[31] Commenting on the Democrat slate, Conkling remarked,

> For example, both the senators from Ohio [Sherman and Pendleton] were put on one and the same committee, the judiciary committee, in order probably that the great State of Ohio might not only give the country the land of the law but the law of the land. (Laughter.)[32]

Giving "the country . . . the law of the land" could have very reasonably referred to the favor Rockefeller had won in Ohio. Conkling was implying that it was premature to take that Ohio idea and apply it to New York's railroading difficulties. For one thing, many New Yorkers did not want to go in that direction especially in handling the difficulties raised by Gould's consolidation of three telegraph companies.

The tables were turned. While it was popular to charge that Conkling could not rise above a postal or customs position, it seemed Garfield could not rise above spoils for Ohioans. Trying to make the Senate hospitable for the Adams bill now waiting in the House had very poor support. Adams's book came out in 1878, but the 1879 New York state convention had not adopted a plank to support his view, nor had the national platform of 1880. In his letter of acceptance Garfield had decided not to mention railroad matters. No less important, in recent weeks both the press and popular opinion had been decidedly against it. If Garfield ever learned of Conkling's comments, he could have either smiled or winced. Later, among his friends Conkling would laughingly refer to "The United States of Ohio."[33] Ohio, smartly boasting of its new oil trust that quashed all competition, would not provide the model for railroading in New York, the heartland of competition at the port and throughout the canals.

Monday the 14th also brought the surprising announcement of Mahone's shift to the Republican side. Most surprised was Ben Hill of Georgia, who was on the pending Democrats' slate for judiciary. Hill had been out of town for a few days and on arriving back on Monday, he must have at once realized that the Republicans would organize the committees. Hill would fail to win a seat on the prize committee and not take a place in the cartel elite.

Hill was furious. He went to the Senate floor and made a venomous attack on Mahone, putting the Virginia Readjuster under cross-examination, even before he had voted on anything, shocking many members. The Virginian made a powerful response. Senator George Hoar of Massachusetts, probably recalling the prewar episode when a southerner had caned Charles Sumner, retorted:

> I think it is due to American manhood to express my emphatic indignation at the exhibition which the senator from Georgia has made so degrading as it seems to me to the character of this body . . . in whatever part of this Republic we may dwell no slave master or plantation overseer is to wave his whip over the heads of American senators.[34]

Even Democrat Daniel Voorhees of Indiana condemned Hill, saying, "I hope that no such scene as we have witnessed this afternoon will ever occur again."[35]

The Prospects for Biracial Politics in Virginia

Hill's attack had its own repercussions. The next day Mrs. Garfield sent Mahone flowers from the First Family greenhouse. For a moment, things looked up for Gorham! Virginia Democrats responded next with flowers for Hill. More importantly, on March 15th in Petersburg, a statewide gathering of black Republicans, which John Syphax had called, announced that they were thrilled by Mahone's response to Hill. They accordingly cast their votes for Mahone's course.[36] The Petersburg declaration was electric and gave promise of other southern states doing the same; the response was precisely what Gorham was looking for. The declaration held that:

> Principles and not names must guide our conduct; and in seeking good government here, for the good of all, we feel that we are not recreant to any duty properly incumbent upon a true Republican. Those who differ with us in this supreme moment of our fate are respectfully asked if they will not refrain from efforts to baffle us in this endeavor to improve our condition as men and as Virginians. We think we can see the dawn of a brighter day.

Gorham responded:

> They cannot be used by selfish schemers to forward the interests of a few place-hunters, claiming to be Republicans, nor can they be made to desert their noble and tried friend, General Mahone, in his great contest with their Bourbon enemies. The colored race of Virginia have set their faces against the handful of false leaders who desire to use them for false

and mercenary purposes, and have resolved to follow the lead of the man they have helped to send to the Senate. . . . The thirty odd thousand Democrats who are known as Readjusters are a standing army in favor of political rights for all. To their standard the colored race has rallied.[37]

Gorham had seen a "standing army" before. During the war in California, where many pioneers had sympathy for the South, the law exempted California males from the draft. As a home guard, they could counter any movement to take the state to the Confederate side. Now, in 1881, the white Readjusters of Virginia would serve as a standing army keeping the racist Bourbons from overwhelming the freed slaves in exercising their franchise.

The "new departure" was easy to understand. In southern states Afro-American Republicans would declare support for a white independent with a following. Together they could make a new majority against the white-supremacist Bourbons. The movement could have swept from Virginia into Tennessee and North Carolina, threatening the Solid South. Of course, that would have meant that some of the currently seated Democratic senators would lose their next elections. Now, with Mahone's help, the Republicans in the Senate would take over the committee organization and, in one fell swoop, would win not only chairs of committees but also office space in the Capitol. Who in the Republican caucus could complain about that? Since Gorham had worked so long in bringing Mahone to the Republican side, he shone as the benefactor. In both New York and Virginia, the stalwarts proved their skills in arousing timely public and editorial support for the cause of their friends. In public relations they left the monopolists far behind.

Collis P. Huntington Opposes Gorham for Re-election to Senate Office

That day, Gorham's foes began to plot his defeat. To begin with, he had no support from California railroaders. In 1876 he had sent the state legislature a lengthy, carefully developed opinion supporting the authority of the state to regulate rates,[38] an opinion anticipating Chief Justice Morrison Waite's decision the next year on *Munn v. Illinois*. In 1879 the California railroaders had taken control of the state Republican Party, and Gorham appeared on the scene to help save the provisions in the new state constitution for regulation.[39] A constitution party was founded which the Democrats later endorsed. Gorham was falsely accused in the campaign of deserting to the Democrats. Overlooked was his support for all the Republican candidates for Congress. As a result, the party leaders dropped him from the National Republican Committee, a post he had held since 1868.[40] On January 31, 1881, Reid wrote Garfield that:

> I asked Mr. Huntington privately what he thought of Mahon *[sic]*. He declared him to be an unscrupulous and utterly treacherous demagogue, and that nothing good could be gained from him in any way.

Mr. Huntington attributed the whole Mahone movement to the desire of George Gorham's to secure his vote in the Senate, and believed that Gorham was trying to use you to the same end.[41]

Another southern Republican might have entered the Senate. Democratic Party factionalism in Tennessee gave promise of sending one, but the plan fell through. Garfield's agents had not managed the options well. If they had succeeded, the Republicans would have had a majority in the U.S. Senate from the outset, and Mahone's place would not have become an important question.

Reid again wrote Garfield that California railroader Huntington claimed he was "a great friend of Conkling's. His associate of last summer [Gorham] is the reverse."[42] Californians understood the hostility. The *San Francisco Chronicle* three years later noted, when Gorham once again tried to regain the secretaryship, that the Central Pacific was his most prominent foe.[43]

Blaine was ready to move against Gorham at the first opportunity. He had intimated that he would do nothing to "build up Conkling, Cameron, or Gorham." On March 14, just as the Republican caucus began to take over committees, Secretary of State Blaine wrote the editor of the *Tribune*, probably referring to Gorham's recent comments about the *Tribune* on the appointment of Windom, "I believe the *Tribune* can beat Gorham. You see he never misses a chance to dig at you."[44] That is, since Gorham was making such remarks as he had, he might just "dig" the wrong person, say, some senators or even the president.

Blaine assumed that the *Tribune* should not come under Gorham's criticism. The paper had taken an extraordinarily preeminent role in American journalism. Monopolist Jay Gould, whose chief ally in Washington was Secretary of State James Blaine, owned it. Gould let Blaine supervise Whitelaw Reid, the editor. Finally, the President's fealty to the paper appeared in *Tribune* reporter E. V. Smalley taking a desk in the White House. Other editors must have observed this seating of the *Tribune* reporter. Their protest was virtually nonexistent.

This was the paper well known for the shenanigans it perpetrated. In the January refunding debate, it had warned that the Carlyle amendment would ruin resumption. Almost immediately about 140 banks withdrew from the national system. Again, the editor and the nominee for secretary of State may have promoted A. M. Gibson, Garfield's nemesis from the *Sun,* for a job in the new Department of Justice.

Mahone's Cautious Entry into the Senate and onto Committees

As an initiate in the U.S. Senate, Mahone moved cautiously. He sidestepped a joust over chamber seniority by taking his oath of office, as the *Congressional Record* shows, a day after the other newcomers took theirs. Above all, he could not afford to squander his prestige of having helped the Republicans gain control of the Senate. The new Senate majority, of course, would recognize the importance of his help, but it would not continually reward him. That would leave the impression that he was continuously throwing his weight around. No. Such good works while deserving recognition would be rewarded by only one prize in return. Mahone, therefore, had to be very careful about waiting for the right one. He wanted to see Gorham in the secretaryship and Riddleberger as sergeant at arms using their patronage to help him in the coming summer's campaign. Mahone certainly did not use his reward by taking more than the average of four committee seats, despite some claims that he took five.[45] (One incoming freshman, Joseph Hawley of Connecticut, unnoticed by historians, did take five seats beginning with the chair of civil service. The caucus might have allowed Hawley the extra seat for his helping negotiate committee assignments among the rest of the freshmen.)

Mahone would take the chair of the committee on agriculture. The committee's status was not very high since the Department of Agriculture did not have a cabinet seat. In addition, he took the chairmanship of agriculture on a condition. In a surprisingly deferential move Mahone yielded claims going with the post. As the chair of the agriculture committee, one would suspect that he would have had some discretion over appointment of the commissioner of Agriculture. The record, however, suggests that in entering the Senate he showed continued caution and relinquished that right. Ten New Englanders from the five coastal states wrote Garfield asking him to name a new commissioner of Agriculture, and Mahone must have agreed.

The New Englanders' candidate for commissioner of was former congressman George B. Loring of Massachusetts, a horticulturist. The incumbent, General William G. LeDuc from Minnesota, simply had to go. Not only was he a poor administrator, but he had little grasp of the rigors of agricultural experiments.[46] For patriotic reasons he had urged the domestic growth of sugar, a prospect causing institutional strain among the New England shipping interests. LeDuc's plan for domestic sugar would cut into their international trade.

During his four-year term, LeDuc published enough books and pamphlets to provide every American with almost eighteen pages, giving him great popularity among farm organizations. Prospects of his termination led some farm organizations to ask the president to retain him.[47] The New England senators, however, apparently wanted to return to their constituents at the ports with the news that the president had dropped LeDuc. For the long term, since sugar import fees comprised a large portion of federal receipts, LeDuc's policy would have required finding new revenues for the federal government. That would have certainly stirred things up.

On March 16th, the news appeared in Gorham's paper that ten New England senators had written to Garfield, asking him to name Loring commissioner of Agriculture. On the same day, Gorham also cryptically asked elsewhere on the editorial page, "Is this the *pons asinorum*?" The term refers to Euclid's fifth proposition and the attempt of dull-witted people to get over it. From Gorham's view, the petition exhibited a complete lack of political savvy. The reason? The New Englanders were asking Garfield for a favor--he would probably not grant it unless they reciprocated. The exchange, Gorham foresaw, would build a bridge to stupidity. The Boston *Globe* chided Gorham about his remark, but he in turn replied that he had said enough.

New England Senators Form a Hegemony over the Committees

In March 1881 it was the New England senators who cut the biggest swath in the caucus and not Mahone or Conkling as some authorities have thought. Collectively, the New England states faced the greatest imminent institutional strain in the federal system. A year later national bank charters were up for renewal--important in their region, which had the largest banking franchises. Since some Democrats and the greenbackers were agitating for abolishing national banking, the New England senators had a special responsibility. In some manner they had to influence the opinion of western party members or hazard another split.

The New Englanders advanced an arrangement of the committees they had first applied in the second session of the 45th Congress (December 1877). It would bring to bear the principles of durability and redundancy. It was a discipline that senators had used earlier to arrange the committees on the Pacific Railroads seating two members from each of three specified committees. More recently, senators used the same discipline in bonding the committees of commerce, judiciary, and foreign affairs by relying on two members from the upper Mississippi valley to sit with Conkling on those three committees.

In 1881 the New Englanders had a new twist. They placed each of seven western seniors—heads of their state delegations in the Congress—on no fewer than two of their committees. The westerners included Roscoe Conkling of New York, John Sherman of Ohio, Thomas Ferry of Michigan, William Allison of Iowa, Angus Cameron of Wisconsin, John Ingalls of Kansas, and John Jones of Nevada.[48] John Logan of Illinois would sit under Edmunds on judiciary and under Allison on appropriations. That meant that two New England senators were looking over the shoulders of each of these westerners including Logan who sat under one as well as under Iowan Allison, a member of the New England hegemony. [As for a discipline among New Englanders, Richard E. Welch, Jr., Hoar's biographer, has a different view.[49]]

243

The Chief Clerk read the list, as follows:

STANDING COMMITTEES.

On Privileges and Elections—Messrs. Hoar, (chairman,) Cameron of Wisconsin, Teller, Sherman, Frye, Saulsbury, Hill of Georgia, Vance, and Pugh.

On Foreign Relations—Messrs. Burnside, (chairman,) Conkling, Edmunds, Miller, Ferry, Johnston, Morgan, Hill of Georgia, and Pendleton.

On Finance—Messrs. Morrill, (chairman,) Sherman, Ferry, Jones of Nevada, Allison, Platt of New York, Bayard, Voorhees, Beck, McPherson, and Harris.

On Appropriations—Messrs. Allison, (chairman,) Logan, Dawes, Plumb, Hale, Davis of West Virginia, Beck, Ransom, and Cockrell.

On Commerce—Messrs. Conkling, (chairman,) McMillan, Jones of Nevada, Kellogg, Conger, Ransom, Coke, Farley, and Vest.

On Manufactures—Messrs. Conger, (chairman,) Hale, Sewell, McPherson, and Williams.

On Agriculture—Messrs. Mahone, (chairman,) Blair, Plumb, Van Wyck, Davis of West Virginia, Slater, and George.

On Military Affairs—Messrs. Logan, (chairman,) Burnside, Cameron of Pennsylvania, Harrison, Sewell, Cockrell, Maxey, Grover, and Hampton.

On Naval Affairs—Messrs. Cameron of Pennsylvania, (chairman,) Anthony, Rollins, Miller, Mahone, McPherson, Jones of Florida, Vance, and Farley.

On the Judiciary—Messrs. Edmunds, (chairman,) Conkling, Logan, Ingalls, McMillan, Garland, Davis of Illinois, Bayard, and Lamar.

On Post-Offices and Post-Roads—Messrs. Ferry, (chairman,) Hill of Colorado, Platt of New York, Sawyer, Mahone, Maxey, Saulsbury, Farley, and Groome.

On Public Lands—Messrs. Plumb, (chairman,) Hill of Colorado, Blair, Van Wyck, McDill, Jones of Florida, Grover, Walker, and Morgan.

On Private Land Claims—Messrs. Bayard, (chairman), Jonas, Call, Edmunds, and Allison.

On Indian Affairs—Messrs. Dawes, (chairman,) Ingalls, Saunders, Logan, Cameron of Wisconsin, Coke, Pendleton, Walker, and Slater.

On Pensions—Messrs. Teller, (chairman,) Platt of Connecticut, Blair, Mitchell, Edgerton, Groome, Slater, Jackson, and Camden.

On Revolutionary Claims—Messrs. Johnston, (chairman,) Jones of Florida, Hill of Georgia, Anthony, and Dawes.

On Claims—Messrs. Cameron of Wisconsin, (chairman,) Frye, Teller, Hoar, Conger, Pugh, Jackson, George, and Fair.

On the District of Columbia—Messrs. Ingalls, (chairman,) Rollins, McMillan, Hawley, McDill, Harris, Butler, Vance, and Gorman.

On Patents—Messrs. Platt of Connecticut, (chairman,) Hoar, Mitchell, Edgerton, Coke, Call, and Williams.

On Territories—Messrs. Saunders, (chairman,) Kellogg, McDill, Sawyer, Butler, Garland, and Vest.

On Railroads—Messrs. Kellogg, (chairman,) Teller, Saunders, Hawley, Sawyer, Sewell, Lamar, Grover, Williams, Jonas, and Brown.

On Mines and Mining—Messrs. Hill of Colorado, (chairman,) Jones of Nevada, Van Wyck, Miller, Hampton, Fair, and Camden.

On the Revision of the Laws of the United States—Messrs. McMillan, (chairman,) Platt of Connecticut, Hale, Davis of Illinois, and Pendleton.

On Education and Labor—Messrs. Blair, (chairman,) Morrill, Burnside, Edgerton, Mahone, Maxey, Brown, George, and Fair.

On Civil Service and Retrenchment—Messrs. Hawley, (chairman,) Rollins, Jones of Nevada, Hill of Colorado, Butler, Walker, and Williams.

To Audit and Control the Contingent Expenses of the Senate—Messrs. Jones of Nevada, (chairman,) Platt of Connecticut, and Vance.

On Engrossed Bills—Messrs. Saulsbury, (chairman,) Call, and Conkling.

On Rules—Messrs. Frye, (chairman,) Hoar, Sherman, Call, and Gorman.

On the Improvements of the Mississippi River and Tributaries—Messrs Mitchell, (chairman,) Kellogg, Van Wyck, Frye, Jonas, Cockrell, and Jackson.

On Transportation Routes to the Seaboard—Messrs. Harrison, (chairman,) Cameron of Pennsylvania, Blair, Platt of New York, Beck, Voorhees, and Camden.

Joint Committee on Public Printing—Messrs. Anthony, (chairman,) Hawley, and Gorman.

Joint Committee on Enrolled Bills—Messrs. Platt of New York, (chairman,) Rollins, and Pugh.

Joint Committee on the Library—Messrs. Sherman, (chairman,) Hoar, and Voorhees.

Joint Committee on Public Buildings and Grounds—Messrs. Rollins, (chairman,) Morrill, Cameron of Wisconsin, Jones of Florida, and Vest.

Source: *Congressional Record* 47th Congress, March 18, 1881.

In the 47th Congress, committee assignments were as follows for senior Republicans who came from outside New England.

New York's Conkling chaired commerce and took seats on foreign affairs under Burnside of Rhode Island and on judiciary under Edmunds of Vermont.

Ohio's Sherman chaired library and took seats on rules under Frye of Maine, on privileges and elections under Hoar of Massachusetts, and on finance under Morrill of Vermont.

Michigan's Ferry chaired post offices and sat on finance under Morrill of Vermont and on foreign affairs under Burnside of Rhode Island.

Iowa's Allison chaired appropriations, and his two other assignments were on finance under Morrill of Vermont and on Private Land Claims under Edmunds of the same state.

Wisconsin's Cameron chaired claims and sat under Hoar of Massachusetts on privileges and elections, under Dawes of Massachusetts on Indian affairs, under Rollins of New Hampshire on public buildings and grounds, and under Hale of Maine on tenth census.

Kansas' Ingalls chaired District of Columbia and sat under Dawes of Massachusetts on Indian affairs, and under Edmunds of Vermont on judiciary.

Finally, Nevada's Jones chaired audit and control and sat under Morrill of Vermont on finance and under Hawley of Connecticut on civil service.

The most practical consequence of the arrangement was that each of these westerners knew that he was subject to being stopped anywhere in Washington by a New Englander for a conversation. They could be stopped not only in the Senate chamber or committee rooms, but also in the hallways, in the hotel lobbies, or by chance on the street. The New Englander would have initiated the conversation especially if he needed to back up information suggesting that some harm might come to New England interests. Likewise, each of these westerners could expect to hear from the two New Englanders he sat under if they thought that he held the wrong ideas on finances.

For the next thirty-five years, western senior Republicans would find themselves in this continuing relationship with New Englanders, i.e., each senior westerner seated under at least two chairs from New England. For example, twenty years later, John C. Spooner of Wisconsin and James McMillan of Michigan were both members of the Senate's "Big Four," along with Nelson W. Aldrich of Rhode Island and Orville H. Platt of Connecticut. The two westerners, in all of their secondary assignments, sat exclusively under other members from New England who served either as committee chairs or as ranking minority members.

These relations were well managed. The committee slates for the Congresses subsequent to 1881 show that when a New England senator left, the redundant channels with the westerner(s) who sat under him were maintained. Another New England senator would simply fill in the vacancy in the hegemony. If a western senior left the Senate, the junior senator from the same state moved up to replace him by taking seats under at least two New England chairs. This arrangement kept the New England elite well informed of the burgeoning economy in the Old Northwest, especially with its shipping traffic on the Great Lakes where, on any summer day, one could see a hundred vessels plying the waters. Further, this arrangement of the facts and this explanation suggests that historian Charles Beard in his conviction that the "northeast fixed poverty on the South and the West" may have missed only slightly the fact that New Englanders in the U.S. Senate had a firm fix on the Republican caucus.

The new relations in the Senate were important in the evolution of national banking. "Resource deployment strategy within the private sector," according to Laumann and Knoke, "is more important than resource mobilization within the public sector in explaining the resource flow."[50] That is, businesses do transfer or elevate their resources to the government. While the bankers had been inactive at the time of the silver bill, by the time of the 1878 fall election, they had called on every member of Congress and then had taken part in the campaign itself. Again, in 1880 bankers were notable in their support of the Republican ticket. Subsequently, the senators from New England elevated themselves over western peers so that they could monitor them, showing how the resource mobilization of the bankers finally became the stewardship of the New England delegation to the Senate, an arrangement that continued to 1913. In that year, the resource deployment was turned over from the Senate to the new Federal Reserve System, and the New England senators were relieved of their monitoring duties.

The New Englanders' ambition to have better information in the Senate also appears from another statistic. In the 47th Congress, with the Senate executive session opening in March 1881, enough contrasts with previous Congresses appeared to make a story. One way to measure the new ubiquity of New Englanders on committees is to count the number of committees seating no New Englander and those seating two or more, then to contrast that set of figures with the New Englanders' experience in the 43rd Congress, at the outset of President Ulysses S. Grant's second term, following the independents' bolt.

Table 9. *Distribution of New England Senators among Committees in the 43rd Congress compared to the 47th Congress, 1873 and 1881.*

	43rd Congress	47th Congress
Number of Committees Seating:		
No New Englanders	12 (36%)	6 (15%)
Two or more New Englanders	4 (12%)	17 (43%)
Total number of Committees	33	39
Source: CR, 43rd Cong., Spec. Sess., Vol. 1, p. 48, and 47th Cong., exec. Sess. Vol. 12, pp. 33f.		

While New England had but one-twelfth of the nation's population, and half of the population now lived west of the Alleghenies, in 1881 the New Englanders in the U.S. Senate placed two members on almost half the committees, seventeen committees in number, up from four committees in the 43ʳᵈ Congress. Correspondingly, the New Englanders in 1881 failed to take seats in six committees, down from twelve committees in the 43ʳᵈ Congress.

In committee meetings the principles of group dynamics would likely prevail, favoring the New Englanders. Two well-informed members supporting a point can often win a majority. Further, if western members wanted their chairs' support for their projects, they would more likely first accede to their chairs' interests. Weinstein shows that the New England regional interest was apparent in 1876 and strong thereafter.[51] The evidence fits well with the hard-money scenario developed here. In that period the region turned strongly to the gold standard. Subsequently their senators, when arranging committees, would assume a discipline forcing them to give careful attention to their western peers, to make their own demands on them. That would greatly limit the chance of a party schism, such as had occurred during the silver debate of 1877–78. The New Englanders arranged the Senate committee system as hegemony in the sense of *realpolitik*, since senior westerners could no longer initiate their own collaboration without New Englanders knowing about it. They had enough members to do so, something a single actor like the allegedly "powerful" Conkling would never have been able to do. The subject needs further study. William Aydellotte, quoted above, has said that:

> A formal quantitative arrangement of the evidence forces upon the investigator's attention the discrepancies between theories and observations, the points at which they do not correspond. Robert K. Merton says, the quantitative anomaly, unlike many qualitative ones, cannot be easily evaded. "The very nakedness of the results, the intolerable character of the discrepancy of this kind, is a stimulant to reformulation and may also give a good indication of the direction in which it can be attempted.[52]

As Gretchen Ritter put it, "The national hegemony of the Republicans placed a premium on cross-sectional unity which constrained the emergence of Republican greenbackism in the Midwest."[53]

John Sherman's Comments in 1878 about National Banking May Have Restricted His Committee Choices in 1881

In the Republican organization of Senate committees in March 1881 the leadership seems to have taken pains to isolate greenbacker John Sherman of Ohio from having influence in the rest of the Senate. Between the 38ᵗʰ and 44ᵗʰ Congress, he rose to chair the committee on finance. In 1877 he became Secretary of the Treasury under President Hayes. The next year, in testimony before congressional committees, Secretary of the

Treasury Sherman had shown himself an apostate on national banking. He had suggested that if a choice were forced between banknotes and greenbacks, the latter would prevail. In 1881 the New Englanders appear to have exacted a price for that comment from Sherman. When he returned to the Senate he failed to regain the chair of finance. New Englander Justin Morrill of Vermont, the Republican ranking member, simply would not yield.[54] Furthermore, in all his secondary assignments he was seated only under New Englanders. On the rules committee he sat under Frye of Maine, on privileges and elections, under Hoar of Massachusetts, and, most disconcerting to him, on finance under Morrill. In spite of his great record at Treasury in guiding the nation to the resumption of species payment, he was given the chair of the committee on library. From that post he could have hardly developed alliances with any other committee chairs except those from New England. Fellow westerners would be out of reach.

These committee arrangements allow the surmise that the New Englanders wanted no difficulty from Sherman, a greenbacker in 1878, as they looked forward to passage of national bank rechartering in 1882. The New England senators probably realized that banking leaders in their region did not want Sherman taking a significant part in the national banking debate. So the New Englanders in the Senate put Sherman out to pasture. While seated under Morrill on finance, Sherman could come up with plans for the much-needed expansion of library facilities and win Morrill's support. The Vermonter would have welcomed more work for the quarries of Vermont. The library would come to completion after both Sherman and Morrill left the Senate.

Gorham's Plaintive Appeal to President Garfield for Help in His Re-Election to the Senate

If the hard-money advocates brought most of the Republican seniors under their inspection, and also set aside Sherman for his mild part in the 1878 elections, little wonder if they did not forget Gorham for what he had said at Newark in 1878. In March 1881, Gorham foresaw the coming juggernaut. At first, things looked promising for him in the new administration. Both Garfield and Gorham had worked on the Indiana November election. In December, as a member of the bi-factional delegation that had gone to Mentor, Ohio, he read aloud to Garfield the fifty-seven-page statement from Mahone on the Virginia debt. He then became editor of the party paper, largely owned by Thomas Brady of the postal contract office. By the midmonth clamor over the telegraph consolidation, he realized that he occupied a vulnerable spot. His only help could come from the president, and he probably saw Garfield one more time before the inauguration. The relations between the two probably chilled, as Garfield realized that Gorham's taking the editorship and then retaking the Senate office would give him the advantage, along with his campaign skills, of building an alliance in the Senate. Gorham could retain that post as long as the Republicans retained the control of the Senate, while Garfield would have to face renomination and re-election in four years. That would put Garfield in the position of looking for favors from Gorham. The president would leave no one confused about his journalistic preferences when he allowed E. V. Smalley of the *Tribune* to take a desk at the White House.

Somewhere along the line, the two men may have discussed the differences that had arisen between them in the 1878 campaign. Familiar enough with each other to adopt nicknames, Gorham turned to the literature of Charles Dickens. He dubbed himself Wilkins Micawber, a profligate character, and dubbed Garfield David Copperfield, among the most circumspect.

With the new administration in place, Gorham's column on March 18, 1881, carried a plaintive appeal inferring that he had asked Brady to sell him the paper, but had had no luck. Gorham explained,

> Mr. Micawber has not been heard from for some days. But he has not been idle. He has been making a personal examination of the various situations to which fate, or the president, might have called him, for he believed to the last that something would turn up. But, copying his illustrious predecessor, he has now written to his young friend Copperfield as follows:

> My Dear Young Friend: The die is cast. All is over. Hiding the ravages of care with a sickly mask of mirth, I have not informed you that there is no hope * * * Under these circumstances, alike humiliating to endure, humiliating to contemplate, and humiliating to relate, I have discharged the pecuniary liability contracted at this establishment by giving a note of hand, made payable fourteen days after the date at my residence * * * When it becomes due it will not be taken up. The result is destruction. The bolt is impending, and the tree must fall . . . This is the last communication, my dear Copperfield, you will ever receive.

> From
>   The
>   Beggard
>   Outcast
>   Wilkins
>   Micawber

Does the President appreciate Mr. Micawber's condition? [55]

Gorham felt the hard-money influences against his apostasy as much as Sherman had, and that bespoke collective action on that side of the line among parties most concerned about passage of the national bank bill.

Unfortunately, Senate observers did not note the hard-money hegemony at the time. Later, one prominent student, Woodrow Wilson, sought a hero in the body, but was disappointed. *The Congressional Quarterly* explained:

> When Conkling resigned his Senate seat in 1881. . ., the Senate reverted to its old independent ways. "No one," wrote Woodrow Wilson in 1885, "is the senator. No one may speak for his party as well as for himself; no one exercises the special trust of acknowledged leadership. The Senate is merely a body of critics." [56]

But Wilson's comment was only a conjecture about Senate leadership. The comment has more to suggest about Wilson's hankering for the heroic and finding it wanting.

Beneath Conkling's grasp of leadership the New Yorker showed that he appreciated the Senate practice of relying less on heroes than on a reliable method of information management. Senators before Conkling, especially in arranging the committee on Pacific railroads, had relied on the principles of durability and redundancy. Conkling did likewise in linking upper Mississippi valley interests to the port of New York. After he resigned, the New Englanders continued to apply the same principles. Yet Wilson's view remains strong to this day. That view assumes that the heroic vision in which Conkling led by his individual strength did not have to rely on a network of information-sharing allies. While Wilson's heroic view prevailed in popular analysis, the members of the Senate probably paid only passing attention. They probably liked what the young academic had written from his base in Calvinistic melodrama. The view added to outsiders' confusion and let the Senate proceed with less interference. To use Wilson's words, if any network developed a "special trust of acknowledged leadership," it was the New Englanders from 1881 onward, who rose to that status and kept abreast of most key westerners seated under them.

The Republican-Organized Senate Judiciary Committee

In March 1881 Republican senators made another marked change. While the New Englanders appear to have arranged seating to protect national banking, the Senate caucus would hardly prove as friendly to railway consolidation. Instead they agreed that western senators could help provide an answer. The Democratic plan for the judiciary committee on March 10 had slated three railroad specialists—two from Ohio where Rockefeller's new trust had made a great impression—but in the Republican plan for that committee, those three names were nowhere to be seen. The Republicans would drop Hill of Georgia, the railroad attorney; Pendleton of Ohio, the railroad president; and Sherman of Ohio, the statistician. While the weakened Adams bill had surfaced in the House—meaning it was headed for the Senate—the cartelists could not now count on smooth sailing for their proposition in the Senate. Ohio would not have one seat on judiciary.

The Republican plan for judiciary greatly illuminated the schism in the party over regulation policy. Where the Democrats had put forward members on the committee pleasing to the cartel, the Republicans put forward members pleasing to the anti-monopoly movement. The most marked change came from dropping Ben Hill of Georgia, known for his stand in the Supreme Court against the Thurman Act. The Republicans looked in exactly the opposite direction for a replacement. *In Hill's place was a granger, Samuel McMillan of Minnesota, who had served on the state court from 1864 and became chief justice ten years later. In that year the court issued its decision finding the state granger law constitutional.* [Italics ours.] *(John D. Blake and others vs. Winona & St. Peter Ry. Co, Minnesota Reports, 1872–73*, pp. 362–376.)[57] In comparison to the Democrats' nomination of a corporate attorney for the committee, the Republican nomination of granger jurist McMillan was probably as diametrically opposed to Hill as one could get. The Republican Senate caucus had allowed its judiciary committee to quarantine the senators from Ohio, the president's state. McMillan would be valuable to the committee due to his standing as having been a chief justice of a state court; he could enlist such people to testify. (Our emphasis.)

The popular press most likely helped in the choice. Francis Thurber, the leader of the New York–based Anti-Monopoly League, had begun a revival of grangerism, which the *Times* furthered in its rebuke of Leland Stanford's defense of monopolism. In addition, Thurber had circulated Henry Demarest Lloyd's *Atlantic* article about how the Hepburn committee had examined the collusion between Vanderbilt and Rockefeller. Already well known as the financial editor of Medill's *Chicago Tribune*, Lloyd had written an article so popular that it went into several printings. Such a surge of anti-monopoly activity may explain why the Republican judiciary committee gave two seats to the men from Illinois, Logan and Davis, and nothing to Ohio. Ohio seemed to shelter resources for the monopolists, such as Pendleton from Cincinnati, the connection at Toledo between Gould's Wabash Railroad and Vanderbilt's New York Central, and Rockefeller's operation near Cleveland. By contrast, the state of Illinois sheltered resources for the anti-monopolists. They included Lloyd on the *Chicago Tribune* staff; independent David Davis, who could speak up against corporate behavior; and Governor Shelby Cullom, who had taken steps to strengthen the granger laws and had support in a consequential terminal city. Further, Logan, an advocate of the Hennepin Canal, would have had a local constituency favoring the water route to the Mississippi, forcing competition on the railroads. Logan, although later opposed to Cullom's legislation for interstate commerce, like McMillan, would have been sensitive to people concerned about the competition between rails and water routes.

Not to be overlooked, the stalwarts seemed much more skilled in making use of the press, a suggestion taken from the fact that the three men nominated for Senate office all had press responsibilities. For secretary was Gorham at the *National Republican;* for sergeant-at-arms was H. H. Riddleberger of Woodstock, Virginia, where he edited a paper; and for chief clerk was Charles W. Johnson of Minnesota, a correspondent for the

St. Paul Pioneer Dispatch, this latter name continuing the integrity of the New York–upper Mississippi valley alliance. Concurrently, in March members of the cartel and supporters were just beginning to talk among themselves about better press beginning with articles placed in the magazines that had recently carried anti-monopoly articles.[58] Finally, considering the quality of the legislation waiting in the House of Representatives to come to the U.S. Senate, the Republican plan for the judiciary committee was warranted. The so-called Adams bill of 1881 was more appearance than reality. As the Massachusetts commission had written the New York Chamber of Commerce at the beginning of the year, the proposed legislation in the House was but a shadow of the law that the Bay Staters were currently practicing. If that was the proposal that was to come before the U.S. Senate, the people around Conkling were quite justified in arranging a committee that would examine whatever the cartel leaders had in mind. If the plan had received a better journalistic examination in January when it was first proposed, it might have been laughed out of court, and by March 1881 be of no further concern. But that did not happen, and the cartelists pressed forward with their proposition.

The collapse of the Democratic gambit for judiciary rippled on into the Democratic plan for foreign affairs. While the Democrats had slated three freshman friends of Blaine, the committee would now include, in addition to Conkling, two other Republican seniors, Ferry of Michigan and Edmunds of Vermont, and only one freshman, Miller of California. Ferry had served with Blaine on rules; Edmunds had served with Conkling on judiciary, thereby perpetuating the alliance; and Miller of California needed help to win adjustments in the China treaty. Blaine's loss of his friends on foreign affairs and the three railroad senators on judiciary most likely outraged him.

The Railroad Lobby's Retreat after the Republican Organization of the Senate

The changes in judiciary from the Democratic plan to the Republican plan amounted to a dramatic loss for the railroaders. The important antepenultimate step was to win a hospitable reception in the U.S. Senate by stacking the judiciary committee: From the time of (a) Vanderbilt's announcement in September 1879 of his legislative goals and willingness to confer with business leaders, to (b) Lloyd's writing that the big three would dictate that the Adams plan be adopted, through (c) the threats during the national convention to suppress public discussion, and (d) the *Times'* December 1880 complaint that it had no hint what the railroaders might present for legislation, to (e) the House committee on commerce finally including the Adams bill in a package of three options, they would still have to win Senate approval and adjustment with the House. But the railroaders did not understand how to lobby their case, let alone negotiate for the naming of committee members. Their effort proved to be an unmitigated disaster. In the entire history of Washington lobbying, the episode stands out as one of the clumsiest episodes ever. Yet, despite the railroaders' poor lobbying, it is easy to imagine that the railroad executives in several company offices in New York City reading the Republican slate for judiciary on the front page of the paper would have been aghast. What they read was that the men

Adams had suggested to the Democrats were out, completely replaced. Most startling to them would have been that the Republicans had dropped Ben Hill, the corporation attorney in the sinking fund case, and substituted William McMillan, a granger from the Minnesota state supreme court. With the other two, Sherman and Pendleton, also dropped, it meant that Ohioans were excluded from the judiciary committee.

The cartel now had no convincing help to process the Adams plan through the U.S. Congress. If they took it before the Republican committee on the judiciary, the committee could have conducted a more open hearing than the railroaders wanted. They had already eschewed that course by the defeat of Grant, followed by the announcement of an alleged gag rule, and they would not return to it now. Laumann and Knoke point out that the final phase of a policy scenario includes selecting the agenda of a sufficiently respected agency where a vote can finally settle the dispute. The railroaders had selected the Senate judiciary committee, but only on their conditions and without an agreement with the anti-monopolists. Once the judiciary committee came under Republican control, they had to retreat. Vanderbilt had looked for legislation from "Congress first." But no more! The Republican plan gave the consolidators a greater legislative challenge than they could meet. After consultation, the cartel leaders must have decided to take it as a loss that had to be overcome. The value of Laumann and Knoke's concepts rests in their capacity to lead the reader precisely to this point in the legislative process, identifying where the cartelists lost control over the scenario.

The moves on the political stage were dramatic. Popular opinion had likely led to reversing the make-up of the judiciary committee. The New York Chamber of Commerce's August survey of the questionnaires returned from peer organizations showed strong opposition to monopolists' practices. Those boards of trade around the country were much more favorable to the Reagan bill. Later, in November 1881, federal statistician Joseph Nimmo confirmed Lloyd's earlier criticism that the railroads had tried to dictate the course they wanted. In the midst of the long rate war among the railroads, Nimmo wrote:

> [I]t is impossible at present to pass final judgment upon pooling organizations. As yet they are tentative and on probation. Too little is known by the public in regard to their practical workings and the methods employed and the expedients resorted to in carrying them into effect to justify State governments or the National government in conferring upon them *at once and unconditionally* the attributes of legality.[59] (Our emphasis.)

The cartel had tried to play king-of-the-hill all the way to organizing a Senate committee. The faulty estimate they had taken of their opposition would show in time. Nimmo mentioned that the cartel was on probation. That probation would end for the cartel six years later when, in the voting on the ICC legislation, merchants from throughout the country showed up at Washington and successfully lobbied against the pooling of rates.

From 1881 until that law was passed, business leaders throughout the country could recall that the cartel had tried surreptitiously to press the case for its legislation, and needed watching.

In 1881 the railroaders had built up a head of steam, looking to the Garfield administration to pass the Adams bill "at once and unconditionally." They dropped the ball and, due to the stand taken by the Republican judiciary committee, believed they were out of the picture. Adams himself had warned, more than two years earlier, that the process of national consolidation "is unlikely to prove a rapid one, for order is not easily established in any community, which has been long in a state of anarchy."[60] In the long history of railroad lobbying, that interest would never again try to gain what they thought in March of 1881 was their due. Most strange is that of all the criticism that befell Conkling, no one criticized him for frustrating the cartel's legislative program. It is as though the rest of the criticism of the senator, for whatever reason, served to distract attention from the most painful loss he forced the capitalists to suffer. The first evidence of the cartel capitulating came in April 1881 with comments Adams made in the *Nation*. The Senate had proven inhospitable to his plan, and Adams seemed to write with some defensiveness, suggesting that the failure was his. (Four years later Adams had another explanation––Reagan would not compromise[61]—and in his posthumously published autobiography, he would have still another reason.) Adams also thought that, after the failure in 1881, he was due at least a consolation prize. He wrote,

> Now, in dealing with the railroad corporations of this country, the passionate denunciation in which the orators of the Anti-Monopoly League are wont to indulge is not going to accomplish much. . . . What is needed, it seems to me, are continuous pressure, and the steady building up of legislation, which can only come through the employment of trained specialists—a class politicians despised, but of which the railroads avail themselves with good results to them. . . .

> I am so far from wishing to have any "employers" at all, or caring for their opinions, that there is but one possible position connected with the working out of this railroad problem which I covet. I should like for the next ten years to represent the United States officially in the discussion, which ought to take place; just as during ten of the last twelve years, I represented Massachusetts. There would then be, as far as I, at least, should be concerned, no terrible grapple with a great monopoly—no life-and-death struggle for popular liberty—nothing, I fancy, even remotely resembling that sort of thing. There would, though, be a good many tedious investigations—a great deal of rather intricate discussion—the gradual exposure of a large number of abuses; and, finally some very prosaic suggestions of laws calculated to correct them. It seems to me blood and thunder is a little

out of place here, though I dare say it may serve its purpose for a party leader almost in despair in his long hunt after a taking political issue.

I have no idea that either through myself, or any other more or less competent than I, the course I have indicated will be pursued. The dislike and distrust, not to say the contempt, felt for all specialists and specialist work in our political circles is so marked that it is ten to one the country will have to wallow through this difficulty, as it has wallowed though so many others.[62]

With the practical defeat of his bill, Adams now *volunteered himself in the place of a tribunal* as the single investigator of troublesome railroad matters. Adams wanted the special consideration that Joseph Nimmo enjoyed. Within the previous five or six years, Congress had found Nimmo, a trained engineer, so helpful to William Windom's committee on transportation routes to the seaboard that they created a new position for him at Treasury as the chief of the bureau of statistics. Subsequently, he issued a number of reports on railroading helpful to all sides. Now Adams wanted Congress to do as much for him, authorizing him to examine critical railroad problems laying the ground for legislation.

This was not the first time such a thought had occurred to Adams. In February 1878 Garfield had introduced HR 3384 for Adams, covering the use of the Army Corps of Engineers in quickly investigating railroad accidents.[63] Garfield could have asked for as much in his presidential inaugural address, or even earlier in the lame-duck session. Instituting the plan would have demonstrated the kind of work experts could do to analyze problems and offer recommendations. Adams would later complain that the popular mind had no appreciation of experts, but he lost a chance to show the public how they worked. Such a piecemeal approach to new law was not possible, because the cartel in their impatience wanted the whole thing "at once and unconditionally."

The absence of a rate war for almost two years hardly meant that everyone was satisfied. Rather, just the opposite. The cartel's failure in the Senate may have infected the harmony among the cartel members. Gilchrist writes:

The rate structure made shippers restive and dissatisfied. As early as February 1881 Fink looked ahead to a time of trouble . . . once the roads entered the season [when lakes and canals would be used] when their capacities were not fully occupied. By June, as he had predicted, the whole system was demoralized because the "pooling arrangements were incomplete and violated."[64]

Comparing this appraisal by cartel manager Fink with developments in the U.S. Senate suggests that the monopolists had hoped to win a favorable judiciary committee. That might have given the cartel members an incentive to keep their discipline.

255

The railroaders having lost in the U.S. Senate, additional evidence of their retreat came when cartel manger Albert Fink on April 7, 1881, joined the New York Chamber of Commerce, as did Mr. Blanchard of the Erie. Commenting on these new members, the *Times* said, "In waging the fight for the people the Chamber of Commerce is doing all it can to draw out and engage at close quarters the champions of the railroads."[65] As players in a policy scenario, Fink and Blanchard served as redundant channels between the cartel and the Chamber. They were likely preparing to "run up the hill again" in order to win later legislative approval of their plan, and they now sought allies. Such a course is the case in many appeals to Congress. It can often take several Congresses to get something settled and each new attempt can bring forth new allies. Fink and Blanchard's joining in April 1881 might well have helped, but a more critical time for the railroaders to have joined the Chamber would have been earlier in mid-1879, shortly after the Hepburn hearings. The *Times* had hoped then for an "ordeal of thorough discussion" to begin, and now it could. That they did join the Chamber at this point suggests that earlier, they were either asked to do so or considered doing so, but discarded the idea. Matters got off to a hectic start. For example, a Chamber of Commerce meeting a little later, to which Garfield had declined an invitation, and mention of Conkling's name aroused some hisses. By that time, however, lines were clear, cartel members were welcome and the Produce Exchange, Francis Thurber's base, had recently voted to support Conkling in his re-election bid at Albany.

At the end of his life, Adams may have returned to the subject of his lobbying efforts and concluded that they had failed. In his autobiography, published posthumously in 1916, Adams reflected,

> At forty-four, I resigned from the railroad commissionership, having achieved success, to become, first the Chairman of the Board of Arbitration of the Trunk Line Railroads [cartel], and then, immediately afterwards, the President of the Union Pacific. These were both natural sequences from what had preceded. The Trunk Line Arbitration was not a success. The time for it had clearly not come. Just the right man in the position held by me might possibly have worked out very considerable results; but I doubt it; and, certainly, I was not the man to do it. *The whole thing depended on Colonel Albert Fink. I was merely his instrument;* and I gravely question whether conditions were at that time ripe for a successful development on the lines Colonel Fink contemplated. Nevertheless, that I was tendered, and for three years held the position I then did, was sufficient proof of the standing I had attained. Unconsciously I had now come to the parting of the ways. I knew it, thoughtfully pondered it— and took the wrong road![66] (Our emphasis.)

Adams was recalling his lobbying for the railroad trust. He must have had to take his cues from such men as Fink and Vanderbilt who had less lobbying experience than he had. The importance of Adams's confession is that he recognized that the failure rested in the poorly developed lobbying effort. Adams also wrote in his autobiography about his work with the cartel. "I made some mistakes of judgment, and bad mistakes. Frequently, I proved unequal to the occasion. More than once, I now see, I was lacking [in] firmness, and even in courage. I did not take the position I should have taken."[67]

In 1881 covering over these shortcomings led to faulting someone else. No one had the nerve at a particular window of opportunity to confront Conkling and to retain some of the railroad experts whom Adams promoted for the Senate judiciary committee. The Republicans might have retained Democratic nominee Ben Hill of Georgia and given Conkling and Edmunds a good match in committee discussion. If the committee had just retained Hill, the revenge against Conkling perchance would never have occurred. On the other hand, perhaps Senator John Ingalls of Kansas, the only new voice for the corporate legal position, tried to urge Conkling to accept someone from among the new nominees on the Democrat slate but failed. That may explain why Ingalls became so angry with Conkling.

Chapter IX

Drawing the Line in Organizing Both the Cabinet and Senate Committees, March 1881

[1] Laumann, Edward O., and David Knoke. *The Organizational State.* Madison: University of Wisconsin Press, 1987, pp. 320–342.

[2] A report Senator Sherman provided the Senate in 1890 on money supply showed that in October 1880 the total circulation of money amounted to slightly over a billion dollars. A fourth of that was in gold coins; 2 percent in silver dollars and a 4 percent in subsidiary silver; 7 percent in gold certificates; 12 percent in silver certificates; and, finally, a third in U.S. notes (greenbacks), and a third in bank notes. In the next ten years both gold and silver certificates would greatly increase along with gold coin while national bank notes would decline slightly. *CR,* Vol. 21, pt. 6, 51st Congress, 1st sess., June 5, 1890, p. 5613.

[3] *The Nation,* July 15, 1880, p. 37.

[4] *The Nation*, September 23, 1880, p. 211.

[5] Taylor, John M. *Garfield, the Available Man.* New York: Norton, 1970, pp. 305f.

[6] *NR,* March 8, 1881.

[7] *NYT,* June 10, 1880.

[8] Lloyd, Caro. *Henry Demarest Lloyd.* New York: Putnam, 1912, Vol. 1., p. 62.

[9] *NYT,* February 17, 1881.

[10] Adams, Henry. *Novels,* etc. New York: Library of America, 1983, p. 120.

[11] Peskin, Allan. *Garfield.* Kent, OH: Kent State University Press, 1987, p. 554.

[12] *CR,* 43rd Cong., spec. sess., Vol. 1, March 17, p. 57.

[13] Benson, Lee. *Merchants, Farmers, and Railroads.* Cambridge, MA: Harvard University Press, 1955, pp. 216–217.

[14] Adams, Charles F., Jr. *The Federation of the Railroad System, Argument...before the Committee on Commerce...February 27, 1880, pp. 23f.

[15] *NYT,* February 26, 1882.

16 *United States Reports, Supreme Court,* Vol. 99. October Term, 1878, Reported by Wm. Otto, Vol. 9, Boston, 1879, p. 718. Available in most law school libraries.

17 Klein, Maury. *Life and Legend of Jay Gould.* Baltimore: Johns Hopkins University Press, 1985, p. 331.

18 For Hill's visit with Garfield, see Gorham, 1888.

19 *NYT,* January 5, 1881. In an editorial on regulation in Pennsylvania, Governor Hoyt characterized the provision in the state constitution as "so obviously just and right as to preclude question or debate." The editor noted: "The difficulty with us [New York] has been that the policy to be adopted is subjected to so much question and debate that it has been, thus far, impossible to reach any basis for action."

20 *NYT,* January 23, 1880.

21 *The Commercial and Financial Chronicle,* March 5, 1881, p. 247.

22 *NYT,* March 10, 1881.

23 *NYT,* March 10, 1881.

24 Jordan, David. *Roscoe Conkling of New York: Voice in the Senate.* Ithaca, NY: Cornell University Press, 1971, p. 407.

25 *Chronicle,* March 12, 1881, pp. 247f.

26 *NYT,* March 9, 1881.

27 Brown, Harry James, and Fredrick D. Williams, eds. *Garfield Diary.* East Lansing: Michigan State University Press, 1981, Vol. 4, p. 557.

28 *NYT,* March 15 and 30, 1878.

29 Gorham, 1888.

30 *NYT,* January 24th, 1881.

31 *CR,* 45th Cong., December 18, 1877, p. 266,

32 *CR,* 47th Cong., spec. sess., U.S. Senate, Vol. 12, March 14, 1881, p. 18.

33 Foraker, Julia Bundy. *I Would Live It Again: Memoirs of a Vivid Life.* New York: Harper and Brothers, 1932, p. 228.

34 *CR,* 47th Cong., spec. sess., U.S. Senate, Vol. 7, March 14, 1881, p. 25.

35 *CR,* 47th Cong., spec. sess., U.S. Senate, Vol. 7, March 14, 1881, p. 28.

36 *NR,* March 17, 1881.

37 *NR,* March 17, 1881.

38 Gorham, George. "The Power of the Legislature, etc.," 1876. Author's copy.

39 Davis, Winfield J. *History of Political Conventions in California, 1849–1892.* Sacramento: California State Library, 1893, pp. 404–408.

40 *NYT,* November 9, 1879.

41 Reid to Garfield, January 31, 1881, *Reid Collection, LC.*

42 Reid to Garfield, February 21, 1881, *Reid Collection, LC.*

43 *San Francisco Chronicle,* December 6, 1883.

44 March 14, 1881; *Reid Collection, LC.* See also March 13, 1881, an editorial Blaine sent to Reid for use in the *Tribune* against Gorham.

45 De Santis, Vincent P. *Republicans Face the Southern Question: The New Departure Years, 1877–1897.* Baltimore, Johns Hopkins University Press, 1959, p. 145.

46 *NR,* May 6, 1881; *NYT,* May 24 and August 1, 1881.

47 *NR,* April 8, 11, and July 1, 1881.

48 *CR,* 47th Cong., spec. sess., Vol. 12, March 18, 1881, pp. 33f.

49 Welch, Richard E. Jr., *George Frisbie Hoar and the Half-Breed Republicans.* Cambridge, MA: Harvard University Press, 1971, p. 90.

50 Laumann and Knoke, p. 368.

51 Weinstein, Allen. *Prelude to Populism.* New Haven, CT: Yale University Press, 1970, pp. 112–114, 119, 193, 194, 215.

52 Aydellotte, William O. "Notes on the Problems of Historical Generalization," in *Generalizations in the Writing of History, A Report of the Committee on Historical Analysis of the Social Science Research Council,* Louis Gottschalk, editor. Chicago: University of Chicago, 1963, p. 175.

53 Ritter, Gretchen. *Goldbugs and Greenbacks.* New York: Cambridge University Press, 1997, p. 149.

54 Sherman, John. *Recollections of Forty Years in the House, Senate and Cabinet, An Autobiography.* Chicago: Werner, 1895, Vol. 2, pp. 839–841.

55 *NR,* March 18, 1881.

56 Staff of the Congressional Quarterly, *Origins and Development of the Congress,* 2d Ed. Washington, D.C.: Congressional Quarterly, 1982, p. 225.

57 A biographical sketch of McMillan is in the *National Cyclopedia of American Biography* (James T. White, 1897).

58 Benson, pp. 224–225.

59 *NYT,* November 12, 1881.

60 Adams, Charles F. *The Railroads: Their Origin and Problems.* New York: Putnam's, 1878, p. 193.

61 Benson, p. 235.

62 "Correspondence. Mr. Adams and Mr. Thurber," a letter by Adams to the editor of *The Nation*, April 28, 1881, pp. 294f.

63 *NYT,* February 26, 1878.

64 Gilchrist, D. T. "Albert Fink and the Pooling System." *Business History Review,* Vol. 34, p. 42.

65 *NYT,* April 8, 1881.

66 Adams, Charles F. *Autobiography.* Boston: Houghton Mifflin Co., 1916, p. 191.

67 Ibid., p. 174.

Chapter X

Revenge among the Republican Factions

In settling conflicts between institutions, and so in organizing legislative committees, leaders face two questions: What is the problem the leaders have to solve? And,
who--by appointment--should take part in solving it? Getting answers can prove difficult.
Railroad industry leaders wanted only experts to handle their interests, to the exclusion
of help from others. Further, they had a plan and were ready for Congress to adopt it.
They apparently thought, however, that the president could steer the plan through to
completion. They underestimated the importance of negotiating with shippers, business
groups, canal advocates, and states as well as with leading lawmakers. In a nutshell, the
railroad leaders presumed a proprietary claim on transportation policy, and apparently
thought they were entitled to what they wanted.

The leaders of national banking had much better fortune. The banking system, operating for twenty years, had staunch supporters in the Senate along with unconditional
support from the president. The less interested senators and those who wanted other currencies were more likely to acquiesce. Concurrently, the proponents managed to sideline
soft-money advocates, giving the gold bugs a much better chance than the railroaders.

The railroad leaders had come to treat intruders with impunity. While they had
won control of the New York senate, they went on to the 1880 Chicago convention
where no important plank on railroading was adopted. When it was apparent that former president Ulysses S. Grant could not win, the railroaders' allies in New York City
announced that a new regimen for lobbying was in order. In no uncertain terms they
would suppress public discussion of their business. Shortly thereafter, advisors to candidate James Garfield persuaded him not to mention the topic in his letter of acceptance.
Railroaders also won an agreement involving Whitelaw Reid, editor of Gould's paper,
on a procedure for nominating candidates for the Supreme Court. Then, to watch over
their affairs, James Blaine, who was known as "Gould's errand boy," was selected as secretary of State, whereupon some called him "the premier." Conkling caught the tenor of
the new administration early on when during the campaign he warned against adopting

a superior attitude. It was a posture that Blaine later persuaded Garfield was quite appropriate by distinguishing between the good men and the bad men. With the president saying that he would not call the House into session, the administration proceeded to discourage public discussion. Indeed, *Tribune* correspondent E. V. Smalley, from his White House desk, a convenience that virtually made him a diarist for the president, argued that business needed protection from the politicians. On whether to open up discussion on corporate matters, Smalley wrote in the March 27 *Tribune,*

> The political profit of the session would in all probability accrue to the Democrats, who would have no responsibility to bear for the loss it would occasion to business interests, and who would be able to get the ear of the country for demagogic attacks on the *banks* and for cunning effort to stir up for their benefit the latent feelings against great *corporate monopolies.*[1] (Our emphasis.)

By this statement in the *Tribune,* the president gave credibility to the rumored alleged gag rule of June 9th after Grant lost at Chicago. The solutions for transportation and banking problems were to be left in the hands of those institutions. In matters of transportation, in case anyone failed to understand the source of all the corporate objections, that was found, for example, in Lloyd's widely popular article in the *Atlantic* on the Rockefeller Empire, appearing in mid-February. The new anti-monopolists coming to the fore had but to read Henry Poor's 1881 annual report on the railroads. They had conjured with the fierceness of his attack on the Hepburn hearings that he claimed went "to the foundation of their [railroads'] right to property."[2]

In order to fortify the administration against unwanted intrusions, the principal resource Garfield had was the power of nomination. On several occasions he managed to name people to office in the cabinets, the courts, and the departments. He tended to favor candidates who would help quell popular discussion of both banking and monopolism.

When such a group as the railroaders, moving toward a policy solution to their complaints, succeeds in crossing one intersection after another with intermediate gains, they can easily imagine that they will prevail all the way. From the railroaders' perspective, the canal was an irritant. John Logan of Illinois and Samuel McMillan of Minnesota, now on the judiciary committee, were nothing but grangers touting an outdated opinion. The dominant lobbyists attended to the commonplace of punishing any opposition who had failed to mind them. It did not occur to the cartelists that their opponents could find a way to draw a line, muster strength, and in the combat win a round. Should the anti-monopolists prevail in one response, they could tilt matters their way for a long time to come.

What the anti-monopolists finally did came in August. The railroad cartel's opponents, chiefly merchant organizations, mobilized around the free canal question. Among the canal supporters had been Roscoe Conkling, Rufus Hatch, Francis Thurber, the Chamber of Commerce, a number of others, and some newspapers, particularly the *Times* and the *Commercial and Financial Chronicle*. In time, they made such a strong showing in the policy scenario through a state election that nationally the railroaders had to make a serious adjustment.

While in 1879 the *Times* had suggested that the parties had to go through an ordeal—a head-to-head discussion—to settle matters, they failed to do so. The players certainly knew what the paper had meant. In the early 1870s, Congressman Garfield had conducted a series of committee meetings that in a manner met the *Times'* standard. His discussions in the early 1870s about appropriations and the census had been like seminars. He had followed up by writing some articles winning critical acclaim. However, between the convention of June 1880 and his inauguration in March 1881, he did not resort to the seminar method in addressing hazards facing the transportation industry. He could have called for a two-day colloquy including such leading lights as Nimmo, Depew, Fink, Hatch, Thurber, Black, Sterne, Reid, Reagan, Adams, and others, to produce an agreement on salient matters. Dividing up the topics between those that could gain immediate attention and those that required more development might have had an appeal. Salient topics would have included whether the Army Corps of Engineers should investigate railroad accidents, how to calculate the costs of railroad investment on a per mile basis, requiring a minimal courtesy of advanced announcement of rate changes to shippers, and agreeing on the character of New York's transportation structure. Since Adams and Reagan conversed down to early January 1881, the deadline for the House report, an experience in a wide-ranging discussion before then might have given them a greater basis for conciliation. A study group had been used on the Virginia question. Garfield had showed no reticence to working with a bi-factional Republican group at the end of December in clarifying the problems with the Virginia debt and independent William Mahone's proposed cooperation with Senate Republicans. In that case, some information meeting Garfield's standards was pursued and helped settle the matter. Railroading could have received the same attention.

On his way home from the inauguration, former president Hayes was in a railroad accident. Garfield, urging a federal solution for investigating accidents as Adams and he had earlier promoted, might have won a popular response. Adams's main complaint was that the popular prejudice against experts meant that the country just stumbled along. By contrast, experts quickly examining the railroad accident involving Hayes could have greatly improved the cartel's case before the public. Nothing was done during the lame-duck session since legislation was in the hands of the cartel. A virtual blackout prevailed. Since the president-elect apparently approved the Adams plan for consolidation and the cartelists wanted to go ahead, as Nimmo later observed, "at once and unconditionally," his duty was quite different from that of leading a seminar. Rather, on behalf of the railroaders, he could not seriously entertain options and had to watch that no one else of consequence did either. Beyond not engaging serious opposition in a dialogue, the president's main role seemed to be one of getting rid of the opposition. Garfield had acquiesced to the cartelists and surrendered his own prerogative in managing information for developing policy options.

Arranging a committee reception for the Adams plan in Congress in March 1881, the railroaders had bungled their lobbying effort by failing to win an early compromise with Congressman John Reagan. Then they failed to discuss committee arrangements with their opposition. Now, if they had to face the Republican judiciary committee, they might find themselves caught up in hearings reminiscent of the Hepburn meetings, with all their disclosures and humiliation. Rather than collecting themselves and preparing to make another lobbying assault in the next session of Congress, they laid their unhappy condition at the feet of just one man, Senator Roscoe Conkling of New York. Two years earlier, he may have approved of the Hepburn hearings, and then recruited state convention delegates who gave the party a platform of the same species. Further, he had supported Alonzo Cornell for governor, and written a letter of acceptance turning the light of day on the corporations' responsibility to the state. Most recently, he had objected to railroad experts on the Senate judiciary committee and frustrated the plan for a national railroad trust. He would have to pay, and what the railroaders expected from Garfield was that he would exact the cost.

In business and politics, the players can develop skills to a fine point for administering punishment. Anyone could recall those childhood experiences of being taken to the woodshed for a whipping, so examples among grownups were quite vivid. When national banks had objected in January to a Democratic refunding bill, they resorted to punishment by pushing the economy to the brink of panic. About 141 banks summarily dropped out of the system, and the rest administered their whipping by raising their interest rates to one percent per day, until President Hayes vetoed the bill. That little business crisis should have given Republicans pause, lest they fail to attend to bankers' interests. Next, when Jay Gould consolidated the telegraph industry, a two-sided punishment arose. Blaine immediately suggested a postal scandal that would put the culprits on the defensive in a trial by newspaper. Further, when Gould learned of any newspapers supporting competition for his telegraph company, he administered a whipping by cutting off their Associated Press services. Shortly before the inauguration, William Windom, the apparent incoming secretary of Treasury, had warned of just such threatening behavior by the new telegraph consolidation. Even in government, Thomas Brady at the Post Office Department showed no remorse in cutting services to any member of Congress opposed to his requests for additional appropriations.

Blaine's Strike against Conkling with the Robertson Nomination

In the view taken here, the railroaders were now likely upset over seating on the judiciary committee and must have looked to James Blaine to correct matters. Five days after the Republicans adopted their slate of committees, "the premier" made an unannounced evening visit at the White House, taking Garfield away from the dinner table. Plausibly he wanted the president to administer punishment to Conkling.

265

What was missing in this policy scenario was a high consequential voice calling for action to effect transportation policy. In the 1860s, there would have been no work on a transcontinental railroad if the party platform had not called for it. In the 1870s, there would have been less likely been better waterways to further cheap transportation if President Ulysses S. Grant had not called for it. Now in 1879 two credible voices arose. Vanderbilt had called for regulating the railroads by Congress first, but the Republican Party meeting at Chicago passed a platform without following up. In 1880 the high financiers exempted themselves from any obligation to the 1879 New York platform on state regulation. The second voice arose out of the Hepburn hearings. Next, they apparently interpreted Grant's loss as permission to reverse the 1879 state platform and proceeded clandestinely with their own. While the party could have moved forward without a platform from the national convention, the stronger, victorious faction decided after the fact to advance without such procedural niceties.

Here were signs that the bonds of the nation's political ethos were breaking apart and spinning toward factionalism. Up until 1873 the spirit of economic liberalism had bridged the differences between major groups, as Nugent noted, but that consensus was snapped by the market troubles of that year. Nothing had replaced the old doctrine while the ethics of Darwin's "survival of the fittest" gained popularity. By 1879, Nugent wrote, everything was awry.[3] This new, disparate society caught up with the Republican Party at its 1880 national convention, where delegates were still shaken by the railroad strike and fears for the sensitive currency settlement. The one group managing to win were the adventurers in capital, who had their own notions of how to run the nation, principally with a strong man, a Caesar. Grant could have done it, but not without bringing along too many undesirables from the old stalwart camp. Blaine could have done it, but he had antagonized too many outside of the new technology important for cartels and trusts. The national convention was simply too weak to pass the kind of strong platform that could provide marching orders for the diverse legions of loyalists.

It all came down to Garfield organizing his cabinet and the U.S. Senate organizing its committees. Those who won at Chicago proceeded surreptitiously to win what they had not even tried to achieve in national platform—a railroad trust. Nor did they encourage the candidate to express views on regulation. This possibly explains the extreme amount of jockeying in the making of the cabinet. The maneuvering, with each side reading the motives of the other in a pejorative fashion, served as a functional alternative to the absence of strong party leadership at Chicago. The condition would not last long.

In 1881, during the state of suspended indirection over committee organization, on the personal level Blaine was probably chagrined by his failure to place either a number of senators on judiciary or his friends on the foreign affairs committee. It fell to one man, James Blaine, secretary of State, who was now in a pit and needed a high step out, to give strong direction to affairs of state. As in the crisis of his nomination of 1876, Blaine was again ill, but he rose to the occasion. The timing of his special call on the president, however, likely betrayed his priorities. He probably could have come a few days earlier and urged President Garfield to negotiate with party leaders to keep some of the Democratic nominees on the judiciary committee, perhaps keeping attorney Benjamin Hill of Georgia. However, Blaine was not a team builder. Where the vacuum appeared, he took his own opportunities, whether for personal retribution or for the railroad monopoly. So Blaine let an opportunity pass and waited until the following week to warn Garfield, just before the nomination of his nemesis—Gorham—came up. Furthermore, Garfield would have had more than a passing interest in the prospects for Adams's work, since he had helped him on other legislative matters. Now that the prospect of a national railroad trust was at stake, all the niceties of "courtesy of the Senate" could be suspended in order to remove the great obstacle, Roscoe Conkling. By Blaine waiting until the last minute, he left the president little time to consult with others. Garfield had laid down no rule that his cabinet would first review all nominations before they were submitted.

Gorham's Prospects for Winning Re-election to His Old Senate Office

One of the oddest quests for office in Washington, D.C., was Gorham's effort to return to the secretaryship of the Senate. He had entered the post in 1868, when the radicals were in the ascendancy, but since then patterns of influence changed in Washington, influence that hardly favored the old office holder. Among those who could not warm up to Gorham in 1881 were the railroaders, looking to form a national trust, and the gold advocates, beginning with the president and New England delegation, looking toward the rechartering of national banks. Their new strategy consisted of discouraging public discussion and Gorham was hardly the man to concede to such a demand. By personal disposition and now, as editor of a party paper, Gorham was inclined to discuss any matter that came along. Because Virginia's Mahone made the difference in organizing the Senate for the Republicans, and he wanted Gorham to occupy his old office to give strength to his Virginia organization, and after the encouraging Petersburg meeting of Afro-American Republicans, the caucus agreed to support him. Certainly, they also wanted the right to name chairs to committees, occupy capitol building offices, and have clerks. Most freshmen members of the caucus would benefit since in those days they also won chairmanships. Above all, Senator Henry Dawes had won election as assistant majority leader. (Majority leader Henry Anthony of Rhode Island was convalescing.) The *Post* commented on May 7th, "Dawes is in command by virtue of Mahone's vote, and Mahone's vote never would have been had if Gorham hadn't negotiated for it and secured it."[4] Thus, every time Dawes or any Republican committee chair looked at Gorham, they saw a man whom they had to regard as their benefactor.

On the downside, Gorham's newspaper was an unprofessional product making it an embarrassment. He made no attempt to model the editorial page after his neighbor's work at the much more modest *Post*. Shareholder George Bliss on February 21, 1882, wrote Gorham complaining that the paper "has absolutely no trained and skilled newspaper man to it." (Bliss to Gorham, *Gorham Collection,* State Library, Sacramento) Gorham's job was to write the editorials, but that did not make him editor-in-chief, as some called him. The editorial page failed to carry a masthead detailing all the assignments. Someone else must have had charge of that, and much of its content was the stuff of roasts, the kinds of comments reserved for hilarious party dinners. Gorham likely made his contribution from time to time.

Any incumbent in the office of secretary of the Senate serves as the Senate's formal liaison with the White House, especially in conveying documents back and forth. Whether Garfield relished the idea of having Gorham dropping in at the White House now and then is not known. With *Tribune* reporter E. V. Smalley settled at the White House, a constant recognition of Gorham as the Senate emissary, while editor of a stalwart paper, would have been something of a miracle in the midst of signs of factional division all through the party.

While Garfield had been with Gorham at times during the campaign and again at New Year's to discuss Mahone, Gorham's becoming editor may have put a chill on their relations. Later, Gorham apparently declined an offer to work under the supervision of an editorial board. Discipline of Gorham moved to the president. Of course, as the vote on rechartering national banks in 1882—another issue not mentioned in the platform—grew closer, Garfield could not likely forget Gorham's outspoken views in favor of a greenback circulation and the abolition of national banks in 1878. The new Senate elite was steered by the New England senators. Garfield himself must have felt the influence of the banking community to deny Gorham the prestige of office that would have given him opportunity to exercise his influence.

It was a clumsy proposition. Gorham's poignant appeal for Garfield's assistance had no effect. It became much clumsier, however, when Gorham was thrown into the role of defender of the star route contractors against the Department of Justice. Although he could show how well he defended his friends, that loyalty was no qualification for re-election to a Senate office.

When "the premier" called on Garfield, the secretary of state had his own reasons for opposing Gorham. Gorham's good work in winning some southern delegations to the last summer's national convention to vote for Grant had robbed Blaine of support he had had in 1876. Now the resentful Blaine had the chance to retaliate. He probably saw the opportunity.

Blaine Closes the Door on Conkling and Gorham

The opportunity would also allow Blaine to strike against Conkling. The Senate carried over Gorham's nomination for the secretaryship. The next day, Garfield's nomination of Robertson for collector of customs at New York—a shock to Conkling—arrived at the Senate. Years later, Lee Benson, thoroughly immersed in the New York side of the story, wrote that the Robertson nomination "was obviously intended, and taken, as a deliberate declaration of war."[5] In a matter of weeks, Garfield would expressly state such a condition of party affairs. Allowing that in nominating Robertson, the president was responding to new conditions in the political landscape, I suspect one thing prompting Garfield was that the Senate would not handle the Adams bill. If the Senate did take it up, the scene would likely remind one of the earlier open discussion in the 1879 Hepburn hearings. His own association with Adams also probably prompted Garfield, as did Blaine's disparaging of the stalwarts as the "bad men." The leader of the "bad men" had checked the legislation that its supporters had never asked the national convention to endorse. As the *Post* had said in early February: "The Republican Party must become either all Blaine or all Conkling—all Cossack or all Tartar . . . There is no man colossal enough in intellect or legs to stride the gulf already formed between them." The gulf was not over personalities but over the conflict between those supporting competition and those opposed.

From the viewpoint of information management, the nomination of a foe of Conkling as collector of the port cut to the heart of Conkling's practices. Some thought that Garfield should not have nominated such a man without first consulting with Conkling and other New York party leaders as he had promised privately and even in public statements. Some thought that the nomination ought to have been withdrawn after Robertson claimed it was "reward" for his services at Chicago. Its importance was that Conkling himself would likely no longer be welcome at the customs house prior to a state convention to line up votes for his particular propositions. He had done that as recently as 1879, even using former collectors Arthur and Murphy to help him. The prohibition against the use of civil servants in party management was not yet securely on the books, but the Robertson nomination was a step in that direction.

Garfield sending the Senate the Robertson nomination created a new situation, putting Gorham's nomination on hold, waiting for some settlement about Robertson. Having missed the opportunity at Chicago to reconcile their factions on several substantive points, the Republicans suffered from serious divisions, and in March 1881 the senators were not about to go into executive session, where the Democrats would have gladly widened the split. The window of opportunity for the Republicans to harmonize had closed, and they would have to live with it. The Republican caucus could not heal its split in an administration frowning on substantive discussion.

On March 22nd Lucretia Garfield wrote in her diary about Blaine's visit that

> While at dinner today one of the ushers brought a card to the President saying that Secretary Blaine desired to see him for one moment only. He left the table, and after staying away through two or three courses came back looking very pale, but composed. A hush fell on the entire table and no one had quite the courage to ask why; nor did the President yield to the inquisitive eyes that were centered upon him from all sides. After we had gone to our room he said to me, "I have broken Blaine's heart with the appointments I have made today. He regards me as having surrendered

to Conkling. I have not but I don't know but that I have acted too hastily. Perhaps I ought to have consulted with Blaine before sending in some of those New York appointments."

The General was in real distress over Mr. Blaine's feelings and could not sleep. He had decided, on account of the Secretary's anxiety, to send in another batch of appointments tomorrow which will very thoroughly antidote the first. These the President did not intend to send so soon, but urged by Mr. Blaine have concluded that now is the time.[6]

If Garfield excused himself from the dinner table for such a long time only to assuage Blaine's feelings, his apologies to his family would have hardly been convincing. Plausibly, the men had had enough time to fume about the loss of experts suggested by Adams's criteria on the judiciary committee. Not only that, but the railroad consolidation would have to face more public exposure to win congressional approval. The two men probably took more time for Blaine's solution, to nominate Robertson, reasonably adding to Garfield's sleeplessness that night. He also put at risk a relation with the Adams brothers, looking to reform in the patronage system. Henry Adams had hosted him in the family home, and he had followed up by promoting some of Charles Adams's plans for legislation, but now he would take steps that caused the brothers to have their doubts.

Garfield may have found that in order to keep the Senate from moving forward on Gorham's nomination to his old post, he had to act quickly on the Robertson nomination. A possible threat from Blaine may have also added urgency to the matter. Blaine had become a patron of A. M. Gibson without Garfield's knowledge, and could use him now to expose the Reid-Garfield correspondence about judicial nominations. That suggestion came up over a year and a half later. On December 31, 1882, the *Sun* told Garfield's contemporaries the story of his bargain with Reid over campaign funds in exchange for judicial nominations. Years later, after the Garfield collection was opened, historian Robert Marcus would develop the story. The accuracy of the *Sun's* story when checked against Marcus's later findings, taken together with the record of Blaine and Reid's treachery involving Gibson, puts credibility in the *Sun's* additional claim. The newspaper said that Garfield "was informed by telegraph that if Robertson's name was not sent to the Senate the letter relating to the appointment of Stanley Matthews would be published." If donors in New York threatened blackmail, it was important to submit the nomination promptly and overlook the courtesies the Founding Fathers had made necessary in relations between the two branches of government.

Garfield had promised Conkling to confer with him before making New York nominations, and he owed courtesies to Secretary Windom, who had jurisdiction over Customs Houses, and to Postmaster General James, the New Yorker on the cabinet. However, he bypassed all three.

The monopolists' impatience with Conkling may explain the president's indecent handling of the nomination. Around the monopolists were plenty of people who wanted to rewrite the rules anyway. In addition to impatience with Conkling, they were discontented with the strictures of the Constitution. They soon won recognition for their views from the *Times*. The founding document had fallen into bad repute and, without apology, the editorial of April 19th stated,

> The power of appointment to office was given to the President, and not the Senate, and the provision that all appointments should be submitted for confirmation to the Senate was merely designed to act as a check upon the president in case he should appoint objectionable persons. *The nation has long since outgrown the Constitution,* and the character of the Senate has wholly changed. It is well understood that the chief duty of senators is to select persons to fill various Federal Offices and to submit their names to the President, who must immediately approve them. The Senate is really the appointing power, and the President is the clerk who registers appointments.[7] (Our emphasis.)

Except for that old document, the New York half-breeds could move much faster in seizing the leadership they sought. Concurrently, in New York City the new money and the old money were sparring and may have counted the shifting scene in Washington for support of one side or the other.

The Massachusetts party would soon propose to fix the matter. In the early winter of 1881–82, Senator Hoar elaborated the problem in an article in the *North American Review*. Then the state party convention adopted a plank reading: "The needed reform will comprehend these aims—viz.: The maintenance of the constitutional prerogative of the President to make nominations upon his solid responsibility."[8] Unfortunately, all this support came long after Garfield's sleepless night.

Massachusetts advocates of the change had pressed the idea for some time; their only problem was that they lobbied it poorly. Just as the half-breeds had miscalculated when bringing the Adams bill to Congress, so now there was not the proper broad support for changing the president's power of nomination. Henry Adams should have been taking more initiative. Garfield had first met Adams in 1869 and, in all likelihood, kept abreast of anything he wrote. As a descendant of two members of the Constitutional Convention, John Adams and Nathaniel Gorham, Henry would more likely than many others have thought the matter through. While he had eschewed ancestor worship and adopted an attitude of nonchalance, if not distaste, he did so because he believed that while the founders had achieved much, what they had done was now largely irrelevant. Henry Adams thought that the Civil War had changed everything. Darkness remained, hovering over the debris of the republic left from the exhausted federalist and Jacksonian structures. In *The Education of Henry Adams,* he would write that:

The whole government, from top to bottom, was rotten with the senility of what was antiquated and the instability of what was improvised. The currency was only one example; the tariff was another; but the whole fabric required reconstruction as much as in 1789, for the Constitution had become as antiquated as the Confederation. Sooner or later, a shock must come, the more dangerously the longer postponed. The civil war had made a new system in fact; the country would have to reorganize the machinery in practice and theory. . . . The political dilemma was as clear in 1870 as it was likely to be in 1920. The system of 1789 had broken down, and with it the eighteenth century fabric of *a priori*, or moral principles. Politicians had tacitly given up. Grant's administration marked the avowal. Nine-tenths of men's political energies must henceforth be wasted on expedients to piece out,—to patch,—or, in vulgar language, to tinker,—the political machine as often as it broke down. Such a system, or want of system, might last centuries, if tempered by an occasional revolution or civil war; but as a machine, it was, or soon would be, the poorest in the world,—the clumsiest, —the most inefficient.[9]

The Adams brothers may have influenced Garfield on the matter. Henry wrote in *Education* that:

The most troublesome task of a reform President was that of bringing the Senate back to decency. . . He meant to support the Executive in attacking the Senate and taking away its two-thirds vote and *power of confirmation, nor did he much care how it should be done,* for he thought it safer to effect the revolution in 1870 than to wait until 1920. (Henry Adams, *Library of America,* New York, N.Y., 1983, p. 947.) (Our emphasis.)

With such an attitude espoused by a member of the Adams lineage, it easily proved popular at the *Times* and at the White House. The ends would justify any careless means and the administration would launch itself on uncharted waters.

Of course, Conkling was aghast when he learned of the Robertson nomination. He had seen Garfield just the Sunday prior, and on May 11 Gorham asserted, "No third party was present."[10] Now he knew that everything was off. The president could not be trusted. Conkling's experiences with Garfield showed him that rather than presenting a steady course, Garfield was arbitrary, if not capricious. The evidence had been accumulating. In his letter of acceptance on the currency question, Garfield had touted the equality of the dollar whether as gold, silver, or paper. Then in his inaugural address, he said that the Court would likely find paper money unconstitutional. In a February meeting with Garfield, with Hayes' nomination of Matthews dead in committee, Garfield told Conkling that he would not resubmit the name–only to hear on March 14 the president had resubmitted it. Then a discussion about Judge Charles Folger turned against

Conkling's expectations. Worst of all, during his campaign Garfield had promised that he would always consult New York leadership about any federal appointment, but submitting Robertson's name broke that promise. In his inaugural address he made only a passing comment for civil service reform and elaborated on it by noting the need for "protection of incumbents [from] intrigue and wrong."[11] Garfield was hardly behaving as Jared Sparks had characterized George Washington, who did not hold out "expectations which he did not intend should be realized."[12] Garfield owed Conkling some apologies and explanations, but they were neither asked for nor given. The current issue of *Robert's Rules of Order* (1875) stated that rules were necessary to keep the leaders from being capricious and the followers from being captious; Garfield had been arbitrary and could only expect criticism.

Conkling found Robertson's nomination galling because, early in 1880, Robertson had pledged at the coming summer's convention that he would observe the unit rule. He then proceeded to break the pledge! He could hardly join Robertson in preparing for a state convention. Indeed Robertson likely would not have wanted him to anyway. Conkling had announced his code for political leaders in his October campaign addresses: "The higher obligations among men . . . reside in honor and good faith." How else could the party leader of New York have operated? Now, just two weeks into the new administration, such a spirit seemed impossible. Conkling foresaw four years of a shell game. He was heard to say of the president, "I can never tell where that lizard is going to turn up." Whether Garfield planned such a course is debatable, but the tactic made the stalwart leader bristle. In the absence of party discipline and an appropriate platform at the convention, common courtesies among its leaders, and the constraints of the constitution, a higher order justified what he had done. The course Garfield took survived in a melodramatic atmosphere, in which the good men were free to treat the bad men as they wished and, in the end, they would fault the bad men. What an easy way out!

Alexander Hamilton's Cautions

While no one in the 1881 dispute came to the defense of the founding fathers, except for Conkling making his stand on their principles, it is worth mentioning that Hamilton had warned against a president rewarding factions. Hamilton had written that

> Several disadvantages . . . might attend the absolute power of appointment in the hands of that officer [the president] . . . To what purpose then [should the Constitution] require the co-operation of the Senate . . . It would be an excellent check upon a spirit of favoritism in the President . . . The possibility of rejection would be a strong motive to care in proposing. The danger to his own reputation, and, in the case of an elective magistrate, to his political existence . . . could not fail to operate as a barrier . . . He would be both ashamed and afraid to bring forward, for the most distinguished or lucrative stations candidates who had no other merit than

273

... being in some way or other personally allied to him ... the supposition that he could in general purchase the integrity of the whole body [Senate] would be forced and improbable.[13]

Hamilton thought that naming favorites would not only raise resistance but also put the president at risk. The fearless Garfield, however, would trump such cautions and proceed. The postwar generation had outgrown the Constitution.

While Henry Adams and the *Times* found the Constitution no longer applicable, what is most surprising in reading accounts of this dispute is that neither side mentioned the views from *The Federalist Papers*—either to approve or disapprove them. Garfield's 1877 *Atlantic* article hardly met the points that Hamilton had raised. He had not done his homework on the question, noting in his diary on March 27th: "The President is authorized to nominate, and did so ... I stand joyfully on that issue—let who will, fight me."[14] If the president's wife's diary gave a glimpse into First Family conversation, good judgment was apparently at a premium as she wrote on March 29th that, in Conkling, she saw "no true loyalty to Right, nor patriotism ..."[15] With such an attitude loose in the White House, little wonder that any sanctions against Conkling were worth considering.

Hamilton would have probably urged retaining General Merritt at the Customs House, as he had also written,

> It has been mentioned as one of the advantages to be expected from the co-operation of the Senate, in the business of appointments, that it would contribute to the stability of the administration. ... Where a man of any station had given satisfactory evidence of his fitness for it, a new President would be restrained from attempting a change in favor of a person more agreeable to him by the apprehension that a discountenance of the Senate might frustrate the attempt, and bring some degree of discredit upon himself.[16]

Gorham's Initial Responses and His Detractors

Gorham's first response, on March 24, 1881, was congenial and sympathetic and did not deal in doctrine. While several scholars have recognized Gorham that unsettled Garfield, the editor often opened his column with severe language, but usually arrived at a calm and collected point to state his case. He wrote that:

> The President feels bound to do the handsome thing for the New York men who participated in his nomination at Chicago. A President's life is not a happy one. If he pleased one side today he must please the other tomorrow. And then each is displeased with him for having recognized the other. The effort to please all is most amiable, but always results in displeasing all.

Gorham praised the other nominations of William Chandler for solicitor-general, William Walter Phelps for minister to Austria, Solicitor Phillips for the Court of Claims, and General Sheldon for governorship of New Mexico. Then the editor closed his comments by spoofing the nomination of Thomas M. Nichol, founder of the Honest Money League, for commissioner of Indian Affairs. Gorham wrote, "We do not see how either the Poncas or the Utes can resist the arguments of Mr. Nichol on the subject of 'honest money.'"

The next day, Gorham suggested a deal.

> There is to be an election of the Governor [in New York] in 1882. The New York Republicans would no doubt take most kindly any suggestion the administration might see fit to make, through its accredited representatives in the State, as to the selection of a candidate. The election there of a man who might be deemed, more than any other, acceptable to General Garfield's administration would be proof of the harmony which the President will have established by his judicious nominations for office.

By March 26th Robertson had announced that his nomination was a "reward," and Gorham explained what he had been talking about: "We have expressed our opinions in riddles because we thought it likely there might be some change of the situation." He went on to add that Robertson

> has spoken in a serenade speech since his nomination of having been appointed by the President as a "reward" for his exploit at Chicago. This is perhaps the severest comment that could be made on the appointment. The conferring of office as "a reward" for partisan services has for years been the subject of much objuration in the quarters which most exult over the present illustration of it. The President may deem it for the best that his action in the premises be reconsidered . . . To set up [Conkling's] most pronounced enemy in the custom-house to reward another as he claims to have been rewarded is an attempt to *create a leadership by external force,* to which the party will never submit. (Our emphasis.)

Gorham would subsequently develop the same points: a) the nomination as a reward, b) the approval from parties who had previously criticized such practice, and c) creating new party leadership in New York by external force. On the latter point, he had already raised the question in January whether Garfield would be used as a makeweight "against the party itself."

The editor will forever be linked to the Garfield administration because of his criticisms of it. He answered his critics March 31st as the White House hubris rode high by writing:

Some people make the mistake of supposing that because *The Republican* has loudly protested against a certain appointment of the President it is, therefore "fighting the administration." Nothing can be farther from the truth. We are sincerely desirous for the success of the administration. Its failure would peril the cause of liberty and law, on which the Republican Party is based. Our fidelity to the President is not lessened when we warn him of a pitfall in which it seems to us he is about to step. He has been greatly deceived if he has been made to believe that there has been any understanding concerning the succession among those who opposed him at Chicago. He has had no more unselfish or reliable supporters than the friends of General Grant. They have no candidate for 1884, as others may have who are apparently more trusted. The opinion entertained by the Grant leaders has been that if the present administration shall be successful before the party and the country it would naturally be continued a second term, and that if it failed its successor would be Democratic.

At the risk of being charged with "fighting the President," we say it is our earnest conviction that the welfare of the country and the party, and the success of his administration, all demand that he desist from the war upon the Republican Party of New York.[17]

In another six weeks the president's declaration of "war" on the Republican Party in New York would be clearly stated for all to understand. That Gorham saw it this far in advance was to his credit.

Gorham's failure in politics was in part due to his practice in editorials of holding up a mirror to public figures and not knowing when to quit! Early in the deadlock, he used this contrivance against the Democrats and only managed to offend them. He came off the Senate floor one day with the sounds of Democrats exasperated over Mahone still ringing in his ears and wrote for April 6th:

[Mahone] has, among other rights, the right to vote on all questions just as he pleases, and to have his vote counted just as it was cast. This is the point at which the Bourbon intellect in the Senate is confused. They never count votes enough against themselves at home to do any harm to their side if they can avoid it. They live politically only by suppressing enough of the majority to change it to a minority. They are bothered about this idea of Mahone's that he may vote his own way instead of their way. "Never!" roars Hill. "It must not be," said Brown. "It is outrageous," blusters Hampton. "It is treachery!" says Johnston. . . [18]

It was two weeks before Gorham found a way to retrace his steps, writing on April 20th:

Republicans believe that the Democratic Party thrives and wins at the South by its disregard of the Fifteenth Amendment, to which at the same time it professes cheerful obedience. It cannot well be that offense can always be avoided in the discussion of vital questions of fact. And it is mainly as to the fact that the two great parties differ. The struggle is largely one of discrediting testimony, and hence the necessity for all possible good temper. We may not always be able to practice as we preach, but will do the best we can.[19]

Garfield's Political Resources during the Senate Deadlock

Conkling's friends sought to reconcile him with the president and were prepared to keep an appointment. As they were about to depart for the White House, a wire arrived from Governor Cornell, already giving signs that he was in the Gould camp, urging Conkling not to object to the Robertson nomination. The senator muttered something about not being "a place seeker" and broke off his appointment, leaving Garfield waiting and fuming. No attempt was made to reschedule the meeting, and each of the men withdrew to muster his resources.

Garfield had a letter from ten New England senators, asking him to name George Loring, a former Massachusetts congressman and a horticulturist, as Commissioner of Agriculture. Their letter could provide some leverage. If they wanted Loring, they would have to help win the Robertson nomination. Further, taking on the role of autocrat, he could require "letters of introduction" from senators who did not agree with the Robertson nomination, letting them cool their heels. Garfield had no concern about rousing the "discountenance of the Senate." The device possibly came to his attention when plans were laid to shepherd the Adams bill through Congress. Since the bill, however, did not even make it out of the House, he could apply the tactic to senators to win support for Robertson. Of course, he could also scandalize the star route service and defame the campaign leaders of 1878.

Conkling's Apparent Familiarity with Hamilton's Thought

In his letter of resignation on May 17, widely scoffed at, Conkling showed familiarity with Hamilton's point:

The avocation of Mr. Robertson and his legislative and professional experience and surroundings, do not denote superiority in the qualities of knowledge, business habits, and familiarity with revenue laws and system of the United States, which make him more competent than General Merritt to collect the vast revenues and administer the vast business pertaining to the port of New York.

277

In the place of an experienced officer in the midst of his term, fixed by law, it is proposed suddenly to put a man who has had no training for the position and who cannot be said to have any special fitness for its official duties.[20]

In New York City merchants were lining up to sign a petition to retain Merritt.[21] The *Times* on May 10th also weighed in on that side: "The business community of this or any other city would never have dreamed of naming [Robertson] for any such position."[22]

The curiosity of those times was that Conkling's most vociferous foes accused him of the wrong transgressions. Gorham reminded his readers that Senator Conkling had "resisted the removal of Arthur, Cornell, and Merritt without cause," He, however, was totally misinterpreted, "and for this he is denounced as a patronage seeker."[23] Since Conkling had never paid a call on the Hayes White House, for four years he had never requested any patronage, and anyone should have easily understood that. Some of the press, however, would create the image of Conkling they thought appropriate.

A Long Branch neighbor of Ulysses S. Grant related that the former president had said much the same thing about the senator. John F. Henry told the *Sun* that Grant told him:

> Conkling never sought but one appointment from me, and that was of a minor character. He visited me freely, but gave no advice unless I asked for it. When Senator Conkling called on me I used to tell him that such and such men were pressing such and such men for office in his State, and asked him concerning their qualification. He gave me his opinions. He always seemed to be governed by what he thought was best for the interest of country. His conduct stood in marked contrast with that of many other senators. They were governed mainly by personal consideration; they were plausible and importunate. Conkling was the soul of honor, and apparently had the interests of the country, which were my interests, solely at heart.[24]

In his resignation, Conkling wrote, "We have not attempted to dictate, nor have we asked the nomination of one person to any office in the State."[25]

Over the decades the historical convention has supported the half-breed case for the integrity of the Garfield administration. Its foundation rests in citizens recoiling at the thought of the assassination of a president. Many find the psychic pain so severe that for relief they assign blame to the person who last contended with the deceased. Thus, Garfield's death by assassination has immortally ensconced the melodrama and cast the stalwarts as the evildoers. Overlooked are any failures of the political parties to require interest groups to produce platforms and enforce the courtesies required to reach that point. Overlooked in all the criticism of Conkling is the one fact––that he blocked the cartel leaders from having specialists on the judiciary committee. Forty years later, Depew would continue to claim that Conkling had tried to dictate appointments. Depew would never mention Conkling's part in frustrating the Adams plan, nor, for that matter, Conkling's denial in his resignation of the charge that he had dictated appointments.

Only the *Indianapolis Journal* speculated on Garfield's original motive in nominating Robertson.

> Senators Conkling and Platt have not resigned out of pique for nothing. Mr. Garfield succeeded to the Presidency by means of the vote of New York. Surely it cannot be said that Mr. Conkling contributed nothing to the Republican success in that State and in the Nation. The appointment of Judge Robertson was not recognition of the Blaine party in New York, or of the independents, or anybody else. It was solely, purely, an attack on Mr. Conkling—so conceived, so understood, so expressed by every one. It is only those who believe that Senator Conkling should be punished for some undefined and indefinable offense who can by any possibility indorse the action of the President in the matter.

The sequence of events and the persons involved would warrant the surmise that Garfield executed the punishment of Conkling for a reason. He had frustrated the cartel plans to name friends of the railroaders to the Senate judiciary committee, friends whom Charles Francis Adams, Jr., had set criteria for selecting.

The Tenor of the Senate Democrats in the Deadlock Suggested Some Implied Threats

The Senate deadlock lasted about six weeks and centered on money matters. The president did not disturb the Robertson nomination, but continued sending in others. In other Senate business, the southerners blocked the vote that would let Gorham resume his old Senate post. In 1879, when the Democrats took over the Senate, the suggestion was made that, if the Republicans again became the majority, they could again put Gorham in the secretaryship. But what he had done in the meantime--bringing a southerner, Mahone, to the Republican side--could hardly have sat well with them.

The Mahone movement's response to Gorham's help did show an improving attitude toward civil rights in the South. Ulysses S. Grant, speaking in Warren, Ohio, had told the crowd that he had found, in his recent tour of the South, many white residents ready to come up to the new constitutional standards and turn their back on tradition. They were looking for a "pretext," he said, to make the change. In a June 17th editorial the *Times* noted the same positive attitude among southerners.

> It becomes more and more evident every day that the Readjuster party in Virginia is engaged in a cause that is broader than that State and deeper than the debt question . . . The new party promises to remove

unjust restrictions and discriminations by which the rights of citizens are curtailed, to protect all in the exercise of their privileges, and to promote a liberal policy in substantial accord with the principles of the Republican Party of the North. . . . Candor compels us to say that we have little respect for the financial integrity on either side of this particular controversy, but the local debt issue is the occasion for a political division which seems to us to promise results of greater import not only in Virginia, but throughout the South. . . . The success of Mahone and his party in Virginia would encourage the liberals of other States to form an independent organization and carry on the contest for equal rights, just laws, and the adoption of national spirit in the section so long and perversely alienated.

The senators from the South had to know of this improving national attitude among their constituents, and they apparently were willing to follow the march—but for a price. In the deadlock they found a way to present their demand.

The 1881 Senate deadlock debate had settled down to the topics of public finances, banking, state debt, repudiation, and the like. Conkling, who had frequently spoken in the Senate before the Robertson nomination, was now silent. Benjamin Hill, who had exploded over Mahone's head on March 14, also had little further to say. Rather, leading the debate on the Democratic side were the virulently anti-bank James Beck of Kentucky and Joseph Brown of Georgia.

Beck and Brown each had assignments on committees that also included seats for either Republicans George Hoar of Massachusetts, the leading national banking state, and/or Justin Morrill of Vermont, chair of the finance committee. There is a suspicion here suggested by that fact. The fact was that the longest addresses in the Senate during the deadlock came from all of the Democrats who sat with Beck and Brown on their committees, facing Republicans Hoar and Morrill. Of the 37 Democrats in the Senate, 18 gave comments extending over ten pages or more of the *Congressional Record*. Among them were Beck and Brown and 13 others. The question was "Why this concentration of oratory from the members on those particular committees?" Forward thinking would allow the surmise that the next year Hoar and Morrill would have to muster support from across the Senate for the renewal of the twenty-year charters of the national banks. If so, the question is: "Did the concentration of oratory from that group of Democrats now seated on the committees of those two New Englanders constitute a warning about the prospects for rechartering banks?" Were the Democrats implying that if Gorham was returned to his former Senate post where he could help manage the spread of Mahoneism from Virginia into the South, they, the Democrats, would trouble the New Englanders on next year's national banking bill? If so, the suspicions were a tribute to Gorham, and they wanted none of it.

The Democratic fusillade on those two New Englanders presented a plausible Democratic reconnaissance, preparing for a full assault the next session of the Senate.

The Democrats had before them the prospect of a good old Jacksonian parliamentary battering of the fortress of New England banking. It would begin in this session with the seating of Gorham as secretary of the Senate, a position from which he could further Mahoneism in the South. Then, in the next session, they would begin the counteroffensive, once the Republicans introduced the bill to recharter the national banks. A great skirmish would be had by all.

A deal was plausibly in the making. If they had to give up their southern white governments, the New Englanders might have to sacrifice national banking in whole or in part. Therefore, in the institutional and sectional adjustments that had to be made, Gorham presented a handicap to the Republicans and could be sacrificed. Or the caucus could delay Gorham's re-election until after the vote on national banking the next year. That option, of course, depended on Garfield being part of such a deal. His options may have been implicit in the length of his remarks on racial matters in his inaugural address. That is, he had his own plan for the South and could do without Gorham.

Senate Filibustering

Parliamentary procedures experienced a terrible setback from the six-week Senate deadlock of the Garfield administration. Democrats discovered that under the Constitution they could tie up procedures by having a mere one-fifth of the Senate ask for votes on rules, voting that could go on repetitiously. During the 1881 deadlock, Senator John Sherman, long experienced in the upper chamber, remarked:

> Suppose this idea had existed during the war when we had session after session night after night, when some of the most vital measures of the war, upon which rested and depended the fate of this country, were pending, and a small but very able minority of men had exercised their right to call the yeas and nays and to interpose these dilatory motions. As I said yesterday, we sat through many a weary night to hear them out, but they never resorted to that expedient. I have heard the senator from Delaware denounce over and over again some of the acts that we have passed, some that have been approved by the Supreme Court of the United States, some that were considered vital and necessary in the reorganization of State governments when reconstruction commenced, as unconstitutional, null, and void, dangerous to the public liberties, and all the other words and phrases that he could heap upon the measures of the opponents, but he never and his associates in those days never thought of resorting to this expedient. [21]

Thus, the Democrats, on the question of civil rights strategies, came out of the deadlock in the Senate much stronger than the Republicans. The recollection of the deadlock must have hung over the Senate for decades as a cautionary tale.

Reid Sends John Hay a Midnight Dispatch and Alvord's Trick

The news of the Robertson nomination would have its different effects in different quarters. It would take a few days for the differences to emerge—allowing enough time to lapse for some parties to jump too quickly to a happy, but unfortunately wrong, conclusion. What happened was that the press in its laziness had reported too quickly on the legislature's response, and when the story was straightened out, it was the *Times* that reported how the legislature had come to retrace some steps. At stake was the question whether the president's nomination of Robertson would win unanimous approval of the New York legislature. That was important because some of Garfield's supporters were ready to interpret a unanimous vote as evidence that the new president had the power to intimidate legislators at Albany. If they wanted his consideration, they would have to show support for his first request.

In the state senate a combination of Republican independents and Democrats carried the day for Garfield. Next, the resolution was sent over to the assembly, where Speaker Sharpe happened to be out of the chair and a man known simply as Alvord, a Democrat, was taking his place and played a trick. Alvord recognized the motion, called for the "ayes," and then ventured into a trick of parliamentary sleight of hand. Alvord, *failing to call for the "nays," declared a unanimous vote!* Third, the newspapers of the country, overlooking the parliamentary ruse, picked up the story saying that the legislature—both houses—had unanimously approved Garfield's nomination. Some historians, unfortunately, have picked up the story at this point and gone no further.

As it turned out, numbering among those who jumped to the same conclusion was none other than Whitelaw Reid. But the facts would not warrant it. He thought that everything was going his way. He wired a message to John Hay at the State Department, a wire that Hay would take to the White House to be read to Garfield. First, he thought he had the evidence that in both houses of the state legislature party members had *voted unanimously* in favor of Garfield's nomination of Robertson. At the moment, however, he concluded that the president had intimidated party members, and, he further concluded, the legislature would adhere to the administration line. What he next told the president was that he should not back down. Presidents Lincoln and Grant had both made mistakes on occasion, and sometimes at the urging of congressmen they would "retrace their steps." In the current crisis, such recommendations came to Garfield. Edwin Godkin wrote, "It is not yet too late for (Garfield's) own fame and success to retrace his steps and abandon the plan of governing through the corrupt use of the public service."[26] Reid nonetheless barreled ahead not realizing how flimsy was his evidence. He wired Hay that:

> I wish to say to the President, in my judgment this is the turning point
> of his whole Administration—the crisis of his fate. If he surrenders now,
> Conkling is President for the rest of the term and Garfield becomes a laugh-
> ing stock. On the other hand, he has only to stand firm to succeed. With
> the *unanimous* action of the New York legislature Conkling cannot make

an effectual fight. That action came solely from the belief that Garfield unlike Hayes meant to defend his own Administration. The assembly is overwhelmingly Conkling, but they did not dare go on the record against Robertson so long as they thought the administration *meant business . . .* We can surely get enough Democratic senators to offset anything Conkling can do. In one word, there is no safe or honorable way out now but to go straight on. Robertson should be held firm, and if a change is made in the survivorship the new man should suit Robertson. Merritt would do perfectly for the place since he is a good subordinate, or some other good man could be found. But it is indispensable that the surveyorship should be kept in our own hands.

Boldness and tenacity now insure victory not merely for this year but for the whole term. Whenever pressure on Platt or James is wanted, let us know. Beware of James' soft, insinuating way. He is again wholly under Conkling's influence, but a stern, sharp admonition will *bring him instantly to his bearings.* He ought to have had that the morning after his serenade speech. (Our emphasis.)

Reid saw that the Garfield organization was now unmistakably rolling forward with such authority that anyone standing in the way, including assembly members, had to be ready to get out of the way or be hurt. "The administration meant business." The same term came to mind when Mrs. Blaine, in a letter to her daughter on March 24, asked, "Did you notice the nomination sent in yesterday? They mean business and strength."[27] She may have been referring to well-calculated punishments in private that, as Reid said, bring a person to his "bearings," probably recalling the kind of childhood whippings that make a victim wince. For adults the phrase "meant business" probably stood for sternness, no foolishness, and loyalty to the top half-breeds.

From the outset Gorham noted on April 1 and 4, "*The New York World* and the *Washington Post* clamor loudly for Democratic senators to sustain Robertson."[28] To him, this suggested that half-breeds would have outside help and that all stalwart responses were foolish, and set on lesser loyalties, hardly qualities of respect yielding to negotiations. They would have a splendid little Republican Party split—and the Democrats might well profit.

Matters soon changed. Reid in Albany had sent his telegram over the weekend to Hay at the Department of State, and it was read to the president. By Tuesday, however, Garfield, and the public in general, would have new information contradicting the earlier press reports about a unanimous vote.

Over the weekend Republicans at Albany found that they had second thoughts and the sleight-of-hand of the alleged unanimous support for Robertson at Albany went up in a puff. The Tuesday *Times* would note that on Monday a new characterization, contradicting what Reid had telegraphed privately, came from none other than "Speaker Sharpe (as he explained to the assembly) . . . that the vote was only taken on the affirmative side on Friday and declared carried unanimously. No one had voted against it." The journalists and some historians covering this business in the legislature, including editor Reid of the *Tribune,* had missed such parliamentary tricks, and then misled the nation into believing that Garfield had gained unanimous support for the Robertson nomination. Garfield was simply not that fortunate. The state legislature had not voted unanimously in favor of the Robertson nomination. That's all there was to it. That day in Albany editor Reid and leader Sharpe probably had no words to exchange.

At that moment, the temper of the assembly was not difficult to understand. After all, in the 1879 convention, when he ran for the governor's nomination, Robertson had received only a quarter of the state convention votes. Furthermore, in the state senate Robertson had held up the regulation bills that the assembly had passed. In preparation for the recent national convention, he had agreed to abide by the unit rule but weeks before the meeting he found reasons to lead a bolt against the state delegation, an action leading to Grant's defeat. He really could not be regarded as a widely popular legislator. Later in his resignation notice, Conkling held that "sixty of the eighty-one Republican members of the legislature, by letter or memorial, made objection"[29] to the Robertson nomination. Robertson was in the minority.

Reading Sharpe's comments and criticizing the quick response of the national press about "the unanimous action of the New York legislature," Gorham picked up the story on Robertson, writing on March 30 that:

> He can confidently rely upon the uncompromising opposition of both senators. His friend Alvord, by the trick of not putting the nays in the New York Assembly last Thursday, when only a few voices had responded aye, gave him the temporary benefit of an apparent indorsement of that body. On Monday *the resolution of indorsement was rescinded and tabled,* only four Republicans voting with the Democrats against such action.[30] (Our emphasis.)

One Democrat had voted with the 43 Republicans. The final tally in the assembly to table the resolution was 44 in favor and 31 against. The premise of Reid's wire to Hay, unanimity for Robertson, was without supporting evidence. The assembly's retraction blew away Reid's announcement that "with the unanimous action of the New York legislature Conkling cannot make an effectual fight. That action came solely from the belief that Garfield unlike Hayes meant to defend his own Administration." On Monday the Republican members of the assembly demonstrated that Garfield's nomination of Robertson had certainly failed to intimidate them. On Tuesday, reading the front page account in the *Times,* Garfield may have wondered what these two cartel proponents, Reid for Gould and Hay for Rockefeller, were trying to do with him.

In early January 1882, someone leaked the midnight dispatch to the *Herald*. The *Tribune* acknowledged it within days, saying that the leaker would be punished.[31] There was no mention of the moral question of having tried to use the false report to put backbone into Garfield. Gorham took another dig at Reid. The dispatch "was a pretense by Whitelaw Reid that Garfield was a man of putty, who could be molded and managed. . . . It was based on the assumption that the President was wavering, and dealt with him as though he had been a weak and vulgar inferior, should be stiffened up by an appeal to his vanity and his timidity."[32] Reid, in authoring the dispatch, feared that any yielding would lead observers to say, "Conkling is president." He would become the laughingstock. Gorham, however, took the opportunity to spoof Reid; by noting his use of the word "we" meant that he himself, an independent in 1872, had finally achieved the status of "co-president."

Little wonder that Hay wrote Reid after the disclosure in 1882 that he could not understand how a copy of the midnight dispatch had been leaked. Due to Sharpe's reversal of the vote, Reid and Hay had to be embarrassed with their effort to interpret legislative events. Hay explained to Reid that the original was in his safe in Cleveland. Indeed! Both of the men must have seen the correction made by the *Times* and suffered a twinge of embarrassment for their having so impulsively cheered the president on his course.

Godkin's Review of Garfield's Course in Civil Service Reform.

In mid-April Godkin at the *Nation* showed that the president had forsaken any prior commitment to civil service reform, a topic he had pursued for years and a stand he had most recently taken in his inaugural address. The April 21st edition of Godkin's paper quoted at length from the inaugural address and asked several questions:

> . . . President Garfield has, within one month after he has taken office, proceeded to remove one of the most important subordinate officers in the Government in the middle of his term . . . as everyone in and out of Congress believes, in order that he may use the place either to reward one set of politicians or inflict injury on another. When, therefore, he comes to ask Congress to protect "those who are entrusted with the appointing power against the waste and time and obstruction to the public business caused by the inordinate pressure for place," and to protect "incumbents against intrigue and wrong," . . . he will expose himself to some very embarrassing questions. Asked whether Mr. Merritt applied to be removed from the Customhouse in the middle of his term, he will have to answer no. Asked whether Mr. Robertson applied for Mr. Merritt's place, he will have to answer no. Asked whether any improvement in administration is likely to be effected by Mr. Robertson which Mr. Merritt could not or would not have carried out, he will have to answer no. Asked whether any law or usage of the service called for Mr. Merritt's removal in the middle

of his term, he will have to answer no. Asked whether this removal does not indicate that he himself does not believe in his own remedy, he will have to answer that this construction may undoubtedly be placed on it. Asked how he came to recommend to Congress to provide by law for the prevention of things which he, while a perfectly free agent, committed the very first moment he had it in his power, he will have to be silent. All his recommendations about civil-service reform will be so discredited that he will not only accomplish nothing by them, but he will, for the sake of his own peace and dignity, have to drop the subject, just as General Grant and Mr. Hayes dropped it, and acquiesce in all the abuses against which he has for years been inveighing. . .

After an indictment like this, it remains an amazing fact that Garfield's legacy became one of promoting civil service reform.

Suspicions of tyranny cropped up on both sides. In Washington evidence appeared of attempts at negotiations that failed to materialize largely because of Conkling's objections. The Republican caucus granted him a private hearing, where he spoke in his excellent and bitter oratorical fashion. He thought that he could embarrass the president for his having relied on donations from federal employees, but that fell flat. Then the caucus committee met with the president but his afterthoughts showed no yielding. He wrote in his diary that Conkling had bulldozed them. For the melodrama to play out, the hero had to keep pressing the evildoer. The term "bulldoze" referred to a new type of pistol recently used in the South to terrorize freedom-loving Afro-Americans. In the president's use, it matched his tactics against the Senate. Each was intimidating the other. He saw that Conkling was bulldozing the committee while he was expecting "letters of introduction" from senators who stood by Conkling.

On May 11, 1881, Gorham wrote that

> The most amazing element in all this is that those who applaud these performances the loudest are those who have for years been engaged in tearing down the Republican Party because they said it was based on the "spoils system." They dreaded "imperialism" under Grant. Now they see a President dictating to the Senate that it shall confirm men appointed by him in payment of political debts, and his chief organ's correspondent writes from his own table at the White House that men are to be selected for office who will set up the political machinery for Garfield's renomination in 1884.

In mid-January, Robertson thought he saw imperialism, and in May, Gorham was sure that he saw it.

Chapter X

Revenge Among the Factions

[1] *New York Tribune*, March 27, 1881.

[2] Benson, Lee. *Merchants, Farmers, and Railroads.* Cambridge, MA: Harvard University Press, 1955, p. 161.

[3] Nugent, Walter, *Money and American Society 1865–1880,* pp. 176, 266–268.

[4] *Washington Post*, May 7, 1881.

[5] Benson, p. 285.

[6] *The Diary of Lucretia Rudolph Garfield,* March 1-April 20, 1881, included in *Garfield Diary,* Vol. 4, edited with an introduction by Harry James Brown and Frederick D. Williams. Lansing: Michigan State University Press, 1981, p. 632.

[7] *NYT,* April 19, 1881.

[8] *NR,* April 10 and 26, 1882.

[9] Henry Adams, *Novels,* etc., pp. 947, 976.

[10] *NR,* May 11, 1881.

[11] Taylor, p. 307.

[12] Sparks, Jared. "Character of Washington," in McGuffey's *Sixth Eclectic Reader, Revised Edition.* New York: American Book, 1880, p. 442.

[13] Hamilton, Alexander. In *Alexander Hamilton, James Madison, John Jay: The Federalist Papers.* New York: Mentor, 1961. Paper # 76, pp. 456–458.

[14] *Garfield Diary*, March 27, 1881, p. 565.

[15] *Garfield Diary*, Vol. IV, p. 635. Entry in wife's diary of March 29, 1881.

[16] Hamilton, p. 459.

[17] *NR*, March 31, 1881.

[18] *NR*, April 6, 1881.

[19]   *NR,* April 20, 1881.

[19]   *NR,* May 17, 1881.

[20]   *NYT,* April 6, 1881.

[21]   *NYT,* May 10, 1881.

[22]   *NR,* May 25, 1881.

[23]   *NR,* May 25, 1881.

[24]   *NR,* May 18, 1881.

[25]   *NR,* May 18, 1881.

[26]   Beale, Harriet S. B., *Diary of Harriet S. Blaine*, Vol. 1, p. 197. Chicago: Micro Library Collection, 1971.

[27]   *NR,* April 1 and 4, 1881.

[28]   *NR,* May 17, 1881.

[29]   *NR,* March 30, 1881.

[30]   *NR,* January 9, 1882.

[31]   *NR,* January 14, 1882.

[32]   *NR,* May 11, 1881.

CHAPTER XI

President Garfield Sees Victory Through a Scandal

In mid-January 1881 Senator James Blaine, Secretary of State–designate, urged president-elect James Garfield to take a firm stand on the suspected corruption in the postal contract office that distributed the mail out West largely by stagecoach owners and river steamer operators. With the increasing migration, the business had been growing swiftly. Two years earlier Congress had examined the service and finally approved appropriations.

The prospect of a serious investigation in 1881 would have had plausibly different appeals to Blaine and to Garfield. Behind Blaine's desire could have been benefits for Gould since the recent telegraph consolidation. Opening an investigation could help raise doubts in the public mind whether the Post Office Department was fit to run a competing telegraph business. If it could be shown that the department could not manage the star route services, one could conclude that the department certainly would not qualify to embark on a new telegraph service. The payoff would be less public clamor for the government to compete with Gould's new consolidation.

The benefit that Garfield might have seen in the scandal could accrue to national banking. He had been through the midterm campaign of 1878 just before resumption of specie payments (having enough gold at the Treasury to back paper dollars) and in one important sense the conditions in 1882 would be the same just as rechartering of national banking arose. At campaign time there would be much less party discipline than in a quadrennial, presidential election when everyone worked for the top of the ticket. Abandonment of hard-money principles would be difficult to curb. In 1878 several departments helped raise money for the campaign, which came to have a greenback hue to it. Garfield could have decided that in the run-up to the midterm campaign of 1882 he could not trust those department employees still employed since 1878. Playing it safe, Garfield apparently decided in 1881 to remove workers lest the next year they lobby on the wrong side of the currency question. A scandal would justify his dismissing several department heads.

If an investigation of the department were to have full impact as a scandal, and encourage whistle blowers, it would have to be well publicized.[1] It certainly would take the assistance of a well-known newspaper. Since the *Times* had achieved such splendid results in publicizing the Tweed scandal, it looked as if it was the paper for the job. George Jones, editor of the *Times,* was invited down to the White House to make an April 1st visit with Garfield. They agreed upon the project. The administration would provide the newspaper with a mountain of information for editor Jones to feed day after day into the seven columns of the front page and beyond. That, however, may not have been the only matter discussed. Within a few days after the first news of the investigation, a *Times* editorial, plausibly suggested by Garfield, expressed fears of a greenback menace during the next year's campaign season.[2]

Having reached an agreement with Jones, Garfield was in a position to command more attention for the Robertson nomination to the collectorship. The day after he met with Jones, he began letting visiting senators know that any members of the Senate not supporting the Robertson nomination would have to submit "letters of introduction." That put a new cast on party relations, discounting their elections, as they had to wait on the president's favor.

The two actions--the opening of the scandal and the corralling of senators--had the common character of drawing attention to affairs in New York. Steady newspaper coverage of the scandal would certainly demand public attention for postal reform, while requiring letters of introduction from senators would have caught the lawmakers' attention. Together the new demands on the Senate and in departments due to the scandal sounded like a prescription right out of Machiavelli. Garry Wills states the injunction for a prince: "Stun your subjects . . . with extravagant kindness or severity, but get their attention."[3]

Garfield's back-to-back actions aimed, as it became clear in May, at shaking up the New York organization. The star route contractors had a house in New York that served as their office, and in the city the scandal about their work would darken their reputation. Taken together with a new appointment for collector, the New York organization had to be on the defensive. In one editorial in January Gorham had wondered whether Garfield would become a makeweight against the party itself. Then as early as March 26th Gorham in another editorial characterized the tone of the new administration when he wrote that the president, by nominating Robertson, was seeking to change the leadership of the New York party by "external force."

At the moment, the half-breeds were under threat. Rufus Hatch had taken Gould to court over the Western Union telegraph consolidation, followed by public outrage against the capitalist and the spectacular growth of the Anti-Monopoly League. Garfield's actions had the marks of a factional leader bent on eliminating opponents. Gone were the attempts by party leaders looking to discuss, negotiate, and compromise on substantive matters, thereby getting everyone through the next election. The *Post* had already said that the gulf between the factions was too wide for anyone to close. The national convention had come and gone and party leaders had lost the opportunity to set forth guidance. Without that guidance the damage about to be done was anyone's guess.

Garfield possibly took a page from J. B. Harrison's recent works. In 1878, just before the November election, Harrison, writing a rather opaque article in the *Atlantic* entitled "Certain Dangerous Tendencies in American Life," called for stronger community leadership. That was followed in an 1880 volume with the same title and a clearer statement. Harrison reported that he had interviewed several greenbackers and concluded that offsetting leadership was needed in every community. He urged community business leaders to talk to their ministers about mentioning in their sermons the perils facing the hard-money agenda.

Getting some momentum into Garfield's effort required a realistic assessment. Thomas Nast had kept alive the fear of greenback resurgence with his March 19 cartoon when the Republicans took over the Senate. The cartoon showed ravenous wolves going after rivers and harbors appropriations. It also showed that "the people's national banks" were at risk. It made the cartoonists' view of the Republican politicians about as uncomplimentary as the bankers' view had been in January.[4] Next, the prospect of the politicians' liaison would gain strength from the results of an early April Michigan election. Even though the state's greenback party was smaller than the older parties, the figures of its turnout, as *Appleton's for 1881* would later report,[5] compared to the November 1880 turnout, showed a very high level of commitment. Hard-money advocates had to consider that if the greenbacker commitment evident in 1881 remained as strong a year later in the midterm elections, some Republican candidates might appeal to the soft-money supporters, leaving the national bank advocates vulnerable to losses. Garfield had stated his worry in his Resumption Day address in Chicago when he had said that the

> most dangerous indirect assault upon resumption is the attempt to abolish national banks, and substitute additional greenbacks in the place of bank notes. The effort will call to its support the sentiment, which to some extent prevails against moneyed corporations [railroads]. Should the attempt succeed it will inevitably result in suspension of specie payment [at the Treasury].[6]

With the Michigan election returns in hand, the president probably knew that he had correctly suspected greenback troubles ahead. He could feel warranted in cleaning out the greenback bureaucrats with assurance. Four days after the Michigan election, on Saturday, April 9, 1881, Postmaster General Thomas James and Special Agent P. H. Woodward showed Garfield a comparative tabulation of the alleged extravagances of the star routes. Garfield wrote, "Great frauds have been practiced, and I will clear out the Contract office."[7] One person notably absent from the meeting was a representative for Attorney General MacVeagh, who later found the cases quite difficult to develop.

The scandal had been on the back burner for some time--ever since Blaine had first intimated it, following the news in the third week in January of donor Gould's telegraph consolidation. In the first week of February, Reid and Blaine had discussed moving Democrat A. M. Gibson to the fore.

Editor Gorham, with his own access to the rumor mill, had gotten wind of the impending investigation. Now the matter went into full gallop. The only trouble not worrying the planners was whether any case could be won for the contractors. Before long, the suspects would be roasted in the daily press.

The New York State Senate Fails to Pass the Canal Bill

Different centers of political reality were in the game. While Garfield moved against the greenbackers, the New York legislature was taking up transportation policy. On the table in the state senate were the railroad commission bill and the bill for improvement of the canal. Trying to enhance canal services, state senator William Astor submitted a bill to promote steam towing by adding railroads on the canal banks, but it failed. Under an April 7, 1881, dateline from Albany, the *Times* reported,

> The Canal Committee of the assembly will consider today the bill providing steam towage on the canals. The bill failed in the Senate owing to the preponderating influence in that body of the great railroad corporations who are naturally opposed to anything that looks like cheapening of transportation.

Public sentiment for free canals now stirred. The *Times* had not always sided with the free canal position. In 1879 the paper had asked anyone to "explain how anything short of a bonus for water transport could divert to the lake and canal boats the carriage of flour."[8] By 1881 the paper had joined the canal camp. On April 14th, a week after Astor's failure, the *Times* echoed his complaint:

> It is getting to be generally conceded, by intelligent men, that the canal policy of the State of New York for the past 15 years has exhibited such a lack of foresight and common sense, to say nothing of statesmanship, as would disgrace a fourth-rate Commonwealth.

> The constitutional amendments that were ratified by the people in 1874 by a vote of 3 to 1 are a perpetual bar to all further progress or improvement. These amendments should have been entitled "An act to fetter, obstruct, and strangle the Erie Canal preparatory to its final abandonment for the benefit of railroad corporations." A suspicion is beginning to creep abroad that the people of this State have been badly hoodwinked by these severe constitutional restrictions, which they have been persuaded to place around their canal—that they were, in fact, concocted by designing men

for a specific purpose. That purpose could have been none other than to tie up and hamper the canals in the interest of the railroads. . . . The same railroad influence is still visible if the strict construction is given to these amendments, and the opposition that is made to all improvements of the Erie Canal by paid attorneys of the railroads, who are also legislators.[9]

Adding to the poor reputation of corporate attorneys out West, where they had hoodwinked the grangers, they got a poor reputation among many New Yorkers for holding up action on the canal. The list of complaints against them included the comment earlier in the year from merchants who did not believe "that only railroad attorneys and experts are capable of forming an intelligent opinion upon [regulation]."[10] In retrospect, the *Times*' complaint was that activity in the state legislature had brought canal matters to the brink of an impending slippery slope.

The Merchants Oppose Letting Railroad Advocates Take Over All the Departments

Concurrently, the New York City anti-monopolists let the president know that transportation matters were on their minds and, as reported in the *Times* on April 8, 1881, two thousand businessmen petitioned favoring the retention of the current collector, William Merritt, who was only halfway through his four-year term. The cover letter to the merchants asking for their signatures pointed out Robertson's

> delaying and killing the bill to prevent the recent [telegraph] consolidation after it passed the assembly . . . this nomination taken in connection with that of Hon. Stanley Matthews to the Supreme Court and Mr. Elliot F. Shepherd [Vanderbilt's son-in-law] to the District Attorneyship indicates a settled purpose on the part of the railroad interest to push their advocates into influential places until they become the dominant power in all departments of the government . . .

Garfield had in 1873 used similar language about the corporations' heavy-handedness in "pushing their advocates into influential places," but in 1881, he made no mention in his diary that the merchants disliked the practice. While in 1873 he had said all that was proper in objecting, in 1881 his greater interest was to do the handsome thing in helping some consolidators get on with their task.

Conkling's Courtesy to the Matthew Carpenter Family

In early April 1881, a chance came for the stalwarts to measure western opinion. On April 8, Senators Roscoe Conkling, John Logan, John Jones, and Democrat Francis Cockrell of Missouri departed for Wisconsin to accompany Matthew Carpenter's ashes home.[11] Carpenter had been very popular and a huge crowd showed up. Eager to learn whether the dispute in Washington had stirred up opinion, the delegation found little interest. The affiliation of senators from the upper Mississippi valley with men from the port of New York had not brought new aid to Conkling.

The Rate War of 1881

Rates for the railroad cartel had been falling since the second quarter of 1881. New York merchants seemed to benefit, but in reality the rate war had locked some merchants into rates higher than those their competitors later obtained, making them suffer accordingly. In his brief history of the three cartels, Ulen writes:

> The collusion's record during 1880 was, for the dead freight pool from Chicago, one of unbroken success. A year-end review of trunk line traffic from the *Commercial and Financial Chronicle* held the year to have been one of untrammeled success for the cartel and its members and noted that passenger traffic showed its first marked improvement since the Panic of 1873. *The Railway Age* in the fall had remarked, "rail rates, thanks to the eastbound pool, have remained firm all summer at a reasonable figure."

> The first quarter of 1881 continued to be successful for the Joint Executive Committee. The rate war on immigrant traffic, which had begun in mid-December, was over by mid-February. All three members of the pool restored the tariff to $14, which had fallen as low as $3 for New York–Chicago passage, in late winter. Passenger rates both east and west bound improved.

> Matters began to go sour for the dead freight pool in the early spring. From a level of 35 cents/100 lbs. of grain, Chicago to New York, a level that had been maintained since November, secret cuts were reported in early April. By the end of the month the prevailing rate was restored to 30 cents, the Chicago Board of Trade criticizing the fact that the cartel failed to give shippers the customary ten days' notice of a change in the tariff of rates.

The usually conservative Chicago Board of Trade, in its April 26 complaint, betrayed obvious annoyance at the recent rate change, saying it was an "abuse of power, and as calculated to visit undeserved and unavoidable hardship and loss upon the general trade of the West whenever the whim of this secret conclave shall choose to exact it." [12] Ulen continues:

> Adherence to the 30-cent rate continued through May, but rumors of discounts of 25 cents filled the railroad press in the first weeks to June. The commissioner's office announced that the former rates might be restored at any time without the customary ten days' notice, which announcement

was taken as an admission that secret cuts were going on. In July further cuts were discovered in eastbound freight, passenger and immigrant rates. Westbound freight and passenger rates were not affected. The official immigrant rate was reduced to $9 from New York to Chicago from the last winter $14, the reduction presumably matching the secret rate. By the end of July, a further official cut was made to $7. The disarray in freight rates on eastbound traffic took the market rate to 15 cents. The general freight agents of the roads from Chicago assembled in Commissioner Fink's office to resolve the differences, but no common policy could be formulated. The rate stayed at 15 cents through the end of September with periodic discounts below that level being recorded.[13]

Passenger fares were another battleground. Try as they might, the corporations did not succeed in restoring rates to their previous levels.

In August, Gorham described the cartel's rate-setting process as something of a merry-go-round.

> The grand pool combinations, whereby all railroad lines were to exact the last penny from the shipper's pocket which could be taken without driving him away from the use of the railroad altogether—the monopoly feature of railroading, which kills competition—failed in the desired object. The robbers are robbing each other. "Cutting of rates" means that the law of competition is in operation. Whenever it is proposed to regulate rates of toll on railroads by law the corporations flunkies, who write for such scrubby newspapers as the *New York Tribune*, immediately sing in unison that competition will regulate the railroads rates best, as it does all other business. Then the competing lines go into partnership and employ Mr. Fink to equalize rates and business, all to prevent competition. Then the partners cheat each other by allowing drawbacks to freighters and selling tickets to scalpers, and Mr. Commissioner Fink tears his hair and despairingly cries out for laws to stop these interruptions of his fascinating game. Then comes the *Tribune* to the rescue of the railway chiefs against the assaults of their servant. Mr. Fink seems to be devoted to the cause of honesty among railway thieves. He is in earnest in his pool making, honest in his endeavor to keep all the parties to the pool up to their extortions to which, under his direction, they have agreed. He wants to make the conspirators rob the people fairly. He wants laws to punish competition, from which the railway managers have "swore off."[14]

Gorham was distinguished in leading anti-monopoly thought. In 1885 Thurber characterized the opposition on the same point. The railroaders, Thurber told the Cullom committee, "appeal to the National Government for legislation to enforce their agreements upon each other and enable them to tax the commerce of the country to sustain these fictitious values."[15]

Blaine Suggests to Reid to get the Press to Toe the Administration Line

Public opinion was hard to shape in these matters—whether concerning the canal, the Robertson nomination, or railroad regulation. The railroaders had in their hands the tools to meet the situation. Shortly after Garfield nominated Robertson, Blaine decided that the president was not getting enough press support. The alleged gag rule of June 9, 1880, had held that the corporations could influence the press with "free passes, advertisements, and other favors . . . extended to the press more freely than ever before." Blaine now thought it was time to bring the press into line. On March 31, 1881, he wrote *Tribune* editor Whitelaw Reid that:

> We feel the need here sadly of a "little more grape" in the editorial columns of the *Tribune* on the great pending issue. The *Times* is very ugly and John Campbell Young is tramping [?] around [?] very [?] in the *Herald* . . . One blast from the *Tribune* bugle is needed terribly . . . I have reason to believe that the enclosed in Saturday's *Tribune* would be an exceedingly valuable contribution to the cause at this end.[16]

Reid complied and in less than two weeks David Davis, independent senator of Illinois, noted in the *Times* that the press had suddenly come under the influence of the corporations. Davis wrote a friend in a letter that soon became public that

> Great corporations and consolidated monopolies are fast seizing avenues of power that lead to the control of the government. It is an open secret that they rule states, through procured Legislatures and corrupted courts; that they are strong in Congress, and that they are unscrupulous in the use of means to conquer prejudice and to acquire influence . . .

> Leading newspapers, recognized as Republican and Democratic organs, are owned and directed by grasping monopolists to subserve their selfish schemes, and to restrain opposition to them in either party. Their only politics is greed of gain.[17]

This condition would endure in early 1884. Gorham, writing for the *San Francisco Chronicle*, added to the dismal picture of the American press, saying, "The metropolitan press is too much of it in the toils of our corporation masters to hope much from it."[18]

Reid's *Tribune*, known as the administration organ, could win compliance from other papers. Across the country railway agents could read local papers daily to discern whether they were conforming to the views of the daily *Tribune*. If they noted that any local paper did not toe the line, they could consider depriving the paper of paid advertising.

The bugle blast from the *Tribune* plausibly meant that the other papers had to start looking at their incomes.

With Blaine's call for a blast, the fate that befell Conkling is better understood. Biographer Allan Peskin asserts, "Garfield was winning the battle for public opinion. Even in Conkling's home state 94 newspapers supported the President, while only 18 defended the senator."[19]

The Blaine-Reid correspondence, however, raises a question about an intervening variable. Since the half-breeds in their alleged gag rule had declared that they would corrupt the press, the question arises as to the meaning of the statistics. Did the figures measure Conkling's loss of popularity or Reid's success in persuading the press to support the administration?

Judge Davis's comment helps explain the sharp censure that would follow Conkling for years to come. By the time Garfield died, the railroad agents placing their ads in local papers on cue from Reid could have furthered the politically correct view of blaming all on Conkling. All Reid had to say was that Conkling was "always the villain of the piece," and he could expect that to be followed by a ripple across the nation's press with similar comments. This surmise about the effect of the *Tribune* on other daily papers during the 1880s presents a testable hypothesis.

The *Times*, while pursuing the postal scandal, continued its opposition to the Robertson nomination. Senator Daniel Voorhees of Indiana had voiced Garfield's view that the position of New York collector was too important to be regarded as anything less than a national office. The Hoosier believed that the office of the collector could not be regarded as a mere appendage to the local politics of a single state. However true that might have been, in early May, 1881, the *Times* wondered,

> Why, in the name of common sense, does [Mr. Voorhees] fail to see that the President insists on making the office just such an appendage by bestowing it without any pretense of public necessity on an adroit local politician who did him a very opportune service.[20]

If the office was of national importance, Garfield should have nominated someone of national importance.

The Star Route Scandal Breaks Just as Greenbackers Have a Victory

On April 25th the *Times* broke the story of the postal investigation across the front page. The coverage continued day after day, filling the seven front-page columns and boosting Garfield's popularity. Thomas James asked James Brady for his resignation, leaving the public to think that an announcement of charges would follow. Certainly virtue was about to strike at evil!

On the same day the *Times* broke the story the *National Republican* carried a story, front, top, and center, about the growth of the greenback cause. From Philadelphia came the story about greenback leader General James B. Weaver's reception on his current tour. Weaver told his audience that:

> I have been speaking since the 15ᵗʰ of last month in different States, and my meetings were remarkable. In Pennsylvania, particularly in the oil regions, the meetings were immense. I tell you the tide is rising throughout the country, and will soon reach the large cities.

Such greenback advances would be Garfield's targets.

The Hard-Money Press Comes to the Aid of National Banking

On April 30, 1881, both the *Times* and cartoonist Thomas Nast made the same point by coming to the defense of national banks. In a *Times* editorial that could have come directly from editor George Jones's early April interview with the president, the paper envisioned longer-range worries about the vote of 1882 on national banking. In the recent Michigan election, the greenbackers' turnout testified to their discipline. The *Times* may have seen in the Michigan results a prospect of a greenback surge. The editorial read that:

> The question which is of special interest to the believers in sound finance, is how far this movement [the greenbackers], supported in part by recruits from both the old parties and partly by men who sincerely hold its ideas, can enforce those ideas in the legislation of the country.

> This is a question to which the answer is necessarily conditional. It depends very much upon what the financial situation of the Government may be at the time when the Greenbackers should reach sufficient strength, if they should ever, to determine legislation. *Two facts make it impossible to look forward to such a contingency without some apprehension.* One is that the Greenbackers and those who sympathize with them can fall back on the actual exercise of the Congressional right to authorize the issue of legal tender paper currency in time of no special emergency. The legal tenders now out are an awkward argument for the issue of more, which circumstances may make it extremely difficult to meet. The second fact is that the national bank charters are approaching their limitation; that the bank-notes now furnish the only paper currency open to no legal and constitutional objections, and that the spirit of hostility to the banks has been very considerably encouraged by the leaders of both the old parties. The Greenbackers, whose first and constant idea is war on the national banks, may find in these facts an amount of strength, which they will not be slow

to avail themselves of. The considerations to which we have briefly called attention are such as deserve the careful study of our political leaders. They show that greenbackism as an independent movement has a possible future that cannot safely be ignored, that forces are working silently, but steadily and constantly, in its favor which may have to be reckoned with by the time that another national contest approaches.

In sum, hard-money advocates preparing for the 1882 midterm election had to prepare for the greenbackers. The sooner the greenbackers faced discouragement, the better. Garfield now had two birds in the hand and one in the bush. The New England senators had established an alliance among themselves making it much easier to spot apostasy on the currency question among their western peers. In addition, the developing star route scandal gave the president a plausible reason to clean out the federal employees who had helped in the 1878 campaign, lest they revive the links between Republican senators and local greenbackers.

Nast's cartoon of April 30th, which ran on the same day as the *Times* editorial, caught the turn of events, detecting the implicit connection between the greenbackers and the "star route thieves." The cartoon showed a "politico" toppled and resumption secure and rising.[21] The new administration had now revealed its heroism; with the scorn against the politicians, the possible link between the anti-bank sentiment and the anti-monopoly sentiment was damaged. Politicians would no longer be able to profit by stirring up the subject. There also soon appeared frequent editorials in the *Times* suggesting how bankers could give their customers better services. Together they suggested a list of complaints the president had assembled that he thought the banks should pay attention to and correct. Garfield may have picked up these suggestions for improving bank services and believed the time was right for sharing them.

Garfield Names Hard-Money Advocates to Head Some Departments

Once the postal investigation became public, Garfield proceeded to remove department heads known for raising funds in the 1878 campaign coordinated by Gorham. William LeDuc of Minnesota, commissioner of Agriculture in 1878, had circulated a subscription list in his department. At the behest of New England senators, Garfield replaced him with former congressman and horticulturist George Loring of Massachusetts, doubtless a hard-money advocate. For the post of commissioner of Indian affairs, vacant since inauguration day, Garfield first nominated Thomas Nichol, founder of the Honest Money League, who shortly withdrew. Then Garfield named banker and railroad president Hiram Price of Iowa, a former congressman. In the Post Office Department, Thomas James won a resignation from Thomas Brady, another fundraiser in 1878. Also dropped was Jacob McGrew of the Sixth Auditor's Office. Hard-money advocates could take confidence that, in the forthcoming banking debate, the department employees would not blindside them, as Gorham had in 1878 with his Newark address.

The most prestigious greenbacker of 1878 had been John Sherman, then secretary of the Treasury and now again a senator from Ohio. In 1878 he too had circulated fundraising subscription sheets through the Treasury Department, known for its factions of hard and soft money. In the 1881 Senate, Sherman found himself, by his committee assignments, thwarted from cooperating with anyone except New Englanders. The suggestion is that the word was out among department employees that Garfield "meant business" on the money question and that the new administration would frown on any traffic that Treasury employees had with greenbackers.

The Opening and Closing of the Postal Scandal

Although most accounts would have readers remember that the Garfield administration initiated fraud charges against the postal contractors, part of the story is missing. Those accounts fail to mention the final outcome. In the end the Department of Justice had nothing to show for all of its work. The campaign had opened with asking Brady to resign and then further insulting him by not telling him of any charges. The fact is that after all that newspaper coverage and special investigations, seventeen years after the charges were raised (1898), the Department of Justice finally dropped the cases. There had been no evidence. So the government gained neither convictions of malefactors nor the recovery of funds. One of the early casualties was George Gorham, largely because, as an editorial writer, he criticized the president for the investigation. The day after the scandal broke in 1881 Gorham wrote for his readers that there was no evidence--just as the Department of Justice in 1898 would have to report. As the papers continued to cover the matter, he criticized them and the administration for the "trial by press" and exceeded propriety in doing so, just as Blaine predicted. Consequently, he had to watch his hope of returning to the Senate office fade. Blaine knew Gorham well enough to suspect that he would probably trip himself up.

Over the years one administration after another had continued the cases, only to end up with prosecutorial headaches. Under Garfield, the criminal case moved slowly since Attorney General MacVeagh was not able to pull matters together. Garfield finally decided to take a hand in the process. The Arthur administration employed better staff, and the court heard the one case against Stephen Dorsey, but the jury acquitted him. Where one would have thought that the Cleveland administration (Democrat) would have had the most to gain, it failed to do so. In 1886, Brady came to Washington, telling his friends that he was writing a book about the trials in order to publish "the true inside history of these events . . . to place several alleged statesmen in the public pillory. [The] moral saints with a 'holier than thou' cast of countenance, I shall impale on the corroded points of their own corruption."[22] During the Harrison administration, District Attorney Hoge, after consultation with the attorney general, advised the criminal court to clear the docket of twenty-four cases, as the government had failed to secure a conviction in the main case. Therefore, charges were dropped against John W. Dorsey, Stephen W. Dorsey, William Pitt Kellogg, John R. Miner, Thomas J. Brady, H. M. Vaile, A. O. Buck, and

John M. Peck.[23] Handling the so-called scandal and hoping for results similar to those from the investigation of the Tweed Ring would prove disappointing. The aging George Jones of the *Times* would die in 1891 with nothing to show for his effort.

The McKinley administration brought a civil case against the star route "thieves" to recover about $500,000 in misappropriated funds, plus interest since 1882. It proceeded to examine the work of postal contractors in some western mountain regions. Such an investigation would be far removed from questionable Washington juries. The promoters of the scandal may have thought that they had a better chance in winning a case. The effort, however, came to naught. In 1898, with a San Francisco dateline of March 19, the *Times* ran the following item on the front page:

END OF STAR ROUTE CASES.

Old Suits to Recover for Frauds on Mail Contracts Dropped.

Assistant United States District Attorney Knight says telegraphic instructions have been received from Washington to dismiss the star route cases. These old suits were begun by the government to recover about half a million dollars, with interest from the year 1882. The principal sum was alleged to have been obtained from the government by systematic frauds practiced in the charges by mail contractors and sub-contractors for the carriage of the mails.

These suits went to the Supreme Court of the United States in 1887 on demurrer, and slumbered there for three or four years. Mr. Knight says it would be useless to prosecute them, as the Government has *no evidence* on which a judgment could be obtained. The routes were in Montana, Nevada, and adjacent territory.[24] (Our emphasis.)

This Department of Justice decision in 1898 provides any latter-day investigator with the end-point for reviewing the entire work on the case. Any investigator who reports the opening of the "scandal" and/or its course through the courts without reporting this favorable judgment for the defense simply leaves an undeserved favorable judgment on the Garfield administration. Certainly Garfield was a scholar of some repute. Certainly he was an attorney who showed that he was familiar with properly conducted investigations. That record, however, cannot save him in the task in hand and from a reputation of carelessness in this particular matter and having made a great mistake. Neither his position nor the manner of his death should obscure how poorly he handled it. Subsequent generations betray their love for the hero of melodrama by overlooking the outcome of 1898 and readily give credit where it is not due. What the public should expect is that they read historians rather than melodramatists, expecting them to catch up with what actually happened. They would do better to admit that Garfield made a mistake, detail his missteps, honor his critics, and hope that future leaders would be more circumspect. At the time, however, there was no Government Accountability Office and editor Gorham served as a functional alternative.

In addition, the following October 1898 Second Assistant Postmaster General W. S. Shallenberger, in his annual reports from the Post Office Department, severely criticized the contracting system under him. He charged that the two-tiered contracting system of major contractors and subcontractors was inefficient, wasteful, and sometimes unfair.[25] Without further examination, one might conclude that the arrangements for the delivery of western mails in the past two decades had not improved whatsoever. What emerged was a system that the operators knew how to work without making a misstep. Although the department did not report to either one of the two controllers at the Treasury, its own systems of accounting had turned out to be adequate to the task. Apparently, Treasurer Spinner's 1871 warning could have alerted observers to avoid scandal. The warning may have led postal administrators to become especially circumspect. One would have thought, since President Garfield had spent so much time on the matter, that to honor his memory Congress would have corrected the system, but apparently neither reformers nor Congress saw reason to do so.

The *Times* and the *Nation* in 1881 had both sharply condemned the star route system, and in 1898 they had nothing to say. The papers' silence probably meant, under the concepts of policy settlements, that they conceded to the authority of the Department of Justice, turning their attention to other, more current matters. Also, in 1898, Thomas L. James, active in public life from his position at Vanderbilt's Lincoln National Bank, offered no comment about the end of the star route cases.

At the outset of the scandal in 1881, on the field of political combat, the opponents on the currency question were still trying to outflank one another. Then hard-money advocates in the East could have seen in the opening of the postal scandals that the Garfield administration was making a perfect target: those "bad men" in the West. Add to that fervor the anti-tax sentiment of those favoring "retrenchment," and a volatile brew was always in the wings. But by 1898 the characters on stage had changed. The *U.S.S. Maine* had sunk in the Havana harbor and war with Spain loomed. An investigation was under way, and the reticent President William McKinley had yet to send a report to the Congress. The "war faction" among the Republicans had the advantage. The Spanish were now the "bad men." The "good men," who had worried in 1881 that the "bad men" among the stalwarts would find political advantage in Caribbean expansion, found that they had quite a proper cause to support!

The Republican hard-money message in 1896 had driven many western party members from their ranks. Since the midterm elections of 1898 were coming up, removing the threat hanging over the western stagecoach operators would have softened the image of easterners' hostility. The quiet on the editorial front may have helped the former contenders to more gracefully abandon their old duel. The judgment remained: the Department of Justice had nothing to work with. All the hoopla Garfield had urged the

Times to raise had helped the paper in the circulation wars, but it also slandered some perfectly good civil servants.

For the newspapers the irony was precious. The papers had argued that the publicity on the star route allegations needed endless attention like the successfully relentless attention given the Tweed Ring scandal. In the long run, however, the coverage of the alleged star route villainy proved only to be "yellow journalism," a practice of treating a subject in the news melodramatically and severely slandering some party to a dispute. Now in 1898, the case was dropped just at the moment when a more productive campaign of "yellow journalism" was under way, centering on Cuba. A new melodrama was simply too seductive to pass up. Hearst and Pulitzer were now in the lead in the press coverage. Burrows and Wallace observe, "Hearst stirred fact with fiction and poured the resulting prose into a mold of pure melodrama."[26]

Good melodrama requires that it follow a course that monopolizes the arena. No other melodrama may arise from another quarter competing for equal attention. In 1898 the star route cases could hardly compete with the alleged Spanish misbehavior, and so were dropped. The efforts in each case could have been written off as a joke, but for the damage they did. Before McKinley gave his report, men who knew about sinking ships asserted that the bomb blast on the *Maine* had bent the metal outward. The blast had to be internal, not from a mine or a torpedo. Never mind. War was wanted and those who wanted it got it! To curb such corruptions of the public mind, the promoters of scandals ought to be required to post bond, before they start their drumbeat, to be divided among the victims if the charges prove false.

The Place of Gorham's Criticism of the President

Gorham's critics at the outset of the star route scandal focused on his style and apparent personal interests, rather than on the substance of his comments. He was one of the "bad men" whom Blaine sought to drive out. After all, the critics only had to remind readers that Brady was a principal stockholder in Gorham's paper, inferring that, as editor, he had to provide the stockholder with a corrupt service. Further, Garfield's complaints were read with an ear to the office he held and, later, to the manner of his death. Defense of the postal system was quite difficult under the circumstances.

When Postmaster General James asked Brady for his resignation, and Brady complied at once, James failed to follow up the next day with any announcement of charges. Instead, the well-primed newspapers went forward with their ceaseless coverage. The *Times* opened the coverage with its front page, seven columns wide, devoted exclusively to the allegations. Then, having a glut of 93 star routes to review, it followed up day after day with as much attention.

Gorham at first claimed that there was no evidence for the charges, and then concluded that the purpose of the coverage was to create a "trial by press," or character assassination. Remembering that in early 1881 the administration had shown a melodramatic penchant for setting the "good men" against the "bad men," Gorham, with tongue in cheek, on April 17th, summarized the smear of Stephen Dorsey:

> J. W. Dorsey had a mail contract some years ago. Service was expedited and compensation increased. His brother, Stephen W., must therefore be a *bad man*. Miner and Peck had a mail contract. Service was expedited and compensation increased. Peck's brother-in-law, Stephen W. Dorsey, must therefore have done something wrong. Not a word of *evidence* that the increase was ill advised. It certainly was lawful. Not a word of *evidence* that Stephen W. Dorsey had any more interest in the matter than has James A. Garfield. Yet, to read some papers, one would suppose he had been caught in the act of stealing. Such enterprising newspapers! Such decent officials, to feed them with rotten scandal! [Quoting Garfield, Gorham added:] Has Dorsey got back from Indiana?[27]

Gorham also resorted to an analogy. However true it was, it was offensive, as it drew an image from a new vogue in New York crimes of passion. In separate cases, two young men had viciously attacked women who had jilted them. In each case, the young man ambushed his woman and threw lye into her face, leaving lifetime scars. The young ladies could never appear as attractive again, and suitors would less likely call. The attacks had been acts of character assassination. The New York legislature quickly raised the penalty for the crime.[28] The language soon slipped over to Washington politics in defense of the stalwarts. In mid-April 1881 some ambitious New York detective had subjected Conkling to character assassination and Conkling referred to it as "vitriol throwing."[29]

Eight days later, Gorham used the senator's figure of speech in the political realm, applying it to the postal scandal. He inferred that the investigation had no greater purpose than destroying reputations. At the end of one of his editorials, while the *Times* was day after day running the scandals, Gorham inquired, "Who desires the credit for this infamous vitriol-throwing enterprise, the Postmaster General or the President?"[30] Gorham implied that the new administration was attacking the celebrity of its own supporters, because it no longer wanted their support. The same reading was apparent in E. V. Smalley's explanation of the Robertson appointment, that the Customs House was needed to assure Garfield's reelection, implying that he did not expect the stalwarts to support the incumbent.

Of course, Gorham's analogy from the crime brought an immediate reaction. About five weeks earlier, Blaine had suggested to Reid that Gorham would "dig" the wrong person, implying that the Senate support for him would weaken. The first to criticize was Senator Joseph Hawley of Connecticut.[31] Meanwhile, Postmaster James kept up a good front by making some righteous statements.[32] Of James, Gorham demanded, cutting into the melodrama, "Give us something more honest and not so good!"[33] Gorham knew it would take a long time to win back his Senate office, so he retreated to pricking the pretenses of the half-breeds. It was altogether out of the question to try to get them to change, or even make a move toward change.

Gorham, of course, would have done well to raise the point about character assassination more felicitously. He could have cited Garfield's *Atlantic* article, in which he had warned that "criticism [of office holders] may degenerate into mere slander, and put an end to its power for good by being used as a means to assassinate the reputation and destroy the usefulness of honorable men."[34] Quoting that, Gorham could have written, "Since we know of the president's disgust with character assassination, we expect evidence will soon drive the matter to a grand jury or some other remedy be found." Gorham, however, apparently had not tried to become thoroughly familiar with Garfield's writings.

Gorham Chides the Times Over the Postal Scandal

The *Times,* not having any specific charges to back its coverage, nonetheless took offense at Gorham's criticism and, on April 30, 1881, Gorham printed the paper's complaint:

> And yet day after day the man publishes in the newspaper which he directs the most scurrilous innuendoes in regard to the President of the United States, and the most wanton abuse of all who are helping the President to discover the amount of the steal which, by the connivance of General Brady, has been perpetrated on the government of the United States.

Knowing a questionable crowd, "all who were helping" in the investigation, Gorham on May 2 replied:

> It is a base libel to say that any steal whatever has been perpetrated on the Government by the connivance of General Brady. The *Times* has no grounds for saying that the President believes that there has been any. Some chiffoniers of journalism, who prowl about the gutters for news and hurl ordure at those who will not drop pennies into their hats, banded together with the harpies who cannot enter the Departments, made up an indictment against Brady, and, as it was sensational, no newspaper could afford to deny it to its readers when the others were sure to print it. Publishers must consult the public taste and they show their estimation of the public by what they serve them. For our part, if General Brady had been a stranger to us, we would only have published the trash to denounce it. We do not believe the American people are savages, or that they enjoy brutality like that being practiced on General Brady.

On May 2, Gorham was in attack mode. He behaved just as the Carson City *Daily Appeal* had described him in 1867, when campaigning for governor of California:

"Opposition brightens him and makes him a terrible enemy." Gorham first made an appeal to Garfield through his admiration for the English historian Macaulay, writing:

> Alluding to Francis North, Chief Justice of the Common Pleas under the reign of Charles II, in connection with the infamous Titus Oates, Macaulay, the historian says:

> He has sense enough to perceive from the first that Oates and Bedloe were imposters under the Parliament and the country was greatly excited: the government had yielded to the pressure, and North was a man not to risk a good place for the sake of justice and humanity. Accordingly, while he was in secret drawing up a refutation of the whole romance of the Popish Plot, he declared in public that the truth of the story was as plain as the sun in heaven, and was not ashamed to brow beat from the seat of judgment the unfortunate Roman Catholics who were arraigned before him for their lives.

Macaulay had charged the government with lying about the Catholics and knew it was doing so, while Gorham, by inference, was saying that Garfield was lying on the "star route" matter and knew that he was doing so.

Elsewhere on the editorial page, Gorham went after the Postmaster General:

> A reformer must be a man of unbounded stomach as a motive to action. He must be possessed of a mien calculated to captivate those who are searching for a moral expert. He must have face of brass, a heart of stone, and conscience of gutta-percha. Moral sense would be drawback, because it would involve a love of justice, which all trained reformers know would be a sad impediment in the way of real yard-wide all-wool reform . . . They think it is right to stick the accusation upon somebody, and then raise an outcry which will preclude any explanation. Reforms have failed sometimes by reason of a slight pause in the outcry.

> An average reformer and a good detective can work up any office or bureau of the Government in forty-eight hours to such a corrupt condition that its head may safely be subjected to the lynch law, without requiring testimony, (and) boil the offender over the live coals of newspaper wrath. . . . What our party wants is to be able to prove that for Virtue's sake it can be cruel.[35]

Once the charge was applied, it was terribly difficult to remove. Blaine had discovered the same thing from the charges about his alleged railroad corruption that stayed fastened to him no matter how much he sought to shake them off.

When the *Times* labeled Gorham a star route apologist, he replied that he was simply "charging willful libel upon those who are willing to bear false witness at second hand on the procurement of Postmaster-General James' superior officer, Woodward."[36] Brady's attorney, at Shellabarger and Wilson, asked for copies of all the reports that the Post Office had given to the *Times,* but the paper refused, leaving Brady unable to counter the "trial by newspaper."

Gorham began considering a course to bring down the Garfield presidency. The president's perfidy with Conkling and the methods of the postal investigation went beyond propriety. On May 4, 1881, Gorham wrote a piece about the French journalist, Emil De Girardin, who with abandon had entered politics for the period of 1830–72, sometimes attacking and sometimes supporting the government.

May 2nd
Frank Pixley Arrives from California; Garfield Refuses to Support Gorham; Chittenden Complains; Washington Snobbery Is Exposed

The railroaders did not miss a chance to attack their opposition at its most vulnerable points. They apparently decided to attack Gorham for the pains he took in 1879 to come to the aid of the California anti-monopolists in saving their recently adopted state constitution and its provisions for regulation.[37] In May 1881 a firsthand report arrived in Washington in the person of Californian Frank Pixley,[38] who chaired the state convention of 1879 and at the recent national convention had seconded Blaine's nomination. One of Gorham's longtime nemeses in California politics, Pixley edited a weekly journal, *The Argonaut*. A well-known white supremacist, he often referred to Gorham simply as "black and tan." Pixley paid a call on Garfield, and shortly thereafter, on May 2nd, Garfield declared that he would not support Gorham for the secretaryship. He wrote Dawes, "I will not aid any arrangement, which includes in it, the advancement to a post of political honor, a man who as Editor in Chief of a newspaper is daily assailing me and my administration." The contents of the president's letter were not made public.

On May 5th Gorham answered through his column.

> The *National Republican* has energetically discussed the nomination of Robertson as collector of the port of New York, believing it to be one of those blunders said to be worse than a crime. We stand by every syllable we have said on the subject. We believe, if persisted in, it will either destroy the administration or the Republican Party in New York. So believing, it is our right and duty to say it.
>
> The President may bestow or withhold official patronage, and is, therefore, supposed to be powerful. If he asks Senators to punish the editor of this paper for daring to differ with him, the inference will be that he presumes upon this power to enable him to direct them in their votes for

307

their own officers. . . . The editor of *The Republican* must not be expected to submit his opinions to an executive censor before publication in order to be eligible to the place. . . .

The *Sacramento Bee* observed that:

> There is not much good feeling between Garfield and Gorham. The Mentor man says he cannot so degrade himself as to assist in the elevation of a man who is constantly defaming him--referring to Gorham's abusive articles in the Washington *Republican*. But if it shall be proved that Gorham told only the truth in this Brady-Garfield matter, what then?[39]

The railroaders, working out of the three dozen or more New York City railroad offices, were likely quite happy upon receiving the news of Garfield opposing Gorham. Now the railroaders would not have to bother with the prospect of a secretary of the Senate who was an industry analyst editing a party paper. Now they could not help strutting in high feather, disdaining their opposition. By the same token, many committed anti-monopolists in New York must have felt chagrined at the loss of Gorham. L. E. Chittenden, president of the Anti-Monopoly League, found the monopolists ready to resort to "personalities." The day after Garfield declared his opposition to Gorham, Chittenden complained:

> The railroad companies can never entirely control the country till they control the United States Senate and Supreme Court. The issue is made on Senator Robertson's confirmation between the railroad interests and the anti-monopolists. We meet the monopolists at every turn. They attack us on personal grounds. They never attack our principles.[40]

Chittenden's comment perfectly characterizes what naturally transpires in policy scenarios. Two opposing sides are bonded by a common fate. If either side finds the opportunity to smear its opposition with character assassination, it can thus avoid substantive discussion.

On the same day that Gorham responded to rejection by Garfield, the president also withdrew several New York nominations from the Senate. He feared that the Senate might try to finesse their passage and postpone further attention to Robertson until the next session. Garfield drew the line, forced consideration and got it.

Social Snobbery in Washington

While such a leader as Chittenden in New York could recount the monopolists' insults on the street, in the Washington social circles, matters were no better. "The cabinet ladies were not returning calls in person or by card from ladies other than in official life," Gorham wrote. One of the leaders of Washington society, Mrs. Sarah Dahlgren, told Gorham that the ladies of the administration were shunning the leading local residents. She came to Gorham's office and showed him some galleys for her new book on etiquette for the capital city. Gorham quoted her further.

> While it is not to be denied that official life constitutes a leading element in Washington society, yet the official, however brilliant, is after all so very ephemeral that in real solidity of social importance the resident society must always form an essential feature, and be classed as the very elite . . . . If ladies whose husbands occupy positions here fail to recognize with due consideration the resident social circle, it is to be feared that sufficient reasons will not exist to induce this society to add the charm of its lifelong training to their more transitory existence. [41]

The long and the short of it would be that the newcomers in town brought in by the administration—unless they started behaving themselves—would find a surprise. When the next regular session of Congress opened, they would not be invited to the old-timers' affairs. While Chittenden could meet verbal abuse from railroaders on the New York streets, in Washington the permanent residents would halt their social traffic with the administration's elite. If in New York City the "old money" and the "new money" were in a standoff, in the nation's capital a parallel prevailed.

May 11th
The Tribune Registers Confident Suspicions about Gorham

Shortly after Garfield withdrew support for Gorham, the New York *Herald*, May 11, ran a five-column, anonymously authored article detailing the troubles in the Garfield administration. The *Tribune* immediately claimed that Gorham had written it, as did Garfield.[42] Since once such a charge is made, it is hard to shake it off, some of the standard accounts assume its accuracy and leave the matter there.*

The question, however, naturally arises whether Gorham responded to the allegation. He did. On May 14 he denied authorship.

> George C. Gorham did not write, suggest, or have any knowledge, prior to the publication, of any of the matter which has appeared in the *Herald* concerning the President. Senator Conkling declares that he neither furnished nor inspired the matter alluded to, and has no knowledge of its authorship.

A content analysis confirms Gorham's denial; the article carried some long strings of adjectives, which was not Gorham's style.

The *Tribune's* charge had much more to say about its own editors than it did about Gorham and Conkling. The *Tribune* had an unfortunate penchant for seeing Gorham's hand in almost anything that gave Garfield a bad press. Earlier, on May 6th Gorham noted: "The *New York Tribune* meanly alludes to the publication of the Garfield-Hubbell letter as 'Mr. Gorham's harmless thunderbolt.' Mr. Gorham had no more to do with its publication than had Jay Gould or E. V. Smalley." So, here were two incidents in which Reid's paper got things wrong.

Did the White House's well-known distrust of Gorham say more about the White House than about Gorham? Were the half-breeds now obsessed by unfounded suspicions of the very men they sought to destroy? Was Reid's mental state influenced by his own complicity in advancing the employment of A. M. Gibson, ending up in the "star route" investigation? Was this mentality traceable back to the party's failure in the last national convention platform to clarify the great issues of the day and announce the guidelines that it expected the president and Congress to follow?

Later, when Guiteau was arrested, a copy of the *Herald* article was found in his collection of clippings. The *Tribune* seized on the fact to state that Gorham had written it and that, therefore, he had provoked Guiteau. The *Tribune* never published Gorham's denial. Journalism was a rough business. The game played by Reid was to issue disinformation damaging to another's reputation, that is, slandering Conkling and Gorham. By enough repetition, the *Tribune* could build its case that Conkling was "always the villain of the piece," and help Blaine with an example of the "bad men's" behavior. It was good melodrama. Garfield made no note of Gorham's defense in the matter, meaning either that he had long since ceased reading Gorham's paper or would just as soon let the libel stand. The *Herald* article may have proven a powerful elixir in Guiteau's mind, and without Gorham ever having written anything, Guiteau would still have carried out his attack on Garfield.

May 12th
The New York Times and Washington Post Define the Situation

The fate that Garfield would suffer derived not only from the mental imbalance of the assassin and partisan struggles but also from some economic factors, chief of which was the declining volume of commerce at the port of New York and the stance taken by the railroad cartel. There had been clear and early indications that New York City, along with other east coast cities, was clearly losing maritime traffic to New Orleans. In March two east coast senators had joined the committee on improvement of the Mississippi, apparently in order to keep on top of trends that could become a slippery slope. New Orleans, for the year ending August 1, 1879, shipped a total of 4,617,825 bushels of corn, and twelve months later the number was 9,863,790. The shipments of wheat rose for those two years from 1,868,084 to 5,344,510 bushels. These great increases had resulted from J. B. Eads' work, with encouragement from Ulysses S. Grant, in opening the mouth of the Mississippi River. A Board of Trade representative, J. J. White, had toured the Mississippi valley and on May 12th reported that he had seen a building boom in barges.

He attributed the increase in New Orleans traffic to the fact that from St. Louis to New Orleans the rate per bushel was five cents compared to the rate from St. Louis to New York, which was twenty cents. White said,

> The consequence of this is our port is full of freighters and many of them go in ballast from here to New Orleans to get cargoes. It is evident that a concerted movement is on foot to divert to New Orleans all the export trade of the Mississippi Valley. The great trunk lines between the West and the East are firmly bound by contract to their pool freights at such rates as the Pool Commissioner has fixed or may fix. The rates fixed are so high as to be prohibitory, and *both the rolling stock and the train crews of the railroads which bring freight from the Mississippi Valley to the East are lying idle and are without occupation.*

> Recently some of the railroads belonging to the pool became restive under this ridiculous state of affairs, and knowing that the freight may be hauled at a profit at much less rate than the pool rates, they broke the contract and began taking freight at reduced rates. The news of this cutting of rates reached the ears of the bears in the stock market, which immediately availed of it to decline the price of stocks. It did not suit the purpose of Mr. Vanderbilt to have stocks decline, therefore he called a conference of the railroad magnates, and the result of the conference, as announced, is that the pool rates are restored, and to this day they remain firm, but *no merchandise is being brought to New York, and therefore our export trade is suspended.*[44] (Our emphasis.)

Given the effect of the alleged gag rule and the impropriety of discussing the behavior of the great railroad financiers, White, a courageous observer, mentioned that railroaders were not getting the rates they wanted and had brought their rolling stock to a standstill. The picture is difficult to imagine, but it should not be. The rate war did not simply involve one company undercutting another. It also involved the cartel pool refusing any transport at rates lower than it had set. One had only to look at the freight yards, where the railroad steam engines and the freight cars were standing idle day after day.

The next day, May 13, the *Washington Post* commented on White's report, painting an unhappy picture. This second editorial appearing within a day of the first added a special character to the issue. The joint back-to-back coverage for the moment qualified the topic as achieving high rank in the hierarchy of announcements.

> The city of New York . . . is in danger of permanently losing the western export trade . . . (T)he great river system of the Mississippi Valley . . . can never be competed with successfully by railway lines to eastern cities. The trade is destined to follow longitudinal lines to the sea—the

311

natural, free and cheaper routes—rather than the lines of latitude that have been artificialized at an immense cost and passed into the control of closed corporations. [Mention was made of White's statistics, including the difference between rates from St. Louis to New York and St. Louis to New Orleans.]

> The cause of this extraordinary difference in rates is largely attributable to extortionate policy of the railroads and the unadulterated despotism of their pools, whose charges are held far above a legitimate and paying tariff . . . . *The great metropolis is completely at the mercy of the pool commissioner,* which in his sphere is a more absolute autocrat than the Czar of Russia . . . . Mr. Eads, by building the jetties, has rendered this commercial revolution possible. The West, by wise, concerted legislation in the future, may consummate it and realize at no distant day her dream of an inland empire, unrestricted in any of her rights or interests by sectional and oppressive monopolies.[45] (Our emphasis.)

Pool Commissioner Albert Fink saw things differently. In April 1881, he told the Joint Executive Committee:

> They [the shippers] will appeal through Board of Trade meetings to the prejudices of the people, and complain that the action of the railroad companies in their efforts to establish and maintain a reasonable and properly adjusted tariff throughout the country, is arbitrary and wrong, and should not be permitted.[46]

Fink added at an August meeting "since June 17 eastbound traffic had been carried for less than one half the average cost of transportation." [47] Part of the problem was that agents were free to offer shippers any bargain they thought necessary. Such discretion was the spark that ignited many rate wars. Vanderbilt and other owners were in a curious position. They knew that their agents sparked at least half the rate wars, but when, as owners, they had troubles with the public, they scapegoated the politicians who presumably had always misled the public.

May 17th

Conkling's Resignation from the Senate

On May 17, 1881, Conkling and Platt resigned from the Senate, stating,

> The appliances employed to effect results set up new standards of responsibility, and invade, as we believe, the truths and principles on which the separate and co-ordinate branches of Government stand. A senator has his own responsibility. . . . he is to be exempt from Executive menace or

disfavor on the one hand and Executive inducement on the other.[48][Later, Gorham would hold that the president's behavior might stand as an impeachable act.]

Conkling also complained that he was now cast as "the enemy." It was Gilded Age melodrama through and through, and Conkling knew where he stood—on the outside.

Gorham met the matter in an editorial, entitled "Robertson's Confirmation."

> In all lands, from the earliest foundation of governments, rulers have been found who were corrupt. Gifts have perverted judgment and offices have been marted for gold. The prostitution of high official station to base uses, whether of avarice, ambition, or revenge, has ever consigned to infamy the prince or ruler to whose door it would successfully be brought. Bacon was destroyed because he received gifts from suitors, even though he decided adversely to them. The great name of Henry Clay was unjustly stained because his acceptance of office under John Quincy Adams was vaguely connected in men's minds with the fact that he had been an important factor in the latter's election. This was declared to be presumptive evidence of a corrupt bargain.

> Through years of Republican rule we have indignantly repelled the idea that offices were gifts to be made, rewards to be bestowed, or merchandise to be sold. In 1868, when President Johnson attempted to remove a cabinet officer for his own political purposes, a Republican Senate said no, and when, in contempt of the Senate, he ordered a removal, Congress by a two-thirds vote passed over the President's veto the tenure-of-office act to restrain the Executive will and preserve the constitutional power of the Senate. The people approved the action of the Senate and of Congress, and condemned the President.

> And now, in 1881, . . . [Garfield nominates Robertson who claims it as a reward] "for my work at Chicago." And the President, instead of withdrawing Robertson for making the shameless confession, makes him a whip and cracks it about the ears of the Senate until, for the sake of peace and to save themselves from Executive tyranny and proscription, that body yields to his unlawful usurpation of the power. Indelibly stamped upon the history of the country and darkly staining what might have been its brightest page, our children will read that President Garfield threatened personal hostility to any senator who should vote against, and inferentially promised his friendships to any who would vote for the confirmation of the man he had determined to pay for his vote at Chicago. The work is done. Robertson was confirmed yesterday. It was not willingly done by

the Senate. Next week the State of New York will comment on this in the election of senators.

Gorham was overly optimistic. Matters would not go well at Albany.

May 18ᵗʰ
An Exchange of Nominations: Robertson at the Customs House for Loring at Agriculture

Arrangements for the Senate vote on Robertson were Byzantine. The petition from the ten New England senators supporting Loring for commissioner of Agriculture remained on Garfield's desk, making the irony of a visit from Dawes quite precious. As Dawes pressed Garfield to drop the Robertson nomination, they both knew of the petition favoring Loring, and Garfield could well have asked, "Am I to be the registering clerk of the Senate?" Was he as president simply to wait until senators brought him suggestions for office, and then agree with them? Or was he permitted to distribute the offices according to his own designs? The New Englanders had urged the president to nominate Loring, while he asked for the Senate to approve his nomination of Robertson. Garfield's point was not lost on Dawes. The senator left the meeting, announcing that the president would nominate Loring for commissioner of Agriculture––meaning that Dawes also would support Garfield's nomination of Robertson. The connection between the two nominations rested in the fact that on the calendar they were back-to-back. One day (May 18) Dawes and Hoar agreed to support Robertson, and the next (May 19) Garfield asked LeDuc for his resignation as commissioner of Agriculture, allowing him to fill that vacancy as soon as the Robertson vote was taken.[49]

The Loring nomination had taken a circuitous route. Gorham, with caucus approval, had enlisted Mahone,[50] who then gave the Republicans control of the Senate. Then the Virginian had accepted the chair of the committee on agriculture, but with limitations, relinquishing his discretion over the commissioner of Agriculture as ten New Englanders petitioned the president on behalf of Loring. Then the president used the petition on behalf of Loring to muster support against Conkling. Gorham, the stalwart leader, had suggested that no good could come of that petition when he asked, "Is this the *pons asinorum?*" The stalwart wedge for the Virginian that had turned the Senate over to the Republicans soon led the New Englanders against the stalwarts.

May 24ᵗʰ
Garfield Announces His Goal of Remaking the New York Party

In Garfield's unfolding dispute with Senator Conkling over the nomination of a new collector of customs, he made himself quite clear regarding his intentions. Conkling had stymied him in arranging a judiciary committee congenial to his pushing the Adams bill through the Senate. With Conkling and Platt having vacated their Senate seats, Garfield could now make up his earlier loss and urge the Albany Republicans to fill both places with "administration" candidates, members who would support the Adams bill in the

U.S. Senate. The *Tribune* even printed the announcement. The announcement proves to be startling if not frightening--but unfortunately the standard accounts have not included it.

It is to be recalled that several hints had appeared that traced an emerging point of view favorable to the railroad industry. Certainly, the industry was large and important and expected attention. What they wanted above all else from the government was the permission without much further discussion given by Congress for the railroads to become a national trust. The notion, most fully explained by Charles F. Adams, Jr. for the last three years, had seized the imagination of railroad leaders. They very likely hoped that by applying the Rockefeller model and ending competition in the industry their railroad industry would catch up to what Rockefeller had achieved.

From December 1880 forward into the new administration, the hints kept appearing. First, Blaine in December, justifying the exclusion of others from discussion, had written the president-elect about the "good" men and the "bad," those who would be either "in" or "out." Then, Gorham observed that it would be hoped that the president would not want to be a makeweight against the party itself. When news spread that Gould had consolidated the telegraph service, within hours not only did Garfield have a dream suggesting that New York was no place for him to go but also Levi Morton of New York knew that he would not become a member of the president's cabinet.

Anyone raising a hand to halt the new momentum had to heed serious warnings. When legislative activity stirred about government competition for the new telegraph and Gorham endorsed the House bill, the *Post* carried a warning, sounding much like Blaine, to wit, "Our neighbor the *Republican*, while running with Garfield, bays with Conkling. This will not do. There is no man colossal enough in intellect or legs to stride the gulf already formed between them. The Republican Party must become either all Blaine or all Conkling—all Cossack or all Tartar." That comment meant that an entire month prior to the inauguration, in the minds of some important leaders the party split was actual, in full force, and irreparable.

Continuing in March, stalwart leader Roscoe Conkling observed some seating for Democrats on the committee on judiciary. One nominee was corporate attorney Senator Hill and another was railroad president Pendleton, newly elected, from Ohio. A third was a Republican from Ohio, John Sherman. Conkling tried to make light of what he saw and commented that it looked as if the law of Ohio would become the law of the United States. That was a very likely reference to applying the Rockefeller model to the railroad industry. In the Republican organization of judiciary the two Ohio senators and the one corporate attorney were replaced, making it more difficult for the trust legislation to go forward. About a week later, possibly in retaliation for falling behind two seats on judiciary, the president sent in the name of Vanderbilt attorney William Robertson, Conkling's nemesis in the New York party, for the collector's post. Gorham soon after commented in an editorial that it seemed to be the president's view that he should try to change the leadership of the New York party by "external force."

Finally came the surprising announcement removing all doubt about the president's intentions. On May 24th, a week after Conkling and Platt resigned from the Senate, the Albany legislature was getting down to the business of filling the two vacancies. The *Tribune* set forth the president's attitude toward the party in the state of New York, marking the outset of a new, clear course to be followed.

THE PRESIDENT'S MEANING

Why men not hostile to Mr. Conkling were

Nominated to Federal Offices in New York.

(By Telegraph to the *Tribune*.)

Washington, May 22. —Some expressions of dissatisfaction have reached here from New-York because the President did not send in the names of men hitherto anti-Conkling for the five offices to which nominations were made on Thursday. Those who complain of this course do not comprehend the president's policy nor the principles upon which it is based. He is not seeking in the least to ostracize the Republicans who have been Mr. Conkling's followers and supporters in the past. On the contrary, it is evidently the intention of the President to have it fully, distinctly, and widely known from Buffalo to Brooklyn that the object of his administration is to abolish factions in New-York and to have one grand, united, harmonious, enthusiastic republican party in the State. Of course this end cannot be attained by sending Mr. Conkling back to the Senate to wage relentless and vindictive war on the Administration, and those who aid in sending him will of course put themselves in the attitude of determined foes and enemies of the Administration and of Republican successes. To have been with Mr. Conkling in the past is one thing, but to join Mr. Conkling in his new crusade of anger and revenge is quite another thing. There is room in New York for one Republican Party, to be led by the Administration. There is not room for another Republican party, to be led by Mr. Conkling. The Administration invites all shades and sects and schools of the party to rally under its banner for the good of the whole. Mr. Conkling asks the maddened, the disappointed and the reckless members of the party to join him in fighting and embarrassing the Administration. Every Republican in New-York can choose which leader he will follow.[16]

What Garfield aimed at on the immediate, practical level was a majority in the Republican caucus at Albany for his candidates. Many legislators went home weekends and learned what their constituents were thinking. Often the vote tallies would change the following Monday.

If the replacements for Conkling and Platt were for Garfield's faction the Adams bill would have clearer sailing in the U.S. Senate. There would be no compromise. Vanderbilt in 1879 had said that the legislation should come from "Congress first." The added prize would be that in the end Garfield would have charge of the convention delegation in 1884. In May of 1881 the standoff could be expressed in melodramatic fashion and the President decided to do so: There was the target, the violence, and the prospect of everything coming out happily.

The next day from Washington, editor Gorham answered the new announcement by Garfield.

The President's Apology

The New York half-breeds having made a disturbance in the administration camp because of the appointment of a few thorough-bred Republicans to unimportant offices after the conclusion of the Robertson outrage, the faithful spokesman of the President telegraphs to the New York *Tribune* an apology for this unexpected conduct. He says:

Those who complain of this course do not comprehend the President's policy nor the principles upon which it is based.

Well, they cannot be blamed for not being able to discover either policy or principles in the President's course. Again:

He is not seeking the least to ostracize the Republicans who have been Conkling's followers and supporters in the past.

Certainly not. He is anxious to buy some of them to defeat Mr. Conkling in the present. He continues:

It is evidently the intention of the President to have it fully, distinctly, and widely known, from Buffalo to Brooklyn, that the object of his administration is to abolish factions in New York and to have one grand, united, harmonious, enthusiastic Republican party in the State.

The intention "to abolish factions" will be fully carried out if he succeeds in his efforts to destroy the party itself. He is trying to scuttle the ship, in order to drown those of his shipmates who do not suit him. But, as all are on one ship, how could he himself escape making of himself what Mr. Mantilini called a "demnition moist, unpleasant body?" The President will not be allowed to scuttle the ship. [The passage is from Charles Dickens' *Nicholas Nickleby* and about a character on the verge of suicide.]

The continuing problem for Garfield, however, was that time would show that he did not understand the Empire State. He had hardly visited there to understand its unique economy. The greatest source of difficulty would come from the unregulated railroads and popular complaints about their behavior. Currently they were not getting the rates that they wanted and much of their business was closed down. Cartel members were not making matters any easier for the president; in fact, they were undercutting him. Gorham chose to emphasize this aspect of the scene. In a June 7th editorial, the one describing the railroaders' influence at the 1880 convention, Gorham challenged his detractors.

> To those who are impatient with the indignant words which we now choose when we discuss the President we say: dispute a word of the above if you can; and you shall have room in our columns for the purpose. We invite discussion. And if you cannot deny what we have said, what words (are) too warm in which to denounce the course the President has since seen fit to pursue? What has he done? He has forgotten the country and the party. He has called to his counsels the deadly enemies of those most potent in its ranks, and has with them organized a conspiracy to degrade, ostracize, and destroy the latter. He has turned his back upon the Republican Party, which made him President for one term, and made him the head of a faction who have no aim but his re-election. He has not even sought for this selfish purpose the friendship of any who opposed him on the final ballot at Chicago. He has assumed the hostility of these and put forth his decree for their annihilation. He has torn down the powerful Republican Party in New York, led by Roscoe Conkling, in order to erect a new one, with custom-house patronage as a foundation, which will pack the New York delegates for him in 1884. He has violated the Constitution by soliciting the votes of senators through favors and coercing them by threats. He has set in motion the mills of slander and detraction against friends and placed the weapons of his mightiest power in the hands of a malignant Democratic partisan.

June 3rd

Blaine Cuts Off Mahone

Meanwhile, Blaine continued his relentless personal vendetta to make sure nothing was done to "build up Conkling, Cameron, and Gorham."[51] He cut off Gorham's work for Mahone in Virginia by seeking out the chair of the Democratic National Committee, former Connecticut Senator William Barnum. Blaine told him that in exchange for Democrats' votes for Robertson the administration would withhold patronage for Mahone. Gorham closes this letter describing the Blaine-Barnum agreement with the statement, "Of course, General Harrison would be at liberty to show this letter to Mr. Blaine and to Mr. Barnum." [52] This story first appeared on Gorham's editorial page on June 3, 1881. In another seven years, he would finally make public all the details.

Some Democrats were busy supporting the Robertson nomination. Senator Butler of South Carolina told constituents, "Those New York petitioners who opposed Robertson did not do so because they were interested in public service. Personal and political grounds had probably influenced them entirely. Such parties had never been friends of the South, nor had they ever been identified with practical measures for the good of the country."[53] In short, Butler thought that it was a waste of their time to think that his constituents might have some common cause with New Yorkers.

June 10th

Parallels with the Star Chamber under King Charles

In a June 10th editorial, Gorham gave the "star route" investigation the full treatment as a parallel with the Star Chamber of the Tudors and Stuarts even in the provision for a special room for the investigators. The *Sun* would come to the same view in November. Gorham would now reach a new high in journalistic excellence, a level that has often been missed by his successors in both journalism and historiography. Missing it comes from a retreating into melodrama, picking the good and the bad, rather than following a discipline for investigation and reporting. Gorham wrote,

> As the Star Chamber Court tried acts "which could not be brought under the law" because they were not contrary to any law, so the Court of Number Fifty-nine [the number on the door in the Post Office Department where the star route investigation took place] . . . is calculated to inspire men's minds with the idea of executive rather than of judicial authority and power, and, like that, is also in its investigations and conclusions "less tied to any rules of pleading or evidence than the ordinary courts of law."

> In the Star Chamber Court of our president men are sentenced without being themselves "privately examined." . . . The sentence in our day is not whipping or cutting of ears, but it is the pillory. The pillory which was in use for six hundred years in England was simply a board nailed to uprights, with holes through it for the head and hands. It was abolished in 1837 as being a relic of a barbarous age. The pillory to which Gibson, MacVeagh, Woodward, and James are now empowered by the President to sentence citizens without trial is the newspaper. The most expert defamer of modern times [A. M. Gibson] is a member of the court. The correspondents of newspapers are alone allowed to know any of the secrets of the Star Chamber. Of these they divulge such as are furnished them. *Care is taken, of course, to give out only such portions of facts as will, in the absence of the remainder, injure and wound the persons connected with them.* The old pillory only disgraced a man in the estimation of the few passers-by who saw him in durance vile. The modern pillory so gibbets its victim that his

319

punishment is seen by the millions who read the newspapers, the columns of which are daily supplied by telegraph from the great reserve of calumny at Number Fifty-nine . . . .

Arbitrary as was Charles I, the Star Chamber could not live through his reign, but was abolished eight years before he was beheaded. If its infamous copy can live in this country during the four years of official life of a President who seems to emulate the spirit of the Stuarts, then we shall not be worthy of our English ancestors. As between "a King resolved to be absolute and a people resolved to be free," the King went to the wall. Here in our day we laugh at the thought of arbitrary power, and yet it stalks abroad at noonday. It slimes its victim before devouring him. Bye and bye it will become careless, and neglect to first make the public hate the objects of its malevolence before it reaches out to destroy. Then it will become itself the object of public rage, and the equilibrium of justice will be restored.

It is this trick of developing biased facts which assures the continued life of a melodrama in journalism and historiography. Unfortunately, the standard accounts of the Garfield administration are heavily supplied with instances of biased facts, or, more precisely, with serious omission of facts. No mention is made that the state assembly did not give unanimous support to the Robertson nomination. No mention is made of Garfield's special plans for the New York faction. No mention is made that the star route inquiry failed to turn up evidence of a crime. No mention is made that Garfield had an association with Charles Francis Adams Jr., of the cartel staff, nor of Conkling's devotion to the Erie Canal as a regulator. All of these oversights in the story only demonstrate how *"Care is taken . . . to give out only such portions of facts as will, in the absence of the remainder, injure and wound the persons connected with them."* What purpose did the omission of facts serve? They were merely a cover for a poorly lobbied bill to establish a single railroad trust, the sponsor's withdrawal from an "ordeal" of further head-to-head discussion, and the vindictiveness that followed. (Our emphasis.)

Chapter XI

President Garfield Sees a Victory through a Scandal

1   *NYT*, June 25, 1881.

2   Garfield *Diary*, April 1, 1881, p. 567.

3   Wills, Garry. *Certain Trumpets: The Call of Leaders*. New York: Simon & Schuster, 1994, p. 231.

4   Keller, Morton, *The Art and Politics of Thomas Nast.* New York: Oxford, 1968, Cartoon number 233, printed in *Harper's* March 19, 1881.

5   *Appleton's for 1881*. New York: Appleton & Co., p. 577.

6   *NYT*, January 3, 1879.

7   Garfield *Diary*, pp. 572 and 573.

8   *NYT*, July 22, 1879.

9   *NYT*, April 14, 1881.

10   *NYT*, January 8, 1881.

11   *NR*, April 6, 9, and 14, 1881.

12   *NYT*, April 27, 1881.

13   Ulen, Thomas Shaman. *Cartels and Regulation: Late Nineteenth Century Railroad Collusion.* Ph.D. diss., Stanford University, 1979, pp. 187–189.

14   *NR*, August 10, 1881.

15   Benson, Lee. *Merchants, Farmers, and Railroads.* Cambridge, MA: Harvard University Press, 1955, p. 243 .

16   Reid Collection, LC.

17   *NYT*, April 13, 1881.

18   *San Francisco Chronicle*, January 7, 1884.

19   Peskin, Allen. *Garfield.* Kent, OH: Kent State University Press, 1978, p. 569.

20 *NYT,* May 10, 1881.

21 Keller, Morton. *The Art and Politics of Thomas Nast.* New York: Oxford University Press, 1968, Cartoon 234.

22 *NYT,* September 15, 1886.

23 *NYT,* June 29, 1898.

24 *NYT,* March 20,1898.

25 *NYT,* October 31, 1898.

26 Burrows, Edwin, and Mike Wallace. *Gotham.* New York: Oxford University Press, 1999, p. 1214.

27 *NR,* April 27, 1881.

28 *NYT,* Jan 20 and March 9, 1881. *Tribune,* May, 4, 1881.

29 *NR,* April 18, 1881.

30 *NR,* April 26, 1881.

31 May 5 & 6, 1881. Hawley had nominated Grant at the 1872 convention and in 1880 had protested Grant's third term bid. In 1881 he and Burnside of R. I. may have nominated Gorham for secretary of the Senate in the Republican Senate caucus.

32 *NR,* April 26, 1881, November 2 and 5, 1881.

33 *NR,* April 29, 1881.

34 *Atlantic,* July 1877, found in John M. Taylor, p. 299.

35 *NR,* May 2, 1881.

36 *NR,* May 3, 1881.

37 *NR* May 4, 1881, *Star,* April 18, 1881.

38 *NR,* May 6, 1881, quotes from the *Golden Era,* San Francisco, and the *Carson City (Nev.) Appeal.*

39 *NR,* June 1, 1881.

40 *NYT,* May 6, 1881.

41 *NR,* May 3, 1881.

42 *New York Herald,* May 11, 1881; Garfield *Diary,* May 12, 1881.

43 *New York Herald,* May 11, 1881; Garfield *Diary,* May 12, 1881.

44 *NYT,* May 12, 1881.

45 *Washington Post,* May 12, 1881.

46 Gilchrist, "Albert Fink and the Pooling System." *Business History Review,* v. 34 (1960), p. 42.

47 Gilchrist, p. 42.

48 *NYT,* May 17, 1881.

49 Garfield *Diary,* April 30, 1881, Vol. IV p. 584; May 19, 1881, Vol. IV, p. 596. For accounts by several members of the LeDuc family during May 1881, see *LeDuc Collection,* St. Paul: Minnesota Historical Society.

50 *NR,* May 7, 1881.

51 Gorham to William Mahone, March 19, 1888, *Mahone Collection*, Durham: Duke University. In 1881, Blaine apparently told Chandler, "I am not going to do anything that will build up Conkling, Cameron or Gorham."

52 Gorham to John C. New, February 8, 1889, *Gorham Collection.* Sacramento, CA: State Library.

53 *NR,* June 2, 1881.

Chapter XII

The Rev. Henry Beecher Trumps President Garfield's Melodrama

After resigning from the Senate, Conkling did not immediately rush off to Albany—contrary to some reporters' accounts who hoped to appeal to their readers by lying about him. Conkling remained a few days in Washington and then headed for New York. He had resigned on May 17, and arrived in New York on May 21.[1] Ex-Senator Thomas Platt had preceded him. Vice President Chester Arthur waited in Washington until adjournment and headed out a few hours later.[2] Conkling then went on to Albany.

Preparing for the coming contest, the *Tribune* admitted, "The followers of Conkling have undoubtedly a majority of the Republicans of the legislature." The paper went on to add, "The friends of the administration think they can show that Republicans are under no moral obligation to enter . . . a caucus."[3] Therefore, they didn't. Instead, they held open meetings or "conferences." There was an important difference. In a caucus, the rules called for their voting by secret ballot, and after each tally dropping the candidate(s) with the fewest votes. That's how Cornell was nominated for governor at the 1879 state convention on the first ballot. In July 1881, Gorham wrote, "Had the stalwart demand for a caucus been heeded before members had sold themselves for plunder and for place, Conkling and Platt would have been easily renominated and on the 1st of June re-elected." Benefiting such an assortment of onlookers as curious outsiders, well-heeled lobbyists, and the press, the new rule at Albany for open meetings made it easier to keep an eye on the legislators. The new practice was actually a throwback to earlier times that had lasted in the less democratic Connecticut until the 1830s when town meetings revoked the rules requiring standing votes and introduced the secret ballot. At Albany in 1881 the irony was that the corporations, which did not want anyone looking over their shoulders in the conduct of their businesses, were demanding such privileges in looking over the shoulders of the legislators as the latter took up balloting to fill the state's vacancies in the U.S. Senate.

Several candidates entered the contest at Albany, leaving the action open to an increased number of interpretations. The *Times* noted that only a third of the legislators voted for Conkling and drew the inference that therefore two-thirds of the Republican members opposed him. Gorham countered by observing: "More than seven-eighths of the Republican members are opposed to each one of the half-breed candidates." The most fortunate half-breed candidate was corporate attorney and cartel president Chauncey Depew. Gorham found it curious that the *Times* supported him since the paper also supported the railroad commission bill opposed by Depew. Gorham believed that if the *Times* could persuade Depew to support the bill it would pass in an instant, but there seemed to be no inclination at the paper to go in that direction.

Gorham Interprets the Tribune about Party Leadership at Albany

As the balloting began at Albany, some troublesome signs attracted Gorham's attention. Since his Sacramento days, when he worked with the owners of the Central Pacific, he knew how to size up lobbyists. Now in 1881 at Albany, what struck him was that the railroad lobbyists wanted to bribe New York legislators. Indeed, they had been quite open about such prospects. The previous June upon Grant's failure to win on the first ballot at Chicago rumors held that the financiers whenever necessary would rely on bribery to win votes. The alleged gag rule had emphasized that unfriendly candidates would be beaten "wherever money can accomplish it."[4] But now money would be used to swing those candidates who had won office.

Profits in the railway industry were good in many cases; bribery, therefore, should have been expected. Tweed at the outset had thrived on the new technology of piping water to the city and turned to bribery. The postal contractors thrived on the increasing migration to the West and were presumed to have thrived in the same way. The railroaders since resumption had an eye on a vast expansion. Confirming the promise, speculators rushed to build new rail routes, hoping that the older lines would buy them out.

To get the bribery operation under way at Albany, men of experience had to be brought to the fore. Therefore, the *Tribune* called for new party leadership. The paper left little doubt about the kind it required. Editor Reid was advancing none other than William Woodin and Loren Sessions, two men who, two years earlier, had managed the bribery for the Tweed Ring. At the time Reid had denounced them. Since then, however, they had joined Robertson as independents at the Chicago convention. Gorham figured that his readers would regard them as knaves and that in the fall elections they would be defeated. The story was too good to pass up. The task he had before him was to make sure that the voters understood what was happening. On May 19, 1881, Gorham made another dig at the *Tribune*, writing that:

> (S)ince it has been proved that the President will use offices to serve his personal purposes the direct road to office is by serving those purposes. In short, "Who'll buy?" being ascertained, "Who'll sell?" will soon appear. Forewarned is forearmed. The men who can be bribed by the administration have not been on the same side with Conkling. There is no man

in the State of New York, of whatever party, who will not feel a burning sense of indignation at the thought that the *New York Tribune* believes the President can corrupt the Legislature in electing slaves of his instead of representative men for the State.[5]

As the *Tribune* trumpeted its two new leaders, Gorham drew his readers back two years to earlier quotes from that paper. Gorham had often employed this method, casting his comments as though he were once again watching proceedings in Judge Field's California court. He would quote at length pertinent original source material and then discuss it.

As Robertson must soon retire into the custom house and distribute the places he has promised in the interest of Reform, all good men will look to Woodin and Session to continue at the old stand the business of keeping the Legislature honest, and this will make people more anxious to know what manner of men Woodin and Sessions are. Let us put the *New York Tribune* on the stand as our witness against them. We shall find upon the testimony of the once-righteous and rigidly truthful *Tribune* that Senators Woodin and Sessions are sorry masqueraders. Instead of being men of stern virtue, battling for principle, they are rotten birds of prey. The picture of them so drawn less than two years ago is one at which the gorge rises. We quote the following from the *New York Tribune* of September 22, 1879 when Cornell was the Republican candidate for Governor and Roscoe Conkling was, as usual, the leader in the contest.

In 1877, [Woodin] did not even live, as a candidate, [in his district] through the campaign. Tweed's testimony confirming the strong popular conviction that he had been Tweed's senator and had taken Tweed's money drove him from the field and the district was only saved by the choice of another name.

This subject is not a pleasant one. Let us dismiss it with an expression of the hope that there will be no more such offenses against the good name of Republicanism. The Republican Party is not made up of men like Mr. Sessions and Mr. Woodin, and does not deserve the reproach of being represented by them.

In 1881, the railroad lobbyists had advanced so handily that they could have become too exhilarated to reverse course due to anything Gorham might write. When private interests spend a huge amount of money on legislators, they can easily over-reach themselves. They believe for the moment that they also write the rules and even conclude that they own the legislators. Their assured dominance can become more evident in the confident stonewalling of their critics. After all, just as half-breeds objected to naming

William Windom secretary of the Treasury, and editor Gorham had dissected their intentions, James Blaine, a staunch friend of railroad leaders, took offense at seeing Reid's paper come under criticism. He became even more determined to sideline Gorham.

Gorham Wonders Why Robertson Delays Taking Office

The story of the political season was all about the president nominating Robertson for the collectorship. From the way in which the White House had pressed the matter, one would have thought that as soon as the Senate confirmed the man for collector, he would have moved into the post. Following the Senate vote, however, Robertson did not move, suggesting that there had never been any urgency. Gorham, therefore, found it hard to fathom Garfield's earlier insistence. Garfield could have avoided the standoff in the Senate, waited until the end of a shorter executive session, and then made an interim appointment. Had he done so, he would not have raised so much public comment. Gorham had to conclude that the entire episode was only aimed at disturbing Conkling. As it turned out, Robertson stayed in the state senate for another month, until after the state legislature had elected new U.S. Senators. He entered the Customs House on August 1, 1881.[6] Gorham further figured that the president wanted to keep Robertson at Albany, preventing Conkling from precipitating some mischief like urging passage of the state regulation bill.

Meanwhile, Godkin considered that Garfield was paying a price for his having nominated a new collector, placing a blemish on his own reputation. The *Nation* on May 26th carried the editor's report of disappointment:

> As matters stand, [Garfield] gets only half-hearted support, even from those who most dislike Conkling and his ways. In approving what has been done they are compelled to acknowledge that in doing it General Garfield has diminished their respect for his character, because they are not ready to admit that any man fitted to fill the office of President of the United States can deliberately repudiate professions made up to the very hour of his entering on office, without the existence of some serious defect in his moral character.

If some derided Conkling, Garfield also had a share of the crowd deriding him.

Thurber's View of American History

While Godkin saw the course of the president violating common-sense civil service reform, the opponents of Conkling thought that it was a bold exercise against bossism. Thurber, sensitive to the boiling sentiment for anti-monopolism, saw it differently, touching on popular participation in government. Thurber, the editor of his own specialist newspaper, *The American Grocer,* entered foreboding comments. He wrote in his May 28, 1881, issue:

Recent political events concerning corporate designs have induced the National Anti-Monopoly League to call attention to some significant facts, indicating the settled purpose on the part of the great railway and telegraph monopolies of the United States.

The decision of the Supreme Court in the Granger cases which affirmed the right of the people through their legislatures, to control corporations, was one of the most important declarations of public rights since the Declaration of Independence, and indications have since been frequent that the monopolists have decided on a settled program to: 1st. Elect a President in their interest. 2nd. Reconstitute the Supreme Court, and reverse the Granger decisions. 3rd. Pack the Senate of the United States.[7]

Under this vision, the New York anti-monopolists had good reasons to think seriously about options, one of which amounted to asking the electorate to pass a free canal amendment. A free canal would not only assure competition for the railways. It would require a popular vote. That would set an historical benchmark in popular influence over corporations, exactly the prescription allowed under *Munn versus Illinois*. The most visible mark of popular views would next come in the passage of the ICC legislation in 1887 when members of boards of trade showed up in Washington and successfully lobbied against the pooling of rates. One consequence was that the cartel was no longer referred to as a "pool" but now as an "association." Thus, there was a stream of events here beginning with the naming of Waite as Chief Justice, followed by passage of the free canal amendment, and then by the restriction on pooling. Cullom reported in his autobiography that in 1899 he was ready to introduce the legislation for the rate board but the other members of his committee, mostly with railway interests, refused to go along and the proposition was not realized until 1906 with a great assistance from President Theodore Roosevelt. The inference is usually left that John Sherman's Anti-Trust Act of 1890 initiated the anti-trust movement. It seems, however, that their earlier activities created a strong environment for that movement.

Garfield Learns of A. M. Gibson's Employment

Another matter soon embarrassed the new Garfield administration. Gorham believed that the half-breeds had the president under their thumb, and on June 1, 1881 he wrote that

The *New York Tribune* is said to have its old Credit Mobilier charge against the President in type, ready to be inserted at any time when he may deviate from the line marked out for him. This is probably the reason why the *Tribune* has never retracted the calumny referred to.

Gorham's comment came none too soon. Two days later, the *Washington Capitol* reported that Garfield's calumniator, A. M. Gibson, had surfaced, working on the postal investigation for the Attorney General. The news would leave the president chagrined, wondering who let the journalist onto the payroll.[8] The *Capitol* had long been a defender of Garfield against Gibson's charges but now stated,

> The President has employed him to reform his administration, thereby certifying to his good character . . . . If Gibson is a trustworthy detective to put on the track of Dorsey, Brady, and others, he must have been a trustworthy detective when on the track of Garfield from 1872 to 1881.

The *Capitol* wrote, and Gorham repeated the passage in the *National Republican*, that

> The issue is the simplest one that could be framed in language. If Mr. Gibson is not a libeler, you [President Garfield] are a bribe-taker, thief, perjurer, and a suborner of perjury and forgery. If you are not a bribe-taker, perjurer, thief, and suborner of perjury and forgery, Mr. Gibson is a libeler under the criminal statute. One of you ought to be in the penitentiary; and that upon your own respective showings of record. Both of you cannot be at large without an outrage upon the principles of justice.[9]

That day, June 6, Garfield wrote in his diary that:

> In the evening, I sent for Mr. Woodward, Post Office inspector, to find what was being done in the Star route investigation and know why Gibson and Cook had been employed. I am not pleased with these men. The first has been a vile calumniator of public men and the second appears to have an unsavory reputation. I find there is much feeling among my friends that such men should not have been employed without first consulting me.[10]

Garfield probably would never learn that Blaine had shown an interest in advancing Gibson. The Secretary of State very likely had helped lift Gibson out of his old job and had him placed where he thought he could do the most good. The appointment compares with Garfield nominating Robertson without first consulting Windom, James, and Conkling. Now some insiders won Gibson a place in the Department of Justice. The instance seems to have been another case of a non-consulting elite acting first and explaining later.

Were journalists gaining acceptance who had been critical of the president? Hardly! Garfield would abide Gibson, but no one from the White House sent Gorham word that all was forgiven. Garfield probably opposed Gorham, not simply because of the editor's criticism, but because Gorham had once pressed for a quite different policy on the currency. He also continued to press for a different policy on corporate governance. Another matter could not be overlooked: Extending Mahonism in the South might cause

Democrats the next year to retaliate and weaken the banking bill. Presumably, what the president needed was to keep a lid on all these matters. Further, he probably could not abide the prospect of returning such a vocal man as Gorham to office with open tenure that could carry him beyond his own term of office and that of many senators.

At the moment, the president failed to examine the circumstances emerging around him. He would not reverse his course on the Robertson nomination. He failed to examine the reasons why Gibson was employed. He had not followed Gorham's denial of writing the May 11 *Herald* article. Most of all, he was supporting a specious investigation of a government department. In short, he gave no evidence of wanting to retrace his steps. Godkin had urged him to do so, and Gorham on May 12th and 16th would write,

> Now is the one opportunity in President Garfield's life for him to be great by conquering the weakness of willfulness. The public sense of fair play demands that he retrace his steps in New York matters, and take counsel of his own good sense and self-imposed obligations when next he moves.

> . . . It is the smallest exhibition of weakness when we adhere to a false position because of the fear of what men will say.[11]

Gorham soon converted this observation into a taunt by printing a mock edict against himself signed by "James the Weak." The Senate Democrats had refused to concede to his election. He failed to recognize that Garfield needed them if the banking bill were to succeed the next year. In the best of circumstances installing Gorham in his old office called for a delay. Short of Gorham winning office and helping Mahone with his summer campaign, several northern papers soon endorsed Mahone. The endorsement suggests that several senators went home and spoke to their editors—all of which seemed to have made a difference in Virginia on election day. Mahone knew what he needed and he got it one way or another.

Gorham Forewarns of More Bribery at Albany

At Albany, the two men whom the *Tribune* had once exposed now won its praise. Gorham wrote,

> We ask our readers to compare this with the daily eulogies of these Messrs. Session and Woodin in the same *Tribune*, while all three are engaged in slandering and belittling the great statesman of the Empire State. It must be a vile cause which requires or can command such instrumentalities. We submit that the *Tribune*'s present copartnership with the men it knows to be corrupt is the best evidence of its own corruption. Let us hear from its most brazen Bohemian on the subject of Senators Woodin and

Sessions. And let the president see it practice its best efforts at swallowing its own words.[12]

With the evidence of bribery at Albany, Gorham asked on June 9, 1881, "Will the President sign Robertson's commission after the terrible scandal, and thereby father the bribery and corruption resorted to by his avowed and especial adherents at Albany?" The same day, Garfield wrote in his diary that he had heard of the charges of bribery at Albany. He, however, made no remark about taking steps either to put an end to it or to repudiate it. If he had wanted to make a public statement about the Albany bribery, it would have gone to the *Tribune* through the paper's reporter, E. V. Smalley, stationed at a White House desk. Garfield must have thought better of that. It was Smalley's boss, editor Reid, who was helping choreograph the bribery at Albany! Rather, the half-breeds took another course and seemed to disparage and discount the reports.

On June 11, Gorham wrote,

> In view of the high market rate of legislative votes on the senatorial question, it will occur to most people that Vanderbilt is a very generous supporter of the president or that he will pay a very high price for the defeat of the assembly bill now pending in the Senate to create a railroad commission. We shall see before the end comes whether it is true that "corruption wins not more than honesty."

Gorham returned to the *Tribune*'s treatment of Sessions two years earlier (May 21, 1879), when the *Tribune* had written:

> Every man who is at all familiar with the political history of the State knows what the record of Mr. Sessions is, in the lobby and out of it, and knows also that it was a great mistake even to have him sent to the Senate—a mistake which his constituents are not likely, let us hope, to repeat.

The next day, Gorham quoted from two years earlier—the June 30, 1879 edition of the *Tribune:*

> It is indeed a little irritating to find Mr. Loren B. Sessions at this late day claiming the consideration that is awarded to men who have lived clean lives. Mr. Sessions has been known for many years to the people of the State; he is notorious in Washington and in Albany; and we have heard many emphatic opinions expressed about him. We have never heard an honest Republican speak of him with confidence.[13]

A month after Gorham had first raised questions about bribery, the president now seemed to have a hand in it. At the moment of Conkling and Platt's resignations, it appears that Garfield had asked John Davenport to go to Albany. He was to offer a leading stalwart a position in exchange for voting for Depew. Gorham added,

> If this rumor is substantiated it will be [that] the stalwart state Senator Robert Strahan [said he] was asked to accept a marshal's [position] and considered [it] a corrupt solicitation on the part of the Executive to control the United States Senate which is an impeachable offense . . . Therefore, . . . articles of impeachment will be presented in the next House of Representatives.

Given the low regard in which many in Washington held the Constitution, Gorham's faith in the impeachment process was unusual. Guiteau believed the section where it gave the conditions for the Vice President succeeding the President, but held little stock in the provisions for the impeachment process. He saw the matter as one of merely "removing" the president.

Gorham Predicts the Next Election

Gorham was convinced of William Vanderbilt's influence in Albany affairs, and wrote on June 20th:

> The people will at the polls next fall find a way to substitute their own will for that of a railroad corporation and a customhouse. We are rejoiced to see the issue presented. The New York Central has been very insolent of late. We shall see whether it can rule the State of New York. We hear much of anti-monopoly. The time has not yet come for legislative remedies against the abuses of corporation monopolies, and cannot come until the legislative power shall have been wrested from the control of those very corporations.

Gorham finally got the picture of what had occurred in the new administration. He had dealt with the alleged Post Office scandal with some insight, some foolishness, and some severe language. However, now he finally saw the connection between the scandal, on the one hand, and Garfield's excluding New York supporters of former president Ulysses S. Grant, on the other. Gorham did not know who had made the initial suggestion for the scandal, but he now saw its connection to getting Brady's resignation. He wrote that

> It is loudly claimed by some that the element in the party recognized as its leader General Grant and Senator Conkling were to be tabooed by the incoming President, and no member of the cabinet would be in sympathy with those gentlemen. The *Republican* always assumed such a prediction to be false, and made every effort to allay the jealous feelings they were

calculated to foster. We insisted up to the last that he would be just to all elements and faithful to his assurances voluntarily given. The cabinet was not such as to sustain those cheerful predictions. The *Republican* was not in favor at court. It had said too much in behalf of the stalwarts to make its course doubtful when their slaughter should commence . . . . We were suspected of enmity from the time we predicted that General Garfield would be fair toward the stalwarts, who, though opposed to him at Chicago, had contributed all in their power to his election. The old Democratic slanders on Brady were brought out from the mud heap and put in readiness if we should openly rebel when occasion came. The knife being applied to the New York Republicans, we espoused their cause. After three weeks of preparation for stage affect the blow descended and General Brady retired. The colored lights were then turned on in the press, and for two months the public have enjoyed the play.

This political melodrama had won applause across the nation. Gorham, however, was mistaken in believing that his becoming editor had turned the new administration against the stalwarts. Rather it was very likely the specific editorial in support of a publicly owned telegraph system that served to turn the new administration against Gorham.

What Gorham and others did not consider was that the June 9, 1880 alleged gag rule had forecast the two-pronged strategy. At that time the financiers were still smarting from the Hepburn hearings, and they did not want such people as Simon Sterne, L. E. Chittenden, and others to urge the politicians to place the Western Union under the glass of legislative inspection. What they had not expected was that by spring of 1881 popular opinion against the financiers would be in such a boiling state that the legislature would be ready to move on behalf of the anti-monopolists. Among the politicians, the state of affairs would have translated into Blaine's fears. Blaine had predicted that the stalwarts would do everything to have Grant win in 1884; though they would start off kindly enough in 1881, they would soon show their true loyalties, loyalties to the growing popular sentiment.

What actually happened was that the New York half-breeds, viewing the turnout at meetings and the provocative articles, finally understood that they were but a small segment in New York politics. They could have figured that what they lacked in numbers, they could make up by outrage over a postal scandal, distracting a goodly segment from concerning themselves with corporate management. Therefore Robertson advised, in the face of rising protest over the telegraph consolidation, that Garfield place none of the Grant men from New York in the cabinet. It was important not only to keep merchant opinion out of the cabinet, but also to assure that they strengthen a new leadership over both the party and the city. Once Conkling failed to bend a knee to corporate interests by frustrating progress on the Adams trust, all pretenses were off. The factional fight came front and center stage, and the president announced that he wanted to remake the New York party. The norm of business non-competition, following the Rockefeller model, was the right way to go, and any other course abhorrent. That would have kept the Rockefeller model relevant in paving the way for final adoption of the Adams plan and a trust in the railway industry.

Charles Guiteau Begins to Stalk Garfield

Guiteau believed that his 1880 campaign speech had turned the tide and he had come to Washington to collect his reward but found a divided party that shifted his attention to another problem to be solved. Gorham would testify at the trial that Guiteau's speech was only average. If Guiteau had taken the pains to seek out corroboration of his own judgment, he might have saved himself, the president and the country a lot of trouble. First, he sought out Garfield for a job. Then he camped out at the State Department and pestered Blaine in his comings and goings to the point of exasperation.

Guiteau's behavior was evident a full month before he followed the president to the railroad station. Even the foreign press was aware of it. The London *Daily News,* as reported by Gorham on June 2nd, said that seekers of foreign posts were "strangely disproportionate to their fitness for undertaking the duties." Gorham, though disgusted with the president, ran the item from the English paper, which could have helped Garfield:

> President Garfield might take a lesson from his great predecessor, Lincoln . . . An indefatigable lobbyist used to pester Lincoln with application for Foreign Service. At last one day Lincoln told his importunate acquaintance to learn the Spanish language and come to him again. For a long time Lincoln saw his friend no more. But when some months had passed away he turned up again and told Lincoln that he was now a complete master of the Spanish tongue. "Then," said President Lincoln blandly, "You had better read Don Quixote in the original at once. You will find it most delightful." If President Garfield adopted such a plan with his would-be ministers he might find their number would rapidly diminish.[14]

Later, at his trial, Guiteau testified that he had turned against the president on learning that Garfield was requiring "letters of introduction" from senators not favoring the Robertson nomination.[15] At the next point, however, he wrote Garfield that he could be free of Blaine and still win the next election. Guiteau's shifting views did not make him any less sane than the shifting views of any policymaker reflected on his sanity.

Guiteau feared that in the 1884 election the Republican Party would split and the Democrats would take over the government. All that was needed, Guiteau concluded, was to stave off the party split by changing the person at the top, ousting Garfield in favor of Arthur. He was hardly aware that commerce was shifting from eastern ports to New Orleans. That would end up shifting New York opinion toward the Democrats.

In fact, what would happen was that the Democrats would win the next two state elections, well before winning the presidency in 1884. Guiteau proved about as dense as the half-breeds, who were so paralyzed by the prospect of who would go to the national 1884 convention that they did not even consider what would happen in the state election in 1881 and in 1882.

What Guiteau would have had to notice about Gorham's editorials was that the editor had made some uncanny predictions. Gorham had written on March 26 that the Robertson nomination aimed at trying to change party leadership in New York state *by external force.* Again, Guiteau would have had to read that on May 24, a week after Conkling and Platt resigned, according to the statement in the *Tribune* that " . . . the President (wants) to have it fully, distinctly, and widely known . . . that the object of his administration is to abolish the factions in New York . . ." According to that view, the stalwart faction would be totally repressed in favor of a more congenial political alliance. Gorham had tracked the consistent policy of the president. Garfield would find, however, that he had not gained the support of some of the most influential people in New York.

From his reading, Guiteau paid more attention to party leadership, probably learning of Ulysses S Grant's alarm over Garfield's treatment of his friends. Grant had written Senator John P. Jones how disgusted he was with the developments in New York patronage. "When it comes to filling the most influential office in their State without consulting these senators it is a great slight. When he selects the most offensive man to be found, it becomes an insult, and ought to be resented to the bitter end."[16] Grant had added that Garfield could retrace his steps.

In Chicago, a reporter interviewed the former president and asked about the Robertson nomination. Grant replied, "I don't believe it would have ever happened if Mr. Blaine had not been in the cabinet." A month later rumors arose that Grant would go to Long Branch, where Garfield was vacationing, and arrange a compromise. However, a friend of Grant told a reporter that:

> General Grant would not walk across the street to see President Garfield
> unless he was invited, and I doubt very much whether he would go then.
> His feelings are very strongly against a President who would allow him-
> self to be made an instrument of revenge in the hands of such a man as
> Blaine.[17]

Each of the men disparaged the other's motives. Grant's cold attitude at Long Branch, Garfield thought, indicated that his loss at Chicago had stung him badly. This, however, would not be the first time that Garfield misread a stalwart. Grant, indeed, saw Garfield as only serving Blaine's desire for revenge. In effect, Grant had withdrawn his endorsement of Garfield, a matter which may have impressed Guiteau.

Gorham's Appraisal of the Railroaders' Political Position

In the midst of this struggle at close quarters, Gorham took a step back to remind his readers of the larger picture. About the party condition in the face of monopolists' demands for railroading on June 21st he wrote,

> The railroads of the country, which cost an average of less than $20,000 a mile, are made to yield dividends and interest on nearly three times that amount. [Cartel commissioner Albert Fink would later testify before Congress that the cost was $60,000 per mile.]

In 1885 Thurber would repeat Gorham's line of thought and complain to the Cullom committee: "Having thus over-capitalized our transportation system they endeavored by combination to enforce rates which would yield dividends upon the entire capital."[18] Gorham had continued:

> State Legislatures have been chosen expressly to check this enormous extortion, but generally the hired lobby of the railway companies have bought some and confused others, until in despair the people have well nigh given over all hope of being represented by the men they elect. The corporations hire men to clamor for vested rights and to resist all attempts at legislative control. The managers formerly claimed only a fair return for their capital invested, but they now abandon this and fix the rate of freight at "what the goods will bear." This means: "How high a rate would you pay rather than not have your goods moved for you at all?" Mr. Albert Fink, their chief expert, lays down the proposition that a railroad company is entitled to charge as freight an amount equal to the value added to the commodity by moving it. As all surplus productions would be worth nothing unless taken to market, his principle would make the market value of the commodity a reasonable charge for its transportation to market.

Gorham's comment was the same as Thurber had made in his note to Conkling the day of the Robertson nomination, namely that the railroads aim "to obtain supreme control of the affairs of our government. A power which dictates to all production and commerce what share of the profits shall go to the producers and the public . . ."[19] Gorham continued:

> Finding that State Legislatures cannot be relied on to resist the blandishments of the gigantic monopolies, the minds of thoughtful men have for several years been turned toward the General government. But the corporations are alert. The disgraceful exposures at Albany show that they intend to battle for the control of the United States Senate. It is now becoming less a question of what Congress can do to relieve the people of

railroad extortion and tyranny than it is how to prevent a subversion of the government and its complete control by that very tyranny.

> They tell us that vested rights are sacred, and that only an agrarian spirit will attempt to touch them with the profane hand of legislation. [It is] for the people to realize that they have the power to control the question if they have enough intelligence and public virtue to wrest their State and National Legislatures from the control of their oppressors.

That is, an aroused public could wrest control––not in the current legislature but in the next, and follow the course marked out in the 1877 decision of Chief Justice Waite in *Munn v. Illinois.*

The Judge Delays Receiving the Star Route Case until September 1881

With the launching of the postal investigation the nation was treated to much fanfare. By May, however, it was not going well. The administration found that the investigation needed some mid-course adjustments. The *Sun* pointed out that since the president began "requiring his work to be subject to supervision"[19] he apparently had doubts about Attorney General MacVeagh's efforts. Nothing was ready for the grand jury. The judge, looking to a summer recess, waited and finally could wait no longer; he postponed the cases to September.[20] Meanwhile, the defense was held at arm's length. On June 24, 1881, Gorham printed James Brady's letter to his attorneys, Shellabarger and Wilson, to win copies of material from the Post Office Department that it was giving to the *Times*. Brady wanted to "read in them what is not printed in the *Times*." (*NR,* June 29, 1881) The letters were not forthcoming. If that was an admission that the prosecutors were having difficulties, the postal investigation appeared to be nothing but a "trial by newspaper."

The Reverend Henry Beecher Criticizes Garfield's Financial Supporters

Garfield believed that he had to make a manly effort to stand up to Conkling. Friends urged him to keep up his backbone. Playing that theme, the *Tribune* reduced the effort to a mathematical spread of power. "Garfield is President of the United States. Mr. Conkling represents one-seventy-sixth part of one branch of Congress. Mr. Garfield has more power than the *entire* Senate."[21] The observation was in keeping with the declaration about abolishing the factions in New York. Together they went hand-in-hand with both the half-breeds' contempt for the federal process.

In the real world at the moment, since their companies could not get the rates they wanted for shipping merchants' goods, they had brought their business in New York City to a standstill. Hardship soon descended upon many quarters of the city, so much so that the next turn of events would arise from a Protestant pulpit.

Henry Ward Beecher delivered a sermon on Sunday, June 26, 1881. It very likely came to the president's attention and called into doubt all the talk about the president's power. Before Garfield read the sermon he may have felt that he was cock of the walk, but, if his behavior meant anything, not afterwards. He called in friends, especially Robert Todd Lincoln, to discuss assassination for he possibly was scared and flinched in the face of the sermon. (See Robertson, Archie, "Murder Most Foul," *American Heritage*, August 1964, cited in Richard Shenkman & Kurt Reiger, *One-Night Stands with American History: Odd, Amusing, and Little-Known Incidents.* New York: Quill, 1982, p. 152.)

Beecher had long held a position that warranted serious attention, especially due to his service in the Civil War. His warnings about Kansas and his turning British sentiment were both critical of the North. His appraisal of the new Garfield administration would make readers sit up and pay attention.

He had already expressed his disappointment with Garfield. On April 24th, when praising Mr. Gladstone of England as a Christian statesman, Beecher asked: "Have we such a man [as Gladstone] here? No. We have politicians and many of them, but no man of eminence who lives for others. May God send us such a man!" [22]

On Sunday, June 26, 1881, Beecher focused on the well-recognized influences. A month earlier both the *New York Times* and the *Washington Post,* one day after the other, had run similar editorials about the decline in New York City's commerce.

Now Beecher drew together three important facts of the day. The first was his recalling the campaign funding that Garfield had received. Beecher mentioned the same coterie of donors familiar to the public seven years earlier through the Windom report about "four men representing the four great trunk lines . . . reduc[ing] the value of property in this country by hundreds of millions of dollars."[22]

The second fact, as J. J. White had pointed out in May, was what everyone could see in the rail yards: the locomotives and railroad cars were standing idle. With little means of transport, the merchants were losing hundreds of thousands of dollars per day.

Finally, the legislators at Albany representing railroad interests had not only opposed the discrimination bill and the commission bill, but also opposed Astor's plan for canal improvement. They were not only discouraging competition from the canal wherever they saw it but also rebuffing regulation for themselves. The dissonance among the commercial leadership was hardly deniable. They could barely defend their interests. Adding insult to injury, the railroad lobbyists were trying to place cartel board president Depew in the U.S. Senate. On top of this stall in business, the president was calling for the abolition of the factions in the state! In short, Beecher counseled that times were tough but the common man had to hold on and not relent. For the worst thing that could happen to their side would be for the half-breeds to win on some legislative proposition leading to further failure of the middle class position. In a matter of weeks, they would settle on strengthening their control over what was clearly possible: saving the canal by making its tolls free.

In his morning sermon, ever ready to instruct his congregation about taking their Christian witness into the world, Beecher decided to set before the faithful the facts that the believers should find on their pilgrimage. He also addressed the matter of monopoly. His central point was that the present suffering could bring about final good, casting the current course of public affairs in the well-known melodramatic format. He first took several illustrations from public policy and finally focused on the current suffering caused by combinations of money. The sermon appeared in the Monday edition of the *Times,* assuring it a wide readership.

One of the most iniquitous pieces of political triumph ever let loose on the country was the enactment in 1850 of the Fugitive Slave law . . . It was a good thing . . . for we poor scrawny Abolitionists, who had been holding little conventions, and had been cheered on by eggs, which had passed the period of their usefulness. Not a book could be printed in the American Tract Society if it contained anything about liberty, except the liberty, which Christ brought. . . [The new law] was one straw too much . . . The breaking of that Missouri Compromise was the best thing that happened, except the enactment of the Fugitive Slave law . . . . The war itself was a good thing . . . it was a good thing that we lost Bull Run. The long protraction of the war was the best thing for the Nation . . . When the South laid down its arms, it had literally exhausted all its resources. There was absolute poverty in the whole South, and that was the best condition possible for the South. Her people were compelled to learn the dignity of personal labor . . .

There were two dangerous tendencies developing in our time. There was a great peril and danger from the combinations of capital––another element––the power of property. . . . There were the railroad combinations, with five or ten men controlling 10,000 miles of railroads and billions on billions of property. They had *their hands on the very throat of commerce. If they should need to have a man in sympathy with them in the Executive chair, it would require only five pockets to put him there.* There were going out of New York City at least three or four roads that were yet undeveloped dangers to the very existence of incorrupt central government. They were a lion bigger than any Samson ever saw. But the lion would be met and slain, and in the end would be a benefit to the country. The increase of manufactories would make all fabrics cheaper and cheaper, and the railroad and steamship companies would bring them to every man's door, and in the distribution of the world's products by these monopolies there would be benefit to all. Commerce was a winged lion, plying with the products of each part of the world to every other part. *When the coming perils of the monopolies had been met and smitten, the benefits would remain.* (Our emphasis.)

339

The sermon fit the scheme of action and reaction across the broad policy arena. Beecher probably was referring to the financiers contributing to the previous year's presidential campaign. Some donors were members of the railroad cartel, and their business decisions were currently suspending railroading, drying up the city's export business, and hitting merchants in their pockets.

One can imagine that in the rail yards the steam engines and other rolling stock stood idle. The streets were more quiet as the cartmen and teamsters had less employment. Goods on order backed up in business houses and at dockside. Income fell off and, as certain as the sun would rise, the merchants knew that routine payments of taxes and debts would have to be met. Such a crisis had been predicted in March of 1878 when Charles Smith reported on a meeting of political and business leaders. At that time Smith also became chairman of the Chamber's new committee on railroads and launched the effort that became the Hepburn hearings. In 1881, on August 3rd, broker Rufus Hatch warned that the cartel was drying up trade and he warned interest groups to see what was at stake. Hatch would write "The Fink pool has done more to injure New York City than a failure of crops for three years."

The public needed no legislative investigation to explain this. No diversion could distract their attention. America's leading Protestant preacher, a good example for other preachers, had now met the cartel leaders' indifference. His words in the community of the merchants' interests captured the institutional strain facing New York City and its renowned leadership in the nation's commerce. Beecher's status together with the popular knowledge of the problem facing New York commerce made his statement high on the hierarchy of announcements. The term "institutional strain," which we take from Laumann and Knoke, pointed to the possibility of New York as a single commercial institution going over a precipice and down the slippery slope––due not only to the increasing competition from New Orleans but also to the behavior of the cartel.

Beecher's facts and interpretation must have ricocheted into the White House. The minister had drawn together well-known but diverse facts and lined them up logically giving the average interested person "debating points" that would carry in every day conversation. Beecher performed as a consequential leader without a distinctive position at the head of an institution other than being a popular editor. Garfield had not paid much attention to New Yorkers, except for Reid. He was of a mind that the state of New York was a shelter to a great evil and on his mind was defeating its opponents. It was a simple goal and that was the problem. New York City was much more complex. To be honest about the city's circumstances, one had to entertain ambiguity, something seriously avoided in melodrama. Thus, the president, accepting the facts of New York's commercial troubles, topics in the paper for some time, had to realize his view had not been entirely honest, and needed revision. Any revision, however, would entail his creating some space between himself and his donors. Beecher's telling blow was that the monster of monopolism would itself face mortality, a fact indeed to be realized in the Cullom bill of 1887.

In addition, since June 9, 1881, Garfield had known of the bribery charges, but some friends had written them off as no more than rumors. Now, with an authority the likes of Beecher pointing out the cartel's broader misbehavior and inevitable mortality, no one could doubt that the people around the president were up to no good.

More broadly than the transportation shutdown, Beecher was also talking about the close of debate on the issue. He had traveled this path a quarter century earlier when he came to the aid of Kansas. Soon northeasterners were sending rifles to northerners in those territories to fend off slavery. On June 12, 1856, in an editorial entitled "Silence Must Become National," Beecher wrote, "a gigantic conspiracy was developed of which Kansas is a single finger, but whose whole hand is yet *to grip the throat* of the Nation."[23] In 1856 skirmishes in Kansas soon flared, and the inference in 1881 was that the popular revolt against the corporations would soon flare up. (Our emphasis.)

The president, no stranger to changing his views on issues, likely wondered whether he stood on the right side. Back in January he had dreamed of traveling on a sinking ship, jumping ashore and knowing for the first time that he was president. However, his resolve did not last. Senator-elect Harrison had paid him a call and, on returning to Indiana, wrote that he seemed perplexed. Recently, he had taken strength from his friends' urgings to keep up his backbone against Conkling. He had done so by threatening senators with the demand for "letters of introduction" to see him, showing he had "meant business." A month earlier, according to the *Tribune,* shortly after Conkling's and Platt's resignations, he felt so confident that he staked out a new position, "to abolish the factions in New York."

Now suddenly, after a sermon delivered by a great preacher, "the most famous man in America" as some dubbed him, Garfield had to reconsider his view of things, even failing to reach his declared goal for the New York party announced in late May. Garfield had mastered the Senate; it was plausible to some that he could master New York politics. Beecher's choice of words upset such prospects by displaying in one sentence the antagonism between the members of the cartel pool and the merchants, a dispute not among persons but among institutions. While Garfield, Blaine and a few others in their *laissez faire* approach had worked to rearrange New York's leadership, they had deeply violated the commercial community's sense of justice. Beecher's plain speaking now made the cartel into the "bad men." Garfield seemed frozen in his tracks. He probably knew that his friends in the legislature would find their hand weakened while he was bound by the alleged gag rule. Even if corruption was indicated, he could not comment on corporate behavior. While Blaine in December had laid out a melodrama between the "good" people and the "bad" people, Beecher had shown that the melodrama had quickly shifted to the opposite pole––always the risk any player has to run. Garfield could no longer pose as Horatio at the bridge, fending off the Philistines in the New York organization, be they Roscoe Conkling, the star route contractors, anti-monopolists or anyone else. When Grant's negative views of Garfield were combined with Beecher's condemnation, the weight against the president was strong indeed.

Meanwhile, Guiteau was still disturbed over the prospects for the next presidential campaign. Chittenden's comments of February 16—that there would be a "bloody revolt"—had likely reached him. Further, he had likely imbibed the *Herald*'s May 11 article that Garfield thought Gorham and Conkling had written. More recently, he had likely read not only about the cabinet ladies' social snobbishness, but also the insults Chittenden had taken on New York streets from monopolists and Grant's condemnation of Blaine for his influence on Garfield.

On the other side of the policy arena, the administration social set were probably taking comfort that the rule of "senatorial courtesy" was about to expire and the star route "thieves" were about to be taken to jail. That set had to take pause, however, with the attorney general's delay in the star route investigation--a delay supporting Gorham's belief that the investigation could rise no higher than the politics of character assassination. While the half-breeds would have been pleased with "the object of (Garfield's) administration to abolish the faction in New York," they would have encountered rumors of the railroad bribery at Albany. On the other hand, good news came from Albany about the failure of the New York state Railroad Commission Bill. With all of these cross-currents in the news, Guiteau could have become quite excited.

June 29th: The Albany Grand Jury Issues Indictments for the Bribery of State Legislators

On June 29, 1881, five weeks after Gorham made his prediction about imminent discovery of bribery at Albany, big money was now plain to see. On June 29th the Albany grand jury handed down indictments. The jury issued one against Lo Sessions, for the $2,000 he had paid to state Senator S. H. Bradley; against A. D. Barber, for paying E. R. Phelps $12,500 to bribe state officers; against Phelps for the same; and against Charles A. Edwards for receiving from Joseph Dickson $5,000 for bribing state officers. No stalwarts were named. While some at the moment seriously doubted the news of bribery, it would remain persuasive enough to fortify plans that the merchants would take in August.

It is plausible that Garfield had new worries about his personal security. He had announced ambitious goals to "abolish the faction" in New York, and the *Tribune* assured everyone that he had more power than Conkling. His power, however, was apparently not enough to keep his cartel compatriots from giving his effort a bad name. Beecher's words had struck a chord that needed attention. Through his half-breed candidate at Albany, Chauncey Depew, the president of the cartel board, could have told strangling railroaders in the city to relent, but he did not.

Rather, giving an inkling that he himself felt at risk, the next day he called in Secretary of War Robert Todd Lincoln, to talk about the assassination of his father.[25] It was no longer, as Blaine had written in December 1880, a scenario of good men against bad. Nor was it a matter, as Reid had recently cast it, of one man's political power being mathematically greater than another's. Rather, it was a conflict of interests. It now appeared that the anti-monopolists could soon take the higher ground, making Garfield one of the early casualties. He had become so wedded to his half-breed supporters, and had shown them so much sympathy, that he could not attain any objectivity for himself.

The New York State Senate Defeats the Assembly's Railroad Commission Bill

Heightening the sustained political strain in Albany, the Railroad Commission Bill passed by the New York assembly in April was defeated by the state senate on June 30th.[26] With that vote over, Robertson had no reason to remain in Albany. Although thoughts of assassination bothered Garfield, he still felt under obligation to his corporate donors and, with Reid's man E. V. Smalley posted at a White House desk ready to write anything Garfield might have dictated, Garfield said nothing. Stalwarts, of course, were hoping for him to "retrace his steps," but nothing happened. On the other hand, was it simply a matter of letting the business year end at the Customs House and making a clean transfer of responsibilities with a new man?[27]

Gorham Refuses to Let the Tribune Discount the Grand Jury

The *Tribune* sought to discount the news of the grand jury indictments. Conveniently forgetting how two years earlier it had censured Lo Sessions, the paper charged that the members of the jury were Conkling partisans, selected under the supervision of John F. Smythe. Since this explanation could have easily originated at the White House and been passed on by E. V. Smalley to New York, it may have represented Garfield's suspiciousness. Gorham couldn't let that pass, and on June 30, 1881, he published a long discourse on the New York law--probably supplied him by Conkling--that covered selecting the Albany grand jury members and concluded:

> The grand jury was selected by the Democratic board of supervisions in November, 1880, and drawn by law from three hundred names in the box—before the alleged bribery occurred—by John Larkin, Democrat, country clerk; James A. Houck, Republican, sheriff, and T. J. Van Alstyen, Democrat, county judge. Poor, malicious, ignorant *Tribune!*[28]

Little wonder that Reid was forever after Gorham's reputation. When Gorham in 1888 wrote his eulogy for Conkling for the *Herald*, he pointed out that one indictment still stood. In 1881 one serious consequence was that the news of the bribery hardly helped attorney and cartel chair Chauncey Depew's candidacy for the U.S. Senate. Although Conkling's position deteriorated rapidly following Guiteau's attack on Garfield, the legislators who were still loyal to Conkling informed Depew, as he relates in his recollections, that under no circumstances would they deliver him their votes. Depew dropped out of the race. Depew's stall of the railroad legislation, the railroad lobbyists' behavior in bribery, and the lockdown of railroad trains had come back to haunt him.

The Drop in Rail Rates Continues to Hurt Canal Receipts

A drop in some rates soon moved business off the canals to the rails. In early July 1881, the *Times* reported that canal receipts were at less than half the previous year's level. The *Herald* reported weekly figures against the previous year's business and showed the same trend. Through the end of June 1881 tolls for the canal season came to $94,609, far less than the receipts a year earlier, $242,522. By the end of the season, they were no better——$326,151 compared to $736,631 the previous year.[29] The surmise is warranted, since the cartel could not keep members from proceeding with the rate war, and the new lows in rates were aimed at——or, at least had the effect of——undercutting the canal. If that course continued, receipts might not be enough to open the canal the next year——the cartel would have achieved another victory by either intention or default.

Guiteau Shoots Garfield at the Station

In his later testimony Guiteau told the court that on the night of July 1st he saw Garfield and Blaine walking down the street in a

> most delightful and cozy fellowship. Just as hilarious as two young school-girls . . . It proved what the stalwart and liberal papers were saying, to wit: that Garfield had sold himself, soul and body, to Blaine, and that Blaine was using Garfield *to destroy the stalwart element of the Nation* . . . it confirmed what I have been reading for weeks in the newspapers . . . This was positive eye confirmation.[30] (Our emphasis.)

Guiteau's testimony resonated with Garfield's May declaration through the *Tribune* that the president sought to "abolish the factions in New York." As time passed, events gave Guiteau more support for what he wanted to do.

After Garfield died in September the jury trial commenced and its procedure surprisingly fit into the prevailing half-breed insistence on the alleged gag rule. The jury decided that the defendant was insane, easily leaving out the work of tracking the sequence of events up to the shooting. Similarly, while the defendant asked that editors of several papers be called to testify, the request was denied. In the end, the jury's course had the consequence of disqualifying any account not sanitizing Garfield and placed responsibility for the shooting elsewhere. Garfield's declaration overlooked allows an author to look at any number of conditions to explain what happened, but Garfield's declaration admitted requires an author to write that the president shared in the responsibility, making quite a different story.

Throughout the trial Guiteau did raise historical points, such a Garfield requiring of the senators "letters of introduction" leading him to decide to stand with Conkling. If the jury had entered into those issues, it would have put the former president on trial. Passing over the record, they saved some editors, such as Gorham and Reid, from too open an examination. What remains is considerable evidence that the former president was hardly an innocent. The week after Beecher's sermon, Garfield may have recognized as much and discussed assassination with Robert Todd Lincoln and others. He gets credit for knowing that he could not now gain in New Yorkers' good opinion. Beecher's language may have been authoritative and clear enough to keep Garfield from performing some verbal sidesteps.

Public reaction to the shooting was mixed. The nation was horrified and struck with grief. Not surprisingly, the assassin did receive letters of support at his prison cell.[31] Through his trial Guiteau maintained that Blaine and Garfield had been the aggressor. In his testimony, Guiteau said, "I have really saved the nation from another war." [32]

Garfield survived the attack and became a convalescent and a hero. While he needed expert physicians to attend him, none did. Ironically, although his railroad allies insisted that experts handle industry matters, they did not succeed in applying that principle to the health care of the president, leaving him to die of poor treatment as much as from Guiteau's attack. *The North American Review* of December 1881 carried a discussion by four eminent surgeons, one of whom denied that Garfield's death was inevitable.[33] After Garfield's death, Anna Dawes, the daughter of the Senate assistant majority leader, wrote her mother, saying, "When I get home I will tell you what the Drs. from N. Y. and elsewhere I have met here think of the medical treatment—which is summed up in the phrase, 'He needn't have died.' It seems Bliss was Rob't Lincoln's Dr & was upheld by him in everything—which accounts you see."[34]

Gould Hears of the Assassination Attempt on Garfield

On the day Guiteau attacked Garfield, financier Gould was at his country estate. A friend who happened to appear just as he received the news reported his response, which in the circumstances suggested that the financier was heavily invested in Garfield's success.

> One summer afternoon at Lyndhurst Alice Northrop came around the porch and found Jay walking unsteadily toward her, clutching a telegram, his face drained of color and his hands trembling violently. "Alice," he whispered hoarsely, "Garfield has been shot! President Garfield has been shot!" She led him to a wicker chair on the porch where, after a few minutes, he regained his composure. Two things about the incident impressed Alice in later years. Jay's mask of self-control, which she had never seen slip, vanished completely, revealing a man of deep if private feelings. His head sagged back, then snapped forward again. Within moments, the mask had returned and he went inside. "At dinner," she marveled, "no one could have told how that telegram had shaken him."[35]

There is plenty here for speculation. Gould recently must have had important business with Garfield when they met at Reid's home following the August Fifth Avenue

Hotel party conference. That was followed by correspondence with Reid and settling on the courtesies in selecting nominees for the court. In that meeting, mention was probably made of the Union Pacific's delinquency in payments to the sinking fund and that Gould wanted to pay less, something Senator Ben Hill of Georgia might have promoted in the U.S. Senate. Gould was particularly pressed, since the Union Pacific had continued to pay out dividends and had only recently developed the practice of a revolving debt. The men at that August session might also have touched on the plan to consolidate the great rails systems through an Adams bill, an event that would make borrowing easier as well as strengthen resumption. Equally important, Garfield's silence on hearing of the telegraph consolidation benefited the financier. As Garfield's administration had progressed, Gould may have anticipated, in the struggle between new money and old money prevailing in the city, that he would soon enjoy status in the elite. Now, on receiving news of the attack on Garfield, Gould must have seen the skein of welfare unravel that the new administration had woven around him and realized that his particular business plan could come apart. He had every reason to be shaken.

The Prevailing Interpretation of Garfield's Death

For a century and a quarter the prevailing interpretation of Garfield's death easily traces the cause to Conkling's obtuse ego. The grief over a president's death has contributed to the belief in his innocence, a belief sustaining the melodramatic view of events and the inference that he certainly could not have done anything wrong that put himself at risk. In addition, many scholars may trace their own professional lineage, and the advance of civil service reform, back to the educated reformers who found fault with the stalwart leader.

That was an easy way out. It has to be admitted that the president's political situation had deteriorated badly. The party had given him no convention platform to guide his actions on behalf of the interest group that he most identified with. That group had been poor lobbyists for their cause and then expected of him, when they did not get what they wanted, to carry out misdirected punishment against Conkling. The president had managed to control the Senate on their behalf, but the special interest left him undeniably exposed when, as anyone could see, they cut off commerce in New York City. If he had any ambition to "abolish the factions in New York," his alleged half-breed supporters, by continuing to shut down rail traffic in the City, managed to pull the rug out from under him. Not only had U. S. Grant and Henry Beecher withdrawn their endorsement, but also the cartel left him exposed. Not surprisingly, Garfield felt himself at risk and asked Robert Todd Lincoln to talk to him about his father's assassination. Indeed, he had cause to worry about assassination, but not enough to call up U.S. marshals to protect him.

In spite of the facts supporting this scenario, the common interpretation remains the melodramatic one, with evil on one side and innocence on the other, in order to blame the much-hated Conkling and, along with that, to overlook such elements of the total transportation system as the canal in mustering popular sentiment against the cartelists. Rather the picture drawn has been of a contest between individuals––Conkling and Garfield––while there is every reason to expose it as a contest between interest groups––the cartel and the Chamber of Commerce. That portion of the scenario was soon to unfold.

As shall be seen, the cleavage in the party over transportation policy was not effectively overcome until the next national convention when the delegates, tacitly admitting the previous convention's culpability, managed to pass an explicit plank on transportation that led the Congress finally to getting down to work in 1885. In the meantime, the corporate interests managed to deflect attention from their part in the matter and they easily faulted both Roscoe Conkling and a leading editor, George Gorham, for the death of Garfield.

Gorham's Prospects for Returning to the Secretaryship of the Senate

Assured that Gorham would lose political favor by the attack on Garfield, the *Tribune* forecast,

> Some of these results, since they concern the organization of both Houses of Congress and the course of legislation, may be profitably considered. Mr. Gorham has been more coarse, brutal, and unscrupulous than any other adherent of Mr. Conkling in assailing the President. Whether the President lives or dies, the election of Mr. Gorham as Secretary of the Senate has become impossible. The slanderer of a dead Republican President will have as little chance to receive every Republican vote as the slanderer of a living Republican President, and the association of Mr. Gorham with the star-route operators and with Mr. Conkling and his stalwarts will make his election the one thing not to be done. The Republicans of the Senate will find themselves obliged to select new candidates if they have desire to succeed. This will involve not only the elimination of Mr. Gorham, but also a reconsideration of the case of Virginia as presented by the nomination of Mr. Riddleberger.[36]

With the statement about Riddleberger, an ally of Mahone, Gorham's risk greatly increased. In the long term, the trouble with the *Tribune*'s caution about Gorham was that the paper would not learn until 1898 that the allegations about the star route "thieves" were without evidence. Further, the paper failed to say that Conkling had frustrated the railroaders' attempt to stack the judiciary committee. Despite Ulysses S. Grant's and Henry Ward Beecher's criticism of the president, the *Tribune*'s comments would work to the discredit of the stalwarts. Garfield had sustained a pro-cartel stance throughout his administration, and at his death the cartelists, dominating the press, could put whatever spin they wanted on his tenure. They defeated both Conkling and Gorham, two stalwarts

347

who were in vulnerable positions since each was standing for office. The *Tribune* had its railroad interests to protect from the stalwarts and the *Times* was increasing circulation through the alleged postal scandal. Totally missing from the charges against the stalwarts was an admission that Garfield lost any claim to reputed innocence by announcing his plans for the New York factions.

Some offer the rejoinder that the victors get to write the history. One problem with that is that it does not fit: in the policy struggle over railroad regulation, the cartelists would not get the regulated monopoly they wanted.

Chapter XII

The Rev. Henry Beecher Trumps President Garfield's Melodrama

1   *NR*, May 30, 1881.

2   *NR*, May 21, 1881.

3   *NR*, May 25, 1881.

4   *NYT,* June 10, 1880.

5   *NR*, May 19, 1881.

6   *NR*, August 2, 1881.

7   Benson, Lee. *Merchants, Farmers, and Railroads.* Cambridge, MA: Harvard University Press, 1955, p. 296.

8   Garfield, James A. *Diary.* Harry James Brown and Fredrick D. Williams, eds. East Lansing: Michigan State University Press, 1981, June 2, 1881, p. 604.

9   *NR,* June 6, 1881.

10   Garfield *Diary,* June 6, 1881.

11   *NR*, May 12 and 16, 1881.

12   *NR*, June 3, 1881; *Tribune,* September 22, and October 11, 1879.

13   *NR*, June 14, 1881; see also NR, June 17, 1881.

14   *NR,* June 2, 1881.

15   *NYT,* December 12, 1881.

16   *NR*, May 20, 1881.

17   *NR,* June 22, 1881.

18   Benson, p. 243.

19   Benson, p. 157.

19a   *NR*, June 29, 1881.

20   *NR*, June 22, 1881.

21 *NR*, June 25, 1881.

22 *NYT,* April 25, 1881.

23 Clark, Clifford, *Henry Ward Beecher, Spokesman for the Middle Class.* Urbana: University of Illinois Press, 1978, p. 121 and corresponding footnotes.

24 Marcus, Alan I. and Howard P. Segal. *Technology in America, a Brief History.* New York: Harcourt Brace Jovanovich, 1989, p 52.

25 Robertson, Archie, "Murder Most Foul," *American Heritage,* August, 1964, p. 91, cited in Richard Shenkman & Kurt Reiger, *One-Night Stands with American History: Odd, Amusing, and Little-Known Incidents.* New York: Quill, 1982, pp. 152f.

26 *NYT,* June 23, 24, 29, and 30, 1881.

27 The anti-discrimination bill passed the assembly (*NYT,* April 29, 1880), and the Robertson "bolt" was announced (*NYT,* May 7, 1880.) less than a week later. Again, in March 1881, two months after the U.S. House Commerce Committee reported on the Adams bill, at Albany the state regulation bill began moving from the assembly committee. On April 20, 1881, the New York assembly voted 74 to 33 in favor of the commission bill (*NYT,* April 21, 1881); Garfield had nominated Robertson for collector, very likely again emboldening the state senate against the assembly's work, and giving the railroaders' allies in Washington time to launch their plan for federal regulation.

28 *NR*, June 30, 1881.

29 *NYT,* July 2, 1881 and December 2, 1881.

30 Herbert, George B. *Guiteau. The Assassin.* Cincinnati: Forshee and McMakin, 1881, p. 381.

31 Shenkman and Reiger, p. 135. Some of the letters are found in *NYT,* January 22, 1882.

32 *NYT,* January 22, 1882.

33 *NYT,* Nov. 16, 1881.

34 Dawes, Anna L., to her mother, September 20, 1881. *Dawes Collection, LC.*

35 Klein, Maury. *Life and Legend of Jay Gould.* Baltimore: Johns Hopkins University Press, 1986, p. 217.

36 *NR,* July 14, 1881.

Chapter XIII

Among the Changing Scenes of Peril
Decorum Returns

The Course Leading up to the Amendment for the Free Canal

The state election campaign of late 1881 had gotten its start on some of the issues raised three years earlier. In 1878 New York business leaders and city officials met about the troubled finances of the city. For the first time, the leaders singled out the railroads as part of the problem. Since the state had initially issued the franchises to the companies, the legislature assumed the privilege of looking into the matter. The investigation by an assembly committee under Barton Hepburn began its work, charging that the companies were derelict respecting six specific problems. The companies responded by denying the problems and the committee proved them wrong. End of round one for the committee.

At the end of the hearings the issues went before the state conventions of the parties, and won approval of platform planks favoring state regulation. At first the owners were ready to negotiate a solution but then they reneged. They would rather first have national regulation and looked to the coming administration to win such legislation.

Included in the owners' proposal were provisions for making the young cartel into a national trust. Charles F. Adams, Jr., had been describing the effort beginning with his book published in 1878. The railroaders, however, were not sufficiently sophisticated in the protocols of lobbying, and they fumbled the attempt. They further antagonized the merchants when in June 1881 they failed to relent on rates and, for a time, they brought the city's export traffic to a halt.

Along with these troubles, news from New Orleans reported the growing trade that was taking away New York's traffic. The interests had one resource in hand that they could bring into play and that was the canal. If it was used correctly, they could solve more than one problem. By dropping the rates on the canal they could assure, first of all, more traffic. Secondly, dropping rates would bolster their competitive position against the growth of trade at New Orleans. At the moment, their good fortune was that the resolution favoring a free canal had passed its first test in the legislature.

All that was needed now was a clean-up campaign. The resolution had to pass a second time in the next legislature and then win adoption from the electorate. For securing that outcome, voters had to defeat the legislators who too clearly had done the bidding of the railroads. Their campaign was so successful, the route of the railroad legislature so complete, that the electorate turned both houses over to the Democrats for the first time since the war. State regulation was adopted as well as the canal resolution a second time. The public ratified the canal option in November 1882 in a very lopsided vote: 3-to-1 in the state and better than 9-to-1 in the city (see Table 7). For one thing, that meant that the work of the Hepburn investigation was vindicated. It also meant that the electorate had found a role to play in transportation policy.

Over time the culminating event of the vote on the free canal would fade into the fog of the distant past. The standard accounts of the Garfield administration, for example, make no mention of the growing organization of the League in early 1881. Windom's February 1881 letter to a New York meeting discusses the emerging power of Jay Gould over the telegraph system but without a mention of Gould's success in consolidating three wire services in January.

The surmise is that this flurry of activity among the protestors got its start in August 1880 following the Republicans' meeting with candidate Garfield at the Fifth Avenue Hotel, a meeting often mentioned. But there were more. Indeed, later in December the *Times* stated that in August the Chamber had decided to poll their peer organizations. Several hints in the original source material suggest tactics and moves and are worth spelling out. Our surmise is that in August the Chamber sent out the questionnaires and they also decided to enlist authors to write the articles that appeared nationally after the first of the year. Right off, the *Times* in January 1881 carried a long copy of Thurber's statement to the national board a month earlier about the habit of the telegraph companies to unite. It came out just as Gould was making ready to unite three companies. When Gould in mid-January consolidated those wire services, the public was alert, and the incident was like throwing kerosene on a fire, plausibly giving Garfield a bad dream. Just how important these developments were came in a decision for the 1884 election. Some leaders of the League thought that the organization was so successful that it could mount a campaign for a third-party presidential candidate.

The state electoral victories of late 1881 and 1882 showed that the railroaders suffered from a double denial. First, they played down how badly they lost to the anti-monopolists, and did so by focusing on civil service reform and other issues. Secondly, they found most painfully that they could no longer make a proprietary claim on transportation policy. It was not putting it too simply to say that the railroad lobbyists had long discounted much of the arguments forwarded by the anti-monopolists. They had won at the 1880 national convention, vowed to keep their practices out of politics, and employed the new president to stave off most of their opposition.

When the anti-monopolists took the option of supporting the Free Canal Amendment, they did more than secure a means of transportation rivaling the railroads. They let the allegedly misleading politicians sit out the canvass. Under the leadership of the Chamber and exchanges they went directly to the electorate to explain their case and win a decision. The result would settle at least one matter for a long time to come. Either the canal supporters would fail and the railroads would continue to dominate matters; or, they would win, and the railroaders would have to take a different measure of their opposition. How far the railroaders were willing to go was represented in their winning President Garfield's support momentarily for scorning the stalwart faction in the state. In the end, the vote on the free canal gave a massive number of New Yorkers a constructive way to register their disagreement.

The canal would continue to provide the nation with a surrogate in lieu of the federal regulation that would not finally mature for another quarter century.

Conkling's Apparent Support of the Free Canal Resolution

The 1881–1882 campaign for the free canal was kicked off by Rufus Hatch writing in the *Times* with a wake-up call to the city's leaders. A stockbroker, he was known as an activist with stalwart credentials. His circulars had led up to the Hepburn hearings. More recently, he had tried to have the Western Union consolidation examined. That went through several courts and finally failed. Hatch, however, probably realized that in the matter of the canal he had a bird-in-the-hand. The state senate under railroad domination had blocked technological improvements for the canal. In the face of growing news of new competition from the port at New Orleans, Hatch could exploit that error to the benefit of a successful campaign for commerce in New York.

In April 1881, state senator George Forster, a Blaine supporter, introduced the free canal resolution, but it failed to pass. Then the railroad rate war suggested that the canals were at risk. In May the railroad pool aroused more hostility with their halt on commerce and the news of bribery at Albany. The corporations' position at Albany had weakened; one way for the canal advocates to seize the advantage was to press for saving the canals simply by passing off the question to the voters themselves. It was time to arouse popular opinion, and the beauty of the move was that the canal advocates would not expect any reforms by the railroads. More importantly, they sought to rid the legislature of railroad control.

In July Conkling seems to have concurred. He may have told his friends that if the free canal resolution were passed, he would agree to withdraw from his dismal race at Albany for a seat in the U.S. Senate. Conkling had long been a friend of the canal system. As his Senate committee assignments showed, he had long associated with senators from the nation's breadbasket. Their constituencies depended on eastbound traffic by rail and water from the Upper Mississippi states to the New York port. That made him focus not only on the interests of the farmers and shippers of the upper Mississippi, but also on the interests of the New York canalers, brokers, bankers, and handlers of the grain trade in the port. His thought on the canal question may have paralleled the opinion shaped by the *Commercial and Financial Chronicle*.

Although often regarded as a corporation attorney, Conkling had three times spoken of the importance of the canal. In July 1881 he appears to have given his approval for a metamorphosis of the canal in the New York economy. His 1881 attempt at re-election to the U.S. Senate was hardly promising, but his upstate friends may have urged him not to quit without winning some concessions. As a second-generation upstater, his family must have known many of the men who had earlier launched the canal system. Out of this network of old associates between Utica and Albany, some must have stepped forward, while Conkling was cooling his heels. His friends may have told him that if the legislature was not going to re-elect him as senator, it at least could give the state a chance at a free canal. He took the step, and the public vindicated his decision in November 1882. To get to the vote in the state senate, all that the senate leadership needed was to exercise some parliamentary requirements to call up the defeated motion for new action.

In trading his withdrawal from the senatorial race for legislative approval of the free canal resolution, Conkling probably recognized that the influence of his political machine was waning. In making the trade, state leadership now shifted from a partisan political entity to an issue he had often supported.

The leading commodity exchanges of the state, without the benefit of professional political help, would have to go directly to the public. Since a good case could be made that the Garfield administration––through Reid, Robertson, and Depew––was trying to assert a new leadership elite for New York, the commodity exchanges taking up the baton of the free canal cause would also soon qualify to enter that contest and take their portion of the city's leadership role.

The trade-off appeared in a two-day back-to-back episode. On July 21, 1881, two state senators previously opposed to the free canal resolution switched their votes, providing just enough votes to pass it.[1] The next day, the Republicans met alone and Conkling's twenty-five supporters were freed from continually voting for him. Only three were needed to give Eldridge Lapham the win, and he became the party nominee. With a united front, the Republican legislators rejoined the Democrats, and Lapham was elected to the U.S. Senate. The legislature adjourned and the members headed home. Not following Garfield's wish to overcome the factions in the state, the Republican legislators had agreed that one U.S. Senate position be filled by a stalwart and the other by a half-breed.[1]

That evening in New York City, as some legislators arrived by train, a reporter tried to interview Senator Robert Strahan. He wrote, "State Senator Strahan had said, 'Conkling's friends had carried every point which they had set out to carry excepting the election of the ex-Senator.' What points these friends of Mr. Conkling had carried Mr. Strahan did not say. He was in a hurry to get to his home." [2]

A point arrives in a policy scenario when the disputants agree on a respected agency where they will vote up or down on a solution and put the matter behind them. For example, in the late 1870s in the U.S. Senate on the matter of the Pacific railroads sinking fund legislation the company proposal had the support of the Senate committee on Pacific railroads. It was debated and defeated. Then the Thurman solution from the Senate committee on judiciary was introduced, debated and won. That sequence was possibly the course agreed upon beforehand, and they followed through on it.

The next great issue for railroading, national regulation, was hardly handled as neatly. Not only were the steps drawn out over time but they occurred in different geographically separate bodies, the Congress in Washington and the legislature in Albany. In March, the railroaders tried surreptitiously to seat only senators with railroad interests on the committee on the judiciary and failed. Seating an effective committee was stalled for another four years. The party had to speak nationally through a platform plank on the matter before the work could resume effectively in Congress under Shelby Cullom. In the meantime, the New York legislature pre-empted the action by putting the free canal option—a device for national regulation—to the New Yorkers and won. That set the precedent of public participation Cullom employed at the outset of his leadership of a new committee on inter-state commerce.

Following Laumann and Knoke's concept of policy scenarios, the passing of the free canal resolution now moved the drama into its third and final phase with a specific option to accept or reject. The cartel, when the Senate failed to seat senators whom Adams had likely suggested for the judiciary committee, had abandoned its earlier attempt for a vote on the Adams plan in Congress. From a different quarter on the policy scenario sidelines, the canal advocates now successfully entered the fray. Taking over the broader issue of transportation but supporting a much different option, the canal advocates had now set a date, November 1882, the state's next general election, for the final vote. With the cartel having abandoned its position, the canal advocates would work to secure their solution.

Before that canal vote, several different activities would occur. Some were intentionally forward-thinking or strategic, such as organizing a campaign to inform the citizenry and produce the vote. Other activities, however pertinent, were accidental and unexpected, and would arise from railroad behavior, from ancillary political activity, and from reports and editorials, all showing the trend of opinion.

The Auditor's August 1881 Report

In early August 1881, the July canal report, an unhappy one, appeared in the *Times*, saying,

> The receipts of the State canals have seriously fallen off, the tolls
> from the beginning of the season to Aug. 1 amounting to less than half

what they were for the corresponding period last year. The season opened a full month later, but the tolls for July alone were little more than one-half that for the same month in 1880. This is no doubt due in part to the fact that the amount of grain shipped from the West is smaller than a year ago and the cutting of rates on the railroads may have had some effect in diverting traffic from the water lines.

Rufus Hatch Focuses on Saving the Canal, August 1881

Hatch now set the modest goal of not only challenging various groups to understand their interests and preserve the canal but also returning decorum to New York business by challenging the cartel pool. The Chamber and the exchanges were to assume responsibility for the commercial supremacy of the city. With his easy access to the *Times* editorial rooms, his appeal appeared in the paper on August 3rd, just two days after Robertson had assumed his new duties at the Customs House.

> The merchants, real estate interests and businessmen of New York ought not overlook the fact that, while the railroad combination has been culminating, the Canadians have been quietly broadening and deepening the Welland Canal, and a movement is on foot to consolidate all the barges on the Mississippi river under one management. The object is to absorb the western traffic to Europe. The effect is already felt here. With the growth of the country, New York tonnage is steadily decreasing. Freight will find an outlet at the lowest prices of transportation. The Fink pool has done more to injure New York City than a failure of crops for three years.

Hatch's reference to consolidated barge companies on the Mississippi meant that railroaders could easily buy out the barges, beach them, and force all grain traffic onto the rails headed to New Orleans. Any perceptive party in New York could conclude that in their state the same thing could happen. The railroads could buy up all the canal boats, and, by putting them out of use, transfer all freight business to the rails. [Congress would pass a law prohibiting railroad companies from owning river barge companies, thus keeping up the competition between the systems.]

Hatch's mentioning the "Fink pool" pointed to the stall in export trade traceable to the lock-down of the locomotives, a condition Beecher had referred to as the cartel's "hands on the very throat of commerce." Hatch's solution was simple: "The Erie Canal ought to have been made free from tolls five years ago. The city alone could afford to keep it in perfect repair, and thus retain its exporting and importing supremacy."[3] In the face of the real and imagined dangers, that would prove a small cost. Hatch's alert amounted to an additional expression of an option to meet the "institutional strain" gripping the commercial class of New York City.

A week later the *Times* editorialized, raising new warnings that the railroads wanted to close the canal.

> The railroad companies took the precaution in the canvass [of 1879] to secure a majority of the [state] Senate in their own favor. For two years, the hand of the corporation has been on one branch of the legislature paralyzing its action whenever this subject of [railroad regulation] has been before it. *[There are] plain indications of a purpose to break down the competition of the canals.* The senators who were in the service of the railroads succeeded in preventing any action calculated to increase the efficiency of the canals, and the present cutting of rates has no doubt been a part of its incentive and supports the injury it is doing to the business of the canals. (Our emphasis.)[4]

Some have thought that the railroads' superior technology finally put the canals out of business. That conclusion, however, is unwarranted. The battle between the rails and canals was political. An energetic and determined industry and its lobby confronted a disorganized and lethargic public. What was needed was a clear, popular definition of the problem and a challenge to the voters. They, in effect, served as the stockholders of the canal and needed a disciplined campaign to turn out and vote. The interests of the merchants would slowly emerge in the form of a formula: a low-cost canal would increase traffic, make for more business, and keep property values up, and taxes paid. Therefore, the critical step to take was the popular passage of the free canal resolution.

The State Chamber of Commerce, August 1881, Calls a Conference at Utica to Promote a Free Canal

On August 11th, the day of the above editorial, the New York Chamber of Commerce called for a special August 19th meeting at Utica. The call came a week after Hatch's appeal and six weeks after Henry Ward Beecher cast a new melodrama. The Chamber wanted an assortment of business leaders in another week to get down to the particulars of the campaign for the coming legislative election. The aim was the second passage of the canal resolution. From the start the campaign would also serve double duty. It would serve as a referendum on the much-criticized work of the Hepburn committee that had reported in March of 1880. The Chamber's call read:

> *Whereas*, After full investigation, the Hepburn Committee pronounced the charges that flagrant abuses existed in the management of the railroads of this State were "fully proved," and recommended certain remedial measures, the most important of which have been defeated through the absolute control of the Senate of this state by the railroads; and

Whereas, The same interest has sought the defeat of measures looking to the improvement of the canals and it is charged that, under the guise of a war of rates during the season of navigation, the railroads are now engaged in an attempt to cripple if not destroy this most important safeguard against railroad extortion; and

Whereas, The railroads persistently discriminate against the property of the State by charging shippers who patronize the canals in Summer higher rates than others during the Winter; and,

Whereas, It is a matter of record that the railroads of this State are in the habit of contributing large sums to control nominations and elections, the result of which is shown by the action of the Senate last elected in defeating the most important bills recommended by the Hepburn Committee—in persistent hostility to measures looking to the improvement of the canals—in emasculating the Corporation Tax bills and killing the bill passed by the assembly to prevent the consolidation of telegraph companies; and

Whereas, Bribery in our elections and legislation has become notorious, (a senator of this State and others now being under indictment therefor), and the principles upon which our Government is founded thereby imperiled. . .[5]

Among the leaders calling for the meeting was Charles Smith, an early spokesperson for that urban financial strain that led to the Hepburn committee work and chair of the Chamber's committee on railroads. Francis Thurber, leader of the Anti-Monopoly League, also signed the call.

A Parsing of the Chamber's Call

The Hepburn committee in making its 1880 report included *"remedial measures"* addressing the strain that Charles Smith had first mentioned in 1878. Some measures were adopted, but not the bill against discrimination or the bill for the state commission.

The legislature, since the election of 1879, had "Defeated (the two bills) *through the absolute control of the senate of this state by the railroads.*" In 1879 the corporation had promised talks with the merchants. Instead they fended off possible merchant control of the legislature by taking control of the state senate. That frustrated the legislators speaking for the merchants. A promise of progress seemed to rest in the 1879 Hepburn hearings, the state convention and the subsequent exchange of letters between Vanderbilt and the merchants. But then matters turned negative. After helping to defeat Grant at Chicago they appear to have assured themselves that the public would no longer play a role in transportation policy. They most likely took offense at Conkling for not letting the U.S.

Senate give a hospitable reception to the Adams bill. President Garfield, in turn, apparently agreed to frustrate Conkling.

"The same interest has sought the defeat of measures looking to the improvement of the canals" referred to the recent defeat of the Astor bill for steam towing. The railroads, benefiting by the new technology celebrated at the 1876 Centennial Exposition, used their *political* power to thwart technological improvements on the canal. Canal advocates would have little difficulty getting the public to understand what the railroad legislators had done. They would enter the campaign seriously faulting the opposition and win a response.

"(A)nd it is charged that, under the guise of a war of rates during the season of navigation, the railroads are now engaged in an attempt to cripple if not destroy this most important safeguard [the canals] against railroad extortion." The members of the pool crippled the economy by refusing to operate their railroads until they could get profitable rates. They also charged higher rates during the winter to shippers who used the canals in the summer.

"Bribery in our elections and legislation has become notorious, (a senator of this State and others now being indictment therefor)." That referred to the alleged gag rule of June 9, 1880, promising the practice of bribery to control elections. Gorham on May 19 had predicted it. While some parties sought to discount the discovery of bribery, many merchants were of no such mind. Discounters could not finesse away the evidence.

The canal advocates had now seized the high ground. In June 1880, the leading financiers had drawn a line against public participation in a declaration that acted as an alleged gag rule. Now in August 1881, the merchants had drawn a line. They called for maximum participation. They had vaulted the intervening period, going back to the origins of their complaints that had led up to the Hepburn hearings. They picked up where they had left off. They restated their case without mentioning the convalescing President Garfield and all that had happened during his brief term to stifle a move toward regulation. His brief period had ended with his announced ambition to "abolish the factions in New York." The evidence of his meddling in the senatorial election process at Albany probably dampened sympathies for his sufferings. The debating points of the anti-monopolists were so proper that the railroaders had to see that they were in trouble.

Their alertness appeared in the quick shift they made to a volunteer movement from one led by the old politicos. William Robertson took over the customs house on August 1 thus cutting off the institution as a source of campaign workers for the canal cause. Two days later, on August 3rd, Rufus Hatch had his letter in the paper, showing as a matter of strategy that the vacuum in party workers would instead be filled by workers from the exchanges and other interest groups. Hatch's allies did not miss a beat in the pulse of the drive. Interest groups were coming out of the woodwork. There were similarities between two of them. In 1878 after the bankers showed reticence in pressing the hard-money cause and saw the silver bill passed, they finally got going. They visited members of Congress, and, beginning in the fall campaign, won an election for resumption. Likewise in 1881 and 1882 the New York brokers and other commercial organizations would come out in full force to win for their cause. As with the bankers in 1878, it would be enough to "make a cat howl."

Concurrently, cartel leaders brought differences between themselves into the press. They would expose their differences over the extent to which the public should participate in policy-making. Commissioner Fink, having persuaded cartel members to agree on rates, found that they would not comply, and he wanted "legislation to help him control his employers and make them keep faith with each other." Reid, however, was afraid that if the companies gave an inch, the public would take a mile. The *Tribune* replied to Fink, "If asked to interfere to prevent harmful competition between railroads, the voters may take occasion to prevent the earning of any dividends upon present stock." The *Tribune* would rather let the competition and combining continue: "Their own interests will force them to regulate competition in a manner not prejudicial to the public welfare."[6]

The high moral call of the New York Chamber of Commerce laid claim to popular influence on transportation policy. They would not leave such definitions solely to railroad experts and political cynicism. The merchants were making a strategic retreat, expecting the voters of the state not to vote directly on a railroad regulation proposition. The voters were to exercise their own constitutional rights in securing reliable traffic on the canal and reinforce the Hepburn report.

What is most interesting, the New York Chamber of Commerce, a metropolitan organization in the *southern* part of the state, was calling for help for the canal in the *middle* of the state. Some thought that the canal had only upstate support. In addition, the railroads, paralyzed by their rate war, could not impress on the public that they had themselves under control. Charles Adams's work as an arbiter had no effect—the sunshine method simply could not apply. Following the November election, federal statistician Joseph Nimmo, in a passage already quoted, would lay blame for recent troubles on the four-year-old pool:

> (I)t is impossible at present to pass final judgment upon pooling organizations. Yet they are tentative and on probation. Too little is known by the public in regard to their practical workings and the methods employed and the expedients resorted to in carrying them into effect to justify State governments or the National government in conferring upon them at once and unconditionally the attributes of legality. [7]

By contrast, the canal system was quite easy to understand, it was up and running, and it was worth conserving.

Finally, for the meeting site the promoters selected Utica. It was the home of three seasoned politicians: Conkling, Seymour, and Kernan. Perhaps Utica symbolized the bond between those politicians, the upstate canal, and the metropolitan merchants. Whether any of the old politicians appeared in the meeting is not apparent.

Laumann and Knoke suggest that in identifying the elite, numbers now become important. In March 1880 Depew had told the state legislative committee that only ten businesses in New York strongly supported regulation. Thurber raised the number in February 1881 in launching the Anti-Monopoly League. He then had on his side three organizations, each of which brought together many businesses. With the new drive begun at Utica he would have nineteen organizations, each of which was represented by no more than five individuals; one member of each group would become a vice president of the League. These included the following:

F. B. Thurber of the New York Board of Trade and Transportation

Theodore E. Tomlinson of the National Anti-Monopoly League

Darwin R. James of the Kings County Anti-Monopoly League

John F. Henry of the New York Chamber of Commerce

John B. Manning of the Buffalo Board of Trade

Dr. L. L. Wright of the Utica Board of Trade

J. A. Hinds of the New York State Millers' Association

J. C. Hubbell of the Albany Board of Lumber Dealers

Horace C. Smith of the Canal Boat Owners' Association

Allen R. Foote of the New York Cooperative Society

Ambrose Snow of the New York Maritime Association

J. Farley, Jr., of the Rochester Millers' Association

George B. Douglas of the New York Butter and Cheese Exchange

W. S. Wayne of the New York State Grange

Josiah J. White of the New York Produce Exchange

Nelson B. Kilmer of the Milk Association

James F. Denman of the New York Cotton Exchange

General A. S. Devin of the New York State Farmers' Alliance

Harris Lewis of the New York State Dairymen's Association

As shall be seen below, the leaders of some of these same organizations lobbied Governor Theodore Roosevelt over sixteen years later to support canal improvements. Such reappearance of the same organizations, according to Laumann and Knoke, indicates the persistence of an elite. Thus it should be asserted that throughout this entire period, the commodity exchanges shared in a significant portion of the city's leadership. The call to the election read:

> The time has come when a conference should be called of persons interested in the commercial and industrial welfare of the State, together with all citizens who believe that corporate monopolies should be held to a proper responsibility to the public, to consider whether our government is to continue a government of the people, for the people, by the people, or whether it is to be a government of corporations, by corporations, for the benefit of the few.

The leaders of the Utica meeting released an "Address to the People," amazing many readers by listing the names of several legislators who had stalled the railroad regulation and/or canal aid. The critics failed to note that the merchants had issued such a list in previous campaigns. In 1879 it was William Vanderbilt who had complained of a newspaper "announcement of appointment of a committee of merchants to foment agitation upon the support or threaten hostility to legislative candidates unless they will pledge an unquestioning support to whatever furthers this sentiment."[8] The merchants in repeating the tactic apparently were committed to make it work this time around.

Organizing the Merchants for the Fall Campaign of 1881

Although the merchants' tactic of screening candidates had not previously worked well, in the 1881 campaign they tried it again––with much better results. If Conkling is remembered as an operator of a political machine, the New York Chamber, if the truth were known, might have upstaged him. What other method could be used to organize the state is difficult to imagine.

The list of railroad supporters among the legislators included "state Senator Wagner," president of a company that manufactured passenger cars in which Vanderbilt held stock. Also listed was Dennis McCarthy of Syracuse, a manufacturer who had received special rates from Vanderbilt. There were also a few attorneys from communities along the entire length of the railroad, such as William Robertson, now collector of the port. In that group was Loren "Lo" Sessions, recently indicted by the Albany grand jury for bribery. Next the railroads won the support from some senators who had business with the company. Some were contractors and others manufacturers. Another group comprised members who were simply friendly with the railroad lobbyists and did their bidding. Given time, this railroaders' system for recruiting state senate members could expand to include assembly members, making it imperative that the merchants either meet the challenge at the next election or soon suffer defeat.

When Gorham read the Address to the People in the *Times*, he saw the coming struggle that he had predicted in March when the *Tribune* complained of anti-monopolist Windom entering the cabinet. Of the Utica meeting, Gorham asserted that

> It is likely that the address will do well by thus calling public attention to the undue influence exercised by the great corporations in the affairs of

362

government. The question is not what shall the government do about the corporations, but it is, rather, shall the corporations govern the country? The Republican Party will stand or fall as it answers this question. [9]

In the next two state elections, the Republicans experienced a sobering fall. Party members witnessed a fracturing of loyalties as discussion about monopolism and civil service came to the fore. Gorham was not convinced that the Democrats could provide a better answer. Lobbyists could take over both parties.

> In what nobler work could any man be engaged than in arousing the people to the danger they are in of losing their right to govern? They do not govern if they only choose between two sets of corporation tools, differing only in appearances, while really there are two friendly wings of a great railroad corporation organization.[10]

Next, the leaders organized a campaign to match the mandate. While the half-breeds had depended largely on influence through presidential appointments and control of the state senate, the merchants turned to statewide organization.

> To carry out the work of the conference a set of officers was elected headed by General Diven of the Farmers' Alliance. Vice presidents to flank him were chosen from every organization represented at Utica and four secretaries were named to take care of the paper work, distribution of documents, etc. Among them was Frank S. Gardner, a full-time employee of the New York Board of Trade, then concentrating on its efforts on spreading anti-monopoly doctrines. In addition to the regular officers, provision was made for a state committee to consist of one delegate from each congressional district. Creation of this body secured an organizational nucleus throughout the state and constituted a real advance.[11]

After the Utica meeting, the new organization moved well. They had to work with a calendar composed of two phases. First, they had to win the coming November election to seat a legislature that would pass the Free Canal Amendment a second time. Second, they had to have the amendment successfully adopted in the election of November 1882.

News from New Orleans

Once the date was set and an agency selected for a vote--a statewide vote on the canal--the next task was to get a good turnout. Supporters had to draw attention to the issues, chiefly the transfer of business to New Orleans, in a manner that compelled urgency. The state senate helped matters by asking for a hearing to discover how to increase the business of the canals and reduce the cost of transportation. Named to the hearing panel were state senators Williams, Forster, and Murtha. The call for the hearings at once produced a surprising plethora of information. While supporters perhaps had one issue to face, support of the canal, what made it complex was using the one issue to face more than one foe. The railroads had been intractable, to be sure. Equally important was the new inter-city rivalry from New Orleans, a matter Hatch had mentioned in his August statement. They held their hearings on September 14–15, 1881, almost eight weeks before the election, in the offices of the Board of Managers of the New York Produce Exchange. Several witnesses testified.[12]

First was A. B. Miller, chair of the Board of Trade's canal committee and a careful collector of canal statistics over the years. In the Cheap Transportation Association, Miller had served on several committees. In the 1880s he reported the statistics for grain shipments annually for both the canal and the rails. Miller suggested cutting costs by making changes in financial management and improving engineering on the locks.

Providing the longest and most disturbing testimony was E. R. Livermore of E. R. and R. B. Livermore, in the grain business for forty years. Working the harbor, the Livermores were sensitive to the incoming ships with cargo compared to the outgoing ships, either empty or filled with ballast, to New Orleans. He explained the extent of the competition from the port of New Orleans, much as J. J. White had in remarks that even the *Post* repeated. What Livermore had to say was that the city was farther down the slippery slope than many realized. He said,

> As present[ly] conducted, with the toll system prevailing, the grain trade was being surely and rapidly diverted from New York to the advantage of Philadelphia, Baltimore, New Orleans, Boston and Montreal. "The commerce of this City, in fact, is threatened with destruction," averred Mr. Livermore. "There is at present no more momentous question for New York to consider than this one of the attack on our commerce. Our competitors are bent on pushing us to the wall if they can, and it is known that they feel no cause for discouragement. [Elevator capacity in New Orleans had been doubled in the past year.] *With the toll system on our canals, we cannot successfully oppose other ports.*

> The Mississippi route is probably our strongest competitor; many railroads are disposed to carry grain south rather than east. The Wabash people for instance, would much prefer to make shipments from Toledo to St. Louis than from St. Louis to Toledo, and there are other railroads whose interests lie earnestly interested in Southern trade or against New York. Heretofore it has been urged that nothing need be feared from Southern competition, inasmuch as enterprise was lacking there, and, further, that grain shipped to Southern ports would be impaired in value from overheating. Those objections amount to nothing now. In the South

at present, there is decided activity looking to the obtainment of New York's trade, and millions of capital is being operated in this one interest. And the objection to overheating is of no consequence, for all such drawbacks have been overcome by improved facilities. We must not blind ourselves. *The South is awake and aggressive, and unless we abolish tolls on our canals, our grain trade will certainly be lost and our commerce ruined. Unless we take immediate action, our canals will soon be worse than valueless.* If the tolls are continued, enough money will not be collected to pay the wages of the lock-tenders. The tariff in 1875 was 2 cents per bushel; now it is 1 cent. In 1875, 29,000,000 bushels were transported. Four years later, the reduction having taken place, 69,000,000 bushels were carried.

Touching the fact that during the present season, westbound tolls having been entirely abolished, the business of the canals has decreased. Mr. Livermore insisted that special causes had obtained, chief among whom he charged was the influence of grain speculators, and the further fact that the railroads have been waging a bitter warfare among themselves by which rates have been greatly lowered. Mr. Livermore predicted that *if the canals were not made free there would result a depreciation of fully 50 per cent in the value of New York real estate, and thus throw increased taxation upon the country districts.* The import trade, as well as the export trade, he said, would be driven from New York unless the toll was abolished, while with free canals the receipts of grain at New York would be at once doubled. In his opinion, he thought the canals should be increased in capacity as well as made free but the former benefit he believed it would be better to postpone till the great success of "no tolls" had been demonstrated. (Our emphasis.)[13]

Others testified but none surpassed Livermore's remarks. They included F. H. Parker, president of the Produce Exchange; A. R. Gray, in the lighterage business; R. H. Lambeer of the Grain Warehousing Company; S. Edward Annan, of Hazelton and Annan, in the floating elevator business; Capt. H. C. Smith, president of the Boat-Owners' Association; Pilot Commissioner Edward Hinken *(sic)*, a former president of the Produce Exchange; Franklin Edson, a former president of the Produce Exchange; William H. Powers, grain exporter; E. F. Elwell, president of the Maritime Exchange; and E. B. Brooks, long in the canal business. The beloved and elderly T. C. Ruggles presented a copy of his 1879 report for the Produce Exchange as evidence.

Within a week of this testimony, on September 19, 1881, President Garfield died. As he had sought to overcome factions in the city, the most recent reports from New York City would have disappointed him. People with critical interests in commerce were coming to the fore, expressing their fears and urging action. At the death of Garfield, the nation turned to mourning. Alert business leaders in New York paused only momentarily and were soon again addressing the perilous commercial standing of the city.

Livermore's testimony appeared six weeks before the state election. It was clear enough to seal the fate of some state legislators, who suddenly found that they were on the wrong side of the issue. First, in June 1880, a small band of New Yorkers, several of them from the state senate, had arrived in Chicago to block the renomination of Ulysses S. Grant for president--and happily succeeded in their mission. By the next winter, they showed up among the opposition to state senator Astor's plan for steam towing on the canal. They prevailed, and the canal technology was unnecessarily thwarted from logical development. Then came the testimony of White and Livermore about the rapid growth of trade at New Orleans at the expense of trade at New York.

By the early winter of 1881–82, the voters of New York could easily see what had happened at the port. They could appreciate that a band of legislators had put trade from the canal at a grievous disadvantage. Ever since Beecher's complaint in June about the financiers having their hands on the throat of commerce, the condition they most feared had come to pass. Charles Smith had declared in 1878, after that meeting between merchant leaders and officials, that "The time was not far distant when the city would find it hard work to pay the interest on its bonds, and when merchants would have to close their doors and discharge their clerks, porters, and cartmen." In November 1881, poetic justice now dictated the voters overthrow those half-breeds for damaging opportunities in trade whether by thwarting the symbol of increased trade, the canal, or by thwarting regulation of the rails.

There was a deep split in the Republican Party. The factional fight had prevented the party from holding onto at least one house of the legislature. For that they might blame former Senator Roscoe Conkling and the course he took against the naming of a new collector. Not so. Some reason may exist for the dispute between the canal advocates and the railroad leaders as traffic slipped away from the canal. Not so. Underneath the city's troubles was the ominous shift in trade from New York to New Orleans. The success of General Eads in sluicing out the mouth of the Mississippi brought a new flood of New York voters from the Republican side in New York to the Democratic. Unless greater flexibility was gained at Albany the new technology at New Orleans could trump the old technology known as the port of New York with all its record of commercial supremacy. The strategy of Hatch, Thurber, and the Chamber was right on target. They showed that New Yorkers could select their own leadership out of an alliance of several trade organizations. It would not matter whether the president named a new collector and/or interfered with the election of senators at Albany.

By the time of the fall election the Anti-Monopoly League was in full swing, thanks plausibly to the preparations that may have begun shortly after the meeting at the Fifth Avenue Hotel in August 1880. The League formally opened at the New Year and had pursued an unusually aggressive organizing campaign, spurred by Gould's consolidation that would lead to it being reckoned with in the November election. New Orleans might have had energetic promoters and could give New York a good contest. But New York had its advantages. The City had a commercial class of several generations providing experience and intelligence. It had an engineered canal while New Orleans was a victim of the changing Mississippi River that would be years away from a comprehensive taming. Thus, the precipitously slippery slope that the New Yorkers faced was real enough, but the resources that the League could muster would out-match their competitors.

If Conkling and Platt had not resigned from the Senate, might the New York Republicans retain the state legislature? Not likely. The fault for the split in the Republican Party rested, not with the former senators, but with the proprietary attitude the railroads held toward transportation policy that failed to give the state canal sufficient flexibility provided by adding steam towing. Between the stiffness of the railroad leadership and the promise of the old canal in a new day, the League provided the flexibility to meet the circumstances.

The Anti-Monopoly League Examines the Candidates for the 1881 Election

The Anti-Monopoly League had succeeded in organizing every legislative district. The League next examined candidates, throwing its support behind the candidates who repudiated the railroaders' tactics. Agitation was so high that more than half the candidates who had been identified as pro-railroad before election day simply dropped out of the race. According to the half-breeds around President Garfield, this was not the way it was supposed to work. The railroad interests in the state senate were presumably holding the line. Under the influence of the Anti-Monopoly League, however, that defense was collapsing. Not only did Conkling fail to win votes at Albany that would send him back to Washington, but the railroad lobby was also failing. Where the assembly had momentarily been strong for Conkling, soon the state senate would also become freed of the railroaders' excessive influence!

The electorate decided to dump the entire crew. Despite the mourning over Garfield's death in September, the anti-monopoly agitation had aroused New Yorkers. By the November election, one might well have panic in the streets. A year before, such conditions could hardly have prevailed. In January 1881 Reid, Robertson, Blaine and others around Garfield had shown only an interest in the 1884 national convention, and sending a delegation that was not all stalwart. They had nothing to say about the intermediate state elections. In anticipation of November of 1881 they had not foreseen the large number of party members that simply bolted. There was a demand for new direction. It was in that Democratic sweep, the first since the Civil War, that the Democrats won both houses at Albany. Meanwhile, Theodore Roosevelt won his first election to the assembly.

Gorham and Reid Continue to Strike at Each Other

The *Tribune* kept up its campaign against having Gorham reconsidered for the secretaryship. The paper reminded readers that he had campaigned against the Republican Party in California in 1879, defended the star route frauds, and covered Garfield with the most malignant abuse and slander. On October 20th, Gorham answered point for point. First, in the California campaign, because the railroads had taken over the Republican Party, he had joined an independent movement, the Constitution Party, later supported by the Democrats. Otherwise, he had campaigned for all the Republican candidates for Congress. Second, as for the star route frauds, he had favored examination by the courts. That was preferable to trial by newspaper. Third, regarding the Robertson nomination, he had in fact opposed it and "discussed it in such language as is usual and legitimate in such cases." Finally, he had expressed no slander of Garfield except to rehash what was found in the *Tribune* of February 10, 1873, and "that as an attack on that paper, and not on the President."[14] Reid's attacks on Gorham were patently in the monopolists' interests in attempting to discredit a well-informed friend of the anti-monopolists.

The Post-Election (1881) Interest in New York Transportation

After the New York Democrats' victory at the polls in November, Joseph Nimmo, chief of the Bureau of Statistics, supported the broadly held suspicion about the railroads. Nimmo wrote, "One of their main objects has undoubtedly been to counteract, so far as possible, the regulating influence exerted over rates by the great water lines." The new Democratic majority at Albany now assured the water line in New York against such fears. The second passage of the free canal resolution was about to come up in the legislature, qualifying it to go before the public.

As for the competition from the Mississippi River, I. I. Hayes, in his November address to the American Geographical Society, picked up on what Livermore had told the special September state senate committee. He elaborated on how the genius of Clinton had preempted the natural flow of goods in the country. "The Mississippi Valley is the largest in the world, and that natural outlet of the great grain producing region is through the mouth of the mighty river which drains it." Hayes inferred that the Mississippi River was coming into its own as the principal channel for western trading. New Yorkers had better understand their interests.

Nimmo devoted a large part of his report to the growth of exporting from New Orleans. He pointed out that spring ice often clogged the river. At other times the water level dropped so low that boatmen had to carry less cargo. He noted the great activity, especially at St. Louis, exploiting the opportunities of trade to New Orleans.

This increase in shipments by river had swelled from 523,000 tons in 1870 to 820,000 tons in 1880. From 1,297,000 bushels of grain in 1870 to 12,278,000 bushels in 1880. This increase in shipments on the Mississippi by citizens of St. Louis and New Orleans has awakened much interest throughout the entire western and northwestern states, especially from the fact that the reduction in cost of transportation by the Mississippi route appears likely to exert a most salutary influence over the rates charged by the east and west trunk lines, not only at St. Louis, but also at the other primary markets of the West. This regulating influence is in a high degree favorable to and protective of the agricultural interest of the western and northwestern States.

Canal matters remained unsure on other grounds. Nimmo showed that during the recent railroad rate war "grain was carried from Chicago to New York as low as 7 2/10 per bushel. The rate by lake and canal was forced down to 6 1/2 cents, a rate which it is thought yielded little if any profit for the carrier." Six weeks later, the news from the canal auditor was no better. John Place, a state auditor, reported that the deficit in canal operations could well be followed by meager business in the summer of 1882. The canals might not be able to stay open after July 1, 1883. Little doubt remained that the Erie Canal helped regulate the rates on the railroads. The state would have to find a new method to continue such regulation. The logic of the economy virtually dictated that the state remove tolls on the canal altogether, so the Free Canal Amendment made sense. In March 1882 the legislature took up the free canal resolution a second time. The assembly passed the resolution by a vote of 74 to 53, with Democrats voting 55 for and 19 against, and the Republicans voting 19 for and 34 against, with Theodore Roosevelt in the Republican minority. In the senate, the Republican support proved negligible. In favor were 18 Democrats and 4 Republicans; 10 Republicans opposed. Conkling, in supporting the canal, represented only a minority in the party—a minority that included the young Theodore Roosevelt.

Blaine's Tribute to the Anti-Monopolists

In mid-1882, Congress invited Blaine to eulogize Garfield. Without shame he seems to have suggested that the postal scandal was a distraction to protect the monopolists from trouble. He told his audience that Garfield was the kind of player who "often skillfully avoids the strength of his opponent's position and scatters confusion in his ranks by attacking an exposed point when really the righteousness of the cause and the strength of the logical entrenchment are against him." In that one sentence Blaine assembled points favoring his foes. Anti-monopolism was the righteous cause. The weakness of the opponent was alleged star route corruption. Consequently, Hatch's cases against the Western Union consolidation could never get off the ground. Garfield had made a smart move. Over half a year after his death some of his supporters were still amused by what he had done. Blaine, however, made the estimate in March of 1882 and would not yet appreciate the extent of Hatch's work for the free canal. Hatch would swing the

369

anti-monopoly vote right behind the cause. In 1884 Blaine would find that he had to appeal to the same voters.

Massachusetts Republicans Approve a Platform Plank Giving the President Authority in Making Appointments

Massachusetts leaders took up the cause of giving the president more direct authority in filling offices. The late president seems to have relied on the post-federalist thoughts of Henry Adams. The thought was that it was time to enshrine them in the constitution. A year later Garfield's view won support at the Massachusetts Republican convention. Gorham would later note that:

> At the last Republican State convention [early winter, 1881–82] in Massachusetts . . . a series of resolutions were adopted . . . [one of which reads:] "The needed reform will comprehend these aims—viz.: The maintenance of the constitutional prerogative of the President to make nominations upon his solid responsibility . . . The relief of members of the legislative branch from the business of selecting office-holders in the departments of administration.

Senator George Hoar even promoted the idea through an article in the November 1881 issue of the *North American Review*. This meant that shortly after Garfield's death the Massachusetts senator was throwing to the wind Hamilton's cautions about the absolute power of the president in making appointments. They had regarded the clause on "advise and consent" as a "villainous thing," according to Gorham. Under the concepts of a policy scenario, "consequential actors," that is, Hoar supported by Henry Adams, were now preparing to try to amend the federal Constitution. In the sequence of the scenario, that may have been a bit late.

The Transportation Policy Scenario Comes to a Major Close

The New York Democratic victory at the polls in November 1881 gave the anti-monopolists a double win. They now had the legislature. They could proceed confidently with both the Free Canal Amendment and the state railroad regulatory commission. The legislature passed the free canal resolution a second time by April 1882, and in June the commission bill was finally adopted.

The Democratic victory also meant that the half-breed alliance, aimed at saving the railroad cartel, was fast becoming just a memory. The cartel and its friends could no longer enforce their alleged gag rule of June 9, 1880. A stalwart, Chester Arthur, was in the White House, and James Blaine left the cabinet in December 1881. The *Tribune* gave up the privilege of having a special desk at the White House for E. V. Smalley. The circulation of the *National Republican,* especially its weekend edition, swelled, likely making it the Arthur administration organ. Gorham had plenty of time to correct the misconceptions in other papers about what he thought had happened in the Garfield administration, making his paper an original source still largely overlooked in the standard accounts.

All Vanderbilt had to consider were strategic options, except, of course, legislation by "Congress first." The railroad attorney Chauncey Depew wrote in his autobiography:

> As soon as I was convinced that commissions were necessary for the protection of both the public and the railroads, I presented this view to Mr. Vanderbilt. The idea was contrary to his education, training and opinion. It seemed to me that it was either a commission or government owner- ship, and that the commission, if strengthened as a judicial body, would be as much of a protection to the bond and stockholders and the investing public as to the general public and the employees. Mr. Vanderbilt, always open-minded, adopted this view and supported the commission system and favored legislation in its behalf.

Depew had won new insights about the judicial functioning of a state commission. It was not necessary to wait only for federal legislation to provide it. In retrospect the ques- tion arises whether Vanderbilt could have come to this position in September 1879. The *Times* had urged him to begin the "ordeal," but both sides had reverted to the well-known tactics of stacking the state legislature. The monopolists won, kept the legislature from proceeding on regulation, turned against the candidacy of Ulysses S. Grant, discour- aged further discussion of policy, and set their sights on regulation by "Congress first." Vanderbilt could have saved the party and the nation considerable turmoil. Apparently he was angry over the Hepburn hearings, and that anger had locked him and his peers into a solution mixing merit with impatience. The monopolists stubbornly clung to the demand that in railroading all competition had to end. Their lobbying proved clumsy and they unnecessarily turned on those who stood in their way. Rather than learning from their failures, they had pressed for retribution, which exacted its own costs.

With Depew telling Vanderbilt that he had only two legislative options, the attorney took attention away from the older claim of strain, the prospects of bankruptcy. That broke the paralysis that had so long gripped the company's imagination. The success of the Anti-Monopoly League had removed the reasons for Vanderbilt's hesitation. He certainly could no longer blame politicians for misleading the voters. Repudiation of the Republicans in the state legislature was compelling; it was not worth arguing any further whether the public had any place in transportation policy. Aside from ordering press releases against the free canal movement, Vanderbilt was ready to move on. The newly adopted legislation for a regulatory commission would finally bring New York up to a par with two of its neighbors, Massachusetts and Pennsylvania, where arguments that some New Yorkers persisted in raising had long been settled.

The New York legislation provided for three members of the new regulatory com- mission with defined interests. The governor would name one member from the majority party. Another member "shall be experienced in railroad business." Finally, one member would be seated by the majority vote of some specified business leaders. That third member had to have the support of the presidents and executive committees of the Chamber of Commerce, Board of Trade, and National Anti-Monopoly League. Thus the law recognized extra-constitutional organizations. Adams had won a place for a business representative in the Massachusetts Commission. In his advising New Yorkers, he apparently deferred to Vanderbilt by promoting a federal plan only partly mirroring his Massachusetts work. There is no telling what might have happened in 1880 and 1881 if Adams had held firm by requiring that the Massachusetts plan serve as a guide for the federal commission, and had advertised from the outset that a seat would be reserved for a business representative.

When, in January 1881, the cartel plan surfaced in the U.S. House, members of the New York Chamber immediately raised objections due to the absence of merchant participation. The process for the national legislation came to a standstill. In New York an agreement became possible by 1882. From the view of the sociology of the policy process this curiosity in the state legislation shows that the prolonged conflict was about participation. In the end, the participation of the merchants trumped other considerations.

One practical consequence is that the arrangement precluded the leaders of the cartel declaring simply a new variant of "the commercial supremacy of New York." Should they broach that topic, for whatever reason, they knew that at the next meeting of the commission, they would have to defend it face to face and likely accept some modifications. The new feature in the law for the New York commission would help to break the legacy of the non-consulting elites so endemic in the Gilded Age, teaching them to talk before they acted rather than afterwards.

The calendar of gains unfolded slowly. Another three years passed before Congress created the Interstate Commerce Commission. The grangers, who held that under common law the state could require accountability from those to whom it gave franchises, had partially won their point. Later, Depew in his memoirs made no mention that the question of participation had plagued the debate from 1878 to 1882. However, he must have understood the point since he expanded public participation to great advantage on both the board of the New York Central Railroad and the cartel. Vanderbilt would help redeem his reputation by paying for a new opera house.

Senator George Hoar Reverses Himself, Vindicates The Courtesy of the Senate, and Sees Value in the Erie Canal

A persistent belief about the Republican factional fight has been the notion that Garfield's joust with Conkling set aside the rule of "senatorial courtesy." The term refers to the practice in the Senate allowing both members from a state to object to a nomination and win concurrence of all the Senate, thereby defeating the president's nomination. Garfield had trumped "senatorial courtesy" by requiring "letters of introduction" of opponents to the Robertson nomination. In the end, he won. Biographer Allan Peskin writes, "Garfield had, unwittingly, taken the first step toward that steady accretion of presidential power that would in later years transform the whole nature of the office. The path upon which he had been pushed led straight to the twentieth century."

That path proved not quite so straight at the outset. Massachusetts returned to the Hamiltonian twists and turns. First, Arthur made four nominations in Massachusetts, which the two Massachusetts senators supported. He could not, however, continue to count on smooth sailing. In a fifth nomination he sent in the name of Colonel Roland Worthington for collector of the port, only to find that the two senators objected. Worthington was the owner and editor of the *Evening Traveler,* and a self-made business-man. The senators objected, in Gorham's view, because Worthington was a stalwart. Where the Robertson nomination had been obnoxious to Conkling and Platt, now the Worthington nomination would prove obnoxious to Dawes and Hoar. Suddenly the two Massachusetts senators found the federalist position of "advise and consent" handy. They could halt the Worthington nomination. Though they had hoped to override that antique practice, they found they had to sacrifice all the fine thought that went into pre-paring and promoting a constitutional amendment. Gorham noted the change, writing "the 'courtesy of the Senate' is a 'villainous thing' in New York, but it is the eminently 'proper caper' in Massachusetts." In a matter of a year, a procedure considered a tool of darkness in the hands of the "bad" men had quickly become a tool of protection.

Gorham recounted that Senator Hoar had written an article the previous November urging the abandonment of "courtesy of the Senate." Then the Massachusetts state con-vention worked the suggestion into its platform. Gorham added,

> This [platform plank to amend the Constitution] was evidently penned with an eye to Robertson in the rear, and not to Worthington in the front. It was a retrospectively beautiful, but a prospectively unfortu-nate, utterance. The White House can afford to look on and smile while the senators from Massachusetts proceed with their vindication of "the courtesy of the Senate."

It had taken only a year for the Massachusetts senators to abandon their post-federalist views, supported by Henry Adams, and once again revert to the pre-Garfield state of affairs—following Alexander Hamilton—and re-instate the courtesy based on the con-stitutional provision that the Senate should "advise and consent." In an unheralded act, President Arthur had looked at the Massachusetts platform and in effect said: "Hold on! Not so fast!" He set the scene—giving them a nominee as repugnant as Robertson had been to Conkling and Platt—making the rhetoric of the two Massachusetts senators tumble. Garfield had momentarily mastered the U.S. Senate and then looked forward to mastering the New York party. A year later, however, the Senate's recovery of the "courtesy of the Senate" would save all states from such presidential ambition. At the White House, the Arthur administration could afford to look on and smile, even laugh.

Garfield had forced the issue of "courtesy of the Senate." He had, however, been in the Congress long enough to recognize a poorly lobbied proposition such as Charles Francis Adams, Jr.'s bill to consolidate the rails into a trust. He should have stalled it for later handling, saving the party the gaffe of the turmoil over Robertson, let alone saving Conkling from eternal censure. There is no good reason why Conkling should have a lasting bad reputation from the episode. The irony remains: the extensive repetition of half-truths mounted to fault Conkling, and overlook Garfield's ambitions to "abolish the factions," was long supported by such consequential leaders as Chauncey Depew. Their course suggests that the half-breeds knew that they had to cover their own failure in theory, strategy, and tactics, as well as abandon promotion of the railroad trust.

An Exchange Between the Banking Bill and Appropriations for Rivers and Harbors

New Englanders had another issue in the arena, that of national banking. Senator George Hoar of Massachusetts helped lead the cause by a trade. Republicans agreed on support for rivers and harbors appropriations for the South, much to the disgust of New England reformers, in exchange for southern support for national banking. Garfield had mentioned the Mississippi improvements in his acceptance letter two years earlier. Mid-continent transportation became more important as General Eads succeeded in sluicing out the mouth of the Mississippi so thoroughly that oceangoing vessels could now make it all the way to Memphis. Probably to mute excessive demands of the lower Mississippi states, the eastern Republicans made freshman John Mitchell of Pennsylvania chair of the committee on improvement of the Mississippi and freshman William Frye of Maine a committee member. Fortuitously, they began their tenures just a year before the great flood of 1882.

Even Mark Twain lent a hand by launching a long-running series, *Life on the Mississippi*. He made mention that economist Edward Atkinson of Massachusetts favored the Rivers and Harbors appropriation, a matter that Senator Hoar also supported. It could have marked change in eastern opinion. The public opinion in the Northeast became more sympathetic to the flooded Midwest. Only four years earlier in the currency debates, the West had shocked the East with its inflationary theories. Eastern reform leaders soon reacted with the star route scandals and the New England hegemony over western senior Republicans. Now the East's hard heart was softening.

Sounding almost like a Mississippi valley senator, Hoar took the approach that waterways helped keep down railroad rates, mentioning the experience of New Yorkers with the Erie Canal. He wrote that:

> These waterways are not only of vast importance in themselves, but they
> are important also as a check upon its prices charged by the railroads. They

are free. When the waterway is once fitted for transport, it is the property of all mankind.

Railroad competition terminates in railroad combination [Adams]. The only check on the power of the great railroad lines, when in concert, over the commerce of the nation is the competition of the waterways [Conkling and Fink]. When the Erie Canal and the harbors of the lakes freeze in the winter, up go the freights. When canal, lake, and river open in the spring, down go the freights. I do not and cannot overstate the importance of this consideration to the American people, and more especially to Massachusetts.

As the Eastern heart softened, the anti-bank rhetoric for soft money from the West and the South lessened. The political trading for banking went well. When the Democrat senators from the lower Mississippi valley saw the support from the North for rivers and harbors, apparently they decided to mute their objections to national banking. In Congress, the work was well choreographed. The House, more likely apostate on currency issues, passed the banking bill. The bill went to the Senate. The Senate, more conservative on internal improvements, passed the rivers and harbors bill and sent it to the House. The senators from the lower Mississippi states seemed to have obliged in the vote on the banking bill. In several instances one senator from each of their states sat on his hands.

Furthermore, the New England hegemony over Senate committees was put to a test. Whereas in 1878 many Midwestern Republicans had supported inflationist legislation, in 1882 nearly all Midwestern senior Republicans went along with the hard-money committee chairs they sat under. They appear to have persuaded their junior partners, together with their state's delegation in the House to join them.

Even some Democrats felt the discipline. For the moment, enthusiasm for silver may have also declined. Senator Voorhees of Indiana, when asked why he no longer spoke up for the silver cause, replied that if he did, he could not get the patronage he wanted. Among the Republicans only Senator John Jones of Nevada went his own way and voted against the banking bill. Everyone won. Arthur vetoed the rivers and harbors bill, and Congress overrode the veto. Arthur signed the banking bill.

The New Englanders' committee arrangements, which kept them in touch with their Midwestern peers, had an interesting effect. The New Englanders might have laid down standards for organizing western state Republican parties, insisting they make no room for greenbackers. Further, the *Tribune's* editorials could have alerted railroad agents throughout the country to watch for local editorials deviating from the true path. That would have triggered the agents to win appointments with the papers' editors to persuade them to get into line or lose railroad advertising. That the western state Republican organizations eschewed greenbackism is an inference from Gretchen Ritter's point about the Illinois organization:

> In Illinois, the demands of the national party system worked to subvert the discussion of financial issues, particularly for Republicans. The national hegemony of the Republicans placed a premium on cross-sectional unity, which constrained the emergence of Republican greenbackism in the Midwest and limited the movement's overall success in that region.[15]

If New England senators found that some Midwestern politicians had not complied with the mandate to curtail discussion of financial issues, they had the power to discipline the state's senior senator by simply turning a cold shoulder on his requests. Understandably, cross-sectional unity was easy to obtain. The national party could count on the state organizations after 1882 filling their own middle and lower ranks with committed hard-money advocates. Tied by their senior senators to New England senators, Mark Hannah had a disciplined organization already in place in 1896 and 1900 when he picked up the duties of the campaign against the threat of William Jennings Bryan's popular views.

Contrary to Allen Weinstein, the hard-money hegemony quartered in New England did systematically use organization to promote their views.[16]

In 1882, the execution of Guiteau may have distracted the public from expressing any strong opinions on the banking bill. On the editorial front, greenbacker Gorham, still hoping to become secretary of the Senate, had hardly a word to say about the topic. Shortly after the passage of the rechartering bill, the *Times* reported, "greenbackism is played out." Thus, the influence of the-hard money cause was ubiquitous—at least for the moment. In the fall of 1882, Ben Butler ran for governor of Massachusetts on the Democratic ticket, attracted greenbackers, and, much to the chagrin of George Hoar, won the election.

New York Merchants Tighten Up the Campaign Organization, July 1882

In July 1882, New York business leaders had but four months before the vote on the canal. Although a year earlier they had organized at the Utica meeting, they now effected a new permutation.

> The various exchanges appointed representatives to confer and adopt a line of policy for the purpose of promoting the desired object . . . Yesterday . . . they met in conference at the rooms of the Chamber of Commerce, Franklin Edson presiding. The organization represented in addition to the Chamber of Commerce was the Produce Exchange, the Butter and Cheese Exchange, the Mechanics' and Traders' Association, the Maritime Exchange, and the Canal-boat Owners' Association.

On October 1st, William Murtha suggested that "the members of the various exchanges become missionaries in the cause of free canals from this day until the day of the election."

New Yorkers' opinion on the canal had strengthened since the lowering of west-bound tolls in 1877. The idea that the canal was a regulator of the railroads, a view long held by Conkling, became easier to understand. One of its strongest supporters was the *Commercial and Financial Chronicle,* which saw that the state canal was a surrogate to anything the federal government could do. It referred to the subject in a September 1882 piece firing up the commodity exchange members and the merchants to get out the vote. The paper stated:

> The transportation question is still up, and seemingly no nearer settlement than ever, namely: the importance of the canals as a railway regulator. The Advisory Commission [for the canals] has lately reported; the old Reagan bill has been up on Congress; the railroad-regulation bill has been fought over at Albany, and how much progress has been made? [Some wanted to let combination through law take its course; while others wanted enforced competition through law.] Where combination is possible competition is impossible, said Mr. Adams, long ago; but there can be no combination on the free, natural highways of the lakes and canals. Competition will always be unrestricted there. Here is an available natural "thus far and no farther" for railway extortions, as our politicians call them. Carry grain from St. Louis and Cairo to New Orleans by the river for six cents or less per bushel and from Chicago to this port by water for twelve cents or less, and we have a natural law of regulation, which cannot be evaded or nullified. [A law on the books can be evaded or later reversed.] This is the crowning value of the canal system, and is alone enough to justify its maintenance and development. It is perhaps to the growing jealousy of railroad power, and to the gradual recognition of the fact that it will never do to allow this natural regulator to fall into decay, that the present policy in favor of the canals may be ascribed.

> Nothing can be a plainer lesson or experience than that statutory regulation of railroads, whether by States or by the general government, is a very questionable step. It is urged, and by many is expected, that Congress must interfere finally, because the general government alone has the power; but in this easy assumption may be lurking a grave error. Has government the power? It may have the jurisdiction, but that its power goes further than to enact an ineffectual law is certainly questionable. It is, as we have more than once pointed out, one of the most mischievous of popular delusions in this country that the efficacy of government, either to construct, prohibit, or regulate, is greatly overrated, and that

people imagine it needful only to speak the phrase "be it enacted," and the particular trouble at hand is cured. At least, *federal intervention should be the last resort;* and while we have been trying the specifics of special leg-islation [e.g., the Massachusetts commission], *we have not been overlooking the natural remedy within reach in the development of the waterways—not those which lobbyists would build at the public expense, but those already working.* (Our emphasis.)[17]

Horatio Seymour Makes a Timely Clarification

When the city voters went to the polls in November 1882, they brought with them a keen sense of their own interests. Their thinking had gone through more than one permutation. When Charles Smith spoke up in 1878 after a meeting between business leaders and public officials, the thought was that railroads were crowding those who had to pay for the municipal bonds. Next, only a month before the 1882 election, Frank Edson, president of the Free Canal Union and later mayor of New York City, forecast that the strongest support would come from the city. "The heaviest taxpayers of the state," Edson said, "favored the free canals while the lightest taxpayers opposed it." A week later, Edson received a letter from Horatio Seymour that elaborated this point. On October 11th Edson shared the letter with the *Times.* It spelled out the economics of the free canal option in relation to property values, a view that need to be reinforced just as the campaign was closing. Whereas the railroads looked to increases in stock values, Seymour said that the average voter in New York had to look to securing his own real estate values. The paper reported that:

When constructed it was thought the cost of the canals would in-crease taxation in the part of the State remote from their channels, but the reverse proved to be the case, and the city of New York, which was largely benefited by their building, has so increased in its assessed property valuation as to have borne the greater part of the expense. The business success of the State depends to a great extent upon the facility with which its products can be sent abroad. Any tax that tends to increase the cost of transportation is a direct injury. A tariff upon exports could hardly be more injurious at this time than any action that may increase the cost of transportation.

When in 1842 the canal question was so exhaustively discussed, Mr. Seymour became convinced that "the revenue they produced was of very little importance, compared with the importance of cutting down the cost of carrying our products to the market of the world. The result of the opening of the canals proved the wisdom of their projectors by the growth of towns and villages along their lines and *the increase in the valuation of property.*" Now he says: "I am mortified to find that in some instances these people are opposed to making our canals free channels of trade. They will find if they look into this subject, that they are not only harming others, but themselves. Experience proves that they will cut down their share of taxation by the adoption of the amendment, which gives growth and prosperity to New York . . . if the amendment is adopted it will lessen taxation upon all sections and all pursuits."

Canals are not made for the sake of the tolls or taxation which they may draw from the people; on the contrary, they are designed for the common benefit of all parts of the State, and to add to the profits by farmers, mechanics, and other producers by cutting down the cost of getting their products to the markets of the world. The hostile attitude of the State toward canals in providing that the Legislature can make up no deficiency, he says, prevents canal boatmen from building vessels and furnishing sufficient carrying capacity. The policy of the state has lessened the receipts for tolls, and virtually placed the boatmen at the mercy of rich competitors, who will find it profitable to carry for a year at losing rates if they can by so doing "destroy forever the boatmen or the canals by their own rates for carrying the products of the people." Competition thus destroyed, they can then "put up the charges to suit their own interests." For this reason, therefore, if for no other, the canals should be made free. (Our emphasis.)[18]

Seymour's letter appeared just in the nick of time. It appeared only a day before a regular meeting of the Union League Club with long-time president William Evarts in the chair. Current topics in chats for the day likely covered bringing the construction of the Brooklyn Bridge to an end and watching property values increase in expectation of the traffic at the bridge's approaches. Seymour's letter covering the relation of the canal traffic and increasing property values could not have been timelier.

At the Union League Club meeting a vote was taken on the Free Canal Amendment. On some grounds one might have expected that the half-breeds in the club would have supported the monopolists against the amendment. But the club with 150 members present voted unanimously for the Free Canal Amendment. Add that vote to the merchants' unanimous vote for the free canal four years earlier, and figure how long it takes some parties to join the cause! It takes that long to refine the reasoning for the project to win broader support.

The End of the 1882 Campaign and the Vote on the Free Canal

The merchants and brokers continued to concentrate on the relief they sought from a free canal. At an October 26th rally in Bowling Green, former state Senator George Forster told the crowd of almost 2,000 people that "the cost of a free canal would be less than $750,000 annually, a sum less than 2 percent of what the people of New York and Brooklyn annually raise from taxation." In early August 1881 Hatch had said substantially the same thing: that "the city alone could afford to keep it in perfect repair, and thus retain its exporting and importing supremacy." Crowd members signed up to work the polls on election day.

On October 28th, the *Chronicle* returned to a point that it had frequently raised:

> [A]lthough governmental troubles to come, do not get much attention from the mass of people, we must not omit to point out once more that the most burning, difficult and tormenting problem of the day is transportation, involving more which is untried and hazardous, and capable of perhaps leading to more disturbance than any other. The press has written at it; orators of all degrees have wrestled with it; States have pottered over it; and the hasty citizen now wants to unload the problem upon a blind and clumsy giant, the Federal Government. But it may prove too much for him--there is great danger that it will, if he tries it; and a trial is on all accounts to be deplored. Remember, therefore, that the waterways are natural and wholesome regulators, and that in voting to make the canals free you vote as well towards taking the transportation problem not only "out of politics" but out of the field altogether, by the silent operation of natural laws, which, unlike statutes, execute themselves.

Topping off the campaign for the vote was an evening rally. The crowd elected Fred Conkling the chair of the meeting, probably recognizing everything his brother Roscoe had done for the cause as well as his own high rank among officers of the Chamber of Commerce. Plausibly, Fred Conkling held those prestigious posts because they comported with his easy access to Roscoe, who would have wanted to keep abreast of everything going on in the Chamber. For example, when in January 1881 the railroader Leland Stanford had sent an answer to the Chamber's poll, Fred Conkling was made chair of the committee to prepare an answer, and they reported in March. An earlier answer had not been necessary since the *Times* had given Stanford such a strong rebuke. Furthermore, the delay would have given Fred time to consult with Roscoe.

The speaker, who was the "catch" of the evening, was William Evarts, former secretary of State under President Hayes, and one with many reasons to oppose anything Roscoe had supported. A corporate attorney, who helped the legal team against *Munn v. Illinois* prepare their case, Evarts now took the position, supported by the Union League Club, that public ownership was a device for regulation. Evarts most likely explained to his cousin, Senator George Hoar of Massachusetts, just how well the canal functioned in setting rates. As Godkin had said of Conkling in 1881, Evarts could now walk down both sides of the street, the monopoly side and the anti-monopoly side.

In preparing his remarks, Evarts may have seen that Vanderbilt had inadvertently given him a text for the evening. Recently some reporters had interviewed Vanderbilt about business affairs, and he managed only to make his case worse by blurting out, "The public be damned!" He could not have better expressed the June 9, 1880, alleged gag rule. That gave Evarts, in the terms of the policy scenario, an opening to explain the irony of the campaign, in which parties were divided over whether the public should or should not have a say. Most noteworthy, missing from Vanderbilt's invective was any of his usual reference to politicians leading the voters astray. Conkling had been the goat in such faultfinding, but that old excuse would no longer play. The canal advocates had sanitized their campaign by keeping the old politicians out. If the Free Canal Amendment was adopted by a popular vote and without aid in the campaign from the old politicians, also authentic was the anti-monopoly vote three years earlier at the 1879 state convention. That state party convention had much more to do with policy than merely showing a decline in the senior senator's support.

The trouble with the monopolists was they operated under the pretense that the realm of transportation policy was their own and they were going to carry the day. Their string of victories was impressive: Robertson's bolt against the Grant delegation; the alleged gag rule imposed after Grant's defeat at Chicago; the naming of Robertson as collector against Conkling's will; Garfield's decision not to let "politicians profit"; and his more daring declaration that he would "abolish the factions in New York." Now, however, the political revolution could reverse all of those gains. The public had peeled off a segment of the transportation arena, the canal, and aimed at determining its fate. The *esprit de corps* now descended on the anti-monopolists and could only be reinvigorated by Vanderbilt's offhand remark, Seymour's astute explanations, and Livermore's explanation of the threat to the tax base. Comments about Vanderbilt's gaffe very likely passed from person to person, increasing resentment that would register in the poll results. The public would have a voice in policy.

New Yorkers had had enough of exclusion and Evarts's appearance represented a sharp turn. At that last rally, speaking for popular government, Evarts said:

> Now we came to the time when the canal was serving its greatest good in keeping down the monopoly of railroads. There was a new school of narrowists who wanted to choke the canals because they didn't earn enough, although they were earning enough to benefit millions by keeping down the charges of corporate monopolies. The Erie Canal also represented the State of New York in a very serious competition between Canada on the north, and Pennsylvania and Maryland on the south. If we were to ask the people of the neighboring communities to vote on the Free Canal Amendment, would they not vote to keep up the tolls? Suppose we got together all the Presidents and managers and conductors and brakemen and stockholders of the railroads, would they not vote the same way?

> Was the State of New York, standing right in the middle of these competitors, to be the broad-backed ass that was to have no vote and no voice in the management of the canals?[19]

The railroaders' confidence that they owned the policy arena itself was just too much, all of which underscores what Laumann and Knoke observed: that much of the rhetoric heard in a policy process refers to who gets to participate. The philistines in New York, the "bad men," as Blaine had called them in his December 16, 1880, letter to Garfield, or in Evarts' words from the podium, "the broad-backed Asses," would now show their force. And the results would redound to the benefit of the leaders. In 1885 Evarts won election to the U.S. Senate and Edson would serve as mayor!

Later readers of these events may make a too-cursory appraisal by concluding that support for the canal came largely from upstate. Lee Benson, for example, wrote, "The urban vote along the canal route passed the amendment" (p. 171). Hidden behind such assertions is the picture of one of the most astounding votes in the Gilded Age. In fact, the greatest support for the canal came not from the urban vote along the canal but from the urban vote in the bay, that is from the five urban boroughs in New York. And that came from the appeal of the commodity exchanges, who won the honors in regulating monopolism. The canal was giving New Yorkers lower rates at the terminals in the city, and to conserve that advantage against Philadelphia and Baltimore, it was the city voters who most wished to conserve the apparatus of the system across the upper regions of the state. To miss these facts is merely to admit that one does not quite grasp the nature of New York City during the Gilded Age.

Counties.	For Governor.				For President, 1880.				Constitutional Amendment.			
	Folger Rep.	Cleve- land. Dem.	Howe. Grbk.	Hop- kins. Proh.	Gar- field. Rep.	Han- cock. Dem.	Weav- er. Grbk.	Dow. Proh.	Free Canals. For	Ag'st	Judiciary. For	Ag'st
Albany	10,360	20,126	385	.....	16,564	19,624	354	.....	18,096	2,550	10,283	1,005
Allegany	3,718	3,779	350	1,586	6,827	3,482	480	10	741	4,238	1,248	779
Broome	4,955	5,060	109	325	7,173	5,450	168	35	2,517	4,922	1,254	1,805
Cattaraugus	4,631	5,270	462	781	7,401	5,466	672	43	3,471	1,511	1,721	700
Cayuga	4,406	5,850	452	696	9,372	5,976	536	28	3,734	3,084	1,290	2,228
Chautauqua	4,803	6,207	369	826	10,422	5,472	585	64	2,501	5,611	1,590	1,720
Chemung	3,079	5,336	651	78	4,636	4,806	976	3	490	2,856	543	513
Chenango	3,913	4,258	482	574	5,769	4,559	623	92	1,517	4,043	398	2,089
Clinton	4,318	3,560	49	18	6,080	4,250	74	.....	2,419	2,408	120	1,550
Columbia	3,607	6,703	27	92	6,486	5,902	19	.....	3,635	3,115	900	546
Cortland	2,996	3,011	44	379	4,124	2,749	78	13	584	2,305	200	413
Delaware	4,331	4,596	240	334	6,058	5,084	218	32	904	6,688	1,281	1,910
Dutchess	7,321	8,875	58	407	11,045	8,475	26	95	2,938	8,937	374	231
Erie	16,408	23,748	190	1,046	24,199	20,848	442	.....	36,997	509	25,163	403
Essex	2,951	2,150	147	24	4,776	2,775	169	1	1,484	2,286	19	549
Franklin	3,074	2,204	95	23	4,185	2,709	96	3	267	4,931	13	1
Fulton and Hamilton	3,331	3,835	55	335	4,985	3,879	35	26	3,031	1,093	550	1,506
Genesee	2,898	3,518	52	395	4,815	3,481	72	5	3,164	1,076	1,892	177
Greene	2,808	4,481	154	273	3,879	4,405	175	34	2,667	1,155	203	1,117
Herkimer	3,701	5,131	30	625	6,331	5,070	61	69	6,667	953	1,715	1,852
Jefferson	4,483	7,190	47	924	9,439	7,216	31	18	2,223	8,454	935	8,665
Kings	26,148	65,636	988	2,548	51,751	61,002	507	9	80,100	513	58,857	1,328
Lewis	2,447	3,787	11	144	4,036	3,674	11	2	3,797	769	1,803	522
Livingston	3,630	3,966	112	388	5,522	4,242	161	20	2,607	1,921	1,471	480
Madison	3,512	4,328	121	648	6,793	4,683	182	60	3,673	2,864	1,178	1,470
Monroe	11,056	13,143	234	1,364	17,102	13,742	316	11	5,208	1,420	1,748	1,084
Montgomery	3,927	5,374	63	102	5,230	4,947	92	3	4,898	1,944	2,922	654
New-York	47,785	124,014	1,537	684	81,730	123,015	610	26	156,981	875	91,710	2,512
Niagara	3,256	5,834	55	638	6,478	5,937	56	48	6,718	1,273	2,814	2,128
Oneida	8,741	13,673	228	918	14,546	12,000	273	120	19,550	651	4,702	1,223
Onondaga	11,020	11,583	31	621	16,153	11,732	188	49	7,674	7,578	5,088	4,822
Ontario	4,675	5,272	120	294	6,774	5,767	134	25	3,082	2,929	610	1,923
Orange	6,541	8,874	153	553	10,088	9,672	116	50	3,368	7,760	2,493	3,215
Orleans	2,549	3,118	98	648	4,581	3,104	75	18	8,028	1,740	1,083	1,120
Oswego	6,370	6,757	348	503	10,286	6,746	444	61	7,557	1,868	3,034	567
Otsego	4,730	6,848	65	677	7,156	7,184	127	108	1,510	6,660	2,333	2,223
Putnam	1,825	1,691	.....	30	2,114	1,708	.....	2	704	474	1	115
Queens	3,698	8,606	100	200	8,151	10,391	86	13	9,383	409	923	14
Rensselaer	10,468	13,714	151	.....	13,672	13,031	318	22	4,199	6,384	1,351	389
Richmond	2,012	4,370	10	36	3,291	4,815	10	.....	5,729	55	3,593	556
Rockland	1,473	2,771	5	89	2,688	3,415	2	9	2,159	248	649	480
St. Lawrence	9,294	5,220	15	238	13,748	5,835	10	18	968	15,032	492	1,870
Saratoga	6,185	6,277	34	214	8,116	5,808	49	16	2,111	6,319	6	219
Schenectady	2,604	2,836	40	157	3,250	2,628	73	5	1,557	2,442	31	1,008
Schoharie	2,076	4,954	55	175	3,646	5,262	85	24	1,618	3,775	530	3,226
Schuyler	2,171	2,155	70	59	2,790	2,293	112	35	741	2,006	61	118
Seneca	2,554	3,510	40	104	3,304	3,802	45	2	2,410	1,024	64	2,879
Steuben	6,577	8,907	473	1,276	10,245	8,902	554	4	2,543	5,505	752	3,412
Suffolk	3,815	5,287	54	330	6,515	6,061	49	15	6,392	484	1,300	183
Sullivan	2,260	3,451	290	119	3,339	3,718	434	.....	598	2,735	114	493
Tioga	3,143	3,583	374	369	4,750	3,627	189	48	239	5,780	1,037	718
Tompkins	2,690	3,619	458	316	4,896	3,956	363	17	3,907	1,297	701	2,054
Ulster	6,140	8,470	42	635	9,994	9,570	30	32	5,461	4,290	767	1,200
Warren	2,560	2,677	339	76	3,330	2,618	379	7	1,045	2,053	.....	16
Washington	5,929	4,190	50	151	7,779	4,145	59	6	2,398	5,965	318	3,671
Wayne	4,254	4,296	350	641	7,600	5,207	235	30	5,165	2,034	1,256	766
Westchester	6,005	11,473	148	314	11,367	11,858	82	8	13,251	713	1,123	51
Wyoming	2,120	2,909	18	859	4,695	3,309	58	9	2,136	1,456	12	20
Yates	2,501	2,073	134	118	3,432	2,197	97	14	1,018	1,035	207	456
Total	341,523	535,347	11,954	26,606	555,544	534,511	12,373	1,517	405,993	185,708	249,955	79,293

The New York T   *Nov 25, 1882*

A partial report by the TIMES of the returns in the state election of November 1882

The voters supported the Free Canal Amendment by an extremely wide margin. Statewide 646,526 votes were cast on the amendment and 486,105 (75%) were in favor. It won in some metropolitan harbor counties by a vote of 170 to 1. For example, on Manhattan Island the vote was 99.4% in favor; in Kings County, 99.4%; in Westchester, 94.3%. In February 1878 the board of the Chamber of Commerce had acted as one person and voted unanimously for a free canal. Now, four years after members of the Chamber had risen as one person and expressed their unanimity, so did the voters of metropolitan New York.

In all the counties where taxpayers on average paid $9 or more per person in taxes, at least 70 percent of the voters favored the amendment. Among the counties with a lower tax rate, only a fourth (15) voted that strongly. Future mayor Frank Edson had predicted "the heaviest taxpayers of the state favored the free canal while the lightest taxpayers opposed it," and his prediction proved true.

The seven counties giving the strongest support for the canal were Erie, Kings, New York (Manhattan), Queens, Richmond, Westchester, Oneida (Utica), and Monroe (Rochester).

Table 10. Top Nine Counties in Support of the Free Canal Amendment, November 1882.

County:	Yeas	Nays	Total	% Yeas
Erie	36,997	509	37,506	98.6 %
Kings	80,100	513	80,613	99.3 %
New York	156,984	875	157,859	99.4 %
Oneida	19,550	651	20,201	96.7 %
Queens	9,323	409	9,732	95.7 %
Richmond	5,729	55	5,784	99.0 %
Rockland	2,159	248	2,407	89.6 %
Suffolk	6,322	484	6,806	92.8 %
Westchester	13,254	743	13,997	94.7 %

Two remarks are warranted by this table. First, the strongest vote—near unanimity—came from port counties at either end of the system. No conclusion is warranted that the Anti-Monopoly League was weak: just the opposite. Second, throughout this investigation, despite promoting oleomargarine, no report or editorial has emerged discussing this obviously heavy vote. Has such a clearly historical vote escaped the notice of the historians?

Since the 1882 election returns in the harbor counties favoring the free canal were so one-sided, it is not hyperbole to hold that a common view gripped the minds of New York voters. The old canal had returned to celebrity status. Very likely, not only had

Livermore's address hit the matter squarely, but voters themselves moving in the streets could have seen the ships arriving from Europe with cargo and leaving for New Orleans either empty or with ballast. Voters fell back on the mature resource they had, and settled the matter.

A printed report in the daily papers gave an unambiguous statement of the previous day's arrivals and departures. The information was in a column headed "Marine Intelligence." Once Livermore had made his statement in September of 1881 before the Board of Managers, the readers of the daily papers could note the implied day-to-day trends in traffic on the bay. The rule of parsimony came to prevail, that is the rule of economy in the explanation. By November of 1882, there was not much to add to or detract from the case for a free canal.

The leading counties had experienced unusual growth during the previous decade, much of it including immigration from abroad. While the New York State population had grown by 16 percent, the average rate of growth for six of the seven counties was 25 percent. (Westchester had yielded territory to New York and showed a loss in total population.) Such extreme growth and high taxes placed the counties in a relatively overextended position. Not surprisingly, their voters saw the necessity of securing a hedge in the form of a free canal to keep down their own costs and increase traffic.

That had given the free canal movement a new drive. Whereas the anti-monopoly movement had first enlisted city leaders to aid New York farmers opposing the railroads' discriminatory through rates from the West, the movement then became the merchants' movement to protect themselves. By 1881, it flourished into a defense of the urban centers hedging their growing, high-risk position. The thriving railroads may have mistaken their technical and political successes for a green light to take over all the traffic between cities. The canal supporters, however, rebuked them, as they realized that the old canal system had not only spawned many cities across the state, but also kept them strong.

The average business owner who needed to ship products now enjoyed greater reliability from the transportation system. He also enjoyed surer prosperity in flourishing urban areas with quicker access to the market through competitive transportation. The city would have tax receipts for paying on the public indebtedness. Therefore, one could conclude that in saving the canal, the taxpayers were moved by their public indebtedness as much as the railroad owners were moved in making a cartel agreement to manage their corporate indebtedness. Further, with a free canal, as Seymour suggested, wealth came from the improved value of real estate. The half-breeds tended to look to a good return on investment in corporate stock. The rest looked to improved real estate value and knew how to protect it.

What the Vote on the Canal Amendment Meant for New York Politics

New Yorkers had high-quality information before they voted. They had realized, from Albert Fink's 1878 letter to Senator Windom, the critical nationwide service that the canal performed seven months a year by forcing lower rates on the rails. It was a view of events that in 1880 the Hepburn committee reported. The first report of the ICC in 1887 repeated it. Further, the decrepit state of the canal made it easy to understand that the system was underfunded. They could believe that the cartel had robbed its traffic in order to dispose of it. In the meantime, New Yorkers faced national policy-making that moved at a snail's pace. It would not give them much advantage over the new competition from the Mississippi and St. Lawrence rivers. The Free Canal Amendment would drop shippers' costs dramatically, giving them a bird in hand. The voters played their trump card and let the old institution begun by Clinton serve in lieu of or as a surrogate for some federal solution.

All this activity in New York may have had side effects. New Yorkers had given strong support to Grant, a fact that, in part, may be explained by his supporting rivers and harbors appropriations. The *Chronicle* may very well have expressed his views. By comparison, the half-breeds in New York State clustered around the railroad interests, had few allies in the state, and had to look for aid elsewhere––to the U.S. Supreme Court and to any number of outsiders hoping to become presidential candidates. With Garfield in the White House they not only pushed railroad interests to the fore, but they also had visions of bringing the New York party into line. Gorham had seen the prospect from the outset when, in his first comments on the Robertson nomination, he declared it an effort to change party leadership by "external force." The old leadership understood what was going on. From the time of Garfield's death onward they gave the public a simple issue to understand, the free canal proposition. The exchanges organized the state as thoroughly as the politicians ever had and turned out the vote. They had a spectacular win. That meant that those who had campaigned for the free canal now comprised a significant portion of the urban leadership. New York leadership did not simply devolve to the half-breeds, their railroad supporters, and other sources of new money. Even the social structure reflected the shift. In New York Mrs. William Astor would reign for several years as the society leader while in Washington the Camerons of Pennsylvania did the same.

The half-breed "bolters" had won at the 1880 national convention, but two years later, they turned out only insignificant opposition to the Free Canal Amendment, exposing their small numbers in party ranks. For all their efforts to stall state regulation at Albany, to keep Conkling from having influence on the Garfield cabinet, and to use President Garfield to replace the New York party's leadership, the half-breeds did poorly in their own bailiwick a year later. Vanderbilt opened a press office at his railroad station to feed releases to rural papers, but that influence fell far short of what Blaine had been able to do in Washington a year earlier on the railroaders' behalf.

The vote showed that New Yorkers knew their rational self-interest. They were free of any machine arm-twisting in this vote and largely followed the arguments of Conkling's brother-in-law, Horatio Seymour. Not only had the monopolism in business and politics been upset by recent events, but the voters experienced a newfound freedom of thinking on their own. The year 1882 would long stand as a watershed year largely because the old politicians decided that their role was to retreat to the sidelines.

Finally, by tracing the interest in the Erie Canal to the point that the public gave it a new, special status, the value of the work of Laumann and Knoke becomes clear. They hold that a controversy continues about who may participate in policy decision-making. The campaign and victory for the free canal advocates forced upon the monopolists the fact that a new definition now prevailed, showing that voters had a place in the policy arena. Laumann and Knoke write that

> Membership in a policy domain is a continuing collective social construction by the domain actors. *Membership is the outcome of continuous negotiations between the consequential actors currently forming the elite, who seek to impose their preferred definitions and requirements for inclusion,* and various excluded non-elite actors, who seek the right to participate in collective decision-making for the subsystem as a whole. (Our emphasis.)[20]

The monopolists controlled much of the policy course––from the time of Grant's failure at the 1880 convention until a year later, when the New York legislature's first passed the free canal resolution. The tally on the popular vote for the canal amendment had broken the railroaders' proprietary claim over the policy arena. The voters no longer had to play the role of what Evarts referred to as "the broad-backed Asses."

What hastened the change? A combination of weaknesses on the railroad side, including the rate war of the summer of 1881, the halting of domestic and foreign trade, the surge in trade at New Orleans, and the railroaders' record in the state legislature of blocking canal improvements, together with findings of the bribery to win votes for Depew. That all led to their loss of control over the New York legislature. Consequently, it led to an opening for the first passage of the free canal resolution of July of 1881. Garfield died in September of 1881. In November of 1881, the Democrats took a slight edge in the legislature. New York voters broke the railroad lobby's hold on the state legislature, going on to the 1882 election of Cleveland as governor and the stupendous vote for the free canal. That is, the anti-monopolists chose their ground in Clinton's ditch, went into an electoral battle, and impressed upon themselves and the monopolists that the public had a place in the direction of policy.

The policy process helps to establish historical periodization. The counter-Hepburn period lasted just over a year and included the Garfield administration, marked by the sidelining of politicians, like Conkling and Gorham, who provoked public discussion. Unfortunately, when one reads the standard American histories that include the Garfield administration, one does not realize the extent of the hiatus. The impression is left that, with the departure of Conkling and in the fury of the civil service reform movement, the entire stalwart organization and sentiment went up in smoke. A price is exacted.

The standard accounts of the national scene overlook an important sequence. Following Garfield's death, New Yorkers turned to the transportation issue and settled it momentarily with the great vote on the free canal. That was in 1882. A year later, in 1883, the Congress finally passed the civil service reform bill. The standard accounts would leave the impression that the 1883 legislation was a first pure response to the troubles of the Garfield administration. In fact, that point has been so completely and repeatedly made that all sense of the successful reaction of the anti-monopolists in 1882 is totally lost.

Any failure to mention the importance of the struggle over transportation to the state of New York and the place of the canal in that history overlooks the role of the canal in the American history of the rise of business competition. The *Chronicle,* after all, had said, "we must not omit to point out once more that the most burning, difficult and tormenting problem of the day is transportation, involving more which is untried and hazardous, and capable of perhaps leading to more disturbance than any other." The major players had reflected the differences. Democrat John Reagan's report issued just before the 1880 Republican convention had said:

> It is urged by two at least of the ablest representatives of the railroad interests, Mr. Adams and Mr. Fink, that the idea of competition must be eliminated from the railroad problem before it can be satisfactorily and properly adjusted. . . I look upon this as the most dangerous theory, which has been advanced . . .

Over against this view, Garfield had looked to censuring the faction in New York that was closest to favoring competition. His view would lose in New York. The vote on the Free Canal Amendment, beyond being a referendum in addition on the Hepburn hearings, was also a referendum on the place of business competition in America. The rest of the country would take time to adjust.

The wonder is that the story of the free canal has largely faded from public memory, since the railroaders' side has become the conventional view, discounting both the canal and their political opposition. The railroaders had come ever so close to replicating in their industry the business model developed in the oil industry by John D. Rockefeller. They failed to get what they wanted largely because Conkling would not let them have the kind of U.S. Senate judiciary committee that they needed to realize their hopes. As a consequence, they urged on punishment that the president meted out, completely blurring a reasonable sense of the sequence of events based on institutional interests. Nonetheless, many events in this scenario resonated with one another. The question remains, although the larger story has been forgotten, whether the victory of the free canal advocates did have a consequence for national politics in the near term.

The Boys on the Canal Footpath

After the vote on the free canal, the most visible mark of the victory was the sight of the waterways from the windows of the trains traveling through the Mohawk Valley. On July 30, 1883, the *Argus* of Albany reported that:

> It seldom occurs to the observer when he witnesses the barefooted canaler plodding along behind a pair of mules which are towing a canal boat containing 8,000 bushels of grain that the craft contains 240 tons of freight, equal in amount to a train of 24 cars with 10 tons each, and that the canaler with his old pair of mules and sluggish looking craft is running a fierce opposition with Vanderbilt, Jay Gould, and the railroad magnates of this country. Yet, such is the fact.

Chapter XIII

Among the Scenes of Peril Decorum Returns

[1]   *NYT,* July 22 and 23, 1881.

[2]   *NYT,* July 24, 1881.

[3]   *NYT,* August 3, 1881.

[4]   *NYT,* editorial. August 10, 1881.

[5]   *NYT,* August 11, 1881.

[6]   *Tribune.*

[7]   Nimmo, November 21, 1881.

[8]   *NYT,* September 19, 1879.

[9]   *NR,* August 22, 1881.

[10] *NR,* August 5, 1881.

[11] *NYT,* August 19, 1881.

[12] *NYT,* September 15 and 16, 1881.

[13] *NYT,* September 16, 1881.

[14] *NR,* October 20, 1881.

[15] Ritter, p. 149.

[16] Weinstein, Allen. *Prelude to Populism, 1865–1878.* New Haven, CT: Yale University Press, 1970, pp. 88–90, 358

[17] *Commercial and Financial Chronicle.*

[18] *NYT,* October 11, 1882

[19] A final rally addressed by Union League President William Evarts.

[20] Laumann and Knoke, p. 12.

Chapter XIV

Former Governors Enter the Arena

Introduction

In the late 1870s and early 1880s Americans ventured some dramatic steps to add order to the rising industrial society. They usually modified existing legislation to make it more serviceable to the changing scene. Paper dollars, issued during the emergency of the war, were not destroyed but brought up to par with gold. The growing railroad industry, in its interstate business, was not only freed from state regulation but also brought under the interstate commerce provision of the Constitution and a prohibition against pooling of rates. While the Constitution allowed claims against the government, the congressional supervision bogged down into something of a bazaar, and the Congress decided to give the Court of Claims greater independence. Government employment had to meet the reformers' standards of merit rather than win posts through favoritism to friends and family. While President Jackson had driven the federal bank out of business, once the Democrats left Washington to fight the war, the old Whigs invoked a new system and managed to sustain it through the first period of twenty-year charters. By the force of arms the North had maintained the Union and freed the slaves but the new voters soon lost their rights and were thrown back on their own resources.

Each of these changes had its own scenario, including lobbying and making adjustments. The question remains whether new generations have quite heard the story. What becomes evident especially in review of the transportation issue is that some accounts leave the inference that after the popular Hepburn hearings of 1879 public participation in railroad policy lessened while the courts took an increasing role.

Something else actually happened. Cullom tells of his working at first on the proposed legislation without many results. Then the break came, and a great step in popular involvement took place. Cullom relates that:

> When the bill was reported to the Senate, and I was pushing and urging and doing everything in my power to secure consideration, Senator

Allison, always my friend, always wanting to assist me in any way in his power, came to me one day and said:

"Cullom, we know nothing about this question; we are groping in the dark; and I believe that there ought to be a select committee of the Senate appointed to investigate the question, to go out among the people, take testimony, and find out what they know about it--what the experts know, what the railroad officials know, what public opinion generally is, and report their conclusion to the Senate at the beginning of the next session. I am willing to help you secure the passage of a resolution with that end in view."[1]

A surmise is warranted that after the passage of the banking bill in 1882 the New England delegation found the institution secure; they decided to let the railroad question become more subject to popular attention. Very likely, Allison--as a member of the New England hegemony and serving as both the chairman of appropriations and the chairman of the committee on committees--had discussed the course with his New England colleagues, won their endorsement and went to Cullom with his suggestion. What will become evident is that Cullom would make the most of this gesture and, in the end, public participation in passage of the ICC legislation would become quite pronounced.

At the time of naming the committee in 1885 the Senate had in recent history both the statement by President Chester Arthur in his third annual report favoring legislation and the clear plank of the national convention passed in the summer of 1884. Now everything conspired to proceed. In the Senate the discussion before adoption of the new committee covered five pages. Members apparently felt under duress to get on. As Senator Maxey of Texas opined, "The country has seen the course pursued by the Senate and the course pursued by the House on the great interstate commerce bill. It has passed out of Congress; it has gone into the hands of the people, and there if the Senate thought proper to throw down the gauntlet it will be taken up . . ." Again, after the defeat of Harrison in 1892, Gorham complained that the reason lay in the executive's violation of the recent party platform on the tariff.[2] In those days a party platform had enough status to effect discipline on the deviants.

Civil Service Reform, Long Repressed, Comes to Meet the Circumstances

In late 1881 the New York railroad interests, which had throttled legislative progress by control of the upper house, suffered a severe setback. The common recollection is that they had helped promote civil service reform as was seen in the practice of Chauncey Depew, attorney for the New York Central, sitting together at the state Republican conventions with George William Curtis, a prominent civil service reform leader. Together they could be alert to the bossism of stalwarts and come up with the formula that "spoils leads to murder," adding to the recollection that Conkling was the "quintessence of evil."

That formula helped to make the campaign into a revival reminiscent of the days of humiliation in the colonial theocracies. (See Perry Miller in his *Nature's Nation*.) Those old revivals were collective experiences under the guidance of the ecclesiastical court and its clergy aimed at overcoming identifiable sins. Through collective repentance in 1883, that body in the nation known for their "wealth and intelligence" appears to have taken over the matter. Standing in the place of the earlier ecclesiastical courts, they in effect called for the days of humiliation and introspection. The charge linking bossism and murder would have called every citizen to self-examination repenting his old Jacksonian views and their objections to merit appointment. Collectively they laid hold of a new hope of civil service reform. With success, the proponents could not help but be elated. While the act was ostensibly aimed at the patronage of congressmen, it also did its unheralded work of reducing the temptation before presidents in using their power of appointment for punishing their foes.

How the Senate Hedged Against Conkling's Abuses and Conserved His Creative Changes

After Conkling left the Senate some of the senators apparently began expressing their views about how he had exercised his senate power. For several sessions, he apparently followed a rule allowed some senators, due to special conditions in their home states, to make a proprietary claim on committee membership. For example, one of the members from Missouri always took a seat on the committee on improvement of the Mississippi River. If that committee, one can surmise, had not allowed that seating, the Missouri members could certainly have raised a sympathetic audience from the rest of the Senate during any debate on Mississippi River matters. Thus, in order to make the process more efficient, one of the Missourians was allowed a seat on the special interest committee where he could work out details with other committee members and thus not slow down debate on the floor. Similarly with New York. For years New York senators had proprietary seating on no fewer than four committees: finance, foreign affairs, commerce, and judiciary. In the mid-1870s Conkling managed to take seats on three of the four assignments. After he left in 1881, the Senate leaders may have decided that never again would they let any subsequent New York senators take more than two of the four seats. That would make it less likely that any later New York senator might master such a complete information system and assume the degree of authority that Conkling exercised in the upper chamber.

On the positive side, Conkling appears to have introduced some committee arrangements in the Senate that continued. In 1881, the Senate Republicans added three mid-westerners to judiciary: John Logan of Illinois, Samuel McMillan of Minnesota, and John Ingalls of Kansas. That regional allocation would continue down to recent years. It was also long reflected in Conkling's association with both senators from Wisconsin and the frequent association with members from Minnesota, two states that grew the grain that headed to New York. He had said,

Nothing affecting the welfare of any community in the nation can be without influence on this metropolis [New York City]. There is not a state or city in all our borders which can be blighted without shriveling us. The bonds of every State, the bonds of the railroads which gridiron the West and South, are held in great sums in the East and in the North. Whatever wounds any member of the Union, we feel also; whatever fertilizes and enriches the most distant field invigorates this Commonwealth.[3]

He knew that the prosperity of New York depended upon prosperity everywhere else in the Union. So he associated through committees with members from everywhere else.

In another lasting arrangement made in the Conkling period, the committees of judiciary and foreign affairs always shared pairs of members traveling back and forth between them. The practice probably finds an explanation in the fact that the two committees had to consider nominations for the court and foreign posts, positions more likely attracting citizens from the upper classes, more so than did positions for local postmaster. Apparently, the members of the two committees had found it helpful to handle such nominations with care. Thus, they may have seen fit to treat the nominees with the same procedures. In the 49th Congress, after Conkling resigned, the two committees continued to seat both George Edmunds of Vermont and William Evarts of New York. A sampling of subsequent congresses shows the continuity of the practice. In the 57th (1901) the two committees seated Clarence Clark of Wyoming and Charles Fairbanks of Indiana. Later, in the 67th (1921) William Borah of Idaho and Frank Brandegee of Connecticut took seats on both foreign affairs and judiciary. In the 83rd (1953) the two committees seated both Alexander Wiley of Wisconsin and William Langer of North Dakota. Credit plausibly has to go to Roscoe Conkling for initiating this practice of linking the committees on judiciary and foreign relations by pairs.

Gorham's Reflection with his Son, William

After Conkling left the Senate, Gorham had occasion to write his son, explaining his failure to regain his old office as Secretary of the Senate. At the time of the letters, my grandfather was 24 years old, living and working in San Francisco. He was about to move to Portland and then on to Seattle, where he would remain for the rest of his career.

The remarkable feature of the correspondence between father and son was that the latter had the courage and clarity to ask his father to give him an accounting. The courage of that request is not traceable to genes, nor is it transferable to the future descendants. The request stands as a moral act. The same goes for the father who gave a direct answer.

March 1, 1883

You have very much my disposition. You are therefore willing to tell me some of my faults, i.e., things which have impeded my progress. I have been too independent, and realized too little the mutual dependence of men. I have been quick to wrath, and too free of speech. I have offended on occasions which were not worth it. I have been to regardless of money and have banked too confidently on the fair play of mankind. If I were young again and knew what I now know, I would not attack everything wrong, nor use force to compel people to agree with me. I would not join in wrong, but I would be less Quixotic, and not weaken myself for everything by keeping myself in hot water all the time. Tolerance of opinion I would cultivate, for if I am sure of being right, my opponent may feel sure (in his dullness) that I am wrong. Curb your will. Be charitable. Judge men by their standpoint and training and not by your own. Despise the wickedness of rich rogues, but do not let them know you have detected them. The rogue who knows that you know him is a dangerous enemy. It is not your duty to discover them. Of course, if you encounter them in your own work, you would not allow them to interfere with rights entrusted to you. If we had money, it would be grand to be a knight errant and devote oneself to redressing human wrongs; but alas! We must accumulate or we are but semi-civilized.

The reference to "rich rogues" likely refers to Gorham's troubles with railroad magnate Collis P. Huntington, known for his vindictiveness. In his second letter, Gorham wrote,

June 29, 1883

You have waited a long time for this letter, and have very naturally been impatient and hurt by turns at my delay. But for two months past I have been sick most of the time, and not well the remainder. With a stock of malaria brought over from last year, and a succession of mental anxieties and irritation I got in a very poor condition both in body and mind. It would be a long story was I to tell you of my cases and my troubles, and why should you be worried with them. I have been waiting and hoping, ever since I saw you, for some success which would help us all to at least have a sight of each other. All the time you were in that bank, after you first wrote me that you had a strong wish for a different life, I was unhappy with being unable to do anything for you. Two years ago I felt sure of my Secretaryship of the Senate. Then I thought to visit San Francisco, and counsel with you, and try to place you better. Had I been again installed in the place there would have been plenty of sycophants to offer me whatever you wanted. But instead of success I found myself in a heated controversy--against power. I was right, and would do the same again, but it set some strong currents against me. The hatred of Garfield and Blaine sufficed to postpone my election, and the assassination of Garfield made him a martyr, and for the time a saint, and all who denounced his perfidy and arrogance were at a disadvantage. Then the Senate was tied, and the accession of Arthur deprived us of casting vote, and there could be no election of officers. I looked forward to the 4th of March last, with confidence there would be an extra session. That resulted in disappointment. Now I count on success in Dec. Meanwhile *The Republican* changed hands and my salary went down Dec. last from $100 a week to $60, leaving me without sufficient support for the family. This was an outrage which I felt, and has had much to do with my sickness. The labor of writing a column and half a day all the time was a severe strain, and when to that was added the disappointment referred to and ill-treatment where I had a right to expect friendship, my whole system gave way for a time, and liver, heart, kidneys, spleen and stomach, all showed signs of wear and tear. I have done but little editorial work since April 25th, and am here for a little rest [with relatives in Connecticut]. These are the reasons my dear son why you have been so neglected.

Gorham could not prevail in December 1883. Rather Republicans by a narrow majority elected former New York Congressman Anson McCook. McCook could have easily replicated many of the information links Gorham had used. He had had experience in California, and, like Gorham, knew New York politics well. As a friend of Garfield he could have been a fellow member of Nichol's Honest Money League, and put a Garfield face on Senate administration.

How Our Greenbacks Won Standing

During this post-Conkling period, important financial matters moved through the courts; passage of the rechartering bill in 1882 was only part of the hard-money victory. The Supreme Court had to take up the constitutionality of the Ferry Amendment in the Bland-Allison Silver Bill of 1878. It had sought to preserve the greenbacks submitted to the Treasury in exchange for gold; hard-money advocates had wanted those received greenbacks destroyed. Gorham had been so bold as to assert in his 1879 midterm campaign speech that the strong support among the congressional Republicans for conserving the greenbacks constituted a plank in the party platform. On the other hand, in his inaugural address Garfield would mention that the matter had to come before the Supreme Court, and he was skeptical of its success.

In 1884 the Court challenge came in the case of *Julliard v. Greenman*, and the Court sustained the Ferry Amendment. Only Justice Field dissented. One hundred years later, in 1984, Bernard H. Siegan wrote,

> The government's discretionary authority to issue paper money is often associated with Congress's creation of the Federal Reserve System in 1913. While this legislation did provide such authority, it is more accurate to attribute this power to the Supreme Court's interpretation of the U.S. Constitution [in 1884].

> It was 100 years ago this year that the Court ruled in *Julliard vs. Greenman* that Congress had the constitutional power in both peace and war to make government-issued paper--the famous greenbacks of the time--a legal tender in payment of all private debts.[4]

Gold advocates in 1884, of course, were outraged. Thomas Nichol, founder of the Honest Money League of the Northwest and campaign associate to Garfield, had hoped to see a party house cleaning, and could not have been pleased with the Court decision.

The National Republican Party Catches Up with New York Opinion

In 1884 the spirit of self-examination and humiliation seems to have carried over for another great issue. That year the most striking political reality was the reverse in direction at the National Republican Party convention in addressing railroad regulation. They abandoned the approach they had used in 1880 and, in effect, "retraced their steps."

In the Gilded Age when one politician urged another to reconsider the course he had taken, he often suggested he "retrace his steps," using nonjudgmental words to urge that he abandon his mistake, go back to the beginning, and start again. Conkling had told his audience at the 1877 state convention how both Lincoln and Grant had sometimes made mistakes "and they manfully corrected them, and retraced false steps in the presence of the whole people more than once." Gorham would use the same words on May 12, 1881, writing, "and now is the one opportunity in President Garfield's life for him to be great by conquering the weakness of willfulness. The public sense of fair play demands that he retrace his steps in New York matters, and take counsel of his own good sense and self-imposed obligations when next he moves." On the Robertson nomination, Edwin Godkin saw virtue in such a move, writing on May 18th, "it is not yet too late for [Garfield's] own fame and success to retrace his steps and abandon the plan of governing through the corrupt use of public service."

The collectivity of the party managed such a reversal. In 1884 the delegates at the Republican National Convention decided to reverse the mistake on railroad regulation they had made in 1880 and 1881. At those earlier dates nearly everyone was walking on eggshells, fearful they would arouse a furor among the capitalists at any hint of bringing up the recent Hepburn hearings. In 1884 the leadership decided not to take a cue from the 1880 experience. The death of Garfield, the scare over the rising New Orleans traffic competing with New York, and the loss of party control in the New York legislature and elsewhere may have prompted party leaders to proceed in 1884 with more care. The delegates fell back to old practices and reinstituted the hierarchy of announcements. First, at the highest level, they had the executive include the matter in a message to Congress--Arthur included his comments in his third annual report. Second, with the prompting of the Court, they prepared a clearly compelling platform plank. Finally, once the next Congress convened the matter was assigned to a new select committee as its mandate.

In 1880 there had been no explicit plank announcing the aims of the cartel. Further, their surreptitious approach did not work. While years later many commentators claimed that Garfield's greatest achievement was to further civil service reform, it would be more accurate to hold that the greatest event consisted in recognizing the importance of writing a relevant platform. The less such courtesies were followed, the more likely the subsequent administration would bob, weave, and stumble. When 1884 arrived, party leaders did not want to repeat the experience.

In the intervening four years some consequential events had both driven and beckoned the politicians on to a higher level of performance. First, in several states, including New York, there had been serious Republican losses. The *Evening Post* summarized for six states showing a definite shift among voters from the 1880 presidential election to the 1882 off-year election. It was Benson's view that "the issue (in 1882) was sharply drawn as never before between the corporations and the people, with the Republicans representing the 'monopolies' and the 'money power,' and the Democrats on the side of the angels."[5] The Grand Old Party had an image problem. Second, in New York there had been the massive vote on the free canal amendment showing that they were not "broad-backed Asses," not even "bad men," but had a place in transportation policy-making, as disquieting as that might have been for the railroaders.

Finally, there had been the Supreme Court decision, which, when combined with the commitment of Senator Shelby Cullom of Illinois, brought matters to a head. As Cullom later recalled, the Supreme Court had held that:

> A statute of a State intended to regulate . . . the transfer of persons or property from one State to another (is) void. This decision of the Supreme Court was rendered just about the time I was elected to the United State Senate, and I then and there determined that I would make it one of my great aims in the Senate to secure the enactment of a Federal statute regulating interstate commerce.[6]

One might well imagine that from the moment of his arrival in the Senate in 1883, Cullom laid out his work on this great aim. Early on he gained allies, saw that a plank was fashioned, and alerted President Arthur to his purposes. Then he finally won caucus approval to create an entirely new Senate select committee that would join in the work with John Reagan's House commerce committee.

At the 1880 national Republican convention, two years after Adams had written that railroaders intended to consolidate, the monopolists sought no platform plank. They did, however, help keep Grant from a third term nomination. The party skipped over the railroad question, only saying that there should be "no further grant of the public domain . . . to any railway . . . corporation," and insisting "that further subsidies to corporations must cease."

In the 1884 national convention the delegates would have President Arthur's views on railroading, found in his December 1883 report to Congress, a statement made just at the opening of the campaign season, putting all of the hopefuls on a common footing. Arthur wrote that:

> Complaints have lately been numerous and urgent that certain corporations, controlling in whole or in part the facilities for the interstate carriage of persons and merchandise over the great railroads of the country have resorted in their dealing with the public to diverse measures unjust and oppressive in their character.

> In some instances the state government have attacked and suppressed these evils, but in others they have been unable to afford adequate relief because of their jurisdictional limitations, which are imposed upon them by the federal constitution.

> The question of how far the national government may lawfully act in these premises, and what, if any supervision or control it ought to exercise, is one which merits your careful consideration.

> While we cannot fail to recognize the importance of the vast railway system of the country, and their great and beneficent influences upon the development of our material wealth, we should, on the other hand, remember that no individual and no corporation ought to be invested with absolute power over the interest of any other citizen or class of citizens. The right of these railway corporations to a fair and profitable return must be recognized, and to freedom in their regulations, must be recognized; but it seems only just that, so far as its constitutional authority will permit, congress should protect the people at large in their interstate traffic against acts of injustice which the state governments are powerless to prevent.[7]

With real stress and with authorities willing to meet it, the convention delegates could have easily assumed that the meeting would take up the issue as a matter of course.

If reformers and monopolists thought that civil service reform would take the zeal out of the anti-monopoly movement—presumably stirred up by profiting politicians and their hacks in the spoils system—they had to be surprised. At the convention, with Cullom having had a full year in the Senate to prepare his colleagues, and with Theodore Roosevelt heading the New York delegation, the convention produced a strong statement on transportation, thereby catching up, as it were, to the 1879 New York view that the public had legitimate opinions about transportation policy. The 1884 national platform declared:

The regulation of commerce with foreign nations and between the States is one of the most important prerogatives of the general government; and the Republican Party distinctly announces its purpose to support such legislation as will fully and efficiently carry out the constitutional power of Congress over inter-state commerce.

> The principle of public regulation of railway corporations is a wise and salutary one for the protection of all classes of the people; and we favor legislation that shall prevent unjust discrimination and excessive charges for transportation, and that shall secure to the people, and the railways alike, the fair and equal protection of the laws.[8]

Freshman Cullom's over-all effort culminating in 1884 and 1885 demonstrated as much as anything that policy about transportation was an abiding critical problem. It had been a problem in 1879 New York and was a problem at the 1884 national meeting. In between 1881 and 1882, during Garfield's term, conventional views to the contrary; it had been a chief concern.

What Blaine Learned in 1884 in New York

In 1880 delegates not wanting to trouble the angry railroad leaders proceeded fearing they might step on eggshells. They made no attempt to elevate the 1879 New York platform to the national level. By 1884 such circumspection had long disappeared. Rather, after the convention it was James Blaine who found that in New York he was the one who had to walk as though among eggshells. In 1884 Blaine spoke positively to the Anti-Monopoly League members, forever suspending his earlier, laughable melodrama by which he set up Garfield, quarantining the "bad" men in the New York stalwart camp. Those disputants may have reached an agreement. The New York Republicans in the Anti-Monopoly League may have agreed to support Blaine in 1884 in exchange for his support of the explicit national party plank on regulation. Such a turn in high opinion likely amounted to a confession that the alleged gag rule of 1880–1881 had been a mistake.

Unfortunately, in the campaign of 1884, Blaine found that he couldn't rise above his old habits of melodramatic thought. He filled his campaign with warnings that

Democratic victory would lead to a sweep of evils across the country, implying that once again the "plumed knight" would vanquish the foe. The *Times* complained that

> It pleases Mr. Blaine to declare that if the Democrats succeed they would proceed to so indiscriminately cut down the tariff as to upset all protected industries, bring on a general disturbance, reduce wages, drive labor out of employment, and frightened capital from investment. There is not the slightest foundation for these predictions in the professions of the party or of the party leaders or in anything that it has done when in a majority.[9]

Blaine's problem among the New York electorate was in part that the voters had already seen Grover Cleveland, the former mayor of Buffalo, in office as governor for two years, liked what they saw, and scoffed at Blaine's alarms. This was not the first time New Yorkers had met a beguiling melodrama with a yawn. Earlier, the 1876 world's fair had forecast that new technology would displace the old, but the New Yorkers, observing the advantages of both rails and canals, decided with the Europeans that they liked the redundancy in transportation.

New York Republican leaders took different approaches to the 1884 election. During the campaign Conkling wrote editorials against Blaine, and Gorham joined him. Roosevelt, heading the New York delegation, had opposed Blaine before the convention, and after the convention he promised to vote for the candidate. He then came home, and went on vacation without lifting a finger to help. Beecher announced in favor of Cleveland. Simon Sterne, whose speeches in the 1870s had led to the Hepburn hearings, also endorsed the former Buffalo mayor, breaking with several anti-monopolists. Even though Blaine lost New York and the presidency to Cleveland, New York Republicans gained enough votes in the state legislature to send William Evarts to the U.S. Senate.

What Gorham Thought of Blaine's Candidacy in 1884

My files include two newspaper items covering Gorham's views on Blaine's loss of the 1884 presidential election. They were probably first saved by my grandfather, and my mother passed them on to me when I showed an interest in her grandfather.

On the day after the November 1884 election, Blaine made a public statement from his home in Augusta, Maine, and the follow day Gorham made his own observations.

> The South was made solid by Blaine's defeat of the "Force Bill" and Hayes' subversion of the governments of South Carolina and Louisiana in 1877.

> The South thus made solid was broken in 1881 by the Mahone coalition in Virginia despite Blaine's opposition. He summoned all his resources, including his newspaper organs, to drive Mahone and his followers away

from the Republican Party, and to restore the old South by forcing Virginia back into the Democratic fold. After failing in this work in 1882, he finally succeeded in 1883. This year he was quite willing to have Mahone succeed but the wounds he had inflicted proved to be mortal.

As Mr. Blaine omitted these interesting facts from his speech on the Solid South, delivered in Augusta last night, I ask space for this mention of them in the newspaper in which I have so often stated them before.

If Mr. Blaine had been opposed to the Solid South even a year sooner, Virginia would not have been remanded to her previous condition last year, and would undoubtedly have been joined by North Carolina. The twenty-three electoral votes of these two states added to the 182 he received would have given him 205--just four more than enough without New York.

Mr. Blaine's reason for opposing Mahone, as stated by him to one of his leading friends in 1881 [probably stalwart William E. Chandler of New Hampshire], was that he "was not going to build up" certain Republicans whom he named [Conkling, Cameron, and Gorham]. As it turns out he was building up Grover Cleveland and the Democratic Party. All of which shows that a ship cannot be scuttled and sunk for the purpose of drowning a portion of the crew without wetting the others.

Very respectfully, Geo. C. Gorham, New York, Nov. 1(?), 1884.

The Times and *The National Republican* did carry this first letter on November 21st and November 22nd respectively.

At the end of the month Gorham wrote another letter carried by the *Statesman* of Walla Walla, Washington, and by the San Francisco *Argus*. The comments from the San Francisco paper, before and after Gorham's letter, are worth repeating along with his text. The clippings carry no dates.

Mr. George C. Gorham has again been airing his views in regard to Mr. Blaine and the Republican Party. In a published letter—and a letter evidently intended for publication—he says:

My Dear Sir—The defeat of Blaine has put an end to sham Republicanism, which for years has been the concubine of the Democratic Turk. If the republicans who are devoted to justice and equal rights will cease mistaking the false for the true, will cease stoning their prophets and enshrining cheats and prostitutes, there can be a reformed Republican Party. If the Reids and Halsteads and Blaines and the like were still to be our Aarons in the wilderness, then it would be a crime to restore a party in which they can flourish. As for the Negro, he will thrive better by a little wholesome neglect from those who have conspired against him in the South. The Republic has some dark problems to solve, but the defeat of the man who was violently opposed to Mahon and coalition in 1881, 1882, and 1883, and the Force bill in 1875 is surely a step forward. Blaine said he was defeated because Burchard arrested the desertion of Catholics from the democratic ranks. What a confession! He received the votes of one-third the Democratic party of the United States; else he would not have carried ten states, perhaps not six. I shall wait to see whether the party tries to recover strength by building on its disease before I hasten my conclusions as to the future.

Very truly your friend,

George C. Gorham

The Argus does not endorse the views of that letter; it merely exhibits it for the purpose of producing harmony in the Republican Party. The uncommonly strong English of the letter will not surprise those who know that George C. Gorham is one of the very ablest press writers in the United States. With Mr. Gorham's political and personal friendship or antipathies in Republicanism we have no concern, but those whom he scores have scored him.

Most explanations of Blaine's 1884 defeat do not take into account his failing Southern strategy. But Gorham was one of the few observers who had a good grasp of politics in the two states of New York and Virginia. For Gorham candidate Blaine was simply too circumspect about with whom he would associate. Blaine simply did not want any competition from Gorham and Conkling. If Mahone had won his 1883 state election—chilled by the Danville riot—Gorham would have come strongly to the fore in party councils. He might have won his re-election to the post in the Senate that he so deeply desired.

Congress Resumes its Work on Transportation Policy

In 1885, the U.S. House returned to Democratic control, once again giving Texan John Reagan the chair of the House committee on commerce. Republicans retained the U.S. Senate. A few days after Cleveland's inauguration, on March 17th, the Senate passed a resolution authorizing Cullom's new committee. While five years earlier monopolists had set about to exclude the public, and win approval of their plan, as Nimmo had put it, "at once and unconditionally," they now had no chance of keeping the public at a distance. The new committee seated some stable politicians, three of the members coming from terminal cities and with a record of having won elections. Both Shelby

Cullom of Illinois and Isham Harris of Tennessee had been three-term governors. In addition, Arthur P. Gorman of Maryland had just completed chairing the Democratic National Committee in the victorious election of Grover Cleveland over James Blaine for the presidency. The combined campaign skills of Cullom, Harris, and Gorman may explain why there was a successful set of hearings in eight cities and a good turnout in Washington in 1887 for the final passage of the bill.

Other members of the committee included Orville Platt of Connecticut, a firm ally of Nelson Aldrich of Rhode Island. Another was Warner Miller of New York, Tom Platt's successor, and highly involved in the lumber business as an investor, inventor, and shipper. Miller may have been the new committee's answer to Chauncey Depew's 1880 complaint that the Hepburn committee seated no one representing heavy shippers. Among the entire panel there was, however, neither a railroad manager, as the Democrats had proposed in naming George Pendleton of Ohio, nor a corporation attorney such as they had in naming Benjamin Hill of Georgia. Even a chance to name a granger judge such as Samuel McMillan of Minnesota was passed by.

The Senate committee would travel with Reagan's House committee across the country to eight cities beginning in Boston to take testimony. The several stops would have had a popular tone to them, showing that they went precisely in the opposite direction from that which some authorities thought the discussion of policy took. As Allison explained first to Cullom and then to the Senate, the traveling joint committee was to take testimony on "what the experts know, what the railroad officials know, and what public opinion generally is, and report their conclusion to the Senate." The railroad managers and attorneys would make their presentations from the far side of the witness table just as the public would. Such arrangements for taking testimony was much more a reflection of the Hepburn hearings of 1879 than what the cartel leaders had hoped for in 1881.

When the legislation passed in 1887, it was clearly a compromise. On the one hand, the commission was composed of members representing the categories of interests that Charles F. Adams, Jr., had been urging based on several years of the British practice. A couple of categories were added. The arrangement became a model for later regulatory commissions.

On the other hand, the legislation brought an effective end to the cartel founded a decade earlier. The cartel had served the original four member railroads by providing for pooling of rates and receipts; the new law of 1887 prohibited just that kind of service among the seventy companies that were now members. The Democrats had insisted upon ending the pooling. Among many westerners the entire practice of monopolism was an eastern error, and the Congress took the opportunity to honor that western sentiment. Further, the Rev. Henry W. Beecher had given support to that western view when he proclaimed the mortality of monopolies. The Anti-Monopoly League had grown with that sentiment, and with the passage of the ICC legislation the political culture for the coming Progressive Era was well set, three years prior to the passage of the 1890 Sherman Anti-Trust Act. Most of the opposition to the legislation had come from the northeast.

Near the end of his work, Cullom recognized how it all began in Albany. He asked attorney Simon Sterne to write some of the language that went into the 1890 act. Sterne was significant because he had pressed for the New York investigation and then was employed in 1879 by the Hepburn committee to conduct the interrogation of witnesses. Cullom recognized that the ICC had not risen out of whole cloth. Nor were the Hepburn hearings destined to remain an isolated event. Reagan's biographer, Ben H. Proctor, summarized the history of the policy, mentioning that in the twelve years Hopkins of Pennsylvania had thrust on Reagan, which had aggrieved Pennsylvania producers and outraged grangers of the Midwest and upper Mississippi River valley. The Hepburn hearings publicized their outrage, and the Anti-Monopoly League and National Board of Trade had given it direction; now regulation was all that the American people demanded. Proctor asked, "Who is the most powerful? The people or the railroads? Through sheer determination and force of character, through an untiring leadership and indomitable will he had answered the question."[10]

The obvious tone of heroism in Proctor's tribute to Reagan overlooks the Texan's working in a structure of alliances, agreements on deadlines, and so forth. The policy debate was brought to a major conclusion in 1906 when Congress conferred on the ICC the powers of a rate board. Such people as Shelby Cullom and New York's State Engineer Frank Williams recognized that 1906 endpoint, and the end of the role played by the canal.

Passage of the new law in 1906 was not without duress in the political establishment. Aldrich of Rhode Island, titular head of the Senate Republicans, led the opposition. J. P. Dolliver of Iowa led the proponents. His standing in the Senate structure is instructive. As the junior senator from Iowa, he doubtless proceeded with the support of the senior senator, William Allison, who was not only a member of the New England hegemony but also chairman of appropriations and often chairman of the committee on committees. Allison had helped Cullom at the outset in 1885, and then also helped Dolliver. As a result the hegemony would not enforce conformity and Aldrich virtually stood alone in opposition.

Dolliver's biographer, Thomas Richard Ross, detailed the maneuverings, writing:

> The House-Senate Conference report was adopted, and the bill became law on June 29, 1906. Thus, the "fundamental principle of governmental control over the most powerful corporations in the country had been fully affirmed. It was an historical event—the most important, perhaps, in Theodore Roosevelt's public career—and a not insignificant one in our national history." As John Blum has put it: "The Hepburn Act (of 1906) endowed the Interstate Commerce Commission with power commensurate

with its task." Roosevelt, himself, maintained that it represented "the longest step ever taken in the direction of solving the railway rate problem."

When Dolliver returned to Fort Dodge after the adjournment of Congress, the townspeople held a great reception for him at the home of Mayor S. J. Bennett. During the ceremonies the mayor read a telegram from President Roosevelt, saying "Through you permit me to join with the people of Fort Dodge in an expression of hearty good wishes to Senator Dolliver. I particularly and deeply appreciate the admirable work he did in connection with the rate bill and congratulate him and the people of Iowa upon it." Later, Roosevelt, writing of the fight for the Hepburn Act, recorded: "There was one Republican . . . whom Senator Aldrich could not control—Senator Dolliver of Iowa."[11]

The melodrama had entered a new stage. Rhode Island's Aldrich, rather than Conkling, had become the enemy.

Roosevelt had seen this scenario from beginning to end. The effort had arisen out of the response to the Hepburn hearings of 1879 and emerged again at the opening of the Garfield candidacy at the party meeting held in August of 1880, when a counter meeting was apparently held. At that meeting not only were other boards of trade surveyed about monopolism but also apparently authors were enlisted to send journals articles about the issue, which began appearing at the turn of the year. With the souring New York economy during the summer getting only indifference from the cartel, the fall election arrived and shook the state legislature from Republican control. New Yorkers could then move on to state regulation and dropping the tolls on the canal. Frustration with the railroaders continued in other states, the Court curbed the states courts from handling interstate commerce cases, and three-term governor of Illinois Shelby Cullom came to the Senate vowing to get the railway question settled. President Arthur declared in favor of a federal solution and the 1884 convention adopted a plank to cover the matter; Cullom at the next Congress got his select committee and with Reagan's House committee proceeded on a nationwide tour to take testimony. In two years the new law was passed. By 1906 matters were further perfected.

How Concerned was Conkling in Defending his Reputation?

This story was hardly repeated in full, largely due to both the disgust of the railroaders with Roscoe Conkling for the encouragement he had given to the cause and to the senator's own reticence to defend what he had done. He thought that the public would have enough sense finally to figure out what had occurred in his public career, and thought it unnecessary to highlight it himself. In 1876, when newspapers attacked some senators, he told his peers in the Senate chamber "He who attempts to follow up these sinister and false statements, and succeed, must be industrious indeed. For one,

I have spared myself such efforts all these years, and have been willing to trust to the truth and the sense of my countrymen to find it out in the end."[12] Five years later, shortly after Conkling resigned, Gorham touched on the same matter, explaining, "Conkling has been more lied about than any ten other men in America. He never corrects a misstatement concerning himself."[13] These two men's testimony casts a shadow not so much over his political critics as over the integrity of the press in reporting them. Conkling was apparently self-possessed enough to realize what was happening. In his public bearing he had little reluctance in letting anyone know if he did not like him, or whether another responded with similar sentiments. He may have had this experience in mind when discussing the public reputation of the railroads, saying, "It is not a tendency of human nature to run riotously against approved and commended people or things. The tendency is rather to do injustice to those against whom feeling, prejudice and opposition prevail."[14] As time passed, his negatives far outweighed his positives.

A Ruined Stalwart Leaves a Torch to the Progressive Theodore Roosevelt

Conkling would die in 1888, a year after the creation of the ICC. While he recognized Congress's right to legislate for interstate commerce, what he thought of the solution is not immediately apparent. The year 1882 was more pivotal for him since not only had the Court approved his defense in an important corporate case but also the voters had confirmed his beliefs in the canal.

In early 1888, a few weeks before his death, the Buffalo merchants invited Conkling to address them on the canal question, but on February 29, he wrote declining the invitation, yet encouraging them, including some suggestions for them to track in order to keep the system functional.

W. M. Thurston, Esq.

Secretary

Merchants' Exchange of Buffalo

Buffalo, New York

My Dear Sir,

May I beg through you to express thanks to the committee of the Merchants' Exchange and Businessmen's Association for the honor of being invited to address the meeting to be held on Saturday. Although it is not in my power to be in Buffalo, my presence is not needed I trust to attest to my interest in the Erie Canal?

I believe in the maintenance and enlargement of this artery of commerce for reasons too many to be state in a brief letter. Not for Buffalo alone nor for Buffalo and New York together—deep as is the interest of both—but for the State of New York, the whole state and all its sections, it is largely and durably important not only to take care of the canal but to keep it up to the times in the fullness of its usefulness. Not only as a feeder, but as regulator and safeguard, the canal is so needful that the day will be ill-starred when the people or the Legislature shall turn deaf ears and blind eyes to whatever honest demands it makes on the state or its revenues.

Had I vote or voice in the matter, that vote or voice would always be for locks long enough and prism capacious enough for the boat traffic willing to float.

Your obedient servant,

Roscoe Conkling[15]

Conkling would have his own admirers, people not particularly remembered by others. Rufus Hatch, the investor and activist, in 1883 would name a newborn son Roscoe Conkling Hatch. Hatch from the early 1870s had stirred public attention that led up to the Hepburn hearings and followed through helping to win the passage of the Free Canal Amendment. Another admirer, Senator Blanche K. Bruce, a wealthy Mississippi black businessman, who was shunned by his Senate colleague, James Alcorn, when it came time to take his oath of office for the 44th Congress, found a friend in Conkling. The New Yorker observed the incivility and came forward to stand with Bruce in the oath taking. It was a gesture not forgotten, as Bruce would name his son Roscoe Conkling Bruce.[16]

Whether or not Conkling was honored in one circle or another, the pity is that no prominent politician or academician has contradicted the propriety hold which reform interpretation had had over the allegedly poor reputation of Roscoe Conkling, even excluding his stand for the canal and its part in the evolution of competition in the American economy. Conkling's practice on policy was to come right down the middle. As Godkin had observed, he was a monopolist in the courts and an anti-monopolist in politics. In the late 1880s with the passage of the ICC act, followed almost two decades later by additional rate settlements, laissez-faire economics had received a lasting setback in America. Conkling deserves a share of the credit. The entire venture was hardly a melodrama, since the community did not return to its previous state of affairs.

Subsequent to his death, Conkling's reputation would take a terrible beating. Gorham got wind of the plan to slander the New Yorker's legacy, and told of it to the audience in a memorial service at a black church in Washington (see the *Gorham Collection*, State Library, Sacramento). It would all come to fruition when *Scribner's* printed J. Benjamin Andrews's articles about Conkling's meanness toward Garfield with the 1895 articles carrying cartoons to emphasize the point. Andrews at the moment was the president of Brown University and likely enjoyed the association with capitalists at Newport thirty miles away. They apparently liked his writing. Rockefeller was a contributor to the college. In time, the articles were printed in hardcover and likely lodged on the shelves of every high school library in the country.

Andrews made no mention of Conkling's long interest in the waterway. More importantly, Andrews left no record of the senator's interest in open discussion. Least of all, Andrews made no mention that Garfield had hoped to abolish the factions in New York. Thus, he failed to meet Gorham's standard for coverage: "Care is taken, of course, to give out only such portions of facts as will in the absence of the remainder, injure and wound the persons connected with them."

In the same tenor, Cortissoz published his biography of Whitelaw Reid in the early 1920s, adding a new dramatic analogy that Conkling was always the "villain of the piece." Again, Chauncey Depew published his autobiography further raising doubt about the former senator. While these two spokesmen for the railroad industry, Reid and Depew, held the same view, a minority report came from that notable student of railroading, Charles F. Adams, Jr., whose autobiography was published posthumously a half decade before either of the accounts of Cortissoz and Depew. One would have thought that these men would have compared notes and gotten their story straight. Adams, however, makes no mention of Conkling but says that the troubles came from his own doing just what Albert Fink, the director of the cartel, told him to do. One can wonder whether Conkling had become Depew's Ahab. It raises the question whether advancement in the railroad industry depended upon adherence to the views of Reid and Depew.

How Committed Were the Canal Advocates?

As the votes on the Free Canal Amendment in 1882 and the Barge Canal in 1903 suggest, New Yorkers were highly committed to the Erie Canal for that period of twenty years. Organizations that had been advocates in 1882 for the Free Canal Amendment became advocates for the Barge Canal in 1903 with new people in charge. Both times they came largely from the commodity exchanges and the business associations. Both times they saw a threat from the railroaders, and both times politicians took up their cause. Not subject themselves to popular election, the merchant-lobbyists have largely remained free of the condemnation poured out on the politicians.

What was supported all that time was a system of conveyance by waterways that could be operated by semi-skilled people whether they were attending locks or piloting craft filled with grains.

Aside from the exchange members and business association leaders, the system had a broad base among independent operators on the canal. Thus, when such men as Conkling were honored for all they did for the canal, their good reputation echoed down among the working class. But that honor was hardly reflected in academia. One historian even took the trouble of blanking out any good that Conking had done. Benjamin Kendrick, tracking the importance of the Fourteenth Amendment and Conkling's early response to it in Congress, said that the senator only had interests in the manner in which the amendment helped corporate trusts, adding that Conkling "was [never] the friend of the common man, the poor, and the oppressed, especially the Negro."[17] That judgment proves, however, to be another of the many cases of *ipse dixit* that this episode seems to have attracted.

In truth, Conkling's friendship with the canal crowd would have been similar to that of a latter-day senator showing interest in the drivers of independent trucks on the nation's highways. At the time other leaders hardly did as well. Among the new industrial elite were leaders who built steel mills, hired qualified ironworkers, and then proceeded to deskill them so that they would not have to pay them what they were really worth. There were other investors who backed the new electrical utility companies and saw to it that the new inventions were not installed in some areas until all of the old water-powered mills of were abandoned--of course leaving all those skilled mechanics in useless occupations. All that Kendrick has left us with is disinformation. Kendrick's version would have fit neatly into the discounting conducted by Reid, Cortissoz, and Depew that added up to the declaration that the former senator "was the villain of the piece." So the melodrama went on and on.

Gorham Keeps Busy

In 1884 Gorham left the Washington paper. It appears that the presses were not only sold to *The Post,* but that the last editor of the paper soon became editor of *The Post.* He was a friend of Iowa's William Allison, thus putting the paper under the influence of the New England hegemony.

Gorham was not confident that the business elite of the nation could ever make a lasting difference in influencing southerners. The northerners, he said, were raised on trade while the southerners in Congress were raised largely on "whooping niggers," a type the northerners could not stand up to. Later the northerners in the Senate who complained about Gorham's sternness nonetheless nominated Harrison for president, another curmudgeonly type, who managed to alienate voters.

Gorham took up the staff work for Drawbaugh Associates in a contest over patents with the Bell Company. The case went all the way to the Supreme Court. As Edmunds and Conkling were in the audience there is the suggestion that they put up money for their friend Gorham and hoped to profit. Justice Field, long known to Gorham, decided against his friend and Bell kept the patents.

Sometime in the 1890s--according to a diary of his brother Charles in my possession--after the death of Huntington and the departure of Leland Stanford from the Senate, Gorham was again a candidate in the caucus for the secretaryship. While such men as Hoar of Massachusetts were opposed to him, he had the strong support of California

Senator George Perkins, the former governor of California who had once pooled the rates of his steamboat company with those of the railroads. Gorham could not win. In time, he left the party and began associating with William Jennings Bryan.

When in 1898 the Department of Justice announced that it had closed the star route investigation for lock of evidence—the same point that Gorham had made from the very first—his reputation in Washington apparently turned favorable. While he could not win a vote in the caucus, the men at the New York Avenue Presbyterian Church did him the honor of electing them the president of their men's club. He went on to write the two-volume biography of Lincoln's Secretary of War, Edwin M. Stanton. For some inexplicable reason Gorham failed to return the original source material from the Stanton collection to the family. The most marked feature of the biography was Gorham's defense of the attempt to impeach President Andrew Johnson--a defense made three decades later after many others had concluded that the trial had been an error.

Gorham's Continued Lobbying for Human Rights

Statistics about black Americans were in sufficient supply to collect and present them to policy makers. To that end Gorham in 1903 joined with five others, two whites and three Afro-Americans, to lobby the case that the figures presented. Joining him were Rev. Dr. Dean Richmond Babbitt, rector of the Church of the Epiphany of Brooklyn, and the Rev. Dr. Mayo of Boston. The Afro-Americans were Jesse Lawson, President of the International Bible College, and publisher of the proceedings of the National Sociological Society, Professor Kelly Miller, and Daniel E. Murray, all of Washington. As the National Sociological Society, their purpose sought to assist in keeping facts, plans, arguments, and efforts for the solution of the race problem. They declared "As solutions of the race problem we regard colonization, expatriation, and segregation as unworthy of further consideration."[18] As this effort opposed to the policy of segregation followed the decision of *Plessey v. Ferguson,* the surmise is that Gorham had consulted with Associate Justice John Marshall Harlan on that case. The additional record strengthens the surmise since in 1909 at Gorham's funeral Justice Harlan was among his pallbearers.

How Canal Advocates Met Railroad Competition

Grain traffic into New York City took a tumble in the 1890s. In the early 1880s, matched against Boston, Philadelphia, and Baltimore, the rails and canal into New York City carried almost two-thirds of the total. In that period, the canal often carried much more to New York than any of the rails did to the competing cities. But by the 1890s the rails into those three competing cities were together taking half the grain shipments. The New York rails had dropped to 43% of the total and the canal to six percent of the total. Improvements were needed.

In 1895, in a show of resilience, the electorate again proved willing to charge itself for costs of the upkeep of the canal when it approved a $9,000,000 bond issue for repairs and improvements. Little campaigning was required. Only days before the election the presidents of the Produce Exchange, the Maritime Exchange, and the Board of Trade and Transportation ran ads in the papers, giving voters reasons to support the bond issue. A few days later the headlines shouted the election results that the non-canal counties had carried the question. For example, New York County voted seven to one for the bond issue. Thus, in 1882 and 1895, the New York City electorate showed strong support and confirmed a binding solution, that is, one that could not be shaken and upset. The allocation, however, soon dwindled into corruption. The plan had been to follow up the bond issue with one of $15 million, but it soon became apparent that the amount was hardly enough.

After Theodore Roosevelt won the governor's race in 1898, the process of winning support for a barge canal took a propitious course, as he required those who petitioned him to make their case in a careful assessment. The delegation came from a wide range of organizations, many of whom had promoted the Free Canal Amendment in 1882. The return of these organizations over a period of two decades, according to Laumann and his associates, gives evidence of a continuing elite in the life of the New York economy. Among the repeating organizations were the New York Chamber of Commerce, the Board of Trade and Transportation, the Produce Exchange, and the Canal Boat Owners. Other organizations were also probably repeaters but appear to have changed their names. While in 1881 the Buffalo Board of Trade sent delegates to the Utica meeting, in 1898 it was the Merchants Exchange of Buffalo that sent some to meet with Roosevelt. Similarly, at the earlier meeting the New York Maritime Association was represented, and at the later meeting it was the Maritime Exchange. New groups at the second meeting included the Merchants and Manufacturers Board of Trade, the Staten Island Chamber of Commerce, the Merchants' Association, International Paper Company, Port Henry Board of Trade, the Manufacturers' Association of New York, and the two-year-old Commercial Association of New York.

The first meeting with Roosevelt was worth the time, but Roosevelt let them know that he was noncommittal. He thought that the matter needed careful study. In another three months, he appointed an advisory committee—not a commission, but a task force of five men known for their expertise and unmatched interest in the canal. Two were civil engineers. The appointees were Major T. W. Symonds of Buffalo, John N. Satcherd of Buffalo, Frank S. Witherbee of New York City, General Francis V. Greene of New York City, and G. E. Green of Binghamton. They undertook an effort to meet with parties with a variety of opinions. They began their work by visiting the Canadian canal—as the Windom committee had in 1873—to learn how that system was intending to attract more traffic from the West, and then spent time in the "anti-canal" lower-tier counties to hear voters' opinions. Their comprehensive report was ready in December 1899. The governor was quite pleased and in January transmitted it to the legislature. Concurrently, the Schieren report on the troubled New York economy appeared and underscored the need for a better canal. In March, the Produce Exchange took the trouble to sharpen the focus of their cause and launched a committee of five leaders to orient an additional group of 25 business leaders before they went to Albany to lobby. The five included two from New York City, whom Roosevelt had named to his advisory committee, thus closing the information loop in the lobbying effort. They were Francis Green and Frank Witherbee. In May, the Board of Trade proceeded to raise $10,000 for an educational fund. The promotional work was going quite well. In June 200 business leaders attending the second annual meeting of the Commerce Association at Syracuse, preceding any vote in the legislature, voted unanimously for the proposition. Needless to say, this broad participation in such an intense study would likely stand for years to come as an influence on business thinking in New York state.

By the time the legislature finished its work on the bond issue proposition, it had grown from $60 million to $101 million. For a third time, the electorate supported the canal. The electorate statewide carried it by a vote of 61 percent. New York County reported nine to one for it, and again, the metropolitan, non-canal counties gave the large margin of vote. In 1903, the money went for the new Erie barge canal, allowing boats with a 3,000-ton capacity rather than merely 240 tons, making it easier for them to compete with the railroad's larger rolling stock. Who was the winner and who was the loser? The railroads hardly effected Schumpeter's creative destruction. The belief stemming from the Philadelphia Centennial Exposition of 1876, that the old technology could not prevail, simply did not become the common conviction among a majority of New Yorkers. Most important, while they learned from Conkling and Fink that the opening of the canals always lowered rates including those of the rails, they had learned from Horatio Seymour that the increased traffic helped to increase the value of adjoining property. Those private investments in property supported by state investments in the canal system were no less important than private investments in the railroads.

The massive appropriation to build the barge canal stood as a testimony to popular control over the definition of the state's commercial supremacy. The ICC statute of 1887 had precluded the railroads from forming a trust that could have dictated the definition. In 1906, however, the federal law was brought to near perfection, closing the role of the canal as a surrogate for federal regulation. New York State presented the image of a poker player, showing that in its bond issue it had reserves of $101,000,000, challenging the Congress to do its part. In a very short time, by 1906, the Hepburn bill was passed, with Roosevelt's support, bringing the policy scenario to an end.

How Easily New Yorkers Lost the Canal

The barge canal that Theodore Roosevelt had supported came to completion following the Great War, but it remained a political football. An administrative weakness appeared which handed the advantage to the rails. Entering the war brought out the patriotism of New Yorkers; the state agreed to aid wartime transportation and let the canal be taken over by the federal government. But in the enthusiasm to fight the war, the state neglected to stipulate a federal exit strategy for when the hostilities ceased. The agreement was executed early in 1918 and the armistice came seven months later. It would take three years, however, for the federal government to return the canal to the control of the state, and the federal government returned it at a loss.

In earlier days, the question often arose whether New Yorkers could look to federal help for funding. The idea was often turned down for an obviously compelling reason, and that was that management of the canal would likely come under the influence of other quarters, namely the states along the east coast and on the Mississippi River, the very quarters that were in competition with the port of New York for the nation's commerce. What became evident during the Great War was that outside influences obviously had a marked effect. When the canal was returned to the state it was found that movable capital equipment had been transferred elsewhere in the country, thus leaving the canal system weaker than when the state had first responded to the call of patriotism to let it be run under the federal administration. The following account is excerpted from a biography of one of the state's most popular state engineers, Frank M. Williams, written in 1996 by Bill Orzell of Syracuse, N. Y., then editor of the Canal Society journal *Bottoming Out*.

On April 17, [1918] before the canal opened for navigation, the Federal Government took over the entire system and placed it under the control of the Railroad Administration, as part of the war effort. Director General William G. McAdoo announced, "He had decided to construct as quickly as possible and put into operation a line of barges to be operated by the government on the Erie Canal." This event, predicated on the premise of coordinating the shipment of war materials, would prevent the establishment of the new Barge Canal as a primary commercial artery. With this act, railroad interests had placed their own important competition in a position where normal economic laws could be overridden under the guise of national defense. Initially, to the patriots of New York, this situation seemed to make sense in speeding the war effort. Governor Whitman commended "action of the Director General meets with our heartiest approval. It was really done at our request, and we will give the plan our entire co-operation." But the die had been cast, and greed and special interest would rob Frank M. Williams, and all the taxpayers of New York from attaining the dividend of commercial canal success from their great investment.

[In 1919] the United States Government continued to maintain control of the Barge Canal, despite the fact that hostilities had ended the year before. The railroad interests had no intention of releasing the stranglehold on the canal . . .

By 1920 the Barge Canal was beginning to suffer an identity crisis. The railroad interests had effectively rerouted much of the freight that the canal could have economically carried. . .

Mr. Williams and all other State Engineers took great care to ensure that existing commercial canal navigation was never interrupted by the construction of the Barge Canal. They realized that most of the shippers were family-owned operations that would never recover from any suspension of their livelihood. Unfortunately, the federal government, instead of using this brand-new transportation artery to its best advantage, turned the operation of the canal over to its competitors, the railroad interests. The railroad Administration naturally diverted as much traffic as possible away from the canal, and also built themselves a fleet of barges and towboats that no private operator could possibly compete with, since the government-owned fleet could operate at a loss. This drove operators out of business, and discouraged new companies from setting up business on the canal ...

The effort to regain control of the canal and remove federal government equipment took nearly three years, following the cessation of hostilities in Europe. However, the railroad interests managed to kill off all but the most intrepid operations on the canal and relocate their wartime fleet in southern states. This created a dearth of vessels and operators on the new Barge Canal, preventing the waterway from ever reaching full capacity ... (On February 28, 1921) President Wilson signed the joint resolution directing the War Department to return the New York Barge Canal, taken during the war, to the control of the state.

[In 1925 Williams testified] that "with regulation of freight rates by the Public Service and Interstate Commerce Commission the function of the Barge Canal as a rate regulatory factor had ceased."

At the opening of the 1920s strong crosscurrents gave the railroaders a new advantage. The 1906 rate-making bill must have satisfied the members of the commodity exchanges who for a few decades numbered among the canal's strongest supporters. The comments made at the opening of the decade by Cortissoz and Depew about Conkling's views could have wilted any recollection of what he had done. But while the encroachment on the canal was so obvious, it could not outlast the adaptations of technology that appeared in another generation when the St. Lawrence Seaway opened, leaving both the canalers and the railroaders the losers. Perhaps Whitford's second history to focus on the barge canal could not stir up support but turned out to be the last hurrah.

Legally, the regulation largely came to an end with the passage of the Regulatory Reform Act of 1976 and the Staggers Act of 1980. The Anti-Trust Section of the Department of Justice could oversee maintaining competition.

The Legacy for New Yorkers at Large

Among New Yorkers the proliferation of modes of transportation, first represented in the use of both the railroads and the canals, became a distinguishing mark of the city's culture. There were street transportation, subways, tunnels, elevated railways, and bridges, boats on the harbor and rivers, and so forth. The practical result was that New Yorkers came to prefer rapid movement from one place to another and tended to eschew style and comfort in their modes of transport in favor of quickness. The consequence has been that a larger portion of New Yorkers benefit from business transactions at their destinations rather than from expensive carriage to and from their destinations and consequent congestion.

Chapter XIV

Former Governors Enter the Arena

1   Cullom, Shelby M. *Fifty Years of Public Service: Personal Recollections.* Chicago: A. C. McClurge & Co., 1911, p. 314.

2   Maxey, *CR*, Executive Session, 49th Congress, March 17, 1885, p. 57; *NYT*, Nov. 13, 1892.

3   *NYT*, December 23, 1874.

4   U.S. Supreme Court Reports, Vol. 110-113, Book 28, October Term 1883, *Julliard v. Greenman.* See also *NYT*, March 4, 1884, and Siegan, Bernard H. "The Supreme Court pointed us toward paper money," *Wall Street Journal*, June 18, 1984.

5   Benson, Lee. *Merchants, Farmers, and Railroads.* Cambridge, MA: Harvard University Press, 1955, p. 185.

6   Cullom, p. 312–313.

7   *NR*, Dec. 5, 1883.

8   Law, Robert O. *The Parties and The Men or Political Issues of 1896: A History of our Great Parties . . . A Record of Bygone Conventions and the Various Platforms.* Springfield, IL: Home Education Publishing House, 1896, p. 122.

9   *NYT*, Oct. 5, 1884.

10 Proctor, Ben H. *Not Without Honor: The Life of John H. Reagan.* Austin: University of Texas Press, 1962, p. 260.

11 Ross, Thomas Richard. *Jonathan Prentiss Dolliver: A Study in Political Integrity and Independence.* Iowa City: State Historical Society of Iowa, 1958, p. 212.

12 *CR*, 44th Congress, 1st Sess., March 10, 1876, p. 1218.

13 *NR*, June 16, 1881.

14 *CR*, 44th Cong., 2nd Sess., p. 1282.

15 *Canal Enlargement in New York State.* Buffalo: Buffalo Historical Society, 1909, p.145.

16 Hatch obit, *NYT*, Feb. 24, 1893; Bruce obit, *NYT*, Mar. 19, 1898.

17 Kendrick, Benjamin, *Journal of the 39th Congress, 1865–1867,* p. 187.

18 *NYT*, Nov. 13, 1903.

Glossary

Cartel: A combination of independent commercial enterprises designed to limit competition to avoid bankruptcy (Webster) by fixing prices and disciplining members for violations (Ulen). Contemporary examples include not only the oil cartel but also the NCAA and its control over college athletics. The organization can recognize legitimate members and enforce discipline among them.

Grangers: A number of settlers in the Middle West who met the railroad controversy in the early 1870s by passing state regulations over rail rates, some of which reduced company profits. For legal precedents they looked to English common law, a sentiment that resurfaced in New York in 1881. See John F. Stover, *American Railroads* (University of Chicago, 1961), pp. 127–130.)

Half-Breeds and Stalwarts: The terms "stalwarts" and "half-breeds" arose in the 1870s and did not last much beyond. Stalwarts, at first, were those Republicans most loyal to Ulysses S. Grant, voting for him in 1872, and later the "new departure" for the South. Many of the half-breeds, like Chauncey Depew, who referred to themselves as "independents," had bolted the party in 1872, and some had run for office as Democrats. The stalwarts tended to be identified in 1880–81 with the anti-monopolists and favored the Court decision in *Munn v. Illinois.* They more likely had their wealth in real estate and benefited from the high volume of business peculiar to New York City. The half-breeds were more likely stockholders in railroad corporations and would have favored the Adams plan for a national trust in railroading. The term "half-breed," according to editor Gorham, "is a Westernism, having its original derivation in the issue of a degraded Pocahontas, demoralized for spoils by a camp-follower." (*NR*, May 24, 1881) (See Allan Peskin, "Who Were the Stalwarts, etc.," *Political Science Quarterly,* Vol. 99, Winter 1984–5, pp. 703–716.)

Hegemony: The preponderant influence of one political body over another. (Adapted from Webster.) In this case the term refers to the New England delegation to the U.S. Senate between 1881 and 1913 having a preponderant influence over party members from other states.

BIBLIOGRAPHY

Author's note about the sequence of the bibliography: Since the contention of this study is that tracking the course of public policy requires appropriate research methods, questions are raised about methods of several authors who have delved into the period. In addition, there are volumes by authors who have conducted objective studies of legislative processes that we believe are applicable to the Gilded Age.

Methods of Analysis

Andrews, E. Benjamin. "The History of the Last Quarter-Century in the United States," *Scribner Magazine,* 1895, Vol. XVIII, pp. 267-289. Accompanied by cartoons, this article set the respectable interpretation of Conkling's influence on the Garfield administration.

Aydellotte, William O. "Notes on the Problems of Historical Generalization," in *Generalizations in the Writing of History, A Report of the Committee on Historical Analysis of the Social Science Research Council,* edited by Louis Gottschalk. Chicago: University of Chicago Press, 1963. This author discusses the importance of studying statistics.

Bennis, Warren. "The Coming Death of Bureaucracy," *Think Magazine.* Armonk, New York: IBM, 1966. Bennis provides a management model that might be useful in any age.

Clark, Clifford, *Henry Ward Beecher: Spokesman for the Middle Class.* Urbana: University of Illinois, 1979. Beecher in 1881, at a time when the monopolists were employing the tactic of enforced silence on a public question, employed the same language they had used.

Donald, David. "The Congressional Equation," in *Sociology and History: Methods,* ed. Seymour M. Lipset and Richard Hofstadter. New York: Basic Books, 1968.

Heinz, John P., Edward O. Laumann, Robert L. Nelson, and Robert H. Salisbury. *The Hollow Core: Private Interests in National Policy Making.* Cambridge, MA: Harvard University Press, 1993.

Mackenzie, G. Calvin. *The Politics of Presidential Appointments.* New York: The Free Press, 1981.

Mitchell, Clyde, ed. *Social Networks in Urban Situations: Analyses of Personal Relationships in Central African Towns.* Manchester: Manchester University Press, 1969.

Thomas, Francis-Noel, and Mark Turner. *Clear and Simple as the Truth: Writing Classic Prose.* Princeton, NJ: Princeton University Press, 1994.

Original Sources and Contemporary Authors

The Charles F. Adams, Jr. Literature

1) *The Railroads: Their Origin and Problems.* New York: Putnam's, 1878.
2) *An Autobiography.* Boston: Houghton Mifflin Co., 1916.
3) *The Federation of the Railroad System, Argument... before the Committee on Commerce of the United States House of Representatives on the Bills to Regulate Interstate Railroad Traffic, February 27, 1880.* Transportation Library, Northwestern University, Evanston, IL.
4) *Diary.* Boston: Massachusetts Historical Society.

Adams, Henry. *Democracy, Esther, Mont Saint Michel and Chartres, The Education of Henry Adams.* New York: Library of America, 1983.

Letters of Henry Adams, 1858–1891. Worthington Chauncey Ford, ed. Boston: Houghton Mifflin, 1930.

Appleton for 1881. New York: Appleton & Co.,

Biographical History of Eminent and Self-Made Men of the State of Indiana. Cincinnati: Western Biographical, 1880.

Blaine, *Mrs. James G., Letters.* Beale, Harriet S. Blaine, ed. New York: Duffield & Co., 1908. Chicago: Microbook Library of American Civilization, Library Resources, 1971.

Bundy, J. M., to Col. W. K. Rogers, September 18, 1878. Rutherford B. Hayes Library, Fremont, Ohio.

Canal Enlargement in New York State. Buffalo: Buffalo Historical Society, 1909.

Cole, G. C. "What a Bank Does for a Community," *Bankers' Magazine,* September, 1882.

Cortissoz, Royal. *The Life of Whitelaw Reid,* Vol. 2. New York: Scribner's, 1921.

"Controller of the Currency, Report of the" *Bankers' Magazine,* December, 1880.

Cullom, Shelby M. *Fifty Years of Public Service: Personal Recollections.* Chicago: A. C. McClurge & Co., 1911.

Davis, Winfield J. *History of Political Conventions in California, 1849-1893.* Sacramento: California State Library, 1893.

Depew, Chauncey M. *My Memories of Eighty Years.* New York: Scribners', 1922.

Field, Stephen J. *Personal Reminiscences of Early Days in California,* privately published, 1877, published again in 1893 with a new chapter by George C. Gorham telling of the assassination attempt on Field. Author's copy.

Foraker, Julia Bundy. *I Would Live It Again, Memoirs of a Vivid Life.* New York: Harper and Brothers, 1932.

The Garfield Literature
1) *The Works of James Abram Garfield.* Hinsdale, Burke A. ed. Freeport, N.Y.: Books for Libraries Press, 1970; first published in 1882.
2) Garfield, James A. *"A Century of Congress,"* *Atlantic Monthly,* July, 1877.
3) The Garfield Collection, *LC, Washington, D. C.*
4) *The Diary of James A. Garfield, Volume IV, 1878–1881,* edited by Harry James Brown and Fredrick D. Williams. East Lansing: Michigan State University Press, 1981.
5) *Politics and Patronage in the Gilded Age, The Correspondence of James A. Garfield and Charles E. Henry.* Norris, James D., and Arthur H. Shaffer, eds. Madison: State Historical Society of Wisconsin, 1970.
6) Leech, Margaret, and Harry J. Brown. *The Garfield Orbit.* New York: Harper and Row, 1978.
7) Peskin, Allan. *Garfield.* Kent State University Press, 1978.
8) Krupp, Robert O. *James A. Garfield: A Bibliography.* Westport: Greenwood Press, 1997.
9) Taylor, John M. *Garfield, The Available Man.* New York: Norton, 1970.

Garfield, Lucretia Rudolph, *Diary,* March 1–April 20, 1881. In *Garfield Diary,* Vol. 4, 1878–1881. East Lansing: Michigan State University Press, 1981.

The Gorham literature (in addition to his unsigned editorials in *The National Republican*)
1) Gorham, George C., "The Power of the Legislature of California to Regulate the Rates of Freights and Fares over Railroads within the State," 1876. Washington, D.C.: National Republican Printing House, in *Gorham Collection,* California State Library, Sacramento.
2) Gorham Collection, California State Library, Sacramento.
3) Gorham, George C. "The Greenback Issue," Newark, September 11, 1878, LC

4) Senate Report 427, Gorham's Testimony, 1879.

5) Gorham, George C. "Conkling Vindicated," *New York Herald*, 1888, New York City Library.

Harrison, Benjamin Collection, University Library, Bloomington, IL.

Hayes, Rutherford Burchard. *Diary*. C. R. Williams, ed. Columbus: Ohio Historical Society, 1924.

Herbert, George B. *Guiteau, The Assassin*. Cincinnati: Forshee and McMakin, 1881.

Hinsdale, Burke A., ed. *The Works of James Abram Garfield*. Freeport: Books for Libraries Press, 1970; first published in 1882.

Keller, Morton. *The Art and Politics of Thomas Nast*. New York: Oxford University Press, 1968.

Kendrick, Benjamin B. *The Journal of the Joint Committee of Fifteen on Reconstruction, 39th Congress, 1865–1867*. New York: Greenwood Press, 1969.

Lloyd, Caro. *Henry Demarest Lloyd*. New York: Putnam, 1912.

The New York Times, 1877–1900.

The New York Tribune, 1877–1882.

Poor, Henry. *Resumption and the Silver Question*. (self-published, 1878)

Thurber, Francis. "The Railroads and the People." *Scribner's Monthly*, December 1880.

The Washington Post, 1881–1882.

Whitford, Noble. *History of the Canals*. Albany, NY: State Engineer, 1906.

Wood, Frederic J. *The Turnpikes of New England*. Boston: Marshall Jones, 1897.

Government Publications and Reports

Congressional Globe, Library of Congress (LC).

Congressional Record, LC.

Controller of the Currency, Annual Reports, *Report of the Secretary of the Treasury*, LC.

Hamilton, Alexander, James Madison, and John Jay. *The Federalist Papers*. Introduction by Clinton Rossiter. New York: Mentor, 1961.

Interstate Commerce Commission Report, 1887. Washington, D.C: Superintendent of Documents.

Minnesota Reports, 1872–1873. Minnesota State Supreme Court.

Nimmo, Joseph Jr. *First Report on the Internal Commerce of the United States,* Treasury Department. Washington, D.C.: Superintendent of Documents, 1873.

Senate Report 427, 46th Congress, 2nd Session, *Select Committee to Inquire into the Alleged Frauds in the Late Elections.* William A. Wallace, Pennsylvania, Chair. 1878.

US. Reports, Supreme Court, Vol. 99. October Term, 1878, The Pacific Roads Sinking Fund Case. Reported by Wm. Otto, Boston, 1879.

US. Reports, Supreme Court, Vols. 110-113, October Term, 1883, Julliard vs. Greenman.

Accounts and Sources Authored in Subsequent Generations

Ackerman, Kenneth D., *Dark Horse: The Surprise Election and Political Murder of President James A. Garfield.* New York: Carroll and Graf, 2003.

Ambrose, Stephen. *Nothing Like It in the World: The Men who Built the Transcontinental Railroad, 1863 — 1869.* New York: Simon & Schuster, 2000.

Baehr, Harry W. Jr. *The New York Tribune since the Civil War.* New York: Octagon Books, 1972.

Baltzell, E. Digby. *The Protestant Establishment: Aristocracy and Caste in America.* New York: Random House, 1964.

Benson, Lee. *Merchants, Farmers, and Railroads.* Cambridge, MA: Harvard University Press, 1955.

Burns, Ken. *The Congress.* PBS, 1990.

Burrows, Edwin, and Mike Wallace. *Gotham: A History of New York to 1898.* New York: Oxford University Press, 1999.

Capo Press, New York, 2004.

Dennett, Tyler. *John Hay: From Poetry to Politics.* New York: Dodd, Mead, 1933.

De Santis, Vincent P. *Republicans Face the Southern Question: The New Departure Years, 1876–1897.* Baltimore: Johns Hopkins University Press, 1959.

Ellis, David, et al. *A Short History of New York State.* Ithaca, NY: Cornell University Press, 1971.

Gilchrist, D. T. "Albert Fink and the Pooling System." *Business History Review,* Vol.34, 1960.

Grasso, Thomas X. "Who is the Father of Today's New York State Canal System?" *Bottoming Out, Journal of the Canal Society of New York State,* No. 38, pp. 22–34.

Hoogenboom, Ari. *Outlawing the Spoils: A History of the Civil Service Reform Movement, 1865–1883.* Urbana: University of Illinois Press, 1968.

Jordan, David. *Roscoe Conkling of New York: A Voice in the Senate.* Ithaca, NY: Cornell University Press, 1971.

Josephson, Matthew. *The Politicos.* New York: Harcourt, Brace, 1938.

Josephy, Alvin M. Jr. *The Congress of the United States.* New York: American Heritage, 1975.

Klein, Maury. *The Life and Legend of Jay Gould.* Baltimore: John Hopkins University Press, 1986.

Lavender, David. *The Great Persuader.* Boulder: University Press of Colorado, 1970.

Marcus, Alan I. and Howard P. Segal. *Technology in America, a Brief History.* New York: Harcourt Brace Jovanovich, 1989.

Marcus, Robert D. *The Grand Old Party: Political Structure in the Gilded Age, 1880–1896.* New York: Oxford University Press, 1971.

Martin, Albro. *Railroads Triumphant: The Growth, Rejection and Rebirth of a Vital American Force.* New York: Oxford University Press, 1992.

Mason, Jeffrey D. *Melodrama and the Myth of America.* Bloomington: Indiana University Press, 1993.

McCloskey, Robert Green. *American Conservatism in the Age of Enterprise, 1865–1910.* Cambridge, MA: Harvard University Press, 1951.

Merrill, Horace Samuel. *Bourbon Democracy of the Middle West, 1865-1896.* Seattle: University of Washington Press, 1953 and 1967.

Nugent, Walter. *Money and American Society 1865–1880.* New York: The Free Press, 1968.

Orzell, Bill. "Frank M. Williams, State Engineer and Surveyor," *Bottoming Out,* Journal of the Canal Society of New York State, No. 33, 1996. Pp. 11-30

Proctor, Ben H. *Not Without Honor: The Life of John H. Reagan.* Austin: University of Texas Press, 1962.

Redlich, Fritz. *The Molding of American Banking.* New York: Johnson Reprint Corporation, 1968.

Ritter, Gretchen. *Goldbugs and Greenbacks: The Anti-Monopoly Tradition and the Politics of Finance in America.* New York: Cambridge University Press, 1997.

Robertson, Archie. "Murder Most Foul." *American Heritage,* August 1964, cited in Richard Shenkman & Kurt Reiger, *One-Night Stands with American History: Odd, Amusing, and Little-Known Incidents.* New York: Quill, 1982.

Ross, Thomas Richard. *Jonathan Prentiss Dolliver: A Study in Political Integrity and Independence.* Iowa City: State Historical Society of Iowa, 1958.

Rothman, David. *Politics and Power: The United States Senate, 1869–1901.* Cambridge, MA: Harvard University Press, 1966.

Stover, John F. *American Railroads.* Chicago: University of Chicago Press, 1961.

Tansill, C. C. *The Congressional Career of Thomas Francis Bayard, 1869-1885.* Washington, D.C: Georgetown University Press, 1946.

Taylor, William L. *A Productive Monopoly: The Effect of Railroad Control on New England Coastal Steamship Lines, 1870-1916.* Providence: Brown University Press, 1970.

Tice, James Moore. *Two Paths to the New South, 1870–1883.* Lexington: Kentucky University Press, 1974.

Ulen, Thomas Shaman. *Cartels and Regulation: Late Nineteenth Century Railroad Collusion and the Creation of the Interstate Commerce Commission.* Ph.D. diss., Stanford University. Stanford University Press, 1979.

Weinstein, Allen. *Prelude to Populism, 1865–1878.* New Haven, CT: Yale University Press, 1970.

Woodward, C. Vann. *Reunion and Reaction: The Compromise of 1877 and the End of Reconstruction.* Boston: Little, Brown, 1951.

COPYRIGHT ACKNOWLEDGMENTS

INDEX

ABOUT THE AUTHOR

Ernest Rueter was born in Seattle, Washington in 1926 where his grandfather, William H. Gorham, had settled in 1884. Rueter spent his adult years in the Midwest where he has taught courses in public policy at Indiana University Northwest (Gary) and  has held a volunteer position with the Indiana Council of Churches in legislative and urban affairs promoting civil rights legislation and state court reform. He was employed in several government programs. He has written this book to clarify the public careers of his great-grandfather, George C. Gorham, and his patron, New York Senator Roscoe Conkling, casting it in a policy scenario explicated by Professors Edward O. Laumann and David Knoke in their study of policy in the Carter administration. The discipline of the policy scenario requires of an investigator that he hold more factors in mind than is usually found in coverage of the Gilded Age. Thus, Rueter is able to show that many of the turns in lobbying evident in the 1970s were also evident in the Gilded Age policy disputes over transportation and banking. Rueter, a World War II veteran, graduated with a history major from Carleton College (Northfield, Minn.) in 1950, a divinity degree from Eden Seminary (Webster Groves, Mo.) in 1953, and a master's degree in sociology from Purdue University in 1966. In the summer of 1950 he worked in East Harlem Protestant Parish. Rueter and his wife, Jeanne, now live in Vermont close to the families of two of their three children.